INSIGHT GUIDE

NewEngland

DISCOVERY
CHANNEL

APA PUBLICATIONS
Part of the Langenscheidt Publishing Group

D0519550

ABOUT THIS BOOK

Editorial

Project Editor
Susan Gordon
Managing Editor
Emily Hatchwell
Editorial Director
Brian Bell

Distribution

UK & Ireland
GeoCenter International Ltd
The Viables Centre , Harrow Way
Basingstoke, Hants RG22 4BJ
Fax: (44) 1256-817988

United States
Langenscheidt Publishers, Inc.
46–35 54th Road, Maspeth, NY 11378
Fax: (718) 784-0640

Worldwide
Apa Publications GmbH & Co.
Verlag KG (Singapore branch)
38 Joo Koon Road, Singapore 628990
Tel: (65) 865-1600. Fax: (65) 861-6438

Printing

Insight Print Services (Pte) Ltd
38 Joo Koon Road, Singapore 628990
Tel: (65) 865-1600. Fax: (65) 861-643

©2001 APA Publications GmbH & Co.
Verlag KG (Singapore branch))
All Rights Reserved
First Edition 1984
Seventh Edition 1999
Revised 2001

CONTACTING THE EDITORS
Although every effort is made to
provide accurate information, we
live in a fast-changing world and
would appreciate it if readers
would call our attention to any
errors or outdated information
that may occur by writing to us:
Insight Guides, P.O. Box 7910,
London SE1 1WE, England.
Fax: (44 20) 7403-0290.
insight@apaguide.demon.co.uk

www.insightguides.com

This guidebook combines the interests and enthusiasms of two of the world's best known information providers: Insight Guides, whose titles have set the standard for visual travel guides since 1970, and Discovery Channel, the world's premier source of nonfiction television programming.

Insight Guides' editors provide practical advice and general understanding about a place's history, culture, institutions and people. Discovery Channel and its extensive web site, www. discovery.com, help millions of viewers explore their world from the comfort of their home and also encourage them to explore it firsthand.

A region with such a rich history and culture as New England lends itself especially well to the approach taken by the 190-title Insight series. In this latest edition, we take you around the region's six states, starting in Boston and journeying to historic towns and pristine clapboard villages, visiting serene lakes, forested mountains, lobster shacks and the old lighthouses that dot the coast.

COLONIAL INN 1716 CONCORD

EXPLORE YOUR WORLD

DISCOVERY CHANNEL

an orange bar, at the back of the book, offers a point of reference for information on travel, accommodation, restaurants and other practical aspects of the region. Information may be located quickly using the index printed on the back cover flap, which also serves as a bookmark.

The contributors

The new edition builds on earlier ones edited by Brian Bell and Jay Itzkowitz. This time the editor was **Sue Gordon**, a partner in OutHouse Publishing Services, author of a guide to Boston and, with **Tim Locke**, co-author of another book on New England. Locke, who has written several travel guides, revised and re-structured parts of this book.

The chief updater and contributor of new material was **Kimberly Grant**, a photographer and author based in Boston. She has written or co-written several guides to New England and a number of her pictures appear in the book.

The writers whose text has been adapted from earlier editions are **Mark Bastian**, **Marcus Brooke**, **Tom Brosnahan**, **Kay Cassill**, **Inez and Jonathan Keller**, **Molly Kuntz**, **Sandy MacDonald**, **Julie Michaels**, **Mark Muro**, **Adam Nossiter**, **Norman Sibley**, **Mark Silber**, **Bryan Simmons** and **Peter Spiro**.

Among the photographers who capture New England's visual splendor are **Carole Allen**, **Ping Amranand**, **Marcus Brooke** and **Stephen Trimble**.

Bryony Coleman proofread the book. **Lynn Bresler** indexed it.

How to use this book

The book is carefully structured to convey an understanding of New England and its culture and to guide readers through its sights and attractions:

◆ The Features section, with a yellow colour bar, covers the region's history and culture in lively authoritative essays written by specialists.

◆ The Places section, with a blue bar, provides full details of all the sights and areas worth seeing. The chief places of interest are coordinated by number with specially drawn maps.

◆ The Travel Tips section, with

Map Legend

▬ ▬ ▬	International Boundary
▬ ▬ ▬	State Boundary
▬·▬·▬	National Park/Reserve
▬ ▬ ▬	Ferry Route
❶	Subway
✈ ✈	Airport: International/ Regional
🚌	Bus Station
Ⓟ	Parking
❶	Tourist Information
✉	Post Office
🏛 † ⍭	Church/Ruins
†	Monastery
☾	Mosque
✡	Synagogue
🏰 🏚	Castle/Ruins
∴	Archeological Site
∩	Cave
❚	Statue/Monument
★	Place of Interest

The main places of interest in the Places section are coordinated by number with a full-colour map (e.g. ❶), and a symbol at the top of every right-hand page tells you where to find the map.

INSIGHT GUIDE
New England

CONTENTS

Maps

Old Map of New England   **16**

New England   **98**

Boston   **102**

Cambridge   **127**

Boston Daytrips   **138**

Salem   **143**

Lexington and Concord   **146**

Cape Cod and
Provincetown   **158**

Central Massachusetts
and the Berkshires   **188**

Connecticut   **206**

Hartford   **209**

Rhode Island   **228**

Providence   **230**

Newport   **235**

Vermont and
New Hampshire   **246**

Maine   **302**

Portland   **307**

A map of New England is
on the inside front cover
and a map of Boston and
the MBTA subway on the
inside back cover

Introduction

America's Attic **15**

History

Decisive Dates **18**

Early Days **20**

Birth of a Nation **35**

Decline and Revival **44**

Features

The People of New England......**53**

The Puritan Tradition **63**

The Tradition of Fresh Food **68**

The Maritime Tradition **72**

The Architectural Tradition **81**

Dune-backed
beach at Truro,
Cape Cod

Insight on....

Museum of Fine Arts, Boston .**134**
Newport Mansions **240**
The Shakers **296**
Wildlife of the Forests and
  Mountains **326**

Information panels

Outlet Shopping **153**
Summer Activities **164**
Whale Watching **183**
Sporting Tradition **201**
Pequot Indians and Gambling ..**223**
Skiing **269**
The Fall **292**
Lobsters and Lobstering **312**

Travel Tips

Getting Acquainted **330**
Planning the Trip **331**
Practical Tips **333**
Getting Around **335**
Massachusetts **339**
Connecticut **359**
Rhode Island **368**
Vermont **373**
New Hampshire **385**
Maine **392**
◆**Full Travel Tips index
  is on page 329**

Places

Introduction **97**
Boston **105**
Boston Day Trips **139**
Cape Cod and the Islands **157**
Central Massachusetts
  and the Berkshires **187**
Connecticut **205**
Rhode Island **227**
Vermont **245**
New Hampshire **273**
Maine **301**

AMERICA'S ATTIC

The blending of Old England traditions and New World values

created six distinctive states, each with its own character

New England "is a finished place," wrote Bernard DeVoto in 1936. "Its destiny is that of Florence or Venice, not Milan, while the American empire careens onward towards its unpredicted end… It is the first American section to be finished, to achieve stability in its conditions of life. It is the first old civilization, the first permanent civilization in America."

And, as America's first old civilization, New England has a rich endowment of many of the nation's most cherished memories: Paul Revere's midnight ride, the Battle of Bunker Hill, the charisma of the Kennedys. It was here that the first cries of American Independence were heard, here that the movement to abolish slavery found fertile ground, here that education achieved its fullest flowering, here that American art and literature attained their greatest refinement.

This is America's attic, crammed with marvelous antiques of every description. Here are the homes of Hawthorne, Emerson, Dickinson, and Melville; souvenirs of clippers and whaling ships from centuries past; houses and churches in whose gables and steeples can be read a national architectural history. The countryside abounds with inspiring vistas, enchanted with the bright golds and reds of fall, slumbering beneath winter's heavy snows, bursting with the worshipful energy of spring's ritual rebirth, and joyful in summer's ceaseless flowering.

The alluring variety embraces Maine's coast, its rocky promontories pointing to adventure; New Hampshire's lakes, deep with silent wonder; Vermont's mountains, shimmering in spring's verdant cloak and majestic in winter's whiteness; the Berkshires' captivating forests; Connecticut's celebrated colonial heritage; Newport's well-preserved luxury; Cape Cod's charming villages and rolling dunes; Martha's Vineyard's quirky vision of quaintness; and Boston's vibrant cityscape.

If Boston is a state of mind – a remark variously attributed by the city's contentious academics to Mark Twain, Ralph Waldo Emerson, and Thomas G. Appleton – so is New England to an even greater degree. And it is a state of mind well worth embracing. ❑

PRECEDING PAGES: quintessential fall scenery; sleigh ride on Come Spring Farm, Union, Maine; all the gear for lobstering; sailboats racing on Penobscot Bay.
LEFT: history re-enacted on Hampton Beach, New Hampshire.

THE PORTRAICTUER OF CAPTAINE JOHN SMITH ADMIRALL of NEW ENGLAND

Ætas 37
A° 1616

NEW ENGL

The most remarqueable parts thus na
by the high and mighty Prince CHA
nowe King of great Britaine

Schooters hill

Sandwich

Dartmouth

Jpswich

P. Kent

Snadoun hill

P. Treves

Boston

Poynt Dauies

Hull

Smith Iles

These are the Lines that shew thy Face; but those
That shew thy Grace and Glory, brighter bee
Thy Faire-Discoueries and Fowle-Overthrowes
Of Saluages, much Ciuiliz'd by thee
Best shew thy Spirit; and to it Glory Wyn
So, thou art Brasse without, but Golde within

If so; in Brasse, too soft Smiths Acts to beare
I fix thy Fame, to make Brasse Steele out weare
Thine, as thou art Virtues
John Dauies Heref

SouthHampton

P. Wynthrop

Cape Anna

COGNITA

GENS IN

Bristow
Salem

Baffable

Talbotts Bay

Fawmouth
Charles Towne

Sangus

Franncis Ile

The River CHARLES
Medford

Winnisimet

Towne
Roxberry

Boston
Charlton
Dorchester

Claiborns Ils

P. Salthrstale

London

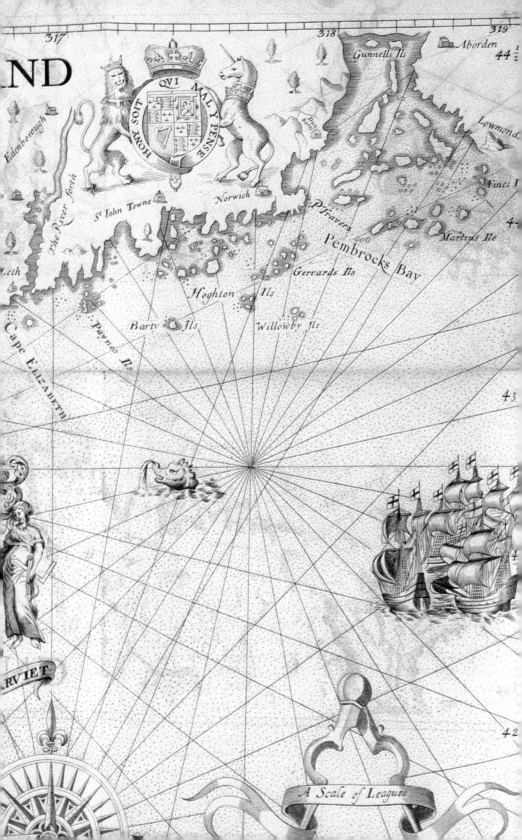

ND

Aborden

44 ½

Gunnells Ils

Lowmond

Edenborough

Finvs I

HONY SOIT QVI MALY PENSE

Drake minit

4:

Maritus Ile

The River forth

St John Towne

Norwich

Pt Travers

Pembrocks Bay

Leth

Gerrards Ils

Hoghton   Ils

Cape Elizabeth

Peirces Ils

Barty   Ils

Willowby Ils

43

RVIET

4

42

A Scale of Leagues

Decisive Dates

9000 BC Earliest evidence of human activity in New England, at Shawville, Vermont.

AD 1000 The Viking Leif Erikson discovers Vinland the Good, the location of which remains unknown.

14th–15th centuries The Algonquin Indians arrive in the region.

EARLY COLONISTS

1492 Christopher Columbus reaches America.

1497 John Cabot explores the North American coast.

1524 Giovanni da Verrazano, sailing under the flag of

the French King François I, journeys as far north as Narrangansett Bay.

1602–6 Bartholomew Gosnold, Martin Pring, and George Weymouth lead successful expeditions to the region. Weymouth returns with five Indians abducted from the coast of Maine.

1607 One hundred adventurers, funded by the Plymouth Company, build Fort St George on Parker's Island, Maine, where they spend the winter.

1614 The surveyor John Smith, also commissioned by the Plymouth Company, returns laden with furs and fish from what he calls "New England."

1620 The Plymouth Company finances a group of 66 Puritans to establish a permanent settlement in North America. They leave Plymouth on the *May-*

flower, and sight Cape Cod just over two months later on November 11. In mid-December they found Plymouth Colony.

1630 The Massachusetts Bay Colony is founded by John Winthrop on the Shawmut Peninsula.

1635 The country's first secondary school, the Boston Latin School, is established.

1636 Harvard College is established. Reverend Roger Williams is banished from the Massachusetts Bay Colony and founds Providence, Rhode Island. War erupts with the Pequots.

1639 The first printing press is set up, in Cambridge.

1675–76 King Philip's War sees the demise of Indian society in New England.

1692 The Salem witch trials take place, during which 400 stand accused of sorcery and other crimes. Of the guilty, 19 are hanged.

1701 The Collegiate School (later renamed Yale) is founded.

1712 Captain Christopher Hussey of Nantucket is blown off course and bags the first sperm whale.

ROAD TO INDEPENDENCE

1764 The Revenue Act, imposed by Britain on the colonists, taxes sugar, silk, and some wines.

1765 The Stamp Act is passed, which taxes commercial and legal documents, newspapers, and playing cards. Demonstrations are held throughout New England.

1767 The Townshend Acts place harsh duties on paper, glass, and tea. Two regiments of British troops land at Boston to impose order.

1770 On March 5, five colonists are killed outside the Custom House by Redcoats in what becomes known as the "Boston Massacre."

1773 On December 16, in the "Boston Tea Party," 60 men (disguised as Mohawk Indians and blacks) dump tea over the railings of three ships in Boston Harbor in protest against taxes on tea.

1774 Britain retaliates against the Boston Tea Party by imposing the Coercive Acts, including the Boston Port Act which closes Boston Harbor. On September 5 the First Continental Congress convenes at Philadelphia and starts to organize an army.

1775 On the night of April 18, Paul Revere and William Dawes ride from Boston to warn Minutemen of the impending arrival of 700 British troops sent to destroy an arms depot in Concord. The following day the two sides engage at Lexington in the first battle of the Revolution. On June 17 the British face their first major defeat at Bunker Hill.

1776 On July 4, the Declaration of Independence is adopted.

BOOM AND BUST

1789 Samuel Slater, apprentice to Jedediah Strutt (partner of industrial innovator Richard Arkwright), is engaged by financier Moses Brown to set up a cotton mill at Pawtucket.

1800 Poor working conditions at Pawtucket lead workers to strike in the nation's first industrial action.

1826 The growing community surrounding the Merrimack Manufacturing Company's showpiece cotton mill is renamed Lowell after its founder.

1831 The Abolitionist William Lloyd Garrison founds the weekly *Liberator* newspaper.

1842 The Wadsworth Atheneum is founded in Hartford, Connecticut.

1871 The Museum of Fine Arts opens in Boston.

1880s Irish immigrants start to dominate New England politics.

1885 Debut of the Boston Pops.

1929 The Wall Street Crash and resultant Great Depression hit New England hard.

1936 The Boston Symphony Orchestra's summer festival is inaugurated at Tanglewood.

MODERN EVENTS

1960 John F. Kennedy is elected President of the United States.

1960s–1970s Boston's urban center is transformed in a major renewal project.

1845–50 The Potato Famine in Ireland. More than 1,000 immigrants arrive in Boston each month.

1852 *Uncle Tom's Cabin*, by Harriet Beecher Stowe, encourages the Abolitionist movement.

1854 The Boston Public Library becomes the world's first free municipal library.

1861 Petroleum-derived kerosene, discovered in Pennsylvania, marks the beginning of the end for the whaling industry.

1870 The first race of the America's Cup is held at Newport, Rhode Island.

1980s New England's economy booms with the manufacture of computers and other precision products.

1989 George Bush, originally from Greenwich, Connecticut, and a Yale graduate, is elected President of the United States. He continues to summer at his compound in Kennebunkport, Maine.

1992 The Mashantucket Pequots open Foxwoods High Stakes Bingo and Casino in Connecticut, a highly profitable but controversial operation.

1990s President Clinton and family vacation on Martha's Vineyard, bringing it worldwide attention.

1990s A multi-billion-dollar public works project (the "Big Dig") to depress Boston's Central Artery and add a third harbor tunnel to the airport is the biggest in American history. Completion due 2005. ❑

PRECEDING PAGES: an early English map of the region.
LEFT: Cotton Mather, Puritan preacher and orator.
ABOVE: a harpooned whale overturns a whaleboat.

EARLY DAYS

The first Indians arrived in the region around 12000 BC, but it was the landing of the Pilgrim Fathers in 1620 that changed the face of America for ever

A crumbling stone wall in the middle of a forest: this is New England. Separating trees from other trees, this wall stands as a reminder of what man can and cannot do, of what the pioneers accomplished and what nature has reclaimed, of what New England was and what it is. The frontier no longer faces technology, and the scholar to study the lessons of the past and plan for the future.

And so the stone wall stands proud. Its people – the newly arrived and those with centuries of American lineage – embody the strength of diversity. Its history – a long trail of advance and retreat – provides an enduring

the rolling hills and woodlands; the Indians no longer hunt and fish undisturbed; the white man no longer clears the forest to eke out a precarious life. Now, spruces and firs tower over this crumbling stone wall, dwarfing the achievements of those pioneers who toiled so hard in the excitement and uncertainty of a new land.

New England's work, for good or bad, has been done; its limits have been met. But its spirit lives on to grapple with the intricacies of a different age. The same urge that impelled the explorer to chart an unknown land, the freeman to stake his claim, and the immigrant to make his fortune, now lead the politician to guide the nation, the engineer to create new

inspiration. And its landscape – the elegance of time-worn peaks, the tranquility of forests that will never be conquered, the lulling crash of the ocean waves – draws countless visitors.

Lay of the land

As defined today, New England encompasses 66,672 sq. miles (172,680 sq. km) including the states of Massachusetts, Connecticut, Rhode Island, Vermont, New Hampshire, and Maine. It is bounded by Canada to the north, the Atlantic Ocean to the east, Long Island Sound to the south, and New York to the west. Moving inland from the coastal lowlands in the south and east, the terrain gradually rises to forested hills and culminates in the weather-beaten peaks of the Appalachian system, represented by the White Mountains to the north and the Green and Taconic Mountains and Berkshire Hills to the west.

Perhaps 2 billion years ago, a vast ocean trough, under the pressure of more than 500,000 cubic miles (2 million cubic km) of sediment, was convulsed upward by an upheaval of the earth's crust. The mountains thus created were ancestors of the Appalachians. Its foundation a great buckling fold, the chain continued to shift and shudder. The intense heat generated by the formation of these mountains metamorphosed sandstone and limestone deposits into the schists and marble now found in the southeastern lowlands and Berkshire Hills of Massachusetts and in Vermont's Green Mountains. Later, streaks of intrusive rocks formed, represented by the granite of Rhode Island, New Hampshire, and Maine, and the reddish rocks found in the Connecticut River Valley.

About 200 million years ago, the thrusts from below the earth's crust stopped. The geologic revolution complete, the Appalachians towered about 30,000 ft (some 9,000 meters), the Himalayas of another time.

The elements went to work on the jagged landscape, until much of southern and central New England was no more than a featureless plain. Some outcroppings fared better against the wind and rain than others, accounting for the few scattered mounts that stand unescorted out of the lowlands – now called monadnocks after New Hampshire's Mount Monadnock. About 8 million years ago, meanwhile, the rest of the flats were gently folded one final time into the hills we see today.

Legacy of the Ice Age

The marauding glaciers of the Ice Age added the finishing touches to the landscape. About a million years ago, a sudden drop in the world's average summer temperature thickened existing ice masses to 200 ft (60 meters). Under this pressure, their foundations spread outward, grasping for new ground, until the glaciers eventually claimed more than one-third of the globe's total area. Ice swallowed up northeastern America on four different occasions during the

Pleistocene Era, retreating and readvancing over the millennia, finally leaving New England about 10,000 to 12,000 years ago.

This last flooding etched the New England landscape we admire today. Although the glaciers left unchanged the land's basic geologic make-up, they did leave reminders of their former supremacy. Working like steel wool, the glaciers – often more than 2 miles (3 km) deep – rounded out slopes and valleys.

Carving scratches (glacial striations) on exposed rock, the glaciers left behind evidence of the path they traveled. Glacial till, the chaff that the ice scraped off the ground, was carried

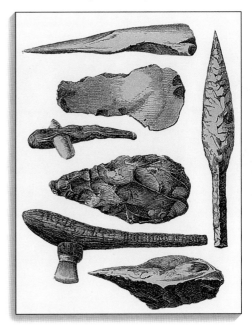

LEFT: a prehistoric inhabitant.
RIGHT: primitve tools unearthed in forests.

TRIASSIC PARK

During the Triassic period, the great swamplands that surrounded the Appalachian core and the hot climate created a perfect habitat for dinosaurs, the rulers of the day. Between 200 and 300 million years ago, dinosaurs roamed the Newark Bed, which runs more or less along what is now the Connecticut River Valley. Such primitive dinosaurs as *coelophysia* (an early two-legged herbivore), *rhychosaurus* (a tusked four-legger with an eery rodent look), and more than 150 other species of reptiles and amphibians, left tracks by the thousands in Smith's Ferry and South Hadley in central Massachusetts, and, of course, at Dinosaur State Park in Rocky Hill, Connecticut.

south. As the glaciers receded, this material was left behind; much of New England's bedrock is blanketed with a thin layer of this till, composed of clay, sand, and broken rock. Rounded hills of glacial till, called drumlins, are found scattered throughout New England, with Bunker Hill in Boston the most famous.

A similar process gave birth to Cape Cod, and the islands of Martha's Vineyard and Nantucket. Other dramatic legacies of the Ice Age include glacial cirques (large bowl-shaped

BEACHED WHALE

In 1848, workers laying railroad tracks in Charlotte, Vermont, a distance of over 150 miles (240 km) from the Atlantic Ocean, unearthed the skeleton of an improbable resident: a whale.

the oceans claimed many areas that are landlocked today. In parts of Maine, Atlantic waves crashed against shores up to 75 miles (120 km) inland from the present coastline; Lake Champlain was a sea which transformed northern New England into an Atlantic peninsula. Evidence of marine activity has been found at more than 500 ft (150 meters) above today's sea level. Hundreds of lakes once thrived where there are none now.

The waters gradually evaporated, and New

M. Lynge lith. Anst. Christiania.

depressions), glacial erratics (boulders, weighing as much as 5,000 tons, dragged for miles by the moving ice), and kettle lakes (crater-like indentations, of which Walden Pond is a good example). Like the towering Appalachians millions of years ago, many of these features are slowly wearing away. The erosion can only be measured in thousands of years, however, and the distinctiveness these features lend to New England's landscape will survive far into the future.

When the glaciers melted in force, they released a vast amount of water, perhaps as much as 8 million cubic miles (33 million cubic km) worldwide. The floods were great, and

England assumed its present configuration. Tundra plants and (later) trees took hold as the ice and sea receded. A flourishing fauna could live once again on the land but, this time, with a new creature in its midst: man.

Frustrated explorers

History remembers success more kindly than it does failure. Although, as the name suggests, it was the English who sowed the seeds of New England's fortune, they were not the first to gaze on these northern shores. Anthropologists gen-

ABOVE: Viking longboats arrived around AD 1000.
RIGHT: an 1876 painting of a native New Englander.

erally agree that the first pilgrims reached North America overland from Asia via the then-frozen Bering Straits, arriving on the continent between 12,000 and 25,000 years ago.

The oldest fossil finds of human activity in New England, uncovered in Shawville, Vermont, and Wapunucket, Massachusetts, date respectively to 9000 and 4000 BC and include a variety of spear points, knives, pendants, and ancient house floors. These early settlers were to witness the landing of the Vikings, the first documented European visitors to North America. In AD 1000, King Olaf of Norway commissioned young Leif Erikson to bring Christianity to the new Viking settlement in Greenland, founded only 15 years earlier by Eric the Red, Leif's father. Despite the winds that blew his *knarr* (Viking longboat) south of his appointed mission, Leif the Lucky lived up to his name and discovered a new land where grapes and wheat grew wild: Vinland the Good.

A few years later Thorfin Karlsefni set sail with several families and a few cattle, intending to establish a permanent settlement in Vinland. At first, the new frontier treated them well. They were impressed by the fertile land, the fish-filled streams, and the game-packed forests.

VINLAND'S LOCATION

The Vikings' visit to North America is well documented, but precisely where Vinland the Good lies on a contemporary map of North America is a matter of much debate. Some claim the stump of a stone tower in Newport, Rhode Island, marks the southernmost extent of their explorations. Other evidence pointing to an 11th-century visit to New England includes a Viking axe found at Rocky Nook, Massachusetts (near Plymouth Rock); early English accounts of blue-eyed natives; and reports that Karlsefni and his band wintered in a place without much snow. Other historians refuse to believe the Vikings ventured south of Nova Scotia.

The skrellings

But the natives proved too strong for the small band. Initial relations between the two groups were good; a cordial exchange system was established where Viking cloth was traded for local furs. All was well, says one saga, until the *skrellings* (Norse for dwarfs) were startled to martial frenzy by a bellowing Viking bull. A fierce battle ensued in which several Vikings fell (including Leif's brother Thorwald). Concluding that "although the country thereabouts was attractive, their life would be one of constant dread and turmoil" because of the natives, Karlsefni and his followers headed home to Greenland. The Vikings did not return.

The Algonquins

The Algonquins were the Indians of the real Age of Discovery and the Indians who were first befriended and then destroyed by European fortune hunters and refugees. Represented as far west as the Rockies and as far south as the Carolinas, the Algonquin tribes were related to one another approximately as the French are to the Spanish. Although intertribal communication often demanded an interpreter, the two languages shared basic grammatical and phonetic constructions.

The Algonquins seeped into the New England forests probably sometime during the 14th or 15th centuries. They did not come in droves; by 1600, no more than 25,000 Indians populated New England, fewer than one for every 2 sq. miles (5 sq. km). Nor did this population comprise a unified culture: the Algonquins broke down into at least 10 tribal divisions. Tribes included the Narragansetts of present-day Rhode Island, the Abenaki of Maine, the Pennacooks of New Hampshire, and the Massachusetts of their namesake, as well as lesser groups such as the Nipmucs, Nausets, Pocumtucks, and Niantics. Some tribes could boast no more than 200 or 300 members.

Far from being the crazed nomads of later characterizations, the Algonquins were agricultural and semi-sedentary, wandering little more than the fashionable Bostonians who summer on Cape Cod. Tribal communities moved with the seasons, following established routes restricted to particular tribal domains. In the winter they occupied the sheltered valleys of the interior, in the warmer months the fertile coastal areas.

But the Indians had to toil year round to feed and clothe themselves. With an excellent understanding of agricultural techniques, they grew crops such as beans, pumpkins, and tobacco, but relied most heavily on maize, the Indian corn. Meat and fish sufficiently balanced the vegetable fare. Plentiful moose and beaver, turkey and goose, lobsters and clams, salmon and bass, along with other delectables, made for an enviably varied menu.

Politics and state affairs were left in the charge of the *sachem*, a hereditary chief who commanded each tribe in much the same way that monarchs ruled medieval Europe. Although men usually controlled the sachemships, there were many cases of women filling the top posts. Sub-*sachems* and war captains, the Indian equivalents of lords and knights, paid material tribute to these rulers and were nominally subject to their will.

The *powwows*, or medicine men, gained considerable political might as the vicars of Indian religion. They combined healing with religion and enjoined their parishioners in intense mystical rites.

In no sense did the Algonquins comprise a nation in the modern European style. Unlike their Iroquois neighbors to the west, no council, senate, or chief-of-chief disciplined the Algonquin tribes toward unified action. Divided into

A WOMAN'S WORK

Everyone contributed to the efficient workings of the typical Algonquin community. While the men took care of the chase, the women sowed and harvested the fields, tended the children, and maintained the portable family wigwams. The Algonquins were, in fact, dumbfounded by the inequity of European sex roles. As one Englishman reported the Indians' reaction to the white female's social function: "They say *Englishman* much foole, for spoiling good working creature meaning women. And when they see any of our English women sewing with their needles, or working coifes, or such things, they will cry out Lazie *Squaes!*"

sachemships, New England's Indians were not simply disunited; they were constantly at each other's throats. "The savages… for the most part," reported the merchant-adventurer George Peckham, "are at continuall warres with their next adjoying neighbor." These conflicts could be extremely vicious, typified by the grotesque torture of prisoners and the parading of a slaughtered adversary's head and hands.

Tribal animosities so hardened by generations of battle would later contribute to the Algonquins' downfall by preventing the tribes from unifying against the advancing white settler, a formidable common enemy.

Columbus's countryman Giovanni Caboto (John Cabot), searching for the Northwest Passage to the East, received slightly better treatment from his patron, Henry VII of England. The first European to visit America's northern shores (at Labrador, historians believe) since the Norse, Cabot was blessed with a huge royal pension of £20 a year after his 1497 expedition. It was a good bargain for the Crown, considering that England based its claim to all America east of the Rockies and north of Florida on the extent of Cabot's exploration.

For most of the 16th century, Spanish conquistadors dominated the New World, where

Path to settlement

The early European explorers of North America were not mere adventurers, but determined fortune hunters seeking an easier passage to the Orient and its treasures. When the Genoese sailor Cristoforo Colombo (better known by the latinized Christopher Columbus) was trying to finance his expedition, he spoke of riches and trade. So when he returned with a new continent, but with no gold or spices, he was ridiculed and disgraced.

LEFT: contact is established with the natives.
ABOVE: French explorer Jacques Cartier.
RIGHT: the Italian Giovanni da Verrazano.

they profitably exploited resource-rich Central and South America. After Cabot's venture, the less inviting and accessible north was largely neglected and the Northwest Passage remained no more than a merchant's dream.

Sailing for the French King François I, Giovanni da Verrazano traveled the Atlantic seaboard in his *Dolphin* as far north as Narragansett Bay. Jacques Cartier laid the foundation for what would later become New France by navigating the important St Lawrence River. The Portuguese joined the French in fishing the teeming waters of the Grand Banks. But, as yet, there was very little talk of settling the then unchristened land of New England.

The English take over

In the closing decades of the 16th century, Elizabeth I's England eclipsed Spain as master of the seas. Recognizing conquest and colonization as a path to power, the late-starting English were to take over from the conquistadors as pioneers of the New World.

In 1583, equipped with a royal charter to discover "remote heathen and barbarious land not actually possessed by any Christian prince or people… and to have, hold, occupy and enjoy" such territories, Sir Humphrey Gilbert was the first Englishman to attempt the settlement of North America. Sailing from Plymouth with

his flagship *Delight* and three other vessels, Gilbert intended to establish a trading post at the mouth of the Penobscot River. But after reasserting English control of Newfoundland, he sailed south to disaster. The expedition never reached its goal: three out of the four ships sank and Gilbert himself lost his life.

The misfortune of Gilbert proved only a temporary inhibition to other pathmakers. The first years of the 17th century saw a renewed interest in exploration. Between 1602 and 1606, expeditions led by Bartholomew Gosnold, Martin Pring, and George Weymouth went smoothly and, although not ambitious enough to plant settlements, these voyages did discover a commercial lure to New England – plentiful sassafras bark, then considered a powerful cure-all. Weymouth also had another interesting cargo – five Indians abducted from Maine.

In 1606, James I granted charters for two new ventures, the Virginia Companies of London and Plymouth, giving the latter rights to found a colony somewhere between North Carolina and Nova Scotia. Directed by luminaries such as Sir Ferdinando Gorges, Raleigh Gilbert (son of Sir Humphrey), and the veteran Pring, 100 adventurers set out from Plymouth in early 1607. Loaded with the usual arms and foodstuffs, some livestock, and trinkets to trade with the natives, the crew built Fort St George on Parker's Island in Maine. There they wintered but, finding no evidence of precious metals, and the weather "extreme unseasonable and frosty," the group left the following spring.

Recognizing the need to plan more carefully, the Plymouth Company next commissioned the experienced surveyor John Smith to take a critical look at the region's potential for settlement and profit. Smith is credited as the first to give the region its name of "New England."

EYEWITNESS ACCOUNT

Early eyewitness descriptions of New England painted an attractive picture. John Smith, in his *Description of New England* (1616), wrote: "And surely by reason of those sandy cliffes and cliffes of rocks, both which we saw so planted with Gardens and Corne fields, and so well inhabited with a goodly, strong and well proportioned people, besides the greatnesse of the Timber growing on Them, the greatnesse of the fish and moderate temper of the ayre… who can but approve this a most excellent place, both for health & fertility? And of all the four parts of the world that I have seen not inhabited, could I have but means to transport a Colonie, I would rather live here than anywhere…"

Answering a higher call

The explorers of the 16th century were driven by the profit motive. Since they discovered neither the coveted Northwest Passage nor gold and diamonds, they couldn't discern the promise of the New World. Decades of work produced no more than a few crude maps and travelogues. The Cabots and Gosnolds and Weymouths were not interested in settling New England; only a higher call would people the new land.

Renaissance Europe could not imagine religious tolerance. Dissent was treason, and heretics mounted the same scaffolds as did traitors. To the Puritans, devotees of more extreme Protestant beliefs, the symbols of papal domination – jeweled miters, elaborate rituals, and power-hungry bishops – were the Devil's work. Satan himself was said to be a representative of the Apostolic See.

Perhaps even more disturbing to the Puritans was the persecution they suffered under Catholic sympathizer James I. The Puritans had enjoyed years of respectability during Elizabeth I's reign. Their followers included highly placed academics and public officials, many merchants, and local clergymen. The

In 1602, a group of several hundred Puritans from Lincolnshire migrated to the college town of Leyden, Holland, but they did not prosper. The exacting Puritans found their travel along the True Path hindered by the fact that "the morals of the people in the Low Countries were loose." And so, the Puritans struck a deal with the Plymouth Company to finance a settlement in the unpopulated north of America. In the early summer of 1620, 66 of the Leyden community sailed with the *Speedwell* to Southampton to prepare for the trials ahead. "They knew they were pilgrims," Bradford wrote, and so they are remembered by history.

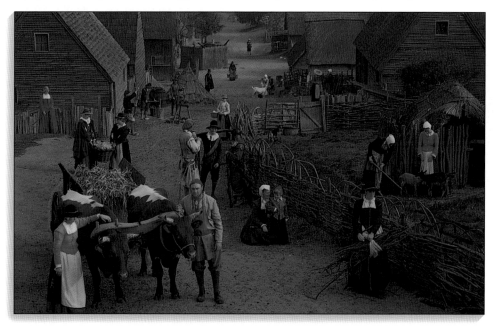

shock of disgrace under James I, therefore, was all the more frightful. The new king wasn't lopping off any heads, but harassment went beyond mere inconvenience. "Some were taken, & clapt up in prison, others had their houses besett & watcht night and day, & hardly escaped their lands," related Puritan leader William Bradford in his oft-quoted *History of Plimoth Plantation*, "and ye most were faine too flie & leave their houses & habitations; and the means of their livelihood."

LEFT: eight-year-old Anne Pollard, the first white woman to set foot in Boston (1630).
ABOVE: "Pilgrims" at Plimoth Plantation today.

Leaving from Plymouth on the 180-ton *Mayflower*, the Pilgrims packed everything they needed to start and maintain a self-sufficient community. The trip itself was no luxury cruise, and after more than two months at sea the travelers "were not a little joyful" to sight Cape Cod on November 11. Deciding that the sandy cape was not the best place to till the land, the group dispatched Captain Miles Standish (who was nicknamed "Captain Shrimp" because of his height) to find a more fertile site. In mid-December, the Pilgrims disembarked at Plymouth Rock.

The first winter was a miserable ordeal, testing fully the hardened Puritan will. Scurvy, pneumonia, and other infections killed more than half of the settlers, including Governor John Carver and the wives of Bradford and Standish. At any one time, no more than six or seven remained in good health. But with warmer weather came better times and the critical cooperation of the local Indians.

As luck would have it, Squanto, one of those brought back to England by George Weymouth, had returned to his homeland and was there to greet the Pilgrims. Squanto persuaded Massasoit, the local *sachem*, to help the beleaguered English pioneers. A treaty of friendship was signed.

A PURITAN ACHIEVEMENT

Like the Pilgrim Fathers, the later Puritan arrivals were determined not only to establish themselves permanently in the New World but also to live fully their religious ideals. "For wee must consider that wee shall be as a Citty upon a hill," Governor Winthrop declared. "The eies of all people are upon us; so that if we shall deale falsely with our god in this worke… wee shall shame the faces of many of God's worthy servants, and cause their prayers to be turned into Cursses upon us till wee be consumed out of the good land." Driven by such heavenly aspirations, these religious refugees fared well with their worldly pursuits. The founding of New England was a Puritan achievement.

Heavenly aspirations

Acknowledging the native contribution, the Pilgrims hosted a feast of celebration nearing the first anniversary of their arrival. In this first Thanksgiving, natives and newcomers enjoyed a meal of roasted game (including turkey), eel, fruits, vegetables, and cornbread. A few weeks later, 35 freedom-seekers, well stocked with provisions, joined the *Mayflower* survivors, and by the spring of 1624, Plymouth was a thriving village of more than 30 cottages.

With tracts such as Edward Winslow's *Good Newes From New England* making their way back to the mother country, more settlers overcame an understandable timidity to join the religious migration.

In 1628 another group of Puritans, led by Thomas Dudley, Thomas Leverett, and John Winthrop, obtained a royal charter as the "Company of the Massachusetts Bay in New England." The next summer, 350 hopefuls arrived at Salem, followed by another 1,500 in 1630. Like the Pilgrims before them, these later settlers suffered many casualties during the early days. But they, too, were determined to succeed in order to become an example for the chosen.

As Charles I and Archbishop William Laud tightened the screws of persecution back home, the Massachusetts Bay Colony grew quickly despite primitive conditions. Some 2,000 immigrants joined the settlement each year between 1630 and 1637, and, to accommodate these arrivals, new communities such as Ipswich, Dorchester, Concord (the first inland village), Dedham, and Watertown sprang up.

In 1636, the Puritan clergy established Harvard College to train future ministers. The General Court was formed to manage administrative and judicial affairs, a governor and deputy governor being indirectly chosen by the colony's freeholders (those who owned Bay Company stock). At lower levels of government, the founders of each town ordinarily convened to confront problems of general interest; this was an entirely practical mechanism of administration given that, even as late as 1700, the average town included no more than 200 or 300 families.

Growth was not limited to the area of the first landings on the Massachusetts shore. The reverends Thomas Hooker and Samuel Stone, along with former Bay governor John Haynes, left Cambridge for Connecticut, where they settled the towns of Hartford, Wethersfield, and Windsor. Londoners Theophilus Eaton and John Davenport soon after established themselves at New Haven. The Plymouth Colony had been operating a trading post on Maine's Kennebec River since 1627, and New World magnates John Mason and Sir Ferdinando Gorges tried to develop vast property grants in New Hampshire and Maine, but these ventures were humbled by the region's inhospitability.

Elsewhere, groups of New Englanders helped pave the frontiers outside the region. Puritan communities transplanted to New York, North Carolina, and Georgia maintained ties with

all worldly pursuits, the rigorous Calvinistic standards made the Puritans far less tolerant of social or theological deviation than their oppressors back in England had been. Indeed, in 1661, the king himself intervened to protect Quakers in the Bay Colony after several were hanged publicly on Boston Common. As has often been the case in American history, tragic deeds of injustice belied the ringing slogans of liberty.

Such intolerances did, however, bear an unwanted but ultimately productive child in the new colony of Rhode Island. In the early years of Massachusetts Bay, the Reverend Roger

their old homes. One such group, originally from Westmorland, Connecticut, continued to send representatives to the Connecticut Assembly long after moving to Pennsylvania.

The social satirist and Revolutionary War general Artemus Ward once observed: "The Puritans nobly fled from a land of despotism to a land of freedom, where they could not only enjoy their own religion, but could prevent everybody else from enjoying his." Dictating rules of conduct not just for the church but for

LEFT: Pilgrims give thanks for their safe landing.
ABOVE: early settlers barricading their house against Indian attack.

Williams, a graduate of Cambridge University, took it upon himself to condemn the shackles of imposed religion, preaching from his pulpit in Salem that "forced worship stinks in God's nostrils." Williams' compatriots in the General Court banished him from the colony in 1636.

But Williams did not return to England. He turned instead to Canonicus and Miantonomi, the two Narragansett *sachems* whom he had befriended in the course of studying the native population. The chieftains saw fit to grant him, *gratis*, a large tract on the Pawtuxet River. Here, Williams founded Providence. Fellow exiles joined him over the next few years – Anne Hutchinson (mother of 15 children) and

William Coddington on nearby Rhode Island (so named because someone thought it resembled the Greek island of Rhodes), and Samuel Gorton in Warwick.

Though the new settlement grew slowly – from fewer than 20 families in 1638 to no more than 1,000 individuals three decades later – the Providence and Rhode Island plantations proved an unholy thorn in Massachusetts' underbelly. No kind words here: Hutchinson, with her "very voluble tongue," lambasted her former parish

SANCTUARY FOR ALL

Aside from outcast Puritans, the new community of Rhode Island welcomed New England's first Jewish émigrés in 1662, along with scores of Quakers and French Huguenots.

descended from a lost tribe of Israel), the Puritans soon assumed the task of converting their new-found neighbors from their heathen ways.

Missionary efforts did show some initial promise. The Bible was translated into the Algonquian language. The Reverend John Eliot set up a string of "Praying Towns," along the Connecticut River and near Cape Cod, in which Christian Algonquins had their own preachers, teachers, and magistrates. During the 1660s and early

with "Call it whore and strumpet not a Church of Christ;" while back in Massachusetts, the ordinarily restrained Cotton Mather continually insulted the colony as the "fag end of creation," "the sewer of New England," and, ever so cleverly, "Rogue's Island." But Rhode Island lived up to its intent, and religious freedom was guaranteed by a 1663 royal charter.

A much worse oppression than Williams had suffered was imposed upon the indigenous population. Although the Puritans owed much to the Algonquins for their cooperation in the early days of settlement, and although they professed no racial prejudice against the Indians (one contemporary theory held that they were

1670s, these communities may have accounted for as many as one-fifth of all New England Indians. But the Puritans were looking for more than religious fellow-travelers; they sought to create nothing less than a breed of neo-Englishmen.

As the historian Alden T. Vaughan concluded, the natives would have had to "forsake their theology, their language, their political and economic structures, their habitations and clothing, their social mores, their customs of work and play" – in short, commit cultural suicide – to please the Puritans sufficiently.

Several Algonquins were sent to Harvard for ministerial training, but only Caleb Cheeshahteaumuck graduated. Many natives took to drinking the "strong water" introduced by the English, and were chastised for their supposed indolence, a cardinal Puritan sin. A few might have made the crossing to "civilization," but to expect all to do so was unreasonable and typical of a profound disrespect for a proud society.

Soon empire-building replaced missionary zeal and led to bloodshed. At first, there was plenty of room for the natives and settlers to coexist peacefully. About a third of the Algonquin inhabitants had fallen victim to a great plague in the early 1600s, leaving their lands

Wampanoag forces, nominally led by Philip (whose real name was Metacom), suffered from chronic tribal disunity and were outnumbered by at least five to one. At the "Great Swamp Fight" near present-day South Kingston, Rhode Island, 2,000 Narragansetts were slain (many of them women and children trapped in burning wigwams) in one of the fiercest battles ever fought on New England soil. The Indian will was broken; for them, the war had been a holocaust.

For the settlers, whose initial ascetic zeal had been diluted, politics, not religion, would be the rallying call of a new era. ❑

underpopulated when the *Mayflower* landed. And, as the English pushed south, the Indians realized that the white settlers intended to expand their holdings.

In 1636 war erupted with the Pequots (a fearsome tribe whose name means "destroyer" in Algonquian), and battles at Fort Mystic and Fairfield, Connecticut, saw several hundred lives lost on both sides. It was King Philip's War (1675–76), however, that marked the demise of Indian society in most of New England. The Nipmuc, Narragansett, and

LEFT: Roger Williams, founder of Providence.
ABOVE: King Philip's War broke the Indians' will.

LAST OF THE WAMPANOAGS

Following the Narrangansett massacre at the Great Swamp Fight in December 1675, King Philip and his allies formed raiding parties, looting and burning towns and garrisons. These attacks spread terror across New England until the settlers began to learn the art of forest warfare and Indian tactics.

These new methods, combined with a policy of withholding food supplies from all but friendly Indians, reduced Philip's forces dramatically until only a few weakened warriors remained. Philip himself was captured in July 1676 and beheaded. Wampanoag land was confiscated and the tribe ceased to exist.

BIRTH OF A NATION

The famous "shot heard around the world" signaled the start of the
American Revolution and the fight for independence

C aptain Preston, a veteran of the Revolutionary War, was interviewed in 1842 by a certain Mallen Chamberlain:

Q: Were you not oppressed by the Stamp Act?
A: I never saw one of those stamps. I certainly never paid a penny for one of them.
Q: Well, then, what was the matter? And what did you mean in going in the fight?
A: Young man, what we meant in going for those Redcoats was this: we always had governed ourselves, and we always meant to. They didn't mean we should.

Politics were not new to New England. But the northern colonies had, for the most part, been left to their own devices from the first landing at Plymouth until the dramatic Stamp Act crisis of 1765. When the mother country attempted to rein in her distant child, the reaction had been quick and biting, a portent of the more drastic rebellion that lay ahead.

Suffering serious political turmoil in the early 17th century, highlighted by the beheading of Charles I and the subsequent ascendancy of the Great Protector Oliver Cromwell, England had little time to attend to the governing of dissident settlers 3,000 miles from London. The Puritans gladly filled the vacuum and took on the responsibilities of *de facto* autonomy.

Even before reaching their destination, the Pilgrims signed the famous Mayflower Compact, creating a government "to enact, constitute, and frame such just and equal Laws, Ordinances, Acts, Constitutions, and offices, from time to time, as shall be thought most meet and convenient for the general good." John Winthrop and his followers carried with them their royal charter when they sailed to Massachusetts, and in 1631 the freemen of the new colony gave an oath of fidelity not to the king but to the Bay Company and its officers. The settlers agreed that if England tried to impose its own governor on them,

"we ought not to accept him, but defend our lawful possessions."

Dominion days

Fifty-five years later, they were given the chance. In 1686, James II unilaterally revoked the northern colonies' sacred charters and con-

solidated English holdings from Maine to New Jersey into a vast Dominion of New England in America. The monarch justified his decision as a security measure, a benevolent protection from the French and Indians. The colonists knew better: who could presume that the Puritans would kowtow to a royally appointed governor? The king's first envoy, Joseph Dudley, an avid Anglican, was scorned as having "as many virtues as can consist with so great a thirst for honor and power."

His successor, Edmund Andros, was ridiculed as "the greatest tyrant who ever ruled in this country." When the new administration extorted taxes, "ill Methods of Raising money

---

PRECEDING PAGES: a Revolutionary re-enactment.
LEFT: the Battle of Bunker Hill, June 1776.
RIGHT: British colonial governor, General Thomas Gage.

without a General Assembly," the disenfranchised populace grew more incensed.

A strong cue from England itself moved New England to action and revolt. At the "Glorious Revolution" of early 1689, William and Mary, in cahoots with Parliament, seized the throne from James II. New England spontaneously erupted; Andros and his cronies were dragged from state house to jail cell. The old powers of self-government were largely restored, along with a certain mutual respect between Crown

MOB RULE

Many of the demonstrations against the Stamp Act were peaceful, but in Boston, mobs ransacked the houses of stampman Andrew Oliver and Governor Thomas Hutchinson.

ridiculed at mock trials. Liberty was buried in symbolic funerals. Citizens of all stripes throughout New England, both of city and country, gathered to decry the new tax. Parliament, led by commoner William Pitt, took the hint and repealed the Stamp Act in March 1766.

But Britain had not learned a proper lesson. In the summer of 1767, with Prime Minister Charles Townshend boasting before the Commons, "I dare tax America," Parliament passed the Townshend Acts, impos-

and colonies. Though only three years long, the Dominion days had nonetheless decisively molded the New Englanders' political instincts.

But Hanoverian monarch George III would have a prostrate America or none at all. Britain's first *faux pas* on the road to losing its New World empire was the Revenue Act of 1764, which imposed duties on sugar, silk, and certain wines. The tax was duly denounced and boycotts proclaimed.

The infamous Stamp Act followed a year later, requiring that all commercial and legal documents, newspapers, and playing cards be taxed. The measure was fiercely assailed. Stamp distributors were hanged in effigy and

ing harsh duties on such imports as paper, glass, and tea. Two regiments of British troops landed at Boston to put some muscle behind Governor Hutchinson's waning control.

A tea party

The Redcoats were not pleasantly received. On the night of March 5, 1770, a crowd of several hundred rowdy Bostonians gathered to taunt a lone "lobster-back" standing guard outside the customs house on King Street (present-day State Street). When shouts turned to stones and snowballs, seven Redcoats came to aid the sentry. One fired into the melee without orders, others followed, and, after the smoke had cleared, three colonists lay dead (including a black man named Crispus Attucks) and two were mortally wounded. The American revolt had its first martyrs, and the growing anti-British element in New England had a field day with the nocturnal showdown.

Tempers cooled after the Boston Massacre. In the early 1770s, economic prosperity returned to the colonies. A once-again pragmatic Parliament struck down the Townshend Acts – all except one, that is. Just to make sure nobody questioned who was still boss – or king – Britain maintained the tax on East Indian tea, a not insignificant gesture given that tea was about as important as bread to the 18th-century diet.

American addicts turned to smuggled Dutch blends or to "Liberty Tea," a nasty brew made from sage, currant, or plantain leaves. The British responded by subsidizing their brand and, in September 1773, flooded the market with about half a million pounds of the "pestilential herb," with shipments to points all along the eastern seaboard. It didn't work.

Boston emerged once again as the focus of resistance. The Massachusetts Committee of Correspondence, an unofficial legislature, and the local chapter of the Sons of Liberty, a fast-growing secret society at the forefront of revolutionary activism, barred the piers and demanded that Governor Hutchinson send home the tea-laden *Dartmouth*.

When he refused, the protesters' reaction was swift and calculatedly theatrical. On December 16, 60 men (among them Sam Adams and John Hancock) disguised as Mohawk Indians and blacks descended on the *Dartmouth* and two sister ships. Boston Harbor was turned into a giant teapot as they dumped 342 crates over the railings.

The Boston Tea Party, as it came to be called, was a display of profound disrespect to the Londoners. Parliament responded with the so-called Coercive Acts. Most infamously, the Boston Port Act sealed off the city by naval blockade. This time, the colonies had had enough. The First Continental Congress convened in Philadelphia on September 5, 1774. Revolution was at hand.

LEFT: the British Redcoats retreat from Concord, defeated by the Minutemen.
ABOVE: the Battle of Lexington.

A shot heard round the world

An uneasy stalemate prevailed from the fall of 1774 to the spring of 1775. British garrisons controlled only the major towns. The countryside became virtually unpoliceable. New Englanders stockpiled arms and ammunition to prepare for the inevitable conflict.

The rebels didn't have to wait long for war. In early April 1775, London instructed Boston commander General Thomas Gage to quash seditious activities in rural Massachusetts, where a Provincial Congress had assumed de facto governmental control. Late on April 18, Gage accordingly dispatched a contingent of 700

soldiers to destroy a makeshift arms depot in Concord, located 20 miles (32 km) west of Boston. At Lexington 70 ragtag colonial soldiers, the original Minutemen, lay in wait for the British by dawn's light, having been forewarned by the daring early morning rides of patriots Paul Revere and William Dawes.

The two forces met on the town common. A musket was fired. Minutes later, eight Americans lay dead. The unscathed Brits continued on to Concord, where the colonial militia triggered, in Ralph Waldo Emerson's words, "the shot heard round the world." The Minutemen made up for what they lacked in numbers by employing unconventional guerrilla tactics, harassing their enemies with crack sniper fire. By nightfall they had knocked off 273 British soldiers.

Sensational accounts of these skirmishes sent settlers reaching for their rifles. "The devastation committed by the British troops on their retreat," reported one, "is almost beyond description, such as plundering and burning of dwelling houses and other buildings, driving into the street women in child bed, killing old men in their houses unarmed." Among the dead bodies, the card of compromise lay discarded.

PAUL REVERE'S RIDE

Henry Wadsworth Longfellow immortalized Paul Revere's ride in his famous ballad: "Listen, my children, and you shall hear/ Of the midnight ride of Paul Revere…"

supply of ammunition. It was for this reason, and not out of bravery, that Colonel William Prescott issued his famous command: "Don't fire until you see the whites of their eyes, men."

Bunker Hill was a costly victory for the Crown, which suffered over 1,000 casualties. Optimism, seen in remarks like General John Burgoyne's "We'll soon find elbow room," was reduced to the doubting reflections of another British officer: "This victory has cost us very dear indeed… Nor do I see that we enjoy one

The first major engagement of the war, the Battle of Bunker Hill, broke out in June on the Charlestown peninsula, across the Charles River from Boston. To consolidate control of overland access to the port city, Continental Army General Artemus Ward ordered the fortification of Bunker's Hill (as it was then known), although it was actually on adjoining Breed's Hill that the Americans dug in.

The British could not allow such a build-up if they were to entertain even the faintest hope of holding Boston. On June 17, Redcoats scaled Breed's slopes twice but were rebuffed. In a desperate third attempt they succeeded, but only because the colonial force had exhausted its

solid benefit in return, or are likely to reap from it any one advantage whatever." Less than a year later, Gage evacuated his troops to Halifax.

A few months later, on July 4, 1776, the Declaration of Independence was adopted by the Continental Congress. Of the proud signatories, 14 came from the charter states of Massachusetts, Connecticut, New Hampshire, and Rhode Island. Except for Newport, Rhode Island, which was not taken from the British until October 1779, the rest of New England had achieved its independence.

Once the Revolutionary War was over in 1781, the magnates of New England's prosperous cities turned to protect their newly established interests as the 13 independent colonies hammered out an integrated union. Concerned that a centralized federal government would prove as insensitive to local sentiment as had the Crown, revolutionary heroes Sam Adams and John Hancock gave only grudging support to the Constitution. Rhode Island, in more than a dozen votes between 1787 and 1789, voted down the Constitution and only ratified it after the Bill of Rights was added.

The industrial age

New England's leaders became increasingly reactionary as they went about guarding their

seas and on the seas that New England's money was made. Codfish and whale products provided a lucrative export to Catholic Europe. New England was at the pivot of the profitable Triangular Trade: in harbors like Newport, a fleet of 350 ships unloaded West Indian molasses and reloaded with rum. From there, the rum was transported to Africa, where it was traded for slaves who were shipped to the West Indies and, in turn, traded for molasses. New England shipyards gained world fame for crafting swift, easily managed ocean-going vessels, a tradition launched even before Pilgrim settlement with the

economic interests. In Massachusetts, poor hill farmers rose against the state government in Shays' Rebellion of 1786, demonstrating that genuine equality remained a dream. In 1812, fearing the loss of a thriving maritime trade, New England firmly opposed renewed and greater conflict with Great Britain.

When not calling comrades to religious or political barricades, the colonial New Englander attended to the more practical pursuit of commerce: it was both out of the

LEFT: whaling was an early source of wealth.
ABOVE: the 19th century saw improvements in transportation, including the Fall River paddle steamer.

construction of the *Virginia* in the short-lived Popham, Maine, colony in 1607.

Although disrupted by the Revolution, maritime trade bounced back quickly, mining the riches of China and India so coveted by the early American explorers. In 1792, Boston's *Columbia* threaded the Straits of Magellan en route to Canton to trade for tea, spices, silk, and opium. The magnates of rival Salem – Elias Haskett Derby, Joseph Peabody, and Billy Gray – preferred to sail east, skirting the southern tip of Africa on frequent and successful ventures to the Orient.

But, unfortunately, the first two decades of the 19th century demonstrated how vulnerable maritime trade was to the whims of international politics. The Napoleonic Wars, President Thomas Jefferson's Embargo Acts, and the War of 1812 ("Mr Madison's War") severely hampered New England's chase after an honest, apolitical dollar. Recognizing that it is best not to put all one's commercial eggs in one flimsy basket, its merchants turned to the herald of a new industrial age.

In the fall of 1789, a teenage Samuel Slater sailed from England to New York disguised as a common laborer. Slater departed in defiance of British laws forbidding the emigration of skilled mechanics. For seven years Slater had

his knowledge to use. Together, they built America's first successful cotton mill on the Blackstone River at Pawtucket.

With underpaid workers kept at the grind for 70 hours a week, Pawtucket became the site of the nation's first strike in 1800. It was left to Bostonian Francis Cabot Lowell (from the family that would later produce a Harvard president, a celebrated astronomer, and a cigar-smoking poetess) to take a more enlightened approach.

During a two-year visit to England, Lowell became an avid industrial tourist and, on his return to Massachusetts, he was determined to duplicate British weaving feats. Putting up

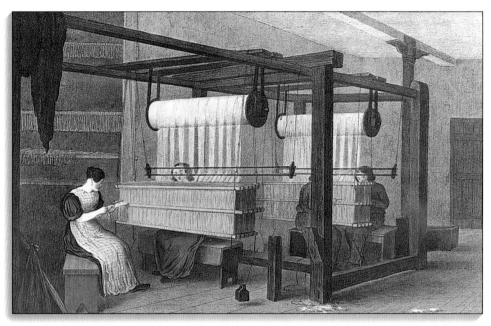

apprenticed to Jedediah Strutt, a partner of the famed industrial innovator Richard Arkwright, and had carefully memorized the specifications of Arkwright's factory-sized, cotton-spinning machine.

In America, the reduction of raw cotton was still being done by the inefficient "put-out" system, where laborers worked in their own homes on individual looms. An early attempt at consolidating the process, a mill at Beverly, Massachusetts, had been a failure owing to the crudeness of its machinery. Arkwright's device, already proven across the Atlantic, was the answer, so Quaker financier Moses Brown engaged Slater to come to Providence and put

INDUSTRIAL CENTER

New England in the 19th century was the center of industrial America. The region boasted two-thirds of the nation's cotton mills, while tiny Rhode Island alone processed more than 20 percent of America's wool. In Connecticut, Sam Colt (of six-shooter fame) and Eli Whitney manufactured the first firearms to have interchangeable parts.

In the paper, shoe, and metal-working industries, New England also stood unchallenged. The Connecticut firm of Edward and William Pattison minted coins for South American governments, while Boston's Frederick Tudor made a fortune exporting ice to places as far away as India.

$10,000 of his own money, he collected another $90,000 from the so-called "Boston Associates" – the families of Lawrence, Cabot, Eliot, Higginson, and others – to establish a small mill (with a power loom and 1,700 spindles) at Waltl......

A "commercial utopia"

Lowell died in 1817, but his plans were realized by his associates under the aegis of the Merrimack Manufacturing Company. In 1820, the mill was moved to a tract on the Merrimack River, just above the village of Chelmsford.

Paying dividends as high as 28 percent, the operation was wildly profitable. Sales went from a respectable $3,000 in 1815 to an unprecedented $345,000 in 1822; 100,000 spindles wove more than 30 miles (48 km) of cloth daily. In 1826, the growing community was named after its founder.

The Merrimack Company took care of its people. Though grievously overworked by modern standards, "mill girls" enjoyed clean, safe dormitory housing and opportunities for cultural enrichment. New England's first company town was, in the words of the English novelist Anthony Trollope, "the realization of commercial utopia."

Life on the frontier

Not everybody shared in the boom. During the second half of the 18th century, the northern areas of New England had enjoyed a dramatic infusion of people, as land began to grow scarce in the densely populated coastal areas. More than 100 new towns were established in New Hampshire in the 15 years preceding the Revolution; between 1790 and 1800, the populations of Vermont and Maine nearly doubled.

On the craggy hillsides, the pioneers set up small farms, built their own houses and barns, and raised wheat, corn, pigs, and cattle to fill the dinner table. These rugged families prided themselves on being almost completely self-sufficient. This was a new frontier, New England's frontier.

But this frontier's potential was limited by nature. The climate was inhospitable: in 1816, for instance, a June snowfall resulted in total

crop failure. Agricultural machinery could not plough the irregular farmland. Property consolidation was difficult, as families jealously guarded original claims; small-scale production could not compete with more efficient new suppliers elsewhere in the United States and around the world. Save for a few scattered industrial concentrations such as Manchester, New Hampshire, northern New England had seen its zenith by 1850.

After that, a slow, sapping decline attacked upland vitality. By the turn of the century, population growth had leveled and agricultural production dived. More than half of New

Hampshire's farmland lay abandoned. Cheese production in Maine, New Hampshire, and Vermont fell by some 95 percent between 1849 and 1919. Young men went off on the more promising Western trails, girls to the Massachusetts mills.

Cultural laurels

Long before the wheels of industry started to turn, New England minds had been establishing a cultural life unparalleled in the New World. In education, the media, the arts, and letters, America looked to New England for guidance and inspiration. Boston led the way in the first flowering of American culture.

LEFT: new textile machinery made it possible to produce cheap cloth using low-skilled labor.
RIGHT: the State House, Boston, around 1801.

As one might expect, New England claimed the laurels of many cultural firsts. Ever mindful of the responsibilities of being God's chosen, the Puritans had hardly built their churches before they set about educating their future clergymen. The nation's first secondary school, Boston Latin, opened its doors in 1635, and Harvard College, destined to join Oxford and Cambridge among the world's finest academic institutions, was founded the next year. New Haven's Yale, established by young Harvard graduates, followed in 1701.

During the 18th century, New Englanders continued to establish colleges that today number among the finest in the country: Rhode Island College, founded in 1764 and later renamed Brown University; Dartmouth College (1769); and Bowdoin College in Maine, which counts among its alumni Nathaniel Hawthorne, Henry Wadsworth Longfellow, Admiral Robert Peary, and President Franklin Pierce.

Libraries, meanwhile, gave ordinary citizens the chance to investigate the issues of their day, and of other days, in greater depth. The Wadsworth Atheneum in Hartford, founded in 1842, and the Providence Atheneum, a haunt of Edgar Allen Poe, provided members with access to impressive collections and cultural events. And in 1854 the Boston Public Library became the world's first free municipal library.

Sophisticated tastes

"High culture," once a preserve of the privileged classes, was similarly opened up to broader audiences in the late 1800s. In 1871 came the Museum of Fine Arts. The Boston Symphony Orchestra, established a decade later by Henry Lee Higginson, took its place among the globe's foremost ensembles and soon gave rise to a less strictly classical offshoot, the Boston Pops, debuted in 1885; the BSO's summer festival at Tanglewood in the Berkshires, inaugurated in 1936, is a mecca for music lovers everywhere.

As a favored tryout spot, New Haven significantly influenced the development of Broadway theater; an experimental counterpart was spawned in a Cape Cod fishing shack by Eugene O'Neill and the Provincetown Players.

Such institutional achievements are impressive. But behind them lay great individual minds, the region's many intellectual and artistic giants. Among these were transcendentalist philosopher and essayist Henry David Thoreau (1817–62), famed for his celebration of nature in *Walden*; poet Emily Dickinson (1830–86); and painter Winslow Homer (1836–1910). The painting of John Singleton Copley, and the prose and poetry of Ralph Waldo Emerson, Henry Wadsworth Longfellow, John Greenleaf Whittier, Nathaniel Hawthorne, Herman Melville, Robert Lowell, and Robert Frost are known the world over. Their lives testify to the spirit of New England. ❑

OFF THE PRESS

In 1639 a printing press was assembled in Cambridge. Its early releases included the *Bay Psalm Book*, the *New England Primer*, and the freeman's oath of loyalty to Massachusetts. In 1690, the colonies' first newspaper, *Publick Occurrences Both Foreign and Domestick*, appeared in Boston but was succeeded by the more popular *Boston News-Letter* in 1704. Other memorable tabloids, including the *Rehearsal*, the *Massachusetts Spy* and the *Independent Advertiser*, kept New England informed, if not always accurately, as the country roared to revolution. By the 1850s, the region hosted no fewer than 424 periodical publications.

LEFT: society life in late 19th-century Boston.
RIGHT: a composite of portraits of the leaders of 19th-century manufacturing and industry.

DECLINE AND REVIVAL

Following the industrial and cultural zenith of the 18th and 19th centuries,
New England faced political corruption and economic recession

By the beginning of the 20th century, New England had done all that it could. It had been America's leader in politics, in economics, in culture. In many ways, New England was America, epitomizing its ideals, drive, determination, and success. Considering the heights attained, however, New England

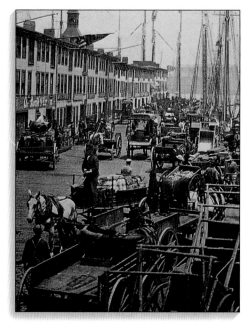

could not help but falter, as other regions competed for political and economic ascendancy.

The symptoms of political decay emerged both at the national level, where New England's influence diminished, and locally, where corruption and social divisions humbled once proud democracy. If only by virtue of America's physical expansion – the great westward surge of the 19th century – New England suffered in Washington. The region no longer represented a physical or psychological frontier; it was not here that battles had to be fought, decisions made, examples set. The White House was no longer the domain of Harvard and the Adamses.

New England turned to the task of managing itself after two last gasps of political pre-eminence: the abolitionist crusade led by William Lloyd Garrison; and the social-reform movements of the late 1800s, aimed at correcting conditions in the nation's prisons, mental institutions, and public hospitals.

Difficulties on the homefront were formidable indeed. Most important, ethnic and religious homogeneity, which had contributed to the political consensus, was diffused as migrating non-Anglo, non-Protestants hit the northern shores. Uprooted by the Potato Famine of 1845–50, the Irish sailed to the land of opportunity. They arrived in Boston at a rate of more than 1,000 a month. Others, primarily Catholic, followed from Italy, French Canada, Portugal, and Eastern Europe. The influx touched every corner of New England; even in backwater New Hampshire, one out of every five residents had adopted, not inherited, the American flag.

Electoral corruption

In the wake of this human shock wave, a predictable, if deplorable anti-immigrant backlash erupted among the established citizenry, whose forebears had fought so hard to achieve democracy and equal rights.

The doors of society were shut to even the most successful of the new arrivals, and their children and grandchildren. Politically, anti-immigration groups campaigned for tightened entry requirements. In the 1850s, the openly racist Know-Nothing Party controlled governorships in Massachusetts, Rhode Island, Connecticut, and New Hampshire. Later organizations such as the American Protective Association and the Immigrant Restriction League gathered substantial memberships in their efforts to contain the electoral power of their upstart neighbors.

Their efforts failed. No matter how unfamiliar the immigrants were with the workings of democracy, they soon learned the power of votes well orchestrated – particularly the Irish. In 1881, John Breen of Tipperary became the first Irish-born politician to take high office as mayor of Lawrence, Massachusetts. His triumph launched fellow Irishmen not only to political influence but also to political domination. Hugh O'Brien won the mayoral election in Boston three years later, and Patrick Andrew Collin represented Suffolk County with a congressional seat in Washington. By the turn of the century, all levels of government were being run by what was, after all, the majority of the population.

> **STATE FOR SALE**
>
> "The political condition of Rhode Island is notorious, acknowledged and it is shameful," deplored journalist Lincoln Steffens; "Rhode Island is a State for sale and cheap."

elected mayor of Boston five times in the first four decades of this century; and governor of the state for one term, 1934–38. The "Irish Mussolini," as his detractors tagged him, undoubtedly improved the economic welfare of his less privileged constituents. His imperious methods, however, left much to be desired. Inspired by New York's Tammany Hall, perhaps the most corrupt political machine of all American history, Curley doled out jobs and money to community leaders who in turn

But with newfound responsibility came insidious corruption. Rhode Island, once again, was the object of biting criticism as "Boss" Charles Brayton and the *Providence Journal* ring bought their way to office. Individual votes cost the political machine between $2 and $5 in normal elections, as much as $30 in hotly contested ones.

Many leaders, vividly embodied in the figure of James Michael Curley, abused the privileges of solid ethnic support. Curley displayed enormous political staying-power: he was

LEFT AND ABOVE: Boston's wharves at the end of the 19th century.

carefully steered their neighborhoods in the appropriate direction when election day rolled around. There was some justice to the critics' call, "This is a Republic and not a Kingdom." When the mayor went to a ball game at Fenway Park, howitzers trumpeted his arrival.

Cultural suppression

In Boston, cultural freedoms came under increasingly harsh attack. Led by Catholic leader William Cardinal O'Connell and the associated Watch and Ward Society, moralists lobbied successfully for prohibitions on such classics as Theodore Dreiser's *An American Tragedy* and Ernest Hemingway's *The Sun Also Rises*.

"Banned in Boston!" sang the crusaders, and the phrase survives in American idiom today.

Days of industrial glory passed. In much the same way that international competition now threatens America's economic might, other regions of the country challenged and overcame New England and its once-proud manufacturers. It was a question of costs, specifically labor costs, and the South underbid New England. Hourly wages in New England averaged 16 to 60 percent higher than those below the Mason-Dixon line. Owners gravitated to the cheaper

BOSTON POVERTY

In 1930, only 81 out of 5,030 apartments in the North End had refrigerators, and only one in two had bathrooms.

quarters. Here, wages plunged by half, and unemployment jumped to almost 40 percent after the Wall Street stock market crash.

Political revival

It took New England a long time to recover from this economic displacement. Employment in textiles bottomed out in the early 1970s and, virtually bereft of natural resources, including oils, the region was at that time hostage to Louisiana, Texas, and the Middle East during the energy crisis.

workforce, in an industrial exodus dramatically illustrated by statistical indices. Up from a mere 6 percent in 1880, the South wove almost half the nation's cotton goods by 1923. Industrial production in Massachusetts alone fell by $1 billion during the 1920s. Unemployment in factory towns left idle a quarter of the total labor pool. Gone, too, were the heady days of Lowell's 28 percent dividends: expenditures in New England mills now surpassed the factories' earnings.

New England felt the brunt of the Great Depression. In Boston it cramped even upper-class lifestyle; hardships were, of course, far more shocking in already squalid working-class

But New England bounced back. On the political front, the "new" New Englander had more than mastered the mechanisms of democracy and readily adopted its spirit. Irish leaders forged a partnership with the old establishment on equal terms; indeed, it was the "Green Brahmins" (Irish successors to Boston's self-appointed aristocracy) who produced one of the nation's mostly highly regarded chief executives, John Fitzgerald Kennedy.

Having more or less cleaned up its own political house, New England returned its attention to national politics with a thoughtful, progressive voice, and commenced playing a prominent role in a number of important grassroots campaigns

– from violence prevention to nature preservation – that it continues to adopt today.

The 1980s saw a resurgence in the region's industrial base. Precision products – computers, electronic and biomedical machinery, special papers and plastics, and photographic hardware – made New England a nexus of the high-tech revolution. Boston became (and still is) the heart of the nation's mutual-fund industry. Hartford's insurance companies, capitalized at

ANTIWAR RULING

In 1970, the Massachusetts Supreme Court, heir to the nation's oldest democratic tradition, ruled that its citizens could not be forced to fight in an undeclared war: a clear condemnation of the Vietnam conflict.

At the millennium

The region's economy continues to be driven by the high-tech and financial services industries. The Boston-based mutual funds is a multi-trillion dollar industry. Fidelity (the largest mutual-fund company in the US), Putnam and MFS are here. Second only to Silicon Valley and perhaps a newly burgeoning Texan high-tech field, New England boasts a thriving technology quarter west of Boston. Graduates from MIT, Harvard

billions of dollars, continued to protect much of American business against damage and risk.

But the recession of the early 1990s deeply wounded the economic complacency that had so long sustained New England. White-collar jobs came under threat. As elsewhere in the world, service industries assumed a new importance as manufacturing industries retreated. In this respect, New England was fortunate. Graced with a unique scenic beauty, it turned to tourism as a major growth area.

LEFT: Bostonian legends: Irish mayor James Curley (left) and John F. Kennedy.
ABOVE: the Boston skyline seen from the harbor.

and other institutions of higher learning fall in love with the place, and don't want to leave. They set up fledgling companies and parlay them into the likes of Digital and Lotus (both of which are in the Boston area).

The so-called "Massachusetts miracle" of the 1990s, which Republicans say was fueled by fiscally irresponsible government spending, marshaled a Republican governor in office in 1990. Although Massachusetts has a higher percentage of Democratic voters than any other state in the country, it elected a Republican governor boasting socially liberal values. Stagnant in the early 1990s, New England's business climate is in a boom cycle again. ❏

THE PEOPLE OF NEW ENGLAND

New England's indomitable Puritan heritage is complemented by the pioneering spirit shared by the region's numerous immigrant ethnic groups

The product of centuries of "plain living and high thinking," New Englanders have long considered themselves the conscience of the nation. New England has contributed more distinguished legislators, writers, teachers, and thinkers to the United States than has any other region. It's true that it had a head start on the rest of America. But even after the other states had caught up in terms of population, the flow of outstanding people produced by this unpromising land never let up.

The Puritan heritage, and the region's harsh landscape and weather, have led New Englanders to view life a bit more seriously than do the residents of more forgiving cultures and climes. Although New Englanders have, as a rule, eschewed frivolity, they're quite in favor of individualism, provided that it enhances self-reliance and does not impinge on others' rights to pursue their own individual vision. This mindset pervades both the opulent enclaves of the ultra-rich and the plainest of rural villages; it even informs the day-to-day dealings of city life.

Most would consider this fierce independence to be a carryover from colonial days. However, the genius of the New England style is that it is an amalgam of all the disparate groups that have settled here and forged common bonds and goals: Native American, English, African-American, Irish, Italian, French Canadian, Latin American, Asian... The list continues to grow.

The Algonquins

New England has been inhabited since about 12,000–10,000 BC. When the first English settlers arrived in the early 17th century, most of the native inhabitants were concentrated in Rhode Island, Connecticut, and Massachusetts. They were divided into tribes with well-estab-

lished rivalries and territorial boundaries. All of Algonquin blood, they had two distinct but grammatically similiar languages, within which 13 different dialects have been identified.

These Algonquins were friendly to the first English settlers, who seemed far too few in numbers to represent any threat. The Mohegans

and Pequots of Connecticut, the Wampanoags of Massachusetts, and the Narragansetts of Rhode Island imparted their age-old hunting, fishing, farming, and canoe-making skills to the newcomers.

But this honeymoon was to last only about 15 years. In 1636, the English waged war against the Pequots in revenge for some real or imagined Indian outrage. The Narragansetts took the fatal step of allying themselves with the English, destroying the possibility of a united native front. When the war was over, the Pequots had been obliterated as a people. By 1670, there were 75,000 English settlers in New England and only about 10,000 Indians. The

PRECEDING PAGES: Irish colleens; outdoor pursuits such as fishing are a major attraction in New England.
LEFT: William Garrett and his Brahmin ancestor.
RIGHT: a Micmac from Connecticut.

natives had sold much of their land, their settlements having been penetrated everywhere. Many had been converted to Christianity and lived in what were called "Praying Towns."

The wars of 1675–76 marked the last desperate gasp of native resistance. In 1675, an alliance to fight the English – formed by the Wampanoag *sachem* Philip with several smaller tribes – was crushed. Philip was caught in July the following year, and was beheaded, his body quartered, and the parts displayed in Plymouth for 24 years.

> **DEADLY DISEASE**
>
> In 1763, during one six-month period, 222 of the 358 natives living in Nantucket succumbed to an epidemic.

The English weren't content until the last threat of a native uprising had been eliminated. After the Pequots and the Wampanoags, it was the Narragansetts' turn. By the time the English were through with them at the end of 1676, fewer than 70 were left out of the original 4,000 to 5,000.

Beginning of the end

The Algonquin's cultural integrity was shattered. Many fled west. Some native groups, like the Narragansetts on Rhode Island, were granted reservations. Those who stayed on the reservations never adopted European farming methods (the notion of private property was entirely foreign to their way of life); instead, they rented out their land, while eking out a meager existence from the manufacture of craft items.

These native-held territories steadily dwindled over the following two centuries; great tracts of land were sold off by the tribes or simply appropriated. Although the reservations were allowed some degree of self-government (they had, for example, their own magistrates or justices of the peace), they were also appointed nontribal overseers, who often administered to the natives' detriment. In 1869 the Massachusetts legislature voted to end reservation status for those Indians still on reservations, and 11 years later the Rhode Island legislature abolished the Narragansett tribe as a legal entity. Their disenfranchised descendants became ordinary US citizens with no special rights – until recently, when activists began mobilizing for the restoration of tribal lands.

Most Indians did not live on reservations, however; they simply merged into the surrounding population at the lowest level of colonial society, assuming menial jobs as indentured servants or day laborers. Some signed on board whaling ships – a grueling and perilous, if colorful, livelihood. In Rhode Island, Indians gained renown for their skill in building stone walls.

For the most part, the 18th and 19th centuries saw a sad, slow decline of the old tribal associations. The colonists' diseases finished what their guns had begun, causing a continual attrition in population. The Algonquin dialects died out almost completely, and Indians in New

SAMSON OCCOM

Although Indians fought bravely in both the Revolutionary and Civil Wars, few outstanding figures emerged from their own ranks to guide and lead them.

An exception was Samson Occom, a Mohegan born in Connecticut in 1723. A brilliant student at Eleazar Wheelock's school for the "Youth of Indian Tribes" (which later became Dartmouth College), Occom became a vigorous Christian missionary. He was bitterly disappointed when his mentor Wheelock moved his school from Connecticut to its present location in rural New Hampshire, where, as Occom pointed out, few indigenous residents remained.

England became so marginal that they faded out of public consciousness.

Native Americans today

Today, there are only about 21,000 American Indians in New England; about a third live on the nine existing reservations. Many are not the descendants of the natives encountered by the Puritans in the 17th century – except in Maine, a great many have relocated from other parts of the country. For most of this century, Indians in New England lived an unobtrusive, unnoticed life. In recent years, however, there has been something of a renaissance.

councils moved into action. They brought suits against their respective New England towns contesting the 1869 law which, in effect, deprived Indians of their reservations. Denied their tribal status in two trials (in 1977 and 1982), the Mashpee Wampanoags, who now number approximately 600, have as yet had no success reclaiming any part of the 10,500 acres (4,250 hectares) which the Plymouth General Court accorded them in perpetuity in 1660. The Gay Head Wampanoags fared a bit better: in 1987, the federal government granted them $4.5 million for the repurchase of 475 acres (192 hectares).

A new consciousness of tribal identity has taken hold in the region. It has found expression in cultural events and in attempts to right some of the wrongs perpetrated by the colonists. Throughout the 1960s, the annual *powwow* of the Wampanoag Indians of Massachusetts, which previously had been a modest affair, grew to include more dances, rituals, performances of music, and meetings with other tribes. In 1972, the Wampanoag communities in Mashpee and Gay Head, Martha's Vineyard, elected tribal councils. Four years later the

LEFT: a park ranger, Ferry Beach State Park Maine.
ABOVE: education is one of the region's big industries.

The Narragansetts – 4,000 to 5,000 people of mixed American Indian, European, and African ancestry in southern Rhode Island – filed a similar suit in 1976; in an out-of-court settlement, they were awarded 1,900 acres (780 hectares). The 700 Penobscots of Maine, the only New England natives who still speak their original tongue, sued the state in 1975 for recovery of 10 million acres (4 million hectares), and reached a compromise settlement three years later. The most unusual case in recent years is of the Mashantucket Pequots in Connecticut, who in 1992 won a Supreme Court ruling to keep open their Foxwoods High Stakes and Bingo, the largest casino in the western hemisphere. The legal battles are far from done, but for the first time in 300 years, New England's Native Americans have begun to recoup some small portion of the losses they suffered at the hands of high-minded colonists.

The proud Puritans

The world has rarely seen a group of immigrants quite like the New England Puritans of the 17th century. Fleeing religious persecution in England, they were fired by an extraordinary sense of mission. As the first immigrants to America, they would create a civilized society in the harsh, inhospitable New England

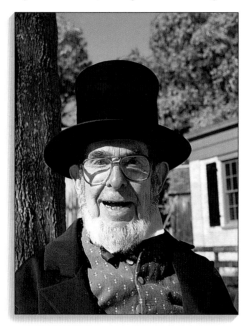

wilderness, and they would set an example of purpose and industry for the rest of the world.

Because their motive for coming to New England was primarily religious and not economic, the Puritans were a socially diverse lot. Although most of these early comers were peasants and artisans, an unusually large number of educated men – ministers, theologians and teachers – were among them. These learned men set a tone for the Puritan community of strict disciplined piety, with religion pervading every aspect of life.

The religious organization of the Puritan church was congregational: that is, members of the community elected the governors of the church. Leaders of church, community, and state were usually the same. From the earliest days of colonization, the Puritan leaders felt compelled to settle the rest of New England. There were two reasons: a high birth rate called for the rapid expansion of the Puritan community beyond the boundaries of Massachusetts; and the churchmen were eager to Christianize the Indians.

For 200 years, New England's settlers consisted of this tightly knit, homogeneous group. What Yale president Timothy Dwight said of Bostonians in 1796 could have been applied to *all* New Englanders: "They are all descendants of Englishmen and, of course, are united by all the great bonds of society – language, religion, government, manners and interest." Having grown from a strictly controlled religious state to a cradle of revolutionary democratic ideas, this community was thought of as a distinctive nation-within-a-nation by other Americans at the end of the 18th century. According to Dwight, New Englanders were distinguished by their "love of science and learning," their "love of liberty," their "morality," "piety" and "unusual spirit of enquiry." Dwight was a New Englander himself and he naturally idealized his origins. For him the typical New Englander was a combination of Ethan Allen, the Connecticut boy who led a daring guerrilla fight against the English in the hills of Vermont; fire-breathing Massachusetts preacher Cotton Mather; and learned statesman and patriot John Adams.

The rest of the country was more likely to characterize Yankees, as they became known, as speculators, entrepreneurs, inventors, or investors. They were men like early 19th-century Boston textile baron Francis Cabot Lowell, who established one of America's first modern factories; or members of a great Boston family that made its fortune in Far East trade.

The "exalted" Brahmins

New Englanders considered themselves the national elite. The self-proclaimed heads of this elite were the Boston Brahmins – rich Boston families such as the Lowells, Cabots, Welds, Lodges, and Saltonstalls, who secured their fortunes in the first half of the 20th century in the railroad, banking, shipping, and textile industries. The Welds, for example, forebears of Massachusetts governor William Weld, had been in 17th-century Governor John Winthrop's entourage and had fallen into obscurity for six generations before they prospered in shipping and railroads in the 19th century. This dynasty carefully nurtured itself at a group of socially select schools and colleges such as Harvard.

Despite this, and despite the fact that many of today's Brahmins hold exalted notions of the extent of their lineage, few descend from the *Mayflower* Pilgrims, from prominent Puritans of the 17th century, or even from rich merchants of the 18th century. For the Boston social system was

> ### HARVARD MEN
>
> Boston Brahmin Edmund Quincy once said of the Harvard Triennial Catalog, which contained a list of all Harvard University graduates: "If a man's in there, that's who he is. If he isn't, who is he?"

Indomitable Yankees

Other Yankees might contest this characterization. President Calvin Coolidge, a famous Vermonter, once declared at Vermont's Bennington College: "I love Vermont... most of all because of her indomitable people. They are a race of pioneers who have almost beggared themselves to serve others. If the spirit of liberty should vanish in other parts of the Union and support for our institutions should languish, it could all be replenished from the

not an aristocratic one; when Brahmins lost their money, as happened to a good many of them at various times in the 18th century, they ceased to be Brahmins.

The Brahmins may think of themselves as European-style aristocrats (some have even adopted family coats of arms), but James Michael Curley, the notorious Irish mayor of Boston, was not far wrong when he remarked acidly that Boston's prominent Yankee families "got rich selling opium to the Chinese, rum to the Indians, or trading in slaves."

LEFT: a Puritan lives again at Old Sturbridge Village.
RIGHT: soaking up the sun by a lake in Vermont.

generous store held by the people of this brave little state of Vermont."

The first inhabitants of the state were hardy trappers, not farmers; and this has contributed to the independent characteristics of the modern Vermonter. Freedom is a personal issue for the Vermonter, not just an abstract historical one, although Vermont has a long tradition of idealism. When neighboring states were laying claim to its territory during the Revolution, Vermont declared itself an independent republic. It maintained this status for 14 years, during which time it declared universal suffrage (excepting women, of course) and prohibited slavery. It was the first state to do so.

New Hampshire Yankees are much like their cousins to the west, but have the reputation of being somewhat less tolerant than Vermonters, and more frugal and stubborn. The Maine Yankee was historically the most isolated inhabitant of the three northern New England states. Roads connecting Maine to the outside were traditionally poor. "Downeasters," as they have come to be called, had to put up with bad weather and unyielding terrain. This may explain why they're commonly characterized as crusty and

quirky; they have a reputation for being down to earth and for saying little beyond what counts.

Rhode Island and Connecticut Yankees are perhaps less distinctive than other old New Englanders. The original populations of these states were the products of the first emigrations from Massachusetts, and today these states tend to be conservative. Unlike those in Massachusetts, the original Yankees here retained political control long after the waves of 19th- and 20th-century immigration greatly reduced their proportion of the areas' total populations.

After the Civil War, New Englanders knew their region was in decline and their numbers were dwindling. Nevertheless, they continue to think of themselves as the essential representatives of the nation's most cherished values and today remain convinced that they symbolize all that is best about their country.

> **MOTHER TONGUE**
>
> Until recently, a form of Elizabethan English was spoken in Washington County's Beals Islands in Maine, as well as in parts of Appalachia and the Ozarks.

African-Americans

The first African-Americans in New England came to Boston from the West Indies in 1638 as "perpetual servants." Within a century, slavery was well implanted in the region: by 1752, Boston's 5,000 African-Americans constituted 10 percent of the population. That percentage declined dramatically during the Revolution, when Tory masters fled the region, removing their entire households. By the end of the 18th century, Massachusetts abolished slavery, and Connecticut soon followed.

In Boston, a thriving black community congregated on the northern slope of Beacon Hill. Though poor, it was organized and ambitious. About 2 percent of the population were doctors, ministers, teachers, or lawyers. Several fraternal organizations were founded to serve as a safety net for the indigent. The most famous, the African Society, founded in 1796 as a mutual-aid and charity organization, mirrored Puritan morality. Black-owned shops served as informal community centers, and black churches helped bring the community together. Ministers were looked up to as leaders, and towering above them were figures such as anti-slavery activist Jehial C. Bemon.

Although blacks in 19th-century Boston rarely lived outside their own quarter, they did mingle freely. Black and white laborers drank together in North End taverns, and after 1855, when schools were desegregated, children of both races studied together. Black students attended Harvard before the Civil War. Freemen laborers could be found in every New England industry, especially along the coast. Often half of crews of whaling vessels were African-American, and black labor contributed largely to the construction of Providence and New Haven.

As the vanguard of the Abolitionist movement, Massachusetts was unique in allowing blacks to stand for a political party (the Abolitionist Free-Soil Party in 1850) in elections to the state legislature. Their ability to excel was never in question, partly because of the accomplishments of such prominent figures as John Swett Rock, an abolitionist, doctor, and lawyer, and Charles Remond, the first black to argue a case before the Supreme Court. Over the past century, Massachusetts has produced an extraordinary number of Civil Rights activists.

Despite such efforts, the decline suffered by the region after the Civil War was particularly devastating to those struggling to subsist as porters, laborers, janitors and household domestics. Even well into the 1950s, few gains were made in improving the lot of this underclass. Although the number of blacks holding white-collar jobs in Boston nearly doubled between

and Charlestown. Adding to the tension is fierce competition for jobs in a local economy hit hard by the recession of the early 1990s. However, the era of equal opportunity, a long time in coming, is quickly becoming a reality, as evidenced by such African-American role models as newscaster Liz Walker and Cambridge mayor Kenneth Reeves.

Connecticut is the only other New England state with a large and long-standing black population. A small number arrived in the colonial days, and a great many relocated from the South in the 1870s to work on tobacco farms. Like Boston, Connecticut cities have had

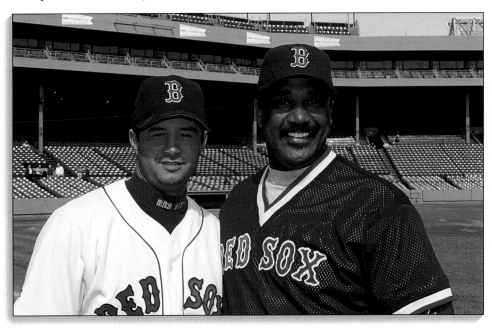

1950 and 1970, the vast majority remained poor and resolutely working class. In recent decades, Boston's black community – now representing roughly a quarter of the population – has made considerable strides, but inequities persist.

To this day, Boston retains vivid memories of ugly race riots touched off by a federal judge's order in 1974 to desegregate schools through busing. Although the situation has calmed down considerably, inter-racial strife is still rampant in Boston's more clannish neighborhoods, such as "Southie" (the Irish stronghold of South Boston)

LEFT: father and son at a Connecticut apple festival.
RIGHT: Red Sox star John Valentin and coach Jim Rice.

their share of racial tensions. Busing met with opposition in New Haven and Hartford, and in the summer of 1967 these and many other towns were shaken by riots. Despite enduring obstacles, blacks are at last making inroads in politics and other areas of influence.

Irish power

The Potato Famine of 1845–50 killed at least a million people in Ireland, and drove another million to seek better conditions elsewhere. Many came to Massachusetts. No precise figures are available, but one statistic claims that by 1860, 61 percent of Boston's population was foreign-born. Virtually all of these people would have been Irish, the only immigrant group to come in large numbers at that time.

The Irish did not receive a warm welcome. Not unlike the British oppressors back home, Yankees showed considerable contempt for Catholicism, and, in turn, the Irish felt little sympathy for the idealism of the reform-minded Yankees. During the Civil War, Irish immigrants in Boston rioted when faced with a draft for the freeing of slaves, a cause in which they had no specific interest.

POLITICAL FAMILY

The political life of the Kennedys began with John F. Fitzgerald, known as "Honey-Fitz," grand-father of John F. Kennedy. He became mayor of Boston in 1905.

The Irish community in Massachusetts grew at an extremely rapid rate. Before long, the Irish went into politics, with great success. The first Irish-born mayor of Boston was elected in 1884, and the first Irish governor took office in 1918. Between the world wars, the Irish controlled both Boston and state politics. Economic as well as political clout was assured once Joe Kennedy, the father of the late President John F. Kennedy, penetrated the Yankee stronghold of finance and banking on Boston's State Street.

Middle-class Irish have long been assimilated into the mainstream of Boston and Massachusetts life. Blue-collar Irish are a different story.

Especially in South Boston and Charlestown, the Irish have fiercely maintained the separateness both of their communities and of their ethnic identity. To this day, many residents identify more with their neighborhoods than with the city as a whole.

In South Boston pubs, Irish-Americans sing a song called "Southie Is My Home Town." This "tribalism," as it has been called, erupted in 1974 when "Southie" rioted over busing. The Irish felt that their neighborhoods were gravely threatened, and busing had been forced on them by upper-class Yankees, their traditional enemies.

Eighteen months after busing began, public schools had lost one-third of their white pupils. In 1980, Melvin King, a black who was then state representative, ascribed racial hatred in Boston to the historical relationship between Irish Catholics and "WASPs" (White Anglo-Saxon Protestants): "The Irish still view themselves as a persecuted minority and therefore don't play the positive role in race relations that one would expect from people who experienced bigotry."

French-Canadians

French-Canadians have been emigrating to New England since the middle of the last century. Although there are more French-Canadians in Massachusetts than in any other New England state, their influence is most evident in New Hampshire, where they make up as much as a quarter of the population; and in Maine, where 15 percent of the people are only one or two generations from Canadian birth.

The Canadians came to work in the textile mills, and (in Maine) as lumberjacks. More than any other group in New England, they have clung to their ethnic identity and maintained a remarkable degree of distinctiveness. They are strongly Catholic, and they still consider French their first language, although most children attend English-speaking schools.

French-Canadians in Maine live together in close-knit communities, have their own radio station, and frequently visit Quebec. Although French-Canadians have been slower than some other groups to move up the social and economic scale, they have a reputation for being hardworking and thrifty, and for keeping to their own.

The Italian and Jewish influx

Italians came to the United States in the first decades of the 20th century, most of them as poor peasants from southern Italy and Sicily. Many of them settled in Massachusetts and Rhode Island. Italians and Irish have traditionally been rivals in Massachusetts, the Italians tending to vote with the Yankee Republicans, the Irish with the Democrats. Despite the incursions of gentrification, Italians – representing a tenth of the city's population – have managed to preserve a distinctive village subculture in certain areas, such as Boston's North End and East Boston.

> **BRANDEIS UNIVERSITY**
>
> In 1948, Brandeis University was established in Waltham, near Boston. This was thanks largely to the fund-raising efforts of the Jewish business community.

The Italians are among the wealthiest ethnic groups in the state, having made their money in law, real estate, construction, and a variety of other businesses. The success of the Italian community in Rhode Island is reflected in the career of John O. Pastore, the first Italian-American governor, later a senator.

Jewish settlers were among the earliest colonists: a community was established in Newport, Rhode Island, in 1658, with the help of Puritan dissident Roger Williams. The first families, from Holland, were Sephardics, descendants of exiles expelled from Spain at the end of the 15th century. Nineteen years after arriving in Newport, they organized North America's second congregation (the first was in New York). Free of the restrictions imposed on them in the Old World, they prospered in Newport.

The Newport community began to dissolve around the beginning of the 19th century as members emigrated to other parts of the country. For 100 years, there was little Jewish presence in New England, mainly because of the intolerance and rigidity of the Protestant Yankees. But by the end of the century, Boston had become a much more ethnically and religiously diverse place, and so Jews from Eastern Europe began to settle there in large numbers.

By 1910, 42,000 East Europeans, mostly Jewish, lived in the Boston area. Ten years later 10 percent of Boston's population was Jewish. Jews have made their mark in Boston, notably in education.

LEFT: capitalism in action at a Grateful Dead concert in Foxboro, Massachusetts.
RIGHT: country cook and friend.

Other late arrivals

New England boasts pockets of small ethnic groups which contribute greatly to the region's diversity. Among the more unusual are the Arabic-speaking Syrian-Lebanese of Rhode Island, Christians who fled the religious persecution by the Turks at the beginning of the 20th century. Portuguese communities exist along the coast, in such fishing ports as New Bedford and Provincetown. These Portuguese arrived in the middle of the 19th century from the Azores, as

whaling hands picked up by American ships. When whaling foundered, they shifted to fishing and into the textile mills.

The 1988 presidential campaign of second-generation Greek Michael Dukakis, though unsuccessful, is just one example of New England's growing acceptance of "outsiders." In the 1990s, among the newcomers making inroads in New England are large numbers of Hispanics and Asians; in Boston, these groups represent 11 and 5 percent of the population.

The transition may not always be easy, but the presence of these groups signals how a region once regarded as inflexible has been enriched by an ever-expanding ethnic diversity. ❑

THE PURITAN TRADITION

The Puritans regarded discipline and hard work as spiritual values, and it was those characteristics which laid the firm foundations of New England

The Puritans did more than settle New England; they created it. Out of the Calvinistic doctrines regarding humanity's inherent evil and the predestination of the soul grew a society that was stern and uncompromising. At its best, the Puritans' was a hard creed, an ultimate faith that required everyone – from the most prominent minister to the humblest child – to strain toward an ineffable God. Puritans argued that humans, in their fallen state, could never know God and could thus never truly know the state of their own souls. Salvation came not through human action, but through God's mysterious grace. Abject though we human creatures may be, we must always examine our conscience, always repent our inevitable sin, always attempt to lead a just life.

Spiritual values

The Puritans' difficult faith stood them in good stead: regarding discipline and hard work as spiritual values, these early settlers labored long for the greater glory of God – and incidentally accumulated wealth and built prosperous communities. At their worst, the Puritans came to identify worldly success with godliness, nonconformity with devil-worship. Their faith found little room for gentleness or pleasure.

The many world-class schools and colleges found in New England stand as tangible reminders of that legacy. Education was essential to the Puritans' vision of what their new society in America was to be. Most of the settlers were well educated; four officers of the Massachusetts Bay Colony – John Winthrop, Sir Richard Saltonstall, Isaac Johnson, and John Humphrey – had attended Cambridge University. For them, the journey to the New World was more than an adventure to a new frontier; it was a chance to transport their old society in purified form to a new land. Discontented in a country where they were persecuted for their

religious practices, they came to America to build an ideal society, their "city on a hill." These men knew that unless they provided for the education of clergymen, they might quickly lose sight of the New (and perfect) England.

In America, as in England, class distinctions were important. But the Puritans, eschewing such worldly signs of status as expensive clothes and fancy carriages, had to devise other more subtle ways of indicating social class. Thus, the title "Master" was reserved exclusively for educated men.

A society in which education established one's credentials before God and the world was destined to develop an impressive school system. As early as 1635, Boston voted a declaration that "our brother, Mr Philemon Pormont shall be intreated to become scholemaster for teaching and noutering of children with us." He established Boston Latin School, the country's first secondary school and still one of Boston's finest high schools. In 1642, the General Court

---

LEFT: guns and God – early settlers go to worship.
RIGHT: John Winthrop, the Cambridge-educated Puritan leader.

of the Bay Colony required every town to see to the education of its youth. By 1671, all colonies but Rhode Island, ever the renegade, had instituted compulsory education.

Higher education

Still, the settlers had yet to provide their colony with an institution of higher learning. In 1636, the Bay Colony's General Court voted £40 toward a public "school or college." What was then the village of Newtowne, across the Charles River from Boston, was chosen as the site for the institution, which opened that same year as Newtowne College. In 1638, a

other Harvard graduates – all Congregational ministers – founded the Collegiate School in Saybrook, Connecticut, in 1701. The school was renamed Yale College in honor of its benefactor, Elihu Yale, when it moved to New Haven in 1716.

Nicholas Brown, who made his fortune in the molasses, rum, and slave trade, founded Rhode Island College as a Baptist school in 1764; it was renamed Brown University in 1804, upon its relocation to Providence. Reverend Eleazar Wheelock founded Dartmouth College in 1769 "for the education of Youth of the Indian Tribes" as well as for "English Youth and Others."

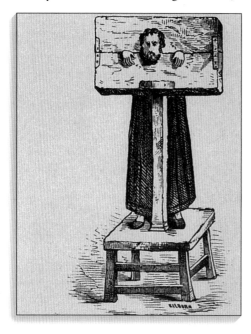

newly arrived young Charlestown minister named John Harvard, a graduate of Emmanuel College at Cambridge, died and left his 400-volume library and half of his estate to the college. In 1638 it was renamed Harvard in his honor, and Newtowne was renamed Cambridge to signify the community's new role.

For the rest of the 17th century, the college served primarily as a training ground for the Puritan clergy. At the outset of the 18th century, however, Harvard, feeling the effects of Enlightenment, liberalized its curriculum and added the teachings of Locke and Newton. Decrying the change in their alma mater's educational philosophy, James Pierpont and several

In 1778, Samuel Phillips and his uncle, Dr John Phillips, complaining of "a growing neglect of youth in our time," founded the Phillips Academy at Andover, Massachusetts. Several years later, Dr Phillips established a similar school, the Phillips Exeter Academy in Exeter, New Hampshire. Exeter's charter illuminates the Puritan mind: the school's purpose was "to promote piety and virtue" in its students and "to learn them the great and real business of living."

Proselytizing through persecution

A far less benign expression of Puritan didacticism emerged in the Salem witch trials of 1692.

Since its founding in 1626, the town (whose name derives, ironically, from *shalom*, the Hebrew word for peace) had never been a bastion of tolerance and good will: it was from Salem that Roger Williams, the founder of Rhode Island, had been exiled for preaching religious freedom.

THE CRUCIBLE

Arthur Miller's celebrated 1953 play, *The Crucible*, is based on the Salem witch trials.

The townspeople's rigid ways took a destructive turn when Tituba, a Barbados slave serving the household of Salem's minister, Samuel Parris, began regaling his daughter, Elizabeth, and niece, Abigail Williams, with vivid accounts of

examine the girls and, after medicine failed to cure them, he diagnosed them as victims of witchcraft.

The Rev. Mr Parris suggested that Tituba might be their tormentor, and the slave was charged with witchcraft. In confessing, under pain of torture, she gave a lurid account of how a tall man from Boston, accompanied by witches, had molested the girls. Satan himself, she claimed, had ordered her to murder the girls, and other witches had beaten her for her refusal to comply; she merely tormented them, trying to abate

voodoo. Fascinated, Elizabeth and Abigail invited a handful of their friends to listen to Tituba's tales. Meetings of such a nature, being strictly forbidden in Puritan Salem, held an illicit appeal that the girls must have found difficult to resist, but no doubt they also found their guilty pleasure difficult to live with, for all soon began to exhibit bizarre behavior: they would crawl on the floor, making choking sounds, and cry out that needles were piercing their flesh. The town doctor was called in to

her own pain. In her stories, she pointed a finger at two women unpopular in the village, Sarah Osborne and Sarah Good, who were charged with everything from bewitching cattle to using voodoo dolls. Enflamed by the oratory of such self-promoting preachers as Cotton Mather, subsequent accusations spread like wildfire. Ultimately, 400 people ended up accused – many of them marginal members of society, whose lack of prosperity the Puritans took to mean a lack of godliness.

Imprisoned in cold, damp cells, several of the accused women died while awaiting trial. Of those found guilty in Salem, 19 were hanged between June and September, and many more

FAR LEFT: a pillory, designed for public humiliation.
LEFT AND ABOVE: the trials of Mrs Hutchinson (left) and George Jacobs in Salem's era of Puritan hysteria.

might have been sacrificed had Governor General Sir William Phips not returned from the north woods, where he had been fighting an alliance of French and Native Americans, and put a stop to the madness. In December 1692, he ordered all the suspects released – including his own wife.

Always ready to discover depravity in someone else, the Puritans sat in eager judgment on the accused. Unrelenting in their desire to purge their world of evil and in their arrogant belief in their own righteousness, they sent innocents to their death. Too late, the Salemites repented of their actions: in 1693, the Salem jurors wrote that they begged the forgiveness of everyone who had been harmed by their actions.

A transcendentalist manqué

The gradual liberalization of New England's colleges in the 18th century gave way to a true intellectual flowering in the 19th century. Flushed with the success of the Revolutionary War and the founding of the nation, growing prosperous from the lucrative China trade, the Puritan temperament was ready for a transformation. Casting off the dour, joyless outlook of their Puritan forebears, New England's intelligentsia readily embraced the sweet optimism

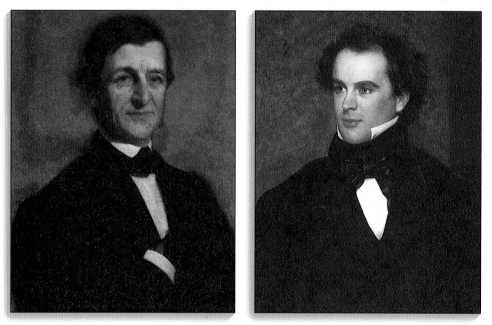

NATHANIEL HAWTHORNE

The descendant of Salem Puritans, Hawthorne grew up with a family legend of a Judge Hawthorne who, as a magistrate at the witchcraft trials, was cursed by a woman he convicted. Hawthorne would later use this story in *The House of the Seven Gables*. In fact, much of Hawthorne's work was drawn from real life. In the 1836 tale, *The Minister's Black Veil*, the protagonist explains: "If I hide my face for sorrow, there is cause enough, and if I cover it for secret sin, what mortal might not do the same." Hawthorne was no doubt familiar with the story of the Rev. Joseph Moody of York, Maine, who, after accidentally shooting and killing a friend on a hunting trip, became morbidly frightened of

having his friend's family and fiancée look upon him, and therefore covered his face with a black handkerchief.

Young Goodman Brown, one of Hawthorne's greatest tales, also draws on his Salem heritage. In what may be a dream, Brown, wandering in the dark forest, comes upon the devil, who leads him to a clearing where villagers are engaged in devil-worship; among the congregation is Faith, Goodman's wife. In this tale, Hawthorne depicts a world sunk in evil: if Goodman Brown's vision is true, the devil rules; if not, and if Goodman has imagined innocent people in Satan's service, he reveals, like the Salem Puritans, the depth of his own corruption.

of transcendentalism, a mystical philosophy which argued the existence of an Oversoul unifying all creation, and which preached the primacy of insight over reason and the inherent goodness of humankind.

The movement spawned several experiments in living, the best known being Henry David Thoreau's solitary retreat on Walden Pond, and short-lived communal farms at Brook Farm in Concord and Fruitlands in Harvard. Led by Ralph Waldo Emerson, the transcendentalist movement attracted some of the brightest minds of the day – including, for a short while, Nathaniel Hawthorne, one of the founding members of Brook Farm. His disillusionment with this experiment reinforced his essentially somber cast of mind, however. Far from being sweetly optimistic, his writing broods on human sin.

Cradle of reformation

As if to live down the small-mindedness of their predecessors, the New England philosophers and legislators of the 19th century stood in the very vanguard of political reform. Having abolished slavery themselves by the end of the 18th century, high-minded New Englanders dedicated themselves to nationwide abolition. William Lloyd Garrison founded his weekly newspaper the *Liberator* in Boston in 1831 (not all shared his views at that time: he was nearly killed by a Boston mob in 1835) and persisted until 1865, when the 13th amendment was finally passed. Joining him in the struggle were writers such as Harriet Beecher Stowe, who delivered one of the Abolitionist movement's most effective tracts in the form of her best-selling 1852 novel, *Uncle Tom's Cabin*. After the Civil War, New England's reformists turned their attention to the labor abuses brought on by the Industrial Revolution and to the role of women in society. The first women's college to open in the US was Vassar Female College, founded in Poughkeepsie, New York, in 1861. By 1879, four outstanding colleges for women had been established in Massachusetts: Smith, Wellesley, Mount Holyoke, and Radcliffe.

Despite this growing willingness to entertain change – reinforced by decades of stability and

prosperity – remnants of the Puritan strain persisted. For the most part, New England remained a deeply moral, and occasionally moralistic, society. At their worst, New Englanders banned books they deemed offensive to public taste (a practice their descendants now deplore among less enlightened, fundamentalist backwaters). They considered theater – and worse yet, actors – a pernicious influence on impressionable minds. Blue laws, first introduced in Connecticut in 1781 to control public and private conduct, especially on the Sabbath, enjoyed regular revivals in the 19th and 20th centuries and linger to this day in

very watered-down form; in Massachusetts, for instance, on Sundays liquor stores are closed and would-be imbibers must wait till noon to be served at a bar.

This seems a relatively small inconvenience to pay as homage to the settlers who, with admirable fortitude if little sense of fun, established so firm a foundation for the New World. And just as the Puritans struggled mightily to maintain a spiritual purity, New Englanders today are in the forefront of the drive to preserve some degree of ecological integrity. The Puritans' conservative zeal lives on – in what has become, ironically enough, one of the country's most progressive regions. ❑

FAR LEFT: Ralph Waldo Emerson.
LEFT: Nathaniel Hawthorne. **RIGHT:** keeping crafts alive at Plimoth Plantation Pilgrims Settlement.

THE TRADITION OF FRESH FOOD

Seafood remains one of the New England classics, but the influence of
immigrants and new traditions are making their mark

The Pilgrims would not have known what to make of our mania for lobster. They considered the crustaceans fit only for pig food, or bait; well into the late 19th century, boatloads of lobsters sold for pennies, and prisoners rioted at the prospect of yet another lobster dinner. New England's lobster harvest

New England's fabled clam chowder got its name from the French settlers of Breton in Canada, who simmered their soups in a *chaudière* (cauldron). Such long, slow cooking is needed to render large hard-shell quahogs (pronounced "co-hogs") palatable. The small and medium-size versions – cherrystones and

is today a $150 million-a-year enterprise. And while creative preparations abound, menus still feature traditional boiled lobsters and "lobster rolls" – toasted hot dog buns filled with chunks of lobster meat, tossed with celery and mayonnaise.

The settlers weren't quite so blind to the appeal of oysters, however. As early as 1601, Samuel de Champlain had singled out the area now known as Wellfleet, on Cape Cod, for its exceptional beds. He named the harbor "Porte aux huitres." And to this day, tiny Wellfleet, as well as the town of Cotuit, also on Cape Cod, is world-renowned for these home-grown delicacies.

littlenecks – are delectable served raw, on the half-shell. Soft-shell, longneck clams – commonly known as "steamers" – are a favored repast all along the coast, dipped first in brine (to wash off the grit), then melted butter. Clam shacks fire up their fry-o-lators to prepare another favorite: clams batter-coated and fried.

Clambakes were once a New England tradition, especially on Cape Cod. The customary procedure was to lay out a stone pit on the beach, build a driftwood fire, cover the hot stones with seaweed, add clams and their accompaniments (typically, lobsters, potatoes, corn on the cob), and then top it all off with more seaweed, a sailcloth tarp, and plenty of sand, leaving the whole to bake for about an hour. Most restaurants these days dispense with clambake *per se*, and just serve what's called a "shore dinner" – steamed.

It was the abundant cod, however, that initially lured English fishermen, and eventually settlers, to this land. Fillet of young cod, called scrod (from the Dutch *schrood*, for "a piece cut off"), still graces traditional menus.

Exposure to European traditions has introduced two relatively new seafood treats. Mussels, long ignored by New England restaurants, are now very nearly ubiquitous, usually served *marinière* or poached in white wine.

Another specialty is available only a few weeks each year. Enthusiasts await late spring to feast on shad roe, from the Connecticut River. As the poet Ogden Nash wrote, "I'm sure Europe never had/A fish as tasty as the shad."

Unlikely elixirs

Cranberries – so named by Dutch settlers who thought the flowers resembled cranes – are one of the few fruits native to North America (among the others are Concord grapes and blueberries, a cash crop in Maine). Native Americans used the sassamanesh – "bitter berries" – as a dye, a poultice, and as food,

pounded with venison to make "pemmican" (meat cakes) or sweetened with maple sap. Long before the need for Vitamin C was recognized, whalers would set off to sea with a barrel of cranberries to prevent scurvy. Today, visitors can tour Massachusetts cranberry bogs and celebrate fall festivals from Plymouth to Nantucket.

Maple syrup

New Englanders have also continued the Indian practice of boiling maple sap into syrup, and Vermont is America's leading producer of maple syrup. The trees of the "sugarbush" are tapped in early spring, when just the right

Seasonal bay scallops have always enjoyed greater gourmet cachet than the larger, tougher sea scallop but, until recently, restaurants invariably threw away the tastiest part, serving only the adductor muscle. Thanks to the efforts of scallop cultivator Rod Taylor of Fairhaven, Massachusetts, bay scallops are now available year-round, and the more adventurous fine restaurants have begun serving them whole, whether on the half-shell or cooked.

LEFT: interpreters at Plimoth Plantation prepare a meal the settlers would have eaten.
ABOVE: Randy Cross prepares breakfast during a canoe expedition.

combination of cold nights and warm days sets the thin sap rising. However modern the equipment, it still takes 40 gallons of sap to boil down to just one gallon of syrup. Visitors can watch the process at dozens of commercial sugar houses.

Beer, wine, and cider

With no access to safe drinking water, the Pilgrims – adults and children alike – had no choice but to drink beer (the alcohol content kept the microbes in check). Today they could travel around New England and never wander far from a microbrewery. Popular regional beer

makers include Vermont's Catamount, New Hampshire's Red Hook and Smuttynose, Maine's Gary's, and Massachusetts' Boston Beer Company (makers of Sam Adams), Ipswich, Harpoon, and Atlantic Coast (home of Tremont brews). Many of these producers open their doors to visitors. In Boston, visitors can join Brew Pub Tours.

It's even possible to find good locally produced wine: New England's notoriously rocky soil is at long last proving good for something. Many vineyards are still in the fledgling stage, but at least three have a proven track record: Stonington Vineyards in Stonington, Connecticut; Sakonnet Vineyards in Little Compton,

Rhode Island; and Chicama Vineyards on Martha's Vineyard, Massachusetts. Some New England vintners are turning other indigenous fruits into novelty wines: sample the Plymouth Bay Winery's cranberry wine or Nashoba Valley Winery's blueberry and apple creations.

Apple seeds, which came to New England with the Pilgrims in 1620, contributed another popular beverage – apple cider. This fresh-pressed apple juice was a favorite drink in colonial times and was also converted into "hard" or alcoholic cider. President John Adams claimed that a tankard of hard cider every morning calmed his stomach and alleviated gas. Hard cider has enjoyed a trendy revival in the 1990s, led by New England brands such as Woodchuck from Cavendish, Vermont. Sweet cider, often served hot with cinnamon or spiked with rum, makes a warming treat after a long day of leaf peeping or traversing the ski slopes.

The classic diner

New England is home to one of the original fast food restaurants – the diner. First created in Providence in 1872 as a horse-drawn lunch wagon, diners grew into a major manufacturing business in Worcester, Massachusetts, in the early part of this century. Many traditional New England diners serve breakfast all day – eggs any style, hash browns, pancakes – while waitresses circle with bottomless coffee pots, asking "Warm it up, hon?" Yet even diners have not escaped gentrification into college hangouts or more upscale incarnations: some diner-style spots mix four types of cheese into the classic baked macaroni dish or spike their French toast batter with amaretto.

Specialty products

A new wave of "back-to-landers" has created a trendy land of plenty, raising deer for venison, goats for farmstead chèvre, trout and salmon for smoking. In Connecticut, the actor Paul Newman has claimed a third of the $3.3 billion salad dressing market with Newman's Own, profits from which go to charity. In Vermont, some 300 specialty food producers whip up everything from "Putney pasta" to salsa and tortilla chips from Stowe; the entrepreneurs behind Ben & Jerry's ice cream empire, in Waterbury, parlayed a $5 correspondence school diploma into a business grossing $500 million a year.

New traditions

Throughout New England, flavors that would previously have been considered "exotic" have entered the mainstream food vocabulary, in part due to the waves of immigration that have brought new culinary traditions to the area. The Italian immigrants who settled in the late 1800s and early 1900s left an indelible stamp on the region's food. Italian-American restaurants serving pizza, spaghetti and meatballs can be found in countless New England towns, while

> **A NEW ENGLAND THING**
>
> The United States currently leads the world in per capita ice cream consumption, and New Englanders are said to eat 14 pints more of the stuff every year than the average American.

Since 1960, almost 80 percent of immigrants to the US have come from Asia, Latin America, and the Caribbean. New England towns boast Chinese, Japanese, Thai, Vietnamese, Puerto Rican, Mexican, Haitian, and many other ethnic eateries, where clams in black bean sauce and lobster sautéed with ginger and scallions blend local ingredients into the classic cuisines of their home countries.

This melting pot of flavors has also turned into more upscale fusion cuisine, where

urban enclaves – including Boston's North End, Providence's Federal Hill, and Hartford's Franklin Avenue – add more contemporary Italian regional cooking.

In several Rhode Island and Massachusetts cities, home to large numbers of Portuguese-Americans, the land of the bean and the cod has been transformed into the home of the feijão and the bacalhau. Doughy sweet bread, spicy linguiça (pork sausage), and all manner of salt cod preparations are among the Portuguese contributions to New England tables.

celebrity chefs are transforming traditional New England products into creative new preparations. Adventurous eaters can indulge in salad of Maine rock crab with lobster knuckles and fried taro, crispy squash risotto cakes, pumpkin ravioli with mussels *marinière*, lightly fried lobster with lemongrass and Thai basil, ginger barbecued skate wing served over spicy jalapeño slaw with Boston baked beans, or seared scallops in cider sauce.

But tradition endures. Those boiled lobsters, that baked cod, and that paper cup overflowing with fried clams, washed down with a cool frappé (that's Massachusetts-speak for milk shake), remain New England culinary favorites. ❏

LEFT: fresh lobster on offer in Rhode Island.
ABOVE: creating a stir with cranberries.

THE MARITIME TRADITION

The sea has always been important to New Englanders – first for transport and trade and as a fishing ground, more recently for recreation

The little ship had been at sea for two months. It was November 1620, in the North Atlantic, not a kind season. The passengers and crew, more than 100 people, had squeezed into this one ship after its sister ship had proven unseaworthy. They were headed for the tiny English colonies in America.

At last, the call came: "Land ho!" The weary passengers who crowded the railings could barely make out the tops of several small islands on the horizon. As the ship drew closer, they discovered that the "islands" were actually hills arising above a long bar of sand. Weary from the months at sea and eager to set foot in the New World, the Pilgrims disembarked at the tip of Cape Cod to rest and reconnoiter. After five weeks on land, they set sail again for Virginia. But, battered by storms that seemed endless, the tiny yet sturdy barque *Mayflower* was driven across Cape Cod Bay and into the mainland at a place the Pilgrims named Plymouth.

A path to the New World

The sea had allowed early New Englanders to escape the spiritual confines of the old country. It had brought them to the New World. But it had not given them any choice about their landing place. Down through the centuries, the sea has written the history of New England and determined its people's destiny.

The sea could move people speedily between continents – or condemn them to a watery grave. It has toppled granite buildings, even torn away the land itself, and it has made men fabulously wealthy overnight. A rich merchant, pillar of his community, might come into his warehouse on Boston's Long Wharf one morning only to find that his entire fleet and all its cargo had been swept away and lost forever, and that he was no better than a beggar. Or a lonesome beachcomber slowly tracing the sinuous miles of Cape Cod's sandy shores might come upon 100 gold doubloons washed up only minutes before by a whim of the sea.

New Englanders have had no choice but to learn the sea's strict laws and abide by them. The sea brought them here, the sea nourished them and, if it did not destroy them, the sea even made them rich. Only one of the six New England states (Vermont) has no maritime coast. For the rest, the outlet to the sea is a source of continuing prosperity.

The first generation of Europeans in America all had the same "baptism by sea:" a two-month voyage across the stormy North Atlantic. Most of the settlers who came were landlubbers; many had never seen the ocean before. Shipbuilding was one of the first enterprises early colonists undertook. Ships maintained the connection to the homeland and provided an income from trade. The vast virgin forests of the New World supplied ready-at-hand materials for their construction. One hundred years after the Pilgrims stepped on Plymouth Rock, New England's coastal shipyards were launching a ship a day. With labor and lumber costs so cheap compared to those in England, American-made ships dominated the market.

For the early colonists, the sea brought news from home, fresh legions of colonists to do battle with the wilderness, and ships involved in the Triangular Trade (the transport of slaves, molasses, and rum between ports in Africa, the Caribbean, and New England). The vast virgin forests of colonial Maine seemed an inexhaustible storehouse of straight, lofty white pines for the masts of the Royal Navy. The fishing grounds along the coasts teemed with marine wealth.

THE "SACRED COD"

The "Sacred Cod" – a wooden effigy presented to the legislature by a Boston merchant in 1784 – was kept in the Massachusetts Colony House, and now hangs at the State House on Beacon Hill.

The whaling boom

The lamps of colonial New England were fired by vegetable and animal oils; candles were made from animal tallow. The light was dim and the lamps were smoky until someone made the discovery that blubber from a beached whale could be rendered, and the oil thus extracted would provide a clearer, brighter light.

Whales beached themselves frequently on the New England shores during the early colonial days, and whaling got its start

One of the first important acts of the Great and General Court of Massachusetts was to set standards for the regulation and encouragement of the fishing industry. Early on, fishing was seen as a prime source of the region's prosperity. In fact, many settlers came not so much to enjoy religious freedom as to catch fish. Codfish, high in protein, iodine, and Vitamin A, nourished and strengthened not just New England's colonists, but those in Mid-Atlantic and Southern towns and even in many ports of Europe.

LEFT: the port of Boston in 1768, before areas of the harbor on either side of Long Wharf were infilled.
ABOVE: a 19th-century lobsterman.

as a shore activity. Teams of townsfolk gathered whenever they saw a whale, tethering the creature to a stake to prevent the tide from taking it out to sea. The blubber was cut away, rendered in the kettles of a "tryworks" set up on the beach and transformed into a high-quality oil which could be burned in the town's lamps or traded for other goods.

The demand for this excellent oil became so great that fishermen, hoping to get rich from the sale of oil, began actively to pursue whales along the shore, thus initiating New England's famous whaling industry. The trade took a great leap forward in 1712, when Captain Christopher Hussey of Nantucket was blown off course into deep water and accidentally bagged the first sperm whale. Although it had teeth in lieu of coveted baleen – bony upper jaw slats useful as stays for collars and corsets – the spermaceti oil proved far superior to that of the already endangered "right" whale (so called because it was the right one to pursue). Nantucket whalers came to specialize in the pursuit of this purer, lighter, and more profitable oil.

Whalers out of Nantucket and New Bedford pursued their mammoth quarry for months, even

SCRIMSHAW

Sailors on the whaling ships whiled away the hours making intricate carvings in whale-bone or teeth, etched in black, known as scrimshaw.

was the world's great proven oil reserve. For a closer look at this fascinating chapter in maritime history, see the last surviving whaler, the Charles W. Morgan, tied up at Mystic Seaport in Connecticut, or visit the whaling museums in Nantucket or New Bedford.

Watery highways

The sea formed the path from England to America, and served as the road system from one point in America to the next. In colonial times, roads were expensive to build and maintain, and the colonies did

years, as far as the Pacific, until their holds were filled with barrels of the oil that would fire the nation's lamps and illumine the capitals of Europe. The whaling ships served as complete processing plants. Once a whale was sighted, men pursued it in small dories, harpooned it, and then braced themselves for the "Nantucket sleighride" that followed. The hapless whale would drag the men in the dory many miles before exhausting itself. Tied up alongside the whaling ship, the whale carcass was stripped of blubber. Rendered in a tryworks right on deck, the oil was then stored in casks in the hold.

Until 1859, when petroleum-derived kerosene was discovered in Pennsylvania, the sea

not have the resources to establish a good system of roads. Nor did they have the need. Coastal freighters and passenger boats carried colonists and their wares from Boston to New York and Philadelphia. Every young American knows the story of Master Benjamin Franklin, a loaf of bread under each arm, arriving from Boston on the docks in Philadelphia, where he would make his fortune.

Dozens of boats out of Salem harbor headed for home with decks full of salt cod. But the enterprising captains headed south, where they unloaded their cod at Philadelphia or Annapolis and took on corn and flour, beans, and barrels of pork, which could be sold at a greater profit at home than could codfish. New England never produced such goods in sufficient quantities; cod it had in great abundance.

Though a boon to New England's maritime economy, the coastal trade, like fishing and whaling, was not an easy way to make a living. Every trip between Boston and ports to the south involved a voyage around Cape Cod, and the weather that had so discouraged the Pilgrims was a constant threat. Ships and men were regularly lost to the ravages of the sea.

Though fishing and the coastal trade helped New England employ its people and pay its bills, the region was not a rich one. Because New England always imported more goods than it exported, ways had to be found to balance the trade deficit. New endeavors were always welcomed, and Yankee ingenuity was always coming up with new ideas.

Merchants and sea captains from New England towns saw themselves as the world's transport agents: if they couldn't produce the goods from their rocky soil and primitive industries, they reasoned, at least they could carry across the oceans the goods produced by others. Like the whalers that roamed the world for years in search of their fortune, New England merchant vessels undertook long and arduous voyages to Europe, Africa, and the Orient. And it was not only the cargoes that were put up for sale: the ships themselves were frequently on the auctioning block, bringing added revenue to their builders back home in New England.

Trade was good to New England. While the pioneer towns of inland America were primitive and rough, New England seaports took on the polish of wealth and culture. Fortunes made at sea were translated into fine mansions and patronage of the arts. From the profits of their voyages, captains brought home art treasures, luxury goods, and curiosities from exotic destinations. The Peabody Essex Museum of Salem is filled with the incredible wealth that came to New England on returning merchant ships.

Clocks, shoes, and ice

As time went by, the new republic developed industries that produced goods for trade. Connecticut's household utensils, machines,

clocks, pistols, and rifles, plus shoes and cloth from Rhode Island and Massachusetts, ultimately made their way around the world.

Perhaps the most ingenious export of all was ice. Cut from ponds, rivers, and lakes, ice was packed in sawdust, loaded into fast clipper ships and sent off to Cuba, South America, and beyond. The rulers of the British Raj in India sipped drinks cooled by ice from New England. In exchange for a commodity that was free for the cutting, New Englanders brought back spices, fine porcelain, silks, and other items.

The volume of New England's trade soon fell behind that of the Southern ports along the

Atlantic and Gulf of Mexico coasts. But trade continued to be important in maintaining the region's economy and its cosmopolitan outlook.

The taming of the sea

The end of the 19th century saw profound changes in the way New Englanders put to sea. The speedy sloops, or clipper ships, with small holds, were economical only for high-profit items (such as ice). For a while, the profits shifted to larger, heavier craft such as the great schooners with four, five, and even six masts. But the magnificent six-masted schooners that could carry huge payloads of coal went nowhere when the wind died, and the

LEFT: mural of Mystic Seaport, Connecticut.
RIGHT: a ship is launched at Bath Iron Works, Maine.

newfangled steamships went anywhere on schedule. Steamships could sail around Cape Cod, ignoring the winds that had caused so much trouble since the time of the Pilgrims.

With the coming of steam came the railroads and the Atlantic and Pacific coasts were finally connected by steel rails. Where once the ships had sailed all the way around South America to reach California, rail transport steamed west in a straight line, undaunted by storms.

Yet transport by sea, for both goods and passengers, hung on in New England well into the 20th century. What finally laid it to rest was not the railroad but the highway.

Safer waves

Today, the sea is still a major source of income – and at a much lower price in lives lost to storms. Although yachts, motorboats, and fishing fleets fill the harbors, disasters at sea are a relative rarity. A century ago whole families, even most of a town, might be lost to a single ferocious storm. There are still tragedies at sea – oil tankers breached, pleasure craft wrecked, swimmers drowned – but stricter safety precautions and radio beacons and radar that pierce the fog help prevent many accidents.

The taming of the sea has allowed New Englanders to put it to other uses. Dependable passenger service by steamship opened up the coasts to vacation travelers in the early part of this century. Newport, Block Island, and Bar Harbor turned into flourishing resorts as soon as they became accessible swiftly, comfortably, and safely by sea.

These newer settlements are not the only ones to have benefited from the taming of the sea. Although the whalers and clipper ships may be gone, excepting a few rare survivors, the beautiful port towns built by the wealth of maritime commerce survive. Tourists come in droves to stroll among the handsome sea captains' houses of Nantucket, Edgartown, Salem, and Newport. Having seen the houses, they then explore in museums the world of the seafaring men who built them.

A salty playground

In other times, a New Englander either went to sea or remained a landlubber. Now every New Englander is part mariner, taking a motorboat or yacht out for a Sunday cruise or climbing aboard a launch for a tour of Boston Harbor. There is a direct service by sea between Boston and Provincetown each summer, and Nantucket, Martha's Vineyard, Block Island, and other islands are all served by ship.

In fact, New England's seacoast has become a major playground, and the variety of maritime sports seems limitless. As in so many other realms, the world of work has become the world of play, and occupations once perilous or tedious are now pursued just for fun. A hundred years ago, for example, "wreckers" used to trudge the beaches of New England with a keen eye for the remains of lost ships. Today, the beaches serve a distinctly different purpose. Forty miles (64 km) of Cape Cod's sandy beaches have been set aside as the Cape Cod National Seashore, one of the great tourist attractions of New England. The beaches of Connecticut, Rhode Island, New Hampshire, and Maine continue to attract visitors from near and far.

The whalers that sailed out of New Bedford and Nantucket are long gone. Or are they? Boats from a dozen New England ports still head out each day in search of whales, but now it's the camera lens and not the harpoon that "captures" the whale for good. Whale-watching cruises are among the most popular summer activities at sea. It's ironic, and heartening, that the leviathans that once made New England "oil-rich" should still be helping its economy.

Cruising the coast

Perhaps the clearest indication of the taming of the sea is this: the perilous voyage undertaken by the Pilgrims in 1620 is now done for sport. Transatlantic yacht racing began in 1866 when the *Henrietta* raced the *Vesta* to England. In 1851, the schooner *America* won the Royal Yacht Squadron Cup, and the America's Cup became the great event of yachting with the first race held in Newport in 1870. The beauty and science of yacht design and racing is pursued passionately in Newport and in dozens of other ports along the coast.

New England's waters are particularly suited to yachting: Long Island, off the coast of Connecticut, protects spacious Long Island Sound; and Cape Cod Bay has provided calm sailing ever since the days of the Pilgrims. With the cutting of the Cape Cod Canal and the establishment of the Intra-coastal Waterway, coastal cruising has been made safer and more enjoyable than ever before.

The highpoint of coastal cruising in New England is undoubtedly the rocky shore of Maine. The jagged coast, cut with bays, inlets, coves, peninsulas, and islands, is some 3,500 miles (5,600 km) long, and blessed with exceptional beauty. One of the most thrilling ways to see it is aboard a windjammer out of Rockport or Camden. Since 1935, these sturdy sailing ships have taken amateur crews out into the cold waters to experience New England's maritime heritage at first hand.

By the late 1980s it had become clear to lawmakers that the New England fishing industry was on its way to over fishing itself into non-existence. Massachusetts fishermen of New Bedford, Provincetown and Gloucester were forced to go farther and farther out to the sea to catch fewer and fewer fish. And those they did find were smaller; mature stocks were dwindling. Although many fishermen – a fiercely independent lot – disagreed, laws were enacted to close and monitor the once fertile fishing banks. Some fishermen trained their sites on more abundant, less glamorous fish: formerly overlooked species began to show up on menus in fancy presentations. Others reluctantly took government subsidies for job

retraining and switched careers. Some sold their boats. Today, it looks as if the regulation is working. Mature stocks are starting to return and fishing banks have been reopened – with strict limits placed on the amount and size of fish that can be caught.

New England's relationship with the sea is changing. The codfish has yielded to the computer as the most important element in New England's economic life; the schooner and whaler have yielded to the yacht and, more recently, sailboard. Over the years ahead New Englanders will no doubt discover new ways to enjoy and profit from the sea. ❑

SCIENCE OF THE SEA

Scientists say we have barely begun to tap the wealth of the sea, and the potential is enormous. To explore that potential, New England has its own world-class research facilities at Woods Hole, Massachusetts, just south of Falmouth. Woods Hole attracts tens of thousands of tourists each summer, most passing through to board the ferryboats to Martha's Vineyard. However, a knowledgeable few come to see what's new at the National Marine Fisheries Service, established in 1871; at the Marine Biological Laboratory, founded in 1888; or the Woods Hole Oceanographic Institute, begun with a $2.5 million Rockefeller grant in 1930.

LEFT: the tide has turned and the future is beginning to look healthier for fishing once more.
RIGHT: a young yachtsman enjoying the ocean.

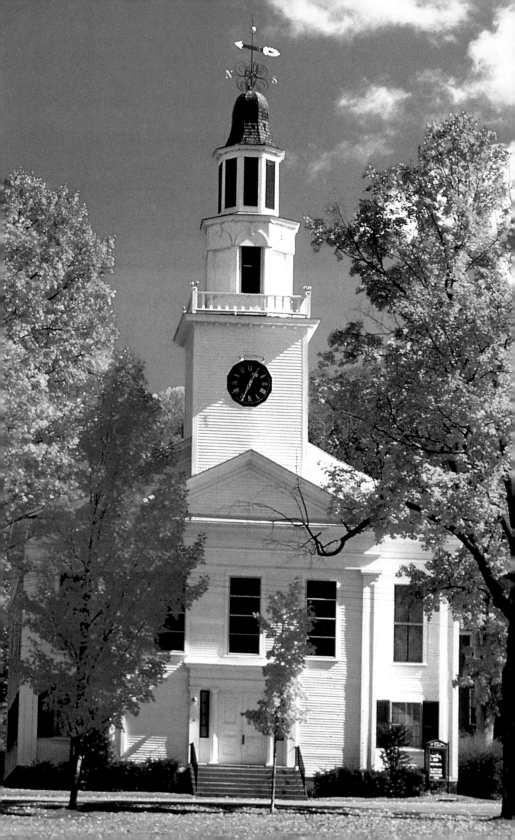

THE ARCHITECTURAL TRADITION

Shingles and clapboards, gables and steeples – the buildings are so graceful
and sturdy that it's no wonder conservation is an important issue

Buildings capture the essence of New England's character; they sum up what was at once noble and humble about the ambitions of the region's settlers. And the charm of the old houses and churches is not lost on today's New Englanders, whose tireless efforts have preserved much of the architectural traditions of the previous centuries.

To learn New England, read its buildings, for they tell rich tales about the lives of their builders and inhabitants. Always aware of its heroic past, New England has retained enough of its architectural heritage to sketch a vivid picture of a distinguished history. Studying its buildings will not only stimulate the mind and seize the imagination; it will delight the eye.

17th-century practicality

Beauty is not a strong point of 17th-century New England homes, although there is something attractive about the stark simplicity of the early one-room dwellings built by the first several generations of settlers. Heavy and medieval though these houses may appear, they are a testament to the unaffected motivations of the Puritans. Stylistic vestiges of English country homes governed building design and construction, but none of these was applied solely for decorative effect: there is virtually no ornamental indulgence in the 1640 Whipple House in Ipswich or the *c.*1641 Wing Fort House in East Sandwich, both in Massachusetts. After all, when one was living for the glory of God and laboring for community good, there was little room for excess.

The Whipple and Wing Fort houses and the handful like them were nothing more than offspring of homes the Pilgrims had left behind in southeastern England. Simple oblong boxes, they were framed painstakingly and filled with the wattle-and-daub that on half-timbered Eng-

lish country homes was left visible. Clapboards, providing a blanket of protection against New England winters, created a stern look, relieved only by small, randomly placed windows. The steep roof and the massive central chimney, shared by the two lower and two upper rooms, crowned the house with an authoritative air.

In very early homes, the upper floor extended slightly beyond the lower. The 1683 Capen House in Topsfield, Massachusetts, offers a marvelous example. This overhang, recalling English townhouses where the lower floor stepped back in deference to the street, was a feature that was dropped as designs began to allow for expansion and reflect the colonists' growing sense of security. Diamond-paned windows were replaced by double-hung ones that brightened the interior and lightened the facade. Roofs were extended, giving additional space on the lower floor in the form of a lean-to addition. The *c.*1675 Hoxie House in Sandwich is a fine example of this "Cape Cod salt box."

PRECEEDING PAGES: Greek Revival Courthouse at Newfane, Vermont.
LEFT: white paint was introduced in the 19th century.
RIGHT: Hoxie House, Sandwich: a Cape Cod salt box.

Many 17th-century meetinghouses, also unadorned and otherwise simple, remain throughout New England. (The Old Ship Meetinghouse in Hingham is a fine example.) The large meetinghouses often served as the village's town hall and religious nucleus, reflecting early ties between church and state.

Coming of age

With a growing sense of confidence and prosperity, the colonists began adding flourishes to their humble homes. At the turn of the 18th century, commerce was growing beyond town borders, and with expanding horizons

England. London burned in 1666, and out of the ashes rose tributes to the ideas of the 16th-century Italian architect Andrea Palladio. Palladio's work recalled the classical architecture of antiquity, restating it in a refreshing, heroic way.

Christopher Wren, among others, championed this Renaissance spirit in London. In the United States, Palladian ideas spread through such design handbooks as Palladio's *Four Books of Architecture*. Guides in hand, the first tentative but unmistakable steps were taken toward the establishment of a conscious esthetic in this new country. Not insignificantly,

there came a more adventurous spirit and a weakening of the religious principles that had dampened individual expression.

The architectural symbols of this change vary according to place and time. Along the coast, where maritime trading and fishing were making their mark, money and exposure to influences from abroad combined to produce splendid mansions. Inland, changes in building style were more subtle and slower to peak.

The Georgian style

The inspiration for the new Georgian style, as the pre-Revolutionary period of 18th-century design is known, stemmed from misfortune in

a style was born that is as often termed Colonial as it is Georgian; the modern American landscape certainly attests to its staying power.

Symmetry, a sense of strength and a quality of ease characterize the Georgian style. (The term Georgian was derived from the three King Georges who succeeded each other in England from 1714 to 1820.) The Georgian house was a simple two-story rectangle, but classical elements gave it definition: scrolled, often broken pediments capped centered doorways and windows; fluted attached columns marked the entrances of houses; and, in the grander examples, bulging cornerstones bracketed the corners of the structures from the eaves to the foundations. Mostly in wood, but sometimes in brick, the elements were carried off with precision by skilled New England carpenters.

Georgian homes, with wood-paneled walls and broad stairways, had larger rooms and more privacy. Four full rooms both upstairs and down were the norm. Two separate chimneys serviced the two, now larger, halves of the house. A massive central chimney was replaced by two leaner towers, adding to exterior elegance and richness while leaving room for a deep hallway where the chimney had been.

As for changes in meetinghouses, Wren-style steeples were added. For two opposite

While the precise Georgian proportions and details exude a calm and assurance, their dark, unpainted clapboards suggest a ruggedness absent in later painted facades. Indians were regularly raiding Deerfield, but when one's eyes rest upon these buildings, there is no sense of trepidation, and the marvelous doorways welcome visitors warmly.

Equally gracious is the 1754 Dwight-Barnard House. This rambling residence is a lovely example not only of Georgian architecture but also of the New England practice of connecting the house, the barn and any outbuilding that had to be reached during the bitter winter.

examples, from plain to elaborate, look to the Old South Meeting House in Boston and the Baptist Church in Providence.

Old Deerfield, Massachusetts, has several charming renderings of early Georgian ideals. At the north end of a marvelous mile of 18th-century historical structures stand the 1733 Ashley House and the 1743 Hawks House.

FAR LEFT: the early colonial (1646) West Parish Meeting House, near West Barnstaple on Cape Cod.
LEFT: 18th-century Georgian houses on Benefit Street, Providence, Rhode Island.
ABOVE: the impeccably Georgian Julius Deming House at Litchfield, Connecticut (1793).

By mid-century, coastal ports were very profitable, as sea captains' and merchants' houses attested. Many of these were later remodeled to keep up with architectural fashions, making it quite difficult to find the purely Georgian. Portsmouth, New Hampshire, is blessed with unsullied originals in its 1763 Moffatt-Ladd House – as handsome as any – and the delightfully understated 1760 Wentworth-Gardner House.

Aspects of Georgian architecture, particularly Palladian motifs, remained in the vernacular of New England design beyond the 18th century, but for the most part the style had run its course by the Revolutionary War. One lovely exception is the handsome town of Litchfield, Connecticut, where pristine homes lining the village green compose the perfect picture of idyllic New England.

Some of the finest homes were built or remodeled after 1780, when the Litchfield China Trading Company brought wealth to the town. The residence of one of the company's founders, a Mr Deming, and the remodeled Sheldon's Tavern are impeccably Georgian, down to the three-part Palladian window not commonly used before 1780. All other buildings in the borough of Litchfield are meticulously preserved, although not necessarily in

The Federal style

Following the revolution, optimism was palpable in the harbors of Salem and Boston. Even inland, whaling, shipbuilding and the expansion of trade brought the sea to many New Englanders as the coastal merchants commanded the goods and natural resources of the whole region. But no country carpenter could rival the skills of Salem's Samuel McIntire or Boston's Charles Bulfinch, whose combined work represents the finest of the period.

In Salem, success in the pepper trade and other undertakings made wealthy men of captains and cabin boys alike. It is fortuitous

their original state. The predominantly white exteriors date from a later 19th-century taste that conveys a feel quite different from that of the original yellow, blue or red hues that comprised a Georgian palette.

No style since the Georgian has lingered so long in New England. Deriving from familiar forms, but with more space and embellishments, New England builders adapted to it with ease. If the Georgian style took a long time to mature into its successor, the Federal, the lag was surely a result of the many preoccupations of a nation in adolescence, rather than an absence of active architectural acumen. The century that followed was to prove that.

that McIntire and Salem developed together, for the local carpenter may otherwise have had no outlet for his self-taught architectural proficiency.

McIntire's work shows the clearest Federal style notations. While New England's roofs had lost some of their cant during the Georgian period, their Federal counterparts virtually disappeared behind delicately carved balustrades. These "widow's walks" provided a vantage point from which a sea captain's wife could scan the harbor for her husband's incoming or departing ship. The effect was urbane, as evidenced by the 1804 Gardner-Pingree house in Salem, a rather neat summation of Federal motifs. Although primarily plain and boxy, its four-square facade is relieved by the semi-circular portico, its refined columns and the arching fanlight over the door – Federal era signatures. The front doorways of Federal houses are often distinguished by their narrow, leaded side windows, too.

McIntire performed his own carpentry with a skill that left him in constant demand up until his death in 1811. His inspiration was Robert Adam, the English architect who raised the art of interior decoration to exquisite heights with his dainty stucco reliefs. McIntire introduced these same embellishments to Salem, as can be

when the sea captains decided to move away a little from the noise and clutter of the port.

Elsewhere in Salem, a 1970s facelift not only turned around a declining city but, in doing so, reversed plans to topple many Federal-era buildings, which have been renovated and put to new use. A similar turnabout occurred in nearby Newburyport, where life and charm have been reintroduced to the dilapidated, deserted commercial buildings.

The brilliance of Bulfinch

The Federal era peaked with the work of Charles Bulfinch, who pursued architecture

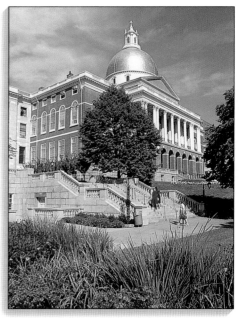

seen inside the Gardner-Pingree house. Classical detailing, free-standing curved stairways and delicate fireplace mantels characterize Federal interior design.

The full impact of McIntire's work on the rest of Salem is best grasped on Chestnut Street, which in its entirety has been designated a National Historic Landmark. Up and down both sides of this majestic street are stunning Federal-style mansions, built in the early 1800s

LEFT: an example of a wooden Federal-style house with typical semi-circular portico and roof balustrade.
ABOVE: a typical Adam-style Federal interior.
ABOVE RIGHT: Charles Bulfinch's State House.

first as a leisure activity and then as a profession. Building – or his speculations in it – bankrupted him twice. One can only surmise, however, that misfortune fired rather than smothered his talents. Unfortunately, many of his more daring buildings have been destroyed, but the jewel among those standing, the Massachusetts State House, rests atop Beacon Hill. Here is as grand a composition as any Bulfinch realized, and to picture it surrounded by open land is to begin to appreciate what a dazzling paean to the promise of government it must have appeared to the Bostonian of 1798.

The classical State House, very Palladian in inspiration, has been extended twice in two contradictory styles. The 1890 addition to the back of the building is a lumpish but highly mannered baroque echo of its opposing side. The second addition of 1914 totally neutralized the first by blotting it out, at least from the front, behind two thoroughly impassive marble wings – dull perhaps, but a mute backdrop to the golden-domed Bulfinch original.

Bulfinch was in on the beginning of Beacon Hill speculation, and the three homes he built for the investor Harrison Gray Otis summarize not only his growth but the maturation of the Federal residential style. The 1796 house, now the headquarters for the Society for the

beautiful cluster of buildings and has protected a rare haven of tranquility in the heart of modern Boston.

Greek grandeur

New England is a peaceful place, and among the emblems of this serenity are scores of white steeples, visible on every horizon as landmarks for travelers. This ubiquitous New England image can be traced back to Asher Benjamin, one of the most influential forces in turn-of-the century New England architecture. It was Benjamin's first of seven widely read architectural handbooks, in which he rendered a

Preservation of New England Antiquities, is the least developed, a harmonious albeit basic expression of Federal-style concepts. In his 1802 house, Bulfinch took a few cautious steps to animate the street facade – the first-floor windows are recessed inside well-defined brick arches. By his third house, completed around 1805, Bulfinch's confidence was established. This Beacon Street residence, of noble proportions and refined detail, set a tone of sophistication for the entire neighborhood.

Bulfinch's contributions to Beacon Hill were recognized in 1955 when residents established the Beacon Hill Historic District. This organization has overseen the preservation of a

steepled church, that became the basis for decades of church design. The simple classicism changed little over time, but the detailing, particularly of the steeple, incorporated changing architectural fashions, giving a clue to the era in which a church was built.

It was Benjamin who, in his final 1830 volume, judged New England ready for the Greek Revival style, a style that elsewhere in America was already vying with the Gothic. The same sense of self-importance that had characterized the Federal era, along with the influence of learning and intellectualism, gave the imposing Greek style a certain snob appeal. New England allowed the style in without totally letting go of the integrity of its previous architectural traditions. Particularly in non-residential examples, the Greek Revival style produced buildings that were a logical extension of the refinements made during the Federal era. The tops of Greek Revival churches were squared-off or had multi-story steeples, but Greek Revival houses proved less successful.

The economy of Greek architecture gives it a superior air, and scale is the key to its grandeur. Civic buildings, institutions and halls of commerce lent themselves to the heroic Greek scale, usually constructed of either marble or granite; houses were dwarfed by it.

colonnaded and handsomely detailed facade. Inside, the two-story, sky-lit interior has been beautifully restored, its cast-iron balconies once again offering an elegant setting for shops.

The most celebrated New England project of its kind, Boston's Faneuil Hall Marketplace, as restored by Ben Thompson & Associates, is now a consumer's cornucopia, with food and specialty stores galore. The renovation was carried out with care and charisma; although the sober Greek references of Alexander Parris's 1826 domed building are generally overwhelmed by their surroundings, it seems fitting that this hive of activity be housed in such splendor.

(There were two residential benefits, however: tall windows and high ceilings.) Although New England is not particularly rich in examples of the style, two exemplary Greek Revival buildings – both marketplaces, temples of commerce, if you will – are among the most clever and renowned examples of recently restored 19th-century buildings.

Providence's 1828 Arcade has been described as "something worthy of London or Paris," an apt compliment to its crisply

The addition of heavy columns and crushing pediments did little, however, for otherwise well-proportioned Federal and Georgian homes. Neither remodeled nor new, Greek Revival houses carry themselves with particular ease, but one of their fundamental features was effortlessly assimilated into the vocabulary of vernacular New England design – the passion for white paint (white being associated with Greek temples). Some unusually fine examples of this style can be found in Grafton, Vermont, a quiet town remarkable less for its architecture than for its rescue by the Windham Foundation, which since 1963 has restored the entire core of this idyllic New England village.

LEFT: Charles Bulfinch's first house for Harrison Gray Otis, 141 Cambridge Street, Boston.
ABOVE: Faneuil Hall, renovated by Bulfinch in 1806.

Enlightened industry

Harrisville, New Hampshire, survives as an unchanged emblem of how pervasive the textile industry was in New England after 1830. The town comprises handsome granite and brick mills, boarding houses and storehouses. Today, these buildings house a weaving school and offer an abridged version of the rapid rise and fall of New England's mill towns, a story that began with windmills and small-town enterprise and climaxed with the building of entire towns designed to support the textile industry. The effects on the social fabric were profound and lasting.

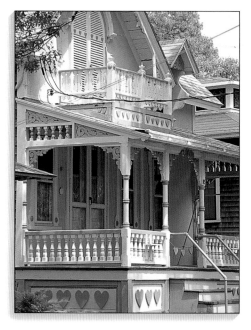

In Lowell, Massachusetts, aggressive efforts preserved an extensive industrial architectural legacy. The Lowell National Historic Park and the Lowell Historic Preservation District celebrate factory buildings designed in the boxy, brick, frugal industrial version of the Federal style. They line the city's intricate canal system, with rows of boarding houses nearby.

Lowell is once again a healthy and active city, a rich visual lesson in the architecture of a tumultuous historical chapter. The mills are among many saved from the wrecking ball and reused for housing, commercial and retail purposes. Towns such as Fall River, Manchester and Pawtucket are the richer for these efforts.

The loss of innocence

The opening of the industrial age marked the closing of an era of architectural innocence in New England. For its first 200 comparatively stable years, New England architecture had been governed by conservative principles that emphasized function first; form existed to serve the central purpose of shelter. While European ideas had clearly dictated design, they had been tempered by restraint. But by 1850, something had changed. Perhaps for no other reason than boredom with symmetry, scale and four-square plans, architecture took off in all directions, most in opposition to the language of the past.

Gothic, Italianate, Renaissance and Romanesque are among the eclectic labels attached to the late 19th-century architectural revivals. The Gothic Capitol building in Hartford is particularly asymmetrical, while the "gingerbread" carpenter Gothic style of Martha's Vineyard cottages represents a more quaint interpretation. Newport mansions exemplify a dizzying range of styles, from the shingled Hammersmith Farm "cottage" to the gilded Breakers (Italian Renaissance), the Victorian Chateau-sur-mer to the beaux-arts Marble House (*see pages 240–41*).

In the hands of architects such as Henry Hobson Richardson (who designed Boston's Trinity Church with Romanesque influences) and McKim, Mead and White (Boston Public Library), these styles could be expressed with uncommon panache. But the spiritual link to New England began growing remote, and these buildings – with massive stones and ornamentation – have only a distant kinship with the carefully proportioned, cautiously decorated creations of New England's early centuries.

Further European grafts have been attempted, with varying degrees of success. Harvard University boasts the only LeCorbusier building in the United States (the Carpenter Center), and Gropius built a model Bauhaus house in the Boston suburb of Lincoln. The future of New England architecture, however, clearly lies in the hands of native architects, such as Graham Gund of Cambridge, who acknowledge the contributions of their forebears even as they strive to break new ground. ❏

LEFT: well preserved Carpenters Gothic cottages can be found at Oak Bluffs on Martha's Vineyard.
RIGHT: Boston's "Richardson Romanesque" Trinity Church contrasts with the 1970s Hancock Tower.

PLACES

A detailed guide to New England, with principal sites
clearly cross-referenced by number to the maps

Meanwhile it occurs to me that by a remote New England fireside an unsophisticated young person of either sex is reading in an old volume of travels... The young person gazes in the firelight at the flickering chiaroscuro of the future, discerns at last the glowing phantasm of opportunity, and determines with a wild heart-beat to go and see it all – twenty years hence.   —HENRY JAMES

There's no need to wait 20 years to see New England, no need to delay at all, for its rewards are well established. It is a region bursting with 300 years of historical sights and influence – considerably more than any other place in America. But it is also a remarkably vital place: attend a town meeting in one of the superficially sleepy rural communities and you'll find that the robust tradition of democracy bequeathed by the founding fathers lives on, making many a town manager's life little easier than the president's.

It is precisely this juxtaposition of past influence and present prestige that is so compelling. Comprising six politically defined states, New England has a thousand states of mind – Maine for solitude and contemplation, Massachusetts for bustle and culture, Vermont for beauty and peace, Connecticut for its carefully kept white clapboard homes, Rhode Island for its renowned sailing, and tranquil New Hampshire, whose bellwether presidential primary every four years suggests the political fortunes that are about to be won and lost.

A trip to New England can mean finding a priceless antique in an out-of-the-way backwoods store, or dining in a sophisticated Boston bistro. It can mean rafting down a Maine river and skiing down a New Hampshire mountain, lounging on a Nantucket beach or picnicking on the harbor in Newport, Rhode Island.

State delineations serve as convenient although somewhat artificial labels for New England's varied regions. In the following pages, each state is explored in depth and treated as a self-contained unit. But Massachusetts, the most populous, has been divided into sub-sections: Boston, Boston Day trips, Cape Cod and the islands of Martha's Vineyard and Nantucket, Central Massachusetts and the Berkshires.

States of mind – calm, contentment, excitement, pride, surprise, intrigue, enjoyment, pleasure – are to be found throughout New England. From the scrub pines on Martha's Vineyard to the granite outcroppings of Vermont's Green Mountains, from the cobbled streets of restored Newburyport to the sleek Boston skyline, from Rhode Island's natural wonderland, Block Island, to the country's history that began in Lexington and Concord, this is New England, home of American dreams, both real and still to be actualized. ❑

PRECEDING PAGES: winter in the White Mountains, New Hampshire; summer in the White Mountains; Back Cove, Maine.
LEFT: Brant Point Lighthouse and Children's Beach, Nantucket.

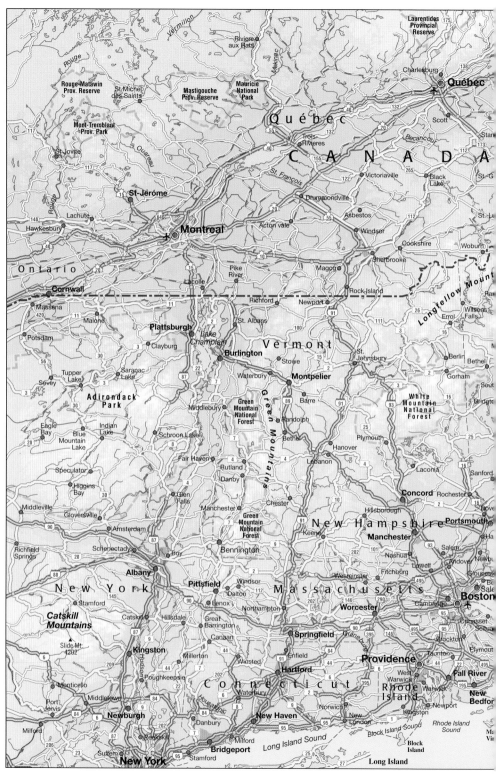

Laurentides Provincial Reserve 175

Charlesburg 138

Québec

Rouge-Matawin Prov. Reserve

St Michel des Saints

Mastigouche Prov. Reserve

Mauricie National Park

Rivière aux Rats

Scott

132

Q u é b e c

132

Trois-Rivières

20

Becancour

Stan

112 173

Mont-Tremblant Prov. Park

117

Ouareau

55

C A N A D A

155

St-G

St-Jovite

117

St François

122

Victoriaville

265

Black Lake

St-L

St-Jérôme

15

Drummondville

20

Asbestos

112

Lachute

148

Acton Vale

55

Windsor

Cookshire

Woburn

Hawkesbury

Montreal

640

10

Sherbrooke

40

O n t a r i o

20

Pike River

Magog

Rock Island

Longfellow Mount

Cornwall

15

Lacolle

Richford

Newport

26

Errol

Wilsons Falls

Ra

Massena 420

11

11

Malone

2

St. Albans

100

91

111

3

16

Potsdam

Plattsburgh

Lake Champlain

V e r m o n t

St. Johnsbury

Berlin

Bethel

56

30

Clayburg

3

Burlington

Stowe

15

Gorham

Sout

Tupper Lake

Saranac Lake

22

Waterbury

Montpelier

2

87

7

A d i r o n d a c k Park

3

Middlebury

Green Mountain National Forest

89

Barre

91

White Mountain National Forest

16

Bridge

Eagle Bay

30

Indian Lake

Randolph

25

Plymouth

25

Blue Mountain Lake

28

Schroon Lake

8

7

Bethel

Hanover

Fair Haven

4

Lebanon

4

Laconia

15

Sanford

Speculator

Rutland

Danby

10

Concord

Rochester

Higgins Bay

30

Glen Falls

Chester

Hillsborough

Dove

Middleville

Manchester

Green Mountain National Forest

91

N e w   H a m p s h i r e

Portsmouth

Gloversville

Keene

9

Manchester

Ha

90

Amsterdam

87

Bennington

202

101

Nashua

93

Salem

Newb

Richfield Springs

Schenectady

Troy

Westminster

Fitchburg

Lowell

Andover

Glouces

20

88

2

Albany

Windsor

M a s s a c h u s e t t s

495

Sale

Boston

N e w   Y o r k

145

Pittsfield

Dalton

112

202

146

290

Cambridge

95

Cohasset

Stamford

90

Lenox

Northampton

Worcester

495

Brockton

Plymout

Catskill Mountains

Catskill

Hillsdale

Great Barrington

Canaan

90

395

146

Slide Mt. 4202

87

9

Springfield

Quinne

Kingston

Millerton

44

91

Enfield

84

Taunton

44

495

6

209

44

7

Winsted

Hartford

44

Providence

22

Fall River

Monticello

Poughkeepsie

22

202

6

West Warwick

6

Rhode Island

Warwick

195

New Bedfor

Port Jervis

Middletown

84

C o n n e c t i c u t

Waterbury

2

395

Norwich

Newport

Milford

84

6

Newburgh

9

Danbury

8

New London

1

Kingston

Rhode Island Sound

Ma Vir

206

87

202

7

Milford

95

Block Island Sound

Block Island

23

Rockskill

95

Bridgeport

Long Island Sound

25

Long Island

Suffern

Stamford

27

New York

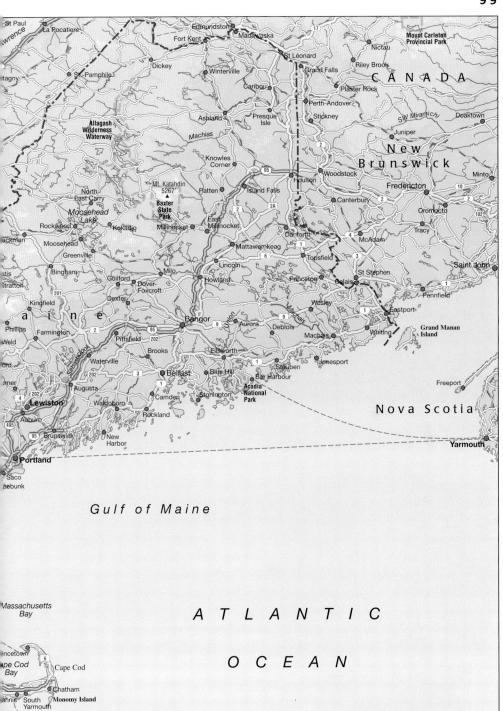

New England

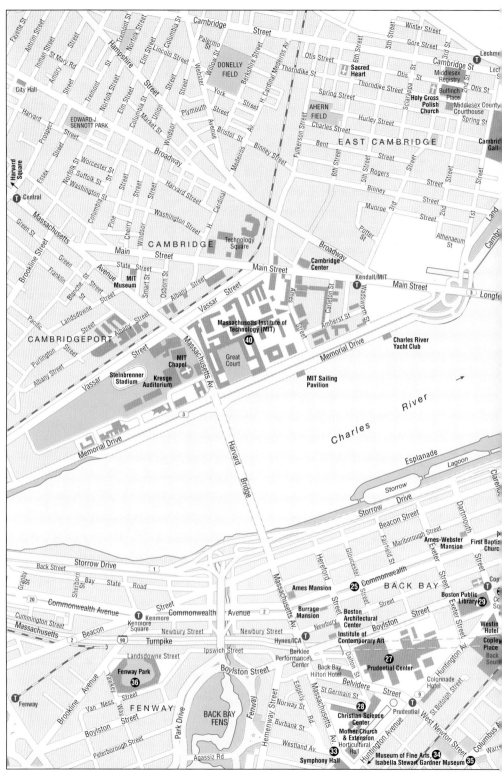

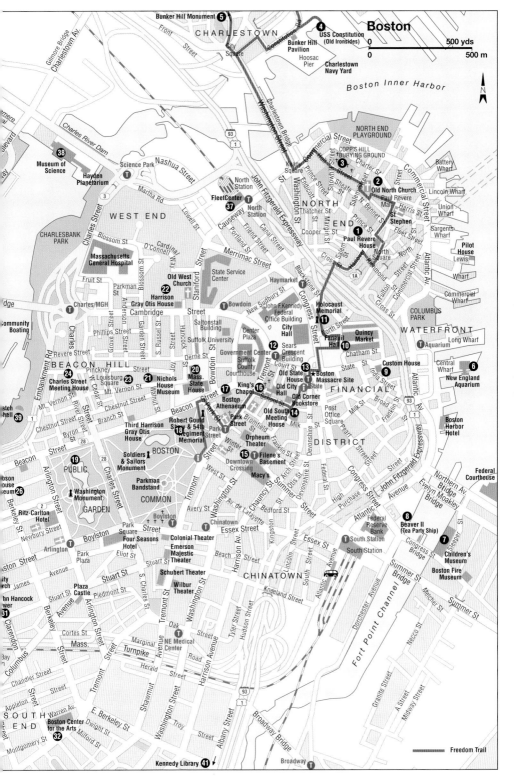

Boston

Boston Inner Harbor

500 yds
500 m

N

CHARLESTOWN

Bunker Hill Monument ⑤
Bunker Hill Pavilion
USS Constitution (Old Ironsides) ④
Charlestown Navy Yard
Hoosac Pier

NORTH END PLAYGROUND

COPP'S HILL BURYING GROUND ③

Old North Church ②
Paul Revere Mall
St Stephen

NORTH END

Paul Revere House ①

Battery Wharf
Lincoln Wharf
Union Wharf
Sargents Wharf
Pilot House
Lewis Wharf
Commercial Wharf

Museum of Science ㊳
Hayden Planetarium
Science Park

WEST END

North Station
FleetCenter ㊲
North Station

CHARLESBANK PARK

Massachusetts General Hospital

Old West Church
Harrison Gray Otis House ㉒

State Service Center

Haymarket

Holocaust Memorial ⑪

COLUMBUS PARK

WATERFRONT

Aquarium
Long Wharf

John F. Kennedy Federal Office Building
City Hall
Faneuil Hall ⑩
Quincy Market ⑩

Central Wharf

Custom House ⑨

New England Aquarium ⑥

BEACON HILL

Charles Street Meeting House
Nichols House Museum ㉓
Mass. State House ⑳
King's Chapel ⑯
Old State House ⑬
Old City Hall
Old Corner Bookstore
Old South Meeting House ⑭

Boston Massacre Site

FINANCIAL DISTRICT

Post Office Square

Boston Harbor Hotel

Boston Athenaeum ⑰
Park Street
Orpheum Theater

Robert Gould Shaw & 54th Regiment Memorial ⑱
Third Harrison Gray Otis House

Soldiers & Sailors Monument

BOSTON

Parkman Bandstand

Downtown Crossing ⑮
Filene's Basement
Macy's

PUBLIC GARDEN ⑲

Washington Monument

Federal Reserve Bank

South Station

Federal Courthouse
Northern Av. Bridge
Evelyn Moakley Bridge

Beaver II (Tea Party Ship) ⑧
Children's Museum ⑦
Boston Fire Museum

Ritz-Carlton Hotel ㉖

Four Seasons Hotel
Colonial Theater
Emerson Majestic Theater

CHINATOWN

Plaza Castle
Schubert Theater
Wilbur Theater

John Hancock Tower ㉛

NE Medical Center

SOUTH END

Boston Center for the Arts ㉜

Kennedy Library ㊶

Broadway

░░░░░ Freedom Trail

BOSTON

The city has always taken itself seriously. But it does, after all, all, have unequaled Revolutionary history, famed universities, vibrant arts, creative cuisine, and the Red Sox

Map on pages 102–3

The poet and essayist Ralph Waldo Emerson, wrote "This town of Boston has a history… It is not an accident, not a windmill, or a railroad station, or a crossroads town, but a seat of humanity, of men of principle, obeying sentiment and marching to it…"

Oliver Wendell Holmes was even more extravagant: "All I claim for Boston is that it is the thinking center of the Continent, and therefore of the Planet." He went on to christen his city "The Hub of the Universe." New York may be more dynamic, Washington more imposing, Seattle more beautiful, but no city in America so nobly mingles its past with its present, tradition with innovation.

Short story of a long history

Founded in 1630 when a band of Puritans who had landed in Salem (north of Boston) went searching for drinking water, Boston early on felt that "the eies of all people are upon us," as their first leader, John Winthrop, said. Driven by this relentless self-consciousness and the certainty that God, too, was watching, the little "Bible Commonwealth" quickly made something of itself.

Prosperity came from the sea. By 1700, thanks to cod fishing and the maritime trade made possible by Boston's natural harbor, the colony was booming: its fleet was the third largest in the English-speaking world, its population the largest in North America.

Success, however, brought attention from home, and in the mid-18th century, the English Crown began to tighten its hold on its precocious offspring, imposing a series of tough new revenue measures which cooled relations between the colonies and the motherland. Tensions escalated; the Boston Massacre of 1770 and the Boston Tea Party (*see page 37*) three years later eventually flared into a brief but famous war – the American Revolution.

The Athens of America

During the high noon of the 19th century Boston took its present-day form. The merchant princes created a great city that would eventually become known not only as "The Hub," but also as "The Athens of America."

Boston's maritime industries surged again with the coming of peace. Piloting swift clipper ships, sea captains traded in ports farther abroad – Java, the West Coast and newly opened China. The Boston fishing fleet increased tenfold between 1789 and 1810, and created a "codfish aristocracy" of fortunes netted from the sea. A seemingly unending flow of gold made Bostonians with names such as Cabot, Lowell, Otis and Hancock incredibly rich. These wealthy mercantilists, adopting the name of the priestly class of the

PRECEDING PAGES: Boston seen from the Charles River. **LEFT:** Acorn Street, Beacon Hill. **BELOW:** George Washington's statue in the Public Garden.

Hindus who performed sacred rituals and set moral standards, emerged as the self-styled "Brahmins".

It was the Boston-designed sewing machine, along with the loom, imported from England, that inaugurated an era of heavy textile and shoe manufacturing in New England.

Growth accelerated as Yankee ingenuity triumphed, and helped Boston lead America into a prosperous Industrial Age. By the century's end, in one of the great testimonies to the American knack for making something from nothing, Boston had tripled its size with landfill.

Boston was also expanding its mind. With its legacy of Puritan high-mindedness, its publishing houses and its fashionable literary salons run by earnest first citizens, Boston suddenly found itself at the radiant center of intellectual America. Henry Wadsworth Longfellow, Robert Lowell, John Greenleaf Whittier, Ralph Waldo Emerson, Henry David Thoreau, Oliver Wendell Holmes, Bronson Alcott, Nathaniel Hawthorne: all were at one time or another citizens of the New England Parnassus; all could be found browsing at the Old Corner Book Store or dictating standards for civilization over seven-course meals at the Parker House, where Emerson convened his luminous Saturday Club.

A whole slew of cultural institutions celebrated and embodied it. Among these were the Boston Public Library, the Boston Symphony Orchestra, the Massachusetts Institute of Technology (MIT) and Boston University, the first American university to admit women on an equal basis with men. Harvard had already ascended to its place among the world's great universities.

The great immigration

BELOW: Boston Public Library.

When the Irish Potato Famine began in 1845, Boston was at the apogee of its gleaming social and cultural pre-eminence. Suddenly, thousands of impoverished Irish immigrants arrived, promptly constituting a new underclass.

As the population exploded – swelled further by additional waves of Italians, Poles and Russians in the 1880s – census figures multiplied thirtyfold during the 19th century to about 560,000 people in 1900. Newcomers and incumbents clashed, and Boston was divided into two distinct cultures. Established Bostonians withdrew into their own carefully defended elite of genealogy and crypto-Puritanism.

Map on pages 102–3

The new citizens became virtual slaves as they sweated in factories and did handwork; they remade Boston in their own image. Once dominated by English names, the Puritan "City upon a Hill" became a predominantly Catholic megalopolis of Irish and Italian names: numbers prevailed, most dramatically in the arena of city politics.

For all Boston's glory and growth during the 1800s, the century's end brought decline, a decline that would continue until the 1960s. New York superseded Boston as a port; the textile mills and shoe factories headed south for cheaper labor and lower taxes. By the 1940s and 1950s, Boston was shrinking.

But then the city woke up. For the first time, Boston's Protestant elite, representing wealth, and its Irish Catholics, representing political power, cooperated in the management of city affairs and began a success story of rejuvenation. The Prudential Center, including what was then the tallest skyscraper outside New York, materialized. Government Center supplanted Scollay Square. Faneuil Hall Marketplace was created from meat warehouses. The waterfront was revived. Suddenly, Boston was a different, altogether exciting place.

Park Rangers have an educational role.

The city further benefited as the Baby Boom generation grew up, went to college, then looked for jobs and apartments. Millions of young people have attended one of the three score colleges in Boston. Many have set up shop and transformed the Boston area into one of the centers of the Technology Revolution. Together with Cambridge, its neighbor across the Charles River, it is at the fore as a seat of learning and as a center for scientific research. Boston of today is young in demographics as well as spirits.

BELOW: festival time in "Little Italy," Boston's North End.

A walking city

Despite urban development, one of Boston's primary charms remains unchanged: its tangled streets and the art of walking them. Boston changes so abruptly in mood and nuance from one street to another that it cries out to be explored on foot. The city is charmingly, perversely bereft of a main drag, and its streets practice the old European vices of waywardness and digression. The visitor should, too. There's no telling what you'll find.

Every day hundreds of visitors walk the red line on the sidewalk that marks the **Freedom Trail**, a self-guided tour that takes in the major sites of the city's momentous Revolutionary history (*see pages 132–3*).

The North End

This picturesque old neighborhood is Boston's original heart, and to walk its streets is to walk among legends. The Freedom Trail threads its way through the North End on its way between Boston Common and the Bunker Hill Monument in Charlestown.

TIP

Look out for the feste, or saint's festivals, on weekends in July and August, when the streets of the North End are spanned by arcs of colored lights and jammed with people surrounding Madonnas bedecked with dollar bills.

The North End is the ethnic heart of Boston: once Irish, then Jewish, and now Italian. Laundry hangs from lines stretched from building to building across the street, and freshly ground sausages are invitingly displayed in storefront windows.

A stroll through the North End can start at the **Paul Revere House ❶** (open daily) in North Square. Built around 1680, it is the oldest building standing in the city, and the period furnishings on display include some items owned by the Reveres. From here, head toward Hanover Street and the Old North Church, but walk at a leisurely pace and take in the sights – and smells – of Old World Italy. Here is a paradise of fresh-baked bread, dried squid, pastries, provolone and braided garlic. Within a few blocks of Hanover Street are dozens of first-class Italian restaurants.

At the end of Hanover Street stands the Revere Mall with its rather comic equestrian statue of Revere looking a tad drunk. At the end of the tranquil, tree-shaded mall, also occupied by a fountain and old Italian men playing checkers, stands Boston's oldest church, the **Old North Church ❷** (officially Christ Church, 193 Salem Street; open daily 8:30am–6pm; Sunday services at 9am, 11am and 5pm), where beneath the graceful spire the sexton Robert Newman famously hung two lanterns on April 18, 1775, on the orders of Paul Revere, to signify to the citizens the British troops' plan to cross by sea rather than by land. Inside, the stately pulpit and a bust of George Washington preside over the original box pews. The beauty of this space finds lovely accompaniment in the "royal peal" of its eight bells, considered the best and sweetest in America. One is inscribed, "We are the first ring of bells cast for the British Empire in North America, Anno 1774."

BELOW: the Paul Revere House.

Behind Old North, between Hull and Charter streets, stand the weathered headstones of **Copps Hill Burying Ground ❸**, where many early Bostonians are buried – including Cotton Mather, the Puritan instrumental in inciting the persecution of the Salem "witches' – and where several gravestones bear evidence of British soldiers using them for musket practice.

Charlestown

Across Charlestown Bridge from the North End a famous bit of history lies at anchor: the **USS *Constitution* ❹** (open daily), the venerable frigate known as "Old Ironsides," built in 1797 and the oldest commissioned vessel in the world (she makes one voyage a year, a ceremonial "turnabout" on the 4th of July); she fought over 40 battles in the War of 1812 and never lost one. The majestic masts soar above the Boston Naval Shipyard, which opened during the War of 1812 and functioned until 1974, up to the latter days of the Vietnam War.

The historic shipyard includes enough to fill a day's visit: the **USS *Constitution* Museum** (open daily) tells the ship's story, while the **Boston Marine Society** within the old octagonal Muster House contains an array of ship models and paintings, and the **Commandant's House** is preserved as it was when last occupied in 1876. Also in dock, the **USS *Cassin Young*** is a World War II destroyer, open for tours. The Bunker Hill Pavilion has a multimedia extravaganza depicting the Patriots' heroic loss to the Redcoats in the second battle of the Revolution.

The Freedom Trail's finale from the Charlestown Navy Yard is less appealing than the rest of the Trail, but it is worth persevering to the very end, to the outsized obelisk of the **Bunker Hill Monument ❺** (open daily), a granite needle 221 ft (67 meters) high, commemorating one of the first major battles of the Revolutionary War. Climb this – be warned that there are 294 steps – and contemplate the complexity of the Harbor, speckled with dozens of islands. Many of these have odd histories, some linked with Native American legends, others – as in the case of Nix's Mate Island – with the visits of pirates such as Captain Kidd. Two islands have supported hospitals, another a prison, and others have been fortified. During the Civil War, hundreds of soldiers trained for the Union Army at Fort Warren on George's Island, and more than 1,000 Confederates were imprisoned there.

The Waterfront

The eastern boundary of the North End is the Waterfront District. If the tall ships – or rather, their modern copies – now appear only sporadically, the great wharves remain, many now recycled as apartments, shopping arcades and upscale restaurants. At the center of it all is the modest Columbus Park; with the completion of a huge project (due for completion 2006) to demolish the I-93 ramp and bury the traffic in tunnels, a much larger park will link the Waterfront with the downtown area.

By Aquarium subway station, Long Wharf is the starting point for harbor cruises, or you can get harbor views for free by walking along the walkway south-

Map on pages 102–3

TIP

In summer the MuSEAm Connection water shuttle links USS *Constitution*, the Aquarium, and Museum Wharf (for the Computer Museum, the Children's Museum and the Boston Tea Party Ship).

BELOW: "Old Ironsides".

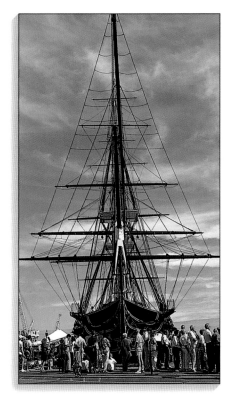

Wind-blown sculpture outside the Aquarium.

BELOW:
Commercial Wharf, the Waterfront.

wards to Rowes Wharf. The **New England Aquarium** (Central Wharf; open daily; entrance fee) has the largest seawater fish tank in the world, a gargantuan three-story, 200,000-gallon (900,000-liter) cylinder in which sharks, sea turtles, moray eels and other tropical species glide in never-ending circles. By its base African and rockhopper penguins play on the Ocean Tray, while other highlights include The Edge of the Sea exhibit, a fiberglass re-creation of a New England shore. You can watch through the window on to the Aquarium Medical Center, a laboratory caring for injured and sick animals. The Aquarium operates "Science at Sea" and whale-watch cruises, with researchers and naturalists on board, from Central Wharf.

Follow Harborwalk southwards past Rowes Wharf and cross Northern Avenue Bridge to find **Museum Wharf** , home of the **Children's Museum** (open Tues–Sun; Fri till 9pm; entrance fee). Housed in a renovated warehouse, it is a hands-on adventure, where children can play shoppers at the Supermercado (based on a real Latino supermarket in Boston), climb a three-dimensional maze, and take their shoes off to enter an authentic Japanese house transplanted piece by piece from Boston's sister city, Kyoto. New England's maritime traditions are reflected in hands-on boating exhibits and an environmental exhibit, Under the Dock, which simulates the underwater landscape of Fort Point Channel and includes a 14-ft (4-meter) fiberglass lobster. Children accustomed to constant warnings of "Don't touch!" and "Be careful!" will find a paradise of things to squeeze, crank, push, pull and explore. On the wharf, an immense milk bottle (a vestige of 1930s advertising kitsch) dispenses ice cream and more substantial snacks.

Nearby, on Congress Bridge, is the **Boston Tea Party Ship** (Congress Street; open Mar–Nov daily; entrance fee), which offers a not-too-serious

ican mythology for schoolchildren of all ages within the *Beaver II*, a full-size replica of one of the three tea ships whose cargo, on that chilly night in 1773, helped make the Harbor into a rather large pitcher of iced tea. You get the chance to participate in a town meeting based on the momentous one that took place in Old South Meeting House, and to hurl a tea chest into the Harbor from the deck.

Map on pages 102–3

Faneuil Hall, Government Center and Downtown

Just west of the New England Aquarium rises the **Custom House Tower ❾**, for many years Boston's tallest building, and today certainly the city's quaintest high-rise (now converted into time-share condominiums), with the 1915 clock tower placed somewhat incongruously on the Greek Revival-style Custom House of 1847. Close by is Faneuil Hall Marketplace, lodestone of the tourist trade and a famed experiment in urban redesign.

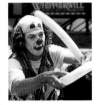

   Faneuil Hall ❿, the fulcrum of the place, was donated to Boston by Peter Faneuil, a French Huguenot merchant who traded in slaves. This future "Cradle of Liberty," where Patriot orators would soon stir the embers of Revolution, was built in 1742 on a site that was at the time, remarkably enough, Boston's Town Dock. In 1976, after 250 sometimes glorious, sometimes scruffy years of service, Quincy Market and Faneuil Hall opened again, after a massive renovation that converted their boisterous, rugged markets into a chic, cleverly remodeled and wildly successful array of flower stalls, jewelry emporia and designer-clothing outfits. In addition, several dozen food stands line the long hall of the central building, tempting strollers with an endless array of classic American and international snacks, from freshly shucked oysters to Italian sausage subs and exquisite French pastry.

Street entertainment in Faneuil Hall Marketplace.

BELOW: reliving the past at the Boston Tea Party Ship (left) and Faneuil Hall.

The New England Holocaust Memorial.

BELOW:
Quincy Market, which attracts over 10 million visitors a year.

The upper floor of Faneuil Hall itself, where the meetings were held, is open daily (tours every 30 minutes) and houses regimental memorabilia of the Ancient and Honorable Artillery Company.

For those who may wonder why all the shopping bags and restaurant menus bear an image of a cricket: when Faneuil gave Boston the hall, he had a large cricket weathervane placed atop its cupola. During the War of 1812, "cricket" became a password and patriot rallying cry of the Boston port. Strangers who could not identify the cricket as the image of the city of Boston met uncertain fates as spies.

Beside Union Street, six glass towers comprise the **New England Holocaust Memorial** ⓫, the "windows" etched with rows of numbers in memory of six million murdered Jews in World War II.

Looming just inland from Faneuil Hall, across Congress Street, is **Government Center** ⓬. Here, in the 1960s, Boston Redevelopment Authority director Edward Logue, Mayor Collins and architect I.M. Pei leveled the colorful tenements of the West End and constructed a city of their own, a radical "New Boston." This was urban renewal on a grand scale – either inspiring or forbidding, depending on your viewpoint. The designers razed buildings and removed streets to create a huge open space – some 56 acres (23 hectares). On this new plaza, they arranged several buildings of imposing scale and abstract design. A massive concrete City Hall designed by Kallmann, McKinnell and Knowles dominates, described as an "Aztec temple on a brick desert."

For a little comic relief, the quirky little Sears Crescent, built in 1816, has been allowed to remain from pre-Pei days. A 227-gallon (1,033-liter) teapot, steaming happily, hangs from a corner of the adjoining 1848 Sears Block building; a late 19th-century advertising gimmick, it lives on as a charming totem for a key government institution, the bureaucrat's breakfast.

To the southeast rises the tall confusion of pinstriped Boston, the banks and office towers along Franklin, Congress, Federal, State and Broad streets. Rising confidently from a primitive warren of jumbled byways, these well-tailored behemoths constitute the Hub of Business. They are evidence that in one way, at least, Boston has not changed much since the 17th century. Even today, it regards money as sacred, a sign of election.

To the southwest beats the throbbing heart of downtown, as well as some buildings illuminated brightly in history. At Washington Street's intersection with Court and State streets stands the **Old State House** ⓭ (open daily; entrance fee) a glorious center of 18th-century public life that today exhibits its heritage of survival by the stubbornness with which it holds the city's predatory skyscrapers at bay; the Bostonian Society has a museum inside, charting aspects of the city's history with changing displays. It was here, in 1761, that James Otis first fulminated against the British Writs of Assistance in a spellbinding speech that prompted John Adams to write that "then and there the child Independence was born." In 1770, the infamous Boston Massacre took place just outside the State House. Some years later, after the Revolution,

Map on pages 102–3

he building served as the meeting place for the Commonwealth Government until the present State House was built.

The **Old Corner Bookstore**, now called the Boston Globe Bookstore, at the corner of Washington and School streets, was once a sort of clubhouse for such writers and thinkers as Hawthorne, Emerson and Thoreau (*see page 148*). Later t was the home of the *Atlantic Monthly* when it was launched in 1857, and of he *Boston Globe*, Boston's journal of record.

Continue down Washington Street to the **Old South Meeting House ⓮** (open daily; entrance fee), from which on December 16, 1773, 60 whooping patriots dressed as Mohawk Indians set off for Griffin's Wharf and the Boston Tea Party. An audio historical display sets the scene. Around the corner at 1 Milk Steet, the house in which Benjamin Franklin was born, is **Dreams of Freedom**, a multimedia show tracing the history of Boston's immigration.

A little further on comes **Downtown Crossing ⓯**, where hordes of suburban shoppers stampede the city's major department stores. Probably the busiest intersection in Boston, it is the location of the phenomenal **Filene's Basement**, the world's most celebrated bargain store. Every day, thousands of sharp-eyed professionals, discerning matrons, and blown-dry teen angels can be seen shoving and elbowing each other as they rummage frantically through this cutrate El Dorado in search of designer seconds, three-piece suits, and household essentials. Goods are progressively marked down until they sell.

Alternatively, at the Boston Globe Bookstore, turn into School Street, pass the Old City Hall, a grand affair that out-Second Empires the French Second Empire, and at Tremont Street turn right to look into **King's Chapel ⓰** (open mid-Oct–mid-Apr, Sat; mid-Apr–mid-June and Sep–Oct, Mon, Fri, Sat;

Free, ranger-led tours of the Freedom Trail start from the Boston National Historical Park office, opposite the Old State House.

LEFT: a bookstore with a history. **BELOW:** the Old State House.

mid-June–Aug, Mon, Thur–Sat; Sun pm). Built in 1754 of Quincy granite, it retains its crisp white box pews as well as Paul Revere's largest bell; its burial ground is Boston's oldest.

Crossing over Tremont Street, head left to the **Old Granary Burial Ground**, a pleasant glade where are found the graves of Peter Faneuil, John Hancock, Samuel Adams, Paul Revere, six Massachusetts governors and the victims of the Boston Massacre. Overlooking the burial ground are the windows of the **Boston Athenaeum** , which in the 19th century became the preserve of wealthy intellectuals and, although anyone is free to walk in, it has retained that atmosphere virtually intact (10A Beacon Street; first two floors open Mon–Sat; tours of entire building 3pm Tues, Thur; reservation required; tel: 617-227 0270). There are reading rooms, marble busts, and prints and paintings, as well as books from George Washington's library. On the top floor there are seven pairs of recessed bays flanking a barrel-vaulted reading room; members can sit out on the balcony and lunch, overlooking the Old Granary Burial Ground.

A few more paces down Tremont lead to Peter Banner's elegant **Park Street Church** (1809) on the corner of Boston Common. Henry James decided it was "perfectly felicitous" and "the most interesting mass of brick and mortar in America." On July 4, 1829, William Lloyd Garrison made his first anti-slavery speech here, launching his far-reaching emancipation campaign.

The Boston Common and the Public Garden

Every metropolis has a great park somewhere in its outline, but only Boston can claim the oldest, the venerable **Boston Common** , a magical swath of lawn and trees and benches bounded by Tremont, Park, Beacon, Charles and Boylston

The song "America" was first sung in Park Street Church on July 4, 1831.

BELOW: the Old Granary Burial Ground.

streets. Sitting in the sun-mottled shade, watching pigeons strut and children frolic around Frog Pond, the out-of-towner can understand how Bostonians might mistake this spot for the very center of the world.

The land that was to become the Common originally belonged to Boston's first English settler, one Reverend William Blaxton. Having fled first England and then an aborted colonial attempt farther south, Blaxton settled in 1625 on the western slope of what is now known as Beacon Hill. There, he tended his orchard and read in peaceful solitude until his serenity was somewhat rudely interrupted in 1631 by the arrival of a band of new settlers led by Governor John Winthrop of the Massachusetts Bay Company. The new Bostonians were nobly determined, as Winthrop had written on the ship, to "be a City upon a hill," and their presence did not please Blaxton. In 1634, he sold his land to the town for around $150 and fled farther into the wilderness.

The 45 acres (18 hectares) he left behind quickly became a versatile community utility. During the next 150 years, it was used as a cattle and sheep pasture and as a drilling ground. And although, as an account written in 1663 says, "the Common was the beauty and pride of the Town, ever suggesting the lighter side of life," it also proved useful as a place to hang people – for stealing, for piracy, for being a Quaker, or a Native American, or a woman who snatched a bonnet worth 75 cents. The whipping post and the pillory stood there, and many a duel took place at dawn. As a military post, the Common put up the Redcoats all through the Revolution, and during the Civil War it provided a backdrop for the tears of recruiting and departures.

Now the Common is an urban oasis, a park and nothing else. Climb the little knolls and walk the meandering paths past bronze statues and dignified

The Emerald Necklace is a 6-mile (9-km) corridor of forests, parks and ponds in and around Boston. Begun in 1881 by Frederick Law Olmsted, it links the Public Garden with Franklin Park in West Roxbury.

BELOW LEFT: the dome of the State House seen from the Common.
BELOW: cooling down in Frog Pond.

fountains. The Common is at its best all year – when the magnolias bloom, or when snow at sunset evokes the impressionist paintings of Childe Hassam.

West from the Common and across Charles Street, the elegant **Public Garden** ⑲ beckons, and, though it continues the pleasant green of the Common, it has quite a different past. Indeed, these variegated trees, meandering paths, and ornate beds of flowers were mere marsh when the Common was well into its second century of tempestuous history. First deeded at the end of the 18th century as a riverside ropewalk – the Charles had not yet been filled here – these 24 acres (10 hectares) at the Common's foot were bought back by the city in 1825 for $55,000. In a series of disputes during the first half of the 19th century, some argued that the valuable land would be best sold. But the park soon began to be laid out, though the destruction by fire of an early conservatory for birds and camellias slowed development. By 1867, the Garden had taken its present graceful shape, complete with weeping willows, a bridge for daydreamers, and a shallow 4-acre (2-hectare) pond.

In summer, one can't overlook the swan boats, those fabled gondolas that carry happy tourists across the placid waters. At the Commonwealth Avenue entrance, an equestrian *George Washington* bronze by Thomas Ball presides, while a row of bronze ducks on the north side pays tribute to Robert McCloskey's children's story *Make Way for the Ducklings*.

Beacon Hill

Back up at the east end of the Common rises the gold dome of the **State House** ⑳ (open weekdays) gleaming atop Beacon Hill. Completed in 1798 when the Old State House became too small, this design by Charles Bulfinch,

Statues in the park include tributes to Edward Everett Hale, author of "The Man Without a Country" (at the Charles Street entrance opposite the Boston Common) and Charles Sumner, who led abolitionist forces in the Senate before the Civil War (at the Boylston Street perimeter).

BELOW: a swan boat in the Public Garden.

with additions by several others, symbolizes the eminence of politics in Boston. The approach to the legislative chambers passes through a series of splendid halls, beginning with the Bulfinch era Doric Hall and leading to the Senate Staircase Hall and the Hall of Flags, both symphonies of fin de siècle marble opulence supplied plentifully with statues, busts, flags and patriotic mottos.

But none of this dulls the eye to the House Chamber in the Brigham extension, a paneled hall under a two-stage dome. Great moments of Massachusetts' freedom decorate the walls in a series of Albert Herter paintings, while above circles a frieze carved with a roll-call of the state's super-achievers. The portentous codfish known as the "Sacred Cod," a sleek, stiff carving in pine that commemorates Boston's great Federal-era fishing industry, was first hung in the Old State House. Without this old mascot, the house refuses to meet.

The State House, now hemmed in by Beacon Hill residences, seems about as centrally located as a building can be, but it wasn't always that way. In 1797, residents of Boston thought that the Wild West itself began on the far side of the Common, hardly a quarter-mile from the State House. Cows still grazed there, and much of the surrounding land had the bucolic air of pastures trailing off into forest. Even Beacon Hill rose, not as a polite demi-hill, but as a rugged mass of wilderness, then called the Trimount because of its triple-peaked summit. The westernmost peak was isolated enough from the Puritan stronghold that it could be put to the purposes suggested by the name Mount Whoredom.

Predictably enough, moving the State House into this setting focused the city's attention on this area and changed things for good. While the Common became a true park, the Trimount became the subject of land speculation. It was quite ingeniously leveled and quickly became the compressed but still

Map
on pages
102–3

The Boston window in the State House.

BELOW: inside the State House.

BELOW:
the gas lamps on
Beacon Hill are
permanently lit.
BELOW RIGHT:
Beacon Street.

idyllic gaslit neighborhood of bow-fronted townhouses now known as "The Hill." At first, everyone expected that the new residences of Beacon Hill would be urban estates along the lines of Bulfinch's No. 85 Mount Vernon Street, which is to this day one of Boston's most majestic houses. But the mansion plans were quickly scaled down to the smaller blocks one sees today. At No. 55 Mount Vernon, the **Nichols House** ㉑ (open Tues–Sat pm; tours every half hour; entrance fee) offers a more typical example of Beacon Hill building. Also a Charles Bulfinch project, the house is now a small museum.

To get a sense of The Hill, walk west down Beacon Street from the State House. At numbers 39 and 40 Beacon stand twin 1818 Greek Revival mansions, one built for Daniel Parker, owner of the Parker House, Boston's oldest hotel. At numbers 42 and 43, the Somerset Club, built in 1819 as a mansion for David Sears, was acquired by the most exclusive of Boston social clubs in 1872. At number 45 Beacon stands the third of Harrison Gray Otis's houses, built in 1805. The **Harrison Gray Otis House** ㉒ at 141 Cambridge Street, just outside Beacon Hill proper (open Wed–Sun 11am–4pm; tours every hour; entrance fee), gives a chance to see inside the first of the Otis houses. It has period furnishings, and is decorated with with authentic, period paints and wallpapers,.

Louisburg Square ㉓, developed between Pinckney and Mount Vernon streets around 1840, epitomizes the Beacon Hill style and its urban delicacy. The Square has long stood at the summit of Boston society. William Dean Howells, the novelist and *Atlantic Monthly* editor; Louisa May Alcott, author of *Little Women*; and Jenny Lind, the "Swedish Nightingale," all lived at one time or another in the houses surrounding the Square's elegant green. Lind married her accompanist Otto Goldschmidt at No. 20 during an American tour in 1852.

Another charming example of Beacon Hill's spirit can be found at numbers 13, 15 and 17 Chestnut Street, where Bulfinch built for the daughters of his client Hepzibah Swan three exquisite townhouses in a prim little row. Chestnut Street vies for the title of prettiest street on the Hill, so fetching is the gently animated conversation of its porches and windows, flower-box geraniums and romantic gaslights.

On the west side of Beacon Hill, Charles Street is a prime spot to stroll, shop and snack. Here is Boston's leading concentration of antique stores and a diverse collection of coffee houses, bakeries, florists, cafes and boutiques. DeLuca's Market brims with the smells of ripe melons, fresh sausage and coffee beans. Nearby, Café Bella Vita serves coffee and pastries, but the real draw is people-watching.

The street's principal landmark is the **Charles Street Meeting House ㉔** at the corner of Charles and Mount Vernon streets. Built first for the Third Baptist Church in 1804, it served as the home of the African Methodist Episcopal Church and later the Unitarian-Universalist Church. At street level, this unpretentious building houses shops and a cafe-scale outpost of the popular New American restaurant, Rebecca's.

Charles Street has dozens of antiques shops.

Wander off Charles on to the shady, peaceful streets that parallel it and lead back up the hill. Many of the houses here are noteworthy either for the talent of their architects or the luminous names of their former occupants. Polar explorer Admiral Richard E. Byrd lived in Nos. 7–9 Brimmer Street, while No. 44 in the same street was the lifelong home of the great historian Samuel Eliot Morison. The Victorian clergyman and philosopher William Ellery Channing lived at No. 83 Mount Vernon Street, next door to the Otis mansion.

BELOW:
Louisburg Square.

Back Bay

From Beacon Hill, it's an easy transition both in distance and architectural feeling to the handsome streets of Back Bay, the area that has come in recent years to epitomize "Old Boston." Don't be fooled by its old-money airs, though. Back Bay literally crawled from the mud into prominence, with a massive program of filling in a festering swampland that, in 1849, was declared "offensive and injurious" by the Board of Health.

The heroic story begins in 1857 when the legislature adopted a grand plan for the Back Bay: there would be long vistas down dignified blocks, and a wide boulevard with a French-style park down the middle. In 1858 the first load of fill, which had been collected with an innovative new tool called the steam shovel, arrived by train from Needham, about 10 miles (16 km) to the southwest. During the next 20 years, some 600 acres (240 hectares) of dry land emerged from the muck that was Back Bay.

And sure enough, as houses began to appear, they were dignified. Despite the vagaries of individual taste and the piecemeal selling of lots, the new blocks went up with a harmoniousness that from the beginning gave Back Bay the stately unity it still possesses. One young man who planned to build his bride a house in Back Bay was icily informed by his prospective father-in-law that he would never allow a daughter of his to live on "made ground." But such qualms were rare, and the new streets quickly became fashionable.

Back Bay presents as great a showing of the Boston domestic architecture of the second half of the 19th century as Beacon Hill does of the first. The verdant mall of **Commonwealth Avenue ㉕** centers things, and the houses along it, as well as those on Marlborough and Beacon, reveal choice architectural cameos.

In 1814 a developer, Uriah Cotting, built a dam across Back Bay, hoping to harness the tidal currents to power as many as 80 mills. But there was less tidal power than expected and only a handful of mills were built.

BELOW:
the rooftops of Back Bay.

Starting at the Arlington Street entrance to the Public Gardens, the visitor may want to cross over to the Ritz-Carlton Hotel, on the corner of Newbury Street. The Ritz-Carlton is the perfect place to fortify oneself with a cocktail or a cup of tea and to observe Brahmin society in its element.

Map on pages 102–3

From here, head north to No. 137 Beacon Street, between Arlington and Berkeley (the cross-streets ascend in alphabetical order). Built in 1860 at the start of Back Bay construction, the **Gibson House** ㉖ (open May–Oct: Wed–Sun, tours 1, 2 and 3pm; Nov–Apr: weekends, tours 1, 2 and 3pm; entrance fee) has been left substantially as it was; it now houses a museum that recreates the feel of Back Bay living in its heyday. Continue to the corner of Commonwealth and Clarendon for a look at the First Baptist Church, a handsome design by H.H. Richardson. Its tower is graced with figures modeled after celebrities of the day – Emerson, Hawthorne and Longfellow.

In the block between Clarendon and Dartmouth, Commonwealth Avenue (known as "Comm Ave" to most of the locals) displays its most memorable structures. The romantic houses that march down this stretch perfectly justify the avenue's reputation as America's Champs-Elysées.

One of several murals along Newbury Street.

Paralleling Commonwealth Avenue on the south are Newbury and Boylston streets, the Back Bay that has been taken over by commerce and the rarefied air of uptown chic. On **Newbury Street**, the hairstyles are elaborate and the clothes are designer. Pricey restaurants, sidewalk cafes and seductive storefronts abound, and a number of fine galleries operate in sleekly converted townhouses. The best of the contemporary galleries – Alpha and Barbara Krakow – are located at No. 14 and No. 10, respectively. Vose's Gallery, at No. 238, specializes in American painting, 1669 to 1940. A fixture since 1897, Vose's is the oldest private gallery in the United States. Five generations of the same family have faithfully maintained the tradition.

BELOW: street café in Newbury Street.

Back Bay has seen the most ambitious building sprees in the past few decades. A controversial project, **Copley Place**, a megaplex occupying over 9 acres (4 hectares) atop the Massachusetts Turnpike, has proved – despite a considerable degree of initial skepticism – an enjoyable addition to city life, with its 11-screen cinema, hotel, and dozens of inviting restaurants and upmarket shops. Although many of the latter are clones of those found in other upscale malls, a few are unique, such as the Artful Hand Gallery (exceptional crafts) and Treasured Legacy (African American literature and art).

Connected to this complex by a "skyway," is Boston's original skyscraper, the **Prudential Center** ㉗ (800 Boylston Street), dating from the early 1960s. It has 52 stories and a **Skywalk** (open daily 10am–10pm; entrance fee) which provides an exhilarating, map-like, four-way view of the city. Envisioned as a bold new look for the city, "The Pru" turned out to be, in fact, a rather graceless development of the sort favored by the builders of the former Soviet Utopia. Developed out of an old railroad yard, the complex encompasses the John B. Hynes Veterans Memorial Convention Center (a striking 1988 design by Kallmann, McKinnell & Wood), a hotel, two department stores, and a lively mix of shops and restaurants spruced up in 1994.

The story of Christian Science

The **Christian Science Church Center**  (Sunday services at 10am and 7pm) occupies the 22 acres (9 hectares) immediately south of the Prudential Center on Huntington Avenue. The complex includes three older buildings – the Romanesque Mother Church (1894), the Italianate Mother Church Extension (1904) and the Publishing Society (1933) – as well as I.M. Pei's recent additions. The expanded center, a happy marriage of old and new architectural styles, makes an impressive Vatican for a religious denomination scarcely a century old.

In the publishing wing, the **Mapparium** (call 617-450 2000 for opening times) is an extraordinary stained-glass walk-in representation of the globe, constructed between 1932 and 1935 to symbolize the Christian Science Publishing Company's worldwide outlook. Illogical it may be – you stand inside the sphere surrounded by the map in concave form, but it is certainly one of the sights of Boston. The weird acoustics compound the hallucinogenic effect.

The founding of Christian Science dates to 1866 when a frail, impoverished 45-year-old woman named Mary Baker Patterson took a severe tumble on the ice as she was walking home from a temperance meeting in Lynn, north of Boston. Several days later, after turning to the New Testament for strength and inspiration, Mrs Patterson was suddenly healed, not only of the injuries she'd suffered in the fall, but of the chronic illness that had plagued much of her younger womanhood.

After several years of Bible study, she set out to heal others. In 1875, she posted a notice on her Lynn house designating it as a "Christian Science Home." She was on her way to establishing a major American religious movement at an age when she might have been expected, in her own ironic words, to be a little

BELOW: the Christian Science Church Center.

old lady in a lace cap. After marrying a follower named Asa Eddy, she moved to Boston, where she continued teaching, writing and guiding the establishment of her church. Since then more than 3,000 Christian Science societies have been established in some 50 countries.

Map on pages 102–3

Copley Square

Follow Dartmouth Street to Boylston for one of the city's most stimulating displays of architecture: Copley Square. First, Charles McKim's **Boston Public Library ㉙** (1895). This simple, serene and high-minded Parnassus might well be the center of the Boston that claims to be the "Athens of America." What better monument to a literary legacy populated by the likes of Emerson, Hawthorne, Thoreau and Alcott? (Bret Hart once observed that in these parts it was impossible to fire a pistol without bringing down the author of a two-volume work.) With more than 5 million volumes, this is one of the great libraries in the world. But it's more than a building of books. There's art everywhere – murals by Sargent, statues by Saint-Gaudens and Daniel Chester French – and, at the center of a maze of stairs and passages, a peaceful inner courtyard. Philip Johnson's massive but compatible 1972 addition completes the complex.

Across the square stands H. H. Richardson's wonderful **Trinity Church ㉚** (1877), a tour de force in Romanesque inventiveness and a striking medievalist contrast to the Public Library's classicism. Inside, what impresses is the wealth of murals, mosaics, carvings and stained glass.

Above everything looms I. M. Pei & Partners' magnificent blue-green mirror, the John Hancock Mutual Life Insurance Tower, built in 1976, topped by the **John Hancock Observatory ㉛** (ticket office at Trinity Place and St James

A "Duck Tour", in a World War II amphibious vehicle, includes a ride on the River Charles. Tours start from the Prudential Center.

BELOW: Copley Square Park.

Avenue; open daily 9am–10pm; entrance fee). At an excellent observatory on the 60th floor with a magnificent view over Boston (a better downtown prospect than the Prudential Skywalk, though visitors cannot see out on all sides), there is also a model of the city as it was in 1776, with commentary.

The Tower initially had a propensity in windy weather to lose the huge sheets of glass covering it; miraculously, no one was hurt when the glass fell. That problem was solved soon after the tower was completed, when all 10,344 panes – some 13 acres (5 hectares) worth – were replaced at a cost of $8.5 million.

The first Boston Marathon, staged in 1897, involved 15 runners. Today, about 8,000 line up for the starter's gun as 1½ million spectators look on.

Every April, on Patriots' Day, Copley Square becomes the destination of the thousands who enter the famous Boston Marathon, perhaps the most celebrated running event on the planet.

South End and The Fenway

To the south and east of the Christian Science Center and Copley Square sprawls the South End, an ethnically diverse, up-and-coming expanse of Victorian bowfront townhouses. Particularly pleasing architecturally are the areas around Worcester Square, Rutland and leafy Union Park Square.

The **Boston Center for the Arts** ㉜, at Clarendon and Tremont streets (tel: 617-426 5000), is almost always hopping: this lively complex encompasses artists' studios and galleries, several small experimental theatres, the Cyclorama (an 1884 dome now used for antique markets and special exhibits and events), and one of the city's favorite bistros, Hamersley's.

From the South End, Huntington Avenue leads southwest past several of Boston's greatest institutions. At the northwest corner of Massachusetts Avenue ("Mass Ave") stands the majestic gable-roofed **Symphony Hall** ㉝ (tel: 617-536 0944 or 800-274 8499; tours by appointment), the acoustically impeccable 1900 building that is home to the renowned Boston Symphony Orchestra and, in summer, its less formal offshoot, the Boston Pops Orchestra. Tickets can be hard to come by, but any amount of exertion will be well rewarded.

BELOW: the John Hancock Tower.

Continuing down Huntington Avenue, one arrives at the spectacular **Museum of Fine Arts** ㉞ (open daily; Wed till 9:45pm; also West Wing Thur and Fri till 9:45pm; entrance fee; reduced admission Wed 4–9pm, Thur and Fri after 5pm). Built in 1909 to house holdings that were bursting the joints of an earlier building situated in Copley Square, Guy Lowell's imposing design affords space for plenty of Impressionists – including the largest number of Monets outside France. This incredible museum boasts the most complete assemblage of Asian art under one roof anywhere; the world's best collection of 19th-century American art; and the finest collection of Egyptian Old Kingdom objects outside Cairo. The latter includes what some consider one of the greatest portraits ever executed by the human hand – a limestone bust of Prince Ankh-haf (2520 BC) that is wholly unearthly in its magnificence.

In 1981, I. M. Pei added a stone-clad, glass-topped new wing that perfectly complements the original building and creates an inspiring, expansive space ideal for a changing array of exhibits.

Within sight of the Museum of Fine Arts stands the **Isabella Stewart Gardner Museum** ㉟ (280 The Fenway; open Tues–Sun; entrance fee) an exquisite 1903 neo-Venetian palazzo assembled by Boston's most flamboyant grande dame. The unstoppable "Mrs Jack" may have scandalized Brahmin Boston (she was known to parade two pet lions down Beacon Street), but she proved a generous and astute patron of the arts.

During the 1890s, she set her sights on such masterpieces as Titian's *Rape of Europa*, Rembrandt's *Storm on the Sea of Galilee*, and Vermeer's *The Concert.* In 1896, when her collection was bursting the seams of two adjoining Beacon Hill brownstones, she commissioned her fantasy palace at the very edge of town, alongside the marshes of the Fens.

The galleries that frame the four-story glass-roofed courtyard remained, by her posthumous order, unchanged until March 1990, when thieves, disguised as policemen, made off with works of art worth $300 million, including the Vermeer, three Rembrandts, five works by Degas and a Manet. To date, none has been recovered. There is still much to see, however, and this eclectic collection, displayed in a charmingly hodge-podge fashion, constitutes one of the great small museums in the world.

North of the museums broods another of Boston's great shrines, **Fenway Park** ㊱ (4 Yawkey Way; tours weekdays 10am–2pm on non-game days only; tel: 617-267 8661 or 617-267 1700) on whose brightly-lit green baseball diamond the Boston Red Sox do heroic, if usually tragic, battle for the pennant. Here, as the world turns slowly during a muggy twilight doubleheader, the out-of-towner can experience first-hand how Boston turns sport into religion. Indeed, such past stars as Ted Williams and Carl Yastrzemski are almost deified.

Map on pages 102–3

TIP

A delightful way to spend a Sunday afternoon in winter is to attend a concert in the Gardner Museum's Tapestry Room. Tickets at the door, or tel: 617-734 1359.

BELOW: the courtyard of the Isabella Stewart Gardner Museum.

Henry Moore's Three-piece reclining figure, draped, on the MIT campus.

The home of the Boston Celtics, one of the success stories of the National Basketball Association, and the Bruins, Boston's major ice-hockey team is the state-of-the-art **FleetCenter** ❼, near North Station.

On the banks of the Charles River

Great cities embrace great rivers from which they are inseparable. This is true of Boston. Here, before the townhouses of Back Bay, the Charles River, having meandered 40 miles (64 km) from its source, widens into a large basin, like a giant mirror held up to the city's profile. It was designed to do just that, by the civic-minded citizens who created the Charles River Dam in 1908. The dam itself is home to Boston's **Museum of Science** ❽ (open daily; Fri till 9pm; entrance fee). Here, visitors can watch simulated lightning, climb into a model of the Apollo lunar module, cower under a plastic Tyrannosaurus Rex, and enjoy a wide variety of ever-changing hands-on exhibits.

In ensuing decades after the construction of the dam, the **Esplanade** was landscaped, a winding park of lagoons, trees and walks. Once a festering, polluted eyesore, the river's edge has become one of the city's favorite places to stretch its legs. Roller skaters wired for sound, joggers, bike riders and sunbathers all migrate here. So do the great crowds that turn out to hear the Boston Pops play under open summer skies at the **Hatch Memorial Shell** ❾.

In Cambridge, but separate from the other sights of Cambridge and across Harvard Bridge, is the **Massachusetts Institute of Technology (MIT)** ❿. Housed in solid, geometrical buildings, as impersonal and mysterious as natural laws, MIT produces Nobel laureates, new scientific advances and White House science advisors with absolute reliability. The Finnish architect Eero Saarinen

BELOW: the Red Sox at Fenway Park.

designed two of its highlights: the inward looking, cylindrical MIT Chapel, illuminated by light reflected from a moat, and the tent-like Kresge Auditorium which rises from a circular brick terrace, its roof apparently balanced by slender metal rods on three points.

Maps: 102–3 & 127

Separate, too, from sights in central Boston but a point of pilgrimage for many, is the **John F. Kennedy Library and Museum** ❹ (Columbia Point; MBTA red line south to JFK/UMass and shuttle bus; or, in summer, boat from Long Wharf; open daily; entrance fee). Set dramatically beside the ocean, the museum makes excellent use of film, videos and recreated settings (including the Oval Office) to recall JFK's life, career, and legacy.

Cambridge and Harvard Square

Elizabeth Hardwick once described Boston and Cambridge as two ends of the same mustache. Indeed, across the Charles lies a separate city that is absolutely inseparable from its companion metropolis. Neither suburb nor next town down the pike, Cambridge is the brains of the act, the nerve center of the body.

At the heart of Cambridge is lively **Harvard Square** ❹, the playground of book stores, coffee houses, and shops to the west and north of the Yard, with a menagerie of horn-rimmed professors, "B School" overachievers and fresh-looking undergraduates in evidence. At its center, as a matrix for all wanderings, is the international **Out of Town News**, housed in a historic kiosk, and beside it, Dmitri Hadzi's gently humorous stone sculpture, *Omphalos*, suggesting that Harvard is, as its supporters have long held, the center (or navel) of the universe.

Opposite Out of Town News is the venerable **Harvard Cooperative Society** ("Coop" for short), a Harvard institution founded in 1882 as an alternative to

The JFK Library is one of nine "presidential libraries," which hold the papers of nine of the presidents since Herbert Hoover. Presidents may establish a library in the location of their choice; this one was set up near the home of Rose Kennedy, JFK's mother.

BELOW: busking in Harvard Square.

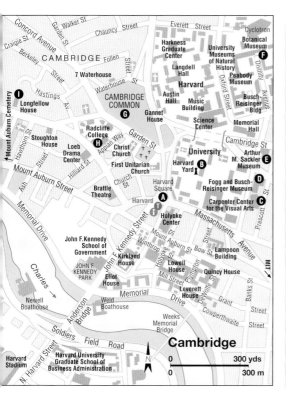

overpriced local shops; today the prices are pretty much at a par (except for affiliated students and faculty, who enjoy a discount), but the full-scale department store is a favorite with tourists for Harvard-seal mementos.

Every block presents some window or door to investigate. Browse the fine bookstores such as WordsWorth and the Harvard Book Store, check the movie schedules at the area's local collegiate-oriented theaters. There's even a great old tobacco store, a dark cave called Leavitt and Peirce, that carries an interesting collection of ruminative games. In fair weather, chess masters invariably hold court – and court challengers – at the Au Bon Pain café within Holyoke Center, a Harvard administrative building that now hosts a corridor of inviting restaurants and shops.

Nearby, on Dunster Street, is a mecca for ice cream fans, Herrell's, and John Harvard's Brew House, an atmospheric brew pub based on the conceit that Harvard's pious benefactor was descended from brew masters.

Standing proudly above the red brick and green ivy, are the spires of **Harvard University**, America's oldest institution of higher learning. Self-confident and backed by enormous wealth, Harvard has been a world index of intellectual accomplishment almost since that day in 1638 when the first 12 freshmen convened in a single frame house bordered by cow pastures. The alma mater of six American presidents to date, Harvard remains a formidable force.

The heart of the place is **Harvard Yard ❸**, withdrawn tranquilly behind the walls that separate it from Harvard Square outside. Passing through the gate that proclaims "Enter to Grow in Wisdom," the visitor enters a hallowed world of grass and trees, ghosts and venerable brick – a living, eminently walkable museum of American architecture from colonial times to the present.

BELOW: Harvard Square and its historic news stand.

Map on page 127

Massachusetts Hall (1720), Harvard's oldest standing building, shows the beautiful simplicity of its period, but its history is complex. While it has always provided students with rooms, the Hall has also quartered Revolutionary troops, as well as housed a lecture hall, a famous drama workshop and, since 1939, the offices of the University president. Nearby stands little Holden Chapel (1744), once described as "a solitary English daisy in a field of Yankee dandelions."

At the Yard's center stands Charles Bulfinch's University Hall, built of white granite in 1815. In front is Daniel Chester French's 1814 statue of John Harvard, the young Puritan minister for whom the college was named after he left it half his estate and all his books. Since no likeness of John Harvard existed, French fashioned an idealized figure for his statue, using a student as his model.

East of University Hall, three massive buildings set off the central green on which commencement is celebrated each June. These are H. H. Richardson's 1880 masterwork Sever Hall, with its subtle brick decorations; Memorial Church (1932), with its Doric columns; and the monumental Widener Library, fronted by a broad flight of steps and 12 stone columns. Given by the mother of one Harry Elkins Widener, who died on the *Titanic*, the library is the center of Harvard's network of 92 libraries, which together house over 12 million volumes, America's third largest book collection.

Chess is traditionally played in Harvard Square.

Around this historic core, the university sprawls throughout central Cambridge. The Harvard Houses (1930), between the Yard and the Charles, represent a return to the Georgian traditions of the 19th century. These are the residences of sophomores, juniors and seniors. To the east of the Yard stands the **Carpenter Center for the Visual Arts ⓒ** (1963), a cubist, machine-like design that represents the only American work of the great French architect

BELOW: a regatta at Cambridge Boat Club, on the Charles River.

Map on page 127

TIP

Admission to the Harvard University Art Museums is free on Saturday mornings 10–12am.

BELOW: Longfellow House, Brattle Street.
RIGHT: students with founding father John Harvard.

Le Corbusier. Harvard extends even beyond the banks of the Charles; the Business School is across the river, and the Medical School is near the Museum of Fine Arts.

Of special interest to visitors are the university's museums. Just outside the Yard to the east are the **Fogg and Busch-Reisinger Art Museums** ⓒ (32 Quincy Street; open Mon–Sat, Sun pm; entrance fee except on Sat am). The Fogg's massive holdings include such masterpieces as Van Gogh's *Self-Portrait*, Renoir's *Seated Bather*, Fra Angelico's *Crucifixion* and several early Picassos. It also owns a world-class collection of Chinese cave paintings and archaic Chinese jade. Adjoining the Fogg, Werner Otto Hall houses central and northern European art. Housed in the same building, the Busch-Reisinger has outstanding examples of German expressionism and Bauhaus artifacts. Along the street, the **Arthur Sackler Museum** ⓔ (open Mon–Sat; Sun pm; entrance fee except on Sat am) houses the Ancient, Islamic and Oriental collections.

A few blocks north on Oxford Street stands a huge complex housing four science museums. The displays are old-fashioned – they are university collections, after all – but a major draw is the **Botanical Museum** ⓕ (open Mon–Sat; Sun pm; entrance fee), with its famous "Glass Flowers," a collection of true-to-life models of more than 700 plant species executed by Leopold Blaschka and his son Rudolph in 19th-century Dresden. In the same building, the **Museum of Comparative Zoology** includes George Washington's pheasants (inevitably in stuffed form) as well as the world's oldest reptile eggs. Also on the site are the **Mineralogical and Geological Museum**, and the **Peabody Museum of Archaeology and Ethnology**, which has an interesting shop reflecting its anthropological collections.

On July 4, 1775, George Washington assumed command of the Continental Army on **Cambridge Common** ⓖ. A trio of cannons abandoned by the British when they left Boston in 1776 stand close to a bronze relief of Washington on horseback under an elm tree; the elm enclosed by a fence is a token replacement of the original "Washington's elm." On the south side of the Common, just across Garden Street, Christ Church (1761) was used as a barracks by patriots, and its organ pipes were made into bullets. Close by is an entrance to **Radcliffe College** ⓗ, the women's college that merged with Harvard in 1975.

In the 18th century Brattle Street was home to so many British loyalists that it was known as Tory Row. There are numerous houses the visitor can admire from the street, including No. 90, designed by H. H. Richardson of Trinity Church fame, and No. 94, the 17th-century Henry Vassal House. The yellow clapboard **Longfellow House** ⓘ (105 Brattle Street; open May–Oct; tours Wed–Sun; entrance fee) was the idyllic wedding present given to the poet Henry Wadsworth Longfellow and his wife, Fanny, by her father in 1843. Little has changed inside; Longfellow's library and furniture are here, including a chair made from the "spreading chestnut-tree," which stood at No. 56 Brattle Street and was immortalized in Longfellow's poem *The Village Blacksmith*. Unhappily, Fanny was fatally burned in the house in 1861. ◻

Map on pages 102–3

CANADA

Boston

THE FREEDOM TRAIL

Given the dense traffic, it's simpler to walk in Boston than to drive. Taking advantage of that fact, this signed route provides an easy way of absorbing the city's revolutionary history

The shot heard round the world – the starting gun of the American Revolution – was fired in Lexington, just west of Boston, on April 18, 1775. In the months and years that followed, until the war for American independence from Britain ended in 1781, Boston would continue to play a leading role in the conflict. The "midnight ride of Paul Revere" (made famous in the poem by Henry Wadsworth Longfellow), the Boston Tea Party, the Battle of Bunker Hill – all are part of Boston's colorful Revolutionary past.

In Lexington and Concord, which today are suburbs of Boston, national parks preserve the legacy of the conflict's beginnings. And in the heart of Boston, a cleverly designed 2½-mile (4-km) footpath, the Freedom Trail, invites visitors to experience Boston as it was in the Revolutionary era, to visit historical sites associated with the war, and to walk where the founders of the country walked more than 200 years ago. It is estimated that some 3 million people visit the Freedom Trail each year.

Although most of the trail follows city streets, it is not advisable to drive it: Downtown Boston is famously hard to negotiate with a car, and parking spaces are hard to find and pricey. The Freedom Trail is easy to follow as a self-guided tour – just follow the red brick road (or more accurately in many places, the red painted line). At some sites, costumed interpreters and docents greet trail-walkers.

It takes an hour or so to walk the length of the trail at a brisk pace, but to appreciate the history of its 16 official sites, you should allow at least a half-day. Detailed brochures and guidebooks are available at the information booth (tel: 617-227 8800) at the start of the trail on Boston Common at Tremont Street.

Walkers may begin anywhere along the Trail, but the logical starting point is the Common, itself a mustering ground for Colonial militia before and during the Revolutionary War. Today, the Common is one of the most beloved public spaces in Boston – a 45-acre swath of green that is overlooked by the gold dome of the State House.

From Boston Common, the Freedom Trail leads to the Old Granary Burying Ground adjacent to the Park Street Church on Tremont Street. Revolutionary heroes such as Samuel Adams, John Hancock, Paul Revere, and James Otis are buried here.

Nearby is King's Chapel, built of granite in 1749 and containing the largest bell ever cast in Paul Revere's foundry. Revere, one of the best-known patriots of the Revolution, lived in the North End and was a silver- and metalsmith by trade. Among those buried in the King's Chapel Burying Ground (the city's oldest graveyard) is William Dawes, the lesser-known of the two Lexington messenger-riders who

BELOW: Paul Revere as portrayed by John Singleton Copley in 1768.

carried the warning that the British were on the march. (Dawes's name is less well known than Revere's in part because he took a longer route to reach Lexington and so arrived later than his compatriot did.)

At the 1729 Old South Meeting House, one of the most notable sites of the Revolutionary era, a small historical museum includes a scale-model diorama depicting Colonial-era Boston. A crowd of 5,000 rallied at Old South on December 16, 1773 to oppose the British tea tax. Following the meeting, the Sons of Liberty headed off to dump a shipload of British tea into Boston Harbor in a famous protest, an incident later known as the Boston Tea Party.

From here the trail leads to the Old State House. Boston's oldest public building was built in 1713 to serve as the center of political life in the emerging Massachusetts Bay Colony. The proclamation of the Declaration of Independence was read to Boston citizens on July 18, 1776. Afterward, in a gesture of elated defiance, two leftover symbols of British rule – a lion and a unicorn – were removed from the roof of the State House and burned. Today, the landmark Old State House is dwarfed by towering financial center buildings.

Wending its way through Faneuil Hall Marketplace (a key meeting point for Boston's revolutionaries), the Freedom Trail heads into the North End. The North End is the oldest section of Boston: its narrow, crooked streets were laid out over what were originally cow paths. Here, at 19 North Square, is the steep-roofed wooden house that belonged to Paul Revere. Already almost 100 years old when Revere bought it in 1770, the little peaked house where the patriot lived for some 30 years is the oldest structure in Boston.

Not far away, on Paul Revere Mall, a statue of Revere on horseback in front of the Old North Church is one of Boston's most-photographed sites. A pair of lanterns hung in the Old North (whose steeple has since been replaced) on the eve of the war signaled that the British forces were leaving Boston (then almost an island) by sea, rather than by land.

From the North End, the Freedom Trail crosses the Charlestown Bridge to Charlestown. (An inexpensive water shuttle runs between Charlestown and Long Wharf, near the trail, making it possible to go one way on foot and the other by ferry.) Here a 221-foot (66-meter) granite obelisk commemorates the June 17, 1775 Battle of Bunker Hill. Here, on what is actually Breed's Hill, the Colonials hastily built an earthwork fort in anticipation of a British attack. During the ensuing battle, which was ultimately a British victory, the revolutionaries managed to strike a resounding blow by wounding or killing about half the British force.

"The Whites of Their Eyes," a half-hour audio-visual presentation on the battle, is shown in the Bunker Hill Pavilion near the Charlestown Navy Yard. Berthed nearby is the frigate USS *Constitution* – not part of Boston's Revolutionary past, but famous as the oldest commissioned warship afloat in the world. Her first mission after being launched in Boston in 1797 was to guard the new country's commercial interests in the Caribbean against the French. During the War of 1812, she earned the nickname Old Ironsides, by which she has been known ever since. ❏

The Freedom Trail is self-guided and can be joined at any point.

BELOW: the Bunker Hill Monument, Charlestown.

THE MUSEUM OF FINE ARTS, BOSTON

Few museums in the world rival the MFA for the quality and scope of its decorative and fine art collections. Every one has something exceptional

One of the first museums in America, the MFA opened in 1870 and in 1909 moved into the present building. Cyrus Edwin Dallin's bronze equestrian statue *Appeal to the Great Spirit* (left) was placed in the forecourt in 1913.

The highly cultured citizens of 19th-century Boston were keen collectors. Many were passionate about things Asian, and their treasures in due course came to the MFA, forming the nucleus of an outstanding collection. Others travelled to Europe, and the museum acquired one of the foremost holdings outside Paris of Impressionist painting, in particular works by Monet, Pissaro, Sisley, Renoir and Manet. It has nearly 70 works by Jean-François Millet. The American art collection is one of the best in the US; the European and American decorative arts rooms display superb silver, porcelain, furniture and musical instruments. The Nubian and Egyptian collections are unrivalled in the world.

There is so much to see, the first-time visitor would be well advised either to pick out just one collection, or take a (free) tour that highlights the best from all the collections. *See also page 124.*

▽ **AMERICAN DECORATIVE ARTS**
The museum is strong in decorative arts from pre-Civil War New England. Below: a Paul Revere teapot, *c.*1760–5.

△ **THE JAPANESE GARDEN**
Tenshin-en, "The Garden of the Heart of Heaven," is one of three gardens in which visitors may draw breath (beside the West Wing; open spring through early fall).

▷ **THE IMPRESSIONISTS**
Renoir's *Dance at Bougival* (1883) shares wall space with equally important works by such European painters as van Gogh, Degas, and Gauguin.

◁ LANDSCAPE ART

The New England landscape is captured in works by such American artists as Winslow Homer and Edward Hopper. Left: Edward Hopper's watercolour *Lighthouse and Buildings, Portland Head, Cape Elizabeth* (1927)

△ AMERICAN ART

The Letter by Mary Cassatt (1890). More formal are the portraits by colonial painters Gilbert Stuart and John Singleton Copley, and society portraitist John Singer Sargent.

▽ THE ASIAN COLLECTION

A highlight of the excellent Asian collection is this little 12th-century AD (Jin Dynasty) Chinese buddha, made of lacquered wood with painting and gilding.

THE ANCIENT WORLD

For 40 years from 1905 Harvard University and the Museum of Fine Arts collaborated on an archeological excavation in Egypt, based at the Great Pyramids at Giza. From this, the museum acquired a world-famous collection of Egyptian treasures. Among many Old Kingdom sculptures is this beautiful statue of King Mycerinus, who built the Third Pyramid at Giza, and his queen, dated to *c*.2548–30BC.

Other treasures include gilded and painted mummy masks, and some amazingly well preserved hierglyphic inscriptions. The Giza expedition's director, Dr Reisner, also worked in the Sudan and brought home a dazzling collection of Nubian artifacts, the best in the world outside Khartoum. Particularly awe-inspiring is the exquisite gold jewelry, inlaid with enamel and precious stones, and the sculptures, varying in size from huge statues of Nubian kings to tiny shawabtis.

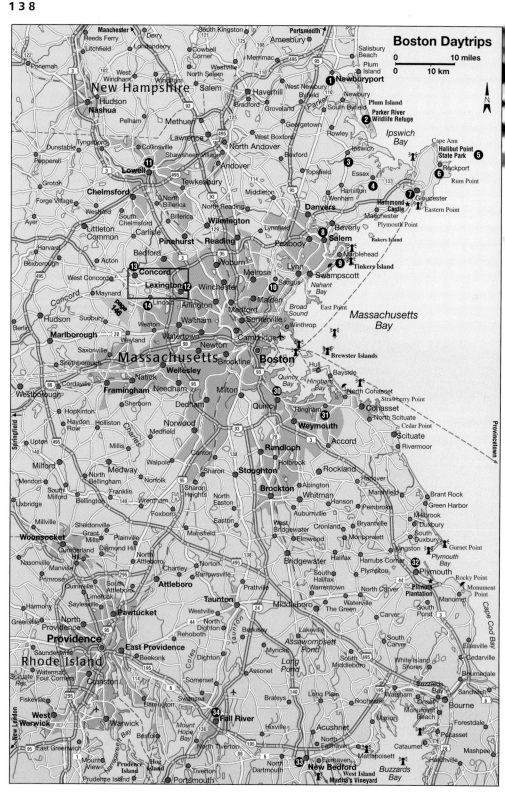

Boston Daytrips

BOSTON DAYTRIPS

We've either read them or we've read about them: the witches of Salem, the Pilgrims of Plymouth, the Patriots of Lexington, and the writers – Alcott, Emerson and Thoreau – of Concord

Map on page 138

E ven Boston's most committed devotees would concede that one of the city's strengths is its scope for daytrips, from the hugely popular cultural epicenters such as Plymouth to offbeat delights such as a Gropius house in suburban Lincoln. Public transportation from Boston makes many of the places described easy to reach; frequent commuter rail services from North Station serve Concord, Salem (for buses to Marblehead), Rockport, Manchester, Gloucester and Ipswich, and there are buses from South Station to Plymouth, New Bedford, Fall River and Newburyport; the T Red Line goes to Quincy Center. Providence (*see page 230*) is another easy daytrip by train from South Station, and buses from South Station serve Newport (*see page 233*).

The North Shore

Once home to a magnificent merchant fleet and a thriving shipbuilding industry and now busy with yachts, **Newburyport ❶**, 35 miles (56 km) north of Boston, has benefited from careful preservation to retain a period flavor. The town survived a devastating fire in 1811 – after which numerous handsome brick buildings were constructed. But by the early 20th century, the arrival of freighters had reduced the proud shipbuilding industry of "Clipper City" to an aging relic. The **Maritime Museum** (Derby Street; open daily; entrance fee) within the former Custom House tells the story.

However, an exemplary renewal program begun in the 1960s has restored Newburyport's beauty and popularity. The **Market Square** district is a symphony of brick and bustle, with fine shops and restaurants, plus live outdoor entertainment in good weather, when strolls along the boardwalk can be enjoyed. Whale-watching trips are big business.

On High Street successful sea captains built their Greek Revival and late Georgian palaces, some with the symbolic "widow's walks" atop the roofs, where anxious wives strained for a glimpse of their husbands' return to port. **The Cushing House**, (open May–Oct Tues–Sat; entrance fee) at No. 98 High Street, belonged to Caleb Cushing, a 19th-century lawyer (Newburyport's first mayor) and the first US Ambassador to China. Visitors to the house, now home to the Historical Society of Old Newbury, can view the exotic booty he brought back.

Just 3 miles (5 km) away via Water Street from Newburyport is the **Parker River National Wildlife Refuge ❷**, known simply as **Plum Island**. Depending on the season, the 6 miles (10 km) of sand dunes and ocean beach yield a riot of false heather, dune grass, scrub pine and delicious wild beach plums and cranberries. Geese, pheasants, rab-

PRECEDING PAGES: Annisquam, Cape Ann. **BELOW:** Newburyport.

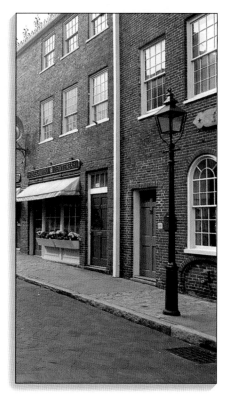

bits, deer, woodchucks, turtles and toads roam freely over the preserve. In March and October the skies are black with migrating geese and ducks. Fishing, hiking and bird-watching are encouraged. Only a limited number of visitors (350 cars; parking fee) are allowed into the refuge at one time.

City and country meet about 4 miles (7 km) out of town in the **Spencer-Pierce-Little Farm** (Route 1A; tours June–mid-Oct Wed–Sun; entrance fee), a manor house built around 1675–1700 and now owned by the Society for the Preservation of New England Antiquities. A distinctively sturdy building for its day (built of stone and brick, instead of the customary wood), it is today, with its layers of structural alteration, a prime site for architectural archeology. Its farmland has been under three and a half centuries of continual cultivation.

The road to Ipswich

Route 1A leads out of Newburyport toward Ipswich along a lazy, tree-lined road, where hand-built stone walls (too low to keep people out but high enough to keep sheep in) give way to quaint roadside stands proffering eggs, apples, ice cream, fresh fish and lobsters-to-go. There are some fine antique bargains to be found along these roads, too.

The old streets of the town of **Ipswich ❸** are lined with restored 17th- and 18th-century houses. On Main Street, the 1640 **Whipple House** is a fine example of a Puritan homestead, furnished in period style and with a colonial herb garden. Out of town, adjacent to the Great House, a breathtakingly showy Stuart-style 59-room mansion (occasionally open for tours) is the **Crane Memorial Reservation**, with 4 miles (7 km) of glorious sandy barrier beach that can be explored by an interpretative trail.

TIP

In the fall, after Labor Day, visitors to Plum Island are allowed to pick beach plums and cranberries – three quarts per person, no rakes permitted.

BELOW: queueing for fried clams at Woodman's, Essex.

Despite local claims to grandeur, Ipswich is perhaps best known for its humble clams, an obsession it shares with the neighboring town of **Essex ❹**, 5 miles (8 km) southeast on Route 133, where, folk legend has it, the fried clam was born. Raw clams had been a staple of the New England diet since pre-Colonial days, and they're still a regional delicacy. It was at **Woodman's** restaurant (tel: 978-768 6451) that clams were first dipped in batter and fried.

Cape Ann

Named for the mother of England's King Charles I, Cape Ann is practically an island, compact enough to explore in a day. From Annisquam, at the mouth of Ipswich Bay, to Pigeon Cove, the landscape is quintessential New England – quaint fishing villages and a rockbound coast.

The area has witnessed some violent behavior. A gang of pirates led by one John Phillips terrorized Gloucester during the 1720s, until one day a fishing crew gained the upper hand and sailed into Lobster Cove, near Annisquam, with Phillips' head hanging from the mast. Today, life is more sedate and visitors enjoy the vistas of sea, shanty and rugged landscape that have lured such great American artists as Winslow Homer to this lovely peninsula.

An alluring nature reserve can be enjoyed at **Halibut Point State Park ❺** in the quarries that once provided granite for Boston's buildings. Within the granite-strewn dwarf woods, the original quarry is now a huge pool edged by sheer cliffs; trees open out into heathland and scrub to reveal views over the rocky shore towards Plum Island.

The granite was shipped to ports around the world in the 19th century, from **Rockport ❻**, a bustling former fishing village-turned-artists' colony and tourist

Map on page 138

On a hot July day in 1915, restaurateur Lawrence Woodman was frying potato chips and complaining to a fisherman friend that business was slow. "Toss some clams in with those chips," suggested the friend. Woodman did, and thus created the first fried-clam.

BELOW: the much-painted harbor scene at Rockport.

Gloucester was the setting for "The Perfect Storm", Sebastian Junger's 1997 best-seller recounting the loss of the "Andrea Gail" fishing boat in 120-mile-an-hour winds.

TIP

See page 183 for more information on whale-watching trips.

BELOW: Gloucester's most famous fisherman.

attraction. In the early 18th century, the Cape Ann fleet roamed as far south as Havana and as far east as London. The seagoers' cottages crowded on to Bearskin Neck have found a new use as tourist-oriented shops. The fishing shack on the harbor has become known as Motif No. 1 because it is said to be more frequently painted and sketched than any other building in America. Signposted off Curtis Street on the edge of the village, the **Paper House** (open July–Aug daily; entrance fee) is an endearing oddity, built entirely of rolled up newspaper reinforced with glue and varnish. Begun in 1924 by an inventor of office supplies (whose wife made the magazine-paper curtains), the project took some 20 years, and includes a desk made of copies of the *Christian Science Monitor*, of which the print is still legible.

Gloucester ❼ is one of the oldest seaports in the United States. Here, Leonard Craske's famous statue of the *Gloucester Fisherman* grips the wheel and peers oceanward, a moving tribute with the legend "they that go down to the sea in ships." The city still has an active fishing fleet, and the catch is processed in plants near the waterfront. Every year, the fishermen, who are predominantly of Portuguese and Italian ancestry, participate in the Blessing of the Fleet ceremony. The town was the setting for Sebastian Junger's best-selling *The Perfect Storm*, which chronicled the climatic perils that lie in wait for fishermen.

Landlubbers get into the act, too, by taking one of the whale-watching cruises that leave daily from the Cape Ann Marina. To learn more about the heyday of whaling, visit the **Cape Ann Historical Association** (Pleasant Street; open Tues–Sat; entrance fee) for its small but select collection of furnishings and artwork, ranging from 19th-century painter Fitz Hugh Lane's rather sentimental seascapes to semi-abstractions by modernist Milton Avery.

Facing Gloucester across the harbor are two intriguing examples of mono-maniacal nesting instincts. On Eastern Point Boulevard, the early 1900s **Sleeper-McCann House** also known as "Beauport" (open May–Sept daily; Oct weekdays; entrance fee), is a romantic labyrinth of cottagey rooms, using architectural fragments from other buildings. It served as a setting for the summer parties of collector and interior designer, Henry Davis Sleeper. The themes vary entertainingly: one bedroom is in chapel style, the belfry is rich in chinoiserie, and the book tower has wooden "damask" curtains that originated from a hearse.

Just south of Gloucester, off Route 127 on Hesperus Avenue, stands **Hammond Castle** (open Thurs, Fri, Sat; Sun am; entrance fee) the 1920s fantasy abode of organ inventor John Hays Hammond Jr, Hammond plundered Europe for elements to work into his dreamhouse, including a medieval village facade to overlook the indoor pool. The entire castle was built around the monumental 8,200-pipe organ (the largest such instrument in the US in a private home). Some of Hammond's other electronic creations are on show.

Westwards along Route 127 is **Manchester**, a lovely resort town that some still call Manchester-by-the-Sea. The town features stately mansions and Singing Beach, where a bare foot scraped across the hard-packed white sand produces an almost musical squeak.

Salem

Though the scandalous witch trials earned **Salem ❽** enduring notoriety (*see page 144*), the area has much else to recommend it. Salem (on Route 1A south of Route 128; 40 minutes' train journey from North Station) owes its grandeur, now carefully restored, to its former prominence as a seaport. A red line along

Maps:
Area 138
City 143

Bewitching Salem.

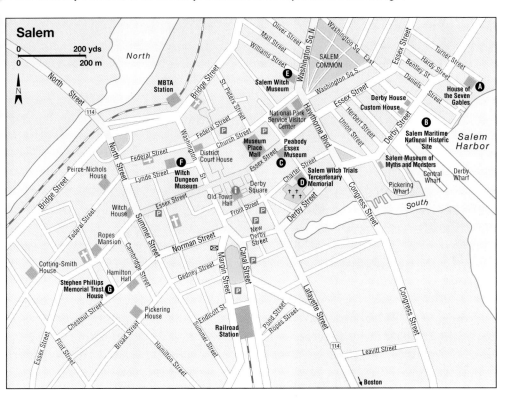

A ship's figurehead on display in the Peabody Essex Museum, Salem.

BELOW: Salem's Witch Museum.

the sidewalks marks the route linking the historic sites, which are also connected by trolley services.

On Turner Street is the forbidding-looking **House of the Seven Gables Ⓐ** (open daily; entrance fee), which inspired Hawthorne's novel of that name; he lived in a smaller house in the grounds – his cousin owned the main house – and worked for a period at the Custom House, now part of the **Salem Maritime National Historic Site Ⓑ** (open daily). Here visitors may tour the Derby Wharf and a replica of a 19th-century brigantine, the *Republic*, the Custom House, and Derby House, a merchant's mansion built in 1761.

No visit should omit the **Peabody Essex Museum Ⓒ** (East India Square; open mid-May–mid-Nov, Mon–Sat; Sun pm; mid-Nov–mid-May, closed Mon; entrance fee), which features excellent displays related to the maritime trade – particularly memorable are the ships' figureheads, maritime paintings, views of old Salem and a superb collection of artifacts brought back from the Far East.

On Essex Street, the Essex Institute preserves six houses that span two centuries of New England architecture, from the Colonial/Georgian through to the Federal styles. On the institute's grounds is a museum displaying exhibits of period furniture and local memorabilia.

Salem's maritime glory notwithstanding, most visitors will want to tour the scenes of the infamous witchcraft trials of 1692, no mere instance of "hysteria," as it has so often been described, but essentially an act of political repression. The accusations and trials capped off an intense battle for power and property between the conservative, established gentry and an individualist faction. The gentry, personified by the convicting judges, fell back on the time-honored method of attacking political and social upstarts as moral deviants.

THE SALEM WITCHES

There's a certain grim irony that Salem now makes sweet economic hay out of its dark and witchy past. All year round – but particularly during October, leading up to Hallowe'en – the old seaport touts occult events. Salem's web site (www.haunted-happenings.com) fleshes out gory details on "Terror on the Wharf" and where to purchase a "Fright Pass," for admission to three haunted houses!

Although Salem has a self-proclaimed "resident witch" (Laurie – she's easy to spot), and although the civil rights of witch practitioners have been upheld in Massachusetts, witches weren't always so welcome. Three hundred years ago, when Puritans were self-appointed arbiters of both law and religion, hysteria swept through Salem. Fourteen women and five men were executed (by hanging or pressing with stones) and hundreds were imprisoned. Several more died in jail. The trials grew from the feverish imaginations of adolescent girls who, in January 1692, became swept up in tales of voodoo and mysticism as told to them by Tituba, a slavewoman from Barbados.

Jealousy and greed between townspeople stoked the fire, as one after another pointed an accusing finger at his or her neighbor. The frenzy didn't end until May 1693, when the Governor issued a pardon to those still in jail.

Most moving, for all its silent subtlety, is the **Salem Witch Trials Tercentenary Memorial** , a stark granite court adjoining Charter Street Burying Point, the final resting place of Witch Trials Court magistrate John Hawthorne. Incised along the paving stones and walls are passages from the accused women's pleas of innocence. The **Salem Witch Museum** (Washington Square North; open daily; entrance fee) reenacts, in a rather sensationalist fashion, key scenes to a recorded commentary, while the **Witch Dungeon Museum** (Lynde Street; open daily; entrance fee) is another live show evoking the persecutions, with a look at some reconstructed dungeons.

Chestnut Street ranks among America's finest shows of domestic architecture. Open to the public is the **Stephen Phillips Memorial Trust House**, furnished with the belongings of sea captains.

A short detour from Salem, **Marblehead** makes for a refreshing day trip. A former port, it abounds in Federal captains' houses, including the **Jeremiah Lee Mansion** (Washington Street; open mid-May–mid-Oct, Mon–Sat; Sun pm; entrance fee); the pre-Revolutionary Old Town section invites strolling.

Echoes of the work ethic

At 244 Central Street, **Saugus**, the **Saugus Iron Works** have been reconstructed as they were, with furnace, forge, slitting mill, iron house, ironworks house and blacksmith's shop (open daily; tours at 9.45, 11.15, 2.15 and 3.45; entrance fee). The site was established in 1640 by John Winthrop Jr, who established a "Company of Undertakers of the Iron Works in New England," selling shares to English investors. However, the works were unprofitable owing to high costs and debts, and a shortage of skilled labor.

Maps:
Area 138
City 143

The word Salem derives from the Hebrew "shalom", meaning peace.

BELOW: Salem Harbor.

The one-time model mill town of **Lowell** ⓫, long an industrial dinosaur, is enjoying a renaissance as a major tourist attraction. Sightseeing ferries ply the old canals, trolleys clang through the streets, and looms pound again at the **Boott Cotton Mills Museum** (Market Street; open daily; entrance fee) operated with the Lowell National Historical Park Visitor Center. The many ethnic restaurants are reason enough to go. Added incentive is offered by the **New England Quilt Museum** (Shattuck Street; open Mon–Sat; Sun pm; closed Sun Nov–May; entrance fee) showcasing outstanding piecework, antique to contemporary, and by the **New England Sports Museum** (Shattuck Street; open Mon–Sat; Sun pm; entrance fee) with exciting hands-on displays of all things sporting.

Lexington and Concord

The Minutemen were armed civilians who were prepared to fight at a minute's notice .

The route of the British advance in 1775 through **Lexington** ⓬ to **Concord** ⓭, where the opposing ranks met in battle, is designated the **Battle Road**, which although mostly a highway has a number of historical attractions along it, many part of the **Minute Man National Historical Park**. It is sometimes forgotten that the colonists' uprising was a truly conservative revolution, fought largely by well-to-do landowners concerned with a growing British bite out of their profit margins as well as with theories of liberty and participatory democracy.

In the 19th century the town of Concord was a seedbed of literary output. It is remarkable that so many of the cultural giants of America lived within a short stroll of each other. Route 126 out of Concord to **Lincoln** ⓮ passes further points of literary and architectural interest.

BELOW: a Memorial Day procession, Concord.

Chronologically, a visit to the Battle Road sites should go east to west. South of Lexington, the **Museum of Our National Heritage** ⓯ (Marrett Road; open

Mon–Sat; Sun pm) exhibits items of American history, with a section on Lexington. The **Munroe Tavern**, a russet-colored building of 1635 on the left side of the Battle Road, served as headquarters for the Redcoats and as a hospital on their retreat from Concord. At the heart of Lexington a statue of Captain John Parker stands on **Battle Green** ⓰, where on April 19, 1775, the first shot was fired (possibly by a nervous 14- or 15-year-old Minuteman whose gun went off accidentally); of the Minutemen, vastly outnumbered, eight were killed.

Maps: Pages 138 & below

At the 1690 **Buckman Tavern** (Bedford Street; open Mon–Sat; Sun pm; entrance fee) now restored to its original appearance, Captain Parker and his 77 Minutemen sipped beer while awaiting Paul Revere's warning; a bullet hole is visible in one door. The **Hancock-Clarke House** ⓱ (Hancock Street; open May–Oct Mon–Sat; Sun pm; entrance fee) where John Hancock and Samuel Adams were woken by Paul Revere on the eve of the battle with news of the British advance, contains period furnishings as well as the drum on which William Diamond sounded a warning to his fellow patriots.

At the **Ebenezer Fiske House Site**, a historical trail explains the course of the fierce fighting that broke out there; a section of the Battle Road here is unpaved and closed to traffic, giving an idea of its original appearance.

The **Battle Road Visitor Center** ⓲, part of the National Park, has a movie showing the events of 1775, and there are talks and guided walks. Just to the west is the **Paul Revere Capture Site**, where Revere was taken but Prescott escaped to give the warning to those in Concord. Restored to its condition at the time of the battle, the **Hartwell Tavern** ⓳ hosts re-creations of colonial life.

As you enter Concord the theme digresses into literature. **The Wayside** ⓴ (455 Lexington Road, Route 2A; open May–Oct Thur–Tues; entrance fee) links

The American flag still flies on the Buckman Tavern in Concord, where the Minutemen were warned that the British troops were on their way.

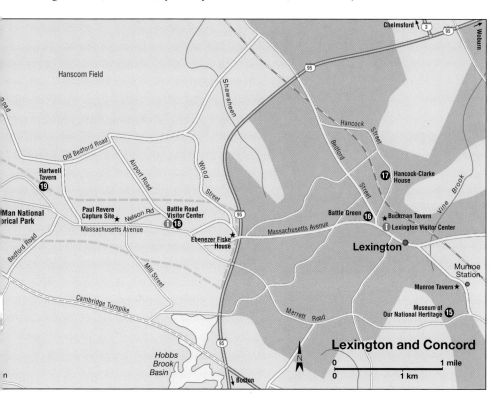

Transcendentalist thinker Henry David Thoreau.

BELOW:
Walden Pond today.

the battle with the literary figures, for here Samuel Whitney, the muster master of the Concord Militia, lived during the Revolution. From 1845 to 1848 it was home to the Alcotts, and was purchased in 1852 by writer Nathaniel Hawthorne – he added the tower, but found it unsatisfactory for working in, and declared that he would happily see the house burn down.

Close by, the Alcott family lived from 1858 to 1877 at **Orchard House** ㉑ (Lexington Road, Route 2A; open Mon–Sat; Sun pm; closed Jan 1–15; entrance fee) where Louisa May Alcott penned her first novel, *Moods*, as well as the hugely popular *Little Women* and *Little Men*, and hospital sketches of the Civil War, which became serialized. The Alcotts were initially a poor family, whose fortunes were reversed by the revenue from Louisa's writings. Her father, Bronson Alcott, founded the Concord School of Philosophy next door, which functioned from 1880 to 1888; the building still stands.

Near the junction of the Battle Road with Route 2, **Concord Museum** ㉒ (200 Lexington Road, Route 2A; open Mon–Sat; Sun pm; entrance fee) has – in addition to samplers, period rooms and costumes – excellent displays relating to Revolutionary and literary Concord, including one of the two lanterns hung by Robert Newman in Old North Church in Boston. The gallery devoted to Thoreau has the largest collection of artifacts associated with the great author and naturalist, including furnishings from his cabin by Walden Pond. Ralph Waldo Emerson's study has been transferred here in its entirety for fear of fire, brought from the **Ralph Waldo Emerson House** ㉓ (28 Cambridge Turnpike; open May–Oct Thur–Sat; Sun pm; entrance fee) just across Route 2, where Emerson resided from 1835 until his death in 1882 and wrote his transcendentalist works. Most of the furniture is Emerson's.

LITERARY CONCORD

If there were a Hall of Fame for 19th-century New England authors, it would have to be in Concord, Massachusetts. In this upper-middle class, rural town about 20 miles (32 km) northwest of Boston, some of the brightest lights of American fiction, poetry and philosophy during the transcendentalist years of the 1870s and 1880s lived and worked. Most are buried in Concord as well, on Author's Ridge in Sleepy Hollow Cemetery.

Ralph Waldo Emerson, Henry David Thoreau, Nathaniel Hawthorne and Louisa May Alcott all spent time in Concord, where they played host to a cavalcade of other literary luminaries that included Henry Wadsworth Longfellow, Henry James, Oliver Wendell Holmes, Walt Whitman and James Russell Lowell. Unlike some authors who work in relative obscurity and then become famous posthumously, the Concord writers were celebrities in their own time – so much so that Alcott (the popular author of *Little Women*) satirized the public's adulation and its fascination with Concord, suggesting (with tongue in cheek) that a hotel be built for the tourists and furnished with "Alcott's rustic furniture, the beds made of Thoreau's pine boughs, and the sacred fires fed from the Emersonian woodpile."

Sleepy Hollow Cemetery ② is the resting place of most of the Concord big names, among them Hawthorne, the Alcotts, Emerson and Thoreau. **The Old Manse** ㉕ (Monument Street; open mid-Apr–Oct Mon–Sat; Sun pm; entrance fee) was built by minister William Emerson around 1770, and was used as a sanctuary for women and children in the battle. It became home to his grandson Ralph Waldo Emerson, who wrote *Nature* (1836) here, and was rented for three years to Nathaniel Hawthorne. Thus it preserves layers of history, with mementos of both these great men – a huge book collection and Hawthorne's desk.

At **Old North Bridge** ㉖ (a replica) where General Gage's British troops, crowded into the narrow pathway, were easily routed by the ragtag Americans, an obelisk marks where the first British soldier fell. Cross the bridge, pass Daniel Chester French's *Minute Man* statue, unveiled for the centennial of the famous fight, and walk up to the North Bridge Visitor Center.

South of Concord off Route 126, Thoreau spent 26 months in a one-room cabin (no longer in existence) by **Walden Pond** ㉗ living in experimental self-sufficiency and recording the progress of nature through the year, all of which he recounted in *Walden* (1854). The pond is now the focus of a state park.

At Lincoln, off Route 126, is the **Gropius House** ㉘ (68 Baker Bridge Road; open June–mid-Oct, Wed–Sun; mid-Oct–May, weekends; entrance fee), built in 1938 by the seminal Bauhaus architect; it is now the most modern of the historic homes preserved by the Society for the Preservation of New England Antiquities. The **DeCordova Museum and Sculpture Park** ㉙ (off Route 2 or Route 128; open Tues–Sun; entrance fee) shows contemporary work in a turreted 1880 mansion; the grounds house oversize sculpture (often playful in mood) and an outdoor theater ideal for a summertime series of jazz concerts.

Map on pages 146–7

The Minute Man *statue, by Daniel Chester French, on Old North Bridge, Concord.*

Below: Old North Bridge, Concord.

The South Shore and Plymouth

Within 8 miles (13 km) of Boston, the **Adams National Historical Site** (Adams Street; open daily; entrance fee) at **Quincy** 30 includes the house built in 1731 and repeatedly enlarged, home to four generations of the illustrious Adams family, among them a unique father-and-son presidential pair, John Adams (second President of the US), and his son, John Quincy Adams (the sixth). High points of the tour are the stone library, packed with 14,000 volumes, and the formal garden, especially appealing when the daffodils are in bloom. The Adams birthplaces, 17th-century saltbox farmhouses, also form part of the National Historical Site.

Further down the coast is **Hingham** 31, beautified by Frederick Law Olmsted, creator of Boston's Emerald Necklace (*see page 115*) and Central Park, New York; his handiwork here is the **World's End Reservation**, a 250-acre harborside estate that is a protectorate of the Trustees of the Reservations. Also noteworthy, at the center of town, is the **Old Ship Meetinghouse**, the oldest wooden church in America in continuous use. Built by ship's carpenters in 1681, the interior resembles a giant hull turned upside down.

Enclosing Hingham Bay and curving toward Boston like a beckoning finger is the sandy spit of **Nantasket**, a long-time summer playground (note the 1928 Carousel under the Clock) grown tacky over the years but still offering, from the tiny town of Hull at the tip, an optimal view of Boston Light, said to be the oldest operating lighthouse in America. The **Hull Lifesaving Museum** (1117 Nantasket Avenue; open June–Sept, Wed–Sun; Oct–May, Fri–Sun; entrance fee) gives a good idea of the heroic measures required when the lighthouse warnings didn't succeed in staving off disaster.

Abigail Adams is remembered today not only as the wife and mother of a president (a unique distinction), but as the mother of American feminism; in 1776, she urged her husband to "Remember the Ladies" at the fateful Continental Congress where independence was declared.

BELOW: the Adams Homestead, Quincy.

Directly southward lies **Plymouth ㉜**, which proudly claims the distinction of being "America's Home Town." Earlier attempts at colonization had been assayed, but, thanks to the Pilgrims' grit and determination, this was the first to make a go of it. The very rock they landed on (or so the story goes, passed down to the next generation) enjoys a place of honor under an elaborate portico overlooking the harbor.

The **Pilgrim Hall** (Court Street; open Feb–Dec daily; entrance fee), the first custom-built museum in the US, designed in 1824 by Alexander Parris, gathered the more outstanding relics of Pilgrim life early on (though they are rather unimaginatively displayed), and several houses from the period still survive in town, tucked in haphazardly among younger contenders. Actually, it's two fairly recent replicas that give the best sense of what early colonial life was really like.

Docked in the harbor, the *Mayflower II* (Water Street; open daily; entrance fee) is a full-scale replica that was built in England and sailed to Plymouth in 1957; actors on board portray the original passengers and field visitors' questions with accuracy and wit.

About 3 miles (5 km) south of town, on Route 3, **Plimoth Plantation** (open daily; entrance fee) is a painstaking reconstruction of the 17th-century Pilgrim village; its every detail has been meticulously researched. It is inhabited by actor/interpreters who so convincingly enact the quotidian rituals of the original village that visitors can easily lose themselves in the fantasy of those heady days full of hardship and dreams.

Plymouth town also possesses a number of historic houses to visit. The oldest is the **Richard Sparrow House** (42 Summer Street; donations) built in 1640,

Map
on page
138

Playing the part at Plimoth Plantation.

LEFT: Plimoth Plantation.
BELOW: *Mayflower II.*

Map on page 138

and still retaining its diamond-shape leaded windows; the **Howland House** (No. 33 Sandwich Street; open late May–mid-Oct) originated in 1667 as a home for the son of one of the original Pilgrims. The **Mayflower Society Museum** (4 Winslow Street; entrance fee) a house built in 1754, has a graceful flying staircase and a variety of period rooms.

Moving on further south again, pause at **New Bedford** to explore the narrow cobblestone streets of the old town – the busiest fishing port on the East Coast. Here the outstanding sight is the **Whaling Museum** (Johnny Cake Hill; open daily; late May–early Sept, Thur till 8pm; entrance fee), the best place to find out about this aspect of New England's maritime past. In addition to informative sections evoking the lifestyles of the whalers and fishermen, there is a huge show of ship models – most memorably the *Lagoda*, a half-size replica of a whaling bark – and some fine paintings on the theme, plus examples of scrimshaw, intricately carved out of whalebone by members of the ships' crews on their long voyages.

At the mouth of the Taunton estuary, 9 miles (6 km) east from New Bedford, **Fall River** ❹ is dominated by the huge mills that act as reminders of the long-defunct cotton industry. Some of these Victorian relics now house the thriving factory outlet stores that have put the town on the map. Another reason for coming is for **Battleship Cove** (open daily 9am–sunset; entrance fee), a collection of World War II vessels berthed on the river – among them the submarine USSS *Lionfish* and the 46,000-ton battleship USS *Massachusetts*. Virtually adjacent, the **Marine Museum** (open weekdays; Sat and Sun pm; entrance fee) is packed with nautical paraphernalia, including a model of the doomed *Titanic* and more than 150 steamship models. ❑

BELOW: going fishing.

BOSTON HARBOR ISLANDS

Until recently, few Bostonians even knew that their harbor had islands. But look on a map and there they are, some 30 of them, sprinkled within the embracing peninsular arms of Winthrop and Hull. They range from little more than piles of rock (The Graves) to 214-acre (85-hectare) Long, which stretches out into the middle of the harbor from the town of Quincy. For centuries, the islands served no more purpose than a dumping ground or shelter for Boston's sick or homeless. As for the harbor, it was little more than a cesspool for the city's waste. But thanks to a $3.5 billion clean-up, Boston Harbor is clean enough now on most days for swimming. And in 1996, Congress created the Boston Harbor Islands National Recreation Area to support ongoing local and state efforts to turn the islands into valuable recreational space for the city. Already, you can catch a ferry from downtown Boston or Hingham to Georges Island, which serves as a nucleus for the recreation area. Free water taxis travel to other islands, some of which feel as remote and unspoiled as those off the coast of Maine – except for that great view of the Boston skyline. For specific information about reaching the islands, or about camping, call 617-727 7676.

Outlet Shopping

Kittery and Freeport, ME, are both scenic coastal towns, but for many their names are more synonymous with outlet shopping than beaches. This was not always so. Factory outlets once referred to shops within factories that sold discounted wares to employees. The modern concept of New England factory outlets began in the mid-1970s in Fall River, MA, when the Anderson-Little clothing store opened a retail outlet.

Anderson-Little no longer exists, but outlets are here to stay. Fifty stores now occupy the original granite-faced Fall River mill buildings, and the popularity of outlet shopping has grown well beyond this industrial city. The outlet malls in Freeport and Kittery are now among Maine's most popular tourist destinations, and North Conway, NH, and Worcester, MA, also harbor large outlet malls advertising 20 to 70 percent discounts on products ranging from clothing to housewares to books. Many shoppers come armed with maps and strategies, and entire books have been written on the most productive way to shop.

There are three kinds of stores: national outlets for single brands selling in-season merchandise at a discount; regional value outlets carrying name-brand and designer merchandise; and manufacturer-owned clearance centers with discontinued and irregular merchandise at sharply reduced prices.

The Fall River Factory Outlet District (800-424 5519), also known as the Heart District, consists of three independently owned malls. Big draws are Bugle Boy, Levi's, the Burlington Coat Factory, and the L'eggs, Hanes, Bali, and Playtex Outlet. The district is at the junction of I-195 and Route 24 South, about one hour from Boston and 20 minutes from Newport and Providence, Rhode Island. Farther west in Massachusetts is Worcester, home to Worcester Common Outlets (508-798 2581), the only fully enclosed outlet center in New England. Anchors here are Filene's Basement, Off 5th–Sachs Fifth Avenue, Sports Authority, BB and Beyond, and Media Play.

One hour north of Boston, at Kittery, ME (888-KITTERY), 14 outlet centers with 120 stores line over a mile of Route 1 (Exit 3 from I-95). Farther north on I-95, at Exit 20, is Freeport, home to the never-closed headquarters of L.L. Bean. The outdoor outfitter's store is now flanked by 170 shops and outlets, and L.L. Bean draws over 2.5 million customers each year (800-865 1994).

L.L. Bean also has a store in North Conway, NH, two hours' drive north of Boston, along with 200 other outlet stores. Two large outlet malls, Settlers' Green OVP. (603-356 7031) and the Tanger Outlet Center (603-436 6277) are the anchors, with about 100 stores. Dozens of smaller outlet centers in stand-alone factory stores are also strung along Route 16, creating long traffic jams.

Vermont also chases tourists intent on parting with greenbacks. Goods in Manchester's high-end outlet shops are generally more expensive than factory stores but still less than retail. If the notion of a "perpetual sale" gets your heart fluttering, you'll be moved by such purveyors as Calvin Klein, Timberland, Baccarat, Giorgio Armani, Cole Haan, Dansk, and Brooks Brothers. ❑

RIGHT: L.L.Bean's "Maine Hunting Shoe."

CAPE COD AND THE ISLANDS

This is a sandy summer playground with fine clam shacks, historic B&Bs, undeveloped National Seashore beaches, and a lively arts scene – plus two sharply contrasting little isles

Map on pages 158–9

Shaped like a bodybuilder's flexed arm, Cape Cod extends 31 miles (50 km) eastward into the Atlantic Ocean, then another 31 miles to the north. Well forested up to about the "elbow," then increasingly reduced to scrub oak and pitch pine, this sandy peninsula is lined with more than 310 miles (500 km) of beaches. The crook of the arm forms Cape Cod Bay, where the waters are placid and free of often treacherous ocean surf. Lighthouses guide mariners plying the cold Atlantic waters. Geologically the Cape is relatively new, a huge mass of debris dumped after the melting of a vast ice sheet.

Bostonians consider Cape Cod their own private playground, but its fame has spread so far that it attracts international travelers. In high season (July and August), lodgings are filled to capacity, traffic on the Cape's few highways is heavy, and local merchants work hard to make the profits that will carry them through the all-but-dormant winters. (The pleasures of the Cape off-season, however, are a well-guarded secret not likely to remain a secret much longer.) Even at the height of its summertime popularity, when the roads, restaurants, and beaches tend to be jammed, Cape Cod manages to preserve its wild charm and dramatic beauty.

Much of this quality is protected within the boundaries of the Cape Cod National Seashore, a vast 27,000-acre (11,000-hectare) nature reserve established by foresighted legislators in 1961. Precisely because it has not been commercially exploited, this huge expanse of untouched dunes – a natural phenomenon created by geological forces about a million years ago – survives as one of the Cape's most alluring features.

PRECEDING PAGES: old coastguard station at Eastham. **LEFT:** looking out to sea, at Douse's Beach. **BELOW:** waiting for the waves.

Getting your bearings

Note the nomenclature. "Upper Cape" refers to the portion nearest the mainland; "Mid-Cape" is roughly from Barnstable County eastward to Chatham and Orleans, where the "arm" bends; "Lower Cape" is the "forearm" jutting northward to Eastham, Truro and Provincetown.

Itineraries on the Upper and Mid-Cape offer a choice of speedy, featureless highways or scenic, meandering roads. Those intent on reaching the Outer Cape in a hurry generally opt for Route 6, the four-lane, limited-access Mid-Cape Highway; those headed for Falmouth and Woods Hole can take the equally speedy Route 28. Anyone wishing to get a true sense of the Cape, however, will be well rewarded by taking the prettier non-highway counterparts. Roughly parallel to the Mid-Cape Highway, two-lane Route 6A starts in Sagamore and runs eastward through old towns full of graceful historic houses, crafts and antique shops. The same can be said of Route 28A,

hugging the shore en route to Falmouth. As Route 28 veers northeast-
ward from Falmouth to Chatham it's
marred by recurrent stretches of
overdevelopment but, again, one has
only to venture off the main road a bit
to discover such towns as Osterville
and Centerville, Harwich Port and
Chatham itself. Once Route 28 and
Route 6 merge in Orleans, Route 6
north is pleasant all the way to
Provincetown, if traffic-clogged.

For those wishing to avoid the
drive, there are ferries between
Provincetown and Boston, Provincetown and Plymouth, and flights into
Hyannis (*see page 169*).

Simple pleasures

The first hordes of tourists arrived in
the late 19th century, brought by
steamship, railroad and – eventually
– automobile. Escaping the summer
heat of Boston, Providence and New
York for the cool sea breezes along the
shore, they found low prices, inexpensive real estate and simple pleasures in abundance.

Before the advent of modern
transport, Cape Cod was a hardscrabble area peopled by the Wampanoag tribes, hardy Yankees and
industrious immigrants from the
coasts and islands of Portugal. Since
the land was too poor to farm for
more than local consumption, most
people earned their living from the
sea. Fishing, saltmaking, whaling,
ship-building and "wrecking" – scavenging the beaches for the flotsam and
jetsam of ships lost at sea – provided
the local people with a livelihood,
however uncertain.

In 1602, Bartholomew Gosnold, a
British mariner sailing by this long
arm of sand, noted a great many codfish in the waters and added the name
"Cape Cod" to his map. In 1620, the
Mayflower pulled into the harbor of
what is now Provincetown and, before
debarking to explore, its passengers
drew up the Mayflower Compact,
whereby they constituted themselves

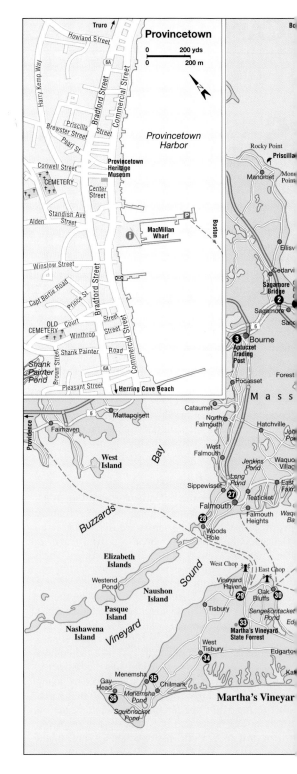

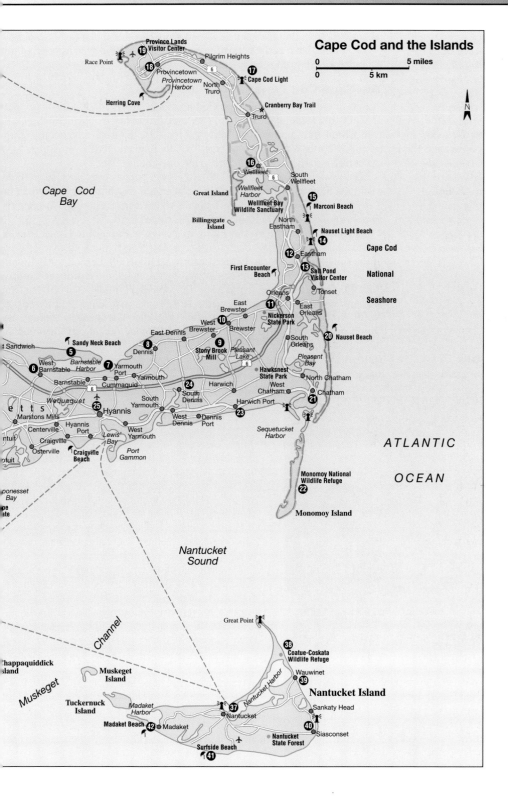

Cape Cod and the Islands

0   5 miles

0   5 km

N

Province Lands Visitor Center — 19

Race Point

18

Pilgrim Heights

Provincetown

Provincetown Harbor

North Truro

17

Cape Cod Light

Herring Cove

Cranberry Bay Trail

Truro

Cape Cod Bay

16

Wellfleet

South Wellfleet

Great Island

Wellfleet Harbor

Wellfleet Bay Wildlife Sanctuary

15

Marconi Beach

Billingsgate Island

North Eastham

Nauset Light Beach

14

12

Eastham

Cape Cod

First Encounter Beach

13

Salt Pond Visitor Center

National

Orleans

Tonset

Seashore

East Brewster

East Orleans

11

West Brewster

10

Nickerson State Park

East Dennis

Brewster

Sandy Neck Beach

8

Dennis

9

Stony Brook Mill

Pleasant Lake

South Orleans

20

Nauset Beach

Sandwich

5

West Barnstable

6

Barnstable Harbor

7

Yarmouth Port

Barnstable

Cummaquid

Yarmouth

Harwich

Pleasant Bay

North Chatham

West Chatham

Hawksnest State Park

Wequaquet

25

Hyannis

South Yarmouth

24

South Dennis

Harwich Port

21

Chatham

Marstons Mills

Hyannis Port

Centerville

West Yarmouth

West Dennis

Dennis Port

23

Sequetucket Harbor

ATLANTIC

Craigville

Lewis Bay

Port Gammon

OCEAN

Osterville

Craigville Beach

Monomoy National Wildlife Refuge

22

ponesset Bay

Monomoy Island

Nantucket Sound

Great Point

38

Coatue-Coskata Wildlife Refuge

Channel

Chappaquiddick Island

Muskeget Island

Wauwinet

39

Nantucket Island

Muskeget

Tuckernuck Island

Madaket Harbor

37

Nantucket

Sankaty Head

Madaket Beach

42

Madaket

40

Nantucket State Forest

Siasconset

Surfside Beach

41

The Cape Cod National Seashore Trail, found at the northern tip of the Cape, is a spectacularly sculpted landscape of sweeping dunes descending into green hollows of scrub brush and stunted forest, with the sea all around to provide invigorating breezes.

BELOW: going clamming.

as a "civil Body Politick" and vowed to work together under just laws for the good of all. This early "constitution" grew into the government of the Commonwealth of Massachusetts.

The Cape Cod Canal

Purists could actually call Cape Cod an island, for in 1914, after five years of work, the Cape was effectively severed from the mainland by the **Cape Cod Canal ❶**. Improved and widened in 1927, the canal is a boon to ships travelling north–south along the coast of New England, for they no longer have to venture into the stormy Atlantic to circumvent the Cape.

Expressways funnel traffic to the two access bridges over the Canal. To the east is the **Sagamore Bridge ❷**, a graceful arched structure with one foot in the Cape town of Sagamore. Route 3 comes south from Boston and crosses the Sagamore Bridge to join Route 6, the Mid-Cape Highway.

Just past the bridge on the north side are the **Pairpoint Glass Works**, where glassblowers give demonstrations daily. Near the southwestern end of the Canal is the Bourne Bridge, leading to Route 28, headed for Falmouth and Woods Hole. West of the bridge and by the canal, the **Aptucxet Trading Post ❸** (open July–Aug, daily; May–June and Sept–mid-Oct, Tues–Sat; Sun pm; entrance fee) is a replica of the first English-speaking trading post in North America, set up in 1627 to trade with the Wampanoag Indians, the Dutch in New York and the Plymouth settlement. There are views of the third great span over the canal, the 270 ft (82 meters) high and 540 ft (165 meters) long Buzzards Bay Vertical Railroad Bridge, which is left raised, and lowered to allow trains to cross.

CAPE COD RAIL TRAIL

In the Cape's early heyday, summertime visitors arrived by train – an option still available to a limited number of towns in July and August from New York City (Amtrak's Cape Codder, tel: 800-872 7245). Otherwise, with a singular lack of foresight, most of the train network has been dismantled. However, at least one lengthy section of roadbed has been put to an energy-saving, pleasure-making use: the Cape Cod Rail Trail is a 28-mile (45-km) paved recreational path ideal for bicycling, skating, walking and jogging. Along the way, it passes lakes and marshes, woods and a harbor. The most scenic or dramatic sections are the National Seashore spur trails in Eastham and Wellfleet that terminate at the Atlantic Ocean. The trail runs from just off Route 134 in South Dennis through Nickerson State Park and on to Wellfleet.

You can rent bicycles at a number of places along the way, including Barbara's Bike & Sport (tel: 508-760 4723) at the trailhead, Idle Times Bike Shop (tel: 508-896 9242) on the edge of Nickerson, and Little Capistrano Bike Shop (tel: 508-255 6515) across from the National Seashore headquarters in Eastham. If you forget to pack a lunch there are a few places along the way where you can get a sandwich or fried seafood.

The Bayside: Sandwich to Brewster

This region gained world renown for its glass after Boston merchant Deming Jarvis founded a glass factory in **Sandwich ④** in 1825.

Map on pages 158–9

By taking advantage of local resources (sand shipped in from the Outer Cape, local timber to stoke the furnaces, and salt marsh to pack the delicate product) and using mass-production techniques, Jarvis put glassware – formerly a rare and precious commodity – within the reach of ordinary people. His Boston and Sandwich Glass Company factory thrived until threatened by coal-powered plants in the Midwest; that, and a strike by exploited workers, shut the enterprise down in 1888. However, examples of their output, in an astounding range of styles, can still be found in the **Sandwich Glass Museum** (Main Street; open Feb–Dec, daily; entrance fee), and in the antique shops that line this historic old route.

Sandwich was the first town to be founded on the Cape, in 1637, and today – with the factories long since razed and the groves of trees regrown – it's one of the prettiest, and best-preserved. At its center stands the restored **Dexter Mill and the Hoxie House**, dating from colonial times (Water Street; open mid-June–mid-Oct, Mon-Sat; Sun pm; entrance fee).

For more glimpses into the American past, follow the signs – past a lovely historic cemetery overlooking **Shawme Pond** – to **Heritage Plantation**, a spacious museum complex whose grounds, in spring, are awash in the vivid pinks and purples of flowering rhododendrons (Grove Street; open May-Oct, daily; entrance fee). Several buildings display extraordinary collections, from children's toys (including a working carousel) to military artifacts and artwork. A round stone barn (copied from the Shaker original in Hancock, Massachusetts)

Exhibits at Sandwich Glass Museum.

BELOW:
the carousel at Heritage Plantation, Sandwich.

houses an outstanding array of early cars, including one particular beauty, Gary Cooper's 1931 Deusenberg.

Motoring east, into the county of Barnstable, you'll pass a 6-mile (9-km) barrier beach, **Sandy Neck** , which is a favored habitat of the endangered piping plover. Hikers and swimmers are welcome to explore this sandy spit, provided they don't disturb the birds' nesting sites. Whale-watching cruises depart from Barnstable Harbor (it's a shorter trip to Stellwagen Bank from Provincetown, but for those who don't mind some extra time out on the water, this departure point is just as good).

Just up the hill from the harbor is the **Trayser Memorial Museum** (3353 Route 6A; open mid-June–mid-Oct, Tues–Sun pm), the former Custom House, which now houses Native American artifacts, children's toys and other bygones. In **West Barnstable** ❻, West Parish Meetinghouse, built in 1646, is an outstanding example of early colonial architecture and has a Paul Revere bell cast in 1806.

East of Barnstable, **Yarmouth Port** ❼ is a delightful village with fine old houses to tour, including the **Captain Bangs Hallett House** (Strawberry Lane; open June–Oct, Sun pm; July–Aug, Thurs pm; tours on the hour; entrance fee), an 1840 Greek Revival showcase house now owned by The Historical Society of Old Yarmouth, and the **Winslow Crocker House** (250 Route 6A; open June–Oct, Sat and Sun; entrance fee), a Georgian manse from around 1780. For a pleasurable glimpse of more recent history, stop for an ice cream soda at **Hallett's**, a well-preserved 1889 drugstore.

In the town of **Dennis** ❽, follow signs for the Scargo Hill Tower, a stone turret from which it's possible to see, on a clear day, Cape Cod laid out like a

TIP

You'll find more fine old houses lining the section of Route 6A around Yarmouth Port – once called Captains' Row – than anywhere else on the Cape. South Yarmouth was settled by Quakers in the early 1800s and many of their lovely houses remain.

BELOW: the Town Hall and Dexter Mill, Sandwich.

map, with Provincetown easily visible at the northern tip. Dennis is home to America's oldest, and most outstanding, professional summer theater: aspiring thespians such as Bette Davis (an ambitious usher) and Henry Fonda began their careers at the Cape Playhouse (Route 6A; tel: 508-385 3838; performances late June–mid-Sep), founded in 1927 by Raymond Moore, a renegade from Provincetown's "little theater" movement. Productions here are skilled and lavish, and movies at the adjoining Cape Cinema are a sensory treat: the cinema features leather armchairs with antimacassars and Art Deco frescoes by Rockwell Kent.

Map on pages 158–9

The **Stony Brook Mill** ❾ (Stony Brook Road southwest off Route 6A) grinds cornmeal several days a week; there's a small museum upstairs. Each spring, from mid-April to early May, the mill hosts an eye-catching event: here, in a timeless ceremony similar to a salmon run, schools of alewives (a fish resembling herring) leap up a series of ladders to spawn in the freshwater pond behind the mill. Besides its fine old houses and inns, **Brewster** ❿ has a variety of attractions. The **Cape Cod Museum of Natural History** (Route 6A; open daily; entrance fee) explores the local habitat with hands-on exhibits and a small network of nature trails. The **New England Fire and History Museum** (1429 Route 6A) has large collections of vintage fire-fighting equipment and memorabilia.

Vintage exhibit at the New England Fire and History Museum.

Railroad magnate Roland Nickerson once owned 2,000 acres (800 hectares) of open land in Brewster and held them as his personal hunting and fishing preserve. In 1934 his widow donated most of this tract to the state; today **Nickerson State Park** ⓫ (Route 6A), is a popular spot for camping, swimming, picnicking, and walks.

BELOW:
the New England Fire and History Museum, Brewster.

Summer Activities

New England's summer season may be short, but locals savor every balmy day that July and August bring. And although May/June and September/October may not qualify as "summer," the fine if less predictable weather of these "shoulder" months makes for excellent outdoor adventuring without the mid-summer crowds.

With 400 miles (640 km) of coastline, Rhode Island looks to the sea for recreation. Newport, known as "The Sailing Capital of the World" for its years hosting the America's Cup, is a good base for harbor sailing or learn-to-sail vacations.

At America's oldest sailing school, Boston's Community Boating, skiffs cruise the Charles River against a backdrop of brick bowfronts and downtown office towers. For longer adventures, many head for the Maine coast, where several outfitters offer multi-day sailing expeditions.

Maine has also become a center for sea kayaking, wiith over 2,000 coastal islands

and their protected waters, The Maine Island Kayak Company (*see Travel Tips*) offers sea kayaking lessons and tours. Rhode Island kayakers are rewarded with seaside views of Newport's grand Ocean Drive estates.

West of Boston, canoeists on the lazy Sudbury and Concord Rivers can visit Revolutionary-era sights, while on Cape Cod, naturalist guides lead canoe tours of salt marshes and tidal rivers. Along the Deerfield River in western Massachusetts, visitors can rent canoes and take whitewater rafting trips.

Connecticut's Housatonic River is a favored destination for canoeing and rafting. North American Whitewater Expeditions (*see Travel Tips*) organizes trips on the Housatonic and on Maine's Kennebec and Penobscot Rivers.

Swimmers will find beaches on Cape Cod or Nantucket Sound warmer and calmer than those on the Atlantic. The Atlantic, however, sometimes offers reasonable surfing, especially after an offshore storm.

Fishermen head for the trout-filled Battenkill River, near Manchester in Vermont, where the Orvis Company runs a fly fishing school. Orvis also teaches saltwater fishing on Cape Cod. Near New Hampshire's Mount Washington, Great Glen Trials (*see Travel Tips*) offers introductory fishing classes and arranges guided fly fishing excursions.

There's hiking for all abilities, from leisurely strolls on conservation land – such as the 11 self-guided nature trails within Cape Cod's National Seashore – to rugged mountain climbs. The 2,000-mile (3,200-km) Appalachian Trail crosses Maine, New Hampshire, Vermont, Massachusetts and Connecticut on its way south to Georgia. Serious hikers also follow the Long Trail, 445 miles (712 km) across Vermont's highest peaks. The Appalachian Mountain Club has a network of overnight huts for walkers in New Hampshire's White Mountains.

Many ski resorts have become summer mountain biking centers, including Vermont's Mount Snow and Killington. The self-guided Franconia Notch Bike Tour in New Hampshire starts at Echo Lake, passes the Old Man of the Mountain, to end at Loon Mountain's ski area.   ❏

LEFT: Cape Cod and Acadia are two areas that offer excellent, easy cycling.

The National Seashore and the Outer Cape

The Cape Cod National Seashore extends along the Atlantic coast of the Lower Cape all the way to Provincetown. Its glorious sandy beaches are backed by high dunes; by contrast the (western) bayside has calmer, warmer waters and marshy inlets.

The town green at **Eastham** ⓬ has a 1793 windmill. For a deeper side trip into Cape Cod's history, head west to **First Encounter Beach**. It's here that a Pilgrim scouting party out of Provincetown first encountered a band of Indians, who, wary after earlier encounters with kidnappers, attacked the Pilgrims and were rebuffed by gunfire. This uneasy meeting is among the reasons the Pilgrims pressed on to Plymouth. Today the historic site is a peaceful town beach (which, like most, charges a parking fee in summer).

Further up Route 6A is the **Salt Pond Visitor Center** ⓭ (open mid-Feb–Dec, daily; Jan–mid-Feb, weekends) of the Cape Cod National Seashore. Interpretive films and exhibits explain the ecology of the Cape, and a bicycle trail (bikes can be rented nearby) winds through pine forests and marshes to end at **Coast Guard Beach**, where, in the 1920s, Henry Beston wrote his classic *Outermost House*; further north is **Nauset Light Beach** ⓮, graced with a picturesque lighthouse.

At **Marconi Beach** ⓯, Guglielmo Marconi set up the first wireless station in the United States and transmitted the first trans-Atlantic wireless message to Europe in 1903. The **Atlantic White Cedar Swamp Trail**, starting from the Marconi site, is especially beautiful.

Famous for its oysters, **Wellfleet** ⓰ is one of Cape Cod's most appealing towns, full of fine galleries and fun restaurants, and surrounded by inviting

 Map on pages 158–9

 TIP

The best beaches in the area are Nauset Beach and Skaket Beach, both in Orleans (see page 168), and Nauset Light, Coast Guard and First Encounter Beaches, all in the vicinity of Eastham.

BELOW: Nauset Light Beach.

Cranberries are a Cape specialty.

wildlife areas. Just south of town, off Route 6, the Audubon Society maintains the 700-acre (280-hectare) **Wellfleet Bay Wildlife Sanctuary** (off Route 6; open 8am–dusk, daily; entrance fee); to the west of town is Great Island (part of the Cape Cod National Seashore), which reattached itself to the mainland and became a barrier beach.

Farther north, the landscape becomes ever more wild and barren. Scrubby vegetation gives way to desert-like sand dunes. East of Truro, the **Cranberry Bog Trail** (within the Cape Cod National Seashore) offers a look at the natural habitat of the tiny red fruit that proved such a boon to Cape Cod agriculture. Another road east leads to **Highland Light**, towering over **Head of the Meadow Beach**.

Cape Cod Light ⓱, also known as Highland Light, is one of the much-photographed landmarks of the Cape; erected in 1857 it is the peninsula's oldest lighthouse.

Provincetown

BELOW: a trio of transvestites in Provincetown.

Contrast the subtle beauties and serenity of the National Seashore lands with the raucous and sometimes tawdry atmosphere along Commercial Street in **Provincetown** ⓲. Sidewalk artists will run off a pastel portrait, or perhaps a cartoon caricature. Shops emblazoned with advertisements sell fine works of art, bad works of art, kitsch souvenirs and an infinite variety of snacks. There are good restaurants and bad ones, delightful old inns and inexpensive guest houses, tacky shacks and beautiful landscaped captains' mansions. The artiness of "P-town" (a term *never* used by the locals) has coincided with its status of one of the most overtly gay capitals of the East Coast.

Map on pages 158–9

With its well-protected harbor, Provincetown started out as a natural fishing port – long before the Pilgrims came along. So it remains to this day. Portuguese fishermen, many from the Azores, came here in the heyday of the whaling trade and stayed on for the good fishing. Their descendants still make up a sizable proportion of the town's year-round residents. Led by painter Charles Hawthorne, who in 1899 founded the Cape Cod School of Art, hordes of artists and writers from New York's Greenwich Village flocked to Provincetown in the early decades of the 20th century, drawn partly by the area's stark beauty and largely by the cheap rents and food to be found here (thanks to the tourist boom they inspired, the latter are of course history).

Among the innumerable notables who passed through here, if only briefly, are dramatists Eugene O'Neill and Tennessee Williams, and writers Sinclair Lewis and John Dos Passos. Perhaps the best-known recent writer-in-summer-residence is Norman Mailer. A dozen or more illustrious painters, such as Robert Motherwell, have left their mark, with new contenders cropping up year after year in such cutting-edge galleries as the Long Point and Bertha Walker. A number of galleries now specialize in Provincetown art going back to the beginning of the century.

Other places to catch outstanding early work are the **Provincetown Art Association and Museum** founded in 1914 (460 Commercial Street; open Sun–Thurs, pm; Fri and Sat, 8am–10pm); the relatively new **Provincetown Heritage Museum** (356 Commercial Street; open daily; entrance fee), which also harbors a half-scale model of a fishing schooner; and the poorly-lit corridors of the 1878 Town Hall, where concerts and performances are held throughout the year.

TIP

A good way to see the principal sights is to take the Provincetown Trolley which runs along Commercial Street and continues on to the National Seashore. The main pick-up point is outside the Town Hall.

BELOW:
Provincetown Heritage Museum.

PROVINCETOWN ART COLONY

Bay and ocean, sand and sky: the natural beauty of Provincetown at the tip of Cape Cod has attracted artists since the town was little more than a fishing pier at the end of a sand spit. Today, Provincetown boasts dozens of art galleries, many of which specialize in contemporary works by local painters, photographers, and sculptors such as Joel Meyerowitz, Paul Bowen, and Paul Resika.

The artists who live and work in Provincetown today are drawn to the area by its pure, Mediterranean-like light – the same light that nearly a century ago inspired a group collectively known as the "Provincetown Art Colony," as renowned as those in Taos in New Mexico, Carmel in California, and East Hampton in New York State.

The colony began in the late 1800s, when a new railroad bed made Provincetown more easily accessible to artists in search of inexpensive lodging and studio space. In 1899, impressionist painter Charles Webster Hawthorne opened the Cape Cod School of Art, which was soon followed by the Summer School of Painting.

By the summer of 1916, more than 300 artists and students – associated with six schools of art – were thriving in the tolerant town, leading the *Boston Globe* to dub it "the Biggest Art Colony in the World."

Just keeping an eye on things.

The lofty Italianate tower looming above the town is the **Pilgrim Memorial** (off Winslow Street; open Apr–Nov, daily; entrance fee), built early in the century to ensure that Provincetown's place in colonial history would not be overlooked. The determined climber (there's also an elevator) will be rewarded with a panoramic view of the town and the entire Cape. At the monument's foot is the **Provincetown Museum** (off Winslow Street from Bradford Street; open July–Aug, daily till 7pm; entrance fee), with intriguing local history exhibits. Spoils from the *Whydah*, a pirate ship discovered off Wellfleet in 1984, are displayed at **Exhibition Whydah** on MacMillan Wharf (open Apr–mid-Oct, daily; June–Aug till 7pm; mid-Oct–Dec, weekends; entrance fee).

The very tip of Cape Cod – which is almost entirely within National Seashore boundaries – is unusual and fascinating. Two vast beaches, **Race Point** and **Herring Cove**, invite exploration: by bike, on horseback, on foot, and off-road vehicle tours. For information, call in at the **Province Lands Visitors' Center ⓭** (open mid-Apr–Nov, daily), which has a good viewing platform.

The Sound: Chatham to Falmouth

A popular base for touring the Cape, **Orleans** offers in the form of **Nauset Beach ⓴** one of the Cape's finest stretches of coast. The settlement was called by its Indian name of Nauset until it was incorporated in 1797 and renamed for the Duke of Orleans (the future king of France), a recent visitor. Orleans has another "French connection" – it was the stateside terminus for a transatlantic telegraph cable to Brest in France. Hooked up in 1879, the cable performed well for decades before it become obsolete, and is now commemorated in the **French Cable Museum** on Route 28 (South Orleans Road).

BELOW:
the Hyannis ferry to the Nantucket and Martha's Vineyard.

Cape Cod's southern shore, from Chatham to Falmouth, is a zone where the battle for – and against – commercialization has raged for the past few decades. Some pockets of subdued gentility still reign just off the honky-tonk stretches.

Chatham ㉑ numbers among the aristocratic enclaves. The handsome Chatham Bars Inn was built as a private hunting lodge early in the century. The nearby Fish Pier is a perfect spot to watch the fishing fleet bring in the daily catch. The **Chatham Railroad Museum** (153 Depot Road) is housed in the town's ornate Victorian railroad station, out of commission for several decades. **Chatham Light**, yet another picturesque Coast Guard lighthouse, overlooks South Beach.

Bird fanciers will want to make a visit to **Monomoy Island ㉒**, a stopping point for hundreds of species of birds traveling the Atlantic Flyway. Protected as the Monomoy National Wildlife Refuge, it is accessible only by boat; both the **Audubon Society** (tel: 508-349 2615) and the **Cape Cod Museum of Natural History** (tel: 508-896 3867) offer cruises.

Picturesque Harwich and **Harwich Port ㉓** are the last peaceful settlements before the Cape's commercial belt. From West Harwich to Hyannis, Route 28 is lined with motels, restaurants, businesses and amusements. It's a long, tawdry stretch, where traffic usually crawls all summer.

Map on pages 158–9

South Dennis ㉔, perversely north of West Dennis, has on Old Main Street a typical shingled Full Cape house (*see panel*) of 1801, known as **Jericho House** (open July–Aug, Wed and Fri pm only). Look behind the house for an 1810 barn filled with farming implements, plus a remarkable "driftwood zoo" of carved flotsam created by Sherman Woodward in the 1950s.

Hyannis ㉕, the Cape's year-round commercial center, boasts more than a score of worthwhile restaurants and nightclubs, the **Cape Cod Melody Tent** (for intimate concerts featuring top-name talent; West Main Street; tel: 508-775 9100), and, in the old Town Hall, the **John F. Kennedy Museum** (397 Main Street; open Mon–Sat, Sun pm; entrance fee) featuring photos and mementos of the President who summered in adjoining Hyannis Port. (Although the Kennedy Compound is the object of many a pilgrimage, it is not open to the public and very little of it can be seen from the road.) A small park dedicated to Kennedy's memory adjoins Veterans Beach, on Hyannis's harbor.

West of Hyannis, the tide of commercialism subsides occasionally to provide glimpses of Cape Cod's signature beauty. Make a southward detour for Centerville, where relatively warm-watered **Craigville Beach** (parking fee in summer) has drawn Christian "camp meetings" since the mid-19th century, and for affluent Osterville, a rarefied village surrounded by awe-inspiring seaside mansions.

Heading on toward Falmouth, take a side trip north to **Mashpee** ㉖, located amid Wampanoag tribal lands which in recent decades have been carved up by development. The **Old Indian Meetinghouse**, the oldest church building on the Cape, built in 1684, is well worth a look (Meeting House Road at Route 28; call for hours; tel: 508-477 208).

"Full Cape" denotes a shingle-hung house with two windows either side of the door. Three-quarters Cape means two windows on one side and one on the other, while a Half Cape has the door on the left and two windows to the right.

BELOW: Spohr's Garden, Falmouth.

*A bird box in
Trinity Park,
Martha's Vineyard.*

Falmouth **27** is like a microcosm of Cape Cod life. The town green – a Revolutionary militia training ground – is among the prettiest on the Cape; it's ringed by fine old houses, including several delightful B&Bs, and the **Falmouth Historical Society Museums** (Palmer Avenue on the Village Green; open mid-June–mid-Sept: weekdays pm; mid-Sept–mid-Oct: Tues and Thurs am; entrance fee). Falmouth Harbor is filled with pleasure craft; swimmers and windsurfers favor the beaches and guest houses of Victorian-era Falmouth Heights, overlooking Nantucket Sound.

One of the most pleasant activities in Falmouth is to rent a bicycle and follow the old railroad bed, now a bike path, down to **Woods Hole 28**. This small town is devoted almost exclusively to maritime activities. Most travelers pass through here merely to board the ferry for Martha's Vineyard, a 45-minute voyage away. But Woods Hole itself warrants a stopover. The world-famous **Woods Hole Oceanographic Institute** (School Street; open Tues–Sat; Sun pm) maintains a visitor center to describe its fascinating research; visitors can also tour the **Marine Biological Laboratory** (MBL Street at Water Street; reservations must be made in advance; tel: 508-548 3705), and the small but intriguing **National Marine Fisheries Service Aquarium** (open weekdays). Though no larger than a couple of city blocks, this tiny town supports a number of superb casual restaurants, where the specialty, naturally, is seafood.

BELOW: Quissett
Harbor, worth a
detour off the road
from Falmouth to
Woods Hole.

The island of Martha's Vineyard

Over the decades, Vineyard residents have grown blasé about the celebrities in their midst, and precisely because of that laissez-faire attitude, the roster just keeps growing. World-renowned actors, musicians, writers, and public figures (including the late Jacqueline Onassis) have felt comfortable here. It took a Presidential visit – the Clintons' during the mid-1990s – to shake things up a bit, but, despite the hordes lining the roadways, most people went about their business, and leisure, as usual.

Islanders have worked too hard to create and preserve a relaxed way of life to let a little glitz and glamour throw them. For many, the island represents a true escape from the pressures of city life and the stresses of high-powered careers. Though the price of admission may be high, once one has arrived, a kind of barefoot democracy prevails.

Like Cape Cod, Martha's Vineyard is a geological remnant from the last Ice Age. Two advancing lobes of a glacier molded the triangular northern shoreline, then retreated, leaving hilly moraines, low plains and many-fingered ponds. And Martha herself? She was the daughter of Thomas Mayhew, who in 1642 bought a large tract of land, including Nantucket Island, for the sum of £40. (Mayhew named Elizabeth Islands after another daughter.)

Vineyard Haven, Oak Bluffs and Edgartown, the three protected harbor towns of the northeastern portion of the island, were always active and prosperous, and to this day represent the commercial half of the island, although the main order of business is no longer shipping and whaling, but tourism and summer homes. By contrast, the sparsely populated "up-island" towns of West Tisbury, Chilmark, Menemsha, and Gay Head remain determinedly rural and non-ostentatious, despite a number of famous residents.

It may come as a disappointment to many visitors to find that, as a rule, Martha's Vineyard's extensive beaches are not accessible to outsiders but have been reserved for homeowners; the major exception, beyond the placid Joseph Sylvia State Beach on the bay side, is South Beach, fronting the rolling Atlantic south of Edgartown; other public beaches are Katama (good for surfing and for strong swimmers), Moshpu, Oak Bluffs and Menemsha.

Vineyard Haven, Oak Bluffs and Edgartown

Long before the Cape Cod Canal provided a shortcut between Boston and ports south, boats had to travel around Cape Cod to make a coastal journey. As traffic on this route and the routes striking out to the West Indies increased, the harbor at the tip of the Vineyard grew in importance as a shelter and a source of supplies.

Known until 1870 as Holmes Hole, **Vineyard Haven** ㉙ (the official name of the town is Tisbury, but everyone calls it by the name of its primary village) blossomed into a busy port during the 18th and 19th centuries, with both maritime businesses and farmers profiting from the constant movement of ships in and out of the port. Today, the homey **Black Dog Tavern** (open weekdays), with its offshoot bakery, store, and catalog business, enjoys a similar relationship with the legions of vacationers who arrive by ferry from Woods Hole.

Vineyard Haven has a no-nonsense, matter-of-fact quality about it, with little of the preciousness of Edgartown or the cuteness of Oak Bluffs. Handsome

Map on pages 158–9

Bikes and blades for rent.

BELOW: Oak Bluffs, Trinity Park.

houses dating from the years before the great fire of 1883 can be found on Williams Street, a block off Main Street.

Nearby, the collection at the **Old Schoolhouse Museum** (Main Street; open July–Aug, weekdays, am only) includes ivory carvings, schooner models, and early island photographs. At the western end of Main Street (bicycle or take the car) stands the **West Chop Lighthouse**.

Religion tinged with tourism produced an unusual community in **Oak Bluffs ㉚**, a town renowned for its engaging cottages built in "carpenter gothic" style. In 1835, Methodists took to the backwoods out of Edgartown in search of a suitable site for a camp meeting, a place where the faithful could come for a short period of spiritual replenishment. They found a secluded circle of oak trees, named it Wesleyan Grove, and conducted the first summer camp meeting on the site. Twenty years later, there were more than 320 tents and many thousands of people. Small houses soon replaced the tents, laid out along circular drives that rimmed the large central "tabernacle" where the congregation assembled.

Today this camp meeting site is known as **Trinity Park**. Tiny gingerbread cottages are a riot of color and jigsaw carvery, with all manner of turrets, spires, gables and eaves. Yet the park remains remarkably serene and intimate. The huge cast iron-and-wood theater in the center of the campground, built in 1870, still hosts community gatherings. **Illumination Night**, held every August, recreates the camp's traditional closing-night ceremony, when colorful glowing lanterns were strung up throughout the park. Circuit and Lake Streets mark the hub of town and the site of the 1876 **Flying Horses**, one of the oldest merry-go-rounds in America (Circuit Avenue; open mid-Apr–mid-Oct, daily).

Oak Bluffs was one of the first resort communities where black visitors were welcomed openly. Film director Spike Lee bought a summer house here and one resident, Harlem Renaissance author Dorothy West, set her novel "The Wedding" in the town.

BELOW: Edgartown.

South of Oak Bluffs on Beach Road, **Edgartown** is the oldest settlement on Martha's Vineyard. In 1642, missionary Thomas Mayhew, Jr, son of the Watertown, Massachusetts, entrepreneur who bought the islands off the Cape for a pittance, arrived at Great Harbor, now Edgartown, and set about converting the island's native population. Relying on fishing or farming, the town grew at a slow pace until the 18th century, when it became a capital in the worldwide whaling trade, vying with Nantucket and, later, New Bedford. The captains who made their fortunes from the sea left behind a treasure: their elegant Federal and Greek Revival houses, especially those lining North and South Water streets.

The most dignified Edgartown residence is that built in 1840 by whale-oil magnate **Dr Daniel Fisher**, who once supplied all US lighthouses with Edgartown oil. His house (open late May–mid-Oct, 11am–2pm daily; tours available; entrance fee) sits on upper Main Street, next to the imposing Greek Revival **Old Whaling Church** of 1843, whose enormous pillars and soaring tower are a rare instance of monumental scale in Edgartown. Tucked behind the church is the **Vincent House** (1672), an example of the popular 17th-century Cape design (open late May–mid-Oct, pm, daily; entrance fee). At the corner of Cooke and School streets is **The Vineyard Museum** (open June–mid-Oct: Tues–Sat; Nov–May: Sat and Wed–Fri pm; closed last two weeks in October; entrance fee), whose collections include whaling items, artifacts from daily Vineyard life and the famous French-made Fresnel lens, which until 1952 cast the warning beam from Gay Head Lighthouse.

A stone's throw away from Edgartown, across a narrow neck of the harbor, is **Chappaquiddick Island** , which hit the world's headlines as a result of the 1969 accident in which Senator Edward Kennedy drove his car over a bridge on the island, drowning his 28-year-old passenger, Mary Jo Kopechne. The island's native name means "The Separated Island," which it steadfastly remains, although the *On-Time III* regularly ferries cars (a few at a time) and clusters of pedestrians over the 200-yard (180-meter) crossing (tel: 508-627 9427). The main attraction on "Chappy," several miles from the ferry landing, is the **Wasque Reservation** and **Cape Poge Wildlife Refuge** at the island's eastern front.

Up-island escape

Should you tire of the enticing stores and restaurants to be found down-island, you need only retreat to the tranquility of up-island life (although the drive west from Edgartown, leading through forests of pine and oak, starts the transition to a vineyard where nature still decisively holds the upper hand).

The 4,000-acre (1,640-hectare) **Martha's Vineyard State Forest** – laced with walking and bridle paths and containing the island's only youth hostel – brings the scent of pines to the outskirts of **West Tisbury** center. This modest and unassuming village traditionally has been a center of small industry (including woolen and flour mills). Quirky attractions such as the Field Gallery (where Tom Maley's fanciful sculptures frolic in a field) and the Granary Gallery at the Red Barn Emporium (showcasing the historic

Map on pages 158–9

TIP

Christmas visitors to the Old Whaling Church can attend Handel's "Messiah". Films, lectures and concerts are presented in the 500-seater church as well as services.

BELOW: the ferry to Chappaquiddick.

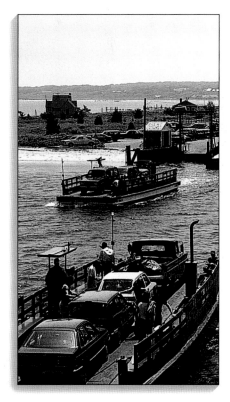

photos of the late Alfred Eisenstaedt, a summer regular) draw more attention these days, but the county fair is still a high point of the summer.

Of the three parallel roads traveling from West Tisbury to Chilmark, Middle Road traverses the most rugged, interesting glacial terrain. At **Chilmark Center** is Beetlebung Corner, a stand of tupelo trees from which "beetles" (mallets) and "bungs" (wooden stoppers) were once made.

Nearby **Menemsha** ⑤ is a tiny fishing village on Vineyard Sound, famed for its appearance in *Jaws* and prized for its Technicolor sunsets.

The most spectacular natural sight on Martha's Vineyard is at its westernmost tip, looking away from the commotion of the domesticated island and out to the untamed sea. From Chilmark, follow the single hilly road that at several points offers breathtaking views of Menemsha Pond northward and Squibnocket Pond to the south. At the end, a lighthouse marks the western terminus of the island and the location of the stunning, ancient geologic strata that compose the cliffs at **Gay Head** ⑥ (newly renamed Aquinnah). Clays of many colors – from gray to pink to green – represent eons of geological activity: fossils found amid the ever-changing contours of this 150-feet (46-meter) promontory have been dated back millions of years.

Gay Head is one of only two Native American communities in Massachusetts; it has been more successful than the Mashpee settlement in asserting its rights, and remains a cohesive social entity, over three centuries since the advent of colonizing forces.

On Indian Hill Road, heading back toward Vineyard Haven, is the site of Christiantown, settled by "praying Indians" in 1659; a plaque fixed to a boulder honors Thomas Mayhew's missionary efforts. At the end of the road, the

Playwright Lillian Hellman and actor John Belushi are buried in Chilmark Cemetery. Belushi's simple stone, which fans sometimes adorn with a beer can, is set up in front, but his body lies in an undisclosed plot.

BELOW:
Gay Head cliffs
and lighthouse.

Cedar Tree Neck Wildlife Sanctuary provides a commanding view of the Vineyard Sound, across to the Elizabeth Islands, and a fine spot for strolling and contemplating nature.

The island of Nantucket

In 1830 the whaling ship *Sarah* returned home to Nantucket island, carrying 3,500 barrels of valuable whale oil after a voyage of nearly three years. On the island, stately mansions, decorated with silks and china from faraway lands, awaited the returning captains. Schools, hotels, a library and the commercial activity on Main Street were indications of a prosperous people.

These were the halcyon days of little Nantucket island, the shining moment in its turbulent past. Although its fortunes soon declined, time has stood still on Nantucket, and the intimate scale and refined taste of its heyday have survived to the present day to endow the island with its charm, beauty and magnetic appeal.

Nantucket may never again know the excitement and adventure of the whaling trade, but its new industry – tourism – has brought an equal amount of fame and fortune. Like the earliest settlers, who came to escape the Puritan lifestyle, people today come to Nantucket to leave behind the harsh realities of life on the mainland.

Chasing the whales

Since its earliest days, Nantucket has been populated by determined and spirited people. The first colonists, who arrived from Massachusetts in 1659, were taught "onshore" whaling by the native Algonquins; they traveled out in open boats to chase and harpoon whales sighted from land. By the beginning of the

Map on pages 158–9

TIP

The ferry to Nantucket leaves from Hyannis and the trip takes around two and a half hours. Call (508) 540 2022 for schedules.

BELOW: cocktails by the harbor, Edgartown, Martha's Vineyard.

18th century, offshore whaling had begun and, with each generation of larger, more seaworthy craft, the whaling industry grew.

The natives, however, lost out. Although they sailed on whaling boats, their way of life on the island was irreversibly changed by the colonists. By 1855, disease (introduced to the country from Europe) and alcohol had taken the last of Nantucket's original residents.

By the time of the Revolutionary War, Nantucket had a fleet of 150 whaling ships. But Quaker pacifism and Nantucket's interest in London markets for whale oil divided islanders' loyalties, and their ships suffered greatly at the hands of the Tories and Revolutionaries alike. No sooner had they rebuilt their fleet than the War of 1812 erupted; by the conflict's end, their whaling empire had once again been left battered and exhausted.

Tenacity brought Nantucket back to life. Nantucket ships again sailed throughout the world and brought back record quantities of oil from their catches. It was during this period that the town acquired much of its urbanity, but the islanders' prosperity was destined to be short-lived: the Great Fire of 1846 razed the port, and in the 1850s kerosene replaced whale oil. Too heavily dependent on whaling, Nantucket was left high and dry.

BELOW LEFT: Great Point Lighthouse, Nantucket.
BELOW RIGHT: a former sea captain's house, Nantucket

From a peak of around 10,000, Nantucket's population dropped to 3,200 in 1875. Those who remained applied their ingenuity to a new venture, one that thrives today and continues to capitalize on the gifts of the sea. Tourism took off toward the end of the 19th century, as the arrival of the steamboat made the island more readily accessible. Land speculators built hotels and vacation homes. Quaint Siasconset, linked to the town by a narrow-gauge railroad built in 1884, was especially popular, drawing such luminaries as actress Lillian

Map on pages 158-9

Russell. The railroad is gone now (it was used for scrap metal during World War I), but tourism lives on.

An Indian word meaning "that faraway land," Nantucket isn't too far away for the thousands of people who visit each year by ferry and airplane. The winter population of 7,000 – lower than that recorded for the peak of the whaling era – increases sevenfold when the "summer people" take over the sidewalks of town and give it its cheery aspect.

In sharp contrast to Martha's Vineyard, Nantucket's mid-island moors and miles of beautiful, unspoiled beaches are open to visitors, most of whom use the preferred island mode of transportation: bikes (several shops stand ready to equip tourists near the ferry dock). Though smaller residential neighborhoods dot the island's coast, the harbor town of Nantucket, centrally located on the north shore, is unquestionably the focal point of the island.

The pleasures of Nantucket town

One can spend days walking through the town of **Nantucket** ❸ and always be sure of seeing something new. The community is a gem of 18th- and 19th-century architecture, from the dominant clapboard-and-shingle Quaker homes to the grandeur of the buildings lining **Upper Main Street**. And while the town may seem a maze of narrow streets, it is actually very ordered in its own cluttered way: early in the 18th century, its center was laid out in lots that ran roughly east–west from the harbor.

Nevertheless, it is best to tour with a street map (available from the bike shops, or in the free local newspapers distributed on the ferry), for the twists and turns can prove disorienting.

Information point for visitors.

BELOW:
Nantucket Town.

The waterfront is certainly the spiritual center of town. Several wharves extend into the harbor, the most central of which – **Straight Wharf** – is an extension of Main Street. First built in 1723, rebuilt after the 1846 fire, and renovated in the late 1950s to accommodate shops and restaurants, it's now like a small village unto itself, surrounded by luxury yachts and sailboats, some of which are available for charter. (The untouched barrier beach of Coatue is an ideal destination.)

Old South Wharf has also been spruced up and rendered tourist-friendly with boutiques and cafés; it's possible to rent tiny but picturesque wharfside cottages here.

Along Main Street up from Straight Wharf, a picturesque shopping district lines the gently rising cobblestone street. Although the square-mile (2.5 sq. km) National Landmark Historic District contains some 800 pre-1850 buildings, the red-brick facades lining Main Street are relatively "young," post-fire replacements. With its tree-lined, brick-paved sidewalks, Main Street is always a hub of activity in the summer months, offering every kind of distraction from collectibles to edibles. Among the more noteworthy emporia are the Main Street Gallery (actually, just off Main, on South Water Street) and Espresso Café, a lively place with the look of a classic ice-cream parlor.

Nantucket is justly proud of its history, especially its grand old homes and museums. The Nantucket Historical Association oversees more than a dozen properties (one ticket gains entry to all of them; tel: 508-228 1894).

A walk down South Water Street to Broad Street leads past three important institutions. Located at the corner of Lower India Street, the Greek Revival **Nantucket Atheneum** (constructed by local architect Frederick Brown Coleman

TIP

A good rainy-day stop in summer is the Dreamland Theatre, on South Water, which shows first-run films. It started life in the mid-1800s as a Quaker meeting house.

BELOW: the tools of a gardener's trade, Nantucket town.

in 1847) represents the intellectual flowering that accompanied the island's era of prosperity: Ralph Waldo Emerson gave the inaugural address and was followed by the leading thinkers of the day. Now a public library, this temple of learning contains interesting exhibits relating to island history. Also on Broad Street, the **Whaling Museum** (housed in a former spermaceti candle factory) commemorates Nantucket's seafaring days in a highly dramatic manner, with impressive displays (open May–Dec, daily; entrance fee).

Nearby, the **Peter Foulger Museum**, also on Broad, mounts temporary exhibits deriving from the research conducted upstairs by the Nantucket Historical Association (open daily; entrance fee). There's also a small **Life Saving Museum**, paying tribute to the work of the United States Life Saving Service (Polpis Road; open daily; entrance fee).

A bracing walk out of town, to the corner of South Mill and Prospect streets, leads to the **Old Mill** (1746), where, on windy days, visitors can watch corn kernels being ground into fine powder.

A few blocks away, at the corner of Vestal and Milk streets, is the **Maria Mitchell Science Center** (call for opening hours; entrance fee; tel: 508-228 9198) honoring the local savant – and Atheneum librarian – who discovered a comet at the age of 29 in 1847, garnering international acclaim. She went on to become the first woman admitted to the American Academy of Arts and Sciences, as well as the first female college professor in the United States (she taught astronomy at Vassar).

The somewhat scattered complex comprises five facilities open to the public, including the Mitchell House, her childhood home; the Hinchman House, a natural history museum; the Science Library, located in a former school house;

Map on pages 158–9

TIP

One of the island's better kept secrets is the subterranean Brotherhood of Thieves, an old whaling bar on Broad Street. It has no listed telephone number and doesn't take credit cards, but serves good pub food and chowder by candle-light.

BELOW: the Wauwinet inn, Nantucket.

Doorknocker, Jared Coffin House.

the Loines Observatory, located farther along Milk Street; and, on Washington Street, a small harborside Aquarium geared to children.

Further out on Vestal is the **Old Gaol**, built in 1805 and in use until 1933 (open mid-June–Sept). It looks like a normal house on the outside but is shockingly crude within; especially dangerous prisoners were confined in an iron-walled cell. But the island has never had much of a crime problem, and in any case prisoners were allowed to spend their nights at home.

The oldest house on Nantucket is the **Jethro Coffin House** (1686) on the northwest edge of town on Sunset Hill Lane (open mid-June–Sept). This plain saltbox design reflects the austere lifestyle led by the island's earliest settlers. In contrast, the three-story red-brick Jared Coffin House, at the corner of Centre and Broad streets, made its 1845 debut as the showiest dwelling on the island; within two years it became a hotel, and to this day it remains one of the island's finest inns.

Two more Coffin residences (the family was so prolific, it accounted for half the island's population by the early 19th century) stand at No. 75 and No. 78 Main Street, examples of the brick Federal style of architecture.

Farther up Main Street are the "**Three Bricks**," architectural triplets built by wealthy whaler Joseph Starbuck for his three sons. Across the street, and worlds apart in style, stand the "**Two Greeks**," Greek Revival mansions built by Frederick Coleman for two Starbuck daughters. One, the **Hadwen House** (96 Main Street; open mid-June–mid-Sept, daily; entrance fee) is maintained as a museum by the Nantucket Historical Association.

No. 99 Main Street, with its detailed and finely proportioned facade, is one of the most handsome wooden Federal-style buildings on Nantucket; it was

BELOW LEFT: Jared Coffin House.
BELOW RIGHT: on the beach near Surfside.

built by forebears of Roland Macy, who left the island to seek his fortune and founded a well-known namesake store.

Overlooking the harbor from **Brant Point** is one of America's oldest lighthouses. Visitors departing by sea often toss the traditional penny into the water off Brant Point to ensure that they'll return to the shores of Nantucket.

The rest of Nantucket island

"Nantucket! Take out your map and look at it," urged Herman Melville in his whaling adventure classic *Moby Dick*. An inspection of the map reveals an island with hamlets and hideaways sprinkled across its 14-mile (23-km) length. Despite some mid-island development in recent decades, about one-third of the island is under protective stewardship, thanks to the intercession of the Nantucket Conservation Foundation; although environmental restrictions limit activity on dunes, moors and other fragile areas, much of the land can be explored.

Stretching to the northeast from the town of Nantucket is a 6-mile (10-km) inner harbor, protected from Nantucket Sound by **Coatue**, a thin spit of land with flat white beaches accessible only by boat or four-wheel-drive vehicles (driven around the Head of the Harbor). This sweep of land, encompassing the **Coatue-Coskata Wildlife Refuge** ㉟, extends north to **Great Point**, where a lighthouse – a solar-powered 1986 replica of the 1818 original, swept away by a 1984 storm – warns boats away from the sandbars of Nantucket Sound.

Residential neighborhoods extend along the south side of the harbor. Monomoy, the nearest to town and the most populous settlement, affords spectacular views from its bluffs.

Map on pages 158–9

TIP

The Nantucket Trustees of the Reservations (tel: 228 6799) offer a three-hour over-sand tour of the Coatue-Coskata Wildlife Refuge. Pick it up in the Wauwinet Inn parking lot.

BELOW: much of Nantucket is protected from development.

Map on pages 158–9

A seaside treat.

BELOW: a Siasconset cameo.

From here, the Polpis Road leads across the rolling and delicate **Nantucket Moors**, which are carpeted with bayberry, beach plum, heather and other lush vegetation – a lovely green and flowering pink in summer, brilliant red and gold in the fall.

Wauwinet ㊴, a tiny community of cottages tucked amid the beach grass at the head of the harbor, is home to the ultra-elegant (and ultra-expensive) Wauwinet, a finely refurbished 1850 hostelry within splashing distance of both ocean and harbor. (It's located on the "haulover" where fishing boats used to avoid the long trip around Great Point.)

Tourists discovered **Siasconset** ㊵ (pronounced "Sconset"), the easternmost and second-largest town on Nantucket, in the 1880s. Theater people from the mainland mingled with local fishermen; the resulting architecture ranges from Lilliputian cottages to large rambling shingle-style houses along the bluffs.

Nantucket's most popular beaches are located on the flat, windswept south shore, open to the cold, spirited waters of the Atlantic Ocean. At **Surfside Beach** ㊶, a colorful Victorian lifesaving station serves nowadays as the island's only Youth Hostel. Surfers favor the beach at **Cisco**, a bit more remote, at the end of Hummock Pond Road, while **Madaket Beach** ㊷, at the southwestern tip of Nantucket, is popular for swimming, fishing, and, especially, sunset-gazing.

The northern coast east of Madaket Harbor, heading back toward town, offers the gentle surf of **Dionis** and **Jetties** beaches. The latter gets its name from its proximity to the West Jetty, which protects the channel leading into Nantucket Harbor. **Children's Beach**, tucked well inside the West Jetty, near Steamship Wharf, is especially placid and enhanced by a playground. ❑

Whale Watching

Destination: Stellwagen Bank, a shallow underwater deposit of sand and gravel off the coast of Massachusetts, to which pods of gentle humpbacked whales return yearly after spending the winters breeding in the West Indies. Sightseers are hot on their tails, for it's truly breathtaking to see these huge (often endangered) spectacles lunge, breach and flipper in the open ocean.

It's so rare for visitors not to see whales during a trip that most companies offer a "rain check," good for another trip. More often than not, the boats approach to within 50 ft (15 meters) of these magnificent mammals.

The world's largest concentration of whales (both in numbers and in species) are drawn to the fertile feeding grounds of Stellwagen Bank by huge quantities of plankton and an infinite number of small sand eels. The vast majority of the 500 or so whales who summer here are humpbacks, but their number also includes minkes, finbacks and a few endangered right whales (so called because, being slow swimmers, they were the "right" whales to hunt). Hundreds of frolicking dolphins and immense basking sharks will be close by, too.

The humpback is basically a bulk feeder, diving deep below schools of sand eels and lunging upward through the school with its mouth open. On the way up, it engulfs large quantities of fish and water, while its rorquals (folds of skin that begin at the chin and stretch to the navel) balloon to double its oral capacity. This allows the whale to catch hundreds, perhaps thousands, of fish with every lunge.

Whales also breach – that is, leap from the water, and flipper-roll on to their sides and lift their long white flipper out of the water before slamming it down hard on the surface.

Experts recognize individual humpbacks, which often reach lengths of 40–50 ft (12–15 meters) and weights of 30 tons, by their body markings, especially those on their tail flukes.

Whale watching was popularized in 1975 by Captain Al Avellar, a deep-sea fisherman from Provincetown, who invited Charles Mayo, a Provincetown-based marine biologist, to act as a guide on his first trips. Today, whale-watching excursions, all with experts on board, attract over 100,000 visitors annually.

Sightseeing boats generally depart two or three times daily in summer and on weekends in spring and fall. Trips last about three hours. Take jackets and seasickness pills, even on calm and seemingly warm days.

Many companies are based in Provincetown on Cape Cod: the Dolphin Fleet (tel: 508-349 1900, 800-826 9300) has an on-board biologist from the Center for Coastal Studies. In mid-Cape's Barnstable Harbor, call Hyannis Whalewatcher Cruises (tel: 508-362 6088).

From Boston, the New England Aquarium (tel: 617-973 5277) sponsors whalewatching trips, as does Boston Harbor Cruises (Rowes Wharf; tel: 617-723 7800).

On the North Shore in Gloucester, call Cape Ann Whale Watch (415 Main Street; tel: 978-283 5110, 800-877 5110) and Yankee Fleet Whale Watch (Route 133; tel: 978-283 0313, 800-942 5464). In Plymouth, Captain John Boats (tel: 508-746 2643, 800-242 2469) and Captain Tim Brady and Sons (tel: 508-746 4809) leave from Town Wharf. ❏

RIGHT: dolphins frolic alongside.

CENTRAL MASSACHUSETTS AND THE BERKSHIRES

Map on page 188

Famed outdoor museums recall the past and students enliven the present. In the west, art, dance, music, literature, and crafts flourish like nowhere else in New England

New England's legacy of rural beauty and industry lives on in Central Massachusetts. Whereas Boston belongs to the modern world of cosmopolitan cities and the Berkshires to the Gilded Age tradition of opulent leisure, the Commonwealth's mid-section harkens back to an earlier, mostly agricultural era when the living was hard and plain, the rewards what ready hands and determined souls could create.

The vigor and sincerity of early Americans' social vision is on display from mid-May to mid-October at **Fruitlands Museums** in the little town of **Harvard ❶**, an hour or so west of Boston via Route 2 (Prospect Hill; open daily; entrance fee). In the mid-19th century, transcendentalist Amos Bronson Alcott, father of Louisa May Alcott (author of *Little Women*), left his Concord home with political activist Charles Lane and a group of followers to found an anti-materialist utopian community on the 18th-century Fruitlands farm.

Vegetarianism, asceticism and a philosophical return to nature were their mandates but, despite their inspiring view of the beautiful Nashua River Valley, the commune soon dispersed. Today, however, the farmhouse has been transformed into a transcendentalist museum with presentations on Alcott, Emerson, Thoreau and others; its tearoom offers the same view of the Nashua Valley, and is surrounded by several other small museums.

Some 19th-century utopian experiments enjoyed greater longevity than that of Fruitlands. The most notable was that of the chaste and fervent Shakers, who persisted in Harvard from the late 18th century until 1918 (other New England Shaker settlements are intact to this day, although the sect is now virtually extinct; *see pages 296–97*). Fruitlands' 1794 Shaker House contains their crafts and furnishings which bespeak a lifestyle of studied simplicity.

The Indian Museum has a fine collection of artifacts, and the Picture Gallery displays folk portraits by itinerant artists and landscapes by such Hudson River School artists as Asher Durand and Frederick Church.

Ski center

Farther west, off Route 62 between Westminster and North Rutland, **Wachusett Mountain State Park ❷** has chair lifts and trails leading up to one of the state's highest summits (2,006 ft/649 meters), with views of the Boston skyscrapers. It doubles as the nearest ski and snowboard center to Boston, particularly geared to beginners and families, and has 100 percent snow-making; booking on busy weekends (tel: 978-464 2300).

To the southeast is **Worcester ❸**, the state's

PRECEDING PAGES: fall in the west of the state. **LEFT:** at Old Sturbridge Village. **BELOW:** in the Indian Museum at Fruitlands Museums.

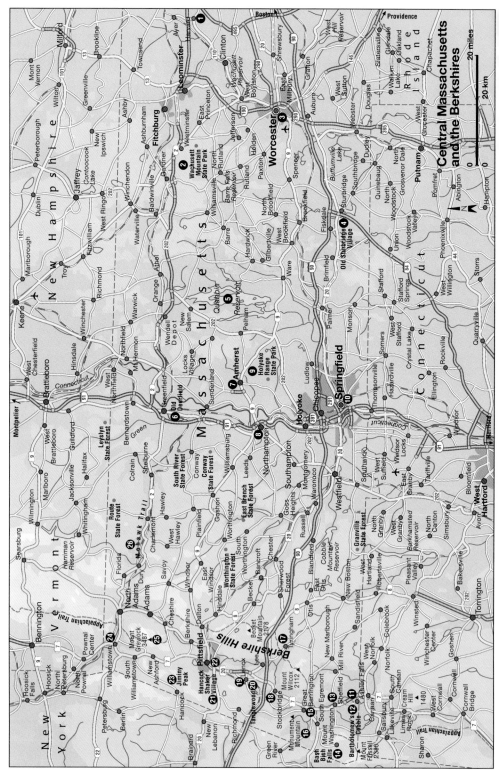

Central Massachusetts and the Berkshires

second-largest city. Where would America be without Worcester? This gritty industrial city spawned the country's first park, first wire-making company, first steam calliope, first carpet loom, first diner, first Valentine, and (suitably enough) first birth-control pill, not to mention the beginnings of liquid-fuel rocketry, female suffrage and the Free Soil Party, now known as the Republican Party. Notable residents have included abolitionist-composer Stephen Foster and socialist leader Emma Goldman; Sigmund Freud gave his only US lecture at Clark University.

The humorist Robert Benchley grew up in Worcester, as did the notorious 1960s radical Abbie Hoffman, and no doubt both owed their unfettered freedom of speech to publisher Isaiah Thomas, a Son of Liberty who fled Boston in advance of the British Army in 1770 and continued to publish his rabble-rousing revolutionary newspaper, the *Massachusetts Spy*, from Worcester. Thomas went on to become one of the wealthiest men in America, establishing the American Antiquarian Society on New York's Park Avenue in 1818; the original Worcester headquarters, on Salisbury Street, now serve as a research library.

Robert Benchley's bomb-proof quote: "The surest way to make a monkey of a man is to quote him."

The city, though left somewhat depressed in the wake of Masschusetts' industrial boom, is itself a trove of antiquarian delights. The **Worcester Historical Museum** (30 Elm Street; open Tues–Sat; Sun pm; entrance fee) is chockful of interesting memorabilia; the museum also maintains the splendid 1772 Georgian Salisbury Mansion. Awe-inspiring in its scope, the **Higgins Armory Museum** – the legacy of a local steel magnate – features a vast collection of medieval armor, as well as armaments dating back to 6th-century BC Greece (100 Barber Avenue; open Tues–Sat; Sun pm; entrance fee).

BELOW: interpreting the past at Old Sturbridge Village.

The **Worcester Art Museum** (55 Salisbury Street; open Wed–Sun; entrance fee) is the second largest in New England and perhaps the most adventurous: its sponsorship of excavations at Antioch, Syria, in the 1930s yielded a remarkable collection of 2nd-century AD Roman mosaics. The museum contains many other valuable antiquities along with fine collections of European and Eastern art. But perhaps most ppealing is the extensive gallery of 17th-, 18th- and 19th-century American art, including paintings by Winslow Homer, John Singer Sargent and John Singleton Copley. In their portraits and landscapes, one can trace the gradual emergence of a distinctly American culture.

Worcester Common (tel: 508-798 2581) is an all-in-one covered factory outlet mall in the heart of the city, with some 90 stores; there are direct buses from Boston South Station.

Reliving the past

Off Route 20, **Old Sturbridge Village** ❹ – a recreated community encompassing some 40 period buildings scattered over 200 acres (80 hectares) – offers a "you are there" take on early 19th-century rural life (Route 20; open May–Oct, daily; Nov–Apr, Tues–Sun; entrance fee; tel: 508-347 3362).

Visitors are given illuminating explanations, couched in modern parlance, as the interpreters go about the daily business of farm and town life: tending their animals, making tin lanterns, or leading prayers.

Map on page 188

Though a delight any time of year, Old Sturbridge is especially captivating in winter, when the crowds are sparser and the harshness of New England weather that so shaped the early settlers' moral and physical fiber can be experienced firsthand. Of special interest is the Pliny Freeman Farm, where, depending on the season, workers in period dress engage in making soap, shearing sheep, and laboriously building stone walls. Concepts of political freedom and discourse grew, in part, from the emergence of a free and vibrant press, and the activities of the Isaiah Thomas Printing Office are designed to show how printed communication became an integral part of the new nation's growth.

Continuing west, through rolling hills verdant in spring and summer, an explosion of color come fall, travelers reach the huge **Quabbin Reservoir 5**, 128 sq. miles (331 sq. km) of flooded valley that holds 412 billion gallons and supplies the drinking water to Greater Boston. Four towns were flooded in 1939 to create this great body of water; the **Swift River Historical Society** in New Salem preserves mementos of these vanished communities. More than a water source, Quabbin is prized as a place to fish, hike and admire the rare bald eagles that breed by the reservoir.

The pioneer heritage

The well-preserved pioneer village of **Old Deerfield 6** – where 14 museum houses are preserved as **Historic Deerfield**, off Route 5 (Main Street; open daily; entrance fee) – has a fascinating history that dates from its settlement by farmers in 1669. The Pocumtuck, who had been using the fertile valley to raise pumpkins, corn, and tobacco, were not pleased to see their land usurped, and massacred the entire population (by then 125 strong) in 1675. That

It is not excelled by anything I have ever seen, not excepting the Bay of Naples.

— JOHN QUINCY ADAMS, WRITING OF DEERFIELD'S MAIN STREET

BELOW: Old Sturbridge Village.

Map on page 188

deterred settlers for the next seven years, but the lure of the land was irresistible, and the interlopers eventually won out, despite another raid in 1704 in which half the village was burned, some 100 colonists were abducted into slavery, and another 50 slaughtered.

Tomahawk marks can still be seen on one sturdy wooden door, but the town's lurid history is not what attracts most visitors. The draw is an extraordinary architectural cache: the carefully restored Colonial and Federal structures along "The Street," Deerfield's mile-long main thoroughfare. The treasures inside the houses, representing decades of changing decorative styles, easily equal the exteriors. Among the more interesting of the buildings open to the public are the Ashley House (1730), a former parson's home with intricately carved woodwork and antique furnishings; the Asa Stebbins House (1810) with early paintings, Chinese porcelain and Federal and Chippendale furniture; the Dwight Barnard House (1725), immediately recognizable by its handsome carved door, behind which is an 18th-century doctor's office; and the Hall Tavern (1760), where Historic Deerfield maintains its information center.

The Pioneer Valley: a cultural nexus

About 10 miles (16 km) south of Old Deerfield, along the region designated as Pioneer Valley (the Massachusetts section of the Connecticut River Valley), is the town of **Amherst ❼**, long a hotbed of intellectual vigor and social independence. Noah Webster, creator of the American dictionary, lived here, as did a reclusive genius of the English language.

Visitors to the **Emily Dickinson Homestead** can experience the spartan environment that housed a sensitive, self-confined soul, who poured her

I never lost as much but twice,
And that was in the sod;
Twice I have stood a beggar
Before the door of God!

– EMILY DICKINSON,
REFERRING TO THE DEATH
OF TWO YOUNG MEN WHO
INFLUENCED HER WRITING

BELOW:
Amherst Common.

Beinfield Flea Market, held three times a year, is the world's largest outdoor crafts show, with more than 5,000 dealers.

BELOW:
canoeing on the Connecticut River.

emotions solely into her poetry (280 Main Street; tours by appointment; tel: 413-542 8161). Just off the spacious central green, **Amherst College's** stately fraternity houses flank a campus quadrangle that is a classic of early 19th-century institutional architecture; American and European works are exhibited at the college's **Mead Art Museum** (call for hours; tel: 413-542 2335).

Down Route 9 and across the Connecticut River is **Northampton ❽**, which can also boast a taciturn celebrity. Calvin Coolidge (1872–1933), the governor of Massachusetts who went on to serve as 30th US President, began his law practice in Northampton and eventually died there. His reputation as a man of exceptionally few words once prompted a determined matron at a society banquet to coax him: "Mr President, I have a wager with a friend that I can persuade you to say more than two words." Coolidge's reply: "You lose."

Surrounded by colleges (Amherst, Hampshire, and the University of Massachusetts – known to all as U-Mass – to the east, Mount Holyoke to the south, and Smith, right in town), Northampton has benefited from the youthful, energetic company it keeps. Once drab and dull, it now hosts a lively mix of fashionable stores and international restaurants, earning it the sobriquet of "Noho." With a sophistication level equal to that of New York's SoHo district, Northampton has attracted hundreds of artisans and artists, who showcase their wares at craft shops such as the Ferrin Gallery and Pinch Pottery and at the fine-art Hart Gallery.

The **Smith College Museum of Art**, one of the finest collections in the country, with a special focus on French impressionists, is on hand to lend inspiration (Route 9; tel: 413-585 2760); the college's Lyman Plant House, a delicate 1896 greenhouse, makes a lovely rainy-day retreat. In complete con-

trast is the **Words and Pictures Museum**, which pays homage to the art of comic books (140 Main Street; open pm only Tues–Fri; Fri till 8pm; Sat 10am–8pm; Sun pm; entrance fee).

Holyoke Range State Park ❾ has some of the best scenery in the Pioneer Valley. A road climbs up from Route 47 at Hadley to a viewpoint that was immortalized in Thomas Coles's 1830 painting, *The Oxbow*, with New Hampshire's Mount Monadnock is in sight. Just down the road in nearby South Hadley the **Mount Holyoke College** campus, designed by the famed landscape architect Frederick Law Olmsted, is the loveliest of the five colleges.

Bouncing back: Springfield

Springfield ❿ is one of those large American cities that just seem to lack pizzazz – or at least it did, until recently. The problem was an insensitive highway project, I-91, that chopped up neighborhoods and cut the city off from its most valuable natural asset, the Connecticut River. Now its banks have been reclaimed for the populace, in the form of a refreshing Riverfront Park, where summertime concerts are held.

Close by is the **Basketball Hall of Fame**, a lively, interactive museum dedicated to the game invented in 1891 by Springfield YMCA instructor Dr James Naismith (1150 West Columbus Avenue; open daily; entrance fee). Visitors have an opportunity to experience the fast-paced thrills in the "Shoot-Out," where a conveyor belt moves participants along a line of hoops.

Among the other "firsts," Springfield is known for its role as the nation's original arsenal (George Washington chose the site in 1779). The **Springfield Armory National Historic Site**, home of the first American musket, now

Map on page 188

YMCA instructor James Naismith nailed up a pair of peach baskets to keep his charges occupied; the game was more absorbing, they discovered, once the bottoms of the baskets were removed. And so basketball was invented.

BELOW LEFT: the Connecticut River Valley.
BELOW RIGHT: at the Basketball Hall of Fame.

houses a museum featuring one of the largest collections of firearms in the world (Armory Square; open Wed–Sun; entrance fee).

Springfield supports four more outstanding museums, all clustered around "the Quad" – the **Springfield Museum Quadrangle** on State Street.

The **George Walter Vincent Smith Art Museum** (open pm only Wed–Sun; entrance fee) features oriental decorative arts, from Persian rugs to Japanese netsuke and Chinese cloisonné (the largest collection of the latter in the Western world). The **Science Museum** contains the first American-built planetarium and plenty of intriguing, hands-on exhibits (open pm only Wed–Sun; entrance fee). The **Connecticut Valley Historical Museum** showcases artifacts – from folk paintings to fine furniture – chronicling several centuries of regional life (open pm only Wed–Sun; entrance fee). The **Museum of Fine Arts** (open pm only Wed–Sun; entrance fee) has an impressively broad collection, including portraits by the noted itinerant painter Rufus Porter; contemporary shows are also mounted.

Springfield's rich cultural life is reflected in the musical offerings, ranging from classical to popular, of the Springfield Symphony Orchestra, and in the sophisticated stagings of **StageWest** (tel: 413-781 2340). And no visit to the city would be complete without a pilgrimage to the **Student Prince and Fort Restaurant**, a colorful 1935 redoubt of German beer and sauerbraten (8 Fort Street; tel: 413-734 7475).

Across the river, in **West Springfield**, are the 175-acre (71-hectare) fairgrounds for the **Eastern States Exposition** (the "Big E"), New England's major agricultural fair and one of the nation's largest (tel: 413-732 2361). Every September, prize livestock and top-name talents entertain the crowds. Permanently ensconced on the grounds is the **Storrowton Village Museum**, seven trans-

Springfield's federal armory produced its first musket in 1795 and was still turning out rifles in World War II. It finally closed in 1968.

BELOW: small farms like this one in the Berkshires often offer bed and breakfast facilities.

planted 18th- and early 19th-century buildings where traditional crafts are demonstrated (Route 147; open late June–Aug Mon–Sat; entrance fee).

Map on page 188

The Berkshires

Making up western Massachusetts, Berkshire County – sometimes called the American Lake District – encompasses a landscape that provides almost every variety of beauty – valleys dotted with shimmering lakes, rolling farmlands punctuated by orchards and wheatfields, deep forests abundant with deer, powerful rivers that cascade into waterfalls under the bluest of New England skies.

Everywhere one turns in this corner of Massachusetts, the horizon is piled and terraced with mountains. Though less dramatic than the White Mountains of New Hampshire or the Green Mountains of Vermont, these gentle ranges have nonetheless provided the Berkshire Hills with an insularity that has historically set them apart from the rest of the state.

The Dutch, who settled New York in 1626 and moved north into the Hudson Valley, were prevented from further advancement by the stony resistance of the Taconic Range. Similar difficulties were met by the English, who found their progress west from the Connecticut River Valley blocked by the Hoosac Mountains – a wall of granite later dubbed the Berkshire Barrier.

Contained within this natural barricade, the Berkshires remained a wilderness until 1725, when Matthew Noble traveled through its dense forests to build a cabin in what is now the town of Sheffield. In the years that followed, farmland was cleared and towns were established along the Housatonic River and its tributaries. During the 19th century, the Industrial Revolution brought prosperity to the Berkshires: its iron foundries melted ore for the country's first railroads, while marble quarried from its hills graced the dome of the Capitol in Washington, DC.

BELOW: fall in the Berkshires.

As big business lured succeeding generations to the cities and better land beckoned farmers farther west, the Berkshires receded into a sleepy silence. But city dwellers seeking pretty scenery and respite from summer heat have periodically rediscovered the Berkshires. During the 1890s, for example, the county became a playground for such wealthy families as the Carnegies and Vanderbilts, who built their mansions in the hills surrounding Stockbridge and Lenox. More recently, visitors have come for the renowned summer music festivals, the splendor of fall foliage, or the challenge of winter skiing.

The first settlers reached the Berkshires through the Housatonic Valley from Connecticut. The modern traveler can do the same, following US Highway 7 north along the Housatonic. Many of Berkshire County's best-known attractions are located along Route 7 (or just a short distance from it).

The South Berkshires

Just inside the Connecticut border on Route 7A is **Ashley Falls** ⓫, a village surrounded by hayfields and dairy farms. The village was named for Colonel John Ashley, a prominent lawyer and major-general of the Massachusetts militia during the Revolutionary War. The **Colonel John Ashley House**, built in 1735, is the oldest structure in Berkshire County. It has been restored as a colonial museum (off Route 7; open June–early Sept; pm only Wed–Sun; entrance fee).

Also located in Ashley Falls is **Bartholomew's Cobble** . This natural rock garden, with hiking trails that meander along the banks of the Housatonic, is a bird-watcher's paradise and an excellent place to search for the trilliums and trout lilies of early spring. It contains more species of fern than any other area in the continental United States.

Sheffield ⓭, established in 1733, is the oldest town in Berkshire County and boasts two of the best-preserved covered bridges in Massachusetts. Traffic still travels over the larger, a narrow, barn-red structure that spans the Housatonic just east of town, on the road to New Marlborough.

At the far corner of the county, 2,000 ft (600 meters) up and teetering on the edge of New York State, is the tiny hill hamlet of **Mount Washington**. The smallest town in the Berkshires, Mount Washington offers some of the finest fall-foliage viewing in New England.

Continuing along the Mount Washington road, the traveler arrives at **Bash Bish Falls** ⓮, a 275-ft (84-meter) natural waterfall where, legend has it, a Native American maiden jumped to her death after being spurned by her lover. When the moon is full, her ghost, it is said, may be seen walking through the mountain laurel to wade in the pool beneath the falls.

The Berkshires' true beauty lies in its backroads and small villages. **New Marlborough** and nearby **Mill River**, small communities that prospered in the heyday of the Industrial Revolution, are gems. At the Old Inn on the Green in New Marlborough, once a stagecoach stop en route from New York to Boston, visitors can dine on fresh lamb or breakfast on blueberry muffins.

TIP

There is excellent blue-berry picking to be had on Mount Washington.

BELOW: capturing the Berkshires on canvas.

Great Barrington ⑮ offers an excellent base from which to explore the towns and villages of the southern Berkshires. Although it does not have the architectural treasures of towns farther north such as Stockbridge and Lenox, Great Barrington does have a homey quality. The Housatonic River courses through the center of town, and it was here, at a natural ford in the river, that the Mohicans built their Great Wigwam. It was also here that William Stanley (later to found the General Electric Company) first successfully demonstrated the use of alternating current; in 1886, the town became one of the first communities in America to be lit by electricity.

Great Barrington has been home to a large African-American community since before the Civil War, when fugitive slaves traveled to Massachusetts on the Underground Railroad. Socialist and scholar W. E. B. DuBois was born here in 1868.

A literary and artistic heritage

North of Great Barrington is **Monument Mountain** ⑯, a craggy peak whose summit is a pleasant half-hour hike from the parking lot at its base. The mountain is a Berkshire literary landmark of considerable repute. The poet William Cullen Bryant sang its praises while practicing as a local attorney in the 1830s.

The tiny village of **Tyringham** ⑰, where a community of Shakers settled in the 19th century, is unspoiled. In the early years of this century, the beauty of the landscape transformed the Tyringham Valley into an artists' colony. Today, in summer, Tyringham Art Galleries, founded in 1953, continue to operate out of the fairy-tale Gingerbread House, a former sculpture studio.

Stockbridge ⑱ was incorporated as an Indian mission in 1739. Its first missionary was John Sargeant, a young tutor from Yale who lived among the

Map on page 188

Many poets and writers have visited the Berkshires. Longfellow once hiked these trails, as did Emerson and Thoreau. Henry James visited often and, more recently, Berkshire County has been home to Thornton Wilder and Norman Mailer.

BELOW: the historic Sargeant House, Stockbridge.

Fall colours.

natives for 16 years. He slept in their wigwams, shared their venison and spoke their language, while introducing them to the colonists' ways. Eventually, Sargeant helped them establish a town, build homes and cultivate the land. Some among the Mohican tribe held public office, serving alongside whites in the town government. The Stockbridge Mission was so successful that it became a model of cultural adaptation; but the experiment was not to last. As more colonists moved into the area, the tribes were slowly deprived of their land. By 1783, the mission was history, and surviving Indians were forced to settle on the Oneida reservation in New York State. All that remains is the **Mission House**, now a museum on Stockbridge's Main Street (open late May–mid-Oct; entrance fee).

If the stately mansions and quaint shops located along Route 102, the Main Street of Stockbridge, look familiar, it may be because their New England essence was captured on the canvases of that remarkable illustrator of American life, Norman Rockwell. Rockwell, who created more than 300 covers for the *Saturday Evening Post,* kept a studio in Stockbridge and made his home here for a quarter of a century, until his death in 1978. Located on Route 183, the stunning **Norman Rockwell Museum**, designed by Robert A.M. Stern, showcases his oeuvre and even recreates his Stockbridge studio. No visitor, however sophisticated, should miss this display: reflecting a time when American ideals were simpler, Rockwell's portraits capture an age of innocence with humor and modesty (open daily; entrance fee; tel: 413-298 4100).

The Red Lion Inn, located in the center of Stockbridge at the intersection of Routes 7 and 102, is one of the *grandes dames* of New England country inns. Its flower-laden front porch, complete with rocking chairs, is a place of pilgrimage for Berkshires travelers.

Naumkeag, 2 miles (3 km) north of Stockbridge, is a Norman-style mansion designed by Stanford White for Joseph Choate, US ambassador to Great Britain in 1899; the furnishings and gardens are unusually lavish (Prospect Hill Road; open late May–early Sept daily; weekends until mid–Oct; entrance fee). **Chesterwood**, the summer home of sculptor Daniel Chester French, is 3 miles (5 km) west of Stockbridge (off Route 183; open May–Oct daily; entrance fee). It was here that he created his masterpiece, *The Seated Lincoln*, focal point of the Lincoln Memorial in Washington, DC. Casts are displayed in the house.

In **Lenox** ⑲ is **The Mount**, novelist Edith Wharton's grand Italianate 1890s mansion (Routes 7 and 7A; open late May–Oct Tues–Sun; entrance fee), now the headquarters of the theater troupe Shakespeare & Co (see below). Here she wrote *Ethan Frome*, set in the Berkshire town of West Stockbridge.

Map on page 188

The sounds of music

Is it possible to vacation in the Berkshires without stopping at **Tanglewood** ⑳, summer home of the Boston Symphony Orchestra? This 200-acre (80-hectare) estate, located on Route 183, 1½ miles (2.5 km) west of Lenox, has been a haven for performers, students and music lovers since the orchestra first began its outdoor concert series in 1931. The 6,000-seat Music Shed, designed by architect Eero Saarinen, has excellent acoustics; but many visitors prefer to pack their dinners, come early and picnic on the lawn. They need blankets and plenty of warm clothes to counter the cool night air.

During the summer, near Tanglewood's lawn, a replica of the little red cottage where Nathaniel Hawthorne lived and wrote *The House of the Seven Gables* and *Tanglewood Tales* can be visited.

TIP

The BSO Tanglewood season begins in late June and runs through August, with concerts on Fridays, Saturdays and Sundays (tel: 413-637 1600).

BELOW: a Housatonic potter at work.

CULTURE IN THE BERKSHIRES

Tanglewood is the best-known of several summer festivals in the Berkshires. The South Mountain Concerts (tel: 413-442 2106), featuring chamber music on weekends, take place south of Pittsfield, on Route 7. For Renaissance and Baroque music head for the Aston Magna Festival (tel: 413-528 3595), in Great Barrington; performances on original instruments are given at St James Church on weekends in July.

When the Jacob's Pillow Dance Festival (tel: 413-243 0745) was launched in the early 1930s, modern dance was in its infancy and many viewed the likes of Martha Graham and Merce Cunningham as a passing fad. Today, Jacob's Pillow (in the hilltown of Becket, southeast of Pittsfield on State 8) is a national institution.

Also impressive is the Williamstown Theater Festival (tel: 413-597 3399), which stages some of the finest summer theater in the country. Running the gamut from Greek tragedy to Restoration comedy, and from Chekhov to Pirandello, the festival also has a fine company of actors.

At Berkshire Theater Festival (tel: 413-298 5536), in Stockbridge, the emphasis is on American classics. For fans of the Bard, there's Shakespeare & Co (tel: 413-637 3353), which performs outdoors at The Mount in Lenox.

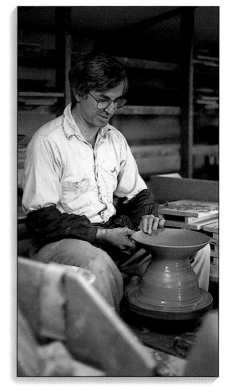

Map on page 188

The simple Shakers

"'Tis a gift to be simple," says the old Shaker hymn. A visit to **Hancock Shaker Village ㉑**, on Route US 20, 3 miles (5 km) west of Pittsfield, is testimony to the virtues of simplicity (tel: 413-443 0188; open daily; entrance fee).

The Shakers (*see pages 296–97*) settled in Hancock during the late 1780s. The community prospered through farming, printing, selling garden seeds and herbs and manufacturing their distinctively designed furnishings. The elegance and functionalism of Shaker architecture is exemplified by Hancock's famous 1826 round stone barn. It enabled one farmhand, standing at its center, to feed an entire herd of cattle. Shakers lived in Hancock until the 1950s, when the community had dwindled to a few staunch survivors, celibacy and changing times having led to their decline.

Returning to Route 7, the northbound traveler passes through **Pittsfield ㉒**, the Berkshire County seat and largest city (population 52,000) and the town that General Electric built. Writer Herman Melville lived here and completed *Moby Dick* (1851) while at **Arrowhead** (Route 7; open May–mid-Sept daily; mid-Sept–Oct Fri–Mon; entrance fee); there is Melville memorabilia at the Berkshire Athenaeum.

Williamstown and the north Berkshires

BELOW: on the Mohawk Trail: "Hail to the Sunrise" recalls the Mohawk Indians.

North of Pittsfield, **Jiminy Peak ㉓** is a ski area with night skiing. It offers something to suit all levels of skill; in summer an alpine slide operates, making an exhilarating drop down the mountain, and fishing, tennis, putting and swimming are on offer (tel: 413-738 5500).

In the state's northwest corner **Williamstown ㉔** is among the most beautiful of New England villages. It is home to **Williams College**, founded in 1793. A major reason to come to Williamstown is for the exceptional **Sterling and Francine Clark Art Institute**, located on South Street just west of the town center (open Tues–Sun; entrance fee). Between World War I and 1956, the Clarks amassed a superb private collection of European and American paintings, including works by Botticelli, Goya, Gainsborough and Fragonard. But the museum is best known for its Impressionist collection, which includes many works by Monet, Degas and Renoir.

Rising to 3,491 ft (1,064 meters), east of Williamstown, **Mount Greylock ㉕** is the tallest peak in Massachusetts. Hardy travelers can ascend on foot, while those less energetic can drive to the summit via a steep and winding access road. From the top, writer Nathaniel Hawthorne looked down upon Williamstown – "a white village and a steeple set like a daydream among the high mountain waves."

The **Mohawk Trail ㉖** (Route 2) winds eastwards from Williamstown, across the top of Berkshire County. An old Indian path-turned-roadway – as recalled by a number of roadside stores selling "Indian" souvenirs – it offers some of the most rugged and romantic scenery in the Berkshires. It is a popular leaf-peeping route in the fall. The best of the views are around Hairpin Turn, east of North Adams. ❑

Sporting Traditions

Ever since football was introduced to the nation on Boston Common in 1862 and basketballs were first stuffed into baskets in Springfield, Mass., in 1881, New England has been a sports trailblazer. Long before expansion became the buzz word, Boston was one of the only cities to boast major league teams in baseball (Red Sox and Braves), basketball (Celtics), and ice-hockey (Bruins). The Braves decamped after 1952; football expansion led to the 1960 appearance of the Patriots; and in 1979 the Hartford Whalers entered the major ice-hockey arena.

Yet it seems the fate of New England fans nearly always to follow losers. Only the Celtics have bucked the trend by winning 16 National Basketball titles, more than any other team. But their last pennant was in 1986.

Admittedly, the Red Sox won the first World Series, in 1903, and clinched it four times between then and 1918, but never since then. In the 1986 World Series, they were within a heart-beat of winning, but they lost that game and the decisive seventh and, with it, the title. In 1988, 1990, 1995 and 1998 they made it to the playoffs but never got to compete in the World Series. The Bruins have won the coveted Stanley Cup five times, but the last time was in 1972. In 1990 they succumbed to the Edmonton Oilers in the third period of overtime in the seventh and last game of the Stanley Cup.

The formerly hapless Patriots, who made it to the 1986 Superbowl but were trounced by the Chicago Bears 46–10, turned a corner in 1993 with the arrival of quarterback Drew Bledsoe and coach Bill Parcels. In 1994 they won the AFC wildcard game but got no further; in 1996 they made it to the Superbowl, but were beaten by Green Bay 35–21. In 1997, under a new coach, they won the AFC wildcard game but lost the next AFC division game.

Patience should, but does not, grow thin: there are always demi-gods to worship: Ted Williams and Carl Yastrzemski in baseball; Bobby Orr in hockey and Bob Cousy and Larry Bird in basketball. Some, however, prefer to remember Rocky Marciano of Brockton, Mass., the heavyweight boxer who, when he retired in 1956, was the only world champion to have won every fight (49) of his professional career.

New England's sporting scene is enlivened by teams from its myriad colleges but mostly these have little impact nationally. Exceptions are Boston College (football and basketball) and the University of Connecticut (basketball). Boston University and Harvard often contribute players to the US Olympic ice-hockey squad. And in squash and sailing New England college teams are often in the fore. Since 1965 oarspeople from around the globe have come to Cambridge in October for the Head of the Charles, the world's biggest one-day regatta.

In spring, thousands of runners, again from all over the world, line up at Hopkinton, Mass., for the start of the celebrated Boston Marathon (tel: 617-236 1652). It's the world's oldest annual marathon, first run in 1896, and is the only marathon to offer equal prize-money, in all classes, to both men and women. The last time New Englanders came in first was 1983, when Gregory Meyer of Wellesley won the Men's and Joan Benoit of Watertown the Women's. ❑

RIGHT: little league baseball in Newton, Mass.

CONNECTICUT

This historic state encompasses Yale University in New Haven, maritime traditions in Mystic Seaport, antiquing and art in the Litchfield Hills – and, unexpectedly, America's biggest casino

Map on page 206

Driving admiringly through the neat-as-a-pin village of Guilford, a one-time resident once remarked: "Connecticut always looks as if the maid has just been in to clean." There, as in so many of Connecticut's picturesque colonial villages, the carefully kept, white clapboard homes and manicured lawns evoke an image of quiet wealth, propriety and old school ties.

Indeed, this state has always had something of a conservative mien. The Puritans who settled here were staunch Congregationalists, little given to the radical ideas of Roger Williams or the autocratic piety of John Winthrop. They may have been farmers and seafarers, but they were primarily involved in commerce; they understood the value of a dollar and the importance of its proper investment.

Though generations have come and gone, this aspect of the Connecticut character has not changed. It has, however, been tempered with pride for the place and a heartfelt sense of its history.

Many visitors make the mistake of traveling non-stop through Connecticut (pronounced *kuh-ned-eket*) en route to vacations elsewhere in New England. Perhaps because its riches are so accessible, people tend to take them too much for granted. For those who exit from the highways and take to the back roads and small towns of Connecticut, there is a wealth of colonial heritage waiting to be explored.

With Long Island Sound as its southern border, Connecticut roughly forms a rectangle measuring 90 miles (145 km) from east to west and 55 miles (89 km) north to south. The Connecticut River, New England's longest, bisects the state; along with the Connecticut River, the Thames and Housatonic rivers were vital in the settlement and later industrialization of the state.

The Constitution State

Adrian Block, a Dutch navigator, was probably the first to understand the possibilities of the region when he sailed along the coast and up the Connecticut River in 1614. Nineteen years later, the Dutch established a trading post near the future site of Hartford, naming their new colony Fort Good Hope.

Beaver and timber had attracted the Dutch first, but it was the British who, lured by fertile land and religious freedom, finally settled the region in 1635. By that time, the original colony of Massachusetts Bay was overcrowded, and newcomers arriving from England had to extend their search for arable land to the upper reaches of the Connecticut River. Added to economic causes were the personalities of strong-willed leaders such as the Reverend Thomas Hooker, who, unwilling to submit to the autocratic theocracy

PRECEDING PAGES: Southbury. **LEFT:** a Middlebury farmer. **BELOW:** Patriot John Wadsworth hides the royal charter in an oak tree.

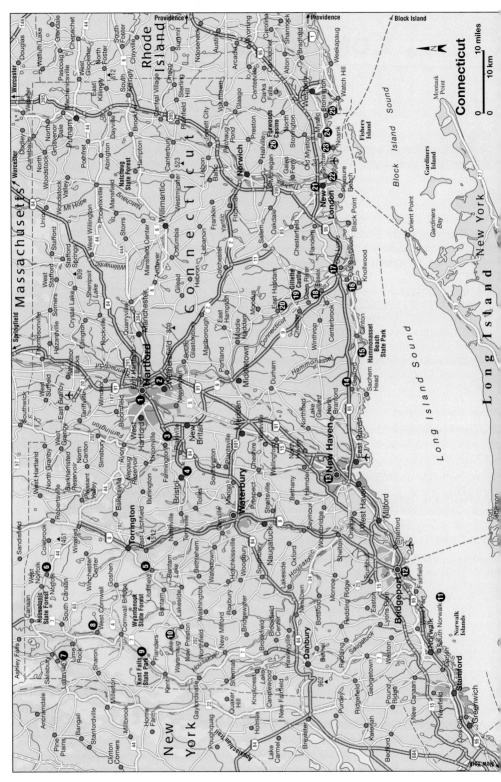

Connecticut

N

0   10 miles
0   10 km

of the Massachusetts colony, chose to lead his congregation to an area beyond the reach of any colonial authority.

By 1636, settlements had been established in Hartford, Windsor and Wethersfield. Calling themselves the Hartford Colony, the three towns adopted the Fundamental Orders of Connecticut on January 14, 1639. This document, sometimes called "the grandfather of the Constitution" is regarded by many historians as the world's first written constitution. From that historical first comes the legend on the license plates, "The Constitution State."

New settlements were organized along the shores of the Long Island Sound. Old Saybrook was first, followed by New Haven, Guilford, and Stamford. Later towns, cleaving to the staunch Congregationalism of their settlers, took such Biblical names as Goshen, Sharon, Canaan, and Bethlehem.

When the time came to fight in the American War for Independence, Connecticut soldiers were eager participants. No major battles were fought on Connecticut soil, but the state had its patriots. Among them were General Israel Putnam and Ethan Allen. Most famous was Nathan Hale, the Coventry, Connecticut, schoolteacher who, when hanged by the British as a spy, uttered the immortal words: "I regret that I have only one life to give for my country."

With the end of the Revolution, Americans returned home to set about building their new nation. But Connecticut citizens quickly realized that they could not make their fortunes in farming. The stony, glacial soil that covered most of the region was poorly suited to cultivation. With the exception of the upper Connecticut valley, where tobacco is still grown under wide, cheesecloth tents, the land could support only small dairy farms and family fruit orchards.

Undeterred, Connecticut citizens turned to commerce, and from the years

Hallowe'en pumpkin.

BELOW:
after milking.

Since the US Patent Office opened in 1790, Connecticut inventors have filed more patents per capita than any other state. Hats, combs, cigars, seeds, clocks, kettles, furniture and firearms – all came out of the factory stamped "Made in Connecticut."

BELOW:
colonial piper in West Hartford.

1780 to 1840, the Yankee peddler reigned supreme. His sturdy wagon, loaded with tinware, soap, matches, yard goods and tools, was a familiar sight up and down the Atlantic seaboard, over the Appalachians into Detroit and St Louis, and even down to New Orleans. Success brought with it the demand for more and more products, and it was here that the Connecticut Yankees made their major contributions to the pioneering American economy.

New products called for new systems of manufacture: Eli Whitney, inventor of the cotton gin, first introduced the use of standardized parts at his firearms factory in New Haven. With the introduction of interchangeable parts came the creation of the assembly line – and the rise of the Industrial Revolution. No longer would manufacturing rely on the talents of a few, skilled craftsmen. Mass production had entered the marketplace, and the American economy prospered accordingly.

Not surprisingly, industry made Connecticut's fortune. In Hartford, entrepreneur Samuel Colt gave his name to the Colt .45 revolver, the "gun that won the West." Winchester rifles were manufactured in New Haven, hats in Danbury, clocks in Bristol, and fine brass in Waterbury.

New industry meant new workers, and the late 19th and early 20th centuries saw waves of immigrants settle in such manufacturing centers as Bridgeport, New Haven, and Torrington. While Connecticut may present a colonial face to the casual traveler, those who remain long enough appreciate the contributions of Italians, Germans, Portuguese, and Eastern Europeans to the essential Connecticut character.

Connecticut's past is also its present, and today the state continues to rely on industry for its economic good fortune. Airplane engines are manufactured in

East Hartford, helicopters in Stratford; nuclear submarines are designed and built in Groton.

Despite its industry, Connecticut has remained a largely rural enclave. With manufacturing concentrated along the South Shore and in Hartford, 75 percent of the state is given over to small towns and deeply forested woodlands. Narrow, winding roads lead the visitor from one charming village to another, to communities proud of their colonial heritage and seemingly untouched by modern times.

Maps:
Area 206
City 209

Capital of Connecticut: Hartford

In any game of free association, the name of **Hartford ❶** immediately elicits the response, "insurance." And, indeed, the skyline of Connecticut's capital city is dominated by the steel-and-glass skyscrapers of the nation's largest insurance companies. Today several dozen are located in the greater Hartford area, together employing approximately 10 percent of the total work force.

The population of Hartford, the state capital, is around 124,000.

The first insurance policy, covering a shipowner's losses in the event his ship didn't make it safely back to port, was written in the 18th century. The early industry served the maritime trade, but, as shipping declined during the 19th century, Hartford's canny insurance companies expanded their coverage to fire and casualty. Their reputation is well founded; from their earliest days, the insurance firms honored their commitments. In 1835, New York City suffered a disastrous fire that destroyed more than 600 buildings. Unable to pay the claims, many New York insurance companies folded. Not so the Hartford Insurance Company, however. Its president traveled to New York and personally guaranteed payment of every claim. Similar incidents in Boston and

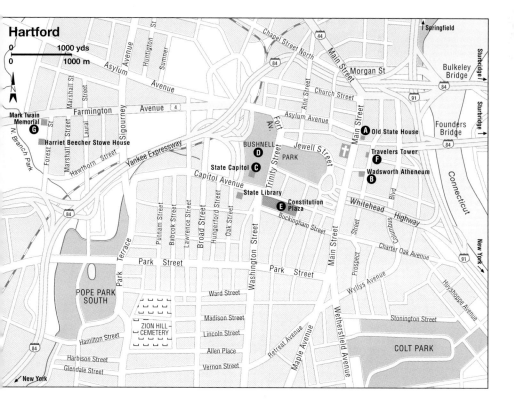

Chicago, as well as the 1906 San Francisco earthquake, bolstered the reputation of Hartford's ambitious insurance companies.

But Hartford means more than insurance companies. It is also Connecticut's oldest city, settled in 1635 by a group of Puritans from the Massachusetts Bay Colony. Its location on the navigable waterways of the Connecticut River has made Hartford a major force in the political, economic and social development of the region. In 1662, a royal charter was drawn up uniting the colonies of Hartford and New Haven, and guaranteeing their independence. Sir Edmund Andros, appointed governor of Connecticut in 1687, had the charter revoked. In defiance of this move, the Hartford patriot John Wadsworth stole the charter and hid it in the trunk of an oak tree at the center of the town. Two years later, on the accession of William III, Andros was recalled to England and the charter was reinstated. A plaque at Charter Oak Place, in the south end of the city, marks the spot where the magnificent oak stood until 1856, when a windstorm felled it. Hartford's museums are filled with items supposedly made from the wood.

As with many US cities, the downtown area was allowed to deteriorate as the middle classes moved to the suburbs; but efforts to control crime and encourage nightlife have been having some effect. Any tour should begin with a visit to the **Old State House Ⓐ**, located at the intersection of Main Street and Asylum Avenue (open Mon–Sat). The nation's oldest state house, it was the first public commission for architect Charles Bulfinch, who would later design the state capitols of Maine and Massachusetts. Neither quite compares to his Hartford creation, which stands as a supreme example of Federalist architecture.

Directly south of the State House, also on Main Street, is the **Wadsworth Atheneum Ⓑ**, the oldest continually operating public art museum in America

In the early days of maritime insurance, ratings were based on the type of wood, as well as the size and number of timbers, used in a ship's construction. Oaks were recommended for the ship's frame, hard pine for the keel, and hard pine, oak or mahogany for the planking.

BELOW:
Connecticut State
Capitol, Hartford.

Map on page 209

(open Tues–Sun; first Thur of month till 8pm; entrance fee). Built in the Gothic Revival style, the Atheneum was erected to house the library and art gallery of Daniel Wadsworth. Numerous additions have been made since, and the museum's collection – which includes paintings by Goya, Rubens, Rembrandt and van Dyck, in addition to works by American masters such as Thomas Cole and John Singer Sargent – remains a proud part of the city's cultural heritage.

The **Connecticut State Capitol** ❻, a Gothic wedding cake of turrets, gables, porches, and towers, was designed by Richard Upjohn in 1879 (tours Mon–Fri am; also Sat Apr–Oct). Though some might question its good taste, there is no doubt that its ornate interiors of hand-painted columns, marble floors and elaborate stained-glass windows were designed to reflect the wealth and prosperity of the community it served. Located on Capitol Avenue overlooking **Bushnell Park** ❼ (which contains an enchanting 1914 carousel; open in summer), the Capitol is flanked by the State Library, which maintains an excellent collection of Connecticut clocks and firearms; and the Bushnell Memorial Auditorium, a center for concerts, ballet, opera and theater.

Constitution Plaza ❽, a 12-acre complex completed in the 1960s, provides Hartford with an open mall, a vast array of shops, office buildings and the starkly modern, elliptically shaped Phoenix Mutual Life Insurance Building, so familiar to the Hartford skyline.

Travelers Tower ❾, the tallest building in the city, has an **Observation Deck**, which offers an excellent view of the Hartford area (tours by appointment mid-May–late Oct weekdays; tel: 860–277 0111). The Travelers Insurance Company was founded in 1683, when Colonel James Bolter insured his life for $5,000 to cover his lunchtime trip from home to the post office.

BELOW: Hartford's Constitution Plaza at Christmas.

Mark Twain (1835–1910) was Hartford's most famous resident. His mansion, now known as the **Mark Twain Memorial** , is at Nook Farm, just north of exit 46 on I-84, less than 2 miles (3.5 km) from downtown Hartford (open daily; entrance fee). Now a busy residential area, it retains little of its pastoral charm. The adjacent **Harriet Beecher Stowe House** is also open to visitors (open late May–mid-Oct Mon–Sat; pm only Sun; entrance fee).

Nook Farm was the intellectual center of Hartford, settled in the second half of the 19th century. Twain's home is easily the largest, a great Victorian mansion designed by Edward Tuckerman Potter in 1874. Exquisitely decorated by Louis Comfort Tiffany and his associates, the house very much reflects the character of its owner. Outdoor porches and balconies give the impression of a Mississippi riverboat, while the interiors are grand and whimsical. Of particular interest is the upstairs billiard room, where Twain did much of his writing.

The riverboat pilot-turned-author spent the happiest years of his life in Hartford. Twain, whose real name was Samuel Clemens, settled here soon after his marriage to Olivia Langdon, and it was in their home at 351 Farmington Avenue that they raised their three daughters, Clara, Jean and Susy. Although Twain originally moved here in 1874 merely to be close to his publisher, he frequently sang the praises of his adopted city. "Of all the beautiful towns it has been my fortune to see, this is the chief…You do not know what beauty is if you have not been here." It was also in Hartford that he penned his most successful novels, including *The Adventures of Tom Sawyer*, *The Adventures of Huckleberry Finn*, and *A Connecticut Yankee in King Arthur's Court*.

The author remained in Hartford until 1891, when poor investments forced him to move to Europe or face bankruptcy. The family always intended to return, but after the sudden death of his daughter Susy in 1896, Twain could not bear to go back to the site of their happiest memories. He sold the house in 1903.

Truth is stranger than fiction, but it is because fiction is obliged to stick to possibilities; truth isn't.

– MARK TWAIN,
PUDD'N'HEAD WILSON'S
NEW CALENDAR

BELOW: Nook Farm, Mark Twain's Gilded Age mansion.

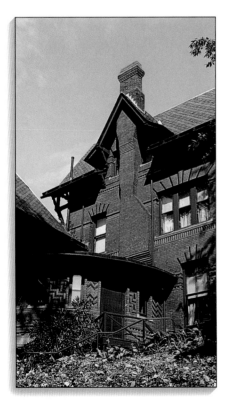

Side trips from Hartford

Wethersfield ②, on the Connecticut River just south of Hartford, is one of the oldest villages in the state. More than 150 of the 17th- and 18th-century homes in its downtown area have been preserved. Look at the 1760 Congregational Meetinghouse on Main Street, and the **Webb-Deane-Stevens Museum** (open May–Oct, Wed–Mon; Nov–Apr, weekends; entrance fee).

Farmington ③, a village situated on the Farmington River just 10 miles (16 km) west of Hartford, is considered by many to be one of the loveliest towns in New England. Certainly, its elegant 18th- and 19th-century mansions display a clarity of architectural detail seldom equaled in the area. **Hillstead Museum** is a particular gem (Mountain Road; open Tues–Sun; entrance fee). Designed by architect Stanford White, the Hillstead was originally conceived as a retirement home for a wealthy industrialist, Alfred Atmore Pope. A self-made man, Pope was a personal friend of the artist Mary Cassatt and a great admirer of the French Impressionist school of painters. Pope's home, which remains as it was in the early 1900s, reflects his taste in art. Scattered throughout the mansion are a number of familiar canvases, including paintings from

Monet's *Haystack* series, Manet's *The Guitar Lady*, and Degas's *The Tub*. Whistler and Cassatt are also well represented.

Bristol ❹, 18 miles (29 km) west of Hartford, was the 19th-century clockmaking capital of the country, producing more than 200,000 clocks in a single year. The neighboring towns of **Terryville** and **Thomaston** were named for Eli Terry and Seth Thomas, craftsmen who at one time put a clock on every mantel in America. The **American Clock and Watch Museum** is located on Maple Street in Bristol, and houses a superb collection of the region's finest and most valuable timepieces (open Apr–Nov daily; entrance fee).

Maps:
Area 206
City 209

The Litchfield Hills

Connecticut's northwestern corner constitutes its wildest forests and mountains, dotted with quintessential New England bridges and covered bridges – an area known as the Litchfield Hills. Through it runs the **Housatonic River**, crystal clear and freckled with trout, and excellent for canoeing. Hikers may want to follow the Appalachian Trail from Kent to Canaan.

Old stone walls recall the days when farmers tried to till the soil; the area was settled somewhat later than the southern reaches of the state. The mountains made access difficult, and many of those who came soon packed their wagons and headed west for the more fertile regions of Ohio and Illinois.

Litchfield ❺ is dominated by a spacious green, graced by the tall-steepled Congregational Church, at the meeting point of the village's four main streets. Lining North and South streets are handsome, white, clapboard houses, which can be toured only on Open House Day in mid-July. On South Street (Route 63) stands the **Tapping Reeve House**, behind which is a small building that housed

Litchfield, founded in 1719, owed its early property to the stagecoaches which stopped there en route from Hartford to Albany.

BELOW: Dixieland comes to the Constitution State.

A barn window in the quiet northwest corner of the state.

the nation's first school of law (open Apr–Nov Tues–Sat; Sun pm; entrance fee). Visitors can see the desks where many a distinguished jurist learned his trade, among them Aaron Burr and John C. Calhoun, two vice presidents of the United States. This simple schoolroom also graduated six cabinet members, 28 senators and more than 100 Congressmen.

Litchfield merchants prospered during the early days of the China trade when their money backed the sailing ships of Mystic and New Haven, but industry faltered when a new railroad bypassed the town center. Commerce was relocated to the more industrialized communities of Waterbury and Naugatuck. Litchfield was left as a sleepy town nestled in the past.

To the north, **Norfolk ❻** is another classic town focused on a green, a summering place for wealthy industrialists, and retaining numerous opulent-looking homes. In summer, the Hillside Gardens (free) on Litchfield Road (Route 272) display a choice range of perennials.

Follow Route 44 west to **Lakeville ❼**, which offers another grand display of traditional 19th-century mansions. The **Holley-Williams House** in downtown Lakeville (Millerton Road; open Memorial Day–Labor Day Tues–Sat) is an excellent example of a Classical Revival house built by one of the area's more prosperous "Iron Barons." To the south on Route 7, in **West Cornwall ❽**, look for the covered bridge, erected in 1836 across the Housatonic.

The Housatonic Valley has one of its most dramatic moments at **Kent Falls State Park ❾**, where water tumbles some 200 ft (65 meters) down a natural stone staircase. A short way south on Route 7, ruins of the Old Kent Furnace recall the discovery of iron ore in the Litchfield Hills during the 18th century. Forges such as this produced pig iron until the discovery of coal in Pennsylvania

BELOW: Litchfield.

made Connecticut's ironworks obsolete. Adjacent to the furnace, the **Sloane-Stanley Museum** is an extensive collection of early American wood and iron tools gathered by the writer and artist Eric Sloane (open mid-May–Oct, Wed–Sun; entrance fee).

To the east just outside New Preston, **Lake Waramaug** is a tranquil hideaway with boating and swimming potential, and ideal shores for picnicking.

The southwestern shore

From the harbors of New Haven, New London, Mystic and Stonington, China clippers and Yankee whalers sailed out to seek their fortunes. Such associations may be merely historical, but people along Connecticut's coast still retain a fondness for salt air and a genuine love of the sea. Most towns have at least one marina, and on a clear summer's day the horizon of the Long Island Sound is filled with billowing sails.

Greenwich, Cos Cob, Stamford, Darien and Rowayton – to the thousands of Connecticut residents who work in New York City, this is a railroad conductor's litany. About an hour away from Manhattan by train, the Connecticut suburbs are among the most luxurious bedroom communities in the nation. Many of New York's wealthiest business executives make their homes here, attracted by the pleasant, countrified locale.

This "**Gold Coast**" has an artistic streak, too, exemplified in the galleries and shops of newly trendy **South Norwalk**, dubbed "SoNo" for its emulation of New York's SoHo district. Once a gritty, run-down neighborhood, it's now a great place to while away a day pleasantly – especially if you spend part at the huge **Maritime Aquarium** (open daily; entrance fee), which has plenty

The Puritans founded a colony in New Haven as early as 1637 but admitted only believers.

BELOW: cooking planked shad in Old Saybrook.

Detail, Barnum Museum in Bridgeport.

of hands-on displays relating to the marine life and maritime culture of Long Island Sound, including boat-building demonstrations and an aquarium stocked with marine species from Long Island Sound. There is a busy events program and an IMAX movie theater.

Bridgeport ⓬, a major industrial center producing everything from clothes to electrical appliances, is an exception to the coast's general aura of ease and affluence. One fun note is the **Barnum Museum**, a showcase for big-top memorabilia connected to Phineas Barnum, with a miniature circus, clown props and items relating to Barnum and General Tom Thumb (820 Main Street; open Tues–Sat; pm only Sun; entrance fee).

New Haven ⓭, settled by Puritans in 1638, was an independent colony until 1662, when it merged with the Hartford settlement. In the early 19th century, the port brought prosperity to the town, and more than 100 ships regularly sailed along the coast to the West Indies and the Orient.

However, it was not until the Industrial Revolution that the town made the big leap to becoming a major manufacturing center. Eli Whitney first instituted a system of mass production in his firearms factory. Since that time, New Haven has pioneered such inventions as the steel fish hook, the meat grinder, the corkscrew, and the steamboat.

New Haven is perhaps best known not as an industrial center, but as a center of learning. It is the home of **Yale University**, which dominates much of the city's cultural life. Founded in 1701 by a group of Puritan clergymen, Yale was originally located in nearby Saybrook. In 1716, the school was moved to New Haven, and two years later it took the name of the wealthy merchant Elihu Yale, its benefactor.

BELOW:
Yale University buildings.

Alma mater to famous personalities such as Eli Whitney, Nathan Hale and Noah Webster, Yale has pursued a policy of commissioning leading architects to design its buildings. But the dominant style on the Yale campus is Gothic Revival – much of it evoking the British universities of Oxford and Cambridge.

Any visit to the university should include its excellent museums and libraries. Start from the **Beinecke Rare Book and Manuscript Library** on Wall Street (open Mon–Fri; Sat am), where an edition of the Gutenberg Bible is on display. Two blocks south is the **Yale University Art Gallery** (1111 Chapel Street; open Tues–Sat; Sun pm), which has well over 100 paintings by patriot artist Jonathan Trumbull, impressive collections of African and pre-Columbian art, as well as canvases by Manet, Van Gogh, Corot, Degas, and Matisse.

Across the street stands the **Yale Center of British Art**, with a vast collection of British paintings (including works by Constable and Turner), drawings and sculpture donated in 1966 by industrialist Paul Mellon (1080 Chapel Street; call for hours; tel: 203-432 2800).

Adjacent to the university, New Haven Green is surrounded by a trinity of churches constructed in Gothic Revival, Georgian, and Federal styles.

New Haven's cultural offerings include the Yale Repertory Theater on campus (Chapel and York streets; tel: 203-432 1234) and the Long Wharf Theater on the downtown waterfront (222 Sargent Drive; tel: 203-787 4282), which mount some of the most interesting productions in the country. The New Haven Symphony Orchestra (tel: 203-865 0831) frequently performs at Woolsey Hall on the Yale campus.

Out at East Haven, the **Shore Line Trolley Museum** has a collection meriting inclusion on the National Register of Historic Places, with some 100 trolleys,

Map on page 206

TIP

For a thorough tour of Yale University, inquire at the university's visitors' information office (149 Elm Street; tel: 203-432 2300). Tours start at 10:30 and 2 on weekdays, 1:30 on weekends.

BELOW: graduation day.

THE IVY LEAGUE

Home to most of the country's oldest and most highly regarded colleges and universities, New England is the region most closely associated with the "Ivy League." The phrase is now used somewhat loosely, referring to the top rank of American colleges, but it originated, with a core of eight prominent institutions, of which four are in New England: Harvard in Massachusetts, Yale in Connecticut, Brown in Rhode Island, and Dartmouth in New Hampshire. (The others are Columbia and Cornell in New York, the University of Pennsylvania, and Princeton in New Jersey.) Harvard, founded in 1636, is the country's oldest college. The eight make up an athletic league whose football games, especially, are among the most hallowed collegiate sporting events in the country

Ivy League schools began as all-male bastions, so the "Seven Sisters" developed as a consortium to provide women the same access. Four are located in Massachus-etts: Mount Holyoke (the oldest, founded 1837), Smith, Wellesley and Radcliffe (affiliated with Harvard). It's likely that the "ivy" refers to the shiny-leaved climbing plant, introduced from Britain in colonial times (precisely when these schools were established), that widely covers the brick and brownstone buildings that dominate the campuses.

Guilford harvest.

BELOW: the
Connecticut River.

the oldest rapid transit car and a rare parlor car (17 River Street; open late May–early Sept, daily; Apr–May, early Sept–Nov, weekends; entrance fee).

Up the coast from New Haven are two of the loveliest communities along this shore, the villages of Guilford and Madison. Of the two, **Guilford** ⓮ is the older, having been settled in 1639 by the Reverend Henry Whitfield. His home on Old Whitfield Street, the oldest stone dwelling in New England, is now called the **Henry Whitfield State Museum** (open Wed–Sun; entrance fee).

Guilford's town green, one of the purest in New England, is bordered by many of its original 17th- and 18th-century homes. Several are museums, including **Hyland House**, a typical colonial salt box of 1660, and the **Thomas Griswold House** of 1774 (open June–mid-Sept, Tues–Sun; mid-Sept–Oct, weekend; off season by appointment; entrance fee), both on Boston Street.

Nearby **Madison** has some of the most beautiful summer and year-round homes in Connecticut. **Hammonasset Beach State Park** ⓯, just 2 miles (3 km) east, is the state's longest public beach. At **Old Saybrook** ⓰, by the western mouth of the Connecticut River, **Fort Saybrook** has storyboards chronicling Saybrook Colony from 1635, and gives fine estuary views, with opportunities for bird-watching from the boardwalk.

Of all the towns on the Connecticut shore, **Old Lyme** ⓱ can boast the richest artistic heritage. There was a time when "a sea captain lived in every house," but later the community came to be known primarily as an artists' colony, thanks in large part to Florence Griswold, the daughter of a sea captain and a devoted, if impecunious, patron of the arts. Her Lyme Street house, now the **Florence Griswold Museum** (open June–Dec, Tues–Sat; Sun pm; Jan–May, pm only Wed–Sun; entrance fee) contains a stunning array of works by her illustrious

American Impressionist boarders, including such notables as Childe Hassam. Some were so moved by her laissez-faire hospitality, they left painted mementos on the doors, mantels and paneled walls.

Map on page 206

Cruising the Connecticut River

Beginning as a mountain stream tumbling from its source near the New Hampshire–Canada border, the Connecticut River travels 410 miles (660 km) through four states and ends its journey to the sea as a broad and majestic tidal estuary. The Native Americans named it "Quinnituckett," which means "the long, tidal river." Throughout history, the Connecticut has linked valley residents with the outside world. A fertile floodplain has made this area a center for agriculture, and water power has generated energy for a variety of small industries.

A tour of the Connecticut Valley can begin near the river's mouth with a visit to **Essex** ⓲, founded in 1645 and a long-time center of maritime activity. Essex developed as an important shipbuilding center during the 18th century. The *Oliver Cromwell*, America's first warship, was launched in 1776 from its docks. Yachts and cabin cruisers still make their berths at various Essex marinas, where tall masts and yards of tackle lend the town a distinctly nautical air. Contained in the dockside **Connecticut River Museum** (open Tues–Sun; entrance fee) is an exact replica of the *American Turtle*, the nation's first submarine. Invented by David Bushnell, a native of the nearby coastal town of Old Saybrook, it was employed in 1776 by Yankee forces to sink an English battleship during the blockade of New York Harbor. Though unsuccessful in its mission, the *Turtle* incorporated a number of engineering ideas that Robert Fulton later adopted in the design of the *Nautilus* (*see Groton, page 221*).

The Old Griswold Inn on Main Street has been in operation since 1776. The rare collection of maritime prints in its tap room warrants a special visit.

Those who want to get a firsthand glimpse of the Connecticut River may take an old-fashioned journey by steam locomotive and riverboat (round trip takes about 2½ hours). Board the 1920s coaches of the **Valley Railroad** at Essex Depot and ride along the river through the villages of **Chester** and **Deep River** (Camelot Cruises: cruises May–Dec; tel: 800-522 7463 or 860-345 8591 for departure times). At Deep River, transfer to a riverboat similar to the hundreds of passenger ships that ferried travelers between Old Saybrook and Hartford more than a century ago.

Those who continue their journey up the valley may cross the river by car ferry at Chester. It is a charming excursion that brings you to **Hadlyme**, home of the spectacularly eccentric **Gillette Castle** ⓳ (open late May–early Sept Fri–Sun; entrance fee). William Gillette (1853–1937) was a much admired American actor whose portrayal of Sherlock Holmes brought him fame and fortune. Gillette was one of the first actors who took to wearing the deer-stalker hat, the distinctive Holmes trademark; and it was he who uttered those memorable words onstage: "Elementary, my dear Watson."

Gillette was born and raised in Hartford and, when he decided to build the house of his dreams, the actor

BELOW: Goodspeed Opera House, on the banks of the Connecticut River at East Haddam.

selected a hilltop aerie that commanded a breathtaking view of the Connecticut River and its surrounding countryside. Work began on the 122-acre (49-hectare) site in 1914, and it took five years and over $1 million before Gillette's architectural vision was completed. The results were whimsical and bizarre. The stone-and-concrete castle is filled with hand-hewn oak furnishings and specialized gadgetry. Javanese mats line the walls, and light fixtures are fashioned from numerous bits of colored glass. The estate grounds are now a state park with fine views and excellent picnicking facilities.

North of Gillette Castle, on Route 82, is the charming Victorian town of **East Haddam** ㉒. Still standing along the shoreline are the great rambling hotels (some now private homes) that served riverboat passengers in the 19th century. Before the railroad came, this was a point of embarkation for the many steamboat passengers crossing the Long Island Sound to New York City.

The **Goodspeed Opera House** (tel: 860-873 8668), which sits so majestically on the banks of the Connecticut River, is a reminder of the heyday of steamboat travel. Countless citizens paused here for a bit of entertainment before continuing their journey downriver. Beautifully restored, the Opera House presents musical revivals, as well as original productions, April–December.

The northeastern shore

New London ㉑, along with Nantucket and New Bedford, was one of the busiest whaling ports in the nation. In the early days of the 19th century, more than 80 ships sailed from its docks and many a vast fortune was accumulated by its merchants. Evidence of this wealth can be seen in Whale Oil Row on Huntington Street, where four Greek Revival mansions were built in the 1830s.

BELOW: approaching Groton on the New London ferry.

When oil was discovered in Pennsylvania in 1859, the whaling industry declined sharply, and manufacturing became New London's chief occupation. But the city maintained its ties to the sea and today is best known as the home of the **US Coast Guard Academy** (Route 32, off I–95; open May–Oct daily; entrance fee).

Across the Thames River from New London stands the city of **Groton ㉒**, known as the "Submarine Capital of the World" – the manufacture of nuclear submarines is the town's major industry. Non-claustrophobes who wish to view the interior of a submarine may visit the USS *Nautilus* Memorial at the **US Naval Submarine Base** (exit 86, off I–95; open Wed–Mon; Tues pm).

The delightful village of **Noank ㉓** has views to Fishers Island, New York. Lobstering is big; shingle-clad Abbott's serves lobsters straight off the boat.

The village of **Mystic ㉔**, an old maritime community of trim white houses, sits at the tidal outlet of the Mystic River. For generations, Mystic was the home of daring mariners and fishermen, and was feared by the British during the Revolution as a "cursed little hornets' nest" of patriots. The village teemed with activity during the Gold Rush days of 1849, when shipbuilders vied to see who could construct the fastest clipper ships to travel round Cape Horn to the boom town of San Francisco. It was the *Andrew Jackson*, a Mystic-built clipper launched in 1860, that claimed the world's record – making the journey in 89 days and 4 hours, 9 hours faster than the famous *Flying Cloud*.

Today, Mystic is best known as the home of **Mystic Seaport**, a living replica of a 19th-century waterfront community during the heyday of sailing ships (open daily; entrance fee; tel: 860-572 0711). Restoration of Mystic Seaport began in 1929 and, since then, the project has expanded to include a complex of over 60 buildings covering 17 acres (7 hectares). It's a big tourist draw, and

Map on page 206

Monument House, in Groton's Fort Griswold State Park, has a collection of Civil War memorabilia assembled by the Daughters of the American Revolution.

BELOW: mural painter, Mystic village.

Map on page 206

a full day and plenty of stamina are required to tour the entire seaport properly.

The restoration imparts a vivid sense of how life was lived by Mystic's residents in the 1860s. Visitors are encouraged to wander along the wharves and streets of the village, and taste the old seafaring way of life. Save time for a visit to the *Charles W. Morgan*, the last surviving vessel of America's 19th-century whaling fleet. Built in 1841, the *Morgan* plied the seas for more than 80 years and made 37 voyages, some of them lasting three or four years. Also board the *Joseph Conrad*, which was built in 1882 by the Danish as a training vessel, and now serves as a student dormitory; demonstrations of sail-handling and chanty singing are scheduled regularly aboard both ships. A major current project is the building of a faithful replica of the slave-trading ship *Amistad*, whose slaves seized control of the ship and eventually won their right to freedom, and returned to Africa from Connecticut; the work will be completed by 2000.

It's also worth stopping at the Stillman Building, a museum with an impressive collection of ship's figureheads, scrimshaw, ship models, logbooks, etc.

Just up the road, near I-95, visit the ambitious **Mystic Marinelife Aquarium**, with extensive indoor and outdoor exhibits spanning sea horses to sea lions, and pools containing Beluga whales (open daily; entrance fee). The Jason Project, to be completed in 2000, will allow visitors to watch a dive to the sea bed through kelp forests and reefs, and to see the resting place of such wrecks as the *Titanic*. The Aquarium operates seasonal seal, eagle and whale-watching cruises.

A few miles further east is the charming old whaling port of **Stonington ㉕**, huddled at the edge of the state near the Rhode Island border. Stonington was once the third-largest city in Connecticut and an important seaport. Although considerably reduced in circumstances, the village remains one of the prettiest coastal enclaves in New England. Its 1823 **lighthouse**, the first government-operated one in the entire state, is these days a museum with artifacts from the Oriental trade, whaling gear and a children's room (open May–Oct Tues–Sun; entrance fee).

BELOW:
Foxwoods Casino.

America's biggest casino

On the Mashantucket Pequot Reservation north of Mystic, the massive **Foxwoods Casino ㉖** has grown within a few years to become the nation's largest casino (*see facing page*). Punters arrive by the busload.

On the same site is the **Mashantucket Pequot Museum and Research Center** (open daily till 7pm; entrance fee), by far New England's largest Native American exhibition. Visitors journey back in time through a simulated glacial crevasse, complete with the sounds of creaking ice and the blast of chill air. The World of Ice sets the glacial scene; then follows the arrival of the first peoples, and has a diorama depicting a caribou kill 11,000 years ago. There are further dioramas evoking Native life 6,000 years back, plus a re-created 16th-century Pequot village, showing daily life up to the first European contact, then a film of the Pequot war. You also see a computer re-creation of a 17th-century Pequot fort excavated on the site. The exhibits lead right up to the present, with a 1970s mobile home and a film explaining how the tribe achieved Federal recognition in 1983. ❑

How the Pequots' gamble paid off

Not so long ago, the eastern Connecticut Mashantucket Pequot Indian tribe was regarded by most New Englanders as part of the area's quaint pre-Colonial past, remembered by tongue-twisting place names such as Wequetequock and Quanaduck that outsiders find all-but-impossible to pronounce.

Then, all of a sudden, the tribe emerged from centuries-long obscurity in the mid-1980s, and its name seemed to be on everyone's lips. The reason was that, taking advantage of new legislation exempting tribal reservation land from local laws against gambling, it began developing hundreds of acres of ancestral reservation land in sleepy Ledyard, Connecticut, into a vast casino-and-hotel complex called Foxwoods.

Incredibly, it now rivals some of the gaming palaces of Las Vegas or Atlantic City. In 1998, just six years after it opened, Foxwoods was the world's highest-grossing casino. In addition to high-stakes bingo, slot machines, and dozens of other gambling games, the resort offers a regular schedule of concerts and performances by Hollywood's entertainment elite, half a dozen restaurants ranging from casual to high-roller high-style, and an ultra-plush hotel.

Most recently, the tribe has added a Mashantucket Pequot Museum and Research Center to the resort complex. With a price-tag of some $135 million, the museum has already earned rave reviews for both its forward-looking architecture and its informative and engaging exhibits on tribal history, including a high-tech recreation of a 16th-century Pequot village that visitors may walk through, experiencing sights and sounds that would have surrounded them long before the era of jangling slot machines and smoky bingo halls.

The success of Foxwoods is unquestioned, but many local residents still decry its presence in the formerly rural area. Driving up the Old Stonington Road (Route 2) into the casino complex, you are confronted with a stunning contrast: rolling countryside, stone walls, and farms versus unabashed glitz. The shining towers of the resort complex, some nearly 200 feet (60 meters) high, appear like an alarming Oz materializing out of thin air.

Meanwhile, just up the road in Uncasville, the Mohegan tribe has opened its own casino, the Mohegan Sun. Smaller than Foxwoods, but similar in its glamorously seductive style, the Sun offers another winning hand: a slick combination of gambling, resort amenities, and Vegas-style concerts by big-name stars.

In the wake of the obvious success of both Foxwoods and the Mohegan Sun, it seemed for a while that every economically challenged small New England city was intent on rolling out a welcome mat for its own Indian-owned casino. Both Fall River in Massachusetts and Providence in Rhode Island flirted with Indian gaming promoters, but widespread local sentiment against more casinos (combined, perhaps, with a recognition that the existing venues might have cornered the market on regional gambling) has shelved such plans, at least for the time being. ❑

RIGHT: a statue inside Foxwoods.

RHODE ISLAND

Map on page 228

Between Providence's downtown, Newport's mansions, sailing in Narragansett Bay, and Block Island's rolling pastures and beaches, this tiny state packs a diverse punch

The smallest state in the nation, Rhode Island has nonetheless managed to hold on to a disproportionate share of wealth and clout. On the map, it may look more like an overgrown port than a genuine state, but that very sea-readiness accounts in large part for its long-term appeal.

Certainly, the millionaires who built their legendary summer "cottages" in Newport at the end of the 19th century recognized natural wealth when they saw it: the dramatic vistas of the Rhode Island Sound, the refreshing westerly breezes wafting in to relieve summer doldrums. The mansions they left behind still gleam atop the cliffs, jewels left over from the Gilded Age.

Centuries earlier, the reclusive Reverend William Blaxton found the area equally attractive. Blaxton, who had been living contentedly as a hermit in what would soon become Boston, fled to Rhode Island when the Puritans he'd invited to share his peninsula proved too proselytizing.

Rhode Island's official founder was a clergyman, Roger Williams. Driven out of Salem in 1635 for preaching religious tolerance, Williams headed south to establish a settlement where all were free to practice their own faith: traveling by canoe with a cadre of followers, he arrived in what is now Providence. Anne Hutchinson followed in 1637, to be joined by other dissidents. In 1663 Charles II granted a charter to the rather wordily named Colony of Rhode Island and Providence Plantations – a name it still officially retains as a state.

Soon people from even farther afield flocked to Rhode Island's shores. A large number of Quakers, fleeing Puritan persecution, made Newport their home, and as early as the 18th century, Jews from Portugal and Holland settled here as well. In the ensuing centuries came Italians, Irish, Russians, Poles, French, Swedes, Greeks, Armenians, Chinese and Cape Verdeans. By 1960 Rhode Island was the most densely populated state in America, with 859,000 inhabitants crowded into 1,214 sq. miles (3,144 sq. km). Today, with a population in excess of 1 million, Rhode Island is a bustling, multicultural cross-section of New England life.

PRECEDING PAGES: Rosecliff Manor, Newport. **LEFT:** sculpture in the Rosecliff gardens. **BELOW:** Villa Marina, Newport.

The Ocean State

As Rhode Island's license plate attests, **Narragansett Bay** dominates the state. Taking a dinosaur bite out of the New England coast, it gives the state a shoreline out of all proportion to its land area. Rhode Island is only 48 miles (77 km) long and 37 miles (60 km) wide, yet it claims 400 miles (644 km) of coastline.

With such an abundance of water at their disposal, Rhode Islanders have long turned to the sea for their livelihood. Two of the nation's leading seaports in the early days of the republic were Providence and

Newport. Using Rhode Island as a base, pirates raided merchant ships in the North Atlantic; the notorious Captain Kidd is rumored to have buried his cache of gold doubloons in Jamestown.

But Rhode Island is a land of contradictions. Despite the state's heritage as a sanctuary for pirates, Newport was the birthplace of the modern US Navy: President Chester Alan Arthur developed a new fleet – built of steel, rather than wood – there in the early 1880s, and enjoyed staging gun drills on the bay. (Though much of the navy pulled out in the mid-1970s, the Naval War College, founded in 1884, remains.) Founded as a haven of religious liberty, it became a world-class slave trade center.

Despite its considerable contributions to the success of the American Revolution, Rhode Island was the last holdout among states ratifying the US Constitution. Notorious for its exploitation of child labor, Rhode Island became a bastion of New Deal social ideals.

Until 1854, it couldn't even decide which city would be its capital. Each year

How the state got its name is uncertain. Some believe it was called after the Greek island of Rhodes. Others think the name derived from a Dutch word meaning "red."

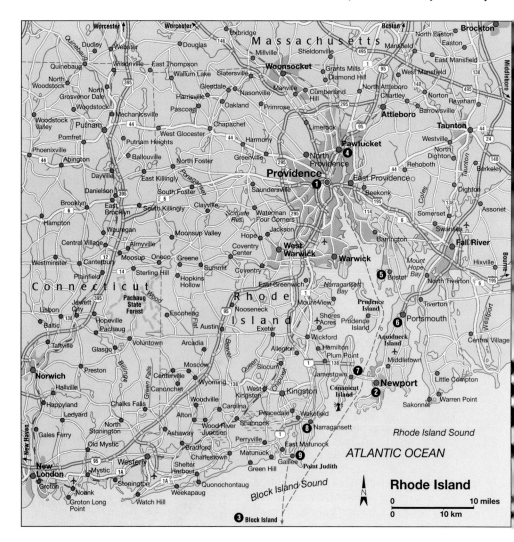

the General Assembly packed up its belongings and moved lock, stock and barrel to one of the five locales contesting for the honor. Eventually, after a raucous battle in 1900, Providence won out over Newport. It remains the capital, but Newporters contend their city is truly the heart of the state.

If little Rhode Island is a land of contradictions, it is also a land of superlatives and firsts. Among the state's distinctions are: the world's widest bridge, in Providence, and the only operational water-powered snuff mill in the United States, in Saunderstown. The state boasts the country's first synagogue, its first department store, and its oldest enclosed shopping mall, built in the early 19th century. And lest it be forgotten, the first two-week paid vacation on record was spent in Rhode Island. In 1524, the Italian navigator Giovanni da Verrazano, on an exploratory mission for the King of France, was investigating the North American coast when he spotted Narragansett Bay. Verrazano was "so enthralled… he lingered for a fortnight."

Rhode Island, in the singular, is actually a misnomer. In fact, there are 35 islands within the state. Within and without Narragansett Bay are the four principal islands of Aquidneck, Block, Conanicut and Prudence; others include Hen, Hog, Rabbitt, Boat, Old Boy, Patience, Hope and Despair. In and about these islands, visitors enjoy boating, sailing, surfing and fishing.

Throughout the state – generously scattered through cities and towns such as Providence, Wickford, Bristol, Little Compton and Newport – are lovely old homes representing the decorative ideals of several centuries. Despite the concentrated population, park lands are plentiful, too. And precisely because the state is so small –it takes less than two hours to drive from one end to the other – it's possible to enjoy its variegated offerings within a short time span. A visitor can walk historic city streets in the morning, picnic in an idyllic grove at noon and savor the delights of the seashore by moonlight.

Adamsville, Rhode Island, claims the world's only known monument to a chicken – the prolific Rhode Island Red.

BELOW:
Narragansett Bay offers good sailing.

Revitalized Providence

Rhode Island's capital has much in its favor: it has outstanding 18th and 19th-century architecture on Benefit Street, an excitingly rejuvenated downtown, and appealingly diverse neighborhoods – Italian, Portuguese, Ivy League university, and funky places such as Hope Street. It's also easily reached from Boston, a feasible day trip by car, train or bus.

In its early days, **Providence ❶** was the port of call for ships engaged in the lucrative Triangular Trade: New England rum for African slaves for West Indies molasses. In 1781, John Brown, one of four brothers whose family would dominate Providence for some years to come, sent the first of many ships to China. The maritime trade began to decline, however, following a series of international wars which resulted in embargoes and protectionism, and public interest and investment shifted toward industry.

As a major manufacturing center in the 19th century, Providence was dubbed "the cradle of American industry." Its huge plants were known worldwide – Brown & Sharpe (machinery and tools), Nicholson (files), Grinnel (sprinkler systems), Gorham (silverware), Davol (rubber goods), and so on.

The 20th century brought hard times. With the Great Depression and the textile industry's exodus to the south, Providence lost its pre-eminence as an industrial center. Although no longer the giant it once was, Providence has enjoyed a revitalization of business in recent decades, and has in turn lavished restorative attention on its variegated downtown. Artists have been given tax-free incentives to set up here; old warehouses and department stores have found new uses; I-195 is to be moved to free up more land for development close to the downtown area; and the ignored river has been beautified and made more accessible.

A city of hills: Providence

Providence is a city best seen on foot. Like Rome, Providence was built on seven hills. Most people remember three: College (officially, Prospect), Federal, and Constitution. The other four – Tockwotten, Smith and two now-leveled hills – seem to have melted in the metropolitan sprawl.

Constitution Hill is pretty much impossible to miss because of the **State Capitol Ⓐ** that dominates its crest (Smith Street; open weekdays; tours am). This imposing 1891–92 McKim, Mead, and White structure is said to have the second largest self-support dome in the world, and contains an historic portrait of George Washington by Rhode Island native Gilbert Stuart. On opposite sides of the downtown area, College and Federal hills are favored haunts of tourists and natives alike.

BELOW: The Arcade, Providence, dating to 1828.

To the south, **Waterplace Park Ⓑ** is evidence of the city's waterside renaissance, where a new Italian-inspired piazza has been created. Once neglected, the riverside has been cleaned up, equipped with walkways and descriptive panels

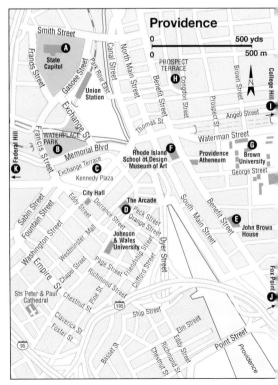

with photos of the old port days. In summer, Venetian-style gondolas offer trips and outdoor concerts take place.

Kennedy Plaza ❸ is overlooked by the art deco skyscraper affectionately dubbed the Superman Building (not that *Superman* was ever filmed here); the Plaza is the arrival point for buses from Boston and elsewhere. To the east stands the restored Providence Station, worth a visit for a glimpse back to the times when train travel was a grand affair. Around the corner from Kennedy Plaza is the **Turk's Head Building**, a 1913 landmark with an ornate stone head over its entrance; and the **Customs House** (1856), with a dome and lantern that once welcomed ships returning from China.

For shopping or snacking and a bit of history, visit the **Arcade ❹** on Weybosset Street. This Greek Revival "temple of trade" and the nation's first indoor shopping mall was built in 1828. Its three-story granite columns (said to be the second largest in America, after those at the Cathedral of St John the Divine in New York) were cut from single pieces of stone, which required 15 yokes of oxen to move.

In historic East Side, **Benefit Street**, the "Mile of History," deserves walking from one end to the other. There are more than 200 restored 18th- and 19th-century buildings (many are now private homes) originally built by sea captains and merchants; many houses, churches and schools bear bronze plaques identifying their original owners and dates of construction. In the late 1960s and early 1970s the street was run down, and nearly demolished as part of a renewal program; only the efforts of the Preservation Society saved the day.

Benefit Street was once a twisting dirt path informally known as Back Street because it led around the back side of homes to the family graveyards. When at

Map on page 230

The dome of the State Capitol, Providence.

BELOW: Restored sea-captains' homes on Benefit Street, Providence.

Sculpture at Rhode Island School of Design.

last a communal burial ground was marked out and ancestral bones duly transferred to it, Back Street was straightened out and "improved for the benefit of the people of Providence."

The First Baptist Church (1775), designed by Joseph Brown, survives as a splendid example of the Colonial style. The same architect designed **John Brown House** ❺, built in 1786 (for his brother) at Power and Benefit streets (2 Power Street; open Mar–Dec, Tues–Sat; Sun pm; Jan–Feb, weekdays by appointment only). John Quincy Adams described it as "the most magnificent and elegant private mansion that I have ever seen on this continent." It displays period furniture, paintings, pewter, silver, porcelain, and mementos of the China Trade; a later resident added an astonishingly showy bathroom. John Brown's chariot of 1782 is the earliest surviving American vehicle.

The **Old State House** (open weekdays) at 150 Benefit Street (between North and South Court streets) is worth a peep, if only to see the modest size of the former capitol, where the Rhode Island General Assembly renounced allegiance to King George III on May 4, 1776.

The bookstacks of **Providence Atheneum** (open Mon–Sat; Sun pm; closed summer weekends) reputedly witnessed the courtship of Edgar Allen Poe and a local resident, Sarah Whitman. She refused to marry him, however, because she claimed he couldn't stay sober. Such literary associations apart, the 1836 Greek Revival structure at 251 Benefit Street is well worth a visit for its collections of rare books, prints, and paintings.

Virtually opposite is the museum of the prestigious **Rhode Island School of Design (RISD) Museum of Art** ❻ with enough major works to fill a day's visit, including paintings by American masters and French Impressionists, a major oriental collection and some fine ancient artifacts (open Wed–Sun pm only; Fri 10am–8pm).

Brown University ❼ dominates this part of Providence (open weekdays). The Ivy League establishment was founded as Rhode Island College; the Brown family were Baptists and intended the college as a Baptist ministry school. The university still holds some commencement ceremonies in the First Baptist Church. University Hall dates from 1770 and was used as a barracks during the Revolutionary War.

Prospect Terrace ❽, on Congdon Street north of the university, is a tiny park that gives a fine view of the city; a statue of Roger Williams, the city's founder (who is buried here), presides. The streets hereabouts are full of imposing 19th-century industrialists' mansions.

The heart of the **College Hill** ❾ shopping area is Thayer Street, four blocks east of Benefit, packed with interesting restaurants, bars, shops, and bookstores.

Continue south down Thayer Street to encounter one of Providence's best-kept secrets: **Fox Point** ❿. Home to the city's Portuguese community, Fox Point speaks with an Old World accent. On holy days, celebrants parade with statues of the Virgin Mary while children dressed in their best suits and crinolines follow along. Early morning brings to Fox Point the tantalizing scent of Portuguese sweet bread wafting from small bakeries.

BELOW:
Brown University.

Perched on **Federal Hill** across the city is Providence's "Little Italy." Wander along Atwells Avenue and enjoy the aroma of crusty Italian breads, cheeses, pastas, herbs and spices. Some people come to stock up on traditional delicacies such as gorgonzola, Romano, homemade pork sausages and prosciutto, others for the restaurants, espresso shops and festive ambience. Without a doubt, Federal Hill is one of the friendliest parts of Providence.

Newport: domain of wealth

During World War II an anti-submarine net was strung across the entrance of the bay guarding **Newport** ❷. It was effective. But then, the elite of the city had long been expert at protecting their privacy. In the halcyon days of the Gilded Age, Newport was the domain of the very wealthy. Huge palaces built on expansive grounds were surrounded by mammoth fences and patrolled by guards and dogs. Now, however, a great many of these fiercely guarded fiefdoms are open to all comers, having become Newport's foremost tourist attractions.

Summering in Newport first became fashionable before the Revolution among Southern plantation owners intent on escaping the heat of Georgia and the Carolinas. After the Civil War, the nation's wealthiest families – Astors, Morgans, Fishers, Vanderbilts – discovered its charms. Arrivistes hoping to legitimize their newfound wealth with indisputable good taste tended to duplicate the palaces and chateaux that had so awed them on their grand tours of Europe. Edward Berwind, for instance, the son of poor German immigrants, managed to enter the ranks of this self-appointed aristocracy with The Elms (*see page 235*). Extravagance became obligatory. Harry Lehr hosted a formal dinner at which a monkey, complete with tuxedo and princely title, numbered

Maps:
Area 228
City 230

TIP

The East Bay Bicycle Path takes a level shoreline route from East Providence to Bristol, along a former railroad track, with good views for much of the way. The total distance is 14 miles (22 km).

BELOW:
Newport marina.

TIP

For more on the
Newport Mansions,
see pages 240–41.

among the guests. James Gordon Bennett, the man who bought a Monte Carlo restaurant when it refused him a table, rode stark naked in his carriage through Newport's streets. The Coogans invited everyone who was anyone to a grand ball to celebrate the completion of their "summer cottage." When no one showed up, the Coogans simply walked out – leaving all the food, drink and furniture – never to return.

There is so much else to see and do in Newport, but a trip must include a tour of at least some of the mansions, the most impressive of which line **Bellevue Avenue** and **Ocean Drive**. Although literally hundreds of these establishments existed during Newport's Golden Age, only 70 remain. Many now house schools and charitable institutions.

The docks reveal a decidedly salty air. Watch boats being prepared and sails stitched in lofts along the wharves; admire the handsomely fitted craft tied up at yacht club slips. As night falls, brush off the sand and head for the waterfront. The parade of strollers on Bowen's Wharf resembles a prep-school reunion. Most action centers on the bars, cafés and restaurants along Thames Street, where the fresh seafood comes accompanied by sea breezes. The White Horse is the oldest tavern in the US.

Newport also has a remarkable legacy of colonial architecture, much of it badly neglected up to the 1960s, but Operation Clapboard encouraged people to buy up and rescue a historic house. Some 200 houses pre-date 1800 – the biggest concentration in the nation.

For a visual feast of Newport's great architectural wealth, tour The Point and the Historic Hill, the oldest colonial sections of the town. By the bayside, **Hunter House** (54 Washington Street; open May–Sept, daily; Apr and Oct, weekends; entrance fee) is a 1748 Georgian home considered an outstanding example of colonial American architecture, and the first building saved by the Preservation Society of Newport County back in 1945. Prominent in the heart of the town, the Brick Market contains the **Museum of Newport History** Ⓐ (Touro Street; in-season Wed–Mon; call 401-846 0813 for off-season hours; entrance fee), with an absorbing collection of local tidbits. **Touro Synagogue** Ⓑ (1763), America's first, in Georgian style, has an impressively lavish interior (85 Touro Street; summer tours Sun–Fri; spring and fall tours Sun pm). In nearby Touro Park stands the mysterious Old Stone Mill, an unexplained open-sided structure formerly said to have been left behind by the Phoenicians, Vikings, Portuguese, or Irish, but now known to be 16th- or 17th-century, and probably built by a Colonial farmer.

A landmark of Colonial Newport is the white clapboard **Trinity Church** Ⓒ (1725–26) on Queen Anne Square, said to be based on the designs of Christopher Wren (open June–Oct daily; Nov–May am only). By contrast the **Redwood Library and Atheneum** (1748–50) took its inspiration from Roman temple architecture; it is thought to be the oldest continuously used library building in the US and contains a noted collection of portraits (50 Bellevue Avenue; open Mon–Sat).

BELOW: Ocean Drive, Newport, facing the Atlantic.

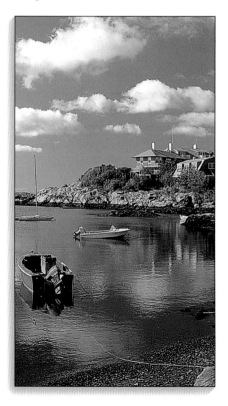

Peruse the offerings of the **Newport Art Museum** on Bellevue Avenue, an 1862 Richard Morris Hunt mansion in the "Stick Style," which has changing exhibitions (open Mon, Tues, Thur–Sat; Sun pm; entrance fee).

The **International Tennis Hall of Fame** is housed in the Newport Casino (194 Bellevue Avenue; open daily; entrance fee) – casino only by name; this has never had anything to do with gambling – America's most exclusive country club when it was built in 1880; its grass courts hosted the first Men's US Lawn Tennis Association tournament, played in 1881. Today they're the only grass courts in America open to the public. Also in this complex is the Casino Theater, designed by Stanford White, where performing arts events are mounted.

Heading along Bellevue Avenue, the first mansion open to the public is **Kingscote** (open May–Sept daily; Apr and Oct weekends; entrance fee), the first of the summer cottages, built in Gothic Revival "Stick Style" – making playful use of asymmetry and varied textures, sprouting a wealth of pendants, lattices and gables. It has glass paneling by Tiffany and exquisite porcelain.

The coal-rich Edward Julius Berwind commissioned **The Elms** (open May–Oct daily; Nov–Apr weekends; entrance fee), built in French Renaissance style, based on Château d'Asnières near Paris. It borrows from a range of styles, including Chinese, Venetian and Louis XIV.

William S. Wetmore built **Château-sur-Mer** (open May–Sept daily; Oct–Apr weekends; entrance fee) in 1852, a confection of Victorian lavishness, and Newport's showiest mansion when it was built. Richard Morris Hunt enlarged it in the 1870s.

The Newport Preservation Society pays the grand sum of $1 a year to rent **The Breakers** (open Apr–Oct and Dec daily; entrance fee). Considered the most

Map below

Touro Synagogue, Newport, the oldest in North America.

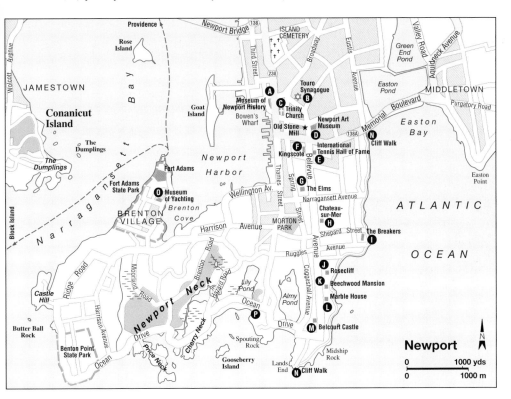

Newport

magnificent of the Newport cottages, this opulent Italian Renaissance palace, completed in 1895, took only two years to build. Cornelius Vanderbilt II commissioned American architect Richard Morris Hunt to design the mansion, whose 70 rooms are extravagantly adorned with marble, alabaster, gilt, mosaic, crystal, and stained glass. The kitchen alone is the size of a small house.

Mrs Hermann Oelrichs hired Stanford White to design **Rosecliff** ● (open Apr–Oct daily; entrance fee), an imitation of Versailles' Grand Trianon. It features a huge French-style ballroom and a heart-shaped staircase.

Caroline Schermerhorn Astor, the "Queen Victoria" of New York society, held court at the Astors' elegant **Beechwood Mansion** ● (open mid-May–Nov daily; Feb–mid-May Sun; entrance fee). Today, costumed actors show you round in your assumed role as a guest of the family.

Marble House ● (open Apr–Oct daily; Jan–Mar weekends; entrance fee), another of Hunt's designs, was built in 1892 for William K. Vanderbilt and styled after the Grand and Petit Trianons of Versailles. With scenes and figures from ancient mythology, it even manages to upstage The Breakers for ostentation, though it is not as large. A Chinese tea house stands in the grounds.

Belcourt Castle ● (open Feb–Dec daily; entrance fee), styled in 1894 on a Louis XIII hunting lodge at Versailles, has the largest collection of objets d'art of any of the mansions, including a full-size gold Coronation Coach.

Strollers can examine the backyards of the Bellevue Avenue mansions from the **Cliff Walk** ●, a 3½-mile (5.5-km) path that overlooks Rhode Island Sound. Crusty local fishermen saved this path for public use by going to court when wealthy mansion owners tried to close it. Visitors who do not wish to walk the length of this path can start at the end of Narragansett Avenue and

Cornelius Vanderbilt II did not enjoy The Breakers for long. He died in 1899, aged 56, four years after its completion. Even though he had given vast amounts to charities during his life, his estate amounted to almost $73 million.

BELOW:
The Breakers.

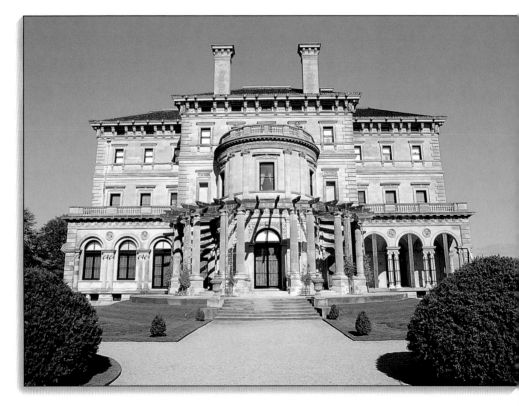

reach the water by way of the Forty Steps; or wander down to Brenton Point State Park on the island's southernmost tip, an ideal place to watch gulls, picnic or just enjoy a sunset.

During the summer, Newport hosts a number of major outdoor music events, such as the Ben and Jerry's Folk Festival and the JVC Jazz Festival, both of which take place in August at Fort Adams State Park. While there, take a look at the **Museum of Yachting** (Ocean Drive; open mid-May–Oct daily; entrance fee), which examines the pursuit through the centuries and across continents. Newport is the scene of many yachting events. The prestigious America's Cup was held in Newport waters 24 times from 1851 through 1983, when the Cup was lost (for the first time) to the Australians.

The 685-mile (1,102-km) Bermuda–Newport Race, held every other year, begins here, and the grueling Single-Handed Transatlantic Race, which starts in Plymouth, England, ends in Newport.

More mansions can be glimpsed from outside along **Ocean Drive** , which makes a pleasant cycle ride; cycle rental is available in the town.

The 28-room **Hammersmith Farm**, on Ocean Avenue, was built in 1887 for John Auchincloss and is much visited because one of his descendants, Jacqueline Bouvier, held her wedding reception there after marrying John Kennedy.

Block Island

When Rhode Islanders want to get away from it all, they head for **Block Island** ❸, a 3 by 7-mile (5 by 11-km) island some 12 miles (19 km) south of Narragansett Bay. Whereas Newport is packed to the gills with hotels, shops, restaurants, and tourists, Block Island remains a hideaway holding its own,

Maps:
Area 228
City 235

TIP

Newport is surrounded by fine beaches. The choice ranges from First, Second, and Third beaches in Middleton (north of Newport) to the more exclusive Bailey's, Hazard's, and Gooseberry.

BELOW: sea kayaking along Ocean Drive.

*Veranda detail,
Block Island.*

quite successfully, against developers and fast-food chains. There are ferry services from New London, Point Judith, and Providence via Newport.

Block Island is the least accessible of the state's islands: although regular or chartered planes fly out of Westerly, R.I., and points in Connecticut (a 10-minute hop), most people take the ferry, a 70-minute trip from Point Judith, R.I. (year-round ferry service; tel: 401-783 4613), or two hours from New London, Connecticut (service mid-June–mid-Sept). A good way to explore is by bicycle; rentals are available on the island.

Greeting visitors to Block Island are fine beaches, popular fishing grounds, tranquility and the romantic allure of aging Victorian hotels with huge verandas and a sense of bygone splendor. A Dutch navigator, Adriaen Block, discovered the island in 1614; the landscape has changed so little, he would in all probability still recognize it today.

The island's claim to fame in maritime annals is the large number of shipwrecks off its coast. Thousands of luckless captains saw their vessels come to misery along the coast of New England, and a great many were wrecked on the submerged rocks and sandbars around "The Block." Scavenging goods from the holds of wrecked ships became such a lucrative trade that some islanders helped engineer more wrecks by setting up lanterns and flares to confuse the ships. Many island place names commemorate the wrecking trade; at Cow Cove, for instance, a cargo of cows from a wrecked ship waded ashore, and on Calico Hill, bolts of cloth collected from another disaster were hung out to dry in the sun.

BELOW: Mohegan Bluffs, Block Island.

Life in the early days was hard. In the turbulent years of the late 17th century, the island was constantly under siege from pirates. During the Revolution,

Map on page 228

islanders – cut off from the mainland – nearly stripped Block Island of its trees building houses and ships.

Tourism arrived in 1842, when the first hotel was opened, and a party of 10 men checked in. The Spring House opened its doors 10 years later and is still accommodating visitors to this day. To spend time in this antique of a summer hotel, with its rambling corridors and simply furnished rooms, is to be caught in a time warp. From its perch high on a hill, one can gaze out over the Atlantic Ocean and breathe the beneficent sea air just as wealthy tourists from New York and Baltimore once did.

The island has several fine sand beaches. The waves are lively at Surfers Beach, as its name suggests; State Beach and others on the east are calmer and attract the most visitors. The westerly strands are windswept and, more often than not, deserted. One trek not to be missed is the hike to Mohegan Bluffs. Here, the entire Mohegan tribe met its doom at the hands of the Manasees, who either enslaved them or drove them over the 200-ft (60-meter) cliffs.

Fishing in New Harbor (formerly Great Salt Pond) can absorb an entire day, as can wandering along the roads and over the hills, looking for wildflowers and Indian relics. Shops in Old Harbor, the island's only town, sell local specialties, such as candles, jellies, and wool watch caps.

Fishermen are attracted to Block Island for its abundant tuna, swordfish, bluefish, mackerel, cod and flounder.

The rest of Rhode Island

Techniques of factory production were pioneered and groundwork for the development of the region's textile industry was laid in 1789, with the construction of **Slater Mill** by Moses Brown at **Pawtucket ❹**, north of Providence. Now fully restored, the mill offers visitors a rare look into bygone industry; together with the Sylvanus Brown House and the Wilkinson Mill these form the **Slater Mill Historic Site** (727 Roosevelt Avenue; open June–Oct Tues–Sat; Sun pm; Mar–May and Nov–late Dec pm only weekends; entrance fee).

At **Bristol ❺** is **Blithewold**, a 45-room mansion with landscaped grounds; a riot of colour in spring (grounds open daily; mansion open mid-Apr–Sept Tues–Sun; entrance fee). The "cottage" was built in a blend of Colonial, Dutch and English manor styles by a Pennsylvania coal magnate, Augustus van Wickle.

At **Portsmouth ❻** a worthwhile visit is **Green Animals Topiary Gardens**, a fanciful Victorian estate where 80 sculpted trees and shrubs represent everything from an ostrich to a camel (Cory Lane, off Route 114; open May–Oct daily; entrance fee).

Take a short detour to **Jamestown ❼** on Conanicut Island. The southern tip of the island offers New England scenery at its most picturesque. Among other notable sights, don't miss Mackerel Cove, the Beavertail Lighthouse, and the view from Fort Wetherhill.

From Jamestown, follow US 1A along the coast. From **Narragansett ❽**, an elegant resort town during the 19th century, proceed south to Scarborough State Beach, popular with Rhode Island's teenage crowd. The sheltered beach at **Galilee ❾**, Point Judith, is a perfect spot for passing a languid summer afternoon. ❑

BELOW: Slater Mill.

NEWPORT'S "GILDED AGE" MANSIONS

Newport, a 19th-century summer playground for the rich and influential, became a showplace for America's greatest architects and designers

With the coming of the railways in the mid-19th century, vacationing became ever more popular, and the delights of Newport, set on an island with a fine summer climate, became readily accessible from New York and Philadelphia. Wealthy and influential families, began to spend their summers here. Many had made vast fortunes from industry and began to lavish unstinting funds on creating opulent summer homes, where they would entertain and impress all those who mattered.

The country's most innovative architects – names such as Stanford White and Richard Morris Hunt – were employed, creating designs that reflect the full range of styles in vogue at the time (*see also pages 235–6*). Building materials and furnishings were often imported from Europe (for Marble House, for instance, different coloured marbles were imported from Italy to be worked by Italian craftsmen in Newport). Interior decor frequently borrowed from European or Far Eastern styles; fine paintings, furnishings and objets d'art collected from around the world filled the rooms.

Eight of these mansions are now maintained by The Preservation Society of Newport County and are open to the public, as is the Astor family's Beechwood Mansion.

▷ THE BREAKERS
The grandest of grand dining rooms: all gold leaf, alabaster and marble – and two 12 ft (3.5 meters) chandeliers .

▽ THE ELMS
The Elms replicates a two-story château near Paris, with the servants' quarters behind the roof balustrade and the kitchens in a cellar.

▷ THE ELMS
The splendid grounds are embellished with statues, fountains, and clipped and shaped trees – but, nowadays, no elms.

THE LEGACY OF THE VANDERBILTS

The Breakers (above), was commissioned in 1893, to replace an earlier house destroyed by fire, by Cornelius Vanderbilt II, chairman of the New York Central railway, a director of 49 other railways, and the head of America's wealthiest family. His younger brother, William, had inherited equal shares in the family fortunes, some part of which he spent building Marble House, on nearby Bellevue Avenue. A serious, modest and gentle man, Cornelius II nevertheless gave free rein and an unlimited budget to Richard Morris Hunt, the architect of Marble House and of the grand Vanderbilt houses on Fifth Avenue in New York. Hunt followed the Italian Renaissance layout adopted for 16th-century palaces, where rooms were grouped symmetrically around a central courtyard. With 70 rooms, 33 of which were for resident staff and visitors' servants, The Breakers is indisputably Newport's largest "cottage".

▽ CHATEAU-SUR-MER
The solid granite 1850s Wetmore home was updated in the 1870s in the latest European fashions, including Arts and Crafts.

△ ROSECLIFF
The glittering ballroom, designed by Stanford White, witnessed many of Newport's most extravagant high-society summer balls.

◁ MARBLE HOUSE
The entrance hall of yellow Siena marble is dominated by a vast Venetian mirror over a bronze fountain custom-made for the house.

▷ THE BREAKERS
Magnificently sited on Ochre Point, The Breakers faces the Atlantic Ocean. Its grounds are skirted by Cliff Walk.

VERMONT

The Green Mountain State is alive with the sound of leaves crunching under foot; the sight of red barns and brick meeting-houses; the smell of country lanes and maple sugar boiling

Map on pages 246–7

Vermont is a great green slice of high ground, a measured wedge of American Pie left over, wrapped up and set aside as a souvenir of the homemade, agrarian utopia that America once aspired to be. Fatally vertical down-west and up-stream, "the land in-between" was a rocky byroad up and away from the parade route of national destiny.

Vermont had its brief, booming share of speculators, cash-croppers, side-wheelers, mother lodes and iron horses. But there was always something wildly tentative about the sweep and dash of its struggle to keep up with the American pageant, something mildly eccentric in its slapdash network of railways, turnpikes and fine rural academies.

Even before the hill towns could settle down properly, the westward exodus kicked in: the farmers' offspring were only too eager to abandon their flinty fields and frowzy home towns in search of more welcoming ground. For all its overlay of tradition, Vermont is a land of transience and experiment, a bottom land repeatedly reclaimed by nature, a country outstripped by the bigger wheels of progress, a land still imperfectly subjugated to human priorities.

PRECEDING PAGES: the Green Mountains. **LEFT:** downhill skiing. **BELOW:** Civil War monument, Newfane.

The Civil War

"Put the Vermonters ahead and keep the column well closed up," said General John Sedgewick at the Battle of Gettysburg. The price of such military strategy was high, for the Civil War decimated Vermont. No other state gave as large a share of its sons to the cause of Union. The year 1865 marked the beginning of its decline in population, which until 1960 grew gradually older and smaller.

The Civil War provided Vermont with one unexpected boon. Mrs Lincoln chose to spend the summer in Manchester in 1863, putting the area on the map (President Lincoln planned to join his family there in 1865, but fate had other plans). Other visitors soon discovered the subtler pleasures of what the 19th-century British historian Lord Bryce described as "the Switzerland of North America."

"Setting and viewing," fishing and strolling among the green hillsides became *de rigueur* during America's Gilded Age; Manchester, Burlington and Woodstock were simply the great places to summer and be seen summering.

At the height of the season, the population approached its pre-war numbers. By putting up city folk, boiling and peddling "sweet water" (maple syrup) and enclosing more of their land for pasturage, some Vermont farmers found a way to lead a somewhat softer life. Some of their neighbors, like marble baron Redfield Proctor and William Dean Howell's

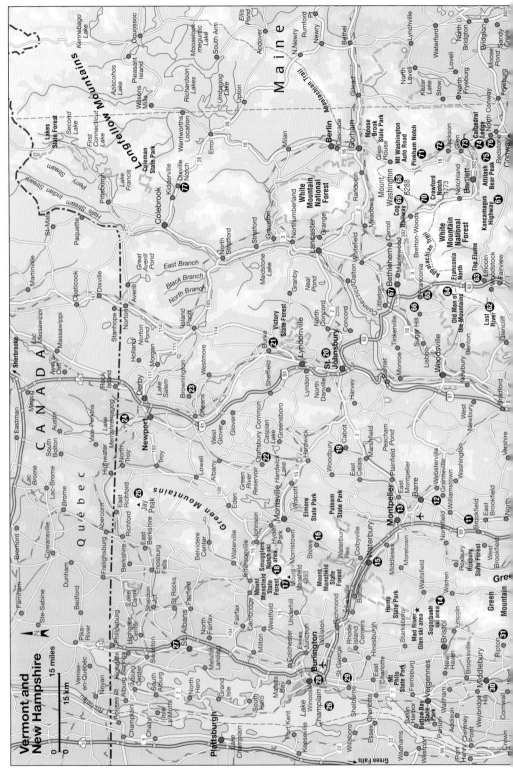

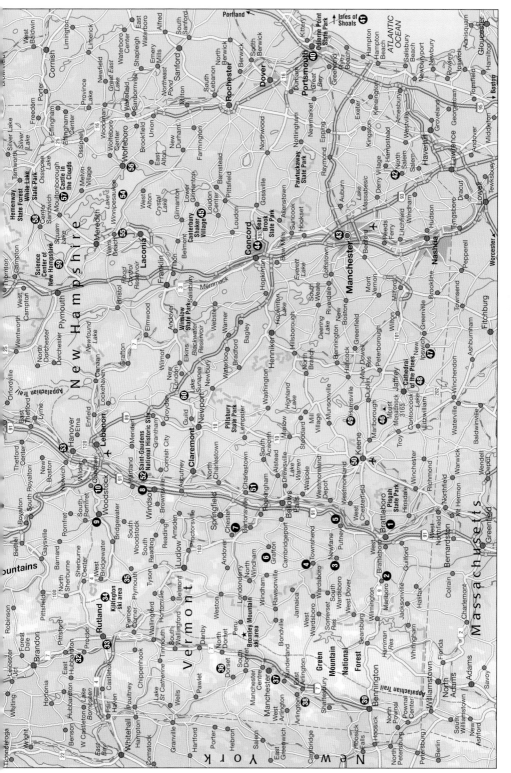

fictive paint king, Silas Lapham, simply turned the fallow land over and made a mint out of bedrock mined by cheap foreign labor. But by the time the railways gave way to the automobile, tourism had become the state's unofficial No. 1 industry.

America's playground

"Vermont, Designed by the Creator for the Playground of the Continent," read a 1911 brochure published by Vermont's state publicity bureau, the first such in the nation. "Development" became the 20th-century battle cry, and roadside attractions outflanked each other from Brattleboro to Morses Line. Natives and visitors alike started grumbling in the 1930s, when rolling pastures and grassy meadows quietly gave way here and there to a lakeside resort, a new rambling "summer cottage," another country club or (finally) the slim interstate highway. Stories began to circulate, about the farmer and his 12-gauge shotgun versus a brigade of the Conservation Corps and their back-hoe. But the lawmakers in Montpelier didn't notice until, nearly overnight in the early 1950s, the ski industry blew land taxes through the rooftop. Suddenly the land of milk and honey was overflowing with New Yorkers from solstice to solstice. The real boom had finally begun.

In 1965, Vermont lost its distinction as the state with more cows than people. Today, few natives make a decent living off the land. But the new gentry – the second-homers with condos or splendid country estates, complete with Morgan horses and 30 head of sheep – are determined to reconstitute and preserve their township's special flavor, its fallow charm, its pastoral innocence, from latecomers. They have formed a shaky coalition with their neighbors – the

It is said that a 1763 picnicking party to Killington Peak gave the state of Vermont its name: instead of quaffing the champagne they brought for refreshment, Rev Samuel Peters broke it on a rock and christened the region "Verd Mont" ("Green Mountain" in French).

BELOW: cows built to survive the harsh Vermont winters.

disgruntled patricians, pillars of their community; refugees from the 1960s, back-to-land artisans of the post-industrial era; the seventh-generation Vermonters, whose trailer homes, pick-up trucks and snowmobiles are emblems of hardscrabble endurance. This is the backwoods elite – the holy alliance keeping the lobbyists and the developers at bay.

One of the toughest anti-pollution stances in the nation, a dizzying array of zoning ordinances, new wilderness designations, a "no off-premise billboards" mandate and even a touch of urban renewal have kept Vermont a superior place to live. Ironically, these factors, together with the protective attitude of its residents, have also made it one of the best places to visit.

The Lower Connecticut River Valley

The long, lazy Connecticut River forms the entire boundary between the states of Vermont and New Hampshire. Covered over by a hydroelectric dam at the southernmost end, Vermont's first permanent settlement – Fort Dummer, founded in 1752 – has been reduced to a mere marker on the shore. A few miles north, however, **Brattleboro ❶**, the town it was meant to protect, enjoyed resort status from 1846 to 1871, when a local physician parlayed its pure springs into a "water cure." In the 1960s and '70s, a new wave of adventurous folk washed upstream and settled right in. The back-to-the-land crowd, not just wandering hippies but dedicated communards, sunk their roots deep into the community, and though it's now their children who sport tie-dyes and flowing hair about town, the hippies managed to set up an economic infrastructure with surprising staying power. They – and a general populace whose tastes have come around – support natural foods markets, alternative shops, and a worker-owned restaurant, **The Common Ground**, which after several decades of broad-based success seems less a restaurant than a cultural touchstone (Eliot Street; open for lunch and dinner; tel: 802-257 0855).

Seek out the Art Deco **Latchis Building**, which houses a movie theater and hotel, and the **Brattleboro Museum and Art Center** (open Tues–Sun, 12–6pm) in the Union Railroad Station. This has a collection of Jacob Estey reed organs that were made in the town in the 19th century.

Naulahka, the ship-shaped manse where Rudyard Kipling wrote the first two *Jungle Books* and *Captain Courageous* in the 1890s, has been recently restored by Great Britain's Landmark Trust (not open to the public, but see Tip in margin). Kipling, an Englishman born in India, came here on his honeymoon in 1892 (his bride's parents had settled in Brattleboro after taking the cure) and he immediately warmed to the life of a country squire; he even enjoyed playing golf in the snow, with balls painted red. His grand airs, however, didn't endear him to the locals, and in 1896 when a property dispute with his roguish brother-in-law hit the headlines, destroying his rural idyll, he and his wife fled, never to return.

Follow US 9 to the west of Brattleboro to reach **Marlboro ❷** – hilltop home of experimental Marlboro College, which every summer hosts the world-renowned **Marlboro Music Festival**, founded

Map on pages 246–7

TIP

Kipling's house, Naulahka, is available for rent by the week from the UK's Landmark Trust. Telephone 802-254 6868 in the US or 0628 825925 in the UK for details.

BELOW: the Art-Deco Latchis Building, Brattleboro.

by the late Rudolf Serkin (book early for tickets; tel: 802-254 2394) – and the ski resort towns of Wilmington and West Dover. The latter two towns are somewhat overdeveloped in places (in the 1950s, the burgeoning Mount Snow ski resort, then the largest, turned these hamlets into veritable boom towns).

State 30 northwest out of Brattleboro follows the West River, past a picturesque covered bridge, to the postcard-perfect town of **Newfane** ❸. Its broad common is lined with shady elms and surrounded by stately Greek Revival public buildings – a white-columned courthouse with Congregational church to match, flanked by a grange, two outstanding inns famous for their culinary offerings, and some worthwhile antique stores. A flea market held summer weekends in a field north of town since the late 1960s has become something of an institution, and a draw for locals and visitors alike.

Further up Route 30 are two equally appealing, low-key villages to explore: **Townshend** ❹ and **Jamaica**, with plenty of unspoiled parkland – including the beach at the West River reservoir behind the Townshend Dam.

A small town directly north of Brattleboro on US 5, **Putney** ❺ predated the social experiments of the 1960s by a good 150 years: in the early 18th century, it was the site of a short-lived but sensational commune espousing free love. The countryside is still populated in part by '60s protesters, some clustered in communes of several decades' duration. Many artists and craftspeople ply their trades in Putney; look for hand-crafted signs announcing sculpture and woodworking studios and potteries.

Scenic backroads dotted with antique shops connect Bellows Falls with Grafton and Chester to the northwest. Purchased in its entirety and renovated by the Windham Foundation, **Grafton** ❻ is a preserved-in-amber Greek Revival

BELOW:
near Putney.

town eerily close to its appearance in the early 1800s: visitors wander about in blissful disbelief, sampling a slice of cheddar at the **Grafton Village Cheese Company** (tel: 802-843 2221), and perhaps claiming a rocker on the porch of the 1801 Old Tavern, whose guests have included notables from Thoreau and Kipling to Ulysses S. Grant and Teddy Roosevelt. **Chester ❼** is a curious little strand of Victoriana on the Williams River. One especially ornate building houses the **National Survey Charthouse**. An 1850s stone village-within-a-village features 30 homes faced in gneiss ledgestone.

The Upper Connecticut Valley

A center of invention during the 19th century and today home of a thriving machine tool industry, the towns of Springfield and **Windsor ❽** form Precision Valley, a living testament to Yankee ingenuity. The **American Precision Museum** on Windsor's South Main Street (Route 12 East; open May–Oct, daily; entrance fee) is chock-full of all the gadgets, whatsits and thingamabobs that not only made the region famous, but helped the North win the Civil War.

Windsor is also famed as the birthplace of Vermont, because it was here in the **Old Constitution House** that delegates met in 1777 to establish the Free and Independent Republic of Vermont, draw up a constitution and create a Council of Safety to protect the new country as much from the other 12 states as from the Crown; the building is now a museum, with material relating to this event (open late May–mid-Oct, daily; entrance fee). On Route 5, the **Catamount Brewing Co.** offers tours and tastings (open Mon–Sat; Sun pm). The **Windsor-Cornish Covered Bridge**, spanning the Connecticut River to lovely Cornish, New Hampshire, is the longest covered bridge in the United States.

Cycling in the forest.

BELOW:
chicken farmer.

"I live in New Hampshire so I can get a better view of Vermont," explained artist Maxfield Parrish from his home in Cornish. He did sneak a considerable piece of that view into most of his paintings, notably Mount Ascutney, which looms south of Windsor. The largest monadnock in New England, **Ascutney** is home to a ski resort (tel: 802-484 7711) and conference center that mounts cultural events in the summer months.

The older money of **Woodstock** ❾ can, from time to time, be heard to lament inroads made by what one observer has called the "suburban gold-coast mink-and-manure set." Upscale shopping sprees along the refurbished downtown blocks of Cabot and French streets may have replaced placid strolls up Mount Tom as the fashionable summer pastime, but in general the enlightened despotism of philanthropist Laurance Rockefeller has preserved the tone of the town much as it must have been in the 1930s, when he met his future wife, Mary French, while summering here.

A passion for maintaining a graceful balance between society and nature has long been the keynote to Woodstock's renown. Mary's grandfather, Frederick Billings, returned from his lucrative law practice in San Francisco in the 1890s to become a pioneer in reforestation and a zealous model farmer. The slopes of Mount Tom and Mount Peg and the restored **Billings Farm Museum** (Route 12 East; open May–Oct, daily; entrance fee) are testaments to his love for rural Vermont. Growing up on the elder Billings' farm in the 1830s, George Perkins Marsh – later to become a noted linguist and diplomat – drafted a landmark treatise, *Man and Nature*, which, over a century after its publication, remains the ecologist's New Testament. In 1998 the Billings family mansion, most recently occupied by Laurance Rockefeller, was opened under the auspices of

BELOW: the Floating Bridge at Brookfield.

Marsh–Billings National Historic Park (Route 12 East; open mid-May–mid-Oct; entrance fee). Tours of the mansion and grounds are offered.

For further glimpses of Woodstock's past, visit the **Woodstock Historical Society** headquarters, nine rooms of period furnishings in an 1807 house – also known as the Dana House (Elm Street; open May–late Oct Mon–Sat; Sun pm; entrance fee).

Map on pages 246–7

The Rockefellers' Woodstock Inn and Resort on the green remains the place to stay – and the Robert Trent Jones golf course and **Suicide Six** ski area (tel: 802-457 6661) offer year-round amusements. On the other side of the green, a covered bridge leads to Mountain Avenue, a redoubt of old summer cottages, and a park at the base of Mount Tom. Trails to the summit overlook a guided floral walk through the Rockefeller estate, and the Vermont Institute of Natural Science maintains the fascinating **Vermont Raptor Center**, a habitat for 26 species of owls, hawks, and eagles unable to survive in the wild (Church Hill Road; open daily; entrance fee).

The hills surrounding Woodstock are horse country. At the fairgrounds in **Quechee** to the east, polo matches are played most Saturdays in July and August. In town, Irish artisan **Simon Pearce** has transformed The Mill at Quechee, an abandoned flannel factory, into a most inviting complex featuring his distinctive glasswork (glass-blowers can be observed at work on weekdays) and a delightful restaurant overlooking the mill pond.

A participant in Woodstock's Wassail Parade.

To the east, **Quechee Gorge** is billed by local boosters as "Vermont's Little Grand Canyon."

Visionaries, religious and commercial

A major crossroads since the days when railroads ruled interstate traffic, **White River Junction** still serves as an Amtrak stop and marks the intersection of Interstates 91 and 89.

"A man can easily hear strange voices," said Kipling of the lonely Vermont winter, "the Word of God rolling between the dead hills; may see visions and dream dreams…" Joseph Smith, founder of the Church of Jesus Christ of the Latter-day Saints, was born in 1805 on **Dairy Mill Hill**, a mile from South Royalton on Route 14. Here Mormon followers maintain a 38½-ft (11.5-meter) obelisk and a museum.

Heading northward, seek out the unspoiled village of **Brookfield** , the geographical center of the state. In 1812, a 320-ft (98-meter) **Floating Bridge**, supported by 380 tarred barrels, was built across the pond at the center of town, and it survives to this day – as part of Route 65 – accommodating one car at a time; it's also popular for fishing. One of the last ice harvests in the east is now the occasion for an annual festival on the lake, held the last Saturday in January.

Between Brookfield and Barre is the town of **Graniteville** , site of the **Rock of Ages Quarry**, one of the largest granite quarries in the world. Mining began in the early 19th century, soon after the War of 1812, and boomed with the influx of skilled immigrant stoneworkers between 1880 and 1910. Fed up with poor wages and working conditions (many died

BELOW: Brookfield's ice festival.

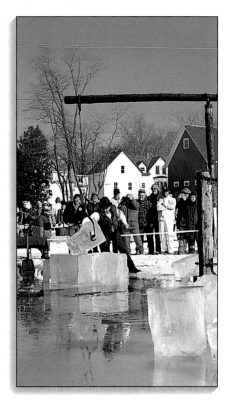

of silicosis), the granite workers managed to elect a Socialist mayor – many decades before liberal Burlington was ready to do the same. Today, the Rock of Ages firm owns nearly all of the quarries on and around Graniteville's Millstone Hill, which provide the nation with one-third of its memorial stones. The operation has long been a tourist-oriented showcase (Main Street; tours June–mid-Oct; entrance fee), with free access to the polishing and sculpting factory, and optional bus tours skirting the fully operational quarry a mile up the hill.

For a more evocative tour, however, visit Barre's **Hope Cemetery** (off Route 14), where the workers commemorated their own, with often touching artwork.

Montpelier was the birthplace of Admiral George Dewey (1837–1917), who became a hero during the Spanish-American War when the US fleet under his command destroyed the Spanish fleet at Manila.

The smallest capital: Montpelier

Home to about 8,200 people, **Montpelier ⑬** is the smallest state capital in the nation. The green ridge of Hubbard Park rises behind the gold-leaf dome of the **Vermont State House** (State Street; tours July–mid-Oct, Mon–Fri). Initially, Vermont's capital rotated through the state, but, with the completion of the original nine-sided building in 1808, the seat of power settled here. When an imposing stone successor, built in 1838, was gutted by fire in 1857, the Doric portico and native granite walls withstood the flames to form a shell for the present structure. The Senate Chamber is rightfully considered the most beautiful room in the state.

The "Steamboat Gothic" Pavilion Hotel – "the Grand Old Lady of State Street," where so many lawmakers bedded down for the January–April session (following an agrarian calendar, legislators go about their ordinary lives the rest of the year) – was demolished in 1966. However, a skillful replica now occupies its place beside the State House Lawn and houses a collection of Vermont

BELOW: Robert Burns stands guard in Barre. **RIGHT:** State House, Montpelier.

icons which once decorated the capitol building. This, the **Vermont Historical Society Museum**, is a rewarding mishmash of Green Mountain artifacts (109 State Street; open Tues–Sat; Sun pm).

   If you spot an unlikely number of chefs' hats about town, it's because Montpelier is also home to the **New England Culinary Institute**, a highly regarded training school that maintains two excellent public restaurants – the Main Street Grill and Bar (lunch, dinner; tel: 802-223 3188) and the Chef's Table (118 Main Street; lunch weekdays, dinner Mon–Sat; tel: 802-229 9202) – as well as an irresistible bakery.

Map on pages 246–7

The Green Mountains

Some 20 miles (32 km) west of Montpelier, the Green Mountain range attains heady heights highly tempting to skiers – as well as to mountain climbers and bikers. South of I-89, the towns of Waitsfield and Warren support two ski areas, the rustic, but challenging **Mad River Glen** and more developed and extensive **Sugarbush ⓬**. Both towns are full of the pleasures – inviting restaurants and cozy inns – that outdoors enthusiasts enjoy in their off-hours.

   Waitsfield boasts an unusual cinema, Mad River Flicks, which offers café-style service and seating in overstuffed love seats. Spectators are also welcome at two summertime sporting venues, the **Sugarbush Polo Club** (the original players, in 1962, used ski poles and a volleyball) and the **Mad River Valley Cricket Club**. To get an unusual perspective on the countryside, consider a vintage airplane ride or soaring excursion out of the Warren-Sugarbush Airport (Route 100; flights May–Oct), or try horse-trekking at the Vermont Icelandic Horse Farm North (Basin Road off Route 100; rides year-round).

BELOW: a street vendor takes things easy.

CRAFTS IN VERMONT

With over 1,500 professional artisans, Vermont has more artists and craftspeople per capita than any other state. Thanks in part to a bucolic setting but also to state support – the Vermont Crafts Council in Montpelier has designated four "Vermont State Craft Centers" – you'll find outstanding creative work in every major town (and minor ones, too). Vermont's non-profit galleries exhibit and sell pottery, woodwork, jewelry, textiles, glassware, quilts and anything else you can think of.

   The largest of these outlets, Frog Hollow, has shops in Burlington, Manchester and Middlebury (tel: 802-388 3177). Over 250 "juried" artisans (those whose work has been judged to be of the highest quality) show their work through this venue. The Vermont State Craft Center at Windsor House, Windsor, features works from 200 juried artisans (tel: 802-674 6729).

   In summer and fall, large craft fairs are held throughout the state (*see Travel Tips*), and on Memorial Day weekend artists participate in a statewide "Open Studio" weekend. The Vermont Crafts Council (tel: 802-223 3380) publishes a free annual studio and gallery guide, and a calendar of fairs. This information, as well as links to member artists, is available on-line at www.vermontcrafts.com.

Ben & Jerry's.

In **Waterbury** N, midway between these peaks and Mount Mansfield to the north, a number of gourmet entrepreneurs have set up shop. Vermont Distillers, "the smallest (legal) distillery in the US," produces vodka, gin, and spicy Tamarack liqueur. And a pair of "flatlander" entrepreneurs have found a great use for Vermont's abundant ice and milk: the **Ben & Jerry's Homemade Ice Cream Factory** on Route 100 in Waterbury is now the largest tourist attraction in Vermont, offering tours (with tastings) daily (tours Mon–Sat; entrance fee; tel: 802-244 8687). Just up the road, you can watch cider being pressed in season, and sample some, at the Cold Hollow Cider Mill, and stop for a nibble at the Green Mountain Chocolate Co., a confiserie run by former White House pastry chef Albert Kumin.

Even before the advent of skiing in the 1930s, when the Civilian Conservation Corps cut the first of Mount Mansfield's precipitous trails, ensuring ascendancy of **Stowe** N as "the Ski Capital of the East," Stowe enjoyed a reputation as a stylish summer place. Three grand hotels were built in the mid-1800s, of which only the 1833 Green Mountain Inn, at the center of town, survives.

Summer or winter, sports opportunities abound, particularly along the **Stowe Recreation Path**, created in the 1980s through community donations and effort. Ideally suited for skiers, cyclists, skaters, wheelchair racers, runners, walkers and stroller-pushers, the 5.3-mile (8.5-km) paved path skirts the West Branch river from town all the way out to the Topnotch resort, passing a number of appealing inns, restaurants, and shops en route. Other notable Stowe inns, such as the Austrian-style Trapp Family Lodge (founded by the Baroness Maria Von Trapp of *Sound of Music* fame) are tucked away in the wooded hills; in summer, the meadows of the Trapp Family Lodge are alive with the sound of concerts and

BELOW:
Ben & Jerry's ice cream factory.
RIGHT: time to think.

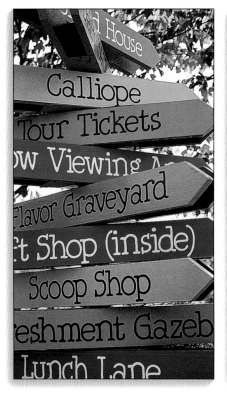

equestrian shows. The Trapp Family Lodge has America's earliest cross-country ski area, which links with three other networks around Stowe to give one of the biggest trail systems in New England.

Map on pages 246–7

On **Mount Mansfield** Ralph Waldo Emerson had a bracing vacation at the Summit House, where, he recounts, his "whole party climbed to the top of the [mountain's] nose and watched the sun rise over the top of the White Mountains of New Hampshire." Hikers still favor this craggy human profile, and two shortcuts are popular: for a fee, the 4½-mile (7.5-km) **Auto Road**, a century-old toll road rising from the Inn at the Mountain on Route 108 (open late May–mid-Oct), offers an easy way to ascend to the "nose," and an eight-passenger **gondola**, the world's speediest (mid-June–mid-Oct; entrance fee), makes fast work of the 4,393-ft (1,338-meter) "chin," the state's highest point. The ski area has some long, challenging and intermediate runs. On adjoining Spruce Peak, the **Stowe Mountain Resort** (entrance fee; tel: 802-253 3000) also operates an alpine slide and the world's first alpine in-line skate park, opened in 1993.

Another big summertime draw is the early August classic car rally, and in mid-January, during the Stowe Winter Carnival, the whole town parties. As the Federal Writers' Project put it decades ago, "Stowe is a 'smart' place to be seen and many snowtime visitors are not skiers."

Wintertime visitors hoping to fit in a visit to the nearby ski area of **Smuggler's Notch** (so named for its role during the War of 1812) are in for a rude surprise: the connecting road is closed in winter, and those who've traveled it in summer will understand why. Hundred-foot cliffs and giant boulders crowd the narrow, winding roadway – a popular staging point for mountaintop hikes. On the other side, the Smuggler's Notch ski resort (tel: 802-644 8851),

BELOW: Balloon Festival, Stowe.

encompassing three peaks (one offers ski access back to Stowe), is popular with families for its well-thought-out children's programs – giving among other things courses for adults on how to teach their children to ski, and courses for children on how to teach their parents to snowboard. The absence of winter through-traffic is a distinctive plus. In summer the attraction is an assortment of water slides – so far, the only such amusements in the state. The town closest to the resort, **Jeffersonville**, has a range of shops and restaurants.

About 8 miles (13 km) east, the sleepy town of Johnson has been all but taken over by the **Vermont Studio Center**, a working retreat for artists and writers that attracts many prominent instructors.

The Northeast Kingdom

North of State 15 is a remote and remarkable region. The Northeast Kingdom is a nearly 2,000-sq.-mile (over 5,000-sq.-km) swath of crystal lakes and climax forests, a region known for greater natural wealth and homegrown poverty than any other area in the state. The counties of Caledonia, Essex and Orleans are sparsely populated and make up Vermont's least industrialized area, except for a scattering of lake resort towns, paper company holdings in the far east corner, and various businesses in St Johnsbury, the Kingdom's unofficial capital. *Where the Rivers Run North* is the title Orleans writer Howard Frank Mosher gave his collection of short stories (it spawned an acclaimed locally produced movie in 1994) in honor of a region known for its backwater quirks.

Increasingly beset by competition from development and government regulation, Vermont's dairy industry has fallen on hard times of late. Not so the 500-odd farms involved with the Cabot Creamery Co-operative in **Cabot** ⓳;

BELOW:
Lake Willoughby.

founded in 1919, the co-op thrives to this day, and offers factory tours, starting with a video recounting the history of farming in the region and ending with tastings of its outstanding Vermont cheddar (open June–Oct, daily; Nov–May, Mon–Sat; closed Jan; cheese is not made every day). Nearby Danville hosts another organization of unlikely survivors: the **American Society of Dowsers**, on Village Green, counts among its members hundreds of firm believers in the powers of the divining rod. Their headquarters, housed in a red clapboard hall, doubles as a store, and their annual fall gathering attracts curious observers.

The city of **St Johnsbury** ⓴ itself remains a vibrant pocket of Victorian charm. From the bank buildings downtown to the Fairbanks mansion on the Plains overlooking the valley, the stamp of architect Lambert Packard and his wealthy patrons is visible everywhere. Thaddeus Fairbanks started making the world's first platform scale here in the 1830s, and he and his sons reinvested the fruits of their precision instrument into the quality of civic life. The St Johnsbury **Athenaeum/Art Gallery** (Main Street; open Mon–Sat; Mon and Wed till 8pm) built in 1871–73, is a tastefully combined library, music chamber and exhibition space dominated by the huge skylit panorama *Domes of the Yosemite* by artist Albert Bierstadt. This is one of the oldest intact art collections in the country ("Welcome to the nineteenth century," reads a sign at the entrance) and one of the most inviting. With a collection of more than 3,000 stuffed fauna and its own vintage planetarium, the Romanesque **Fairbanks Museum and Planetarium** is a little bastion of natural history erected by the Fairbanks family in 1890 (Main and Prospect streets; Mon–Sat; Sun pm; entrance fee).

About 10 miles (6 km) north of St Johnsbury, the still relatively undiscovered ski area of **Burke** ㉑ deserves its promotional billing as "Vermont's Northern

Map on pages 246–7

Bierstadt (1830–1902) belonged to the Hudson River School of painters, the country's first native school of painting. Its earliest leaders worked in the wilderness areas around the Hudson River north of New York, and in nearby New England.

LEFT: old postcard view of St Johnsbury Athenaeum. **RIGHT:** a farmer at Norwich.

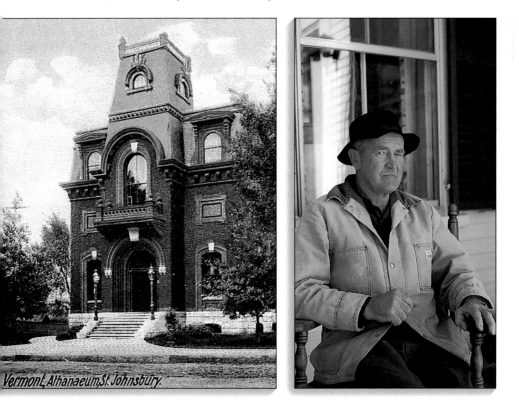

Vermont Athanaeum, St. Johnsbury.

Star." With a challenging array of trails, and affordable lift tickets (tel: 802-626 3305), it's one of the best deals in the Northeast. It also serves as an outdoor campus for Burke Academy, which has consistently turned out Olympians.

Craftsbury Common and Greensboro are among the more moneyed summer communities hidden in these hills. The former has become a magnet for serious athletes – the Craftsbury Sports Center offers dormitory-style accommodation and year-round instruction in sports – and the latter remains a peaceful retreat favored by writers and other intelligentsia (the local general store stocks the *New York Times*).

Every summer, hordes of joyous pilgrims descend on the small town of Glover to partake in the Bread and Puppet Theater's "Domestic Resurrection Circus," a pageant and festival put on by the radical theater group founded by Peter Schumann in 1963 to illustrate the horrors of war and wonders of life. The **Bread and Puppet Museum** is an amazing barnful of fantastical creatures (Route 122; open May–Oct daily).

The **Old Stone House Museum** (off Route 58; open mid-May–June and Sept–mid-Oct, Fri–Tues; July and Aug, daily; entrance fee) at **Brownington** ㉓ is a collection of locally donated miscellenia, housed in the former county grammar school, built between 1827 and 1830 by "Uncle" Alexander Twilight. He was claimed by Middlebury College as the first black college graduate, Class of 1823, and said to be the first black legislator in the nation. Each of the building's 11 rooms is devoted to a particular township.

Once a fashionable watering hole on the Canadian frontier, the vast **Lake Memphrémagog** ㉔ lost most of its following in the 1920s with the retirement of the Mountain Maid and Lady of the Lake steam liners, but none of its inter-

TIP

The date of the Bread and Puppet Theater festival in Glover is not advertised, so as to minimize crowds, but details can be obtained from the Bread and Puppet Museum (tel: 802-525 3031).

BELOW: the Black River Valley near Craftsbury.

Map on pages 246–7

national charm. **Newport**, "the Border City," is a fair-sized town noted for its easy mingle of Canadian day-trippers, contented locals and southerly summerers strung along Cape Elizabeth Bluffs at the lake's eastern shore. Smelt, small-mouth bass and wall-eyed pike are all common catches over the Derby Line.

To the west, Route 242 climbs from Jay to the ski area of **Jay Peak** ㉕ (tel: 802-988 2611 or 800-451 4449), where an aerial tramway runs, transporting skiers, foliage peepers and summer sightseers to its 3,861-ft (1,177-meter) summit. The views into Canada are magnificent.

The northwestern corner

The northwest corner of Vermont's border with Canada, between Alburg and Morses Line, was a favorite route for smugglers in the steamboat era. But the notorious smuggling center of Highgate Spring was known chiefly for its springs (which supposedly had curative powers) until Prohibition, when bootleggers began running their nag brigades and motorcades right into Franklin County.

Over the years since 1609, when Samuel de Champlain discovered the body of water that now bears his name (and spotted a Loch Ness-like monster that has as yet eluded capture), the islands at its northern end have been compared to every place from the Isle of Man to the Louisiana bayou. Just fertile enough to support a few orchards and some grazing Jerseys, and just far enough out of the way to have withstood development, the Four Brothers Islands – Alburg, Isle La Motte, the Two Heroes and Grand Isle – stretch for 30 beautiful miles (48 km) south to the widest reach of **Lake Champlain** ㉖.

"Vermont's Cape Cod" is strewn with arcadian preserves, lakeshore drives and

BELOW: beach scene, Lake Champlain.

TIP

Lake Champlain offers
great scope for cruises.
From Burlington, a ferry
plies from to Port Kent,
NY, and there are scenic
trips on the *Spirit of
Ethan Allen* (College
Street, Burlington
Boathouse,
tel: 802-862 8300).

BELOW: the sun
sets over Lake
Champlain.

sleepy little towns. **Isle La Motte** is perhaps the most satisfying of the islands, with its exquisite marble deposits, "the oldest coral reef in the world" (leftover from 10,000 years ago, when the Atlantic covered the Champlain Valley, it's littered with sunken steamboats and bobbing scuba buoys), and **St Anne's Shrine** (open mid-May–mid-Oct, daily; Sat till 8pm) honoring America's first French settlement (1664).

Franklin County was the center of Vermont's rise to eminence as a dairy state. Although the principal town, **St Albans** ㉗, lacks the vivacity it enjoyed as a major railyard on the way to Montreal, it does host a Vermont Maple Festival in mid-April which officially denotes the long-awaited end of winter. And it was also once the scene of the Civil War's most northerly skirmish: in 1864 a band of Confederates seized the town, robbed the banks and hightailed it to Canada. There they were caught and brought to trial; however, their exploits were excused as "legitimate" acts of war.

Burlington and environs

"The most miserable of one-horse towns," complained the young wife of an Army recruiting officer stationed here in the 1840s. "Startling incidents never occur in Burlington. None ever occurred there, and none probably ever will." Things have livened up along "New England's West Coast" since then. By the Civil War, fiercely competitive steamboat lines and a busy lumber trade were turning **Burlington** ㉘ into a plucky little inland port of entry. By 1900, the wharves were teeming with businessmen, seekers of pleasure and ships' crews.

Today, trendy restaurants and the lively Church Street Marketplace, a pedestrian mall lined with sidewalk cafés and gentrified shops, have further improved Burlington's outlook. But the view remains the same. From Battery Park or the Cliffs, the sunset over Lake Champlain and the Adirondacks is still – as novelist William Dean Howells maintained – "superior to the evening view over the Bay of Naples," and "parties of pleasures" are again threatening to outnumber the workaday commuters who board the evening ferry to Port Kent, New York. In fact, the dock itself has become a tourist attraction, with a lively bar and sailboards to rent, sailboats to charter.

A growing influx of industry – notably, IBM – and the new metropolitan tone mingle to make the core of Vermont's "Queen City" (population 40,000) a commercial and cultural nexus that keeps turning up on polls as being one of the US's "most livable cities." Thanks in part to the presence of the University of Vermont (called "UVM" for its Latin name, Universitas Viridis Montis), the city enjoys a year-round array of cultural events, including annual Mozart and Shakespeare festivals. The **Flynn Theater for the Performing Arts**, a 1930 Art Deco movie palace on Main Street, hosts an impressive line-up of dance, music and theater (tel: 802-863 5966).

There's a lot worth doing within Burlington's widening metropolis. When the city's famous woolen industry moved south, the nearby city of Winooski (straddling its namesake river) went completely bottom up. But in 1978, the huge mill was revamped

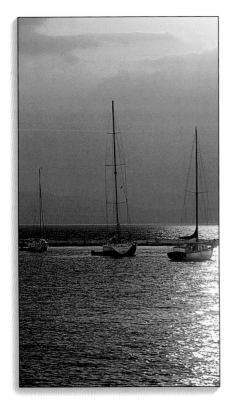

and refitted with an alluring bay of shops as the Champlain Mill Mall. Nearby, **St Michael's Playhouse**, on the campus of Saint Michael's College, has been mounting professional summer theater performances since 1951 (off Route 15; tel: 802-654 2281). Circling back into Burlington from the north, stop in at the **Ethan Allen Homestead Trust**, a restored 1787 farmhouse, for an insight into the exploits of this beloved native son as well as 5,000 years of local history (off Route 127; open mid-may–mid-Oct Mon–Sat; Sun pm; entrance fee).

About 7 miles (11 km) south of the city, at **Shelburne ㉙**, is the **Shelburne Museum**, which has to be seen to be believed (Route 7; tours mid-May–late Oct, daily; entrance fee). Neither a "living museum" nor a fusty historical collection, it's a 45-acre (18-hectare) complex reflecting the tastes of one very passionate and well-funded collector. Electra Havemeyer Webb developed an eye for Americana and folk art long before anyone else was paying attention, and managed to amass some 80,000 exemplary objects – 37 buildings full in all, with some train cars, a carousel and a Lake Champlain side-wheeler, the *Ticonderoga*, thrown in for good measure. It takes more than a casual stroll to do the collection justice; hence admission, though pricy, is good for two days.

Shelburne's other landmark is the Webbs' 100-room Queen Anne-style cottage on the lake. Carved from 22 lakeside farms by Frederick Law Olmsted, designer of New York City's Central Park, this 1,000-acre (400-hectare) estate is now a model ecological farmstead, **Shelburne Farms**, with a farm trail and guided tours (off Route 7; tours mid-May–mid-Oct, daily; entrance fee).

Charlotte, a few miles south of Shelburne, is home to the unusual **Vermont Wildflower Farm**, a 6-acre (2.5-hectare) preserve and learning center that offers delightful strolling (Route 7; open May–Oct daily; entrance fee).

Maple syrup – one of Vermont's specialties.

BELOW: a country store – for maple syrup and much, much more.

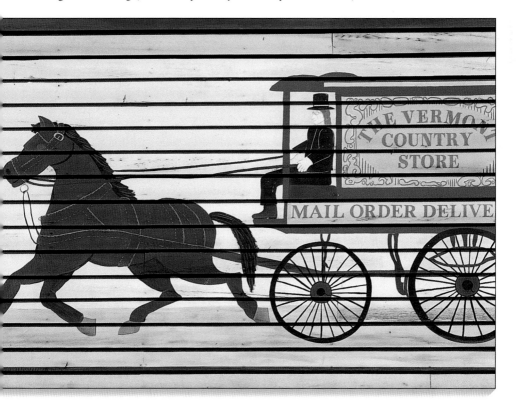

Middlebury and marble

Vermont spawned the world-famous Morgan horse, a barrel-chested steed, which, as one celebrant boasted, "can outrun, outpull, and outlast any other breed, just as you would expect a Vermont horse to do." The **UVM Morgan Horse Farm**, in the village of Weybridge, is a working farm with training demonstrations and tours (off Route 23; tours May–Oct daily; entrance fee).

Middlebury ❸, a few miles southeast, is the ideal college town, a verdant campus of grand, well-spaced 19th-century buildings, accompanied by a lively community of shops and restaurants. The **Vermont State Craft Center** at Frog Hollow showcases the traditional and contemporary work of more than 300 of the state's most talented artisans.

The poet Robert Frost spent his summers writing in a log cabin in **Ripton** ❸, not far from Bread Loaf, home of the prestigious **Bread Loaf Writers' Conference**. The mile-long **Robert Frost Interpretive Trail**, beginning at his home, the Homer Noble Farm, leads to the Bread Loaf campus by way of the cabin, which has been left untouched. For magnificent scenery, continue on State 125, through steep Lincoln Gap, and south through the unspoiled towns on this stretch of Route 100, which bisects the state vertically, and not always prettily.

The town of **Proctor** ❸ is the home of the **Vermont Marble Exhibit** (off Route 3; open mid-May–mid-Oct daily; entrance fee), offering a glimpse of the Vermont Marble Company factory, a sculptor at work, and marble samples from around the world, including the local product – some of which can be seen lining the sidewalks of the more prosperous towns in the region. The abandoned quarries make tempting swimming holes, too, if you can wrest the location from a local source.

BELOW:
Vermont Marble
Exhibit, Proctor.

Map on pages 246-7

The region west of Vermont's second-biggest city, **Rutland ⑬**, was a popular summer spot in the Victorian era, but faded after World War II, when the trains stopped coming. Rediscovered in recent decades by starry-eyed innkeepers and their guests, pretty towns such as Middletown Springs (a one-time spa) and Fair Haven are making a comeback, offering little more than old-fashioned B&B hospitality and plenty of unspoiled countryside to roam. Though they're minuscule in comparison to Lake Champlain, Lake St Catherine and Lake Bomoseen are flanked by state parks and offer sandy beaches.

Rutland itself is rather drab, but it does harbor a hidden gem: **Wilson Castle** (West Road; tours mid-May–mid-Oct, daily; entrance fee), an improbably opulent mid-1800s mansion with 32 rooms, 12 fireplaces and such elegant appointments as a Louis XVI crown jewel case, with manicured walkways covering 115 acres (46 hectares).

New England's largest ski area is **Killington ⑭** (tel: 802-422 3333 or 800-621 6867) in Sherburne Center, which quickly eclipsed **Mount Snow**, expanding to cover seven peaks, and in 1999 was linked up by trail to the adjacent resort of **Pico** as well – the whole complex being owned by the American Skiing Company. It ranks top among the Northeast ski resorts for nightlife. With a 4,241-ft (1,296-meter) peak reached by gondola, for sightseers as well as skiers, the resort is active year-round – the skiing often lasts from October through June and then in summer mountain bikes take over.

Nearby **Plymouth** spawned the US's most taciturn president. The **President Coolidge Birthplace and Homestead ⑮** (Route 100A; open late May–mid-Oct, daily; entrance fee) serves as a hilltop shrine to silent Cal – that self-styled "Puritan in Babylon," and the only President born on the Fourth of July. When

BELOW: spring colors in Rutland.

President Warren Harding died on August 3, 1923, and Vice-President Calvin Coolidge needed to be sworn in as the 30th president, the news had to be conveyed to the Coolidges by hand; true to form, the family did not have a phone.

The picturesque, marble-paved village of **Dorset ㊱** is home to the **Dorset Playhouse**, a rustic barn that served as Vermont's first summer playhouse (tel: 802-867 5777), and to a writers' colony .

Manchester and south: a pre-eminent summer place

Franklin Orvis gave the local tourist industry a boost in 1849 when he began taking in summer guests at his father's house, located next to the famed 1769 Marsh Tavern in **Manchester ㊲**, where Ethan Allen and his "Green Mountain Boys" had plotted the Tories' overthrow. The hotel kept expanding bit by bit until it became the grand Equinox, named for the mountain that presides over the town, and which can be reached 4 miles (6.5 km) south of town via the **Skyline Drive** toll road (open May–Oct, daily 8am–10pm). For all the former farmhands drawn to the metropolis, city-dwellers began to catch on to the attractions of open spaces and fresh air.

Meanwhile, Frank's younger brother, Charles, had a clever idea, too – why not teach the leisured class to catch their supper along the banks of the abundant Battenkill River? Less than 10 years after he sold his first bamboo flyrod, Manchester had become the place to get away from it all.

By the mid-20th century, the Equinox had deteriorated into white elephant-hood, but in the early 1980s it was restored to showplace luster, along with its 18-hole golf course. And the Orvis Company has prospered all the while: today it operates a thriving mail-order business, and the store – with its history-of-the-

BELOW: the Dorset Inn.

art **American Museum of Fly Fishing** (Route 7A; open daily) next door – draws visitors from around the world, as do the company's three-day fly-fishing courses. Orvis's success inspired other upscale companies (Ralph Lauren, Esprit, et al) to open their own outlets here, so the shopping opportunities are unsurpassed in the state.

All this brisk commerce notwithstanding, Manchester Village remains as tranquil and elegant as ever, with its marble-slab sidewalks and showy summer homes, many of them creatively converted into inns and restaurants.

Although Abraham Lincoln never made it to the Equinox (several other presidents did), Mary Lincoln and son Robert cherished fond memories of the mountains; they later returned to build an estate, **Hildene**, which now opens its richly appointed Georgian Revival rooms to antiquity-lovers and its 412-acre (167-hectare) grounds to cross-country skiers and summer strollers (Route 7A; tours mid-May–Oct, daily; entrance fee). Another pleasant place to visit in town is the **Southern Vermont Art Center** (West Road; open mid-May–Oct, Tues–Sat; Sun pm; donations), with contemporary indoor exhibits, outdoor sculptures, and a well-marked botany trail.

On Route 11, 6 miles (9.5 km) east of Manchester, **Bromley Mountain** ski area (tel: 802-824 5522) has a 1,334-ft (407-meter) vertical; in summer you can sled down the Alpine slide.

South of Manchester on Route 7A, **Arlington** ❸ is a former Revolutionary capital and one-time home to five *Saturday Evening Post* artists. The **Norman Rockwell Exhibition** (Route 7A; open daily, except closed January) displays a large number of *Post* covers and lesser-known prints, in which local uncles and grandmas figure largely; some former subjects actually serve as museum guides.

Map on pages 246–7

BELOW: a fall gathering at Peacham.

Map
on pages
246–7

*Bennington Monument,
erected in 1887–91.*

BELOW LEFT:
mountain biking,
Putney.
BELOW LEFT: pre-
Revolutionary
gravestone, Old
First Church.

Local author Dorothy Canfield Fisher needs no introduction to Vermonters: in a series of down-home novels and her glorious *Vermont Tradition: The Biography of an Outlook on Life*, Fisher celebrated the spirit of fairness and community that imbues the state. The Martha Canfield Library, named after Dorothy's grandmother, holds a rich store of the author's memorabilia.

The 1777 skirmish commemorated at **Bennington** by the Battle Monument (open mid-Apr–Oct, daily; entrance fee) actually took place a few miles west, where General John Stark and 1,800 ragtag troops forced the Redcoats back across the Walloomsac River in Hoosick Falls. However, it was a colonial supply dump on this site that General John Burgoyne was after, and his failure to attain it proved a turning point in the entire British campaign.

For an interesting trove of local artifacts, from Revolutionary War mementos to vintage toys, visit the **Bennington Museum and Grandma Moses Gallery** (Route 9; open May–Oct, daily; entrance fee). The self-taught painter's endearing primitives of rural life are exhibited in the schoolhouse she attended as a child in Eagle Bridge, New York.

Old Bennington sprawls east toward Bennington proper, home of Bennington College, among the country's most progressive – and expensive – schools. The older part of town, free of commerce but for the occasional inn, is like an immaculate open-air museum along Monument Avenue. Wander about the green and visit the Old First Church, with its unusual three-tiered steeple. Beside it, in the Old Burying Ground, lie the founders of Bennington, five Vermont governors, and Robert Frost, whose epitaph epitomizes the feisty loyalty endemic to true Vermonters, whether native-born or transplanted: "I had a lover's quarrel with the world." ❑

Ski Fever

Scandinavian immigrants introduced skiing in New Hampshire's logging camps in the 1870s. The Norwegian-speaking Nansen Ski Club was founded in Norway Village near Berlin about 1872; with six other clubs it founded the US Eastern Amateur Ski Association in 1922, and survives to this day.

Ski fever spread to the college circuit after Dartmouth's Outing Club was founded in 1909. Just five years later, Dartmouth college librarian Nathaniel Goodrich was the first to descend Vermont's highest peak, Mount Mansfield in Stowe. This was all without trails, of course, much less the "up-ski" devices – rope tows, J-bars, and ultimately aerial trams, gondolas, and high-speed quads – that came decades later. The sport was essentially confined to "touring" (comparable to today's cross-country), jumping off wooden chutes and the odd foray into the woods. In 1926 Appalachian Mountain Club hutmaster Joe Dodge was the first to hurtle down Mount Washington's Tuckerman Ravine.

By then, skiing was well on its way to popularity. In 1929, fresh from a Switzerland ski trip, Katharine Peckett opened the country's first organized ski school at her family's resort in Sugar Hill, New Hampshire. Soon, the Boston and Maine Railroad began running ski trains to New Hampshire. Then, in 1934, New England's first rope tow was constructed at Gilbert's Hill, in Woodstock, Vermont.

The sport was dormant during the gas-rationing of the early 1940s, but area after area sprouted up in the late '40s and '50s, among them Vermont's Mount Snow (tel: 800-451 4211), Smuggler's Notch (tel: 802-644-8851), Stratton (tel: 802-297 2200), Sugarbush (tel: 802-583 2381) and Killington (tel: 800-621 6867). For current slope conditions, call for an around-the-clock snow report (tel: 802-229 0531).

It was at Killington, in the mid-'60s, that the Graduated Length Method was introduced, easing the way for the general public to approach this often intimidating sport: tyros could start on short skis, gradually increasing the length as their prowess improved.

Just to keep the challenge fresh, though, a Stratton bartender came up with an innovation in the mid '60s that has changed the landscape of skiing. Jake Carpenter started experimenting with "snurfing" (as the underground sport of snowboarding was then called) secretly at night. It would take years, but his Burton snowboard company would become a leader in the field and, in the process, create a "rad" new skiing subculture. Stratton is still the most partial to snowboarders.

Today, Maine's big downhill resorts are Sugarloaf/USA (tel: 207-237 2000) in the Carrabassett Valley and Sunday River (tel: 207-824 3000) in Bethel. Sugarloaf has 43 miles (69 km) of trails and a vertical drop of 2,820 ft (860 meters); Sunday River has 121 trails. Snowmaking is excellent at both. There are almost 20 mountains developed for skiing in New Hampshire, but the two biggies are Loon Mountain, Lincoln (tel: 603-745 8111) and Waterville Valley (tel: 603-236-8311). "Skiophiles" will want to check out the New England Ski Museum, Franconia, NH (tel: 603-823 7177), for a full regional history. ❑

RIGHT: there are resorts to suit all abilities.

NEW HAMPSHIRE

*This solidly conservative state serves outdoor pleasures on a
platter – by way of the dramatic and rugged White
Mountains and dozens of deep lakes*

Map
on pages
246–7

A lthough New Hampshire's primary appeal is its quiet country life and
serene beauty, there are a number of special spots that warrant hitting the
road. There are particularly elegant flourishes of nature, such as the Old
Man of the Mountain, the Flume, the notches, and Mount Washington; there are
examples of human ingenuity and history, like the Cog Railway, Canterbury
Shaker Village, and Mystery Hill. More than half of the covered bridges in
New England are in New Hampshire, including the nation's longest – the
460-ft (140-meter) span crossing the Connecticut River from Cornish.

Isolated until relatively recently, with few links to international industry, New
Hampshire was slow to receive and absorb developments originating elsewhere.
This cultural sluggishness has now paid off: while so much of the country has
progressed into a wasteland of "miracle miles" and economic frenzy, many
parts of New Hampshire have retained a calm, dignified pace and quality.

Here, there are still long, slow days to sit idle on a shaded porch or by the fire;
evenings with the stars clear overhead and the startling silence of the countryside; old farms with pastureland arching down to a barn with a pond beside it;
small towns where everybody is on a first-name basis with everybody else; and
forests where the only signs of the modern age are the visitors themselves.

New Hampshire's town fairs feature ox-pulls and
taffy-pulls, exhibits of handmade quilts, the rapid-fire
patter of auctioneers hawking antiques, beans baked in
a pit in the ground, homespun games involving base-
balls and milk bottles and a prize for the best pig.

Once every four years, New Hampshire trundles
out of general obscurity to perform one of the classic
song-and-dance acts of American politics. The New
Hampshire presidential primary is the first in the
nation, the supposed diviner of political fortunes and,
for many, a make-or-break event.

Though typically disdainful of such ephemeral
trivia as fame and public attention, the people of New
Hampshire jealously guard their self-appointed right
to keep the nation's elections reasonably honest.
Vermont (New Hampshire's perennial competitor for
glories about which no one else much cares) once
hinted it might steal the primary limelight by sneaking
its elections in before New Hampshire's. Retaliation
was swift and decisive: New Hampshire passed a law
stipulating that its primaries be held on "the Tuesday
preceding the date on which any other New England
state shall hold a similar election." So there.

Crafty Massachusetts made its move in 1975,
waiting until only a few months before the 1976
primaries began, to announce that it would vote on
the same day as New Hampshire, the second Tuesday
of March. New Hampshire promptly pushed its date

PRECEDING PAGES:
Franconia Notch,
in the White
Mountains.
LEFT: antique
tractor rally
BELOW: snowgiant
in Hanover.

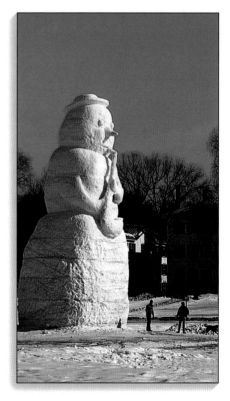

up to the last Tuesday in February, even though this resulted in the inconvenience of voting in the primaries one week and then getting back together for Town Meeting Day the next (the two events had formerly been something of a political double-header). Though it's highly unlikely that many New Hampshirites lie awake nights worrying over the fact that the rest of the nation is reminded of their existence only once every four years, the Presidential primary is their moment center stage and they intend to keep it.

Politics in New Hampshire is definitely a participatory (and contact) sport. New Hampshire's state legislature, the General Court, is the third-largest governing body in the English-speaking world. The United Kingdom's House of Commons has 630 members; legislators in both houses of the US Congress total 485; New Hampshire manages to get by with 24 senators and 400 representatives (roughly, one for every 3,000 residents).

Much of the state's business, however, is conducted by that venerable, fundamentally American institution, the Town Meeting. Each Town Meeting Day, every eligible voter with an opinion on any part of that year's agenda has the opportunity to speak his or her piece and cast a vote. This is politics in the revolutionary vein that first shaped the nation. Without the camouflage of cloakroom deals, press-conference equivocation or media hype, the Town Meeting is pure, simple democracy, out in the open and accessible to immediate response, whether praise or scorn. The signatures of only 10 voters are needed to place an issue on the agenda. It's not a very efficient system, but it is difficult to corrupt.

BELOW:
an old-fashioned
toboggan ride.

It's no surprise, then, that New Hampshire is something of an acid test for Presidential hopefuls. Most of the voters are amateur politicians themselves, and they are not easily fooled. They're also pretty accurate in anticipating the

nation's mood. Since its first primary in 1952, New Hampshire has picked the candidates nominated by both parties nine out of 10 times. In the great majority of the contested elections in the nation's history (George Washington ran unopposed), New Hampshire has voted for the winner.

Map on pages 246–7

All this hands-on governmental process both reflects and, no doubt, fosters the feistiness that is deeply ingrained in the state's collective temperament. New Hampshire has yet to institute a general sales tax or state income tax. Instead, it rather deviously allows outsiders to make sizable donations by deriving over half of its general-fund revenue from tax-free liquor sales, state-run gambling and other "sin taxes." New Hampshire's constitution retains (in its Bill of Rights) the right of revolution when "all other means of redress are ineffectual."

This is not to suggest that New Hampshire is a haven for rampant radicals. In fact, the state is decidedly right-of-center on most issues, yet fervently independent. Though predominantly Republican, New Hampshire has voted for Democratic presidential candidates about one-third of the time in recent decades. The Republican predominance is kept in check by a nearly equal (if not entirely opposite) force of registered Independents. Public opinion falls mostly between the two poles represented, on the one hand, by the arch-conservative viewpoint of the *Manchester Union-Leader*, which is distributed statewide and, on the other, by the more liberal *Concord Monitor*, which is not.

Yankee ingenuity

The rugged individualism which typifies the people of New Hampshire is intricately bound up in both their land and their history. The first settlers came not to escape religious or political pressures, as was the case in many of the other

BELOW: riding low.

ONE LIBERTY IS PROTECTED BY FOUR BOXES:
THE BALLOT BOX AND THE JURY BOX,
THE SOAP BOX AND THE CARTRIDGE BOX.

*"Our liberty is
protected by four
boxes: the ballot box,
the jury box, the
soap box and the
cartridge box."*

BELOW: shopping
the old way.

original colonies, but simply to have a little space in which to apply their Yankee ingenuity productively. They encountered and eventually subdued a land that was obstinate and rugged – with thin, "cold" soil, fresh crops of rock pushing through the surface each year, a forested wilderness that had to be cleared before settlements and farming were possible, and long, hard winters. The Indians, if initially welcoming, soon learned that the arrival of these foreigners was no blessing and began to retaliate.

The main assets of the region at the beginning of the colonial period were the deepwater port and surrounding shores of what is now Portsmouth; and the tall, straight pines, which became highly prized in the construction of ships. Fisheries established along the coast prospered from the sale of salt cod and other catches, hauled from the Atlantic as far north as the Grand Banks off Newfoundland.

The impetus behind these first forays was provided by Sir Ferdinando Gorges, head of the council established by King James to govern all of New England, and Captain John Mason, an early governor of Newfoundland. They obtained grants to an ill-defined territory lining the coast from the Naumkeag to the Sagadahock rivers and extending roughly 60 miles (100 km) inland. Gorges and Mason proposed a variety of commercial enterprises and promised healthy dividends to investors.The venture never really paid off. Lack of supplies limited the scheme's progress, the company eventually collapsed and the settlers simply divided the land up among themselves and proceeded to amass their own fortunes, without giving much thought to the niceties of property laws.

At first, relations with the Indians, primarily Abenakis and Pennacooks, were harmonious and mutually rewarding. In exchange for coats, shirts, kettles, and other goods, and in anticipation of assistance in repelling assaults by other tribes

Map on pages 246–7

and of a market for their furs, the Indians granted the settlers access to the land between the Piscataqua and Merrimack rivers, including the rich fishing bases of the Isles of Shoals. In principle, the Indians were to retain the right to hunt, fish, and farm in the area.

The original deal was reasonably fair to both parties. Soon, however, the settlers became more ambitious. They built dams that obstructed the migration of salmon along the rivers, introduced livestock that wandered into and consumed the Indians' crops, conducted lumbering operations that frightened off game, and clogged the waterways with sawdust from mills. Realizing they had been taken, the tribes of New England banded together in 1675 and unleashed "King Philip's War," named for Philip, chief of the Wampanoags. For one year, they raided settlements and garrisons, and the turmoil continued, on a lesser scale, for nearly a century.

Throughout this period, New Hampshire's commercial reputation and prosperity rested primarily on its supplies of mast pines. They were invaluable to the expanding fleets of England's merchant marine. The best of them were reserved solely for the use of the King, providing in due course one of many motives leading to the Revolution.

Soaring 150–200 ft (46–61 meters), and as much as 6 ft (2 meters) in diameter, the massive shafts of wood used for masts – up to 1,000 years old – required as many as 100 oxen to haul them from the forest.

Settlement and Revolution

Strong-willed settlers, gradually pushing their way inland from Portsmouth and up the Connecticut River from the south, laid claim first to the lush valleys, then to the harsher hillsides and finally to the forbidding mountains in the north. The first man to lend the colony some cohesion was John Wentworth, a prosperous merchant appointed by the King in 1717 to govern the province of New

BELOW: logging.

Hampshire. Though hardly an altruist (his land grants always reserved a portion for himself, a token 500 acres/250 hectares), he did begin the process – later carried on by his son and nephew – of stabilizing the province, encouraging settlement and promoting commerce. Largely through their enthusiasm for gracious living, the Wentworths helped transform Portsmouth into a genteel oasis, traces of which are still evident.

For most of the settlers, however, life was anything but genteel. When not warring with the Indians, they cleared land, produced crops without much help from either climate or terrain and, by sheer obstinance, endured. Matters were not improved by the unresponsiveness of their government, and when the Revolution came, New Hampshire joined early in the fight, moved not so much by political fervor as by a general acknowledgment that change could hardly be for the worse. Savvy in the ways of guerrilla warfare after a century of skirmishes with the Indians, New Hampshire's militia was particularly skilled at battle tactics, which the orderly British were ill-equipped to combat.

Despite its active involvement in all the major campaigns of the war, New Hampshire, alone of the 13 original colonies, was spared the task of fighting the British within its own boundaries.

Among its Revolutionary credits, New Hampshire was the first colony to assert its independence from England (establishing its own government on January 5, 1776) and the first to suggest the idea to the Continental Congress in Philadelphia (in 1775). Late in 1774, alarmed by an edict from the King forbidding the shipment of gunpowder to the colonies, and informed that a British ship was on the way to fortify Fort William and Mary near Portsmouth, 400 New Hampshire rebels invaded the garrison, locked up the British guard and stole 100 barrels of gunpowder, later used at Bunker Hill.

BELOW: many rural farms remain in the southern part of the state.

Following the Revolution, the people of New Hampshire went back to the task of coming to terms with their land. The push inland was by now extending up into the White Mountains, already rich with Native American myth and soon to generate new legends of the courageous settlers. Revolutionary fervor gave way to the more tiresome task of transferring high ideals to workable practice. Given the combination of a terrain ill-suited to plantation farming and an innate resistance to the idea of constraint, New Hampshire resolved the issue of slavery for itself by effectively abolishing it early in the 19th century. An unfortunate pragmatism, however, kept the only New Hampshire-born US president, Franklin Pierce, from advocating Abolition throughout the country. He argued that slavery was morally wrong, but that the issue should be decided by the states practicing it.

By the middle of that century, it was becoming evident that New Hampshire's weak soil and short summers could not support competitive agriculture. Farmland was abandoned as people moved West in hopes of greater success. Textile mills were established and logging operations continued, but the most notable shift in New Hampshire's economy resulted from the discovery that it possessed one asset that promised a good return for relatively little investment or labor: scenery.

Map
on pages
246–7

The summer people

By the 1850s, "summer people" were a well-established industry. Executives on holiday, retired librarians with a nest-egg set aside, and an assortment of temporary bohemians came to sit on farmhouse porches in rocking chairs, dine in the lavish resort hotels newly built in splendid surroundings, or hike the expanding network of trails through the hills and mountains. Others, professedly more serious in intent, came to paint, sculpt, or write. Among them were essayist Ralph Waldo Emerson, novelists Nathaniel Hawthorne and Willa Cather, sculptor Augustus Saint-Gaudens, and playwright Thornton Wilder.

Over the decades, the ranks of summer people have steadily swelled and spilled over into other seasons as well. Autumn draws connoisseurs of vibrant foliage which reaches its peak in early October to the north, then proceeds south. And New Hampshire's heavy snowfalls provide for superb skiing. The state boasts over a dozen ski areas; Cannon, Loon, Wildcat and Waterville Valley are among the largest, each with a vertical rise in excess of 2,000 ft (600 meters). Wildcat boasts cozy gondolas-for-two, and Cannon a roomy aerial tram; both run through the summer for sightseers.

New Hampshire's river, streams and lakes are kept well stocked with game fish: brook trout, smallmouth and largemouth bass, salmon, pickerel, perch, whitefish and shad, among others. Hunters – and, more often these days, photographers – track deer, hare and rabbit, porcupines, raccoons, gray squirrel, ruffed grouse, pheasant, and migratory birds. The lucky few might spot a lynx or wildcat.

In addition to the White Mountain National Forest (of which nearly 700,000 acres/283,000 hectares are situated in New Hampshire, roughly 40,000

BELOW:
covered bridges are found in most New England states.

COVERED BRIDGES

It is surmised that the covered bridges across waterways and railroads throughout New England were designed not to protect travelers from the region's brutal winters, but to insulate the bridges' wooden supports. Other theories hypothesize that horses were more comfortable crossing covered spans than open ones where they could see the water. Although the bridges were covered, people were employed to shovel snow on to the surface since most winter travel was by sled.

Covered bridges were originally made of wood, with sides supported by triangular trestles; hardwood "tree nails" held it together. Today's renovated bridges often have metal roofs. The nation's longest covered bridge connects Cornish, NH., and Windsor, VT., and is a National Historic Civil Engineering Landmark. New Hampshire's oldest bridge, built 1829, connects Bath and Haverhill on Route 135 over the Ammonoosuc River.

New Hampshire's bridges have been more fortunate than Maine's in that 54 have survived fire, floods, ice, and modern traffic. (In Maine, only nine of 120 remain.) Most have been patiently repaired. Although many are open to traffic, most cannot take trucks and are only one-lane. For the official state highway map, tel: 1-(800) 386 4664.

acres/16,000 hectares in Maine), there are 32 state parks in New Hampshire, with some 1,000 campgrounds in the 11 largest. Depending on location, these parks offer swimming, boating, fishing, cross-country and downhill skiing, snowmobiling, hiking, camping, and picnic facilities.

Local enterprise has also resulted in an impressive crop of roadside attractions – compact amusement parks, miniature golf courses, water slides and just about anything else that might possibly be termed "entertainment." Although not always in the best taste, and rarely sophisticated, they do at least ensure that no one can complain of a lack of activities, and most are fun.

A sliver of seacoast: Portsmouth

Portsmouth ⓴ – the state's major seaport, is the jewel at the northernmost edge of its narrow and otherwise predominantly drably developed 18-mile (28-km) coast. Standing at the mouth of the Piscataqua River, a superb natural harbour, the town is the nation's third oldest settlement (after Plymouth and Jamestown). The **Strawbery Banke Museum** (the English settlers named their 1623 colony for the profusion of wild strawberries that greeted them) is an ongoing restoration project that recaptures the look and feel, and some of the activities, of this old seaport neighborhood, encompassing over 40 buildings and covering 10 acres (4 hectares) (Marcy Street; open May–Oct and weekend after Thanksgiving daily; first two weekends in December 3:30–8:30pm; entrance fee; tel: 603-433 1100). A handful of restored and refurnished homes, ranging from humble to grand, illustrate changes in architectural style; the Drisco House has even retained 1950s features. Some feature displays of construction and restoration techniques; others await restoration.

BELOW: tugboats in Portsmouth harbor.

Several of the lesser abodes serve as workshops for artisans whose work harks back to the past: open on a revolving schedule, there are studios for a cabinet-maker, cooper, potter, and weaver. Here, also, one of the oldest boat shops in America continues to produce dories, skiffs, and other vessels, employing archaic copper clench nails. Strawbery Banke is literally an open-air museum: tours are self-guided and open-ended, permitting visitors to proceed at their own pace.

Several other worthy historic manses are scattered about this enchanting, compact town. Among these is the 1763 **Moffatt-Ladd House** (Market Street; mid-May–mid-Oct, Mon–Sat; Sun pm; entrance fee), an imposing three-story mansion topped with a captain's walk and graced with terraced English-style gardens, a splendid carved staircase, a Gilbert Stuart portrait and some choice examples of Portsmouth-made furniture – a flourishing craft in the 18th century. Seek out, too, the 1716 **Warner House** (Daniel Street; open mid-May–mid-Oct, Mon–Sat; Sun pm; entrance fee). America's first house to be registered as a National Historic Landmark back in 1962, it was the first of Portsmouth's many brick houses, and the stair hall is endowed with an intriguing array of early 18th-century murals. Rediscovered in 1852, they include depictions of Mohawk Indians and a British soldier on horseback.

Backroad scene.

Also well worth a visit is the Port of Portsmouth **Maritime Museum and Albacore Park** (Market Street; open daily; entrance fee). The *Albacore* is a grounded 1952 submarine, 205 feet (62 meters) long, which for two decades carried a crew of 55 in sardine-like quarters.

For a more pleasant experience on the water, consider a cruise to the **Isles of Shoals ④** 6 miles (9.5 km) offshore; "barren piles of rock" charted in 1614 by

BELOW: Strawbery Banke, Portsmouth.

Captain John Smith and long haunted by pirates and other nefarious outcasts. Improbably enough, an arts colony blossomed here at the turn of the century, after poet Celia Thaxter, the daughter of an innkeeper, created a miraculous garden on Appledore which inspired no fewer than 400 paintings by the noted American Impressionist Childe Hassam. Whale-watching trips are also on offer from Portsmouth.

The best of the rest of the coast comprises Great (or New Castle) Island, with its old forts and lighthouses, and **Odiorne Point State Park**, where a World War II fort stands amid extensive dunes.

The industrious Merrimack Valley

Driving north from Boston, the first site worth a detour off Interstate 93 (after it crosses the border into New Hampshire) may also be the oldest. **America's Stonehenge** in **North Salem ㊷** (Haverhill Road; open Mar–Nov, daily; July and Aug, till 7pm; call for Dec–Feb hours; entrance fee; tel: 603-893 8300), long known as "Mystery Hill," has purportedly been carbon-dated to about 2000 BC. Though considerably scaled down from its British namesake – its circle of standing stones measure only 3 ft (1 meter) tall – the site is thought to have served much the same purpose as Stonehenge: as a giant calendar tracing celestial movements.

Within the circle are a series of stone buildings and passageways, altars, walls, chambers, and carvings, which have been attributed, variously, to ancient Greeks, Phoenicians, Celts, and Native Americans, or more recent settlers of a mystical or perhaps mischievous bent – take your pick. The identity of the builders and the purpose the site served remain matters of pure speculation. Indeed, much of its charm derives from the fact that questions outnumber answers: your guess is as good as anyone's.

Further north on I-93 is **Manchester ㊸**, which together with Nashua and several other New Hampshire cities, served as centers of textile manufacturing, attracting large numbers of French-Canadian immigrants to work in the mills. Manchester retains the vast red-brick buildings of Amoskeag Mills and much of its French-Canadian legacy, including a large bilingual population and the nation's most comprehensive archives of material on French-speaking Canadians, L'Association Canado-Américaine, founded by a Manchester grocer in 1918. For a précis of local history, visit the Manchester Historical Association, three floors of old-fashioned exhibits spanning Indian relics to a Victorian parlor.

The **Currier Gallery of Art** (201 Myrtle Way; open Mon, Wed–Sun; Fri till 9pm; entrance fee; tel: 603-669 6144) features fine collections of European and American paintings, New England decorative arts, and contemporary crafts; it also offers modern architecture buffs access to the **Zimmerman House**, a 1950 design by Frank Lloyd Wright.

Some 15 miles (24 km) north of Manchester is **Concord ㊹**, where the gold-domed 1819 **State House** (the granite centerpiece was built by prisoners) is fronted by statues of New Hampshire's political

BELOW: a replica of the *Endeavour*, in Portsmouth, with an interpreter in period costume.

Map
on pages
246–7

luminaries – Daniel Webster, Franklin Pierce, General John Stark and others – striking imperial poses in bronze. Its Hall of Flags contains 88 Civil War standards carried into battle (North Main Street; open Mon–Fri).

Its entrance topped by a Daniel Chester French sculpture, the grand **Museum of New Hampshire History** houses the collections of the New Hampshire Historical Society, from furniture and folk art to tools and toys (Eagle Square off Main Street; open Tues–Sat; Tues till 8:30pm). Among the highlights is an original Concord Coach, the 19th-century vehicle known as "the coach that won the West." Also worth a visit is the **League of New Hampshire Craftsmen** gallery in North Main Street (New Hampshire was the first state officially to support its artisans, with the establishment of the New Hampshire Commission of Arts and Crafts in 1931), and the **Christa McAuliffe Planetarium**, dedicated to the New Hampshire teacher/astronaut who perished in 1986 in an explosion aboard the US's first civilian space shuttle (3 Institute Drive, New Hampshire Technical Institute; open Tues–Thurs; pm only Sat and Sun; entrance fee). A fitting tribute to her dream, this highly interactive museum claims to be the most advanced digital planetarium projection system in the world, capable of simulating space travel in three dimensions.

Located in its namesake town, about 17 miles (27 km) north of Concord, **Canterbury Shaker Village** ⓯ (Shaker Road off I–93; open May–Oct, daily; Apr, Nov, Dec, Fri–Sun; entrance fee; tel: 603-783 9511) is an eloquent testament to the ingenuity and gentle faith of the Shakers, one of the religious sects that sought asylum in the New World (*see pages 296–97*). The Shakers believed all should be made welcome, a commitment that continues today as docents, rather than family members, greet each visitor.

BELOW: Canterbury Shaker Village.

The 1½-hour tours of the Village provide a glimpse of the skill and faith of this remarkable community. Crafts on display (some reproductions of which are available for purchase) include basketry, tin-smithing, wood-working and "the sewing arts." In addition, there is the simple grandeur of Shaker architecture, a host of intriguing inventions and a restaurant offering Shaker specialties.

The Mount Monadnock region

More than one local booster is not keen on the marketing monicker "The Quiet Corner", often used for the southwestern corner of the state ("Might as well come right out and call it boring," grouses one). Crowned by **Mount Monadnock** ㊻, a rocky 3,165-ft (968-meter) peak whose 360° views attract record numbers of climbers (the ascent is surpassed in popularity only by Mount Fuji), this is a region of meandering back roads past prim white churches, innumerable antique stores, and historic inns.

In the former mill town of **New Ipswich** ㊼, **Forest Hall (the Barrett House)** of 1800 (Main Street; tours June–mid-Oct, weekends; entrance fee), maintained by the Society for the Preservation of New England Antiquities, is an elegant Federal-style building, erected as a wedding present for Charles Barrett and his bride by his father, and contains many original items, including portraits and musical instruments. It will be instantly familiar to some as the setting of the Merchant-Ivory film adaptation of Henry James's *The Europeans*. The terraced grounds rise to a Gothic Revival summerhouse.

The small town of Rindge hosts the 2,000-seat **Cathedral of the Pines** ㊽, an open-air war memorial chapel with a set of Norman Rockwell bas-reliefs. It began when the Sloane family planned a small chapel to their son, a bomber pilot who was killed in action in Germany in 1944, and later became an interdenominational place of worship and a national memorial. Every President since Truman sent a stone to built the altar, which is backed by a view of Mount Monadnock.

Peterborough, home to the McDowell Colony, the country's most prestigious artists' retreat, inspired Thornton Wilder's famous play, *Our Town*. The **Peterborough Historical Society and Museum** contains intriguing relics and photographs, as well as two mill houses and an early general store (Grove Street; open pm only weekdays; entrance fee).

Bucolic **Harrisville** ㊾ has perfectly preserved its 19th-century mill-town mien; a self-guided tour of its beautifully proportioned brick buildings (one is now a renowned weaving center) is a lovely way to travel back in time. The region's largest town is **Keene** ㊿, where manufacturing companies flourished at the turn of the 19th century. It is said to have the widest street in America.

Along the Connecticut River valley

In **Charlestown** ㈤, about 22 miles (35 km) northwest of Keene, the **Fort at Number 4** recreates a 1746 settlement which, in its day, was the northernmost frontier of colonization (Route 11 West; open late May–mid-Oct, Wed–Mon; weekends only first two weeks of Sept; entrance fee). Within its stockade,

interpreters demonstrate such crafts as candle-dipping, weaving and the molding of musket balls and, at certain dates, re-enact skirmishes.

Some 10 miles (16 km) farther north, in Cornish, is the **Saint-Gaudens National Historic Site** – the summer residence, garden and studios of Augustus Saint-Gaudens, one of America's most celebrated classical sculptors (off Route 12A; open May–Oct, daily; entrance fee; tel: 603-675 2175).

Another 15 miles (24 km) north is **Hanover** ⦿, home of Dartmouth College. One of the bastions of Ivy League tradition (*see page 217*), Dartmouth was founded in 1769, primarily for "the education and instruction of youth of the Indian tribes in this land." The college retains much of its colonial appearance while accommodating such modern touches as the **Hood Museum of Art**, with galleries spanning many cultures over the centuries, and the Hopkins Center, with an impressive performing arts roster (Wheelock Street; open Tues–Sat; Wed till 9pm; Sun pm). Hanover is very much a college town, and for that very reason full of interesting shops and restaurants.

Across the river in Norwich (Vermont), the wonderful **Montshire Museum of Science** – a hit with children – addresses the whys of natural processes to all ages (Montshire Road; open daily; entrance fee). For the extraordinary sight of a row of magnificent Charles Bulfinch mansions, it's worth pressing on to Orford.

The Lakes Region

At the center of the state, north of Concord, is New Hampshire's "Lakes Region," where **Lake Winnipesaukee** ⦿ sprawls in convoluted splendor with 183 miles (294 km) of shoreline and 274 islands, the centerpiece of a cluster of

The schools of Dartmouth College include the undergraduate college, the medical school (1797), the Thayer School of Civil Engineering (1867), and the Amos Tuck School of Business Administration (1900).

BELOW: a Dartmouth College, Hanover.

Flights over Lake Winnipesaukee.

lakes and ponds scattered among rolling hills. According to legend, Winnipesaukee means "the smile of the Great Spirit," the name given to it by Chief Wonotan on the occasion of his daughter's marriage to a young chief from a hostile tribe. Wonotan regarded the overcast sky on their wedding day as a bad omen but, just as the two lovers were departing, the sun broke through the clouds and sparkled over the lake.

Weirs Beach ⑤ (named for the weirs, or fishnets, which Indians once stretched across a narrow channel there) brings a touch of Atlantic City to Winnipesaukee's western shore, with its boardwalk, arcade, marina, and elaborate miniature-golf links. Other attractions include two water-slide parks and cruises on the MS *Mount Washington*.

Wolfeboro ⑤, on the eastern side, can lay claim to being the oldest summer colony in the nation. In 1769, John Wentworth, the last of New Hampshire's colonial governors, built a summer home here, and comfortable old money has been following his example ever since; a stroll around reveals a wealth of architectural styles, including Georgian, Federal, Greek Revival, and Second Empire.

On South Main Street the **Wolfeboro Historical Society** maintains the 1778 **Clark House**, a 19th-century firehouse and an 1820 schoolhouse (open July–Aug Mon–Sat). In nearby Wakefield, two sisters who are inveterate doll collectors have opened an appealing **Museum of Childhood**, complete with an 1890s schoolroom (off Route 16; open May–Oct, Mon, Wed–Sat; Sun pm; entrance fee).

Looking down over the lake from the north, the **Castle in the Clouds** ⑤, near Moultonboro, stands as an imposing monument to one man's rather megalomaniacal vision of a tranquil idyll. Built in an inventive amalgam of styles by eccentric millionaire Thomas Gustave Plant, this 1910 mansion is set in a 5,200-acre (2,100-hectare) estate with waterfalls, ponds, streams, miles of forest trails, and magnificent views out over the surrounding countryside.

Moultonboro, and other towns north of the lake, offer a refreshing respite from the commercialism that has claimed the western shore. Particularly pretty is the predominantly early 19th-century village of **Center Sandwich** ⑤, with several appealing crafts and antique shops.

About 8 miles (13 km) southwest, a visit to the **Science Center of New Hampshire** ⑤ is sure to intrigue: exhibits include a nature preserve for injured animals unable to survive in the wild (Routes 113 and 25; open May–Oct daily; entrance fee). Here's a rare opportunity to observe bears, owls, perhaps even a bobcat; there is a ¼-mile (1-km) trail with wheelchair access, and live animal demonstrations with a naturalist. Squam Lake, where *On Golden Pond* was filmed, is famed for its loons.

Lake Sunapee ⑥, finely set beneath the hills, has a small sandy beach by shallow water, and is popular for canoeing, windsurfing and picnicking. Mount Sunapee State Park includes the ski area, with a chair-lift open year round taking you up to the summit, from where a short trail makes the most of the views across to Mount Washington and other points some 75 miles

BELOW: the Baptist Meeting House Cemetery, Center Sandwich.

(135 km) distance. The League of New Hampshire Craftsmen holds its August fair at the base of the lift.

Map on pages 246–7

The White Mountains

Continuing north, travelers now begin their ascent into the **White Mountain National Forest**, a vast tract encompassing the Franconia Range, clustered along an east-to-west axis, and the Presidentials, running northeast and culminating in New England's tallest peak, Mount Washington. Long a forbidding wilderness, the White Mountains have evolved into an enormously popular region, with an ambience as distinct as the landscape.

Here, hikers can enjoy the serenity of seemingly endless stretches of untrammeled (though no longer quite so forbidding) nature. The region also supports a thriving tourist industry, contained – by law and convenience – in pockets along the major highways. All the rest is reserved (and preserved) for backwoods purists.

A typical trail will lead from a parking lot along the highway directly into the forest, over gradually inclining terrain, maybe taking in a viewpoint or waterfall. Trails are well marked, with color-coded blazes cut into tree trunks at regular intervals, so there's little risk of taking a wrong turn. Eventually, towering trees give way to twisted dwarf pines and lichen-encrusted boulders. Above the tree line are the summits, from which adventurers may gaze down over the world spread at their feet, savoring that peculiar sense of accomplishment that comes from finding oneself on top of the world.

Most of these peaks are not, for all their massive beauty, too demanding. Many summits can be reached with an hour or so of fairly leisurely walking.

Boat tours can be taken on Squam Lake, the setting for the movie On Golden Pond.

BELOW: tranquil scene in the White Mountains.

One of the most rewarding excursions (in terms of view obtained relative to energy expended) is the short (45-minute) romp up Mount Willard, along an old bridle path. Those reaching the summit are rewarded with a magnificent panorama of **Crawford Notch** – particularly splendid at sunrise.

There are too many trails – some 1,200 miles (1,900 km) all told – to attempt even a partial description here; the White Mountain National Forest offices (various locations in the area) and the Appalachian Mountain Club at Pinkham Notch can provide further information. The AMC also maintains a network of "huts" (some are fairly large) offering bunk lodgings and hearty meals; they're often booked up months in advance, so reserve well ahead (tel: 603-466 2727). The AMC's White Mountain Guide is the "walker's bible."

For enjoying the scenery from the car, however, the **Kancamagus Highway ⏥** (Route 112), is hard to beat, and passes numerous trailheads offering anything from short strolls through the forest to major upland hikes. Seek out especially the signed overlooks at the western end (notably Kancamagus, Pemi and Hancock); views are at their best when the fall foliage reaches its most brilliant phase, but then you may find the traffic nose to bumper. Worthwhile short walks include the Champney Falls Trail and the Boulder Loop Trail, while pleasant roadside stopping picnic areas are at Rocky Gorge and Sabbaday Falls.

Continue through **North Woodstock** on Route 12 for the pay booth for **Lost River ⏥**, where a river disappears through a labyrinth of boulder caves and re-emerges. A slow-going trail leads through this remarkable place, discovered by two brothers out fishing when one of them fell into a cave.

Just off I-93 north of **Lincoln** and somewhat easier on the feet, **The**

BELOW: in the White Mountains.

Flume , an 800-ft (243-meter) gorge with granite walls attaining 90 ft (27 meters) and ending at a waterfall, was reportedly discovered in 1803 by 93-year-old Aunt Jess Guernsey, who happened upon it while out fishing. Unfortunately, it's no longer quite as she found it – viewing platforms have been added to accommodate the busloads of sightseers – but some hint of the awe this natural wonder must have inspired remains (open May–Oct, daily; entrance fee). Off the main path is the Pool, another fine waterfall. In winter the wooden walkways are dismantled as the ice forms a massive layer.

Map on pages 246–7

Northward, pull into the parking lot at Profile Lake for a glimpse of the **Old Man of the Mountains** . Noteworthy not so much for its size – it measures 40 ft (12 meters) from top to bottom – as for the fine detailing of its features, the Old Man has generated a sense of reverence over the years. The jutting brow, regal nose, lips slightly pursed as if in meditation and sharp line of the bearded chin all conspire to produce not merely a likeness, but a real sense of character. As Nathaniel Hawthorne described it in his story *The Great Stone Face*: "all the features were noble, and the expression was at once grand and sweet, as if it were the glow of a vast, warm heart, that embraced all mankind in its affection, and had room for more."

The Robert Frost mailbox.

Though credit for its discovery has been ascribed, rather presumptuously, to a road-survey team in 1805, no doubt the region's Indians were acquainted with the Old Man long before then. According to some sources, they saw in it the features of Manitou, the Great Spirit, and reserved for their chiefs the right to view it – and, even for them, only in times of crisis. Legend has it that the face was not always as stern as it now appears, but became so through sorrow over the conflicts and cruelty of the human race.

BELOW: the Old Man of the Mountains.

Directly to the north is **Cannon Mountain** ski area (named for a cannon-shaped rock perched on its ridge; tel: 603-823 5563). An easy year-round means of ascent is offered by the **Aerial Tramway** (a 1980 replacement for the 1938 original) at its base (fee), rising above the timberline and offering a short trail at the summit. Also located here is the **New England Ski Museum**, with historical paraphernalia (such as hand-crafted wooden skis from the 19th century) and various audio-visual exhibits (open Dec–Apr, Thurs–Tues; May–Oct, daily pm only).

Two classic villages await the visitor just past Franconia Notch. **Franconia** was home to poet Robert Frost in 1915–20, where he "farmed a little, taught a little and wrote a lot." Looking out towards his favorite three New Hampshire mountains, the modest **Robert Frost Place** ("R. Frost" still marks the mailbox on Route 116) preserves manuscripts and other assorted memorabilia and hosts a changing roster of worthy successor poets who are amenable to giving readings (Ridge Road, May–Oct Wed–Mon pm; entrance fee).

The small town of **Sugar Hill** , once a magnet for summer manses, is a mecca for maple-lovers. **The Sugar Hill Historical Museum** (Route 117; open July–mid-Oct pm only Thurs, Sat, Sun; entrance fee) contains relics of 19th-century resort life, but most of those who flock here come to feast on

unlimited "seconds" at **Polly's Pancake Parlor**, which produces its own maple syrup (Route 117).

A few miles north of Franconia, US 302 veers eastward, through another handsome town, **Bethlehem** (full of dazzling summer homes, some turned B&B), and southeast toward Bretton Woods, nestled on the western flank of magnificent Mount Washington.

An "awful" peak

Nathaniel Hawthorne (who played an important role in promoting and preserving the region) accurately pointed out that the White Mountains, and particularly the Presidential Range, are "majestic, and even awful, when contemplated in a proper mood, yet by their breadth of base and the long ridges which support them, give the idea of immense bulk rather than of towering height." **Mount Washington** ⓭, at 6,288 ft (1,197 meters), is high enough to qualify as the tallest summit north of the Carolinas and east of the Rockies, and its sheer bulk is impressive, at least from the bottom, but to really appreciate its height, one must tackle the peak.

There are three ways to "climb" Mount Washington: on foot, by car (from Gorham, on the eastern side), or by train. The first option is, of course, the preference of outdoors enthusiasts, but the ascent is not easy and, even in summer, can be extremely dangerous, even deadly. A spectacular and very popular approach is from Pinkham Notch, taking in Tuckerman's Ravine; be sure to ask at the Appalachian Mountain Club headquarters (tel: 603-466 2727) at Pinkham Notch about conditions before setting out. The summit bears several chilling markers commemorating those who, like 23-year-old Lizzie Bourne in

BELOW: Polly's Pancake Parlor.

September 1855, died of exposure only a few hundred yards from the top. The destination she sought, a rustic hotel called the Tip Top House, survives as a small museum; visitors can marvel at the cramped dormitories, where travelers bunked down on crude beds cushioned with moss.

Climatically, the summit is classified as arctic. Its topographic isolation results in alarmingly abrupt changes in weather, including blizzards even in summer. The highest-velocity winds ever recorded – 231 miles (372 km) an hour – were measured here in 1934, and some of the buildings that are part of a weather observatory (founded in 1932) are tethered to keep them from blowing away.

Visitors have access to the Sherman Adams Summit Building, surrounded by a deck with 70-mile (112-km) views, and within it the small but fascinating **Mount Washington Observatory Museum**, which focuses on mountaineering history and on the summit's unusual ecology.

On the east side of Mount Washington it's possible to drive up – provided your car's in fighting trim. The 8-mile (13-km) climb up the **Mount Washington Auto Road**, via endless switchbacks, can be hell on radiators, the return journey tough on the best of brakes (off Route 16; open mid-May–mid-Oct, weather permitting; daily in summer 7:30am–6pm; shorter hours in spring and fall; entrance fee; tel: 603-466 2222). For those who'd rather spare their vehicles the ordeal (and forgo the campy "This Car Climbed Mount Washington" bumper-sticker), there's also a van shuttle service from the base.

Alternatively you can reach the summit by the remarkable 1869 **Cog Railway** ⑩, a testament to American ingenuity in the pursuit of diversion (Route 302; June–Oct, daily; tel: 603-846 5404). The train serves no more noble purpose than that of carting tourists 3½ miles (5.5 km) up and down the

Map on pages 246–7

BELOW: Mount Washington Cog Railway.

The Fall

One of the most revered rituals of New England life is "leaf-peeping" – driving to see the green leaves of summer turn to vivid shades of orange, yellow and red each fall. Droves of dedicated leaf-peepers come by the car and busload from all over the US and the world (advance reservations at inns and even restaurants are essential during October). In the far northern parts of the region, the leaves usually start turning mid-September, farther south a little later; by the end of October, the show is pretty much over.

New Hampshire and Vermont are most often linked with great foliage, but all six states have favored routes for colorful fall vistas. The advantage the northern states have is their mountains: From certain routes through the Green or White Mountains (a misnomer in fall!), the views across valleys to neighboring peaks can be breathtaking.

Each New England state has a toll-free foliage hotline telephone number. There's

even a Maine "leaf lady" whose Web page contains frequently updated photos of the show (access the page through the state's website at www.visitmaine.com).

By trying too hard to pinpoint the absolute peak of foliage, however, you risk missing the majesty of the leaf-changing phenomenon: If you're lucky enough to be in New England in October, you're sure to see peak foliage somewhere, because each tree changes its color according to an inner timetable that's affected by moisture, temperature, and the shorter days of fall. Botanists call the color change "leaf senescence" – the process by which the green pigment chlorophyll is drawn back into the tree to nourish it, permitting other, brighter pigments in the leaves to shine through. Brightest of all are red swamp maples and sumac. Aspen and birch turn yellow, sugar maples a peachy orange.

While it can be fun to drive back roads in search of great fall color, interstates often have the best foliage. Designed to cut through swaths of forest bypassing populated areas, I-95, for example, offers some of Maine's best leaf-peeping in the 75-mile (120-km) stretch from Augusta to Bangor. Similarly, in Connecticut, I-95, from Danielson to Waterford, always puts on a fine leaf show.

Almost any highway route designated as "scenic" on a state map will yield bountiful leaf color. In Massachusetts, one of the best foliage drives is westward along the Mohawk Trail (Route 2, Greenfield to Williamstown) in the northwestern corner of the state. Turn north on Route 7 into Vermont, then east on Route 9 and south on I-91 for an exceptionally pretty loop tour.

New Hampshire's mountains and lakes make it particularly appealing. A 340-mile (550-km) mid-state tour that takes in a little bit of mountain and lake begins at the Massachusetts border on I-93. Take Exit 24 to reach Route 3 south to Route 113 east to Route 16 north. At the Kancamagus Highway (Route 112), go west through the White Mountains National Forest back to I-93.

Foliage hot-line numbers – New Hampshire: 1-800-258 3608; Vermont: 1–800-837 6668; Massachusetts: 1-800-227 6277; Maine: 1-888-624 6345. ❑

LEFT: tupelo leaves and white pine needles.

mountain, but it does so with an admirable inventiveness. The average grade is 25 percent, the steepest 37.4. Relying on a failsafe rack-and-pinion system, the railroad was devised by Sylvester March, a local inventor who hoped to capitalize on the tourist trade attracted to the mountain. He obtained a charter to build the railroad from skeptical Concord legislators (they offered him the right to extend it all the way to the moon) and completed it in three years. It was the first railroad of its kind and has since been emulated, though outdone only once by an even steeper version in the Swiss Alps.

Just beyond the access road to the Cog Railway stands one of the few remaining symbols of New Hampshire's heyday as the home of numerous luxury resorts. Its genteel grandeur still intact, the colossal **Mount Washington Hotel**, which opened in 1902, continues to welcome well-heeled visitors in a manner to which most people could all too easily become accustomed.

Circled by a 900-ft (274-meter) veranda set with white-wicker chairs, and topped with red-tiled turrets, this elongated white-stucco wedding-cake contains some 174 rooms (many marked with plaques commemorating famous former residents) and a voluminous lobby with 23-ft (7-meter) ceilings supported by nine sets of columns and illumined with crystal chandeliers. Without leaving the hotel grounds, guests can enjoy golf (on an 18-hole PGA course), swimming (indoor or out), tennis (12 clay courts), and horseback riding. Though the lovely formal dining room has yet to catch up with an admittedly trend-crazy age, diners can at least console themselves with the thought that, because of the room's intentionally octagonal design, they'll never be relegated to a corner table. And with a band playing throughout the dinner hour, they can work in some dancing as well.

Map on pages 246–7

In the glorious age of the grand hotel, resorts such as the Mount Washington Hotel and the Balsams (see page 295) often had private rail lines. Their wealthy guests would arrive for the season, complete with entourage of servants, in their own rail carriages.

BELOW: Mount Washington Hotel.

Cradle of tourism

From Bretton Woods, US 302 cuts south through **Crawford Notch** , a narrow pass named for two notable early entrepreneurs. The notch was "discovered" in 1771 (more or less accidentally) by Timothy Nash, who was tracking a moose at the time. When Nash informed Governor Wentworth of his discovery, the disbelieving governor offered to grant him a tract of land including the notch if Nash could bring a horse through it and present the animal, intact, at Portsmouth; he was even willing to provide the horse. Nash met the challenge – incidentally opening up the White Hills (as the mountains were then called) to a steady influx of settlers, and eventually tourists.

Among the first to anticipate and capitalize on the area's potential were Abel Crawford and his son, Ethan Allen Crawford. They blazed the first path to the summit of Mount Washington (in 1819), advertised both it and their services as tour guides and established inns to accommodate their clients and other travelers – thereby masterminding the White Mountains' debut as a tourist attraction. Both men were as rugged as the mountains. In his 80s, Abel is said to have hiked five mountainous miles each morning to his son's house for breakfast. He was 75 when he made the first ascent of Mount Washington on horseback. Known as the "Giant of the Hills" – he was nearly 7 feet (2.1 meters) tall – Ethan was fond of wrestling bears and lynx and could carry a live buck home on his shoulders.

Just up the road from Jackson is **Pinkham Notch**, home to the pristine Wildcat ski area, set amid national forest (the gondola welcomes sightseers), and opposite it, the Appalachian Mountain Club's **Pinkham Notch Visitor Center**, which offers lodgings, workshops, and trail information (tel: 603/466 2727).

BELOW:
winter scene.

Map on pages 246-7

Every spring, skilled skiers make the arduous pilgrimage to shoot the headwall at Tuckerman's Ravine, a natural snow bowl affording a precipitous descent; others climb up just to watch.

On Route 16 is the "cross-country capital" of **Jackson 72**, which communally maintains a 90-mile (150-km) network of trails. Its many delightful restaurants are just as appealing in summer, and **Jackson Falls**, a series of cascades trickling toward town past glacial "potholes," decidedly more so. Young children might enjoy a stopover at **Story Land** in **Glen 73**, a small-scale amusement park guaranteed to delight the 10-and-under set (Route 16; open mid-June–Labor Day, daily; Labor Day–Columbus Day weekends; entrance fee).

Reached off West Side Road (itself a useful way of avoiding the jams in North Conway, leaving the Kancamagus Highway as Dugway Road, and joining Route 302 just east of Attitash Bear Peak), by a road climbing up west of North Conway, **Cathedral Ledge 74** is a vertigo-inducing rock-climbers' cliff high above Echo Lake (not to be confused with the other Echo Lake by Franconia Notch). **Attitash Bear Peak 75** has extensive snow-making in winter, but in summer you can mountain bike or take the Alpine slide (summer, daily; late May–mid-June, early Sept–early Oct, weekends; entrance fee).

The bustling town of **North Conway 76** is doing its best to steal some of the mountains' thunder – an odd amalgam of historic structures, rather tacky modern "resorts," and discount outlets. One reason to venture into town is to take a 1-hour, 11-mile (18-km) journey on the vintage **Conway Scenic Railway**, based at an 1874 Victorian railroad station in the center of town (Routes 16 and 302; open May–Oct, daily; Apr, Nov–Dec, weekends; entrance fee; tel: 603-356 5251 or 800-232 5251).

TIP

North Conway's outlet shops are especially attractive because New Hampshire has no sales tax. Be warned that this commercial strip is prone to bottlenecks.

BELOW: cutting strawberries in Franconia.

The North Country

This isolated, sparsely populated region is one of New Hampshire's better-kept secrets. The landscape is as stunning as any in the state, if less than inviting during the long months of winter. Vast stretches of forest cover most of the region and provide its primary industry – logging. A lacework of lakes, rivers, ponds, and streams offers a delicate counterpoint to the craggy hills and mountains. It is up here that the Connecticut River has its source, in a string of lakes just a few miles from the northern tip of the state, in a corner so out of the way that its allegiance was not decided, nor its boundary with Canada fixed (and then, by force), until 1840.

There is one grand old resort up here: **The Balsams** at **Dixville Notch 77**, a sprawling 1866 establishment with some 233 rooms and recreational facilities (golf, tennis, skiing, trout-fishing, canoeing, riding) spread over an area the size of Manhattan Island; it even has its own small ski area. Not the least among its appeals are the groaning buffets set out three times a day.

From here northward to Canada, it's a world of forest, water, scattered hunting camps and occasional towns hugging quiet highways, a world well suited to an exploring spirit. Those prepared to explore an environment such as this one don't need a guide to tell them how to go about it. ❑

THE SHAKERS

*These disciplined people were famous for their
unique way of life, their manner of worship, and a
craftsmanship that permanently influenced design*

The Shakers aimed
for perfection in
life. Devoted to
orderliness and
simplicity, they
were also dedicated
to such progressive
notions as sexual
equality (facilities for men and women were
identical and jobs were shared on a rota), and
they welcomed technological advances that might
improve the quality of their work. They were
inventors (of, for instance, the circular saw and
clothes pegs). They ran model farms and, as keen
gardeners, were the first to packet and sell seeds;
they also marketed medicinal herbs. They sold
their meticulously crafted baskets, boxes, chairs
and textiles. By blending discipline, business
acumen, ingenuity and superb craftsmanship, they
achieved prosperity, both spiritual and financial.

Celibacy was a key principle, but the ranks
were swelled by converts, and orphans were
adopted, Numbers dwindled after the mid-1800s,
however, and today just a handful of "Believers"
remain, in Sabbathday Lake, Maine. The Shaker
ideals of simplicity and practicality live on,
however, in a legacy of architecture, furniture and
crafts. The villages at Canterbury, NH, and
Hancock, Mass., are preserved as museums,
where visitors watch craftsmen make baskets,
boxes and chairs in the Shaker manner. In the
Dwelling Houses (above, at Hancock) they can
see the efficient kitchens, the wall pegs on which
chairs and utensils were hung, and the built-in
cupboards (so no dust
could accumulate on top
or underneath).

▽ **THE ROUND BARN**
Envied by many, the round
barn at Hancock, Mass.,
was a large one, built not
only for its efficiency, but as
a status symbol.

▷ **THE LADDERBACK**
These light but sturdy
chairs were made for
Believers by the thousand.
The woven-tape seat was
a Shaker innovation.

▷ **THE SHAKER BOX**
Shakers did not make
anything unless it served a
purpose. Oval boxes of
every size, with distinctive
"swallowtail" joints, stored
household goods.

THE VISION OF MOTHER ANN LEE

The founder of the Shakers was Ann Lee, born in 1736 in Manchester, England. An illiterate factory-worker, she was a woman of deep convictions at a time of religious persecution. She became the spritual leader of a group of dissidents from the Anglican Church called the "Shaking Quakers" because of the movements they made as the holy spirit took hold of them. Persecuted and sent to jail, she had a vision that she had a mission to teach a new way of life, one where men and women were equal, free from lust, greed and violence, with their lives governed by material and spiritual simplicity. She was convinced that only through celibacy could men and women further Christ's kingdom on Earth. After a second vision, she and eight followers set sail for New York in 1770. It was not until the 1780s, however, that converts were attracted in great numbers. Mother Ann died in 1783, soon after a prosetylizing tour of New England and before the full flowering of Shakerism. At its peak in the 1840s, 6,000 members lived in 19 communities.

△ **SONG AND DANCE**
The Shaker dance was an integral part of worship, instituted as an ordered alternative to the whirlings and tremblings of the early Believers (above). Brothers and sisters danced in perfect unison to the sound of song. In time, thousands of songs were composed, many under divine inspiration.

▷ **COMMUNAL DINING**
The Hancock dining room: believers ate at fixed times, in silence, with men and women at separate tables.

MAINE

Maine is a land of jagged coastlines and vast pine woods, of remote peninsulas, fresh lobster and famed outlet shops – a state inimitably evoked in the soft canvases of Winslow Homer

Even by New England standards, Maine – beyond its heavily trafficked southern coast – remains a mysterious wilderness. Larger in area than the other five New England states combined, but less populous than any one of them, the "Pine Tree State" (nine-tenths of it are covered with forest) bears little resemblance to its comfortably settled neighbors. Winters here can be an endurance test: some joke that Maine has only two seasons, winter and July.

It's little wonder, then, that residents pride themselves on their rugged independence and turn a bemused eye on the strange habits of "summer people" – or "rusticators," as they're sometimes still called. The term dates back to the late 19th century, when the first brave tourists came to reconnoiter this uncharted territory.

Henry David Thoreau explored the Mount Katahdin region in 1846 and came back raving about its savage beauty. "What is most striking in the Maine wilderness is the continuousness of the forest," he mused in Katahdin. "It is even more grim and wild than you had anticipated, a damp and intricate wilderness." Despite the inroads of civilization, vast stretches still fit the description, offering nature-lovers of a Thoreauvian bent the opportunity truly to get away from it all.

For those who prefer to encounter nature on their own terms, with a certain modicum of creature comforts, old-fashioned "camps" are still scattered along remote lakes interspersed among rugged mountains. Long prized by skilled canoeists and kayakers, Maine's wild waterways have been harnessed for the sport of whitewater river rafting. The ocean waters may prove too chilly for all but the most stalwart of swimmers, but sailboats, including majestic restored windjammers, ply the crenulated coastline – only 400 miles (640 km) as the gull flies, but 3,500 miles (5,600 km) if all the coves, inlets, and peninsulas were magically ironed out.

Drowned valleys and Red Paint

Traditionally, the Maine coastline has been the focus of the state's commercial and cultural activity. Geologists refer to it as a "drowned" coastline: the original coast sank thousands of years ago, its valleys becoming Maine's harbors, its mountains the hundreds of islands that cling to the shoreline from the New Hampshire border to New Brunswick, Canada. While the coastline was sinking, receding glaciers exposed vast expanses of granite, which not only gave Maine's mountains their peculiar pink coloration, but provided settlers with a valuable source of building material.

The first known residents, 11,000 years ago, were paleolithic hunters and fishers who lived along the

PRECEDING PAGES: Portland Head Light. **LEFT AND BELOW:** lobstering.

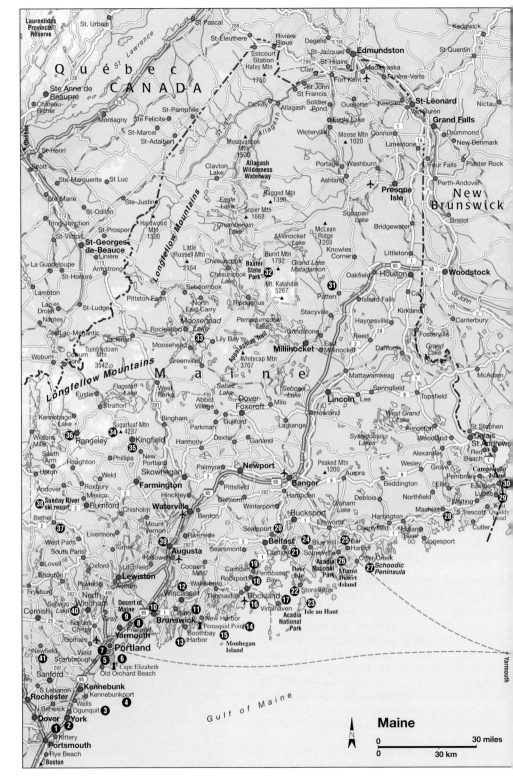

Maine

Map on page 302

coast. Other tribes followed, including a race known as the Red Paint People because lumps of red ocher (powdered hematite), thought to have been part of a religious sacrament, have been found in their grave sites. The earliest European explorers, in the 15th and 16th centuries, were greeted by the Abenaki tribe, whose name means "easterners" or "dawnlanders."

John Cabot visited Maine in 1497–99 (his explorations established all future British claims to the land), but it wasn't until after Captain John Smith sounded "about 25 excellent harbors" in 1614 that the "Father of Maine," Sir Ferdinando Gorges, was granted a charter to establish British colonies. Rival French explorers also claimed parts of Maine and Canada, and territorial disputes eventually led to the French and Indian Wars of the 18th century. Maine became a part of the Commonwealth of Massachusetts and remained so until 1820, when it became, as residents still like to call it, the State of Maine.

Maine's coast has been much battered by the sea. On the map it extends only 228 miles (367 km) as the seagull flies, but it has been calculated than anyone walking the length of its indented shore would have to tramp nearly 3,500 miles (5,600 km).

The South Coast

The best way to see Maine is to start at the southern tip and head northeast along the old coastal highway, US 1. (I-95 is bigger and faster, for those who have a specific destination in mind, but utterly lacking in scenery.) Although, geographically, the coast represents only a tiny fraction of the state, 45 percent of Maine residents call it home, and the overwhelming majority of visitors to "Vacationland" (Maine's license plate slogan) are also headed for the shore.

The southernmost segment, extending from Kittery to Freeport, attracted the earliest settlers and to this day is the most heavily traveled, blending historic enclaves with built-up beaches and discount shopping malls. Just across the New Hampshire border from Portsmouth, is **Kittery ❶**, where **Portsmouth**

BELOW: Long Sands Beach, York, on the South Coast.

Navy Yard – the nation's first, founded in 1806 – is still active; the **Kittery Historical and Naval Museum** (Routes 1 and 26; open June–mid-Oct, Tues–Sat; entrance fee) documents the shipyard's history, from the construction of *Ranger* (the first ship ever to fly the Stars and Stripes, under the command of John Paul Jones) to a more recent focus on submarines. Nearby **Fort McClary** was first fortified in 1715 and rebuilt repeatedly right up until the 1898 Spanish-American War. All that remains is the 1844 hexagonal wooden blockhouse, and the granite seawall – a scenic vantage point from which to view racing yachts in Portsmouth Harbor.

York ❷ was a center of dissent during the Revolutionary era. The local chapter of the Sons of Liberty decided to hold their own tea party when a British ship carrying tea anchored in **York Harbor**. Being Mainers, however, they were much too practical to waste all that good tea by dumping it in the harbor – they hijacked it instead.

The Yorks epitomize that odd blend of historical preservation and beach-oriented tourism typical of the lower Maine coast. The **Old York Historical Society** (York Street; open mid-June–mid-Oct, Tues–Sat; Sun, pm; off–season by appointment; entrance fee) maintains seven historic buildings, including the **John Hancock Warehouse** (a contemporary wrote that the signer of the Declaration of Independence was "more successful in politics than in business"), the 1759 **Jefferds Tavern** and the **Old Gaol**, built in 1719, thought to be the oldest public building in the US. With its 2-ft (60-cm) thick fieldstone walls and tiny windows bordered with sawteeth, the jail served its purpose right up until 1860. It has now been restored to its 1790s appearance, complete with dungeon. The **Elizabeth Perkins House** is a prime example of Colonial revivalism,

BELOW: John Hancock Warehouse and wharf, York.

Map on page 302

an 18th-century farmhouse lovingly adapted by the Perkins, a family that was proud of its New England roots, in the early 20th century.

The other side of York, physically and philosophically, is **York Beach**, a narrow mile-long strip of fine sand, lined with every imaginable type of fast-seafood shack and family-entertainment facility. The Cliff Walk off York Harbor's boardwalk affords beautiful views of the coastline, and of Cape Neddick's 1879 **Nubble Light**.

To the north is Perkins Cove, a quaint fishing village that is now part of **Ogunquit ❸** (whose Indian name meant "beautiful place by the sea"); its 3-mile (5-km) beach is a big draw. Boston painter Charles Woodbury "discovered" the area in the late 19th century, and the word soon spread to other artists, including Edward Hopper and Maurice Prendergast. Where the artists wandered, the gentry soon followed. Today, tourists crowd the countless small galleries and eateries that have taken over the fishing shacks. The **Ogunquit Museum of American Art** (Shore Road; open July–Sept, Mon–Sat; Sun, pm; entrance fee) displays locally produced work, including a sampling by such renowned summer residents as Reginald Marsh. **Marginal Way**, a 1-mile (1.6-km) seaside walk along the cliff is still quite scenic, in spite of its popularity.

Ogunquit itself is a bustling summer colony so thronged with visitors that a quartet of reproduction trolleys offer the easiest way to get around (parking is tight). On fine summer days, the magnet is the 2½-mile (4-km) beach. Night spots abound, and a perennial pleaser is the **Ogunquit Playhouse**, a highly regarded straw-hat theater founded in 1933; Tallulah Bankhead, Bette Davis, and Helen Hayes all trod these boards (Route 1; late June–Aug; tel: 207-646 5511).

Once the shipbuilding center of York County, the town of Kennebunkport

 TIP

To escape the bustle of town, try a contemplative – and educational – walk amid the 3,100-acre (1,252-hectare) Rachel Carson Wildlife Refuge (off Route 9). The pioneering ecologist spent many summers exploring these fertile wetlands.

BELOW: Perkins Cove, Ogunquit.

has long since turned its attention to tourism: the commercial center of **Kennebunkport** ❹, Dock Square, is practically impenetrable in summer, but worth pressing through for a visit to the **Kennebunkport Book Port**, specializing in Maine and maritime titles and housed in a 1775 brick warehouse that served, variously, as a boarding house, post office, harness shop, fish market, and artist's studio. The town's legacy shines on in its stately elms and handsome white houses. To get a closer look at these buildings (a few of which are open to the public), take the architectural walking tour conducted by the **Brick Store Museum**, an old general store now devoted to exhibits about local history (Main Street; open Tues–Sat; entrance fee).

Among the sights not to be missed is the unmistakable 1826 **Wedding Cake House** (Route 53), festooned with elaborate carved wooden scrollwork. Legend has it that a sea-bound captain who married in haste had it built to compensate his wife for the lack of a cake at their rushed ceremony. For intimations of a slower-paced age, visit the **Seashore Trolley Museum**, which showcases streetcars, vintage buses and public transit memorabilia, with rides along a 2-mile (3-km) track through the woods (Log Cabin Road off Route 1; tours late May–mid-Oct, daily; entrance fee).

Further up the coast is **Old Orchard Beach** ❺, a turn-of-the-century seaside resort popular among French Canadians. The 7-mile (11-km) beach is flanked with motels and condos and, at the Ocean Pier, an amusement park and waterslide complex. Eastward, just south of Portland on **Cape Elizabeth** ❻, is the oldest lighthouse on the eastern seaboard, the Portland Head Light, commissioned by President George Washington in 1791. The **Museum at Portland Head Light** (Shore Road, Fort Williams Park; open June–Oct, daily; Nov, Dec, April, May, weekends; entrance fee) documents the history of lighthouses from early Egypt up to the present, when satellites have led to the decommissioning of towers such as this one. With its sweeping views of the bays, it's still immensely scenic – much as it was in Henry Wadsworth Longfellow's day. The Portland-born poet often walked here from town to chat with the keeper and draw inspiration from the surroundings. His *Wreck of the Hesperus* was inspired by an actual shipwreck off Peak's Island in 1869.

BELOW: Wedding Cake House, Kennebunkport.

The phoenix of Maine: Portland

The state's most populous city (with only about 65,000 residents, or 125,000 in the metropolitan area), **Portland** ❼ presides over Casco Bay. Founded as Casco in the middle of the 17th century, the city soon became a center of international commerce. Located more than 100 miles (160 km) closer to Europe than any other major US seaport, and blessed with a sheltered, deep-water harbor, it presented itself as a natural port for trade.

Yet Portland's success has often been choppy and beset by sudden storms. Three times the city was burned completely to the ground – by Indians in 1675, by the British in 1775, and by accident in 1866. Three times the city rose quickly from its ashes, improved and rejuvenated. After the last fire, it was reconfigured. Streets were widened, and an elaborate network of municipal parks instituted. The city stands today as a shining example of urban planning – all the more so with the revitalization, in recent decades, of the atmospheric **Old Port Exchange** Ⓐ district, a salty warren of old brick buildings and cobbled streets, packed with sophisticated shops and restaurants.

Portland remains a thriving cultural crossroads, known for its innovative dance and theater troupes. (Theater stood a better chance here after the repeal of a Puritan statute holding that plays "have a pernicious influence on the minds of young people and greatly endanger their morals by giving them a taste for intrigue, amusement and pleasure.") The city is also home to the outstanding **Portland Museum of Art** Ⓑ, designed by I.M. Pei and strong on such locally inspired artists as Winslow Homer, Edward Hopper and Andrew Wyeth, as well as the internationally renowned Van Gogh, Degas and Picasso (7 Congress Square; open July–mid-Oct, daily; Thurs and Fri till 9pm; off–season: same except Sun, pm only and closed Mon; entrance fee; free Fri 5–9pm; tel: 207-775 6148). Next door, the **Children's Museum of Maine** Ⓒ is imaginatively set up (142 Free Street; open Wed–Fri; Fri till 8pm; Sun pm only; entrance fee).

Several Portland neighborhoods warrant strolling – especially the Western Promenade, a parade of 19th-century architectural styles. The 1859–63 brownstone Italianate villa **Victoria Mansion** Ⓓ (109 Danforth Street; tours May–Oct, Tues–Sat; Sun pm; entrance fee), is by far the most elaborate dwelling in town – with showpiece interiors, featuring painted ceilings and carved walls in the Rococo manner, every square inch seemingly subject to intense ornamentation. By contrast is the somewhat restrained 1785–86 **Wadsworth-Longfellow House** Ⓔ (485 Congress Street; tours June–Oct, daily; entrance fee), built by the Longfellows' grandfather, a Revolutionary War officer, and

Maps:
Area 302
City 307

Which way?

BELOW: decoy carver's stand at a blueberry festival.

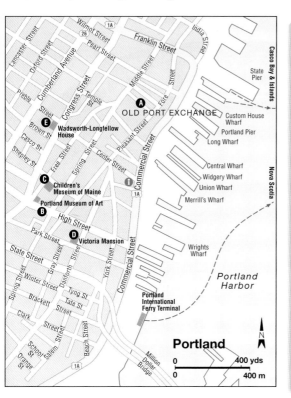

home to three generations of the family. Inside are the parlor where the poet's parents were married and the room where he wrote *The Rainy Day*.

Spread out below are the Calendar Islands – so named because John Smith reported that there were 365 of them, when in fact they number only 136. Cruises to the various islands leave from Portland's State Pier Wharf. The islands range in size from a few square yards of exposed rock to fully functional suburbs like Peaks Island; they tend to get wilder and more beautiful, the farther out to sea. Though rumors of pirate booty have been bruited about for centuries, none – at least on record – has been found so far. Portland's residents and visitors find treasure enough in these peaceful retreats, ideal for biking and picknicking.

Following in L.L. Bean's boots

The little town of **Freeport ❽** on the Bay, attracts customers from around the world – all because, in 1912, a young man named Leon Leonwood Bean decided to build a better hunting boot. In his initial circular, he offered the new, improved waterproof boot with a money-back guarantee. Legend has it that 90 out of the first 100 pairs fell apart: the soles separated from the leather uppers. True to his word, Bean replaced the defective boots with pairs of a newer, improved design and – after absorbing the loss – began building the legendary **L.L. Bean** empire that he controlled until his death in 1967 at the age of 94.

Bean lived long enough to see his store, built in 1951, grow from a humble hunting and outdoors outfitter to a purveyor of casual fashion and recreational sporting goods. The back-to-the-land movement of the 1960s and '70s, along with a boom in mail-order sales, soon prompted expansion into a three-story

Morethan 3½ million visitors a year turn up at L.L. Bean's store in Freeport. World-wide mail order sales exceed $1 billion a year.

BELOW: sign of a seagoing heritage.

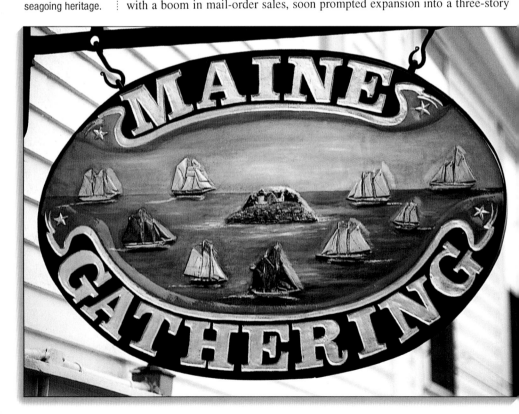

department store (95 Main Street; tel: 800-221 4221), open 24 hours, 365 days a year since 1951 (Bean announced he had "thrown away the keys."). Though a boon to the local economy, Bean's has inspired imitators, so that the entire village is now overrun with discount outlets – tasteful, for the most part, but nonetheless intrusive. In the final irony, Bean's original customer base, the liberally inclined baby boomers, have begun to shun the enterprise because of his daughter's ultra-conservative stance. All the same, ardent shoppers continue to throng here; doing the outlets has become one of Maine's more popular sports.

Map on page 302

A rather peculiar attraction in this area is the **Desert of Maine ❾**, a former farm that was overcultivated, then logged, eventually losing all its topsoil. Sand took over, eventually engulfing entire trees... Amateur mineralogists and children alike will enjoy this overgrown sandbox.

The Mid-coast

Brunswick ❿ is best known as the home of Bowdoin College. Founded in 1794, Bowdoin was originally slated to be built in Portland, but the college's benefactors found that that city offered too many "temptations to dissipation, extravagance, vanity and various vices of seaport towns" for impressionable young minds. Nathaniel Hawthorne and Henry Wadsworth Longfellow were college classmates in 1825.

It was in Brunswick that Harriet Beecher Stowe wrote her 1852 masterpiece Uncle Tom's Cabin, *after having a vision while listening to her husband preach at the town church.*

The **Pejepscot Historical Society Museums** (the Indian name for the Androscoggin River meant "crooked like a snake") provides a good overview of 19th-century life in this region (Joshua Chamberlain Museum; Maine Street; open May–mid-Oct, Tues–Sat; entrance fee; and the Pejepscot Museum, Park Row; open weekdays; plus June–Oct, Sat pm). The campus harbors two worthwhile museums. Bowdoin College's **Museum of Art** houses a small but astute sampling of paintings by such notables as Start, Copley, Homer, Eakins, and Wyeth (Walker Art Building; open Tues–Sat; Sun pm; tel: 207-725 3275).

BELOW: launching the *Arleigh Burke* at Bath Iron Works.

The **Peary-MacMillan Arctic Museum** (Hubbard Hall; open Tues–Sat; Sun pm) heralds the accomplishments of Polar explorers Robert E. Peary and Donald MacMillan, who achieved their objective in 1909. Etched over the doorway is the Latin inscription Peary carved over his shipboard bunk after frostbite claimed most of his toes on a failed 1899 mission: *Inveniam viam aut faciam* ("I shall find a way or make one"). It's also possible to visit the house Peary built on Eagle Island, via cruises out to Bailey Island; inquire at the museum.

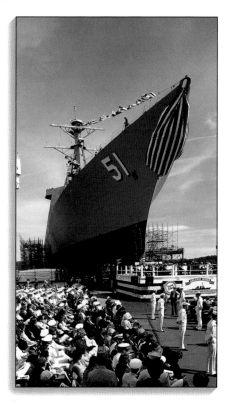

East of Brunswick on US 1 sits **Bath ⓫**, once the state's shipbuilding center, and the nation's fifth-largest seaport. For a time during the 19th century, Maine's shipyards were responsible for one-third to one-half of all ships on the high seas. Timber cut north of Augusta was floated down the Kennebec River to Bath, where the riverbank slopes perfectly for laying keels into the water. The era of the wooden ships ended, however, on the day the iron hull was invented. Not ready to give up a lucrative business, Bath constructed the **Bath Iron Works**, today one of the country's busiest producers of Navy ships. The

Sardines to go at Prospect Harbor.

BELOW: the trail to Popham Beach.

shipyard is off-limits to civilians (except for occasional open houses), but a good view of the towering cranes and other equipment can be obtained from the Carleton Bridge over the Kennebec.

The history of shipbuilding in Bath and other coastal towns is preserved in a beautiful riverside complex, the **Maine Maritime Museum and Shipyard** (Washington Street; open daily; entrance fee; tel: 207-443 1316). Exhibits on nautical tools and gadgets capture the flavor of seafaring days, while a working boatyard demonstrates techniques of different stages of shipbuilding. For a small additional fee, visitors can cruise up the Kennebec to view the Iron Works. The museum also maintains an authentic 142-ft (43-meter) Grand Banks schooner, the *Sherman Zwicker*, which can be boarded, when in port, for a glimpse of the seafaring life.

The town of Bath has restaurants lined up along Front Street and Elm Street.

Directly south of Bath is **Popham Beach State Park** (entrance fee), featuring an unfinished 1861 fort and a 4½-mile (7-km) stretch of sand, one of the prettiest in the state. This was also the site of a failed 1607 colony, of which no trace remains.

Wiscasset ⓬ claims, with some justification, to be the "prettiest village in Maine." It's certainly a contender, with its many grand houses, several of them built by prosperous sea captains. Two are open to visitors: the Federal-era **Nickels-Sortwell House** (Main and Federal Streets; open June–Sept Wed–Sun pm; entrance fee), maintained by the Society for the Preservation of New England Antiquities, and **Castle Tucker** (overlooking the Sheepscot River; open June–mid-Oct, tours Wed–Sun; entrance fee), a prim 1807 Federal building aggrandized in 1860 by Captain Richard H. Tucker and with Victorian furnishings. The 1852 **Musical Wonder House** is an aptly named mansion full of vintage music boxes, player pianos, and other automata from around the world – often playing against one another in improbable euphony (High Street; open late May–Oct, daily; entrance fee).

One of the most picturesque sights in town, oddly enough, is a pair of scuttled World War I schooners, the *Hesper* and the *Luther Little*, mouldering in the mudflats near the town landing. Another offbeat tourist attraction is the **Old Lincoln County Jail and Museum**, an 1811 hoosegow with granite walls up to 41 inches (over 1 meter) thick (Route 218; open July, Aug Tues–Sun; entrance fee). Considered a model of humanity in its day, because prisoners were afforded individual cells, this grim repository was used right up until 1913, and has the graffiti to prove it. On the southeast side of the village **Fort Edgecoomb**, an octagonal fort of 1808–9, is empty inside, but has a great view over the estuary.

Although certainly subdued compared to the commercial excesses of the south coast, **Boothbay Harbor** ⓭ is decidedly touristy. In summer, tens of thousands of visitors throng the streets of this former fishing village to inspect the shops, sample seafood delicacies, and charter boats to explore offshore islands with names such as the Cuckolds and the Hypocrites. There are yacht and golf clubs, flower shows,

Map on page 302

auctions, and clambakes to pass the time. **Boothbay Railway Village** (Route 27; open late May–mid-Oct daily; entrance fee) features a narrow-gauge railroad, encircling a range of reconstructed buildings of yesteryear, including a barbershop, bank and country store.

South of Damariscotta on Route 130 is **Pemaquid Point** ⑭, a rocky peninsula whose Indian name meant "long finger." Early explorers couldn't miss it, and in fact there's some evidence to support a claim – unsubstantiated as yet – that a settlement here may have predated Plymouth. It's known that Pemaquid's settlers provided the Pilgrims with supplies to survive their first harsh winter in the New World; lacking a chronicler like Governor William Bradford, however, Pemaquid's history was never recorded, so details remain hazy.

Its cellar holes filled in by 19th-century farmers, this "Lost City" was entirely unknown until the early 1960s, when Helen Camp, a Rutgers University professor, noticed clay pipes and other detritus in a freshly plowed field. She alerted the Smithsonian Institution; the state bought the land and began excavations. Some 40,000 artifacts have been unearthed so far. The more remarkable ones – such as a 16th-century German jug – are displayed in the state-run museum, **Colonial Pemaquid Restoration**, alongside a diorama recreating the settlement (off Route 130; open late May–early Sept, daily; early Sept–mid-Oct, weekends; entrance fee).

Admission to the museum also includes **Fort William Henry**, a 1907 replica on the site of several unsuccessful stockades. The 1630 original was burned by pirates, and a 1677 replacement, thought impregnable, was destroyed in 1689 by the French Baron de Castin (for whom the town of Castine was named) and his Indian cohorts. A Fort Frederick was built here in 1729, but during the Revolution locals leveled it, lest it fall into the hands of the British.

BELOW: Pemaquid Point Lighthouse.

Lobsters and Lobstering

The colorful lobster buoys dotting the coast of Maine are one of the state's hallmarks. And rightly so – more lobster is fished in Maine than in any other state. Lobstering is a $130 million business in Maine, and in 1997 alone, over 40 million pounds of Maine lobster were consumed throughout the US and shipped all over the world. Yet despite all this, most lobsters in Maine are still caught by independent fishermen in small boats.

A lobsterman's day starts early and goes on late: many head out before dawn, when waters are calmer, and return in the late afternoon. Traps need to be checked at least once a week, and many professional lobstermen – "high-liners" – have 1,000 to 1,500 traps or more, and may need to check several hundred a day. Although proximity to shore makes lobstering safer than other commercial fish-

ing, it is still a dangerous profession, a year-round activity that in the bitter Maine winter can be particularly grueling. Slipping on an icy deck and going over would mean the end, so most high-liners take a helper with them in the form of a "sternman."

On the southern coast of Maine, guided lobstering trips give visitors a gentler taste of a lobsterman's work. In York Harbor, tourists can join Tom Farnum, a retired middle-school science teacher, as he checks traps from his fiberglass skiff. Farnum has been lobstering for 25 years, and, as he leads groups through York River to the mouth of York Harbor, he shares his knowledge of the history of lobstering and the lobster life cycle.

Lobsters are crustaceans whose external skeletons do not grow. Every year they molt, shedding their old shells and growing larger ones. This process happens when the water is warmer, in late June or early July. Conveniently for tourists, molting brings the lobsters closer to shore, making them easier to catch during the peak summer months.

Without shells, the soft lobsters are vulnerable to predators – cod fish and sharks among others – so they migrate to shallow waters for safety. Here, they hide, absorbing sea water and expanding 15 to 20 percent in size. Over four to six weeks, the lobsters produce new shells, then return to deep water, where they shrink again. The lobsters are now known in the trade as "new-shell," or in restaurants as "soft-shell," as opposed to "hard-shell" before molting. A hard-shell lobster's meat can be up to 33 percent of its body weight, while a soft-shell's is only 25 percent; accordingly, hard-shell lobster tends to be more expensive. The taste is slightly different, and each Maine connoisseur has a preference. Some say new-shell is sweeter, some prefer hard-shell for its stronger taste. Visitors have ample opportunity to decide for themselves at the hundreds of lobster pounds along the coast, where lobsters are cooked in seawater in wood-fired barrels.

Farnum's tours leave from Town Dock 2 in York Harbor, Maine; mid-June–mid-Sept weekdays, on the hour 10am–2pm and by reservation at 3 and 4pm; $7.50 per person; (tel: 207-363 3234 5–6pm). ❑

LEFT: at work in Corea Harbor, Down East coast.

At the tip of this peninsula on Route 130 stands the **Pemaquid Point Lighthouse**, built in 1824. With powerful surf constantly breaking on the rocks, the point is a favorite spot for painters and photographers, as well as families who enjoy poking around the tide pools.

Map on page 302

An island in time: Monhegan

An early European explorer, David Ingram, astounded Europe with tales – most rather tall – of the marvelous peoples and cities he encountered on a journey from the Gulf of Mexico to Canada. Lured by such promising reports, a group of Germans settled Waldoboro in 1748, with, as a plaque at the center of town attests, "the promise and expectation of finding a prosperous city, instead of which they found nothing but wilderness." Another Ingram allusion, to "a great island that was backed like a whale," was naturally dismissed as fantasy.

However, the cliffs of **Monhegan Island** ⑮, 12 miles (19 km) south of Port Clyde, do indeed lend the island the appearance of a whale. And yet an other-worldly air still pervades this 700-acre (283-hectare) isle, little changed in the past century. Cars have made no inroads, and virtually all of the cottages – including two out of the three hotels – not only lack electricity, but like it that way. A magnet first for fishing fleets (the abundantly stocked waters attracted European fleets as early as 1605, and possibly the Vikings six centuries earlier) and later artists (the most famous summer resident is painter Jamie Wyeth), most of the island remains undeveloped.

Visitors are free to explore the Cliff Trail circling the island, and the Cathedral Woods Trail, where the island children are in the habit of constructing tiny "fairy houses" out of twigs and moss. Monhegan is served by ferries from both

TIP

For information on Maine's 61 surviving lighthouses, visit the Fishermen's Museum, in the old keeper's residence, next to the Pemaquid Point Lighthouse (open mid-May–mid-Oct daily). *See also page 320.*

BELOW: Monhegan Island meadow.

Boothbay Harbor (Balmy Days Cruises, tel: 207-633 2284; June–late Sept, daily) and Port Clyde (tel: 207-372 8848; May–Oct, daily; rest of the year: Mon, Wed, Fri; the vessel is a rugged mailboat named the *Laura B.*), and though it's possible to make the round-trip in one day, an overnight is advised for those who wish to ease back into a less stressful age. Traditionally, departing visitors are given bouquets of some of the 600 species of wildflowers scattered throughout the island meadows.

Penobscot Bay

On the west end of Penobscot Bay is the town of **Rockland** ⓰, once a great limestone producer and now the world's largest distributor of lobsters. Thanks to the 1935 bequest of "Aunt" Lucy Farnsworth, a frugal spinster who lived in but three rooms of her family mansion and left the town $1,300,000 to start a museum, Rockland has a world-class collection of art. The **Farnsworth Art Museum** (Main Street; open late May–mid-Oct, daily; mid-Oct–late May, Tues–Sat; Sun, pm; entrance fee; tel: 207-596 6457) counts among its holdings many noted 19th- and 20th-century works, including sculpture by Louise Nevelson, who grew up in a Bath lumberyard, and paintings by all three Wyeths – N.C., Andrew, and Jamie. Andrew Wyeth still summers in nearby Cushing. Another pleasant way to pass the afternoon is to peruse the **Shore Village Museum** (Limerock Street; open June–mid-Oct, daily), not big but crammed with a collection of lighthouse artifacts unrivalled elsewhere in the nation, together with other maritime bits and pieces such as ship models and navigational instruments, and straying into Civil War items and costume dolls.

To view an interesting assortment of vehicles, airborne and otherwise, visit the **Owl's Head Transportation Museum**, housed in a spiffed-up hangar at the Owl's Head airport south of Rockland (off Route 73; open daily; entrance fee). The collections range from vintage bicycles to a 1910 Harley, a Model T Ford and a Model F plane (a Wright Brothers prototype). On summer weekends, some of the displays are taken off their blocks and sent for a spin.

A ferry out of Rockland (Maine State Ferry Service, tel: 207-596 2202) serves the large, mostly old-money island of **Vinalhaven** ⓱, where old granite quarries (the stone went into Boston's Museum of Fine Arts, among other edifices) make fine swimming holes and the paved roads are ideal for day-tripping bicyclists.

Up the coast, **Rockport** ⓲ is home base to a fleet of windjammers (sailings late May–mid-Oct; tel: 207-374 5400 or 800-807 9463). These two- or three-masted schooners, sails billowing in the wind, are a throwback to an earlier era, and a wonderful way to discover the coast as the earliest explorers encountered it. Weekend and weeklong excursions may be booked aboard more than a dozen venerable vessels, including the *Stephen Taber*, believed to be the oldest sailboat in continuous use.

Rockport is also a summer mecca for shutterbugs attending the **Maine Photographic Workshops** (tel: 207-236 8581); they can be spotted prowling the town, snapping up picturesque tableaux. A gallery

Map on page 302

with changing exhibits (often by nationally known professionals and teachers) is open to the public.

Camden ⓭ ("Where the Mountains Meet the Sea") has enjoyed a long reign as the ultimate in genteel summering spots. It was here, as a chambermaid at the gracious Whitehall Inn, an 1834 home turned hotel in 1901, that Rockland native Edna St Vincent Millay first began to polish her poetry, and even recite some aloud (one of the guests, noting her talent, arranged for a scholarship to Vassar). One of her verses (*see panel*) was penned after climbing to the summit of 800-ft (244-meter) Mount Battie in the **Camden Hills State Park** (off Route 1), now accessible on foot or via a toll road.

A modern statue of the poet stands watch in a waterfront park overlooking the Megunticook River falls which once powered a half-dozen woolen mills; it's a pleasant place to catch one's breath amid the hubbub of town. Camden is once again in full flower as a summer destination, and the port is packed with restaurants and shops. Many of the grander "cottages" gracing the hilltops have become luxurious B&Bs.

Much quieter than Camden, **Belfast** is starting to attract some fun shops to its Victorian brick storefronts, and its fine houses, too, are turning B&B. **Searsport** ⓴, lined with dazzling white sea captains' homes (nearly 300 lived here in the 19th century), calls itself "the antiques capital of Maine," and the pickings are indeed unusually good. Between 1770 and 1920, this one town produced more than 3,000 vessels, and evidence of its rich history, along with China Trade treasures, can be found at the **Penobscot Marine Museum** (Route 1; open late May–mid-Oct, Mon–Sat; Sun, pm; entrance fee)

Farther along the coastal road and near the mouth of the Penobscot,

All I could see from where I stood Was three long mountains and a wood I turned and looked another way And saw three islands in a bay

– EDNA ST VINCENT MILLAY, ON THE VIEW FROM MOUNT BATTIE

BELOW: looking down on Camden.

Bucksport is dominated by the vast and crumbling Fort Knox, built 1844–69 but never completed.

Detours "down east"

Intent on getting to the justly famed Mount Desert Island, many tourists never veer from US 1 and thus miss one of the most scenic areas in Maine. The peninsulas along the eastern side of Penobscot Bay well warrant some poking around.

Established as a trading post by the Plymouth Pilgrims, **Castine ㉑** became one of the most hotly contested chunks of property in New England: changing hands nine times, it was owned by the French, Dutch, British, and, eventually, Americans (it was a Tory outpost during the Revolution, and the British managed to take it over again after the War of 1812). Plaques around town, as well as a free walking-tour brochure distributed by the Castine Merchants' Association, fill in the details, but it's enough to wander around, beneath a canopy of elms, taking in the array of fine white houses. Some belong to the **Maine Maritime Academy** (one of five such schools nationwide that train merchant marines). Their 1952 troop ship, the decommissioned *State of Maine*, is a floating classroom (hourly tours, mid-July–Aug, daily; Sept–Dec, weekends).

Take a detour off this detour to make a circuit of **Deer Isle**, where the principal occupations are lobstering and fishing, and tourists, though welcome, won't find themselves catered to unduly. On the eastern side of the isle is the prestigious **Haystack Mountain School of Crafts**, whose 1960 "campus" is a cluster of small modern buildings perched precipitously on a piny bank overlooking Jericho Bay (sessions mid-June–early Sept; visitors may be admitted some afternoons and for evening lectures and concerts; tel: 207-348 2306).

BELOW: conductors check their watches on the Belfast to Moosehead railroad.

For a true getaway, take the mailboat from the picturesque port of **Stonington ㉒** to the sparsely inhabited 2,800-acre (1,130-hectare) **Isle au Haut ㉓**. Half is privately owned, the other half part of the Acadia National Park (most of which is situated on Mount Desert Island).

Heading northeast to hook up with US 1 again, one passes through **Blue Hill ㉔**, long the choice of blueblood summerers who didn't care for the showy social season in Bar Harbor. This lovely town attracts craftspeople (especially potters), musicians, and restaurateurs, so the pleasures are varied. One early citizen was the cleric Jonathan Fisher, who served here from 1796 to the mid-19th century and was a man of many enthusiasms. One of his primitive landscapes hangs at the Farnsworth Museum in Rockland, and the 1814 **Jonathan Fisher House** (Routes 15 and 176; open July–mid-Sept, Mon–Sat, pm; entrance fee), which he built himself, is full of his handiwork, from furniture and maps to the wooden clock he made while at Harvard.

Mount Desert Island

The reason there's so much territory to explore in Mount Desert Island is that 35,000 acres (1,414 hectares) of the16 by 13-mile (26 by 34-km) island belong to Acadia National Park, which draws over 5 million visitors a year. "Society" discovered this remote spot in the mid-19th century, inspired in part by Hudson River School painter Thomas Coles. By the time the stock market crashed in 1928, millionaires arriving by steamboat and yachts had constructed more than 200 extravagant "cottages." (Only a few survive, some as institutions or inns: many were destroyed in 1947's devastating fire.) Fortunately, Harvard University president Charles W. Eliot had the foresight to initiate the park in 1916, and

Souvenirs of Down East.

BELOW: Stonington, Deer Isle.

many of his peers contributed parcels. John D. Rockefeller threw in 11,000 acres (4,400 hectares) crisscrossed with 50 miles (80 km) of bridle paths he built to protest against the admission of horseless carriages on to the island in 1905. The trail network makes for great mountain-biking, cross-country skiing, and just plain walking.

Bar Harbor's heyday as a fashionable summer resort was in the 19th century, when a railroad from Boston and a steamboat service lured the wealthy. A forest fire in 1947 destroyed 60 of the grand summer cottages and finally ended the resort's gilded age.

Bar Harbor ㉕ is Mount Desert Island's main town – a bit overcommercialized, but with a pretty town green, a marvelous Art Deco cinema, and some exceptional crafts stores, along with appealing restaurants, and a good choice of accommodations.

Spotting the 17 exposed pink granite peaks of **Mount Desert Island** ㉖, now the main part of Acadia National Park, in 1604, Samuel de Champlain described the place as *"l'île des monts deserts"* – and the French pronunciation still holds, more or less, so be sure to accentuate the final syllable, as in "dessert."

Exploring Acadia

Off Route 3 in Hulls Cove is the National Park's **Visitor Center** (open mid-Apr–Oct, daily; tel: 207-288 3338). Here you can pick up a park map and a schedule of naturalist activities; there are excellent hiking maps on sale. Most visitors will want to experience the view from Cadillac Mountain, whose form dominates the whole park, and to drive or cycle the Park Loop Road, but there are many other possibilities, including horse and carriage tours from Wildwood Riding Stables, kayaking, sailing, and hiking in the less frequented areas. Even the shorter trails tend to be over uneven rock, so suitable footwear is essential.

Car traffic is kept under control by a permit system covering the mostly one-way 22-mile (35-km) Park Loop Road, which makes a clockwise circuit of

BELOW: Bar Harbor.

all the more scenic spots along the eastern coast; the reasonably priced permits are good for a week. Close to the Visitor Center, the **Acadia Wild Garden** shows a range of flora that can be found in a variety of sites within the national park, such as mountain heath and bog; adjacent are the Nature Center, with exhibits on the cultural and natural history of Acadia, and the **Robert Abbe Museum** (off Route 3 and Park Loop Road; open May–Oct, daily; entrance fee). Sweeping views follow, from the Champlain Mountain Overlook across Frenchman Bay to the distant Gouldsboro Hills. The road passes the start of the Precipice Trail, which features iron rungs and ladders for the steep sections, and further on are Sand Beach – edged by low cliffs, and Acadia's one sandy beach – and the Beehive Trail, which gets superb panoramas but involves some potentially dizzying sections. Thunder Hole needs a wind to stir things up; in the right conditions, the spray blasts up through this chink on the coastline. Otter Point provides another memorable coastal outlook before the road heads inland, past Jordan Pond, with walks along the lakeside or on the short trail past Bubble Rock, a huge boulder transported and dumped by glacier, to South Bubble Summit.

Reached by road or on foot, the tallest peak, 1,530-ft (466-meter) Cadillac Mountain, is the highest point along the Atlantic coast north of Rio de Janeiro, and affords glorious 360° views stretching inland as far as Mount Katahdin, Maine's highest summit, and seaward to encompass myriad smaller islands – a particularly lovely vista when bathed in the orange glow of sunset.

On the other side of Somes Sound, the only fjord on the East Coast, the landscape is just as lovely and a bit less traveled. Visit the spectacular seaview **Thuya Gardens**, and stop in Southwest Harbor to try your hand at the "touch

Map on page 302

Wild lupins.

BELOW: biking on one of Acadia's carriage roads.

tanks" and "mystery barrels" in the ramshackle **Oceanarium** (open mid-May–mid-Oct, Mon–Sat; entrance fee). At the most southerly point of the island, Bass Harbor Head Lighthouse is a classic Maine cameo.

To the Canadian Border

In Washington County – also known as "Sunrise County" for its easterly location – tourism takes a back seat to lobstering and growing blueberries and Christmas trees. The patient will be rewarded with a vision of the true Maine, much as it looked 50 years ago. It's worth a detour to the small, unspoiled fishing town of Winter Harbor, and, to the south, **Schoodic Peninsula ㉗**, a little-visited portion of Acadia National Park with fine views of Cadillac Mountain across the bay.

Machias ㉘, about 35 miles (60 km) farther east on US 1, was once a haven for pirates and smugglers. It was also the site of the first naval battle of the Revolutionary War. In June 1775, a month after the Battle of Lexington, the *Margaretta* set anchor off Machias to stand guard over a freight ship collecting wood with which to build British barracks in Boston. After debating their course of action at **Burnham Tavern** (now restored and open as a museum; open early June–Sept weekdays), the townspeople rounded up two smaller ships and successfully attacked. *Margaretta*'s captain died of his wounds when brought back to the tavern, but the crew, nursed back to health there, vowed revenge – and followed through, with subsequent attacks and conflagrations.

Lubec is the easternmost town in the United States, and the easternmost American soil is **West Quoddy Head ㉙**, graced with a candycane-striped 1858 lighthouse surrounded, in summer, by wild roses and day lilies. A walking trail leads along a 50-ft (15-meter) cliff, to Quoddy Head State Park. Having come

BELOW: West Quoddy Head Lighthouse, sited where the rising sun first strikes the United States.

MAINE'S LIGHTHOUSES

With thousands of miles of deep craggy coastline and treacherously rocky shores, it isn't surprising that Maine has 63 lighthouses. What's really surprising is that there aren't three times as many! These sentinels guard the entire coast – from East Quoddy Head Lighthouse on Campobello Island at the Canadian border (accessible only at low tide) to the southern Nubble Light on York Beach. You could easily structure a coastal drive with them acting as a focal point. These picturesque outposts, where sea meets shore, have long represented hope, strength, security and romance in the American imagination. Although several are privately owned, many are open to the public. Portland Head Light, Maine's oldest – built in 1791 under President George Washington's authorization – houses a charming museum in the lighthouse keepers' quarters. Pemaquid Point Light, at the tip of the eponymous peninsula, rises 79 ft (24 meters) above the water from a dramatic rock ledge. (You're guaranteed to spot painters at their easels here.) In 1934 it became the first automated lighthouse. Like others, however, it still relies on a Fresnel lens – a technology designed in 1822 that bends the light into a narrow beam by means of a magnifying lens and concentric rings of glass prisms.

this far, don't miss **Campobello Island** ㉚, only a bridge away from Lubec but officially in Canada. Franklin Delano Roosevelt summered here from the age of one (in 1883) to 1921, when he was crippled by polio. After a self-guided tour of the house, which remains as the family left it, visitors can enjoy 8 miles (13 km) of walking trails, including a 2-mile (3-km) stroll along the ocean.

Map on page 302

The North Woods

Much of the northernmost part of Maine consists of millions of acres of soft-wood forest, owned by a couple of dozen corporations who sometimes admit visitors onto their gravel logging roads for a fee. For an overview of the logging boom that swept the area in the mid-19th century, when papermakers turned to timber in lieu of rags, visit the **Lumberman's Museum** (Route 159; open late May–Sept, Tues–Sun; entrance fee) in **Patten** ㉛, whose 10 buildings of exhibits include a reconstructed 1860s cabin.

To the west, via State 159, is **Baxter State Park** ㉜, the legacy of Percival Baxter, governor from 1920 to 1925. Unsuccessful in his efforts to get the state legislature to purchase and protect this land, he bought and donated a total of 201,018 acres (81,211 hectares), and deeded them to the state, requiring only that the tract remain "forever wild." The park contains 45 peaks over 3,000 ft high, including 5,267-ft (1,605-meter) Baxter Peak, the tallest of Mount Katahdin's three peaks and the second highest point in New England. Baxter is connected to nearby Pamola Peak by a narrow, mile-long strip of rock known as the Knife Edge. Only a few feet wide in spots, the Knife Edge is an acrophobe's nightmare – 3,000 ft (915 meters) straight down on one side, 4,000 ft (1,200 meters) on the other. Would a person fall straight down to the bottom? No, a park ranger

Potatoes are a staple crop in Maine.

BELOW:
a frequent sight in
northern Maine.

reassures: they'd bounce a couple of times. Don't try to cross in high winds.

Pamola Peak is named for the Native American god Pamola, said to have the wings and talons of an eagle but the arms and torso of a man. In *The Maine Woods*, Thoreau warned of Pamola's legendary ire for mortals who reach the top of Katahdin, thus entering the territory of the gods. Those who attempt to scale Katahdin – particularly up the most difficult trails, Cathedral and Dudley, which present the most rugged rock-climbing possible without benefit of ropes and pitons – might well wonder whether Thoreau was right.

Here immigration is a tide which may ebb when it has swept away the pines.

– HENRY DAVID THOREAU
ON CHESUNCOOK

Running northward from the northwest corner of Baxter State Park, the **Allagash Wilderness Waterway** provides 92 miles (150 km) of the most scenic canoeing available in the United States; the trip takes a week to 10 days. South of the park, the Penobscot River's West Branch offers some of the state's most hair-raising whitewater rafting, through granite-walled Ripogenus Gorge. And to the west of the park, accessible only by boat or float plane, is the preserved-in-amber 19th-century logging town of **Chesuncook**. Logged out and left to recover, this lovely little village welcomes outdoors-oriented guests eager to leave the 20th century behind.

BELOW: a successful cast on Maine's St. Croix River.
BELOW RIGHT: rafting on the Kennebec River.

Several dozen such "camps," unchanged for decades, are tucked away in this region pocked with lakes and ponds, where the fish are plentiful and moose and black bear still roam. Many are clustered around **Moosehead Lake ㉝**, the largest body of freshwater in New England, with 320 miles (512 km) of shoreline. The SS *Katahdin*, a restored 1914 steamship, tours the lake out of Greenville on the southern shore (cruises: July and Aug, daily except Mon and Fri; early Sept, weekends; mid-Sept–mid-Oct, Tues, Thurs, and weekends), and the **Moosehead Marine Museum**, which operates the ship, contains fascinat-

Map on page 302

ing displays on Greenville's history, from frontier town to logging capital to turn-of-the-century tourist destination. Another great way to get a full grasp of this mammoth lake is to take a float-plane tour; several operators offer "fly-and-canoe" packages (Folsom's Air Service, Greenville; tel: 207-695 2821).

About 20 miles (32 km) southwest of Greenville as the crow flies (or thrice that distance by car), **The Forks** has turned into a major tourist attraction in recent decades, attracting thousands of amateurs eager to try whitewater rafting along the Kennebec and Dead rivers. Suitable for anyone over the age of 10 and in reasonably good health, these thrilling descents take only a day and alternate roiling rapids with placid floats.

The western lakes and mountains

The ski area at **Sugarloaf ❸**, Maine's second highest peak, has a treeless top offering superb views (including Mounts Katahdin and Washington), and gets more vertical descent (2,820 ft/860 meters) than any other winter resort in New England (tel: 207-237 2000). Snowboarders can try the largest halfpipe in the country. All the runs filter into the one resort village at the base. The 18-hole golf course and abundant wilderness trails for hiking and mountain-biking make Sugarloaf a year-round destination.

A useful base for Sugarloaf is **Kingfield ❸**, which has been a magnet for sporting types since the mid-18th century. It also fostered a family of home-grown geniuses, whose accomplishments are showcased in the **Stanley Museum** (School Street; open Tues–Sun pm; closed Apr, Nov; entrance fee). The twins, F.O. and F.E., invented the Stanley Steamer, which wowed enthusiasts at the first New England auto show in 1898 and set a land-speed

BELOW: winter scene: Sugarloaf and the Carrabassett Valley.

NEXT 9 MILES

Woody Allen built one of his early stand-up sketches around the not uncommon experience of hitting a moose.

BELOW:
a lake camp.

record of 127 miles (203 km) an hour in 1906. Three restored, working samples are garaged in this Georgian-style schoolhouse, which the family built for the town in 1903. Also on display are the photographs of their younger sister, Chansonetta, who had an eye for rural customs now all but forgotten.

About 30 miles (42 km) west is **Rangeley** ㊱, also popular with outdoors enthusiasts for more than a century, and the unlikely home of one-time Freud protégé Wilhelm Reich. His renegade theories on sexual energy ended in his ignominious death in jail – the victim, many believe, of an overzealous Food and Drug Administration. Some of the "orgone energy accumulators" he built stand at his remote home and laboratory, **Orgonon** (Wilhelm Reich Museum; off Routes 4 and 16; open July, Aug, Tues–Sun pm; Sept, Sun pm; entrance fee). The tour is fascinating, the view of Rangeley Lake inspiring.

The **Norlands Living History Center** (open July–early Sept, daily; early Sept–mid-Oct: weekends; entrance fee) in **Livermore** offers a rare opportunity to time-travel back to 19th-century farm life. Most visitors content themselves with a two-hour tour, but true aficionados can sign up for a weekend "live-in" program, in which they'll enact historic characters associated with the farm – and carry out all their chores. **West Paris**, about 12 miles (19 km) west, might prove more attractive to those with "get rich quick" inclinations: Perham's of West Paris, founded in 1919, is a rockhound's mecca, not just for its store, but for the chance to poke around in the five quarries it owns within 10 miles (16 km). Gem-quality tourmaline – striated in a watermelon-like color scheme – is fairly common in these hills, and even gold is not unheard of.

Bethel ㊲ gained prominence as a spa town when Dr John Gehring attracted to his clinic many Harvard academicians suffering from nervous disorders. The hotel he built in 1913 on the pretty town green, the Bethel Inn, is still a restorative treat. Also in town, the **Moses Mason House** (Mason Street; open July–early Sept, Tues–Sun pm; early Sept–June, Tues–Fri pm; entrance fee), an 1813 Federal manse maintained by the Bethel Historical Society, is a treasure house of American primitive painting: the itinerant muralist Rufus Porter decorated the entryway and second-floor landing with, respectively, a seascape and forest tableau.

North of town, the **Sunday River ski resort** ㊳ (tel: 207-824 3000) covers seven mountains, with plenty for intermediates and beginners, and scope for some more challenging black runs, together with the largest snow-making system in New England – virtually guaranteeing good snow conditions. There are also ski programs for the disabled. It is also excellent for views, looking across the highlands of western Maine. There is mountain biking in summer. Nearby is Sunday River Cross-Country Ski Center (tel: 207-824 2410, at the Sunday River Inn), where trails get fine views, and there are some easy ups and downs for novices, as well as more challenging routes.

To the south, lovely **Kezar Lake** is ringed by opulent summer houses, some of them transformed into inns, and the various villages of Waterford, scattered amid the Oxford Hills, present an unspoiled

Map on page 302

reminder of the era when vacation "amenities" consisted largely of cool water, lots of trees, and plenty of fresh air.

Augusta ㊲, Maine's modest-sized capital (population 22,000), stands on the Kennebec River and began its days in 1628 as a trading post. Its gold-domed **State House** (open weekdays) was designed by Charles Bulfinch in 1832, but substantially altered and enlarged in 1909–10. Close by is the **Maine State Museum** (State Street; open Mon–Sat; Sun pm), with displays on "12,000 years of Maine," plus the "Made in Maine" exhibition, which includes a waterpowered woodworking mill and hundreds of Maine-made items. The city's other major sight is **Fort Western**, built close to the river in 1754 and America's oldest wooden fort (City Center Plaza; open late May–early July, daily pm only; early July–early Sept, weekdays and weekends pm; early Sept–mid-Oct, weekends pm; entrance fee). It became a trading post – like the original Pilgrim settlement which preceded it on the same site – and later became the home of its commander, William Harvard. The stockade and block-houses have been evocatively re-created, complete with replica cannons.

With its easy access from Portland, **Sebago Lake** ㊵ is one of the most popular of the Western Lakes, offering swimming, boating, camping, and fishing in the state park at its northern end.

Willowbrook at Newfield ㊶ (off Route 11; open mid-May–Sept, daily; entrance fee) is a reconstituted late 19th-century museum village, between the southern end of Sebago Lake and the New Hampshire border, which captures many of the pleasures of this slower, gentler time, from horse-drawn sleighs to bicycles built for two, from a classic ice-cream parlor to a musty general store. In Maine, none of these pleasures is necessarily confined to the past tense. ❏

Augusta was incorporated in 1797 but was soon renamed after Pamela Augusta, the daughter of the Revolutionary War general Harry Dearborn.

BELOW: canoe expeditions on local lakes are popular.

FOREST, LAKE AND MOUNTAIN WILDLIFE

New England's wilderness areas are one of its big draws. Locals hunt there; visitors have a more benign interest in the animals, birds and plants

It's obvious from the air and just as clear from the freeways: trees cover more than three-quarters of New England, cloaking the mountains of New Hampshire, Maine, and Vermont. These woods and mountains ring with birdsong and are carpeted with wild flowers; particularly enthralling are the alpine flowers on Mount Washington (above and far right).

The most exciting animal to see in the forests is moose. Desperately ungainly, and sporting hairy dewlaps beneath large snouts, they can often be spotted in New Hampshire's White Mountains and in inland Maine, especially in and around lakes and marshes – or licking the salt that runs off the roads in winter. A bull can grow to well over 6 feet (2 meters) tall, with huge antlers on top, and can weigh half a ton (give him a wide berth). You may see moose as you drive around, particularly at dawn or dusk; if not, join one of many moose-waching trips organised locally.

Black bears are also often seen in the forests. They don't normally attack humans, but don't feed them or leave food scraps on the ground. Keep food in sealed containers. Look out, too, for porcupine, chipmunk and stripey-tailed raccoon.

In the lakes and streams that lace the forests, especially in northern Maine, beavers fell trees with their teeth, busily building lodges and dams and creating deep ponds. The lodges, or houses, built of mud and sticks, may be up to 6 feet (2 meters) tall.

◁ **WHITE-TAIL DEER**
White-tailed deer are common in forested areas, and hunting them is a popular pastime in the fall. This faun wears its white-spotted, spring-time coat.

△ **BEAVERS AT WORK**
A beaver dam (above) is an amazingly effective construction of mud and sticks. Sticks stripped of their bark are a give-away sign of a beaver colony.

▽ **THE LOON**
The loon is the state bird of New Hampshire and, some say, the oldest bird on Earth. The diver is often to be seen on Squam Lake, New Hampshire (above).

▽ BIRDLIFE
Waders include American egret (below) and black-crowned night heron. Forest birds include pine siskin, blue jay, golden-crowned kinglet and chickadee.

▽ FOREST FLOOR
In the cool, moist forests, pine seedlings grow up through a silver-gray carpet of mosses and lichens, some of which are native to Arctic tundra regions.

ALPINE FAUNA AND FLORA

Mount Washington in New Hampshire, subjected to three continental storm systems, has some of the worst weather in the world, and the treeline occurs as low as 1,400 feet (420 meters). This arctic zone supports a few mammals – voles and shrews, for instance, living in deep crevices – and some 100 species of alpine plants, many of which grow only here, on Mount Katahdin in Maine's Baxter State Park, and in Labrador and the Arctic. These plants have successfully adapted to dessication caused by biting winds, poor soil, minimal sunlight, and a short growing season. For some, it is 25 years before they flower. It's a fragile ecology. These exquisite plants, growing in and around the lichen-covered rocks with sedges and dwarfed balsam firs, include gold thread, fireweed, alpine bearberry, starflower, arnica, mountain cranberry, wren's egg cranberry, skunk currant and the dwarf cinquefoil *Potentilla robbinsiana*, unique to Mount Washington. Their vibrant colors are best seen mid-June to August.

△ DAWN OUTING
A sunrise canoe trip on a lake or river (look out for advertisements locally in Maine and New Hampshire) is often the time to see beavers and moose.

▷ DRIVERS BEWARE!
A collision with a moose could cause serious damage not only to your car, but also quite possibly to you and your passengers. Go slowly if you see one by the road.

INSIGHT GUIDES
TRAVEL TIPS

TIMBUKTU   KALAMAZOO

AT&T Direct® Service

AT&T Direct Service access numbers are the easy way to call home from anywhere.

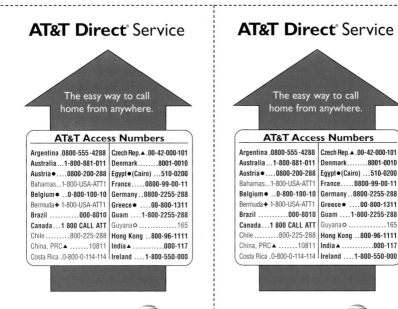

AT&T Direct® Service   AT&T Direct® Service

The easy way to call home from anywhere.   The easy way to call home from anywhere.

AT&T Access Numbers

Argentina .0800-555-4288	Czech Rep.▲.00-42-000-101
Australia ...1-800-881-011	Denmark........8001-0010
Austria● 0800-200-288	Egypt●(Cairo) ...510-0200
Bahamas..1-800-USA-ATT1	France.....0800-99-00-11
Belgium● ..0-800-100-10	Germany..0800-2255-288
Bermuda✛ 1-800-USA-ATT1	Greece● 00-800-1311
Brazil 000-8010	Guam ...1-800-2255-288
Canada...1 800 CALL ATT	Guyana○ 165
Chile 800-225-288	Hong Kong ..800-96-1111
China, PRC▲ 10811	India▲ 000-117
Costa Rica .0-800-0-114-114	Ireland 1-800-550-000

AT&T Access Numbers

Argentina .0800-555-4288	Czech Rep.▲.00-42-000-101
Australia ...1-800-881-011	Denmark........8001-0010
Austria● 0800-200-288	Egypt●(Cairo) ...510-0200
Bahamas..1-800-USA-ATT1	France.....0800-99-00-11
Belgium● ..0-800-100-10	Germany..0800-2255-288
Bermuda✛ 1-800-USA-ATT1	Greece● 00-800-1311
Brazil 000-8010	Guam ...1-800-2255-288
Canada...1 800 CALL ATT	Guyana○ 165
Chile 800-225-288	Hong Kong ..800-96-1111
China, PRC▲ 10811	India▲ 000-117
Costa Rica .0-800-0-114-114	Ireland 1-800-550-000

 AT&T   AT&T

Global
connection
with the AT&T
Network

AT&T
direct
service

The best way to keep in touch when you're traveling

overseas is with **AT&T Direct**® Service. It's the

easy way to call your loved ones back home from just

about anywhere in the world. Just cut out the wallet

card below and use it wherever your travels take you.

For a list of AT&T Access Numbers, cut out the attached wallet guide.

AT&T

Israel 1-800-94-94-949	Portugal ▲..........800-800-128	Israel 1-800-94-94-949	Portugal ▲..........800-800-128
Italy ●. 172-1011	Saudi Arabia ▲ 1-800-10	Italy ●. 172-1011	Saudi Arabia ▲ 1-800-10
Jamaica ● 1-800-USA-ATT1	Singapore 800-0111-111	Jamaica● 1-800-USA-ATT1	Singapore 800-0111-111
Japan ● ▲ 005-39-111	South Africa 0800-99-0123	Japan ● ▲ 005-39-111	South Africa 0800-99-0123
Korea, Republic ● ...0072-911	Spain 900-99-00-11	Korea, Republic ● ...0072-911	Spain 900-99-00-11
Mexico ▽ ● ..01-800-288-2872	Sweden.............020-799-111	Mexico ▽ ● ..01-800-288-2872	Sweden.............020-799-111
Netherlands ● ..0800-022-9111	Switzerland ● 0800-89-0011	Netherlands ● ..0800-022-9111	Switzerland ● 0800-89-0011
Neth.Ant. ▲☺001-800-USA-ATT1	Taiwan 0080-10288-0	Neth.Ant. ▲☺001-800-USA-ATT1	Taiwan 0080-10288-0
New Zealand ● 000-911	Thailand ❰......001-999-111-11	New Zealand ● 000-911	Thailand ❰......001-999-111-11
Norway.............800-190-11	Turkey ●............00-800-12277	Norway.............800-190-11	Turkey ●............00-800-12277
Panama 00-800-001-0109	U.A. Emirates ● 800-121	Panama 00-800-001-0109	U.A. Emirates ● 800-121
Philippines ● 105-11	U.K. 0800-89-0011	Philippines ● 105-11	U.K. 0800-89-0011
Poland● ▲...00-800-111-1111	Venezuela 800-11-120	Poland● ▲...00-800-111-1111	Venezuela 800-11-120

FOR EASY CALLING WORLDWIDE

1. Just dial the AT&T Access Number for the country you are calling from.
2. Dial the phone number you're calling. *3.* Dial your card number.*

For access numbers not listed ask any operator for **AT&T Direct**® Service.
In the U.S. call 1-800-222-0300 for **AT&T Direct** Service information.
Visit our Web site at: **www.att.com/traveler**
Bold-faced countries permit country-to-country calling outside the U.S.

● Public phones require coin or card deposit to place call.
✚ Public phones and select hotels.
▲ May not be available from every phone/payphone.
○ Collect calling only.
▽ Includes "Ladatel" public phones; if call does not complete,
  use 001-800-462-4240.
☺ From St. Maarten or phones at Bobby's Marina, use 1-800-USA-ATT1.
❰ When calling from public phones, use phones marked Lenso.
* AT&T Calling Card, AT&T Corporate, AT&T Universal, MasterCard®,
  Diners Club®, American Express®, or Discover® cards accepted.

When placing an international call *from* the U.S., dial 1-800-CALL ATT.
WW   © 6/00 AT&T

FOR EASY CALLING WORLDWIDE

1. Just dial the AT&T Access Number for the country you are calling from.
2. Dial the phone number you're calling. *3.* Dial your card number.*

For access numbers not listed ask any operator for **AT&T Direct**® Service.
In the U.S. call 1-800-222-0300 for **AT&T Direct** Service information.
Visit our Web site at: **www.att.com/traveler**
Bold-faced countries permit country-to-country calling outside the U.S.

● Public phones require coin or card deposit to place call.
✚ Public phones and select hotels.
▲ May not be available from every phone/payphone.
○ Collect calling only.
▽ Includes "Ladatel" public phones; if call does not complete,
  use 001-800-462-4240.
☺ From St. Maarten or phones at Bobby's Marina, use 1-800-USA-ATT1.
❰ When calling from public phones, use phones marked Lenso.
* AT&T Calling Card, AT&T Corporate, AT&T Universal, MasterCard®,
  Diners Club®, American Express®, or Discover® cards accepted.

When placing an international call *from* the U.S., dial 1-800-CALL ATT.
WW   © 6/00 AT&T

CONTENTS

Getting Acquainted

The Place............................330
Government 330
The Climate 330
Public Holidays 330

Planning the Trip

Passports and Visas 331
Money Matters......................331
Health..................................331
What to Wear 332
Getting There 332

Practical Tips

Media 333
Postal Services 333
Telecommunications 333
Emergency Numbers.............334

Getting Around

By Air...................................335
By Bus and Train 335
By Car..................................335

Where to Stay

Country Inns, B&Bs 336
Hotel Chains 337

Activities

Entertainment 337
Shopping 338
Children's Activities...............338

Boston

Facts and Figures..................339
Where to Stay 347
Cultural Activities 354
Nightlife...............................356
Shopping 358

Massachusetts

Facts and Figures..................339
Where to Stay 341
Where to Eat 349
Outdoor Activities.................357

Connecticut

Facts and Figures..................359
Where to Stay 360
Where to Eat 362
Cultural Activities 365

Rhode Island

Facts and Figures..................368
Where to Stay 368
Where to Eat 369
Cultural Activities 371

Vermont

Facts and Figures..................373
Where to Stay 373
Where to Eat 378
Cultural Activities 381

New Hampshire

Facts and Figures..................385
Where to Stay 385
Where to Eat 389
Cultural Activities 391

Maine

Facts and Figures..................392
Where to Stay 392
Where to Eat 399
Cultural Activities 402

Further Reading

Fiction & Non-fiction 405
Other Insight Guides..............405

Getting Acquainted

The Place

Situation: New England's six states form the northeastern tip of the US, bordering Canada to the north and the Atlantic Ocean to the East.

Language: Although English is the national language, some communities speak other tongues, including French (northern Maine), Portuguese (Gloucester, New Bedford and coastal towns), Italian (Boston's North End). Many notices in the Boston area are printed in English, Portuguese, Spanish, Vietnamese and Cambodian.

Time Zone: New England is within the Eastern Time Zone, which is 1 hour ahead of Chicago and 3 hours ahead of California. On the last Sunday in April the clock is moved ahead 1 hour for Daylight Saving Time, and on the last Sunday in October it is moved back 1 hour to return to Standard Time.

Currency: US dollar.

Weights and Measures: US metric.

Electricity: most wall outlets have 110-volt, 60-cycle, alternating current. If you plan to use European-made electrical appliances, be sure to step down the voltage with a transformer and bring a plug adaptor as local two- and three-sockets are not compatible.

International Dialing Code: 1 (*see page 4* for the codes for each of the six states)

Government

Each of New England's six states has its own political identity, with state senators and representatives in Congress. Each has an elected governor as well, however, and the New England Governors' Council meets regularly to deal with shared interests and conflicts. There are also twice-yearly town meetings, attended by the whole adult population, at which anyone can air their views and the town's business and finances are decided.

Doing Business

Most offices are open Monday to Friday 9am–5pm. Many businesses have free 800 numbers (some in operation 24 hours a day), and virtually all use voice-mail or answering machines. Fax machines are also ubiquitous.

Climate

New England's climate is as varied as its landscape, with large variations from state to state and from season to season:

Massachusetts Pittsfield in the west has an average annual temperature of around 7.2°C (about 45°F), while Boston in the east is about 10.8°C (about 51.5°C) and Nantucket about 9.7°C (49.5°F).

Connecticut Winters are just below freezing, and summers warm and humid. The average yearly temperature along the coast is 10.6°F (51°F), and in the northwest 7.2°C (45°F); for most of the rest of the state the yearly mean is 8.3–9.4°C (47–49°F).

Rhode Island Summer temperatures are moderated by proximity to the ocean, but winters are quite cold. Providence has an average January temperature of about –2°C (about 28°F) and an average July temperature of about 22°C (about 72°F); Block Island has a mean January temperature of about –1°C (about 31°F) and a mean July temperature of about 21°C (about 70°F).

Vermont There is considerable variations in temperature depending on proximity to the mountains (which have heavy snows).Saint Johnsbury, in the northeast, has an average January temperature of about –8.1°C (about 17.5°F) and an average July temperature of about 20.8°C (about 69.5°F); Rutland, in the central part of the state, has a mean January temperature of around –5.8°C (about 21.5°F) and a mean July temperature of around 20.8°C (about 69.5°F).

New Hampshire Concord has an average July temperature of about 21°C (around 70°F) and a mean January temperature of about –6°C (about 21°F); atop Mount Washington, on the other hand, the average July temperature is around 10°C (about 50°F) and the mean January temperature about –14°C (about 6°F). In April 1934, winds of 231 mph (372 kmph) were recorded on the summit of Mount Washington.

Maine As it is on the coast, the state enjoys a maritime climate. Winter temperatures are much milder than those inland, and summer temperatures are cooler. In the north, however, it is extremely cold with a high snowfall. In 1925, Maine's lowest recorded temperature of –44.4°C (–48°F) was observed. The south is the warmest part of the state.

Public Holidays

During the holidays listed below, some or all state, local and federal agencies may be closed. Local banks and businesses may also close on the following days.

- **1 January** New Year's Day
- **Third Monday in January:** Martin Luther King Jr. Day
- **Third Monday in February:** Presidents' Day, celebrating Lincoln's and Washington's birthdays
- **Third Monday in April:** Patriots' Day (Massachusetts only)
- **Last Monday in May:** Memorial Day
- **4 July:** Independence Day
- **First Monday in September:** Labor Day
- **Second Monday in October:** Columbus Day
- **11 November:** Veteran's Day
- **Fourth Thursday in November:** Thanksgiving
- **25 December:** Christmas Day

Planning the Trip

Passports & Visas

To enter the United States most foreign visitors need a passport (which should be valid for at least six months longer than their intended stay). You should also be able to provide evidence that you intend to leave the United States after your visit is over (usually in the form of a return or onward ticket).

Visa requirements

Most foreign nationals (except Canadians and Mexicans) also require a visa to visit the US.

Citizens of the UK, New Zealand, Japan and European Union nations do not need a visa, however, as long as they are staying for less than 90 days and have a round-trip or onward ticket. Before entering the US, they must sign a Non-Immigrant Visa Waiver form, declaring, among other things, that they are not seeking to work during their stay.

Anyone wishing to stay longer than 90 days must apply for a visa. This can be done by mail or by personal application to the US Embassy or Consulate nearest their home. Visa extensions can be obtained in the US from the United States Immigration and Naturalization Service offices.

HIV

Anyone who is HIV positive or has Aids must also obtain a visa (unless they are the spouse, partner or child of a US citizen or have a green card). Although HIV is not grounds for exclusion from the States, the US Immigration and Naturalization Service requires proof of your current state of health, medication and so on. Failure to provide correct information on the visa application is grounds for deportation.

Immunization requirements

Visitors from some countries need to supply proof of immunization against smallpox or cholera.

Money Matters

Travelers' checks

Despite the small fee (generally one percent of the cash value of the checks), travelers' checks are the best way to bring money into New England, as they can be replaced if lost or stolen. These should be in US dollars, as other currencies may be difficult to exchange. Most hotels, restaurants and stores will cash them for you or accept them as payment without charging commission. Make sure you have plenty of small-denomination checks, though, as stores may not cash $100 checks.

Foreign currency

Visitors may encounter problems exchanging foreign currency. A large number of banks throughout New England offer a foreign-exchange service (don't forget to take your passport), but this is not universal.

Banks

Many banks have only one branch in each town. Most banks open around 10am and close between 3pm and 5pm on weekdays, and operate from 10am to 1pm on Saturday.

Banks generally have ATMs that dispense cash and accept most credit cards.

Credit cards

These are widely accepted. If you rent a car, you may have to leave your acard as a deposit.

Health

INSURANCE

Most visitors to New England have no health problems during their stay: sunburn in summer is the main nuisance for the majority. Even so, you should never leave home without travel insurance to cover both yourself and your belongings. It's not cheap to get sick in the United States. Your own insurance company or travel agent can advise you on policies, but shop around since rates vary. Make sure you are covered for accidental death, emergency medical care, trip cancelation and baggage or document loss.

HAZARDS

Lyme disease (borne by deer ticks hiding in high grass) is a potentially life-threatening condition. Starting with a rash, it develops into flu-like symptoms and joint inflammation, and possible longterm complications like meningitis and heart failure. Even though it is statistically

Tourist Information Abroad

There is no American Tourist Office in the UK, US or Australia. If you have a business or visa enquiry, information can be obtained from the US Embassies in each country:
Australia: 21 Moonah Place, Yarralumla, ACT 2600.
Tel: 6 270 5900.
UK: 5 Upper Grosvenor Street, London W1. Tel: 0171–499 9000.
Website: www.usembassy.org.uk

For holiday information, the tourist organisation Discover New England supplies a color brochure with sights, useful telephone numbers and accommodation, plus maps of each state.
UK: Vestry Road, Sevenoaks, Kent TN14 5XA. Tel: 01732 742777 (24 hours).
US: Box 3809, Stowe, Vermont 05672. Tel: 1–802 253 2500.
Website:
www.discovernewengland.com

There is also a Massachussetts Office of Travel and Tourism in the UK at:
Molasses House, Clove Hitch Quay, Plantation Wharf, York Place, London SW11 3TN.
Tel: 0171–978 7429.

rare, precautions are in order. When hiking in grass or brush, wear light-colored pants tucked into socks, and spray the clothing with an insecticide. Inspect your skin afterwards: if a tick has attached itself, disinfect the area with alcohol and visit a doctor or clinic immediately. An undetected bite may result in a red-ringed rash; again, see a doctor. If you suffer any of the symptoms described after exposure to ticks, a doctor can prescribe antibiotics.

Poison ivy is only temporarily discomfiting, but can be avoided by keeping an eye out for the shiny three-leaf clusters and washing immediately upon accidental contact. Camomile lotion is good for soothing the skin.

Tapwater is perfectly safe to drink, but avoid stream water as it can cause serious intestinal problems.

What to Wear/Bring

Clothing styles in New England vary from state to state, and then from region to region. In New Hampshire, Maine, Vermont and the Berkshires in Massachusetts people tend to dress in casual clothes geared towards outdoor life, whereas attire in most other New England cities in Massachusetts, Connecticut and Rhode Island is more traditional.

To cover all occasions, bring a variety of clothing from sportswear to formal attire. For men, a jacket and tie, although not necessarily a suit, is standard dress for more

Customs

Visitors aged 21 or over may bring the following to the US:
● 1 liter of duty-free alcohol
● 200 duty-free cigarettes, or 2kg tobacco or 50 cigars
● Gifts worth $100 if non-US citizens or $400 if US citizens
● up to $10,000 in US or foreign cash, traveler's checks or so on. Any more must be declared.
Import of meat, seeds, plants and fruit is forbidden.

formal restaurants and may in fact be required; women have more latitude, in terms of pants versus dresses, but be warned that even youth-oriented bars and nightclubs may ban jeans.

Some warm clothing, such as sweaters, jackets, and windbreakers, should be packed even during the summer, when evening temperatures tend to dip, especially in the mountains and on the coast. Winters necessitate heavy outerwear, including hats, scarves, gloves and boots.

Getting There

Flying is by far the easiest way to get to New England. If you come overland from elsewhere in the US, cars are the preferred mode of travel. Trains are less frequent than flights and, although buses connect most cities and several major towns, they are not much cheaper than a discount airfare – and substantially longer and less comfortable!

BY AIR

Most major US carriers service the New England states. A variety of discount fares and special deals are offered, so shop around.

Logan International Airport in Boston is the 15th-busiest airport in the world, and smaller airports – many of them served by Delta – are scattered throughout New England, near larger cities such as Hartford, Bangor and Burlington.

Some 15 international airlines fly direct to New England. Alternatively, you can fly into New York and catch one of the many connecting flights to the New England area, or the hourly shuttle to Boston (no reservations required, tickets can be bought just before boarding).

Boston's Airport has a bureau de change and hotel reservation desk (which charges no commission), plus car hire outlets.

During holidays (*see page 330*) it may be difficult to find a flight, especially at Thanksgiving, when most of the US seems to be on the move and discount tickets are virtually non-existent.

Tour Operators

The following companies specialise in tailormade New England itineraries:
In the UK
● North America Travel Service
7 Albion Street
Leeds LS1 5ER.
Tel: 0113–243 0000.
Fax: 0113–243 0919.
Website:
In the US
● Destinnations
572 Route 28
Suite 3
West Yarmouth
MA 02673.
Tel: 508 790 0566.
● Ego Trips
250 Boylston Street
Boston, MA 02116.
Tel: 617 266 5744.
● Tourco
29 Bassett Lane
Hianis, MA 02601.
Tel: 800 537 5378.

BY LAND
Train

Amtrak (tel: 800 368-8725) offers efficient rail services to New England from Washington, DC, and New York, routing through Connecticut and Rhode Island and terminating in Boston; another route extends from New Haven, Connecticut, to Springfield, Massachusetts, to St Albans, Vermont. Various commuter trains serve smaller towns, and seasonal trains – such as the Vermonter from Boston to Brattleboro and on up to Burlington – cater for tourists.

Bus

Large air-conditioned buses connect New England to most other US tourist destinations (*see page 335*).

Car

Driving is by far the best way of exploring and experiencing New England (*see page 335*).

Practical Tips

Media

Newspapers

As well as the US nationals such as *USA Today*, the tabloid *National Enquirer* and financial *Wall Street Journal*, New England has three local newspapers. The *Boston Globe* is a highly regarded daily, the *Boston Herald* a tabloid daily, with listings on Thursday and Friday respectively, and *The Boston Phoenix* is Saturday-only. Foreign magazines and papers are sold on newsstands in the larger cities.

Television and radio

Flick through the channels on both TV and radio, and you'll experience the gamut of American life, from game show to in-depth news. Most hotels receive the three major national networks (ABC, CBS and NBC), several dozen channels, plus many cable networks. The Public Broadcasting System (PBS) has some of the better-quality imported programs. National Public Radio (NPR), at the low end of the FM scale, is a good all-round station.

Postal Services

There is a post office in most New England villages and towns. Opening hours vary between central big city branches and those in smaller places, but hotel personnel will be able to tell you when the nearest post office is open.

If you do not know where you will be staying in a particular town, you can receive mail simply by having it addressed to you, care of General Delivery, at the main office in that town – but you must pick up such mail personally (within 10 days). Check with postal officials about charges and the variety of mail-delivery services available.

Stamps may be purchased from vending machines installed in hotel lobbies, in shops and airports, and at bus and train stations.

To facilitate quick delivery within the States, include the five-digit zip code when addressing communications. Zip code information may be obtained from any post office.

Telecommunications

Telephone

Public telephones are to be found in hotel lobbies, restaurants, drugstores, street corners, garages, convenience stores and other general locations. Long-distance call rates decrease after 5pm, going down still further after 11pm, and are lowest on weekends. Several countries can be dialed directly

Phone Codes

Dail the following codes, preceded by 1, when phoning from a different state or area:
- ● **Connecticut (southwest)** 203
- ● **Connecticut (elsewhere)** 860
- ● **Maine** 207
- ● **Massachussets (west/central)** 413
- ● **Massachussets (east)** 508
- ● **Massachussets (Boston area)** 617
- ● **New Hampshire** 603
- ● **Rhode Island** 401
- ● **Vermont** 802

from many areas in New England, without operator assistance. For all specific information concerning telephone rates and conveniences, simply call the local operator (0) and inquire.

All 800 and 888 numbers are toll-free. For numbers to dial in an emergency, *see over the page.*

Email

Although email is used extensively within the US, there are few public places within New England from where you can use it. You are far better off faxing messages.

Fax

All but the smallest of hotels and B&Bs offer access to a fax machine; there's generally a fee for outgoing faxes (often exorbitant!), but incoming are usually free.

Tourist Information in New England

The following state tourist agencies provide ample information on attractions, restaurants, lodgings, recreational options and events. They can also refer you to local chambers of commerces, if required.

Connecticut
505 Hudson Street
Hartford, CT 06106.
Tel: 860 270–8065/8080.
www.ct.us/tourism/

Maine
State House Station 59
Augusta, ME 04333.
Tel: 207 287–2071/5711.
www.visitmaine.com

Massachusetts
100 Cambridge Street
Boston, MA 02202.
Tel: 617 727–3201.
www.mass.vacation.com

New Hampshire
Box 1856
Concord, NH 03302,.

Tel: 603 271–2666.
www.visitnh.gov

Rhode Island
1 West Exchange Street
Providence, RI 02903.
Tel: 401 222–2601.
www.visitrhodeisland.com

Vermont
6 Baldwin Street
Montpelier, VT 05633.
Tel: 802 828–3237.
www.travel-vermont.com

Alcohol

The legal age for both the purchase and consumption of alcoholic beverages is 21 throughout New England. Alcoholic beverages are sold by package in state liquor stores and by the drink or the bottle at licensed establishments in all the six states. On Sundays, however, no package sales are allowed and drinks are sold only at specified hours.

Often a restaurant without a liquor license will permit customers to bring their own beer or wine; then again, some communities have elected to remain "dry," and if they do, you must, too. If you are driving, keep bottles of alcohol unopened and out of sight in the car.

Medical Treatment

Pharmacies stock most standard medication (though some painkillers that are available over the counter in other countries may be prescriptions only in the US), and staff are trained to help with most minor ailments.

Hospitals are to be found in most New England cities, signposted on highways with a white H on a blue background. Major hospitals have 24-hour emergency rooms – you may have a long wait before you get to see the doctor, but the care and treatment are thorough and professional. Boston's are particularly highly regarded.

Walk-in clinics are also commonplace in cities, where you can consult a nurse or doctor for a minor ailment without an appointment. If cost is a concern,

Taxes

Most of the states levy taxes on meals and accommodation, and some on all sales. When restaurants and hotels quote prices, these taxes are not normally included – so ask, as they can bump up the cost by 11 percent. Ticket prices for transport have the tax included.

Emergency Numbers

● **911** Most of New England is connected to the national emergency number (no money required). Operators hook you up to police, firefighters or medical services.
● **0** If 911 does not work, call the operator, who will connect you to the appropriate local emergency services.
● *Yellow Pages* Another option, time permitting, is to turn to the inside front cover of a local telephone directory, which lists emergency numbers.

turn first to clinics offering free or pro-rated care (look under "Clinics" in the *Yellow Pages*).

Security & Crime

Most of New England is relaxed and crime free – and it is generally safe to walk the streets. Despite the picture presented in the movies, violence is not endemic. But it still pays to exercise caution.
● Keep a firm grip on bags. Don't sling them over the back of a chair.
● Whenever possible, travel with another person, especially at night.
● When not driving, lock your car and never leave valuables in view. At night, park in lighted areas. When returning to your car, have your keys ready before you reach it.
● Never leave your luggage unattended or out of view. Lock your hotel door when out, and never leave valuables in your room.
● Do not carry more cash than you need. Whenever possible, use credit cards and travelers' checks; be discreet when paying cash.

Gay Travelers

Boston has a very active and proactive gay presence, as do, to a lesser extent, other large cities and even rural towns. Northampton, for instance, has in the past few decades emerged as a lively enclave for lesbians, and Provincetown, of course, has long

been a preferred gay summer vacation spot; it even has a gay counterpart to the Chamber of Commerce, the Provincetown Business Guild (tel: 508 487-2313, 800 637-8696).

Information concerning gay-oriented activities and businesses (including gay-owned and operated inns throughout the region) can be found in the Boston-based newspaper *Bay Windows*, and in *One in Ten*, a supplement produced by the alternative weekly, the *Boston Phoenix*.

A good in-town networking source, for those visiting Boston, is the Glad Day Liberation Bookshop, at 673 Boylston St (tel: 617 267-3010).

Travelers with Disabilities

Federal regulations regarding handicapped accessibility have made some inroads, but the work is by no means complete. Larger facilities, especially those of recent vintage, should pose no problem. Many B&Bs, mindful of their elderly clientele, have also done adaptive retrofitting. If in doubt, call ahead.

Tipping

Tip generously or it will be interpreted as an insult – or tourist ignorance. For meals, hairdressers, bartenders and taxi drivers, around 15 percent is the norm (or 20 percent for exceptional waiter service). Give a few dollars to the doorman, bellhop and housekeeper.

Dates

The convention for writing dates in the US is to put the month first, so 2/12/2000 is 12 February 2000.

Smoking

Smoking is banned in most public places and on transport. Most restaurants have a no-smoking zone, some are non-smoking. Some hotels have non-smoking rooms.

Getting Around

Information

The best source of information for travelling around New England is the tourist board of each specific state, which may also be able to book tickets for you (*see page 333*).

By Air

Internal flights are expensive, but if you want to hop from place to place by air, airlines serve the following New England towns and cities:
Massachusetts Boston, Hyannis, Martha's Vineyard, Nantucket, New Bedford, Worcester
Maine Bangor, Portland
Connecticut Bradley Airport (near Hartford), Bridgeport, Groton, New Haven
Vermont Burlington
New Hampshire Lebanon-Hanover, Manchester
Rhode Island Providence

AIRLINES
Major domestic airlines include:
Cape Air Tel: 800 352–0714)
Delta Tel: 800 345–3400
Northwest Airlines Tel: 800 225–2525
USAir Tel: 800 428–4322

By Bus

Most New England cities and tourist sights can be reached by bus. Greyhound has the most comprehensive coverage of the US, and the following companies operate local services:
Bonanza Tel: 617 720-4110. Based in Providence, RI, with connections to New York and Massachusetts, and several routes within Rhode Island.

C&J Trailways Tel: 800–258 7111. Services mainly Maine.
Concord Trailways Tel: 603 228 3300. Services mainly New Hampshire and based in Concord.
Greyhound Tel: 617 526–1800/ 800 231-2222. The most extensive bus network, with offices in Boston, MA, and elsewhere, and long-distance routes throughout the US.
Peter Pan Tel: 800 237-8747. Based in Springfield MA.
Plymouth & Brockton Tel: 617 773–9401. Based in Boston, with routes mainly within Massachusetts and Connecticut.
Vermont Transit Lines Tel: 802 864–6811. The main Vermont service, based in Burlington.

Some bus terminals are in "problem areas," so take care when traveling to and from stations.

By Train

The most extensive train service throughout New England is offered by Amtrak.
Amtrak Tel: 800 368-8725 (*see page 332* for some routes).

Connecticut is served by Metro North, with trains between New York and New Haven.
Metro North Tel: 800 638–7646/ 212 532–4900.

Boston has a commuter line (MBTA) from North Station traveling north and west, with stops at Concord, Rockport, Gloucester and Manchester.
MBTA Tel: 800 392–6099/ 617 374 1234.

By Car

A car offers the most popular and convenient means of getting around New England. Although the network of airplanes, buses, trains, ferries, and taxis is reliable, having your own car is the easiest way to get around (except, perhaps, in the congested heart of Boston), and it also offers the greatest leeway for getting off the beaten path.
Highways A number of well-maintained interstate highways (ranging from four to eight or more lanes) make covering New

England's distances easy. To get an idea of the range, picture a radius from Boston to Burlington, in northwestern Vermont – a trip which, on Routes 93 and 89, would take only about five hours. That radius, extended across New England, would cover all but the northernmost regions of Maine (beyond Bangor).
Secondary roads Travel on secondary roads is time-consuming, but all the more scenic. However, beware of dirt roads – usually represented by a broken line – in mud season (typically, March into May). And note that mountain roads may be closed in winter.

CAR HIRE
Visitors wishing to rent or lease a car after arriving in New England will find offices of all the major US firms at airports (usually more expensive than elsewhere) and other locations convenient to tourists. Toll-free arrangements can be made in advance. The most reputable firms are:
Hertz Tel: 800 654–3131
Avis Tel: 800 331–1212
Budget Tel: 800 527–0700
But it's worth calling around, referring to the *Yellow Pages* (under "Automobile Renting & Leasing"), for the best rates. Sometimes local rental firms may offer lower rates, especially for lower-quality cars (several franchise chains, such as Rent A Wreck, have sprung up to cater for just this market). But be sure to check insurance coverage provisions before signing anything.

Also check with an airline, bus or rail agent or travel agent for special package deals that provide rental cars at reduced rates.

The cheapest rates for hire tend to be from Thursday noon until Monday noon.
Legal requirements
Most car rental agencies require drivers to be at least 21 years old (sometimes 25), to hold a major credit card and a driver's license that is current and has been valid for at least a year; some will accept a cash deposit, sometimes as high as $500, in lieu of a credit card.

Drink Driving

Regulations are very strict. If you fail a breath test after drinking, your license will be removed on the spot. So avoid drinking and keep alcohol out of sight and unopened in the car.

Foreign travelers may need to produce an international driver's license or a license from their own country.

Insurance

Liability is not included in the terms of your lease, so advertised rates usually do not include additional fees for insurance. Collision Damage Waiver (CDW) is strongly recommended, as it covers you if someone else causes damage to your car.

RULES OF THE ROAD

In general, state laws apply to the New England driver. Each state has specific laws and special regulations regarding parking, speed limits and the like; most are clearly posted. Check with the tourism board if in doubt.

Seatbelts

These are obligatory for all front-seat occupants. Children under six must be buckled into safety belts, safety seats or a proper child restraint. Many rental firms supply child seats for a small extra cost.

Fuel

Petrol, or gas, is lead-free and stations are plentiful, with many open 24 hours a day. British travelers should note, however, that the US gallon is 17 percent smaller than the English equivalent.

Special considerations

Rotaries, especially in Boston, pose a particular challenge. The official rule is that the cars already in the circle have the right of way in exiting, but this rule is rarely observed in practice. It's best to proceed cautiously, whether entering or exiting.

Unless otherwise posted, a right-hand turn at a red light is permitted throughout New England. On

sighting a school bus that has stopped to load or unload children, the driver must stop completely before reaching the bus and may not proceed until the warning signals on the school bus have been switched off, or until directed to do so.

Hitching and car-jacking

Hitchhiking is discouraged; so is picking up hitchhikers. Car-jackings are exceedingly rare, but a growing threat. If you are planning to drive, learn what areas of cities to avoid before starting out. Ask questions of your rental clerk when you arrive, or check with tourist offices before taking a drive.

Breakdown

Some highways have emergency phones every few miles. Otherwise, park up with your bonnet raised and a police patrol will soon arrive. The American Automobile Association (tel: 800 222 4357) offers reciprocal breakdown services for some affiliated firms in other countries – check with your company at home.

Parking

You must park in the direction of traffic, and never by a fire hydrant. A yellow line or yellow curb means no parking is allowed. In some towns a white line along the curb shows where you can park.

Speed Limits

New England states maintain their interstate highway system in fine condition. Highway speed is generally limited to 55 mph (89 kph), although along some stretches in certain states – check the roadside signs – a maximum of 65 miles (105 km) is permitted.

On interstates, you may find your fellow drivers will be cruising along at about 10 miles more per hour than the posted limit, on the presumption that such an offense is likely to get them no more than a warning. Join them at your own risk: Enforcement, if sporadic, can be strict, with high penalties.

Where to Stay

New England provides an especially diverse set of accommodation alternatives. The options vary in terms of location, price, amenities, atmosphere and orientation, and can be anything from low-budget B&Bs and youth hostels, through roadside motels, to full-service grand hotels like Boston's Ritz Carlton. For details in each state, see *Where to Stay* sections below.

COUNTRY INNS

Perhaps the most uniquely New England lodging is the famed country inn. If you are tired of motels and hotels, and willing to forego certain conveniences (such as an in-room phone or TV) for more simple pleasures, country inns are a wonderful option. They can be stereotyped only in that they provide year-round lodging and regional fare – some sophisticated.

They range from weathered farmhouses with huge fireplaces and relaxing music, like Vermont's Inn at Sawmill Farm, to the grand elegance of Wheatleigh in Lenox, Massachusetts, to the golf courses and pools of the Spalding Inn located in Whitfield, New Hampshire.

Other country inns offer many or all of these attractions, and often more; the traits they share are high-quality service and hospitality.

In the UK, New England Inns & Resorts specialises in country inns. Tel: 01923-821469. Fax: 01923-827157.

B&Bs

Bed and breakfast accommodation is widespread. Companies specialising in B&Bs include:
Bed & Breakfast Agency of Boston
Tel: 0800 895 128.

HOLIDAY HOMES

UK firms specialising in renting out New England houses include:

Bridgewater's Holiday Homes
217 Monton Road
Monton
Manchester M30 9PN.
Tel: 0161–707 8547.
Massachusetts, all year round.

Four Seasons in New England
Truendle Crockenell
Exeter EX6 6NB.
Tel: 01647 24726.
Houses and inns in all states.

New England Connection
PO Box 218
Dorking RH5 6YZ.
Tel: 01306 877600.
Vermont, New Hampshire and Massachusetts. All year round.

New England Country Homes
Bignor
Pulborough RH20 1QD.
Tel: 01798 869461.
All states all year round.

North American Vacation Homes
86 Turners Mill Road
Haywards Heath RH16 1NJ.
Tel: 01444 450034.
Houses in Massachusetts, New Hampshire, Maine and Vermont. From April to October only.

Hotel Chains

Among the large chains that have hotels throughout the New England states are:

Best Western Tel: 800 528–1234
Comfort Inn Tel: 800 424–6423
Days Inn Tel: 800 325–2525
Choice Hotels Tel: 800 424–4777
Hilton Tel: 800 445–8667
Holiday Inn Tel: 800 465–4329
Howard Johnson
Tel: 800 654–2000
Hyatt Regency
Tel: 800 233–1234
Marriott Tel: 800 872–9563
Quality Inn Tel: 800 228–5151
Radisson Tel: 800 333–3333
Ramada Tel: 800 272–6232
Red Roof Inn Tel: 800 843–7663
Sheraton Tel: 800 325–3535
Super 8 Tel: 800 800–8000
Susse Chalet Tel: 800 258–1980

Where to Eat

"Land of the bean and the cod"
New England's culinary standing made a stratospheric leap in the late 1980s and 1990s. Once bemoaned as the land of "the bean and the cod", Boston started the region's culinary renaissance rolling with a group of world-class chefs who trained their sous-chefs so well that their ranks kept expanding. Where once the highest quality you could expect was provincial and stodgy, now the offerings are fresh and flavorful, the equal of sophisticated fare anywhere.

New England's chefs have not only come up with brilliant new uses and combinations for the area's renowned bounty (especially seafood), they've developed their own network for securing new native delicacies, from farmstead cheeses to locally raised game birds.

Traditional fare revisited
If you've never tried the classics, by all means try them. These range from thick, wholesome soups, to seafood specialties like lobster bisque and shad roe, to old-timers like boiled dinner (a hotpot of boiled beef, cabbage, carrots and potatoes), to wicked desserts such as Indian pudding (a cornmeal bake flavoured with milk, molasses, ginger, cinnamon and raisins), Boston cream pie (custard-filled sponge cake covered in chocolate). For regional traditions see the *Where to Eat* section for each state.

But be prepared for some surprises. New England's ingenious cooks – from executive chefs at the four-star hotels to the hardworking chef/owners at country inns – are having a year-round field day with seasonal specialties, and lucky customers are in for an ever-changing array of treats.

Entertainment

New England offers a wide range of entertainment. Rural areas tend to be more slow-paced and relaxed during the evening, while Boston supports a varied, exciting nightlife. **Boston** outgrew its staid image long ago. At night, the city sparkles with lively and sophisticated activity. The Boston Symphony Orchestra has earned an international reputation; its less formal offshoot, the Boston Pops, also commands a great following.

Music permeates the region, ranging from rural chamber groups to big-city rock and jazz. Comedy clubs are also increasingly popular. **Theater** thrives not only in Boston and New Haven (proving grounds for Broadway) but in myriad regional repertory companies and "straw-hat" summer theaters.

Dance Professional modern dance and ballet can be seen in bucolic settings, as well as in towns. The larger cities have dance clubs where it's easy to meet and mingle. **Listings** For more specific information, check the listings in local papers – especially alternative ones, such as *Phoenix* (various editions cover Boston, Providence, and Worcester), *Advocate* (Pioneer Valley), and *Vanguard* (Burlington, Vermont). See also *Nightlife* and *Culture* for each state, below.

Special Events

State tourist boards will gladly provide detailed lists of seasonal festivals, fairs and other annual events large and small – from teddy bear picnics to antique car rallies. Many are so appealing it would make sense to plan a trip around them – or at the very least commit yourself to a detour.

Shopping

New England provides as great range of shopping as can be found anywhere in the country: large department stores, local country auctions, antique shows, craft stores and bargain factory outlets. Whether you're looking for bargains or one-of-a-kind works of art, the six state have plenty to offer.

ANTIQUES
Antique stores abound and antiquing in these shops can be fun and, depending on the level of the stock, relatively inexpensive.

HANDICRAFTS
American handicrafts are experiencing a renaissance. There are probably more quality craft items being produced now than at any time since the Industrial Revolution. Crafts, whether pottery, weaving, scrimshaw or woodworking, are usually less expensive and higher quality when bought directly from the artisans, at their studios or juried crafts fair.

FACTORY OUTLETS
Discount and so-called "factory outlet" stores are increasingly popular and widespread.
Filene's Basement The world-famous store in Boston (with dozens of branches throughout the country) initiated off-price retailing in 1908. The original store, at the corner of Winter and Summer Streets, is still a wild, potentially lucrative place to shop: you might find a designer original reduced to a fraction of its original price.
L.L. Bean The famous store in Freeport, Maine specializes in outdoor wear and gear, and operates a mail-order business in addition to its outlets.

Children

New England is a veritable paradise for children. They can entertain themselves endlessly with amusements as simple as observing a tide pool, or take in a bit of readily absorbed history at such "hands-on" living museums as Plimoth Plantation or Old Sturbridge Village. Staff members at these sites are skilled at engaging children's interests.

Boston
Boston's Children's Museum is one of the most appealing in the country, and smaller facilities with similar agendas are scattered through the countryside. Other Boston attractions sure to thrill little ones include the Computer Museum (next-door to the Children's Museum, on Museum Wharf); the nearby New England Aquarium, the Swan Boats in the Public Garden; and the view from the 62-story John Hancock Observatory.

Bernice Chesler's excellent book, *In and Out of Boston with (or without) Children* can provide leads on lesser-known but equally rewarding attractions.

Outdoor Activities

Whatever your age and whatever the season, New England offers plenty of active outdoor adventures. From urban walking to thrill-a-minute rafting, from downhill skiing to mountain biking, from fly fishing to gliding a canoe through the salt marshes, New England is an outdoor playground. Within each state are recommendations for outfitters who will help you enjoy the outdoors more fully.

Seaside attractions
Cape Cod might as well be a giant sandbox, and the calm, shallow waters on the bay side offer optimal swimming and splashing for those still acquiring their sea legs.

Children's reaction to the many whalewatch excursions offered on the Cape and along the coast up into Maine is invariably "Awesome!"

Resorts
A number of resorts – most notably Smuggler's Notch in northern Vermont – have made a specialty of catering for kids and the parents they hold in thrall. In summer, this ski area basically becomes a camp for all ages, with waterslides, special outdoors events, and a real sense of camaraderie.

Some of New England's family-oriented resorts, such as The Balsams, in remote northern New Hampshire, date back a century or more, and are attracting a fifth generation for mannered meals and unstructured enjoyment of the great outdoors.

Accommodation
Regrettably, many of New England's fussier B&Bs shun the company of children (though such discrimination is arguably illegal). If you're blessed with particularly well behaved youngsters, you might try pushing the envelope, but then again, it's no fun to go where you're not welcome. Fortunately, there are plenty of inns where their presence is not only tolerated but actively courted.

If in doubt, call ahead or check the detailed listings in *Best Places to Stay in New England*, by Kimberly Grant and Christina Tree.

Restaurants
The fancier restaurants may also exercise their own unpublished strictures regarding children – claiming, for instance, that the place is booked solid when you can see it's half-empty. Here, the best antidote is a reservation. But again, depending on your child, you may enjoy just as pleasant and educational a repast at a ramshackle lobster pound or a nostalgic diner.

Massachusetts

The Place

Known as: The Bay State.
Motto: *Ense Petit Placidam Sub Libertate Quietem* (By the sword we seek peace, but peace only under liberty).
Origin of name: May derive from an Algonquian Indian village meaning "place of big hills".
Entered Union: 6 February 1788, the sixth of the 13 original states.
Capital: Boston.
Area: 10,555 sq. miles (27,337 sq. km).
Highest point: Mount Greylock.
Population: 6 million.
Population density: 570 people per sq. mile (220 per sq. km).
Economy: Financial services; high technology; healthcare; academe.
Annual visitors: 33 million.
National representation: 2 senators and 10 representatives to Congress.
Famous citizens: Samuel Adams, Louisa May Alcott, Emily Dickinson, Ralph Waldo Emerson, John Hancock, Nathaniel Hawthorne, Oliver Wendell Holmes, Edgar Allen Poe, Paul Revere, Henry David Thoreau.

Getting Around Boston

Boston is the only New England city with a subway system (the MBTA, or "T" for short); the cost is low (especially compared to other cities), the transit rapid and the experience generally quite pleasant.

The Boston Passport, offering one, three or seven days of unlimited rides, can be purchased at the Boston Common Visitor Information Center at 147 Tremont St, or call 617 426–3115 for further information.

The Association for Public Transportation advocacy group publishes an excellent and comprehensive low-cost guide called *Car-Free in Boston*, available at newsstands and bookstores; it actually covers, in lesser detail, all of New England.

Where to Stay

BOSTON

Boston Harbor Hotel
70 Rowes Wharf, 02110.
Tel: 617 439–7000/
800 752–7077.
Fax: 617 345–6799.
With 230 rooms, this is a modern beauty with old-world charm, perched on the harbor. **$$$$**

Boston Park Plaza Hotel
64 Arlington Street, 02117.
Tel: 617 426–2000/
800 225–2008.
Fax: 617 426–5545.
A huge hotel with just under 1,000 rooms at the hub of the Hub. **$$$$**

Bostonian Hotel
4 Faneuil Hall Marketplace, 02109.
Tel: 617 523–3600/
800 343–0922.
A mix of modern and historic, overlooking Quincy Market with 152 rooms. **$$$$**

Copley Square Hotel
47 Huntington Avenue, 02116.
Tel: 617 536–9000/
800 225–7062.
Fax: 617 267–3547.
www.copleysquarehotel:com.
Older, centrally located, European-style hotel with 143 rooms; often more affordable than neighboring hotels. **$$$$**

Fairmont Copley Plaza Hotel
138 James Avenue, 02116.
Tel: 617 267–5300/
800 795–3906.
Fax: 617 247–6681. A 1912 grand hotel with 379 rooms and plenty of romance. **$$$$**

Four Seasons
200 Boylston Street, 02116.
Tel: 617 338–4000/
800 332–3442.
Fax: 617 423–0154.
The standard-setter for luxury and service. The hotel has 288 rooms and overlooks the Public Garden. **$$$$**

Hotel Meridien
250 Franklin Street, 02109.
Tel: 617 451–1900/
800 543–4300.
Fax: 617 423–2844.
A modern hotel with 326 rooms built atop a Renaissance Revival 1922 bank; fabulous French service. **$$$$**

Price Categories

A very approximate guide to current room rates for a standard double per night is:
$$$$ = over $200
$$$ = $150–200
$$ = $100–150
$ = under $100

Lenox Hotel
710 Boylston Street, 02116.
Tel: 617 536–5300/
800 225–7676.
Fax: 617 236–0351.
A 212-room hotel well situated for shopping, with Copley Place and Newbury Street on either side. **$$$$**

Omni Parker House
60 School Street, 02108.
Tel: 617 227–8600.
800 843–6664.
Fax: 617 742–5729.
Hawthorne, Whittier, Emerson and Long-fellow used to conduct literary salons at this grand 546-room hotel soon after it opened in 1854. **$$$$**

Ritz-Carlton Hotel
15 Arlington Street, 02117.
Tel: 617 536–5700/
800 241–3333.
Fax: 617 536–1335.
Classic Bostonian white-glove elegance, with the lovely Public Garden at its doorstep and a total of 278 rooms. **$$$$**

Swissôtel Boston
1 Avenue de Lafayette, 02110.
Tel: 617 451–2600/
800 621–9200.

Modern luxury, with 500 rooms and a convenient location for the financial and theater districts, as well as the Common. **$$$$**.
Eliot Hotel
370 Commonwealth Avenue, 02215.
Tel: 617 267–1607
Fax: 800 443–5468.
Fax: 617 536–9114.
Well-appointed hotel whose 92 rooms are all suites with a popular first-class restaurant. Convenient for both Back Bay and the Fenway. **$$$–$$$$**
Gryphon House
9 Bay State Road, 02215
Tel: 617 375-9003.
Fax: 617 425-0716.
www.gryphonhouseboston.com.
Near Kenmore Square and Boston University, this bowfront brownstone has been converted to a small luxury hotel with just eight rooms. Voice mail, fax machines, two phone lines, CD players and other high-tech amenities draw business travelers and technology junkies. **$$$–$$$$**
Tremont House
225 Tremont Street, 02116.
Tel: 617 426–1400/
800 331–9998.
Nicely refurbished 322 rooms in the thick of the theater district. **$$$**
82 Chandler Street
82 Chandler Street, 02116.
Tel: 617 482-0408/888 482-0408.
A five-room B&B in a 19th-century brownstone with bay windows and fireplaces in the revitalized South End neighborhood. Credit cards not accepted. **$$–$$$**

Boston B&Bs

B&B Agency of Boston
47 Commercial Wharf, 02110.
Tel: 617 720–3540/
800 248–9262.
From UK free on 0800 895128.
Fax: 617 523–5761.
This is the largest B&B agency in Boston, with rooms and self-catering apartments in Beacon Hill, Back Bay, North End and near the waterfront.

Meal Guide

● **B&Bs** supply a complimentary full breakfast, often quite sophisticated.
● **MAP** (Modified American Plan) rates include breakfast and dinner
● **FAP** (Full American Plan) rates include all three meals

Harborside Inn
185 State Street, 02109.
Tel: 617 723–7500.
Fax: 617 670–2010.
In a renovated mercantile warehouse all 54 modern rooms have exposed brick and Victorian-style furnishings. Near Faneuil Hall, the financial district and the waterfront. **$$**
John Jeffries House
14 Embankment Road at Charles Circle, 02114.
Tel: 617 367–1866.
Fax 617 742–0313.
Red-brick inn at the foot of Beacon Hill. The 46 rooms are small and simply appointed rooms, but many have kitchens or sitting areas. **$$**
Mid-Town Hotel
220 Huntington Avenue, 02115.
Tel: 617 262–1000/
800 343–1177.
Fax: 617 262–8739.
One of Boston's better deals, a motel-style building with 159 rooms and an outdoor pool, near the Prudential building and the Christian Science Center. **$$**
Newbury Guest House
29 Newbury Street, 02116.
Tel: 617 437-7666.
Fax: 617 262–4243.
A trio of 1882 townhouses converted into a well-appointed Victorian-style inn right on the "street of dreams". With 32 rooms in total, this is excellent value for the location, so book far in advance. **$$**

Brookline
Bertram Inn
92 Sewall Avenue, 02146.
Tel: 617 566–2234/
800 295–3822.
Comfortably elegant Victorian

mansion with a grand staircase and 14 rooms. On a quiet street, convenient for the Green Line MBTA trolleys that go to downtown Boston. **$$–$$$**

Cambridge
The Charles Hotel
1 Bennett Street, 02138.
Tel: 617 864–1200.
800 882–1818.
Fax: 617 864–5715.
A modern hotel with 296 rooms right in Harvard Square, with airy, neo-traditional rooms, some overlooking the river. Home to the popular Regattabar jazz club which draws nationally known jazz performers. **$$$$**
The Inn at Harvard
1201 Massachusetts Avenue, 02138.
Tel: 617 491–2222/
800 458–5886.
Fax: 617 491–6520.
Graham Gund designed this intimate four-story inn encircling a peaceful atrium (114 rooms). **$$$$**
A Cambridge House Bed-and-Breakfast
2218 Massachusetts Avenue, 02140.
Tel: 617 491–6300/
800 232–9989.
Fax: 617 868–2848.
B&B with 16 rooms in a quiet, lavishly restored 1892 Victorian house with carved cherry paneling and immense fireplaces in the common areas. Located about two miles (3.2 km) north of Harvard Square, but only four blocks from a subway stop. **$$$–$$$$**
University Park Hotel at MIT
20 Sidney Street (off Massachusetts Avenue), 02139.
Tel: 617 577–0200.
Fax: 617 494–8366.
www.univparkhotel.com.
Business-class hotel (opened in 1998) between Central and Kendall Squares. Occasional quirky decorating touches in the 210 rooms, such as armoires with circuit board inlays, play up the hotel's location near the Massachusetts Institute of Technology campus. **$$$–$$$$**
Irving House
24 Irving Street (off Cambridge

Price Categories

A very approximate guide to current room rates for a standard double per night is:
$$$$ = over $200
$$$ = $150–200
$$ = $100–150
$ = under $100

Street), 02138.
Tel: 617 547–4600/
800 854–8249.
Fax: 617 574–2814.
www.irvinghouse.com.
Basic but comfortable 44-room B&B, a short walk from Harvard Square. **$$–$$$**
Mary Prentiss Inn
6 Prentiss Street, 02140.
Tel: 617 661–2929.
Fax: 617 661–5989.
Tastefully appointed Greek Revival B&B with a spacious deck. Some of the 18 rooms have antique armoires and four-poster beds. Situated on a residential street between Harvard and Porter Squares. **$$–$$$**

A DAY TRIP FROM BOSTON

Concord
Colonial Inn
48 Monument Square, 01742.
Tel: 978 369–9200/
800 370–9200.
Fax: 978 369–1533.
www.concordscolonialinn.com.
A 1716 inn on Concord's town common with 53 rooms. **$$**
Hawthorne Inn
462 Lexington Road, 01742.
Tel: 978 369–5610.
B&B with seven rooms in the historic district, opposite Hawthorne's Wayside. **$$**
Longfellow's Wayside Inn
Wayside Inn Road, South Sudbury, 01776.
Tel: 978 443–1776.
A mid-18th-century tavern with 10 rooms, close to Lexington and Concord. **$**

Fall River
Lizzie Borden Bed and Breakfast
92 2nd Street, 02721.

Tel/fax: 508 675–7333.
This B&B is the house where the infamous Lizzie Borden allegedly hacked her father and stepmother to death in 1892. The six rooms in the 1845 Greek Revival home are small but feature Borden family memorabilia. **$$$**

Gloucester
Bass Rocks Ocean Inn
107 Atlantic Road, 01930.
Tel: 978 283–7600.
A 48-room motel looking straight out to sea. **$$**
Harborview Inn
71 Western Avenue, 01930.
Tel: 978 283–2277/
800 299–6696.
A comfortable house-turned-B&B near the Fishermen Memorial statue. Some of the nine rooms have an ocean view. **$–$$**

Marblehead
Harbor Light Inn
58 Washington Street, 01945.
Tel: 781 631–2186.
Fax: 781 631–2186.
A formally decorated inn, built around an 18th-century house with a 19th-century addition. Decor in the 21 rooms ranges from traditional to contemporary. **$$$–$$$$**
Spray Cliff on the Ocean
25 Spray Avenue, 01945.
Tel: 781 631–6789/
800 626–1530.
A 1919 Tudor mansion turned B&B with seven rooms. Near the beach. **$$$**

New Bedford
Spouter Inn
One Merill's Wharf, 02740.
Tel: 508 997–7771/

800 691–9066.
Granite building on the waterfront with 17 rooms and a rooftop restaurant. **$$**
1875 House B&B
36 7th Street, 02740.
Tel: 508 997–6433.
Three simple comfortable rooms in the historic district, near the Whaling Museum. No credit cards **$**

Newburyport
Clark Currier Inn
45 Green Street, 01950.
Tel: 978 465–8363.
A dignified, three-story 1803 shipbuilder's home in the Federal mode. Many of the eight rooms feature wide-board floors, pencil-post beds and other antique furnishings. **$$–$$$**
Windsor House
38 Federal Street, 01950.
Tel: 978 462–3778.
B&B in a 1786 house with a British bent (six rooms). **$–$$**
Morrill Place Inn
209 High Street, 01950.
Tel: 978 462–2808.
A Federalist mansion, converted into a lavishly decorated B&B with nine rooms. **$**

Plymouth
Governor Bradford Motor Inn
98 Water Street, 02360.
Tel: 508 746–6200.
A motel with 94 rooms right on the historic (and heavily trafficked) harbor. **$–$$**
Jackson-Russell-Whitfield House
26 North Street, 02360.
Tel: 508 746–5289.
Fax: 508 747–2722.
B&B. B&B in a charming 1782 home with antique furnishings in the three rooms. **$–$$**

Sightseeing in Boston

● **Guided Tours**
You can hop on and off a tram-style wooden bus for a sightseeing tour of the historic parts of the city and most of the Freedom Trail. Start your tour at any stop, buy tickets on the bus and get on and off wherever you wish.

● **Boat Cruises**
Without doubt the most colorful way of doing Boston is onboard a Duck, or renovated World War II amphibious landing vehicle. The tours (with commentary) start in the back bay area and include a mini-cruise on the Charles River.

John Carver Inn
25 Summer Street, 02360.
Tel: 508 746–7100/
800 274–1620.
An immaculate modern hotel, with
79 rooms near the sights. **$–$$**

Rockport
Yankee Clipper Inn
96 Granite Street, 01966.
Tel: 978 546–3407/
800 545–3699.
A total of 27 rooms in three
buildings: a Georgian mansion
(where John and Jackie Kennedy
once stayed) on an ocean
promontory, an 1840 neo-classic
house across the street designed
by Charles Bulfinch, plus a modern
waterside building with large picture
windows; heated saltwater pool.
$$$–$$$$
Eden Pines Inn
48 Eden Road, 01966.
Tel: 978 546–2505.
Fax: 978 546–1157.
A cliffside mansion with dramatic
ocean views. Seven large
bedrooms, many with private
balconies. **$$–$$$**
Seaward Inn
44 Marmion Way, 01966.
Tel: 978 546–3471/
800 648–7733.
A welcoming summer house turned
B&B on a beautifully landscaped
seaside ledge. There are 38 rooms
available in the main inn building,
two nearby houses and adjacent
cottages. **$$–$$$**
Seacrest Manor
99 Marmion Way, 01966.
Tel: 978 546–2211.
A 1911 clapboard mansion turned
quiet, comfortable B&B inn with
eight rooms, well-tended gardens,
sea views, some private decks. **$$**
Addison Choate Inn
49 Broadway, 01966.
Tel: 978 546–7543.
Fax: 978 546–7638.
www.cape-ann.com/addison-choate
Lovely summery decor and a quiet
in-town setting for an inn with six
rooms and two apartments. **$–$$**
Linden Tree Inn
26 King Street, 01966.

Tel: 978 546–2494/
800 865–2122.
A captain's home with 18
reasonably priced B&B rooms and
an innkeeper who loves to bake. **$**
Sally Webster Inn
34 Mount Pleasant Street, 01966.
Tel: 978 546–9251.
Small antiques-filled town inn.
Several of the eight rooms have
wide-board pine floors,
(non-working) brick fireplaces, or
canopy beds. **$**

Salem
Hawthorne Hotel
18 Washington Square West,
01970.
Tel: 978 744–4080.
1920s hotel (89 rooms); harbor
views from top floors. **$$–$$$$**
Amelia Payson Guest House
16 Winter Street, 01970.
Tel: 978 744–8304.
1845 Greek Revival B&B with four
bright, airy rooms. Convenient to
museums and sites. **$$**

CAPE COD AND THE ISLANDS
Barnstable
Charles Hinckley House
8 Scudder Lane, 02630.
Tel: 508 362–9924.
B&B with five period rooms in an
1809 Federal house; lavish
breakfasts. **$$**
Crocker Tavern Bed and Breakfast
3095 Main Street (Route 6A),
02630.
Tel: 508 362–5115/
800 773–5359.
Fax: 508 362–5562.
A 1754 ordinary, tastefully
renovated. The five rooms are
furnished with canopy or four-poster

Massachusetts Trivia

● Commercial electricity was
pioneered in the US in Great
Barrington, Massachusetts,
when inventor William Stanley
installed street lights in 1886.
● US currency is printed on paper
manufactured by the Crane
company at Waconah Mill in
Dalton.

beds, quilts, claw-foot tubs and
antique sinks. **$–$$**

Brewster
Captain Freeman Inn
15 Breakwater Road, 02631.
Tel: 508 896–7481/
800 843–4664. Fax: 896-5618.
A luxurious 1866 Victorian B&B with
12 spacious rooms (some feature
private whirlpool tubs) and an
outdoor pool; healthy and decadent
breakfasts. **$$–$$$**
Bramble Inn
2019 Route 6A, 02631.
Tel: 508 896–7644.
Two houses (1792–1861) offering
eight rooms with a distinctive
decor. **$$**
Old Sea Pines Inn
2553 Route 6A, 02631.
Tel: 508 896–6114.
A 1907 Shingle-style mansion that
once served as a girls' boarding
school; there are 21 rooms and the
modern annex is wheelchair-
accessible. **$**

Chatham
Chatham Bars Inn
Shore Road, 02633.
Tel: 508 945–0096/
800 527–4884.
Fax: 508 945-5491.
A 1914 private hunting lodge turned
grand hotel, now grander than ever.
It even features a private Atlantic
beach, with resort activities. **$$$$**
Wequasset Inn
Pleasant Bay, 02163.
Tel: 508 225–7125/
800 352–7169.
A country club-like setting, with 103
rooms, tennis, pool, bay beach; full-
service resort activities. **$$$$**
Captain's House Inn of Chatham
371 Old Harbor Road, 02633.
Tel: 508 945–0127/
800 315–0728.
The 16 B&B rooms have luxurious
traditional decor; silver-service tea
is served in the garden room, plus
full breakfast. **$$$–$$$$**
Pleasant Bay Village Resort Motel
1191 Route 28, 02633.
Tel: 508 945–1133/
800 547–1011.
An unmotelish complex of 58 rooms
with elaborate gardens. **$$$–$$$$**

Dennis area
Lighthouse Inn
1 Lighthouse Road
West Dennis, 02670.
Tel: 508 398–2244.
Fax: 508 398–5658.
An old-fashioned seaside resort B&B with 61 rooms on a private beach comprising cottages and a 1855 lighthouse-turned-inn. Supervised activities for children in July and August. **$$$–$$$$**

Isaiah Hall B&B Inn
152 Whig Street, Dennis, 02638.
Tel: 508 385–9928/
800 736–0160.
Tax: 508 385–5879.
Stars from the Cape Playhouse favor this charming 1857 farmhouse, with its 10 rooms furnished with country antiques, on a residential street. **$–$$**

Beach House Inn
61 Uncle Stephen's Way
West Dennis, 02670.
Tel: 508 398–4575.
Gray shingled house simply furnished with practical oak and wicker pieces. Seven bright and airy rooms, and right on the beach. No credit cards. **$**

Eastham
Whalewalk Inn
220 Bridge Road, 02642.
Tel: 508 225–0617.
B&B in an 1830s Greek Revival captain's house with 10 luxuriously upscale rooms decorated with breezy panache. Gourmet breakfasts are served, and there are cottages, too. **$$–$$$**

Over Look Inn
3085 Route 6, 02642.
Tel: 508 225–1886.
Scottish hospitality in a colorful 1869 Victorian 11-room B&B near the Salt Pond Visitors Center. **$$**

East Orleans
Nauset House Inn
143 Beach Road, 02643.
Tel: 508 255–2195.
A convivial 1810 farmhouse B&B with 14 rooms and an early 20th-century conservatory) near magnificent Nauset Beach. **$**

Edgartown
Charlotte Inn
27 S Summer Street, 02539.
Tel: 508 627–4751.
An exquisite country inn encompassing five buildings (from 18th century to new) and a total of 24 rooms, all romantically decorated in various styles. **$$$$**

Harbor View Hotel
131 N Water Street, 02539.
Tel: 508 627–4333/
800 225–6005.
A lavishly renovated 1891 shingled grand hotel, with 124 rooms and a heated pool, near Lighthouse Beach. **$$$$**

Price Categories

A very approximate guide to current room rates for a standard double per night is:
$$$$ = over $200
$$$ = $150–200
$$ = $100–150
$ = under $100

Colonial Inn
38 N Water Street, 02539.
Tel: 508 627–4711/
800 627–4701.
Nicely updated and centrally located, this shingled 1911 hotel has 43 rooms and is as vital as ever. **$$$–$$$$**

Point Way Inn
104 Main Street, 02539.
Tel: 508 627–8633.
B&B with 15 rooms in a renovated, now-contemporary, 1840 Federal sea captain's house. **$$$–$$$$**

Falmouth area
Inn at West Falmouth
Off Blacksmith Shop Road, West Falmouth 02574.
Tel: 508 540–6503/
800 397–7696.
Fax: 508 548–6974.
Six rooms in a luxuriously renovated 1898 Shingle-style summer house with tennis court, small heated pool and views of Buzzards Bay. **$$$–$$$$**

Inn on the Sound
313 Grand Avenue South, Falmouth Heights 02540.

Tel: 508 457–9666/
800 564–9668.
Fax: 508 457–9631.
B&B in an 1880 shingled cottage on a bluff overlooking Vineyard Sound. A large porch offers magnificent water views, as do four of the 10 rooms with private decks. **$$**

Mostly Hall
27 Main Street, Falmouth, 02540.
Tel: 508 548–3786/
800 682–0565.
Fax: 508 457–1572.
This six-room B&B is an 1849 plantation-style mansion (built by a seafarer to please a homesick wife) with large, handsome, high-ceilinged rooms, and friendly, knowledgeable hosts. **$$**

Harwichport area
Beach House Inn
4 Braddock Lane, 02646.
Tel: 508 432–4444/
800 870–4405.
Four rooms with all the comforts of home (air-conditioning, television) and then some, right on the beach. **$$$–$$$$**

Augustus Snow House
528 Main Street, Harwichport, 02646.
Tel: 508 430–0528/
800 320–0528.
B&B. Victorian splendor in a five-room B&B in a 1901 Queen Anne mansion near the Sound. **$$$**

Commodore Inn
30 Earle Road, West Harwich, 02671.
Tel: 508 432–1180/
800 368–1180.
A very nearly seaside motel with pretty country decor (26 rooms). **$$**

Hyannis
Inn on Sea Street
358 Sea Street, 02601.
Tel: 508 775–8030.
Fax: 508 771–0878.
B&B with nine rooms in a cheerful inn, made up of two 19th-century houses, a short stroll from downtown Hyannis and from the beach; great value. **$–$$**

Menemsha
Menemsha Inn and Cottages
off North Rd, 02552.

HOTELS IN CAPE COD AND THE ISLANDS

Tel: 508 645-2521.
www.vineyard.net/biz/menemshainn
Peaceful simplicity in 27 rooms and
cottages, on 10 green acres with
water views. $$

Nantucket
The Wauwinet
120 Wauwinet Road, Wauwinet,
02584.
Tel: 508 228–0145/
800 426–8718.
A fabulously refurbished 1850 hotel
with 30 rooms: luxurious, secluded
and very expensive. $$$$
Jared Coffin House
29 Broad Street, 02554.
Tel: 508 228–2400.
A grand 1845 mansion with 60
rooms, and several adjoining
buildings, constitute a popular
island inn. $$$
Martin House Inn
61 Centre Street, 02554.
Tel: 508 228–0678.
Reasonably priced, this 13-room
1803 mariner's home is one of the
prettiest and most congenial of the
many historic B&Bs in town. $-$$

Oak Bluffs
The Oak House
Seaview Avenue, 02557
Tel: 508 693–4187.
A lavish, oak-filled Queen Anne B&B
with 10 rooms overlooking
Nantucket Sound. $$$–$$$$

Provincetown
Watermark Inn
603 Commercial Street, 02657.
Tel: 508 487–0165/
800 734–0165.
An architect-designed contemporary
seaside B&B inn in the quiet East
End. $$$–$$$$

White Horse Inn
500 Commercial Street, 02657.
Tel: 508 487–1790.
An 18th-century captain's house inn
shaped by Provincetown's 20th-
century artistic history. $–$$
Captain Lysander Inn (B&B)
96 Commercial Street, 02657.
Tel: 508 487–2253.
An 1850s captain's house in the
sedate West End (13 rooms). $

Sandwich
Dan'l Webster Inn
149 Main Street, 02563.
Tel: 508 888–3622/
800 444–3566.
Fax: 508 888–5156.
A large 53-room luxury hotel on the
site of a historic tavern. $$–$$$
Inn at Sandwich Center
118 Tupper Road, 02563.
Tel: 508 888–6958/
800 249-6949.
Fax: 508 888–6958.
A 1750s saltbox, with five bright
bedrooms decorated with Laura
Ashley bedding. $$
Wingscorton Farm (B&B)
11 Wing Boulevard, 02537.
Tel: 508 888–0534.
A working farm with four rooms for
B&B located about five minute's
walk from the beach. The 1763
main house with original paneled
bedrooms was once a stop on the
Underground Railroad. $$
Summer House
158 Main Street, 02563.
Tel: 508 888–4991/
800 241–3609.
An 1835 Greek Revival house with
large, airy bedrooms. Most of the
five rooms in this B&B have working
fireplaces. $
Village Inn at Sandwich
4 Jarves Street, 02563.
Tel: 508 833–0363.

National Parks
An extensive selection of
accommodation is available in
and around America's National
Parks. For details of where to
stay in the Freedom Trail area in
Boston and Maine's National
Park, contact:
The National Park Service Public
Inquiry
Department of the Interior
18th and C Streets NW
Washington, DC 20013.
Tel: 800–365 2267.

An 1837 Federal home converted
into a B&B with eight rooms
decorated in a spare, fresh style. $

Vineyard Haven
Martha's Place
114 Main Street.
Tel: 508 693–0253.
A handsome 1840 Greek Revival
B&B with four spacious bedrooms,
immaculately designed. $$$–$$$$

West Tisbury
Lambert's Cove Country Inn
Lambert's Cove Road, 02575.
Tel: 508 693–2298.
A 15-room 1790s farmhouse on
seven pastoral acres with an
English garden. $$–$$$

Woods Hole
Woods Hole Passage
186 Woods Hole Road, 02540.
Tel: 508 548–9575/
800 790-8976.
Fax: 508 540–4771.
1890s carriage house and barn
converted into a romantic B&B with
five room. "Breakfast in a bag" for
early risers. $$

Yarmouth Port
Lane's End Cottage
268 Route 6A, 02675.
Tel: 508 362-5298.
A 300-year-old full Cape in a quiet
wooded setting with three
bedrooms for B&B. $

Wedgewood Inn
Route 6A, 02675.
Tel: 508 362–5157.

Stay in a Lighthouse

Lighthouses sprinkle the whole
New England coast, a memorial to
the area's maritime past. A few of
these are now B&Bs, and at some
of them you can get a taste of how
life was as a lighthouse keeper –
complete with record-keeping jobs!

Contact:

**New England Lighthouse
Foundation**
PO Box 1690
Wells, Maine 04090.
Tel: 800 758 1444.

An imposing 1812 Federal home, with six bedrooms that are at once formal and romantic. **$$**

CENTRAL MASSACHUSETTS

Amherst

The Allen House
599 Main Street, 01002.
Tel: 413 253–5000.
www.allenhouse.com.
Meticulously restored inn of the Aesthetic period, blending Victoriana with Japanese influences. Seven B&B bedrooms. **$-$$**

The Lord Jeffery Inn
30 Boltwood Avenue, 01002.
Tel: 413 253–2576/
800 742–0358.
Fax: 413 256–6152.
www.pinnacle-inns.com/lordjefferyinn.
A traditionalist Colonial Revival-style inn with 48 rooms on the town green, near the Amherst College campus. **$-$$**

Deerfield

Deerfield Inn
81 Old Main Street, 01342.
Tel: 413 774–5587/
800 926–3865.
Fax: 413 773–8712.
www.deerfieldinn.com.
A traditional inn surrounded by historic houses; 23 large rooms furnished with antiques and period reproductions. **$$$–$$$$.**

Greenfield

Brandt House
29 Highland Avenue, 01301.
Tel: 413 774–3329/
800 235–3329.
Fax: 413 772–2908.
www.brandt-house.com.
1890s Victorian B&B with eight comfortable, simply decorated rooms, huge porches and a tennis court. **$$–$$$**

Hadley

Clark Tavern Inn
98 Bay Road, 01035.
Tel: 413 585–1900.
Colonial tavern, originally built in the 1740s, transformed into a romantically appointed B&B.

Amenities in the three bedrooms include canopy beds, working fireplaces, guest refrigerator in the sitting room stocked with complementary snacks, spacious gardens and a swimming pool. **$$**

Northampton

The Hotel Northampton
36 King Street, 01060.
Tel: 413 584–3100.
Fax: 413 584–9455.
www.hotelnorthampton.com.
A handsome traditionally decorated 1926 76-room hotel in the heart of town. **$$**

Northfield

Northfield Country House
181 School Street, 01360.
Tel: 413 498–2692/
800 498–2692.
A grand turn-of-the-century summer home B&B with a swimming pool. The six bedrooms are furnished with Victorian antiques and brass beds, and some have working fireplaces. **$–$$**

Sturbridge

Publick House Historic Resort
The Common, 01566.
Tel: 508 347–3313/
800 782–5425.
Fax: 508 347–5073.
A cluster of historic houses, plus a modern motel-style annex offering 125 rooms in total, close by Old Sturbridge Village. **$$–$$$**

Price Categories

A very approximate guide to current room rates for a standard double per night is:
$$$$ = over $200
$$$ = $150–200
$$ = $100–150
$ = under $100

Worcester

The Beechwood Hotel
363 Plantation Street, 01605.
Tel: 508 754–5789.
A handsome new 73-room hotel overlooking the lake. **$$**

THE BERKSHIRES

Great Barrington

Windflower Inn
684 S. Egremont Road, 01230.
Tel: 413 528–2720/
800 992–1993.
Fax: 413 528–514.
www.windflowerinn.com.
B&B in a late 19th-century country estate with gardens and a pool; 13 rooms with four-poster beds and antiques, some with fireplaces. **$$$**

Elling's Guest House
Route 23, 01230.
Tel: 413 52–4103.
A cozy 1742 frame house offering four bedrooms for B&B. **$**

Lenox

Apple Tree Inn
10 Richmond Mountain Road, 01240.
Tel: 413 637–1477.
Fax: 413 637–2528.
A 22-acre hilltop estate with heated pool, within earshot of Tanglewood; some motel units **$$–$$$$**

Blantyre
16 Blantyre Road (off Route 20), 01240.
Tel: 413 637–3556.
Fax: 413 637–4282.
www.blantyre.com
An opulent mock-Tudor castle on 100 manicured acres with a heated pool, sauna, tennis courts, and croquet lawns. The sky-high prices help ensure luxury and impeccable service in this 23-room hotel. **$$$$**

Canyon Ranch
Bellefontaine, Kemble Street, 01240.
Tel: 413 637–4100/
800 742–9000.
New England's most elaborate spa occupies an 1890s cottage modeled on Le Petit Trianon (120 rooms). **$$$$**

Cliffwood Inn
25 Cliffwood Street, 01240.
Tel: 413 637–3330/
800 789–3331.
Fax: 413 637–0221.
www.cliffwood.com.
An antiques-filled 1890 colonial mansion with seven bedrooms and an outdoor swimming pool on a quiet residential street.

HOTELS IN THE BERKSHIRES

$$$–$$$$
Gables Inn
103 Walker Street, 01240.
Tel: 413 637–3416/
800 382–9401.
An 18-room B&B. Edith Wharton
stayed at this lavish Victorian
mansion while building her own.
19th-century antiques evoke
Wharton's time; more modern
amenities include an indoor pool
and tennis court. **$$$–$$$$**
Rookwood Inn
11 Old Stockbridge Road, 01240.
Tel: 413 637–9750/
800 223–9750.
Fax: 413 637–1352.
www.rookwoodinn.com.
An 1885 "painted lady" B&B at the
center of town. Comfortably elegant
Victorian furnishings in the 21
rooms, creative modern breakfasts.
$$$–$$$$
Garden Gables
141 Main Street, 01240.
Tel: 413 637–0193.
Country charm in this 23-room B&B
in a 1780s house, and one of
Lenox's better deals. **$$**

Youth Hostels

● **American Youth Hostels**
733 15th Street, Suite 840,
Washington, DC 20005.
Tel: 202 783–6161.
Fax: 202 783–6171.
Will supply a list of youth hostels
in New England. The
association's *Hostelling North
America* is available
in bookstores.

The Village Inn
16 Church Street, 01240.
Tel: 413 637–0020/
800 253–0917.
A 1771 inn, with 31 comfortably
furnished rooms. **$$–$$$$**
Walker House
64 Walker Street, 01240.
Tel: 413 637–1271/
800 235–3098.
B&B with eight rooms. A cultural
mecca with private recitals. **$$**

New Marlborough
**Old Inn on the Green & Gedney
Farm**
Village Green (Route 7), 01230.
Tel: 413 229–7924/
800 286–3139.
15 antique-furnished rooms in a
c. 1760 stagecoach inn, plus luxury
suites in a former Normandy-style
cow barn. **$$$–$$$$**

Sheffield
Ivanhoe Country House
254 S Undermountain Road (Route
41), 01257.
Tel: 413 229–2143.
Casual, sprawling, simply furnished
country inn with 11 rooms set in 20
acres. No credit cards. **$–$$**
Staveleigh House
S Main Street, 01257.
Tel: 413 229–2129.
B&B with five rooms in an 1821
parson's home, in spacious
grounds beside the Housatonic. **$**

Stockbridge area
Merrell Tavern Inn
1565 Pleasant Street (Route 102),
South Lee/Stockbridge, 01260.
Tel: 413 243–1794/
800 243–1794.
Fax: 413 243–2669.
www.Merrell-Inn.com.
Nine-room B&B in an authentically
restored 1794 stagecoach tavern,
in a rural riverside setting. **$$–$$$**
Red Lion Inn
30 Main Street, Stockbridge,
01262.
Tel: 413 298–5545/
Fax: 413 298–5130.
A classic old inn (since 1773) at
the center of a Norman Rockwell
town. Many guest rooms in the
main inn are quite small;
accommodations in the adjacent
buildings offer a bit more space. A
total of 111 rooms. **$$–$$$$**
Williamsville Inn
Route 41, West Stockbridge,
01266.
Tel: 413 274–6118.
Fax: 413 274-3539.
www.williamsvilleinn.com.
16-room B&B in a restored 1790s
farmhouse and barn on landscaped
grounds with a summer sculpture
garden. **$$–$$$**

Camping

New England has a large number
of campsites. Government-run
sites (open mid-May to October)
are fairly spartan with flush
toilets and hot showers (at extra
cost). Private campsites (mainly
for RVs) have shops and snack
bars and offer extensive
recreation facilities, including
playgrounds, swimming pools
and even mini-golf courses. Book
well in advance in July and
August, and weekends.

Williamstown
The Orchards
222 Adams Road (Route 2), 01267.
Tel: 413 458–9611/
800) 225–1517.
Fax: 413 458–3273.
A modern hotel with antique
appointments in its 49 rooms,
creating a peaceful, elegant oasis
in spite of its location on an
unappealing commercial strip of
Route 2. **$$$–$$$$**
Field Farm Guest House
554 Sloan Road (off Route 43),
01267.
Tel/fax: 413 458–3135.
This 1948 American Modern
mansion B&B set in over 250 acres
of conservation land has five large
rooms with modern furnishings and
views of the grounds or the hills.
Outdoor amenities include pool,
tennis courts, pond (with fishing
poles available), and trails for hiking
or cross-country skiing. **$$**
River Bend Farm
643 Simonds Road, 01267.
Tel: 413 458–3121.
A 1770 colonial, painstakingly
restored. Furnishings are simple,
even rustic, as befits the colonial

Price Categories

A very approximate guide to
current room rates for a
standard double per night is:
$$$$ = over $200
$$$ = $150–200
$$ = $100–150
$ = under $100

period in this five-room B&B. No credit cards. **$**

Steep Acres Farm
520 White Oaks Road, 01267.
Tel: 413 458-3774.
A four-room B&B on a 50-acre hilltop, complete with orchards and animals. **$**

Where to Eat

BOSTON

Ambrosia on Huntington
116 Huntington Avenue.
Tel: 617 247–2400.
Bold new American cuisine in a dramatic windowed dining room. Are the patrons or the plates dressed more fancifully? Near the Prudential Center. **$$$$**

Aujourd'hui (Four Seasons Hotel)
200 Boylston Street.
Tel: 617 451–1392.
The decor is corporate-opulent, the cuisine invariably artful. The best power tables overlook the Public Garden. **$$$$**

Biba
272 Boylston Street.
Tel: 617 426–7878.
Even after more than a decade, there's no place trendier; owner-chef Lydia Shire is Boston's most resplendent culinary diva. The food may sometimes cross into weirdness, but it's always exciting, and it's served in one of Boston's most intriguingly decorated dining rooms. **$$$$**

Clio
Eliot Hotel, 370A Commonwealth Avenue.
Tel: 617 536–7200.
Creative food but not excessively trendy in a polished spot for business or a night out. **$$$$**

L'Espalier
30 Gloucester Street.
Tel: 617 262–3023.
This ultra-elegant, ultra-romantic and ultra-expensive Victorian townhouse stays two steps ahead of the culinary cutting edge with its prix-fixe French-inspired menu. One of Boston's most popular spots for marriage proposals. **$$$$**

Hamersley's Bistro
553 Tremont Street.
Tel: 617 423–2700.

This pioneer on the now-hopping South End restaurant row remains the standard for other eateries to match. Deft and imaginative touches dress up this excellent, sophisticated comfort food. **$$$$**

Julien
Hotel Meridien, 250 Franklin Street.
Tel: 617 451–1900.
First-class French cuisine, amid the marble grandeur of the former Federal Reserve Building. **$$$$**

La Bettola
480A Columbus Avenue.
Tel: 617 236–5252.
One of Boston's newest star chefs, Rene Michelena, creates Italian-inspired wonders with Asian sensibilities in an unpretentious South End storefront. **$$$$**

Mistral
223 Columbus Avenue.
Tel: 617 867–9300.
One of Boston's hippest dining spots. The New American food, while stylish, is not always as creatively turned out as the dining room and the crowd. But dress up and have fun. **$$$$**

Zinc
35 Stanhope Street.
Tel: 617 262–2323.
Ever-so-chic French bistro serving elegantly updated classics. The menu changes daily but often includes fashionable preparations of lobster and French hangar steak. Off Clarendon Street, one block behind the Hard Rock Cafe. **$$$$**

Rowes Wharf Restaurant
Boston Harbor Hotel, 70 Rowes Wharf.
Tel: 617 439_3995.
Superb harbor views and superior regional cuisine. **$$$$**

Galleria Italiana
177 Tremont Street.
Tel: 617 423–2092.
Sublime modern Italian, including innovative seafood preparations and fresh pastas with inspired sauces, opposite Boston Common. The small, almost spare room, is jammed pre-theater. **$$$–$$$$**

Pignoli
79 Park Plaza.
Tel: 617 338–7500.
A stylish Back Bay haunt for imaginative Italian/Mediterranean creations. Owned by Lydia Shire of Biba fame. **$$$–$$$$**

Sonsie
327 Newbury Street.
Tel: 617 351–2500.
A trendsetter's cafe, with exotic fare. Also a good spot for a light breakfast. **$$$–$$$$**

Aquitaine
569 Tremont Street.
Tel: 617 424–8577.
A happening French bistro and wine bar (although the "bar" is the size of a postage stamp) in the trendy South End restaurant district. **$$$**

Hampshire House
84 Beacon Street.
Tel: 617 227–9600.
Nonpareil jazz brunch with a view of the Public Garden. Above the bar made famous in TV's Cheers. **$$$**

Lala Rokh
97 Mount Vernon Street.
Tel: 617 720–5511.
Refined Persian cuisine in an intimate, romantically appointed Beacon Hill townhouse. The staff are happy to explain the intriguing, comforting dishes. **$$$**

Legal Sea Foods
Boston Park Plaza Hotel, 64

Restaurant Guidelines

● **Prices** are approximate, but for a three-course meal for one (excluding beverages, tax and tip), the following guidelines may prove helpful:

$$$$ = over $40
$$$ = $28-40
$$ = $15-28
$ = under $15

● **Meal tax** varies from state to state, but it is customary to tip 15 to 20 percent on the pre-tax total.

● **Credit cards** The more expensive establishments generally accept credit cards, but call ahead to check just in case.

● **Reservations** Most restaurants, except for the clearly casual, appreciate reservations (some require them).

Arlington Street.
Tel: 617 426–4444.
The freshest of fish, served the
moment it's done. Other Legal
branches are located in the
Prudential Center, Copley Place and
across the river in Cambridge's
Kendall Square. **$$$**

Locke-Ober
3 Winter Place.
Tel: 617 542–1340.
Brahmin (in other words, somewhat
boring) cuisine in an atmospheric
1894 landmark. **$$$**

Ristorante Toscano
41 Charles Street.
Tel: 617 723–4090.
True Tuscan delicacies in a
handsome upscale trattoria on
Beacon Hill. **$$$**

The Ritz Dining Room
Ritz-Carlton Hotel, 15 Arlington St.
Tel: 617 536–5700.
The menu choices may be stuffy,
but this is still the spot for Brahmin-
watching. **$$$**

Sage
69 Prince Street.
Tel: 617 248–8814.
Hidden away on a North End side
street, this barely-room-to-walk
storefront blends warm service and
New Italian cuisine. **$$$**

Tremont 647
647 Tremont Street.
Tel: 617 266–4600.
Adventurous American "melting pot"
cuisine in a hip South End dining
spot. Wear black. **$$$**

29 Newbury St
29 Newbury St
Tel: (617) 536-0290.
A perennially popular bistro, with a

strategic sidewalk cafe for
assessing the passing fashion
parade. **$$$**

Skipjack's, 199 Clarendon St, tel:
(617) 536-3500. Native seafood
with a modernist bent in the
shadow of the John Hancock tower.
$$$

Antico Forno
93 Salem Street.
Tel: 617 723–6733.
A cozy North End storefront serving
hearty home-style Italian. Casual
enough to bring the kids (the brick-
oven pizzas get high marks), but the
grown-ups can savor seafood
linguini, baked rabbit or grilled fresh
halibut. **$$**

Artu
6 Prince Street.
Tel: 617 742–4336.
Friendly, bustling trattoria in the
North End. A good value for fresh
pastas, roasted vegetables or
updated Italian classics. **$$**

The Daily Catch
323 Hanover Street.
Tel: 617 523–8567.
Superb calamari and other seafood
in the North End. The room is tiny
and always jammed, so be prepared
to wait. **$$**

Durgin-Park
Faneuil Hall Marketplace.
Tel: 617 227–2038.
Cheap New England classics
(chowder, pot roast, baked beans),
with good-natured insults thrown in
free. **$$**

East Ocean Seafood
25 Beach Street.
Tel: 617 542–2504.
Fresh-from-the-tanks Hong Kong-
style seafood in a low-key
Chinatown eatery. **$$**

Ginza Japanese Restaurant
16 Hudson Street.
Tel: 617 338–2261.
One of Boston's best sushi spots,
tucked away in Chinatown. The
unusual *maki* rolls are particularly
tasty. **$$**

Sakura-bana
57 Broad Street.
Tel: 617 542–4311.
Nonpareil sushi in the financial
district. **$$**

Barking Crab
88 Sleeper Street, at Northern
Avenue.
Tel: 617 426–2722.
Seaside clam shack transported to
the city. Fried clams and other
simple seafood with great harbor
and city vistas. **$**

Commonwealth Brewing Co
138 Portland Street.
Tel: 617 523–8383.
The pub grub is hearty, the home
brew alluring. **$**

Golden Palace
14 Tyler Street.
Tel: 617 423–4565.
Skip the ordinary dinners here and
come for dim sum on weekend
mornings. Just look at what others
are eating in this loud, jam-packed
room and point at the passing food
carts. **$**

Sultan's Kitchen
72 Broad Street.
Tel: 617 728–2828.
A popular downtown take-out shop
(with a few upstairs tables) serving
fresh Turkish/Middle Eastern shish
kebabs, salads and the Greek
sweet *baklava*. **$**

Cambridge
Chez Henri
1 Shepard Street (off Mass
Avenue).
Tel: 617 354–8980.
Modern French fare with a Cuban
accent in a snug bistro north of
Harvard Square. The spinach salad
fired up with spicy duck tamale is
destined to become a classic.
$$$–$$$$

Rialto
Charles Hotel, I Bennett Street.
Tel: 617 864–1200.
Restaurateur Michela Larson and
chef Jody Adams have earned

Restaurant Guidelines

● **Prices** are approximate, but for
a three-course meal for one
(excluding beverages, tax and tip),
the following guidelines may prove
helpful:
$$$$ = over $40
$$$ = $28-40
$$ = $15-28
$ = under $15
● **Meal tax** varies from state to

state, but it is customary to tip 15
to 20 percent on the pre-tax total.
● **Credit cards** The more
expensive establishments
generally accept credit cards, but
call ahead to check just in case.
● **Reservations** Most restaurants,
except for the clearly casual,
appreciate reservations (some
require them).

international accolades for their flavorful Mediterranean cuisine in a coolly elegant dining room. **$$$–$$$$**

East Coast Grill
1271 Cambridge Street (Inman Square).
Tel: 617 491–6568.
A stylish, wildly popular spot – and deservedly so – for innovative grilled seafood (often topped with exotic spice rubs or fruit salsas), creative salads, barbecue and fiery "pasta from hell". Margaritas help ease the often long waits for a table. **$$$**

Harvest
44 Brattle Street.
Tel: 617 492–1115.
Recently refurbished, it remains one of Harvard Square's most reliably innovative bistros, with a civilized bar. **$$$**

Salamander
1 Athenaeum Street (off First Street).
Tel: 617 225–2121.
Chef Stan Frankenthaler is a rising star in Boston's culinary firmament for his bold, sure hand and international inspiration. His inventive fusion cuisine lights up East Cambridge. **$$$**

Atasca
279A Broadway at Columbia Street.
Tel: 617 354–4355.
Way off the beaten path (between Central and Inman Squares), this tiny storefront brings a satisfying taste of Portugal to Cambridge. **$$–$$$**

Casablanca
40 Brattle Street.
Tel: 617 876–0999.
Turkish/Moroccan menu within reach of student budgets. Go just for David Omar White's murals of the movie, but the comfortable bar is a fine spot for appetizers and drinks, too. **$$**

Green Street Grill
280 Green Street.
Tel: 617 876–1655.
A drab bar in a marginal neighborhood serves hyper-spicy Islands food (especially grilled fish), often with lively jazz accompaniment. **$$**

A Meal with a View

Look out over Boston's night lights when you dine on the 52nd floor at the Top of the Hub restaurant, or the 33rd floor of the Bay Tower Room.

● **Top of the Hub**
Prudential Center
Tel: 617 536-1775.
Seafood is the best bet, and there's a good Sunday brunch.

● **Bay Tower Room**
60 State Street
Tel: 617-723-1666.
Lush plants, piano music, good seafood. Near Faneuil Hall.

House of Blues
96 Winthrop Street.
Tel: 617 491–2583.
Southern to international fare, with musical accompaniment. In Harvard Square. **$$**

John Harvard's Brew House
33 Dunster Street.
Tel: 617 868–3585.
Surprisingly refined pub grub, and made-on-the-premises beers. In Harvard Square. **$$**

Rhythm and Spice
315 Massachusetts Avenue.
Tel: 617 497–0977.
A taste of the Caribbean near MIT. Jerk chicken, curried goat and reggae music. **$$**

Fraser's
1680 Massachusetts Avenue.
Tel: 617 441–5566.
A comfortable neighborhood café between Harvard and Porter Squares serving interesting salads, sandwiches and pastas. Good selection of microbrews. **$–$$**

Algiers Cafe
40 Brattle Street.
Tel: 617 492–1557.
Turkish coffee and tabbouleh for the intelligentsia in Harvard Square. **$**

Charlestown
Olives
10 City Square.
Tel: 617 242–1999.
Avid patrons put up with long lines

and often-deafening hubbub to savor Todd English's first-class Tuscan country cuisine. **$$$$**

Figs
67 Main Street.
Tel: 617 242–2229.
Olives' pizza-parlor cousin, still upscale, only slightly less mobbed. **$–$$**

Somerville
Dali
415 Washington Street (at Beacon Street).
Tel: 617 661–3254.
Robust Spanish specialties (try the signature fish baked in salt) and particularly fine tapas in a lively atmosphere worthy of Hemingway. On the Cambridge/Somerville line. **$$–$$$**

eat
253 Washington Street.
Tel: 617 776–2889.
Creative comfort food – roast chicken, grilled fish with intriguing sauces – in a homey Union Square storefront. **$$**

Redbone's
55 Chester Street (off Elm Street).
Tel: 617 628–2200.
The place to go when you're hungry for massive plates of barbecued ribs. A loud and rowdy Davis Square dive with an extensive beer list and valet parking for bicycles! **$–$$**

The Burren
247 Elm Street.
Tel: 617 776–6896.
Comfortable Davis Square Irish pub draws locals, yuppies and students. Stop in for a Guinness or some fish and chips. **$**

BOSTON DAY TRIPS

Concord
Aigo Bistro
84 Thoreau Street.
Tel: 978 371–1333.
Sophisticated if suburban Provencale. **$$$**

Colonial Inn
48 Monument Square.
Tel: 978 369–2000.
A 1716 inn serving traditional New England fare as well as afternoon tea. **$$–$$$**

Walden Grille
24 Walden Street.

Tel: 978 371–2233.
Contemporary cuisine in an old brick firehouse. **$$–$$$**

Essex
Woodman's
The Causeway.
Tel: 978 768–6451.
Home of the original fried clam, invented in 1915. **$**

Fall River
Estoril
1577 Pleasant Street.
Tel: 508 677–1200.
A white-tablecloth introduction to classic Portuguese fare. **$$**
Tabacaria Açoriana Restaurant
408 S Main Street.
Tel: 508 673–5890.
A casual Portuguese cafe downtown. **$**

Gloucester
Cafe Beaujolais
118 Main Street.
Tel: 978 282–0058.
An upscale bistro with a popular wine bar, blending fresh fish and local produce into intriguing French creations. **$$$**
Evie's Rudder
73 Rocky Neck.
Tel: 978 283–7967.
A rollicking tavern in the Rocky Neck artists' colony. **$$**
White Rainbow
65 Main Street.
Tel: 978 281–0017.
Rich, evolved Continental in a dramatic granite-walled hideaway.
$$$

Lexington
Dabin
10 Muzzey Street (off Mass Avenue).
Tel: 781 860–0171.
Traditional Japanese and Korean fare in a peaceful shelter from the bustle of Lexington Center. A small patio for outdoor dining in warm weather. **$$**
Lemon Grass
1710 Massachusetts Avenue.
Tel: 781 862–3530.
A low-key Thai storefront café where the food is tempered for American palates. **$–$$**

Lowell
La Boniche
143 Merrimack Street.
Tel: 978 458–9473.
An intimate restaurant in a landmark Art Nouveau building serving creative French fare.
$$–$$$
The Olympia
453 Market Street.
Tel: 978 452–8092.
A friendly, family-run Greek restaurant. **$–$$**

Marblehead
The Landing
81 Front Street
Tel: (781) 631-1878.
The food – New England seafood standards – may not be exciting, but the view of Marblehead Harbor is fine. **$$–$$$**
Maddie's Sail Loft
15 State Street.
Tel: 781 631–9824.
Standard fried or broiled seafood in a lively, often-crowded casual room. Located between Front and Washington Streets. **$$**

New Bedford
Antonio's
Coggeshalle and N Front Streets.
Tel: 508 992–7359.
Huge portions of Portuguese classics that draw crowds to this nondescript dining room. Near the intersection of Routes 95 and 18. **$$**
Davy's Locker
1480 E Rodney French Boulevard.
Tel: 508 992–7359.
Traditional seafood preparations, since 1962, right on the harbor near the Martha's Vineyard ferry docks. **$$**

Newburyport
David's
Garrison Inn, 11 Brown Square.
Tel: 978 462–8077.
Formal dining room emphasizing seafood in classic and updated preparations, with a more casual tavern downstairs. Offers childcare and dinner for kids while parents dine. **$$$**
Glenn's Restaurant
Merrimack Street.

Boston Ice Cream

Toscanini's Ice Cream
899 Main Street.
Tel: 617 491–5877.
In ice cream crazy Boston, this is the Mecca. As well as excellent versions of the basics, it serves many more unusual flavors such as mango, green tea and ginger. The flagship store (which often hosts small art exhibits) is just off Massachusetts Avenue between Central and Kendall Squares. Another (smaller) location is on Mass Ave in Harvard Square. **$**

Tel: 978 465–3811.
Creative cuisine in a former shoe factory. **$$**
Scandia
25 State Street
Tel: 978 462–6271.
Small candlelit dining room serving fine New American cuisine with a seafood focus. **$$$**

Plymouth
Cafe Nanina
14 Union Street.
Tel: 508 747–4503.
Italian country cuisine. The deck looks out on the *Mayflower II*. **$$$**
Lobster Hut
on the Town Wharf
Tel: 508 746–2270.
Basic fried seafood on the waterfront. **$**

Rockport
The Glass Verandah
Yankee Clipper Inn, 96 Granite Street.
Tel: 978 546–3407.
Studied and satisfying New American cuisine in a formal setting with ocean views. **$$$–$$$$**
Portside Chowder House
Bearskin Neck.
Tel: 978 546–7045.
A basic seafood hole-in-the-wall in the heart of Rockport's tourist bustle. Specializes in chowder, but serves up sandwiches, burgers and seafood plates, too. **$**

Salem
Grapevine
26 Congress Street.
Tel: 978 745–9335.
A peaceful, elegant spot for northern Italian fare sparked with an occasional fusion influence. **$$–$$$**
Red Raven's Havana
90 Washington Street.
Tel: 978 740–3888.
Funky, upscale and eclectic New American fare in a funky, upscale and eclectic room; in spite of the name, the food is not Cuban. **$$$**
Red Raven's Love Noodle
75 Congress Street.
Tel: 978 745–8558.
A more casual sister restaurant to Red Raven's Havana. **$$$**
Salem Beer Works
278 Derby Street.
Tel: 978 745–2337.
Salem's contribution to the microbrewery fad. Upscale bar food and fresh-brewed beers in a renovated warehouse building. **$–$$**

CAPE COD AND THE ISLANDS
Barnstable
Mattakeese Wharf
271 Mill Way.
Tel: 508 362–4511.
A classic wharfside seafood haven. **$$$**

Brewster
Bramble Inn
2019 Route 6A
Tel: 508 896–7644.
Intimate rooms with interesting decor, and absolutely fascinating food. **$$$**

Brewster Fish House
2208 Route 6A.
Tel: 508 896–7867.
"Nonconformist" seafood, snazzy desserts, long waits. **$$**
Chillingsworth
2449 Route 6A
Tel: 508 896–3640.
The seven-course *prix-fixe* menu (classical French) is among the ultimate dining experiences the Cape has to offer. **$$$$**
Old Manse Inn
1861 Main Street.
Tel: 508 896–3149.
Mediterranean panache; try for the flower-filled sunporch. **$$$**

Chatham
Christian's Restaurant
443 Main Street.
Tel: 508 945–3362.
A lively New American bistro; upstairs, an inviting, library-like piano bar. **$$$$**
Chatham Bars Inn
Shore Road.
Tel: 508 945–0096/ 800)527–4884.
A grand old dining room with French and regional cuisine. **$$$$**
Vining's Bistro
595 Main Street.
Tel: 508 945–5033.
A wood grill with a taste for exotic spices. **$$$**
Impudent Oyster
15 Chatham Bars Avenue.
Tel: 508 945–3545.
International takes on local seafood; popular and packed. **$$**

Chilmark
The Feast of Chilmark
State Road.

Tel: 508 645–3553.
New York-sophisticate cuisine in a loft carved out of a plain clapboard house. **$$$$**

Dennis
Gina's by the Sea
134 Taunton Avenue.
Tel: 508 385–3213.
Hearty classics characterize this lively cafe set amid the Cape's "Little Italy". **$$$**
The Red Pheasant
905 Route 6A.
Tel: 508 385–2133.
Bold New American cuisine in an 18th-century ship's chandlery. **$$$**
Scargo Cafe
799 Route 6A.
Tel: 508 385–8200.
Traditional favorites, plus a few wildcards, in a retro-fitted captain's house. **$$**
Captain Frosty's
219 Route 6A.
Tel: 508 385–8548.
A casual clam shack with exceptional lobster rolls. **$**

Eastham
Eastham Lobster Pool
4360 Route 6.
Tel: 508 255–9706.
Unbeatable fresh fish; no frills. **$$$**

Edgartown
Among the Flowers Cafe
Mayhew Lane.
Tel: 508 627–3233.
Omelets, quiches, pasta and other filling, inexpensive fare. **$**
L'Etoile,
Charlotte Inn, 27 S Summer Street.
Tel: 508 627–5187.
Superlative nouvelle cuisine served in a candlelit conservatory. **$$$$**
The Newes from America
23 Kelley Street.
Tel: 508 627–4397.
Pub grub in a recently unearthed 1742 tavern; a vast range of beers, available in sampler "racks". **$**
Savoir Faire
14 Church Street
Tel: 508 627–9864.
Skillful cuisine with sunny Mediterranean touches in a small, sophisticated restaurant with patio. **$$$$**

Restaurant Guidelines

● **Prices** are approximate, but for a three-course meal for one (excluding beverages, tax and tip), the following guidelines may prove helpful:
$$$$ = over $40
$$$ = $28-40
$$ = $15-28
$ = under $15
● **Meal tax** varies from state to state, but it is customary to tip 15 to 20 percent on the pre-tax total.
● **Credit cards** The more expensive establishments generally accept credit cards, but call ahead to check just in case.
● **Reservations** Most restaurants, except for the clearly casual, appreciate reservations (some require them).

CAPE COD AND ISLANDS RESTAURANTS

Falmouth
The Regatta of Falmouth-by-the-Sea
217 Clinton Ave
Tel: (508) 548-5400.
One of the Cape's most sophisticated restaurants, with elegant appointments and celestial nouvelle cuisine, surrounded by the Sound. **$$$–$$$$**
The Wharf Restaurant
281 Grand Avenue South (Falmouth Heights).
Tel: 508 548-2772.
An early 20th-century seafood restaurant with plenty of atmosphere and sweeping views. **$$**
Clam Shack
227 Scranton Avenue.
Tel: 508 540-7758.
A shack (literally, albeit very picturesque) right on the water. **$**

Hyannis
Baxter's Boat House
177 Pleasant Street.
Tel: 508 775-4490.
Perched over the harbor, a 1950s clam shack with a lively blues bar. **$$**
Starbuck's
950 Route 132.
Tel: 508 778-6767.
Eccentric decor and Mexican-American fare, by the airport. Unrelated to the coffee chain. **$$**
Steamers
235 Ocean Street.
Tel: 508 778-0818.
Mesquite-grilled seafood; live music, and a place-to-be deck. **$$**

Tugboats
21 Arlington Street.
Tel: 508 775-6433.
Fun food and great harbor views, especially at sunset. **$$**
Up the Creek
36 Old Colony Boulevard.
tel: (508) 771-7866.
Boathouse decor; international menu. **$$**

Menemsha
Home Port
North Road.
Tel: 508 645-2679.
Fresh–off-the-boat seafood in a picturesque harbor. **$$$$**

Nantucket
American Seasons
80 Centre Street.
Tel: 508 228-7111.
Adventurous dining amid colorful murals. **$$$$**
Boarding House
12 Federal Street.
Tel: 508 228-9622.
Bold New American cuisine, and the island's most sophisticated sidewalk café. **$$$$**
Chanticleer Inn
9 New Street, Siasconset,
Tel: 508 257-6231.
Classical French cuisine in an opulent auberge-like setting. **$$$$**
Rope Walk
Straight Wharf.
Tel: 508 228-8886.
Seafood with *nouvelle* splashes, on the harbor. **$$$$**
Straight Wharf Restaurant
Straight Wharf.
Tel: 508 228-4499.
Elegant regional fare in a handsome loft space. **$$$$**

21 Federal
21 Federal Street.
Tel: 508 228-2121.
Sensational regional cuisine in a tastefully spare 1847 Greek Revival house. **$$$$**.
Brotherhood of Thieves
23 Broad Street, no phone.
Great burgers, live music and good company in an 1840 whaling bar. **$$**
Espresso Cafe,
40 Main Street.
Tel: 508 228-6930.
Cheap and scrumptious international grazing at a vintage ice cream parlor turned café. **$.**

North Truro
Adrian's
Route 6.
Tel: 508 487-4360.
Irresistible neo-Italian treats; spectacular views. **$$**

Oak Bluffs
Papa's Pizza
158 Circuit Avenue.
Tel: 508 693-1400.
An old-fashioned storefront serving traditional pies at long wooden tables. **$.**

Orleans
Capt. Cass Rock Harbor Seafood
117 Rock Harbor Road, no phone.
No-frills 150s seafood shanty. **$**
Captain Linnell House,
137 Skaket Beach Road.
Tel: 508 255-3400.
Evolved Continental cuisine in a neoclassic 1854 villa. **$$$$**
Off-the-Bay Cafe,
28 Main Street.
Tel: 508 255-5505.
An ambitious bistro menu; jazz brunch. **$$$$**
Land Ho!
38 Main Street.
Tel: 508 255-5165.
A pub known mostly to locals, who keep it packed. **$$**

Provincetown
Cafe Edwige
333 Commercial Street.
Tel: 508 487-2008.
Natural-foods breakfasts, delicious enough to seem sinful; candlelit

Restaurant Guidelines

• **Prices** are approximate, but for a three-course meal for one (excluding beverages, tax and tip), the following guidelines may prove helpful:
$$$$ = over $40
$$$ = $28-40
$$ = $15-28
$ = under $15
• **Meal tax** varies from state to

state, but it is customary to tip 15 to 20 percent on the pre-tax total.
• **Credit cards** The more expensive establishments generally accept credit cards, but call ahead to check just in case.
• **Reservations** Most restaurants, except for the clearly casual, appreciate reservations (some require them).

New American dinners among the best in town. **$$$**
Front Street
230 Commercial Street.
Tel: 508 487–9715.
The cuisine is cutting-edge, the ambiance both intimate and intense. **$$$**
Gallerani's Cafe
133 Commercial Street.
Tel: 508 487–4433.
An appealing bistro with cozy booths and eclectic cuisine. **$$$**
Martin House,
157 Commercial Street.
Tel: 508 487–1327.
A c.1750 shingled house with intimate, rustic dining rooms and a skilled regional-cuisine chef. **$$$**
Napi's
7 Freeman Street.
Tel: 508 487–1145.
A colorful institution built of architectural salvage; the menu spans the world. **$$$**
Sal's Place
99 Commercial Street.
Tel: 508 487–1279.
Classical Italian, romantic. **$$$**
Mews and Cafe Mews
429 Commercial Street.
Tel: 508 487–1500.
On-the-beach elegance; creative cuisine. **$$–$$$**
Cafe Blase
328 Commercial Street.
Tel: 508 487–9465.
A sidewalk café perfect for people-gazing. **$**
Cafe Heaven
199 Commercial Street.
Tel: 508 487–9639.
The best burgers in town; breakfasts, too. **$**
Spiritus,
190 Commercial Street.
Tel: (508) 487–2808.
A pizza mecca, and magnet for the late-night crowd. **$**

Sandwich
Dan'l Webster Inn
149 Main Street.
Tel: 508 888–3622.
Surprisingly sophisticated cuisine for a restaurant on this large a scale. **$$**
Dunbar Tea Shop
1 Water Street (Route 130).

Tel: 508 833–2485.
English tearoom serving pastries, light lunches and, of course, tea. **$**

Vineyard Haven
Black Dog Tavern
Beach Street Extension.
Tel: 508 693–9223.
Inventive neo-American fare in a simple wharfside tavern. Their signature T-shirts are everywhere. **$$$$**

Wellfleet
Aesop's Tables
Main Street.
Tel: 508 349–6450.
Festive and celestial regional cuisine; delightful attic bar. **$$$**
Bayside Lobster Hut
Commercial Street.
Tel: 508 349–6333.
Shore dinners in an 1857 oyster shack. **$**
Painter's
50 Main Street.
Tel: 508 349–3003.
A skilled young culinary artist whips up fine New American dishes. **$**

Woods Hole
Fishmonger Cafe
56 Water Street.
Tel: 508 548–9148.
A lively wharfside café with inventive natural foods and fresh seafood. **$$**
Landfall
Luscombe Avenue.
Tel: 508 548–1758.
Seafood in a loft-like space festooned with nautical salvage. **$$**
Shuckers World Famous Raw Bar & Cafe
91A Water Street.
Tel: 508 540–3850.
The freshest of seafood, to be slurped dockside. **$$**

Yarmouthport
Abbici
43 Route 6A.
Tel: 508 362–3501.
This 1775 house sports drop-dead modern decor and serves knockout Northern Italian cuisine. **$$$$**
Inaho
157 Route 6A.
Tel: 508 362–5522.

Shaker Meals

Hancock is Massachusetts' best-kept Shaker village, now a living museum. You can watch craftspeople at work and cooks preparing meals using herbs from the original-style herb garden. In summer visitors can enjoy candlelit dinners, with dishes from Shaker cookbooks. But guests should take heed: the expression "shaker your plate" derives from the fact that leftover food was frowned upon by the Shakers.
Tel: 413 443–0188.

A superb Japanese restaurant, with the freshest possible sushi. **$$$**
Jack's Outback
161 Main Street.
Tel: 508 362–6690.
Looking for local color? You'll find it here in spades, along with tasty, affordable old-favorites food. **$**

CENTRAL MASSACHUSETTS
Amherst
Amherst Chinese
62 Main Street.
Tel: 413 253–7835.
A casual restaurant known for hearty portions at low prices. **$**

Deerfield
Deerfield Inn
81 Old Main Street.
Tel: 413 774–5587.
The setting is appropriately sedate, the menu surprisingly forward-thinking. **$$$**
Sierna
28 Elm Street.
South Deerfield.
Tel: 413 665–0215.
Distinguished regional cuisine. **$$$**

Northhampton
East Side Grill
19 Strong Street.
Tel: 413 586–3347.
Wildly popular Cajun-influenced grill. The food may not convince you that New Orleans has come north, but the room is always bustling. **$$**

CENTRAL MASSACHUSETTS RESTAURANTS

Spoleto
50 Main Street.
Tel: 413 586–6313.
Italian classics in a lively
contemporary cafe. **$$$**

Springfield
**Student Prince and Fort
Restaurant**
8 Fort Street.
Tel: 413 734–7475.
Stout German cuisine in a
convincing beer hall atmosphere,
since the 1940s. **$$**
Pioneer Valley Brew Pub
Taylor Street.
Tel: 413 732–2739.
Locally made microbrews paired
with surprisingly creative eats. **$–$$**

Sturbridge
Whistling Swan
502 Main Street.
Tel: (508) 347–2321.
New American cuisine in a formal
dining room; more casual fare in a
converted barn. **$$**

Worcester
Charlie's Diner
344 Plantation Street.
Tel: 508 752–9318.
A classic diner, manufactured in
1941 by the Worcester Lunch
Company, located on the East Side
near the Beechwood Hotel. **$**
**Restaurant at Tatnuck Bookseller
Marketplace**
335 Chandler Street (Route 122).
Tel: 508 756–7644.
Located on the West Side in the
city's largest bookstore, this
comfortable café serves interesting

New American fare. **$$**
Shorah's Ristorante
Foster and Commercial Streets.
Tel: (508) 797–0007.
A casual downtown storefront, near
the Centrum, serving Italian dishes
ranging from basic pizza and
calzones to more creative chicken
or veal dishes. **$–$$**

THE BERKSHIRES
Great Barrington
Boiler Room Cafe
405 Stockbridge Road (Route 7).
Tel: 413 528–4280.
Contemporary American/
Mediterranean. **$$–$$$**
Castle Street Cafe
10 Castle Street.
Tel: 413 528–5244.
An American/Continental bistro with
big-city flair. **$$–$$$**

Lenox
Blantyre
off Route 20.
Tel: 413 637–3556.
Contemporary French cuisine in the
formal dining rooms of a Tudor
mansion. Served in the summer
only. **$$$$**
Village Inn
16 Church Street.
Tel: 413 637–0020.
New American artistry in a
venerable 1771 inn. **$$$**
Church Street Cafe
65 Church Street.
Tel: 413 637–2745.
Featuring American bistro fare and
whimsical decor. **$$**
Sweet Basil Grille
306 Pittsfield-Lenox Rd at
Brushwood Farms.
Tel: 413 637–1270.

Updated Italian in a comfortable
restored house. **$$**

New Marlborough
**Old Inn on the Green & Gedney
Farm**
Village Green (Route 7), 01230.
Tel: 413 229–3131.
French auberge-style cuisine in a
c.1760 stagecoach inn. **$$$$**

West Stockbridge
Williamsville Inn
Route 41.
Tel: 413 274–6118.
Gourmet country cuisine with
produce from the garden. **$$$**
La Bruscetta Ristorante
1 Harris Street.
Tel: 413 232–7141.
Dinner only. Traditional, contem-
porary and cutting-edge Italian. **$$**

Williamstown
The Orchards
222 Adams Road.
Tel: 413 458–9611.
Accomplished New American
cuisine in a setting of studied
elegance. **$$$**

Culture

DANCE
Boston Ballet (tel: 617 695–6950),
world-renowned, performs regularly
at the Wang Center for the
Performing Arts.
Dance Umbrella (tel: 617
482–7570) produces modern
dance presentations at theaters
around the city.

CLASSICAL MUSIC
Boston Symphony Orchestra and
Boston Pops are heard at the
acoustic and aesthetic **Symphony
Hall** (tel: 617 266–1492; 301
Massachusetts Avenue).
**New England Conservatory's
Jordan Hall** (tel: 617 585–1100; 30
Gainsborough Street), hosts its own
classical concerts.
**Berklee College of Music
Performance Center** (tel: 617
266–7455; 136 Massachusetts
Avenue, Boston) excels in jazz
performances by faculty and
students, many international.

Restaurant Guidelines

● **Prices** are approximate, but for
a three-course meal for one
(excluding beverages, tax and tip),
the following guidelines may prove
helpful:
$$$$ = over $40
$$$ = $28-40
$$ = $15-28
$ = under $15
● **Meal tax** varies from state to

state, but it is customary to tip 15
to 20 percent on the pre-tax total.
● **Credit cards** The more
expensive establishments
generally accept credit cards, but
call ahead to check just in case.
● **Reservations** Most restaurants,
except for the clearly casual,
appreciate reservations (some
require them).

OPERA

Boston Lyric Opera Company (tel: 617 542–4912; 114 State Street) produces three operas each season.

Berkshire Opera Company (tel: 413 528–4420; East Main Street, Great Barrington) presents full-length operas in English.

ROCK AND POP

Boston Big-name national rock and alternative talent can be heard at **The Paradise** (tel: 617 254–2052; 967 Commonwealth Avenue).

Mama Kin (tel: (617) 536–2100; 36 Lansdowne Street) books a variety of rock bands on three stages.

Beverly North Shore Music Theater (tel: 978 922–8500; 62 Dunham Road, off Route 128) hosts acts from April through December.

Cambridge Try the incomparable Johnny D's (tel: 617 776–2004; 17 Holland Street near Davis Square) for everything from blues jams to Cajun music.

Hyannis Cape Cod Melody Tent (tel: 508 775–9100) hosts national comics and musicians throughout the summer on the Cape.

JAZZ

Sculler's Jazz Club (tel: 617 783–0811; 400 Soldiers Field Road, Guest Quarters Suites Hotel, Cambridge) features blues, Latin and jazz in a cozy setting.

Regatta Bar (tel: 617 864–1200, 617 876–7777 for tickets; Bennett and Eliot Streets, Charles Hotel, Harvard Square, Cambridge) presents more traditional, big-name jazz personalities.

Ryles Jazz Club (tel: 617 876–9330; 212 Hampshire Street, Inman Square, Cambridge) features local jazz talent and a jazz brunch on weekends.

Berkshire Performing Arts Theater (tel: 413 637–4718, 413 637–1800; 70 Kemble Street, Lenox) presents jazz at the National Music Center.

THEATER

Boston's theater district, at the intersection of Tremont and Stuart streets has many first-rate and historic theaters, including the **Wang Center**, **Schubert**, **Colonial**, and **Wilbur**.

Higher-quality drama is found throughout the city, though, with performances at the **Boston Center for the Arts** (tel: 617 426–5000; 539 Tremont Street), the **Emerson Majestic Theater** (tel: 617 578–8727; 219 Tremont Street), and Boston University's **Huntington Theater** (tel: (617) 266–0800; 264 Huntington Avenue), with Boston's largest professional company in residence.

American Repertory Theater Company (tel: 617 495–2668; 64 Brattle Street, Harvard Square, Cambridge), a highly acclaimed award winner, has two stages at the Loeb Drama Center.

On the north shore, the **Firehouse Center for the Performing Arts** (tel: 978 462–7336; Market Square, Newburyport) produces year-round plays, and specializes in children's theater.

Merrimack Repertory Theater (tel: 978 454–3926; 50 East Merrimack St, Lowell) has professional productions.

Cape Playhouse (tel: 508 385–3838; off Route 6A, Dennis) offers some of the best summer stock on the Cape; check local listings for other current shows.

Boston *The Phoenix* (published weekly) contains a large Arts and Entertainment section.
The Boston Globe's pull-out Calendar section (published every Thursday) is devoted to cultural events around the city.

Western Massachusetts
For cultural events, consult the *Five College Calendar of Events*, published monthly, or *The Valley Advocate*, a free weekly newspaper.

BosTix (tel: 617 723–5181), with booths in Copley Square and Faneuil Hall Marketplace, is a major entertainment information center. Half-price tickets can be bought at 11am on the day of the event. Cash and traveler's checks only.

CINEMA

Brattle Theater (tel: 617 876–6837; 40 Brattle Street) and the **Harvard Film Archive** (tel: 617 495–4700; 24 Quincy Street), both in Cambridge, show classic movies, plus foreign, nostalgia and art films. The Art Deco **Kendall Square Cinema** (tel: 617 494–9800; Kendall Square, Cambridge) offers cappuccino with its foreign and art movies.

Sony Nickelodeon Theater (tel: 617 424–1500; 606 Commonwealth Avenue, Boston) shows both mainstream and independent films.

Pleasant Street Theater (tel: 413 586–0935; 27 Pleasant Street, Northampton) runs independent, foreign and art films.

Cape Cinema (tel: 508 385–2503; off Route 6A, Dennis) was built in 1930 as a movie theater and is still true to its mission.

A trip to the **Wellfleet Drive-In** (tel: 508 349–7176; Route 6, Wellfleet) is one of the best remembrances of a sultry, relaxing summer holiday.

COMEDY

Boston's Faneuil Hall Market Place has several comedy clubs, including **Comedy Connection** (tel: 617 248–9700), while **Nick's Comedy Stop** (tel: 617 482–0930; 100 Warrenton Street) is located in the theater district.

ART GALLERIES

Most of Boston's largest art galleries can be found on Back Bay's Newbury Street, while a number of upstarts have moved to the Fort Point Channel area near South Station. Also try Tremont Street in the South End.

Massachusetts Festivals

● SPRING

Spring officially arrives with the **Boston Marathon** (tel: 617 236–1652), held on **Patriot's Day** (the third Monday in April).

Meanwhile, modern-day Minutemen stage **Revolutionary War Reenactments** in Boston at the Paul Revere House (tel: 617 536–4100) and in Lexington and Concord (tel: 781 861–0928).

In late April, a colorful **Daffodil Festival** on Nantucket (tel: 508 228–1700) marks the first stirrings of summer.

In mid-May (and again in July and September), flea-market fever sweeps tiny Brimfield for the three **Brimfield Outdoor Antiques Shows** (tel: 413 283–6149/800 628–8379), mega-swap meets that attract over 1,000 dealers and some serious antiquaries.

● SUMMER

Summer is music time, beginning in mid-June with the **Boston Globe Jazz Festival** (tel: 617 929–2649).

From mid-June to late August, the Boston Symphony Orchestra presides over the world-famous **Tanglewood Music Festival** (tel: 413 637–5165/800 274–8499) in Lenox.

Following roughly the same schedule are two fellow Berkshires institutions: the **Jacob's Pillow Dance Festival** (tel: 413 243–0745) in nearby Becket, and the outstanding **Williamstown Theatre Festival** (tel: 413 597–3400) in Williamstown.

While the BSO is off to the country, the Boston Pops wow the masses with a free **Fourth of July Concert** (with fireworks) at the Hatch Shell on the Charles River Esplanade (tel: 617 266–1492).

Later in July, the Lowell National Historical Park holds the **Lowell Folk Festival** (tel: 978 970–5000), a melange of traditional music and ethnic foods.

Summer is also a good time to catch up with local artisans. Five hundred of the country's very best (including a sizable New England contingent) exhibit in West Springfield at the **ACC Crafts Fair** (tel: 800 836–3470) in mid-June.

A smaller sampling show at the **Old Deerfield Craft Fair** (tel: 413 774–7476) in mid-June and late September.

● FALL

Harvest festivals mark the foliage season, including large-scale extravaganzas such as Springfield's **Big E** (tel: 413 737–2443), and one of the nation's oldest county fairs, the **Topsfield Fair** (tel: 978 887–5000).

Also in October, college crew teams and spectators come to Cambridge for the **Head of the Charles Regatta** (tel: 617 864–8415), while in Salem, the annual **Haunted Happenings** week climaxes on Halloween (tel: 978 744–0013).

● WINTER

Communities across Massachusetts ring in the New Year with **First Night** festivities. Started by Boston artists in 1977, First Night has spread to more than 70 communities nationwide and offers a moveable feast of music, theatre, ice sculptures, parades and fireworks.

Towns in which First Night celebrations are held include the following:
Boston (tel: 617 542–1399)
Salem (tel: 978 744–0004)
several Cape Cod towns (tel: 508 709–2787)
and Northampton (tel: 413 584–7327).

For further information about venues and timings of these events, consult the local tourist offices or newspapers with listings.

The north shore town of Rockport has more than two dozen art galleries, as does Northampton in western Massachusetts.

In Lowell, **Brush Art Gallery and Studios** (tel: 978 459–7819; 246 Market Street) showcases the studios of 12 working artists.

On Cape Cod, head to the towns of Wellfleet and Provincetown and simply wander the streets from gallery to gallery.

Nightlife

NIGHTCLUBS/DISCOS

Boston's Lansdowne Street, behind Fenway Park in Kenmore Square, is the city's largest conglomeration of nightclubs. **Axis** (tel: 617 262–2437; 13 Lansdowne Street), one of the city's largest clubs with a capacity of 1,000 people, has music on several floors.

LIVE MUSIC

In Cambridge, head to **The Middle East** (tel: 617 354–8238; 472 Massachusetts Avenue, Central Square), an eclectic club showcasing nightly jazz, rock and world music on two floors, and **The House of Blues** (tel: 617 491–2583; 96 Winthrop Street, Harvard Square), featuring blues performers and various "all-ages" shows.

The venerable **Iron Horse** (tel: 413 584–0610; 20 Center Street, Northampton) has live folk and jazz music.

GAY & LESBIAN VENUES

Quest (tel: 617 424–7747; 1270 Boylston, Boston) features house music and has gay nights every Monday and Saturday.

At **Avalon** (tel: 617 262–2424; 15 Lansdowne Street, Boston), Sunday is gay night.

Provincetown is the East Coast's Mecca (perhaps tied with Key West) for gays and lesbians. Although it's best to ask around for the current "in" club, you can always count on tea dances at **The Boatslip** (tel: 508 487–1669; Commercial Street), held every summer afternoon on the waterfront deck.

CABARET

Zeiterion Theater (tel: 508 997–5664; 684 Purchase Street, New Bedford), an all-vaudeville theater, stages theme performances.

LATE-NIGHT VENUES

Although Boston is notorious for shutting down early, its large student population usually keeps things rolling, at least on Friday and Saturday. Most nightclubs on Lansdowne St are open until 2:30am, but don't forget: the "T" stops running at 12.30am.

DANCING

Bay Tower Room (tel: 617 723–1666; 60 State Street, Boston) is a beautiful spot for swing-dancing while taking in a twinkling cityscape.

MUSIC

During the summer, Boston has several free outdoor concert series at the **Hatch Shell** on the Charles River Esplanade. Check the *Boston Globe* for listings.

Spectator Sports

Generally, the New England states are represented by Boston's teams – basketball's **Boston Celtics** (tel: 617 523–6050; Fleet Center, September to May), baseball's Boston **Red Sox** (tel: 617 267–1700; Fenway Park, April to October) and hockey's **Boston Bruins** (tel: 617 624–1900, 617 931–2222 for tickets; Fleet Center, October to March).

The major exception is football which the **New England Patriots** (tel: 508 543–8200/800 543–1776 for tickets, Foxboro Stadium, August to December) play in the southern suburb of Foxboro.

For up-to-date information on schedules and locations, check the sports section of any local daily.

Outdoor Activities

BIKING

In Eastern Massachusetts, mountain bikers can explore the trails of **Blue Hills Reservation** (tel: 617 698–1802) in Milton, just south of Boston, or in **Maudslay State Park** in Newburyport on the North Shore. In the western part of the state, **Mount Greylock State Reservation** (tel: 413 499–4262) near Williamstown has a number of mountain biking trails.

Bikers also flock to the **Cape Cod Rail Trail**, a scenic 30-mile (48-km) paved path along the former Penn Central Railway route from South Dennis to South Wellfleet (*see page 160*).

A classic urban bike path is Boston's **Dr. Paul Dudley White Bikeway**, an 18-mile (29-km) loop that follows both sides of the Charles River.

CANOEING/KAYAKING AND RAFTING

In Boston and the nearby suburb of Newton, **Charles River Canoe and Kayak Center** (tel: 617 965–5110) rents canoes and kayaks on the Charles River for an hour or more.

South Bridge Boat House in historic Concord (tel: 978 369–9438) has canoes for rent on the lazy Sudbury and Concord Rivers.

Cape Cod Coastal Canoe & Kayak (tel: 508 564–4051), naturalists lead canoe and kayak tours of the Cape's salt marshes, tidal rivers, bays, and islands.

In western Massachusetts, **Zoar Outdoor** (tel: 800 532–7483), based along the Mohawk Trail in Charlemont, organizes whitewater rafting expeditions for all levels on the Deerfield River. They also run two- or three-day learn-to-kayak or canoe clinics.

FISHING

If you're interested in salt-water fly-fishing, check with **Orvis Saltwater School** (tel: 800 235–9763, Chatham) on Cape Cod. They run a 2.5-day course that teaches basic saltwater techniques. Also on the Cape, **Patriot Party Boats** (tel: 508 548–2626), operating out of Falmouth Harbor, offers deep-sea fishing trips.

The Orleans-based **Rock Harbor Charter Fleet** (tel: 508 255–9757) run fishing excursions as well.

HIKING

Close to Boston, hikers can explore the 150 miles of trails at **Blue Hills Reservation** (see *Biking* above). More ambitious hikers head west to **Mount Tom State Reservation** in Holyoke or **Mount Greylock State Reservation** (see *Biking*), which includes a stretch of the Appalachian Trail.

SAILING

Boston's **Community Boating** (tel: 617 523–1038), America's oldest public sailing program, sells two-day (and longer) memberships for sailing along the Charles River.

Cape Cod Museum of Natural History (tel: 508 896–3867; Brewster) offers nature explorations in Orleans' Nauset Marsh on a motorized catamaran.

The schooner **Bay Lady II** (tel: 508 487–9308) makes two-hour sails from Provincetown into Cape Cod Bay.

SKIING

Massachusetts' best downhill skiing is in the Berkshires. Two of the major areas are **Jiminy Peak** in Hancock (tel: 413 738–5500) and **Brodie Mountain** in New Ashford (tel: 413 443–4752).

But weather permitting, there are options for skiing in the eastern part of the state; the largest area is **Wachusett Mountain** in Princeton, about an hour west of Boston (tel: 978 464–2300/800 754–1234).

The Berkshires are the most reliable for cross-country skiing. **Northfield Mt. XC Center** (tel: 413 659–3715) has 25 miles (40 km) of trails.

Closer to Boston, two smaller but still popular areas are **Weston Ski Track** (tel: 781 891–6575) and in Carlisle, **Great Brook Farm** (tel: 978 369–7486).

Shopping
WHERE TO SHOP
Boston Downtown Crossing, a pedestrian-only zone, is Boston's largest shopping area, complete with outdoor kiosks and street-venders. The popular Faneuil Hall Marketplace has many small shops and foodstands. Boston's version of Fifth Avenue is Newbury Street, 8-block stretch of expensive clothing stores, salons, and art galleries.
Cambridge Harvard Square has over 150 stores within a small radius.
Nantucket As long as you have money in your pocket, the town has a fine and dense concentration of shops.

MALLS
Boston's **Copley Place** (tel: 617 369–5000; Copley Square) has almost 100 upscale stores and restaurants, while **Cambridgeside Galleria** (tel: 617 621–8666; 100 Cambridgeside Place, Cambridge) is a three-story mall with over 100 shops and three department stores. **Cape Cod Mall** (tel: 508 771–0200; Routes 132 and 28, Hyannis) isn't particularly distinctive, but if you're in need of something, it will probably have it.

MARKETS
Boston's historic **Haymarket,** selling inexpensive fruits and vegetables, meat and seafood, is open every Friday and Saturday near Faneuil Hall Marketplace.

Department Stores

Two mammoth retailers worth checking out on Washington Street, Boston are:
Filene's Tel: 617 357–2100 and **Macy's** Tel: 617 357–3000. For bargain hunters the floor below Filene's is the place to head for a unique way of reducing merchandise prices.
Filene's Basement
Tel: 617 542–2011.

FASHION & ACCESSORIES
Chic Newbury Street in Boston is the place for high fashion, with stores such as **Brooks Brothers** at no. 46 (tel: 617 267–2600), **Alan Bilzerian** at no. 34 (tel: 617) 536–1001), and **Ann Taylor** at no. 18 (tel: 617 262–0763).
One of Boston's oldest men's store, **Louis Boston** (tel: 617 262–6100; 234 Berkeley Street) also sells women's apparel now.

BOOKS
Boston and Cambridge are havens for buyers and browsers of new and used books. Apart from the reliable **Barnes & Noble** and **Borders** outlets, check out **Waterstones** (tel: 617 859–7300; 26 Exeter Street; and tel: 617 589–0930, Faneuil Hall Market Place) and **Wordsworth** (tel: 617 354–5201; three stores in Harvard Square, Cambridge).
For travel, nothing beats **Globe Corner Bookstore** (tel: 617 859–8008; 500 Boylston Street, Boston and tel: 617 497–6277; 49 Palmer Street, Harvard Square, Cambridge.)
As for used bookstores, **Avenue Victor Hugo** (tel: 617 266–7746; 339 Newbury Street) and **Trident Booksellers and Cafe** (tel: 617 267–8688; 338 Newbury Street) are both great.
Schoenhof's (tel: 617 547–8855; 76A Mount Auburn Street, Cambridge) sells foreign-language materials, as well as fiction and dictionaries in almost any language.
Tatnuck Bookseller Marketplace in Worcester (tel: 508 756–7644; 335 Chandler Street) is the largest independent bookseller in the state, carrying over 500,000 volumes. Northampton has a particularly dense concentration of shops.

ANTIQUES
Boston's Charles Street has a large number of antique dealers, including the **Boston Antique Co-op** (tel: 617 227–9810; 119 Charles Street). Also try the **Boston Antique Center** (tel: 617 742–1400; 54 Canal Street, near North Station)
On the north shore, Gloucester's

Main Street has lots of interesting antiques shops, and in Essex, you can't help stopping at **The White Elephant** (tel: 978 768–6901; 32 Main St), one of the town's 40 antique dealers.
Antique Center of Sturbridge, 462 Main Street, Sturbridge (tel: 508 347–5150) has dealers on two floors.
On Cape Cod, the whole stretch of Route 6A from Sandwich to Orleans is lined with antique shops. Brewster has the most and generally the best.

CHINA AND GLASS
Fellerman & Raabe Glassworks Main Street, Sheffield. Tel: 413 229–8533. Sells glassware of every shape, size and color.
October Mountain Stained Glass 343 Main Street, Great Barrington. Tel: 413 528–6681. Features stained glass. Both are in the Berkshires.
Martha's Vineyard Glass Works State Road, West Tisbury. Tel: 508 693–6026. Carries an exceptional selection of glassware; you can watch the master craftspeople at work, too.
Pairpoint Crystal Route 6A, Sagamore. Tel: 508 888–2344/800 899–0953. Glassmakers use a variety of techniques developed in nearby Sandwich, which was world-renowned in the 1800s for its innovative glassmaking.

JEWELRY
Shreve, Crump & Low 330 Boylston Street, Boston. Tel: 617 267–9100. One of Boston's oldest and most venerated shops, sells a dazzling array of fine jewelry, as well as exceptional china, crystal and silver.
Tiffany & Co Copley Place, Boston. Tel: 617 353–0222. Always exceptional.

ARTS AND CRAFTS

Society for Arts and Crafts
175 Newbury Street, Boston.
Tel: 617 266–1810.
A prestigious, non-profit institution
with high quality handmade items.

Worcester Center for Crafts
25 Sagamore Road, Worcester.
Tel: 508 753–8183.
One of America's oldest crafts
complexes.

Great Barrington Pottery
Route 41.
Tel: 413 274–6259.
Sells pieces glazed in Japanese
wood-burning kilns.

TOYS

F.A.O. Schwarz
440 Boylston Street, Boston.
Tel: 617 262–5900.
Sells an astonishing variety toys,
both old-fashioned and high-tech,
many at astonishingly high prices.

Children

THEME PARKS

Whalom Park
Route 13, Lunenburg.
Tel: 978 342–3707.
A waterslide, 50 carnival-style rides
and a beach on Whalom Lake.

ZOOS

Franklin Park Zoo
Blue Hill Avenue at Columbia Road,
Boston.
Tel: 617 442–4896.
Has a free-flight aviary, an African
Tropical Rain Forest exhibit and a
whole cast from the animal
kingdom.

Steam Train Journeys
Berkshire Scenic Railway
10 Willow Creek Road, off Route 7,
Lenox).
Tel: 413 637–2210.
Runs train rides May through
October.

THEATER

Priscilla Beach Theater
Rocky Hill Road, Plymouth.
Tel: 508 224–4888.
Presents children's shows on Friday
and Saturday, as well as a
performing arts camp throughout

the summer.
(See also Firehouse Center for the
Performing Arts, Theater.)

MUSEUMS

Children's Museum
Museum Wharf, 300 Congress
Street, Boston.
Tel: 617 426–8855.
A delight, pure and simple, with the
focus combining fun with learning.

Museum of Science
Science Park at the Charles River
Dam, Boston.
Tel: 617 723–2500.
Has hundreds of hands-on exhibits
to spark the excitement of children
aged three and up. Science has
never been so much fun.

New England Aquarium
Central Wharf, off Atlantic Avenue,
Boston.
Tel: 617 973–5200.
A world-class facility that supports
serious marine research as well as
a three-story cylindrical glass tank
teeming with sea life.

Thornton W Burgess Museum
4 Water Street, Sandwich.
Tel: 508 888–4668.
Dedicated to the creator of Peter
Rabbit and many children's books.

Connecticut

The Place

Known as: The Constitution State,
because its delegates played a
crucial role in drawing up the US
Constitution in 1787
Motto: *Qui Transtulit Sustinet* (He
who transplanted still sustains)
Origin of name: probably derived
from an Algonquian Indian term
thought to mean "place of the
long river"
Entered Union: 9 January 1788,
the fifth of the original 13 states.
Capital: Hartford.
Area: 5,544 sq. miles (14,358
sq. km).
Highest point: Mount Frissell,
2,380 ft (725m).
Population: 3.29 million.
Population density: 593 people per
sq. mile (229 per sq. km).
Economy: Hartford is a a major
insurance centre. Also aircraft
engines, helicopters, submarines,
and firearms.
National representation:
2 senators and 6 representatives
to Congress
Famous citizens: Phineas T.
Barnum, Samuel Colt, Katharine
Hepburn, J. Pierpoint Morgan,
Harriet Beecher Stowe, Mark Twain,
Noah Webster, Eli Whitney.

Connecticut Trivia

The following were all invented in
Connecticut:
- Colt revolver
- portable typewriter
- can opener
- tape measure
- vacuum cleaner
- Polaroid camera
- Frisbee.

Where To Stay

AVON
Avon Old Farms Inn
Routes 44 and 10, 06001.
Tel: 860 677–1651/
800 836–4000
Fax: 860 677–0364.
164 modern rooms with traditional furnishings in several red-brick buildings spread across 20 acres. Swimming pool. **$$**

BRISTOL
Chimney Crest Manor
5 Founders Drive, 06010.
Tel: 860 582–4219.
Fax: 860 584–5903.
Six-room B&B in an elegantly appointed 1930s Tudor-style mansion with views of the Farmington Valley, 20 minutes west of Hartford. **$–$$$**

CHESTER
Inn at Chester
318 West Main Street, 06412.
Tel: 860 526–9541/
800 949–7829.
Fax: 860 526–4387.
www.innatchester.com.
Modern amenities in a 44-room inn built around a 1776 farmhouse. Located between Essex and East Haddam. **$$–$$$**

EAST HADDAM
Gelston House,
Main Street, 06423.
Tel: 860 873–1411.
Small elegantly appointed inn, built in 1853, located next to the Goodspeed Opera House. Some of the six rooms overlook the river, others have village views. **$$–$$$$**
Bishopsgate Inn,
7 Norwich Road, 06423.
Tel: 860 873–1677.
Fax: 860 873–3898.
www.bishopsgate.com.
Six-room B&B in an 1818 shipwright's home with six fireplaces. **$–$$**

ESSEX
Griswold Inn,
36 Main Street, 06426,.
Tel: 860 767–1776,
Fax: 860 767–0481.

A haven for wayfarers since 1776. Historical appointments in the 31 rooms include ancient firearms, Currier & Ives prints, and an old popcorn cart. **$–$$$**

FARMINGTON
Barney House
11 Mountain Spring Road, 06032.
Tel: 860 674–2796.
Fax: 860 677–7259.
www.lib.uconn.edu/barneyhouse.
7 rooms. B&B. An imposing 1832 mansion with formal gardens and Victorian greenhouse. **$$**
Farmington Inn
827 Farmington Avenue, 06032.
Tel: 860 677–2821/
800 648–9804.
Fax: 860 677–8332.
A handsomely renovated motel with 72 rooms decorated traditionally. **$$**

GLASTONBURY
Butternut Farm
1654 Main Street, 06033.
Tel: 860 633–7197.
Fax: 860 659–1758.
B&B with five rooms in a 1720 colonial with period antiques, herb gardens and a barn housing goats, chickens (for fresh eggs), ducks, pigs and a llama. **$**

HARTFORD
Goodwin Hotel
1 Haynes Street, 06103.
Tel: 860 246–7500/
800 922–5006.
Fax: 860 247–4576.
www.goodwinhotel:com.
A luxury urban inn with 124 rooms in the heart of town. Significant discounts often available at weekends. **$–$$$$**
The 1895 House B&B
97 Girard Avenue, 06105.
Tel: 860 232–0014.
A bay-windowed Victorian home with three bedrooms in a residential neighborhood. **$**

IVORYTON
Copper Beech Inn
46 Main Street, 06442.
Tel: 860 767–0330/
888 809–2056.
Luxuriously appointed 1890 home

and carriage house; nine of the 13 rooms come with whirlpool tubs. **$$–$$$**

LAKEVILLE
Wake Robin Inn
Sharon Road (Route 41), 06039.
Tel: 860 435–2515.
Fax: 860 435–2000.
www.wakerobininn.com.
A Georgian colonial inn and motel with 38 rooms set in 15 acres. **$$–$$$**

LITCHFIELD
Litchfield Inn
432 Bantam Road (Route 202), 06759.
Tel: 860 567–4503/
800 499–3444.
Fax: 860 567–5358.
Central location is a plus at this new inn, with its 32 rooms traditionally decorated in the Colonial style. The parlor has a baby grand piano and fireplace. **$$–$$$**

Meal Guide

● **B&Bs** supply a complimentary full breakfast, often quite sophisticated.
● **MAP** (Modified American Plan) rates include breakfast and dinner.
● **FAP** (Full American Plan) supply all three meals.

Tollgate Hill Inn
Tollgate Road and Route 202, 06759.
Tel: 860 567–4545/
800 445–3903.
Fax: 860 567–8397.
A romantically appointed 1745 Federal inn supplemented by a renovated schoolhouse; many of the 20 rooms have canopy beds. **$$–$$$**

MADISON
Tidewater Inn
949 Boston Post Road (Route 1), 06443.
Tel: 203 245–8457.
Fax: 203 318–0265.
A former stage coach stop turned

cozy, antiques-filled B&B with nine rooms. Walking distance to Madison village. **$$–$$$**
Madison Beach Hotel
94 West Wharf Road, 06443.
Tel: 203 245–1404.
Fax: (203) 245–0410.
An old-fashioned wooden hotel with a wraparound porch, right on the sound (35 rooms). **$$**

MYSTIC AREA
Harbour Inne & Cottage
15 Edgemont Street, Mystic, 06355.
Tel: 860 572–9253.
www.visitmystic.com/harbourinne.
5 rooms, 1 cottage. Family-friendly pine-paneled 1950s bungalow on the Mystic River, with nautical-themed rooms. Walking distance to the seaport. **$–$$**
House of 1833 B&B
72 N Stonington Road, Mystic, 06355.
Tel: 860 536–6325/
800 367–1833.
www.visitmystic.com/1833.
Five-room romantic, elegant Greek-revival mansion, built in 1833, with a swimming pool and tennis court.
$$–$$$$
Inn at Mystic
Routes 1 and 27, Mystic, 06355.
Tel: 860 536–9604/
800 237–2415.
www.innatmystic.com.
Choose from motel units or 67 elegant rooms in the Colonial Revival mansion. **$$–$$$$**
Red Brook Inn
2750 Gold Star Highway, Old Mystic, 06372.
Tel: 860 572–0349/
800 290–5619.
B&B in a pair of classic colonials on 7 acres. Rooms furnished with American period antiques. Seven of the 10 rooms have working fireplaces. **$$–$$$**
Steamboat Inn
73 Steamboat Wharf, Mystic, 06355.
Tel: 860 536–8300.
Fax: 860 536–9528.
www.visitmystic.com/steamboat.
10 rooms. Dramatic spaces right on the water. **$$$–$$$$**

Whaler's Inn
20 E Main Street (Route 1), Mystic, 06355.
Tel: 860 536–1506/
800 243–2588.
Several 19th-century homes transformed into a homey inn with 41 rooms, clustered near the docks. **$$**

NEW HAVEN
Three Chimneys Inn
1201 Chapel Street, 06511.
Tel: 203 789–1201.
Fax: 203 776–7363.
10-room B&B in a luxurious restored 19th-century urban inn near Yale University. **$$$**
New Haven Hotel
229 George Street, 06510.
Tel: 203 498–3100/
800 644–6835.
Fax: 203 498–3190.
www,nhhotel:com.
A large 92-room city-center hotel with the feel of an exclusive inn for business or leisure travelers. Amenities include an indoor lap pool and hot tub. **$$–$$$.**
Colony Inn
1157 Chapel Street, 06511.
Tel: 203 776–1234/
800 458–8810.
Fax: 203 772–3929.
Located near the Yale campus, this inn features a lobby with a grand chandelier and 86 comfortable guest rooms furnished with Colonial reproductions. **$$**

NEW LONDON
Lighthouse Inn
6 Guthrie Place, 06320.
Tel: 860 443–8411/
888 443–8411.
Fax: 860 437–7027.
Restored 1902 mansion with private beach and 51 rooms. Located a few blocks from Ocean Beach Park. **$$–$$$**
Queen Anne Inn
265 Williams Street, 06320.
Tel: 860 447–2600/
800 347–8818.
Fax: 860 443–0857.
www.visitmystic.com/queenanneinn
10-room B&B in a fanciful Victorian inn. **$$–$$$**

Price Categories
A very approximate guide to current room rates for a standard double per night is:
$$$$ = over $200
$$$ = $150–200
$$ = $100–150
$ = under $100

NEW PRESTON
Boulders Inn
Route 45, 06777.
Tel: 860 868–0541/
800 552–6853.
Fax: 860 868–1925.
www.bouldersinn.com.
An 1895 stone mansion turned 17-rooms B&B or MAP, overlooking Lake Waramaug. **$$$$**
Hopkins Inn
22 Hopkins Road, 06777.
Tel: 860 868–7295.
11 rooms, 2 apartments. An 1847 Federal house with rustic Alpine touches and lake views. **$**

NOANK
Palmer Inn
25 Church Street, 06340.
Tel: 860 572–9000.
www.visitmystic.com/palmerinn.
A grand turn-of-the-century seaside mansion with six rooms in a small fishing village southwest of Mystic. **$$–$$$$**

NORTH STONINGTON
Antiques & Accommodations
32 Main Street, 06359.
Tel: 860 535–1736/
800)554–7829.
Five-room B&B in an elegant 1861 Victorian country house furnished with antiques, many of which are for sale. **$$$–$$$$**
Randall's Ordinary
Route 2, 06359.
Tel: 860 599–4540/
877 599–4540.
Fax: 860 599–3308.
www.randallsordinary.com.
Colonial inn with 15 rooms. On the National Register of Historic Places. Restful rural setting. **$$–$$$**

NORFOLK

Greenwoods Gate
105 Greenwoods Road East (Route 44), 06058.
Tel: 860 542–5439.
Fax: 860 542–5897.
greenwoodsgate.com.
A romantic country hideaway with four sumptuous suites for B&B. Fresh flowers and champagne on request. **$$$–$$$$**

Manor House
69 Maple Avenue, 06058.
Tel/fax: 860 542–5690.
www.manorhouse-norfolk.com.
An opulent 1898 Tudor summer home B&B with 20 Tiffany stained-glass windows. Some of the 10 rooms have whirlpool tubs, fireplaces. **$$–$$$$**

NORWALK

Silvermine Tavern
194 Perry Avenue, 06850.
Tel: 203 847–4558.
Fax: 203 847–9171.
A 1785 country inn with 11 bedrooms set by a waterfall. **$$–$$$**

OLD LYME

Bee & Thistle Inn
100 Lyme Street, 06371.
Tel: 860 434–1667/
800 622–4946.
Fax: 860 434–3402.
A 1756 Colonial home with 12 rooms, set peacefully beside a river. **$–$$$**

OLD SAYBROOK

Saybrook Point Inn
2 Bridge Street, 05475.
Tel: 860 395–2000/
800 243–0212.
Spiffily 62-room nautical luxury hotel, with water views, indoor and outdoor pools and a spa, offering services from exercise programs to massages to facials. **$$$–$$$$**

SALISBURY

Under Mountain Inn
482 Undermountain Road, 06068.
Tel: 860 435–0242.
Fax: 860 435–2379.
MAP with seven rooms offering British hospitality in an 18th-century

Price Categories

A very approximate guide to current room rates for a standard double per night is:
$$$$ = over $200
$$$ = $150–200
$$ = $100–150
$ = under $100

farmhouse. **$$$**

White Hart Inn
Village Green (Routes 44 and 41), 06068.
Tel: 860 435–0030.
Fax: 860 435–0040.
www.whitehartinn.com.
A century-old landmark offering 26 rooms at the center of a timeless town. **$$–$$$**

WASHINGTON

Mayflower Inn
118 Woodbury Road (Route 47), 06793.
Tel: 860 868–9466.
The ultimate in romantic country luxury. A new building with 26 rooms built on the site of an old country inn on 28 secluded acres with gardens, woods, and ponds. Facilities include a pool, tennis courts, health club, and a highly regarded restaurant. **$$$$**

WEST CORNWALL

Hilltop Haven
175 Dibble Hill Road, 06796.
Tel: 860 672–6871.
A stone house on a 64-acre hilltop estate, perched over the village, with lovely views of the Housatonic Valley and Taconic Mountains. Two rooms only. **$$**

WESTPORT

Inn at Longshore
260 Compo Road South, 06880.
Tel: 203 226–3316.
An old-fashioned 11-room inn on the Sound with a trendy restaurant. **$$–$$$**

Inn at National Hall
2 Post Road West, 06880.
Tel: 203 221–1351/
800 628–4255.
Fax: 203 221–0276.
An elegant new inn, styled like an

English manor house, fashioned from a 19th-century Historic District building on the banks of the Saugatuck. 15 lavishly decorated rooms, first-class restaurant. **$$$$**

WETHERSFIELD

Chester Bulkley House
184 Main Street, 06109.
Tel: 860 563–4236.
Five-room B&B in an elegant 1830 Greek Revival home in a historic town 5 miles (8 km) from Hartford. **$**

WOODBURY

Merryvale
1204 Main Street South, 06798.
Tel: 203 266–0800.
A simple rambling 1789 B&B, decorated in an English country style, in Connecticut's "antiques capital". Located on four wooded acres near the Pomperaug River. **$**

Where to Eat

AVON

Avon Old Farms Inn
Routes 44 and 10.
Tel: 860 677–1651.
One of the country's oldest inns (1757); Yankee/Continental fare in a suite of atmospheric rooms. **$$$**

Fat Cat Cafe
Riverdale Farms (Route 10).
Tel: 860 674–1310.
Upscale comfort food, where the motto is "Fine Dining, No Whining". **$$**

Max A Mia
70 East Main Street (Route 44).
Tel: 860 677–6299.
Lively northern Italian spot for pizza, risotto and seafood. **$$**

CANAAN

Cannery Cafe
85 Main Street (Routes 44 and 7).
Tel: 860 824–7333.
"American bistro" innovations. **$$–$$$**

CHESTER

Restaurant du Village
59 Main Street.
Tel: 860 526–5301.
Superb formal French fare in a country auberge between Essex and East Haddam. **$$$$**

EAST LYME
Flanders Fish Market
22 Chesterfield Road (Route 161).
Tel: 860 739–8866.
This humble little roadside
restaurant dishes up ultra-fresh
fish. **$**

ESSEX
Griswold Inn
36 Main Street.
Tel: 860 767–1776.
Traditional fare in a traditional inn.
$$–$$$
The Black Seal
15 Main Street.
Tel: 860 767–0233.
Contemporary grazing, with nautical
touches. **$$**

FARMINGTON
Apricots
1593 Farmington Avenue.
Tel: 860 673–5405.
Creative Continental dishes in a
formal room with river views. More
casual pub fare downstairs.
$$–$$$$

GLASTONBURY
J. Gilbert's
185 Glastonbury Boulevard.
Tel: 860 659–0409.
Steakhouse with southwestern and
Mediterranean influences. Club-like
dining room done in dark woods.
$$–$$$
The Union,
2935 Main Street.
Tel: 860 633–0880.
Contemporary fare – portobello
quesadillas, duck confit risotto,
pan-seared sea bass – and home-
brewed beers in a casually
sophisticated room. **$$–$$$**
Bamboo Grill
875 Main Street.
Tel: 860 633–3446.
Fragrant Vietnamese fare with
ascetic coffee-shop ambiance.
$–$$

GROTON
Fun 'n' Food Clam Bar
283 Route 12.
Tel: 860 445–6186.
Chili dogs, clams, chowder and
milkshakes. **$**

Norm's Diner
171 Bridge Street.
Tel: 860 445–5026.
1950s diner serving breakfast all
day. The cheesecake claims local
fame. **$.**

GUILFORD
Bistro on the Green
25 Whitfield Street.
Tel: 203 458–9059.
Serious French bistro fare with an
American accent. Outdoor patio and
sculpture garden. **$$–$$$**

HARTFORD AREA
Arugula
953 Farmington Avenue,
West Hartford.
Tel: 860 561–4888.
Contemporary Italian cuisine –
roasted eggplant Napoleon, grilled
polenta with portobello mushrooms,
asparagus-filled sun-dried tomato
ravioli, wild mushroom lasagna – in
a small, pampering dining room. **$$$**
Back Porch Bistro
971 Farmington Avenue, West
Hartford.
Tel: 860 231–1922.
Popular, stylish bistro serving
creative American fare: crab cakes,
veal with porcini mushrooms,
upscale pastas. **$$–$$$**
Carbone's
588 Franklin Avenue, Hartford.
Tel: 860 296–9646.
Has been serving Italian classics
since 1938. **$$**
Max Downtown
185 Asylum Street, Hartford.
Tel: 860 522–2530.
Upscale power dining. Menu
emphasizes fish and pasta. Cigar
bar draws a business crowd. **$$$$**

Oasis
267 Farmington Avenue, Hartford.
Tel: 860 241–8200.
1940s-style diner serving
wholesome traditional fare – pot
roast, open-face turkey sandwiches
with mashed potatoes and gravy –
along with a variety of more modern
dishes. **$–$$**
Savannah
391 Main Street, Hartford.
Tel: 860 278–2020.
Blend New England ingredients,
Southern influences, white
tablecloths and African art to serve
up an intriguing dining adventure.
$$$–$$$$.
Trout Brook Brewhouse
45 Bartholomew Avenue, Hartford.
Tel: 860 951–1680.
Historic rubber factory transformed
into a smokehouse and brewery. **$**
Quaker Diner
319 Park Road, West Hartford.
Tel: 860 232–5523.
Restored 1931 diner cooking up
"made from scratch" breakfasts
and homestyle food. **$**

IVORYTON
Copper Beech Inn
46 Main Street.
Tel: 860 767–0330.
Classic French cuisine in a setting
of studied elegance. **$$$$**

LITCHFIELD
Litchfield Food Company
West Street.
Tel: 860 567–3113.
A bakery/deli/café offering great
grazing. **$–$$**
Tollgate Hill Inn
Route 202.
Tel: 860 567–4545.

Restaurant Guidelines

● **Prices** are approximate, but for
a three-course meal for one
(excluding beverages, tax and tip),
the following guidelines may prove
helpful:
$$$$ = over $40
$$$ = $28-40
$$ = $15-28
$ = under $15
● **Meal tax** varies from state to

state, but it is customary to tip 15
to 20 percent on the pre-tax total.
● **Credit cards** The more
expensive establishments
generally accept credit cards, but
call ahead to check just in case.
● **Reservations** Most restaurants,
except for the clearly casual,
appreciate reservations (some
require them).

The superb New American cuisine belies the stark and lovely simplicity of this 1745 tavern. **$$$**

West Street Grill
43 West Street (Route 202).
Tel: 860 567–3885.
Trendy in black-and-white, this citified bistro serves brilliant regional fare. **$$–$$$**

MADISON
Cafe Lafayette
725 Boston Post Road (Route 1).
Tel: 203 245–7773.
Once a church meeting house, now an elegant spot for updated Continental and regional cuisine. **$$$**

MYSTIC
Flood Tide Restaurant
The Inn at Mystic.
Tel: 860 536–9604, Routes 1 and 27.
Fax: 860 536–9604.
Contemporary continental served with water views. **$$$.**

Seamen's Inne
105 Greenmanville Road.
Tel: 860 536–9649.
American seafood; convenient to Mystic Seaport **$$**

NEW HAVEN
Barkies
220 College Street.
Tel: 203 776–0795.
Casual American grill and rotisserie serving up seared chops, chicken, fish and vegetarian sausages. **$$$**

LPika Tapas Cafe,
39 High Street,
Tel: 203 865–1933.
Authentic Spanish tapas elevates group-grazing to a high art. **$$.**

Polo Grille and Wine Bar
7 Elm Street.
Tel: 203 787–9000.

Mystic Pizza

Connecticut cuisine hit the map in rather curious way when the movie *Mystic Pizza* was named after a fast-food parlor in downtown Mystic. Filming actually took place in a lobster warehouse nearby.

Restaurant Guidelines

● **Prices** are approximate, but for a three-course meal for one (excluding beverages, tax and tip), the following guidelines may prove helpful:
$$$$ = over $40
$$$ = $28-40
$$ = $15-28
$ = under $15
● **Meal tax** varies from state to state, but it is customary to tip 15 to 20 percent on the pre-tax total.
● **Credit cards** The more expensive establishments generally accept credit cards, but call ahead to check just in case.
● **Reservations** Most restaurants, except for the clearly casual, appreciate reservations (some require them).

Modern Italian-inspired fare with an extensive wine list. Sophisticated but not stuffy. **$$**

Sally's Pizza
237 Wooster Street.
Tel: 203 624–5271.
The hands-down local favorite. **$**

NEW LONDON
Lighthouse Inn
6 Guthrie Place
Tel: 860 443–8411.
Traditional American fare with a seafood emphasis in a restored Victorian mansion. **$$–$$$**

NEW MILFORD
Adrienne
218 Kent Road (Route 7).
Tel: 860 354–6001.
Chef-owned restaurant featuring New American fine dining in a pretty white country house. **$$$**

The Bistro
31 Bank Street.
Tel: 860 355–3266.
Classic French and contemporary American. **$$$.**

NEW PRESTON
Boulders Inn
Route 45.
Tel: 860 868–0541.
Tasty extrapolations of hearty Continental fare, with a view of Lake Waramaug. **$$$.**

Hopkins Inn,
22 Hopkins Road
Tel: 860 868–7295.
Specializing in Austrian and Swiss dishes (and pretty vistas of the lake). **$$–$$$**

NOANK
Abbott's Lobster in the Rough

117 Pearl Street.
Tel: 860 536–7719.
A classic lobster shack on the water. Summer only. **$**

The Fisherman
937 Groton Long Point Road.
Tel: 860 536–1717.
Seafood, of course (lobster, fried seafood platters, squid, scallops, bouillabaisse), but steaks and a water view, too. **$–$$**

OLD LYME
Old Lyme Inn
85 Old Lyme Street.
Tel: 860 434–2600.
Dazzling seasonal dishes served with aplomb. **$$$$**

OLD SAYBROOK
Cafe Routier
1080 Boston Post Road (Route 1).
Tel: 860 388–6270.
Tiny café serving French bistro fare. **$$**

Saybrook Point Inn
2 Bridge Street.
Tel: 860 395–2000.
Traditionalist decor, contemporary fare, water views. **$$$**

SALISBURY
White Hart Inn
Routes 44 and 41.
Tel: 860 435–0030.
Contemporary American fare in a historic inn. **$$$.**

SOUTH NORWALK AREA
Silvermine Tavern
194 Perry Avenue, Norwalk.
Tel: 203 847–4558.
American classics in an old inn beside a mill pond. **$$$**

Cote d'Azur
86 Washington Street, South
Norwalk.
Tel: 203 855–8900.
A casual, comfortable room offering
up French bistro classics. **$$–$$$**

**Barcelona Restaurant and
Wine Bar**
63 N Main Street.
South Norwalk.
Tel: 203 899–0088.
Savory Spanish "little plates" in a
stylish dining room and sidewalk
cafe. **$$**

Pasta Nostra Trattoria
116 Washington Street, South
Norwalk.
Tel: 203 854–9700.
A convivial contemporary café. **$$**

STONINGTON

Boatyard Cafe
194 Water Street.
Tel: 860 535–1381.
A waterside café with priceless
sunsets. **$$**

Randall's Ordinary
Route 2, North Stonington.
Tel: 860 599–4540.
Reservations required. Authentic
17th-century open-hearth cooking,
serving staff in period dress. **$$$**

VERNON

Rein's New York-Style Delicatessen
Route 30 (I–84, Exit 65).
Tel: 860 875–1344.
The most authentic – and tasty –
noshing north of Manhattan.
Located east of Hartford. **$**

WASHINGTON

G.W. Tavern
20 Bee Brook Road, Washington
Depot.
Tel: 860 868–6633.
A restored colonial tavern honoring
the first president with updated
New England classics: clam
chowder, slow-roasted duck,
homemade cherry pie. **$$**

Mayflower Inn
Route 47, Washington.
Tel: 860 868–9466.
The "country American" cuisine is
far, far from being rustic – it is
every bit as rarefied, in fact, as
this fine country inn. **$$$**

The Pantry
Titus Square.
Tel: 860 868–0258.
A gourmet shop cum café, in a
charming town. **$–$$**

WESTPORT

Acqua
43 Main Street.
Tel: 203 222–8899.
Italian/Mediterranean fare in a
wildly popular, sometimes
clamorous, two-story riverside
villa. **$$$**

Sakura
680 Post Road East.
Tel: 203 222–0802.
One of Connecticut's favorite sushi
spots. **$$–$$$**

Splash
The Inn at Longshore, 260 Compo
Road South.
Tel: 203 454–7798.
An elegant traditional inn serving
elegant, distinctly non-traditional
fare: eclectic Pacific Rim cuisine
with all courses designed for
sharing. **$$$–$$$$**

WOODBURY

Good News Cafe
694 Main Street.
Tel: 203 266–4663.
A cheerful spot focused on local
bounty and luscious desserts. **$$**

WOODVILLE

Le Bon Coin
Route 202.
Tel: 860 868–7763.
Worth seeking out for French
classics. **$$–$$$**

Home of the Burger

Louis' Lunch
261 Crown Street.
Tel: 203 562–5507.
This homely, family-run burger
joint in New Haven holds the
dubious distinction of being
birthplace of the original 1900
hamburger. Today's burgers are
still served in time-honored style
on toast, *sans* frills), amid period
decor and Tiffany lamps. **$**

Culture

DANCE
Hartford Ballet (tel: 860
525–9396; 166 Capitol Avenue,
Hartford) stages both classical and
modern dance productions.

CLASSICAL MUSIC
Hartford Symphony performs at
The Bushnell (tel: 860 246–6807;
166 Capitol Avenue).
New Haven Symphony Orchestra,
the fourth oldest in the United
States, holds a concert series at
Yale University's Woolsey Hall (tel:
203 865–0831; 33 Whitney
Avenue).

CHAMBER MUSIC
The popular **Norfolk Chamber
Music Festival** (tel: 860
542–3000; Route 44 and 272,
Norfolk) features chamber music
and an annual choral concert.

OPERA
The renowned **Goodspeed Opera
House** (tel: 860 873–8668;
Goodspeed Landing, East Haddam)
showcases operas, musicals and
revivals from April to December.

ROCK AND POP
Concerts are held year-round at the
16,500-seat **Hartford Civic Center**
(tel: 860 727–8010; 1 Civic Center
Plaza).
Both Hartford clubs **Voodoo** (tel:
860 525–3003; 191 Ann Street)
and **Arch Street Tavern** (tel: 860
246–7610) feature live acts.

JAZZ
The 880 Club (tel: 860 956–2428;
880 Maple Avenue, Hartford) is the
city's oldest jazz club.

THEATER
Hartford Stage Company (tel: 860
527–5151; 50 Church Street), an
award-winning ensemble, produces
new plays, as well as many
classics.
Theaterworks (tel: 860 527–7838;
233 Pearl Street, Hartford) features
more experimental theater.
The Little Theater (tel: 860
645–6743; 177 Hartford Road,

Connecticut Festivals

● **SPRING**
Meriden's annual **Daffodil Festival** (tel: 203 630–4259) in April is one sign that spring is on the way.

In May, the **Mystic Lobsterfest** (tel: 860 572–5312, (888) 973–2767) draws lobster lovers to the seaport for an old-fashioned outdoor lobster bake.

● **SUMMER**
Summer is arts festival time, beginning in June with New Haven's **International Festival of Arts & Ideas** (tel: 888 278–3325), which showcases world-renowned groups and premieres of commissioned works.

In July, the **Hartford Riverfest** (tel: 860 293–0131) celebrates **Independence Day** with entertainment for all ages, culminating in fireworks over the Connecticut River.

The **SoNo Arts Celebration** (tel: 203 866–7916) in August, a two-day outdoor festival of the visual

and performing arts, draws visitors to historic South Norwalk.

● **FALL**
Connecticut's harvest festivals actually begin in August with the **Brooklyn Fair** (tel: 860 779–0012), the oldest continuously active agricultural fair in the US, followed in September by the **Woodstock Fair** (tel: 860 928–3246), the nation's second oldest. In October, Southington hosts the annual **Apple Harvest Festival** (tel: 860 628–8036).

● **WINTER**
First Night Hartford (tel: 860 728–3089) is the New Year's Eve festival of the arts. In February, skiers head for the Litchfield Hills for the **Salisbury Invitational Ski Jump** and the **US Eastern Ski Jump Championships**, an Olympic-level competition on the site of the nation's oldest ski jumping program (tel: 860 435-9729).

Manchester), Connecticut's oldest theater, presents local talent.

Two Tony-award-winning theater companies reside in New Haven: The **Long Wharf Theater** (tel: 203 787–4282; 222 Sargent Dr) once premiered Arthur Miller's The Crucible and produces many prize-winning shows, while **Yale Repertory Theater** (tel: 203 432–1234; 222 York Street) shows experimental work by Yale students.

CINEMA
Cinestudio (tel: 860 297–2463; 300 Summit Street, Trinity College, Hartford) shows first-run and art films.

COMEDY
City Steam (tel: 860 525–1600; Hartford), a brew pub, features comedians from Boston and New York on Friday and Saturday nights.

ART GALLERIES
"SoNo" (short for South Norwalk and a take off on SoHo in New York

City) has revitalized itself with art galleries, chichi cafés and shops. Also, Kent boasts more than a dozen galleries.

Nightlife

NIGHTCLUBS/DISCOS
Hartford's popular **Bourbon Street North** (tel: 860 525–1014; 70 Union Place) features a large dance floor and encompasses a variety of music styles.

The **"SoNo"** area of downtown South Norfolk contains a variety of tavernlike nightclubs.

LIVE MUSIC
Blue Star Cafe (tel: 860 527–4557; 26 Trumbell Street, Hartford) features live blues, jazz and swing music.

Toad's Place (tel: 203 624–8623; 300 York Street, New Haven) is a popular club which books a variety of major acts.

CASINOS
Foxwoods High Stakes Bingo & Casino (tel: 800 752–9244; Route 2 in Ledyard between I–395 and I–95), housed on what was a small Native American reservation, is the US's largest gambling casino. **Mohegan Sun Resort Casino** (tel: 888 226–7711; Route 2A, Montville), 10 miles south of Foxwoods, has 2,500 slot machines.

Outdoor Activities

BIKING
Winding Trails Recreation Area off Route 4 in Farmington (tel: 860 677–8458) and **Woodbury Ski & Racquet Area** (tel: 203 263–2203) are popular destinations for Connecticut mountain bikers.

For a free Connecticut Bicycle Map, write to the Connecticut Department of Transportation, 2800 Berlin Turnpike, P. Box 317546, Newington, CT 06131–7546.

CANOEING, KAYAKING AND RAFTING
For whitewater rafting or canoeing, head for the Housatonic River. **North American Whitewater Expeditions** (tel: 800 727–4379) organizes Housatonic rafting trips.

Canoe rentals are available at several state parks; call the **Connecticut State Bureau of Parks and Recreation** (tel: 860 424–3200) for details.

Mountain Workshop (tel: 203 438–3640) leads canoeing trips on Connecticut's rivers and lakes.

FISHING
All along the Connecticut coast, charter boats run half-day or full-day fishing expeditions. The best thing to do is get a list of operators from the Connecticut State Tourism Office (tel: 800 CT-BOUND) or head to the harbor where you want to go out and talk to the captains directly.

Catch-and-release flyfishing is popular all along the Housantanic River. As for the Farmington River, home to trout, bass and pickerel, call the **Farmington River Anglers' Association** (tel: 860 738–7327; Winstead) for details.

HIKING

The **Appalachian Trail**, a 2,000-mile (3,200-km) trail linking Maine and Georgia, traverses about 50 miles (80km) of western Connecticut and the Appalachian Mountain Club (tel: 617 523–0636; Boston) provides detailed trail information.

At **Talcott Mountain State Park** in Simsbury, hikers who reach the peak of the one-and-a-half mile (2.4 km) walk are rewarded with panoramic vistas of the Farmington River Valley. On clear days, visibility can be up to 50 miles (80 km).

Macedonia Brook State Park in Kent and **Sleeping Giant State Park** in Hamden also have scenic trails for day hiking.

Contact The Connecticut State Bureau of Parks and Recreation (tel: 860 424–3200) for details.

SAILING

Mystic is a center for sailing activity in Connecticut. The **Offshore Sailing School** (tel: 800 221–4326) conducts five-day learn-to-sail courses in the town.

SKIING

While downhill skiing is not a major sport in Connecticut, the state does have several small downhill areas in the Litchfield Hills region: **Mohawk Mountain** in Cornwall (tel: 860 672–6100), **Mount Southington** in Southington (tel: 860 628–09540),

Connecticut Cruises

Voyager Cruises' Argia (tel: 860 536–0416), a replica of a 19th-century schooner, offers half-day excursions from Mystic to Fisher's Island.
The Mystic Whaler (tel: 800 697–8420), a classic schooner, sails for one- to five-day trips along the New England coast.
Mystic Seaport (tel: 203 572 5351) offers cruises from Mystic on the last coal-fired passenger steamer to sail in the US.

and **Powder Ridge Ski Area** in Middlefield (tel: 860 349–3454, (800) 622–3321).

For cross-country skiing, try the **Woodbury Ski & Racquet Area** (tel: 203 263–2203), **Blackberry River Ski Touring Center** in Norfolk (tel: 860 542–5100), or Farmington's **Winding Trails Cross Country Ski Center** (tel: 860 678–9582).

Shopping

MALLS

Hartford Civic Center (tel: 860 275–6100; 1 Civic Center Plaza) hosts over 60 shops.

New England's largest shopping mall is the **Danbury Fair Mall** (tel: 203 743–3247; Backus Avenue, off of I-84, Danbury) which has 240 shops, including five department stores.

The **Olde Mistick Village** (tel: 860 536–4941; Exit 90 off I-95, Mystic) features 60 Colonial-style specialty shops.

MARKETS

For fresh farm produce, flowers and crafts in Hartford, head to **Main Street Market** (at Main and Asylum Streets).

BOOKS

In Hartford, try the **Gallows Hill Bookstore** (tel: 860 297–5231; 300 Summit Street) and in West Hartford, **Bookworm** (tel: 860 233–2653; 968 Farmington Avenue). Hartford's **Reader's Feast** (tel: 860 232–3710; 529 Farmington Avenue) sells feminist, gay and children's literature.

Yale University Co-op in New Haven (tel: 203 772–0670; 77 Broadway) sells books, as well as Yale sweatshirts and paraphernalia.

ANTIQUES

New Haven sports over 30 antique dealers, among them **Antique Corner** (tel: 203 387–7200; 859 Whalley Avenue).

The Litchfield Hills are often referred to as the "antique capital" of the country (slight hyperbole, but there are an impressive number), with almost every village having

multiple shops. Try **The Bittersweet Shop** (tel: 860 354–1727; Route 7, New Milford) and **Old Carriage Shop Antiques** (tel: 860 567–3234; 920 Bantam Road, Bantam). Both feature over 15 dealers.

Dealers in Mystic and Stonington are on Main and Water Streets.

The large **Old Saybrook Antiques Dealers** (tel: 860 388–1600; 756 Middlesex Turnpike, Route 154, in Old Saybrook) houses more than 100 dealers of 18th- and 19th-century pieces.

ARTS AND CRAFTS

Dozens of pottery and crafts shops are located in the Litchfield Hills; try either of these on Route 128 in West Cornwall: **Cornwall Bridge Pottery & Store** (tel: 860 672–6545) and **Ingersoll Cabinetmakers** (tel: 860 672–6334).

Farmington Crafts Common (tel: 860 674–9295; 248 Main Street, Farmington) features over 200 craftspeople.

Children

THEME PARKS

Lake Compounce (tel: 860 583–3631; 822 Lake Avenue, Bristol), America's oldest amusement park.

CAROUSELS

The Carousel (tel: 860 246–7739; Bushnell Park, Hartford) is a 1914 merry-go-round with hand-carved horses.

ZOOS

Beardsley Zoological Gardens (tel: 203 576–8082; Noble Avenue, Beardsley Park, Bridgeport), the state's largest zoo, features over 120 species, a carousel and a New England farmyard petting zoo.

STEAM TRAIN JOURNEYS

New England Railroad Museum (tel: 203 575–1931; 83 Bank Street, Waterbury) offers a historic ride through Black Rock State Park. **Valley Railroad** (tel: 860 767–0103; Railroad Avenue, Essex) runs an old-fashioned service.

Rhode Island

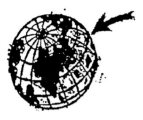

The Place

Known as: The Ocean State.
Motto: Hope.
Origin of name: unknown. Perhaps reminded an early explorer of Rhodes in Greece. Or maybe derived from the Dutch for "red" after the color of its soil.
Entered Union: May 29, 1790, the last of the 13 original states.
Capital: Providence.
Area: 1,545 sq. miles (4,002 sq. km).
Highest point: Jerimoth Hill, 812 ft (247 meters).
Population: 1 million.
Population density: 649 people per sq. km (251 per sq. km).
Economy: manufacturing (fabricated metals, precision instruments, apparel and textiles, printed materials, rubber and plastic items, industrial machinery, primary metals, electronic goods, transportation equipment, chemicals and processed foods.
Annual visitors: 29 million
National representation: 2 senators and 2 representatives to Congress.
Famous citizens: George M. Cohan, Nelson Eddy, Christopher and Oliver La Farge.

Where to Stay

BLOCK ISLAND

Atlantic Inn
High Street, Old Harbor, 02807.
Tel: 401 466–5883/
800 224–7422.
Fax: 401 466–5678.
An 1879 white-clapboard hotel, Block Island's *grande dame*, with a spacious porch on a hill overlooking the sea. 21 pleasant Victorian-style rooms and two tennis courts.
$$$–$$$$
Hotel Manisses and The 1661 Inn
Spring Street, Old Harbor, 02807.
Tel: 401 466–2063/
800 626–4883.
Fax: 401 466–2858.
Victorian inns with ocean views; 38 old-fashioned rooms in the main inns and in cottages and efficiencies. An animal farm on the property is home to llamas and emus. **$$$–$$$$**
Spring House Hotel
Spring Street, Old Harbor, 02807.
Tel: 401 466–5844/
800 234–9263.
www.springhousehotel.com.
A classic 49-room hotel (built in 1852) with Victorian furnishings, a cupola-topped mansard roof and a wraparound porch. Set on 15 acres above the ocean. **$$$–$$$$**

BRISTOL

Bradford-Diamond-Norris House
474 Hope Street, 02809.
Tel: 401 253–7930.
Known as "the Wedding Cake House," this clapboard mansion was originally constructed in 1792 and architecturally embellished over the years. It has four antique-filled rooms, gardens. **$$**
Joseph Reynolds House Inn
956 Hope Street, 02809.
Tel: 401 254–0230.
Fax: 401 254–2610.
Built in 1693 and considered to be the oldest three-story building in New England; now a B&B with suites and cozy guest rooms on a busy street. **$$**

JAMESTOWN

Bay Voyage Inn
150 Conanicus Avenue, 02835
Tel: 401 423–2100.
Formerly a country house in Newport, this 31-room inn was transported across the bay in 1899. It's now an all-suite inn overlooking the harbor. **$$$–$$$$**

LITTLE COMPTON

Stone House Club
122 Sakonnet Point Road, 02837.
Tel: 401 635–2222.
A stone farmhouse overlooking the ocean, now a private club, that rents 15 simply furnished rooms. **$–$$**

Price Categories

A very approximate guide to current room rates for a standard double per night is:
$$$$ = over $200
$$$ = $150–200
$$ = $100–150
$ = under $100

NARRAGANSETT

The Richards
144 Gibson Avenue, 02882.
Tel: 401 789–7746.
An 1884 stone English manor B&B surrounded by gardens. All four antique-furnished rooms have working fireplaces. Private access to the rocky coast. No credit cards. **$–$$$**
Stone Lea
40 Newton Avenue (off Ocean Road), 02882.
Tel: 401 783–9546.
A Victorian summer "cottage" designed in 1884 by McKim, Meade & White, located on a cliff overlooking the ocean. This formal inn B&B – many of the nine rooms have striking ocean views – is set on a broad lawn that extends to the sea. **$$–$$$**

NEWPORT

Cliffside Inn
2 Seaview Avenue, 02840.
Tel: 401 847–1811/
800 845–1811.
Fax: 401 848–5850;
www.cliffsideinn.com.
Near the Cliff Walk, an 1880 Victorian villa, carved into grand, dramatic quarters. The 15 rooms in this B&B are light, airy rooms, and some have working fireplaces and whirlpool tubs. **$$$–$$$$**
Elm Tree Cottage
336 Gibbs Avenue, 02840.
Tel: 401 849–1610/
800 882–3356.
Fax: 401849–2084
www.elm-tree.com.
A six-room "cottage" B&B only in the Newport sense, one block from

Meal Guide

- **B&Bs** supply a complimentary full breakfast, often quite sophisticated.
- **MAP** (Modified American Plan) rates include breakfast and dinner
- **FAP** (Full American Plan) supply all three meals

the water, overlooking First Beach and Easton Pond. **$$$–$$$$**

Francis Malbone House
392 Thames Street, 02840.
Tel: 401 846–0392/
800 846–0392.
Fax: 401 848–5956.
www.malbone.com.
A 1760 Colonial brick mansion B&B on the harborfront. 18 lavishly appointed rooms with period reproduction furnishings.
$$$–$$$$

Ivy Lodge
12 Clay Street, 02840.
Tel: 401 849–6865.
Seven-room B&B in a Victorian home in the mansion district, designed by Stanford White. Dramatic old-English entryway, wraparound porch, and 11 fireplaces. **$$–$$$**

Melville House
39 Clarke Street, 02840.
Tel: 401 847–0640.
www.melvillehouse.com.
A 1750 Colonial B&B on a gas lamp-lit street on Historic Hill. Eight small, but comfortably appointed guest rooms, plus a fireplace suite. **$$**

Victorian Ladies
63 Memorial Boulevard, 02840.
Tel: 401 849–9960.
A pair of vintage lovelies, in period style, offering 11 rooms for B&B. Near First Beach and the Cliff Walk. **$$$**

PROVIDENCE

Old Court
144 Benefit Street, 02903.
Tel: 401 751–2002.
Near the Rhode Island School of Design, an 1863 rectory retrofitted as an elegant Victorian-style inn. 11 spacious rooms with high ceilings,

chandeliers, and (non-working) marble fireplaces. **$$**

Omni Biltmore Hotel
Kennedy Plaza, 02903.
Tel: 401 421–0700/
800 843–6664.
Fax: 401 455–3040.
A 1922 Art Deco-style grand hotel downtown, with 238 rooms nicely restored. **$$–$$$$**

State House Inn
43 Jewett Street, 02903.
Tel: 401 785–1235.
Fax: 401 351–426.
www.providence-inn.com.
An 1880s Colonial Revival home located near the State House. The nine B&B rooms are done in basic Early American style; some have canopy beds and working fireplaces. **$$**

WEEKAPAUG

Weekapaug Inn
15 Spring Avenue, 02891.
Tel: 401 322–0301.
A classic FAP inn (65 rooms) with a wraparound porch sheltering well-heeled families since 1938. On a peninsula surrounded on three sides by Quanochontaug Pond in a coastal village 6 miles (9.6 km) from Westerly. No credit cards.
$$$$

WESTERLY

Grandview Bed and Breakfast
212 Shore Road, 02891.
Tel: 401 596–6384/
800 447–6383.
A comfortable turn-of-the-century house with 12 cozy guest rooms (some with ocean views), gardens and a stone wraparound porch. **$**

Restaurant Guidelines

- **Prices** are approximate, but for a three-course meal for one (excluding beverages, tax and tip), the following guidelines may prove helpful:
$$$$ = over $40
$$$ = $28-40
$$ = $15-28
$ = under $15
- **Meal tax** varies from state to

Shelter Harbor Inn
10 Wagner Road (Route 1), 02891.
Tel: 401 322–8883/
800 468–8883.
Once a working farm, now a luxury 23-room getaway for B&B in a rural setting near the beach. The roof deck has a barbecue grill and a hot tub. **$$**

Where to Eat

BLOCK ISLAND

Atlantic Inn Restaurant
High Street, Old Harbor.
Tel: 401 466–5883.
Prix-fixe seafood and continental dinners. Dress is more casual than the food. **$$$$**

Spring House Hotel
Spring Street, Old Harbor.
Tel: 401 466–5844.
Seafood, pastas and all-you-can-eat barbecues overlooking Block Island Sound. **$$–$$$**

Juice 'n Java,
235 Dodge Street, Old Harbor.
Tel: 401 466–5200.
Funky coffee house serving sandwiches and pastries. Large supply of magazines and board games. **$**

BRISTOL

Quito's
411 Thames Street.
Tel: 401 253–4500.
Casual seafood spot overlooking the bay since 1962. **$–$$**

Aidan's Pub
5 John Street.
Tel: 401 254–1940.
Irish pub serving fish and chips, bangers and mash and other simple fare. **$**

state, but it is customary to tip 15 to 20 percent on the pre-tax total.
- **Credit cards** The more expensive establishments generally accept credit cards, but call ahead to check just in case.
- **Reservations** Most restaurants, except for the clearly casual, appreciate reservations (some require them).

JAMESTOWN

Bay Voyage Inn
150 Conanicus Avenue.
Tel: 401 423–2100.
American standbys – lobster thermidor, rack of lamb, filet mignon – and bountiful Sunday brunch with harbor views. **$$$**

Jamestown Oyster Bar
22 Narragansett Avenue.
Tel: 401 423–3380.
Fresh fish, burgers and quahogs in a popular local spot. **$**

LITTLE COMPTON

Stone House Club
122 Sakonnet Point Road.
Tel: 401 635–2222.
A private club in an old stone farmhouse that is open to non-members for dinner. Traditional American and French-inspired fare. **$$–$$$**

The Commons Lunch
Tel: 401 635–4388.
A downhome diner fit for gentleman (and lady) farmers. **$**

Olga's Cup and Saucer
261 West Main Road.
Tel: 401 635–8650.
A tiny take-away stand at Walker's Roadside selling creative, delectable baked goods: vegetable tarts, intriguing pizzas and delicious fruit pies. Although the little shop is only open seasonally, you can find their goodies year-round at 103 Point Street, Providence, tel: 401 831–6666. **$**

NARRAGANSETT

Aunt Carrie's
1240 Ocean Road, Point Judith.
Tel: 401 783–7930.

Classic seaside clam shack. **$**

Spain
Ocean Road.
Tel: 401 783–9770.
Authentic Iberian cuisine; generous portions. **$$–$$$**

Woody's
21 Pier Marketplace.
Tel: 401 789–9500.
Savory tapas-style appetizers and substantial contemporary entrées. **$$**

NEWPORT

Le Bistro
Banister's Wharf.
Tel: 401 849–7778.
A charming French café in a loft above the bustling harbor. **$$$$**

Clarke Cooke House
Bannister's Wharf.
Tel: 401 849–2900.
A 1790 Colonial with formal, waterview dining. **$$$$**

The Black Pearl
Bannister's Wharf.
Tel: 401 846–5264.
A classic harborside tavern. **$$$**

The Mooring
Sayer's Wharf.
Tel: 401 846–2260.
The former HQ of the New York Yacht Club, serving seafood staples. **$$–$$$**

Le Petite Auberge
19 Charles Street.
Tel: 401 849–6669.
Classic French in a historic home. **$$$**

Puerini's
24 Memorial Boulevard West.
Tel: 401 847–5506.
Affordable, traditional Italian staples, all made from scratch. **$$**

White Horse Tavern
Marlborough and Farewell Streets.
Tel: 401 849–3600.
Reputedly the oldest continually operating tavern in the US (established in 1673), this atmospheric eatery serves classics like grilled lobster and Chateaubriand. **$$**

PROVIDENCE

Al Forno
577 S Main Street.
Tel: 401 273–9760.
Arguably New England's pre-eminent temple of *nuova cucina*. **$$$$**

Capital Grille
1 Cookson Place.
Tel: 401 521–5600.
Premium dry-aged beef, in the renovated railroad station. **$$$**

Hemenway Sea Food,
1 Washington Square.
Tel: 401 351–8570.
Superb seafood, with views of the Providence River. **$$$**

Pot au Feu
44 Custom House Street.
Tel: 401 273–8953.
From bistro-style to neo-classical French. **$$$**

La Locanda del Coccio
265 Atwells Avenue (DiPasquale Plaza).
Tel: 401 273–2652.
Italian regional cuisine using ancient clay cookery techniques in a comfortably upscale Federal Hill location. **$$–$$$**

Rue de L'Espoir
99 Hope Street.
Tel: 401 751–8890.
Contemporary, sophisticated bistro fare in a pretty room near Brow University. **$$–$$$**

Big Alice's Ice Cream
100 Hope Street.
Tel: 401 273–5812.
Providence's premier ice cream vendor since 1980. All homemade, all delicious. Near Brown University. **$**

WATCH HILL

Olympia Tea Room
Bay Street.
Tel: 401 348–8211.
A classic 1916 luncheonette. **$$**

Restaurant Guidelines

● **Prices** are approximate, but for a three-course meal for one (excluding beverages, tax and tip), the following guidelines may prove helpful:
$$$$ = over $40
$$$ = $28-40
$$ = $15-28
$ = under $15
● **Meal tax** varies from state to state, but it is customary to tip 15 to 20 percent on the pre-tax total.
● **Credit cards** The more expensive establishments generally accept credit cards, but call ahead to check just in case.
● **Reservations** Most restaurants, except for the clearly casual, appreciate reservations (some require them).

Rhode Island Festivals

- **SPRING**

In Bristol, the Blithewood Gardens & Arboretum sponsors the **Annual Spring Bulb Display** (tel: 401 253–2707) in April and May; it's one of New England's largest daffodil exhibitions.

- **SUMMER**

In mid-July, Newport's gilded mansions scintillate to classical strains of the **Newport Music Festival** (tel: 401 846–1133).

The season is capped off by two extremely popular harborview events in mid-August: **Ben & Jerry's Newport Folk Festival** (tel: 401 847–3700) – the long-standing folkie Olympus, now sponsored by the ice cream company – and the **JVC Jazz Festival** (tel: 401 847–3700).

Bristol claims the nation's oldest **4th of July Parade** (tel: 401 245–0750). Then, in August, the

Charlestown Chamber Seafood Festival (tel: 401 364–3878) spreads out a "roll-up-your-sleeves" gastronomic *smorgasbord*, including chowder, clam cakes, lobster and more.

- **FALL**

The capital city ushers in the autumn with the five-day **Providence Waterfront Festival** (tel: 401 785–9490) in September, where music, children's programs, an international food court and water activities celebrate the city's maritime heritage and the revitalization of downtown.

- **WINTER**

The 10-day **Newport Winter Festival** (tel: 401 849–8048) in January and February lures visitors with food, music, ice carving and snow sculptures.

but perhaps that's the point.

Art films, old couches from which to watch the flicks and cheap popcorn continue to survive in college towns.

ART GALLERIES

Providence's Wickenden Street has a number of galleries, including **Alaimao Gallery** (tel: 401 421–5360; 301 Wickenden Street) which has an unusual number of prints, playbills and posters.

ALL-IN-ONE

AS220 (tel: 401 831–9327; 111 Empire Street, Providence) caters for so many interests: at various times it is a performance art space, gallery, theater and musical venue for tastes as diverse as techno and folk.

Nightlife

The free *Providence Phoenix* can be found around town in shops and restaurants and is slanted towards a younger, hip crowd.

Thames Street is where it's happening in Newport.

WESTERLY

Shelter Harbor Inn
Route 1.
Tel: 401 322–8883.
Well-priced regional specialties.
$$$

Three Fish
37 Main Street.
Tel: 401 348–9700.
Creative seafood and delectable desserts in a former woolen mill overlooking the Pawcatuck River.
$$–$$$

Culture

The daily *Providence Journal* newspaper has all the up-to-the-minute information on what's happening culturally in and around the state of Rhode Island, as does the glossy *Rhode Island Monthly* magazine.

CLASSICAL MUSIC

Rhode Island Philharmonic (tel: 401 831–3123; 222 Richmond Street, Providence) gives 10 concerts throughout the year.

ROCK AND POP

Providence Civic Center (tel: 401 331–6700; 1 LaSalle Square) hosts big-name touring rock bands.

THEATER

Trinity Repertory Company (tel: 401 351–4242; 201 Washington Street, Providence), always among the country's finest and most innovative, has won Tony awards.
Brown University (tel: 401 863–2838; Leeds Theater, 77 Waterman Street, Providence) stages contemporary to classical and everything In between.
Providence Performing Arts Center (tel: 401 421–2787; 220 Weybosset Street) sets a stage for pre- and post-Broadway shows.
Astors' Beechwood (tel: 401 846–3772; 580 Bellevue Avenue, Newport) stages murder-mystery plays once a week in-season.

CINEMA

Cable Car Cinema (tel: 401 272–3970; 204 S Main Street, Providence) has seen better days,

LIVE MUSIC

Thames Street Station (and Great American Pub) (tel: 401 849–9480; 337 America's Cup Avenue, Newport) has dance music.

On Block Island, both **The National Hotel** (tel: 401 466–2901; Water Street) and **Govern's Yellow Kittens Tavern** (tel: 401 466–5855; Corn Neck Road) have music every night in summer. Govern's is more diverse, with reggae and R&B.

GAY & LESBIAN VENUES

Gerardo's (tel: 401 274–5560; Atwells Avenue at Franklin Square, Providence) is a popular gay and lesbian dance place.
David's (tel: 401 847–9698; 28 Prospect Hill Street, Newport) is primarily a men's bar with a DJ.

LATE NIGHT VENUES

The Hot Club (tel: 401 861–9007; 575 S. Water Street, Providence), aptly named, is a popular waterfront hang-out.

Outdoor Activities

BIKING

The 14½-mile (23-km) **East Bay Bicycle Path** follows Narragansett Bay and winds through several towns between Providence and Bristol. On Block Island and in Tiverton and Little Compton, the relatively little-trafficked roads are popular destinations.

Bikers can also follow Newport's **Bellevue Avenue** and **Ocean Drive** for about 15 miles (24 km) past the mansions and along the shore.

For a free *Guide to Cycling in the Ocean State*, call 401 222–4203, extension 4042.

CANOEING, KAYAKING AND RAFTING

Coastal sea kayaking is popular and the **Kayak Centre** (tel: 401 295–4400 in Wickford or 401 848–2920 in Newport) leads a variety of excursions, including a Newport tour with ocean glimpses of mansions; the company also runs a multi-day trip to Block Island. In Providence, **Baer's River Workshop** (tel: 401 453–1633) rents canoes and kayaks and leads guided tours of local rivers. For information about canoeing the 45-mile (72-km) long Blackstone River, request a free copy of the *Blackstone River Canoe Guide* (tel: 800 454–2882).

SAILING

Newport, known as The Sailing Capital of the World, is a good base for short harbor excursions and learn-to-sail vacations.

Sightsailing of Newport (tel: 401 849–3333) offers harbor sails, rentals and instruction.

America's Cup Charters (tel: 401 846–9886) runs evening sails and half- or full-day sailboat charters.

Other Newport charters include **Flyer** (tel: 401 848–2100), a 57-foot catamaran; **Spirit of Newport** (tel: 401 849–3575); and the 72-foot schooner **Madeline** (tel: 401 847–0298).

Newport Sailing School (tel: 401 848–2266) runs narrated one- and two-hour sailing tours plus classes.

Offshore Sailing School (tel: 800 221–4326; Newport) conducts a learn-to-sail vacation program. **Block Island Club** (tel: 401 466–5939) offers sailing instruction and one-week family memberships.

FISHING

Saltwater Edge (tel: 401 842–0062; Newport) offers fly-fishing lessons as well as guided saltwater fishing outings. Several charter fishing boats are based in Narragansett, including **Persuader** (tel: 401 783–5644).

HIKING

Rhode Island Audubon Society (tel: 401 949–5454) leads nature hikes.

Shopping

WHERE TO SHOP

The Arcade (tel: 401 598–1199; 65 Weybosset Street, Providence) was the country's first indoor mall, built in 1828. Architecturally, it's a beauty to behold. It's still a bastion of consumerism, although styles have changed over the years.

DEPARTMENT STORES

Ley's (tel: 401 846–2100; Long Wharf Mall, across from the visitor's Gateway Center, Newport) is the country's oldest department store, established in 1796.

MARKETS

Route 77 to Little Compton is blessed with many little roadside farm stands offering extra-fresh fresh produce.

BOOKS

Map Center (tel: 401 421–2184; 671 N Main Street, Providence) sells every kind of imaginable map. **Armchair Sailor Books** (tel: 401 847–4252; 543 Thames Street, Newport), purveyors of maritime titles, is appropriately located in this sailing center.

ANTIQUES

In Providence head straight to Wickenden Street and in Newport, you'll find clusters of antiques

shops on Thames, Franklin and Spring Streets.

CHINA AND GLASS

Thames Glass (tel: 401 846–0576; 688 Thames Street, Newport) blows glass in a neighboring studio and sells firsts and seconds from the shop.

SOUVENIRS & GIFTS

Jewelry

Coppacetic Rudely Elegant Jewelry (tel: 401 273–0470; The Arcade, 65 Weybosset Street, Providence) is a determinedly eclectic place, thanks to the diverse work of a very distinct group of artisans.

Arts and Crafts

MacDowell Pottery (tel: 401 846–6313; 220 Spring Street, Newport) displays the work of many state- and New England-wide potters; some work here.

Provincetown Tours

● **On foot** Grab a Walkman for a tour at your own pace, at 21 Meeting Street.
● **Provincetown Trolleys** run 40-minute conducted tours every half hour 10am–4pm from in front of the Town Hall. Hop on and off as you wish.
● **Horse and carriage** tours start from in front of the Town Hall from May to mid-October.

Children

THEME PARKS

Flying Horse Carousel (no phone; Bay Street, Watch Hill), with beautiful hand-carved horses, lays claim as the oldest merry-go-round in the country.

ZOOS

Roger Williams Park Zoo (tel: 401 785–3510; Elmwood Avenue, Providence), a 400-plus-acre park, has an antique carousel, tiny train and lots of animals for kids, and a quiet Japanese garden for adults.

Vermont

The Place

Known as: The Green Mountain State.
Motto: Freedom and unity.
Origin of name: from the French *vert* (= green) and *mont* (= mountain).
Entered Union: March 4, 1791, the 14th state.
Capital: Montpelier
Area: 9,615 sq. miles (24,903 sq km).
Highest point: Mount Mansfield, 4,393 ft (1,339 meters).
Population: 562,800.
Population density: 59 per sq. mile (23 per sq. km).
Economy: once agricultural, now relies increasingly on tourism.
Annual visitors: 7.9 million.
National representation: 2 senators and 1 representative to Congress.
Famous citizens: Ethan Allen, Calvin Coolidge and Admiral George Deweys.

Where to Stay

Many Vermont inns take a break between foliage and the holidays, and again during "mud season", so check first if you plan to visit in the late fall or early spring.

ARLINGTON
Arlington Inn
Route 7A, 05250.
Tel: 802 375–6532/
800 443–9442.
Fax: 802 375–6534.
An elegant Greek Revival mansion with comfortable Victorian-style interior furnishings in the 19 B&B bedrooms. Located between Bennington and Manchester. **$–$$$**

West Mountain Inn
River Road (off Route 313), 05250.
Tel: 802 375-6516.
Fax: 802 375–6553.
www.westmountaininn.com.
A family-friendly 1840s farmhouse turned 18-room MAP with mountain views on 150 country acres. Trails for hiking or cross-country skiing, children's game room and the resident llama ranch amuse all ages. **$$$–$$$$**

BENNINGTON
Four Chimneys Inn
21 West Road (Route 9), 05201.
Tel: 802 447–3500.
French Provincial decor in a grand old manse with 11 rooms for B&B. **$$–$$$**
Molly Stark Inn
1067 E. Main Street, 05201.
Tel: 802 442–9631/
800 356–3076.
Fax: 802 442–5224.
A friendly, homey B&B; the seven cozy guest rooms have New England country-style furnishings, antique quilts and clawfoot tubs. **$–$$**

BOLTON VALLEY
Bolton Valley Resort
Mountain Road, 05477.
Tel: 802 434–2131/
800 451–3220.
Fax: 802 434–4547.
This 143-room Alpine-style family ski resort, with a sports center and 6,000 acres of mountainous wilderness, makes an affordable summer getaway as well. Hotel units are ski-in/ski-out; children under six stay and ski free. **$$–$$$**
The Black Bear
Mountain Road, 05477.
Tel: 802 434–2126/
800 395–6335.
Fax: 802 434–576.
www.blkbearinn.com.
Cozy countrified decor (with bear-adorned quilts) in a lodge located amid the Bolton Valley Resort. 24 rooms. **$**

BRATTLEBORO
Latchis Hotel
50 Main Street, 05301.
Tel: 802 254–6300.

Fax: 802 254–6304.
A 1938 Art Deco hotel, right downtown. Some of the 30 rooms have refrigerators, some have views of Main Street or the Connecticut River. **$**

BRIDGEWATER CORNERS
October Country Inn
Upper Road, 05035.
Tel: 802 672–3412/
800 648–8421.
A cozy MAP farmhouse with 10 rooms on a back road, about 5 miles (8 km) from the Killington ski area. **$$**

BROOKFIELD
Green Trails Inn
Main Street, 05036
Tel: 802 276–3412/
800 243–3412.
A sprawling 13-room inn and lodge B&B, built around 1790 and 1830 farmhouses, on 17 acres overlooking Sunset Lake. The owners maintain 19 miles (30 km) of trails for cross-country skiing and hiking. **$–$$**

BURLINGTON
Willard Street Inn
349 S. Willard Street, 05401.
tel (802) 651–8710/
800 577–8712.
Fax: 802 651–8714.
www.willardstreetinn.com.
Built for a state senator in the 1880s, this stately, formally appointed house (now a B&B with 15 rooms furnished with antiques and down comforters) in Burlington's historic hill section has views of Lake Champlain. **$–$$$**

CHITTENDEN
Mountain Top Inn
Mountain Top Road, 05737.

Price Categories

A very approximate guide to current room rates for a standard double per night is:
$$$$ = over $200
$$$ = $150–200
$$ = $100–150
$ = under $100

Tel: 802 483–2311/
800 445–2100.
Fax: 802 483–6373.
This 52-room MAP is a big, comfy family resort deep in the countryside north of Rutland; outstanding Nordic skiing. **$$$$**

Tulip Tree Inn
Chittenden Dam Road, 05737.
Tel: 802 483–6213/
800 707–0017.
An electricity magnate's 1920s retreat 10 miles (16 km) north of Rutland; five of the eight rooms in the MAP feature whirlpool tubs.
$$–$$$$

CRAFTSBURY COMMON AREA

Craftsbury Outdoor Center
Craftsbury Common, 05827
Tel: 802 587–2514/
800 729–7751.
Fax: 802 586–7768.
A 47-room MAP offering dorm-style accommodation, with skilled training available in various outdoor sports. There are more than 100 miles (160 km) of cross-country ski trails, plus sculling, running camps, mountain biking and canoeing on offer. **$–$$$**

Inn on the Common
Main Street (Route 14).
Craftsbury Common, 05827.
Tel: 802 586–9619/
800 521–2223.
Fax: 802 586–2249.
www.innonthecommon.com.
A 17-room MAP with luxurious decor – including plush carpets, quilts, historic wallpaper reproductions – as well as a swimming pool, tennis court, and mountain views. Ambitious cuisine served dinner party-style. **$$$$**

Craftsbury Inn
Main Street (Route 14), Craftsbury, 05826.
Tel: 802 586–2848/
800 336–2848.
Fax: 802 586–2848.
Country comfort in an 1850 Greek Revival inn, with wraparound verandahs overlooking lavish gardens. 10 rooms just down the road from Craftsbury Common.
$** B&B, **$$ MAP.

DORSET

Barrows House,
Route 30, 05251.
Tel: 802 867–4455/
800 639–1620.
Fax: 802 867–0132.
www.barrowshouse.com.
An 18th-century Federal-style MAP inn and carriage house with homey touches in the 28 rooms and a well-regarded restaurant. Pool, tennis courts. Located 6 miles (10 km) north of Manchester. **$$$$**

Cornucopia of Dorset
Route 30, 05251.
Tel: 802 867–5751/
800 566–5751,
Fax: 802 867–5353.
www.cornucopiaofdorset.com.
Five prettily appointed rooms; pampering services include champagne welcome, marvelous breakfasts (served by candlelight), cozy down comforters or quilts, and terry-cloth robes. **$$–$$$$**

Dorset Inn
Church & Main Streets, 05251.
Tel: 802 867–5500.
One of the state's oldest – and reliably enjoyable – inns (MAP), opened in 1796, with 31 rooms.
$$$–$$$$

Marble West Inn.
Dorset West Road, 05251.
Tel: 802 867–4155.
An eight-room B&B in a marble-columned 1840s Greek Revival manse, elegantly decorated. **$–$$**

EAST BURKE

Burke Mountain Resort
P.O. Box 247, Mountain Road, East Burke, 05832.
Tel: 802 626–3305/
800 541–5480.
Fax: 802 626–3364.

150 condominiums offering a range of modern accommodations on the slopes of Burke Mountain. **$–$$$**

Old Cutter Inn
RR 1, Box 62, 05832.
Tel: 802 626–5152/
800 295–1943.
A small farmhouse converted into a quaint nine-room inn. The restaurant serves Swiss fare. **$–$$**

ESSEX JUNCTION

Inn at Essex
70 Essex Way (off Route 15), 05452.
Tel: 802 878–1100/
800 288–7613,
Fax: 802 878–0063.
A neo-traditional Georgian-style hotel with 97 rooms, a swimming pool and outstanding cuisine (provided by the New England Culinary Institute); convenient to Burlington. **$$–$$$**

FAIR HAVEN

Maplewood Inn
Route 22A, 05473.
Tel: 802 265–8039/
800 253–7729.
A five-room B&B in a former dairy farm with fanciful decor and hearty breakfasts. Located west of Rutland near the New York border. **$–$$**

GRAFTON

Old Tavern at Grafton
Route 121, 05146.
Tel: 802 843–2231/
800 843–1801.
Fax: 802 843–2245.
An 18th-century stagecoach inn (plus several nearby buildings) with 66 bedrooms furnished with country antiques in a lovingly restored town. Swimming pond, tennis courts, ice skating, cross-country ski trails. **$$–$$$**

HIGHGATE SPRINGS
Tyler Place on Lake Champlain
Route 7, 05460.
Tel: 802 868–3301.
www.tylerplace.com.
A family FAP "camp" (50 rooms) since the 1930s on 165 acres of lakefront property. Accommodations include cottages, an 1820 farmhouse, a Victorian guest house, and a modern inn. Extensive activities for children. **$$$$**

JAY
Hotel Jay and Jay Peak Condominiums
Route 242, 05854
Tel: 802 988–2611/
800 451–4449.
Fax: 802 988–4049.
48 simple, ski lodge-style hotel rooms and 120 modern one- to three-bedroom condos, most right on the slopes. **$$–$$$**

KILLINGTON
Cortina Inn
Route 4, 05751.
Tel: 802 773–3331/
800 451–6108.
Fax: 802 775–6948.
97 surprisingly lush and spacious rooms; indoor pool, tennis courts, health club, ice skating, horseback riding. **$$–$$$$**
Inn of the Six Mountains
Killington Road, 05751.
Tel: 802 422–4302/
800 228–4676.
A 103-room modern hotel with a Rockies feel; everything, including the central fieldstone hearth, is lavishly overscale. **$–$$$**
Inn at Long Trail
Route 4, 05751.
Tel: 802 775–7181/
800 325–2540.
Fax: 802 747–7034.
A 1938 rustic 19-room ski inn/B&B built around a huge boulder, which intrudes, picturesquely, into the dining room and Irish Pub (which features Guinness on tap and, often, Irish music). Near the Pico ski area and the Appalachian Trail. **$$**
Mountain Meadows Lodge
Thundering Brook Road, 05751.

Tel: 802 775–1010/
800 370–4567.
www.mtmeadowslodge.com.
A large lakeside farmhouse offering 18 rooms (MAP), with extensive cross-country trails. Child care center with a playground and farm animals. **$$**
(Also at Bridgewater Corners, see page 373)

LOWER WATERFORD
Rabbit Hill Inn
Route 18, 05848.
Tel: 802 748–5168/
800 762–8669.
Fax: 802 748–8342.
www.rabbithillinn.com.
A Greek Revival stagecoach inn (MAP) on 15 wooded acres near Street. Johnsbury. 21 ultra-romantic rooms, a superb elegant restaurant and lots of pampering personal touches. Trails for walking or cross-country skiing; canoes also available. **$$$–$$$$**

LUDLOW
Governor's Inn
86 Main Street, 05149.
Tel: 802 228–8830/
800 468–3766.
Nine-rooms MAP. Formal Victorian decor, romantic ambiance and solicitous hospitality in an early 20th-century building, 10 minutes from the Okemo Mountain ski area.

Well-regarded dining room serving French-influenced cuisine on antique china and sterling silver. **$$$$**

LYNDONVILLE
Wildflower Inn
Darling Hill Road, 05851.
Tel: 802 626–8310/
800 627–8310.
Fax: 802 626–3039.
www.wildflowerinn.com.
22-room B&B. A cheerfully renovated 1796 farmhouse (with modern carriage house annex) great for families; there's a petting zoo, pool and panoramic view. Short drive to the Burke Mountain ski area. **$$–$$$$**

MANCHESTER
1811 House
Route 7A, 05254.
Tel: 802 362–1811/
800 432–1811.
Fax: 802 362–2443.
A Federal manse that has been an inn/B&B for most of its history. 14 spacious, antiques-filled guest rooms. Additional rooms in a separate cottage. Located at the north end of Manchester Village. **$$–$$$**
The Equinox
Route 7A, 05253.
Tel: 802 362–5700/
800 362–4747.

Skiing Tour Operators to Vermont

Companies offering tailormade skiing package holidays to Vermont from the UK include the following:
● **American Dream**
243 Euston Road
London NW1Y 4BS.
Tel: 0171–388 2000.
● **Crystal Holidays**
Cyrstal House
The Courtyard
Arlington Road
Surbiton KT6 6BW.
Tel: 0181–399 5144.
● **Inghams**
10–18 Putney Hill
London SW15 6AZX.
Tel: 0181–780 4400.

● **North America Travel Service**
Suite 2000, 11 Albion Street
Leeds LS1 5ER.
Tel: 0113–246 1466.
● **Thomas Cook**
PO Box 5, 12 Coningsby Road
Peterborough PE3 8XZP.
Tel: 01733 563200.
● **United Vacations**
United House
Southern Perimeter Road
Heathrow Airport
Middlesex TW6 3LP.
Tel: 0181–750 9674.
● **Virgin Holidays**
The Galleria, Station Road
Crawley RH10 1WW.
Tel: 01293 617181.

www.equinoxresort.com.
A grand old hotel with 155 rooms, beautifully refurbished and maintained as a sister property to Scotland's Gleneagles. **$$$$**
Village Country Inn
Route 7A, 05254.
Tel: 802 362–1792/
800)370–0300.
A rambling 33-room old MAP inn with romantic French country decor. **$$$–$$$$**
Wilburton Inn
River Road (off Route 7A), 05254.
Tel: 802 362–2500/
800 648–4944.
Fax: 802 362–1107.
A railroad baron's 100-year-old brick mansion set on 20 acres of lawn, with contemporary outdoor sculpture. The 34 elegantly appointed guest rooms for B&B feature canopy beds, fireplaces and whirlpool tubs; cottages also available. **$$–$$$$**

MARLBORO
Whetstone Inn
South Road, 05344.
Tel: 802 254–2500.
A 200-year-old farmhouse with 12 bedrooms decorated with a mix of Colonial appointments and contemporary Scandinavian furnishings. Pond for swimming or skating. No credit cards. **$**

MIDDLEBURY
Swift House Inn
25 Stewart Lane, 05753.
Tel: 802 388–9925.
Fax: 802 388–9927.

Leaf Peeping

For up-to-date information on where you can catch foliage is at its most magnificent in the fall during September and October, call the states' Autumn Foliage Hotlines on the following numbers:
● Connecticut 800 252–6863
● Maine 800 533–9595
● Massachusetts 800 227–6277
● New Hampshire 800 258–3608
● Rhode Island 800 556–2484
● Vermont 800 828–3239

An elegantly detailed 1815 Federal house with 21 luxurious guest rooms; the Carriage House features spacious suites with whirlpool baths. **$$–$$$**
Middlebury Inn
14 Court House Square, 05753.
Tel: 802 388–4961/
800 842–4666.
www.middleburyinn.com.
An 1825 inn (plus 1827 annex and modern motel extension, offering a total of 80 rooms) overlooking the village green. Dining room serves traditional New England fare. **$–$$$**

MIDDLETOWN SPRINGS
Priscilla's Victorian Inn
South Street, 05757.
Tel: 802 235–2299.
A six-room Victorian home B&B with impressive porches and parlors. Located south of Rutland. **$**

MONTGOMERY
Black Lantern
Route 118, 05470.
Tel: 802 326–4507/
800 255–8661.
Fax: 802 326–4077.
Built in 1803 to house mill workers, now a country-style inn with 16 rooms for B&B near Jay Peak. Several suites have whirlpool baths and fireplaces. **$$–$$$**
Inn on Trout River
Main Street, 05471.
Tel: (802) 326–4391/
800 338–7049.
Fax: 802 326–3194.
A late 1800s inn with 10 rooms for B&B furnished in English and Victorian country styles with down quilts and flannel sheets (in winter). The living/dining room has a large wood-burning stove; the downstairs recreation room has a pool table. Near Jay Peak. **$–$$**

MONTPELIER
Inn at Montpelier
147 Main Street, 05602.
Tel: 802 223–2727.
Fax: 802 223–0722.
A pair of adjoining Federal mansions make a restful in-town retreat (19 rooms) for both business travelers and vacationers. The main inn has a wide

Price Categories

A very approximate guide to current room rates for a standard double per night is:
$$$$ = over $200
$$$ = $150–200
$$ = $100–150
$ = under $100

wraparound porch and a formal sitting room. Both buildings have small guest pantries with coffee makers and snacks. **$$–$$$**

NEWFANE AREA
Inn at South Newfane
369 Dover Road, South Newfane, 05351.
Tel: 802 348–7191.
www.innatsouthnewfane.com.
Six-room MAP. Pretty country decor, a pool and pond, and over 100 acres to roam. **$$$**
Four Columns Inn
230 West Street, Newfane, 05345.
Tel: 802 365–7713/
800 787–6633.
Fax: 802 365–0022/
www.fourcolumnsinn.com.
A majestic white-columned Greek Revival inn beside one of New England's most photogenic greens. The 15 Colonial-style guest rooms have been updated with cassette players, and there is a pool and trout ponds. **$$–$$$**

NORTH HERO ISLAND
Shore Acres Inn and Restaurant
RR1, Box 3, 05474.
Tel: 802 372–8722.
A sedate 23-room lakeside hotel with a vast verandah affording a 40–mile (64 km) view. **$**

PUTNEY
Hickory Ridge House
Hickory Ridge Road, 05346.
Tel: 802 387–5709/
800 380–9218.
Fax: 802 387–5387.
An 1808 brick Federal manor with seven country-style rooms on 12 pastoral acres. Vegetarian breakfasts, with soufflés and homemade breads, are a specialty of this B&B. **$**

QUECHEE

Quechee Inn at Marshland Farm
Clubhouse Road, 05059.
Tel: 802 295–3133/
800 235–3133.
A 1793 farmstead with 24 rooms
(MAP) in a bucolic riverside setting.
Cross-country skiing, hiking,
canoeing. **$$$–$$$$**

Quechee Bed & Breakfast
Route 4 at Waterman Hill, 05059.
Tel: 802 295–1776/
800 628–8610.
Eight-room B&B. Surprisingly
spacious country-style quarters
carved out of a 1795 house. Walking
distance to Quechee Gorge. **$$**

RUTLAND

Inn at Rutland
70 N Main Street, 05701.
Tel: 802 773–0575/
800 808–0575.
Fax: 802 775–3506.
10-room B&B in a renovated
Victorian mansion with views of the
surrounding mountains and valleys.
Traditional appointments include an
ornate oak staircase, carved ceiling
moldings, and botanical prints. **$$**

SHELBURNE

Inn at Shelburne Farms
Harbor Road, 05482.
Tel: 802 985–8498.
Fax: 802 985–8123.
Lila Vanderbilt's turn-of-the-century
Tudor-style mansion (24 rooms,
MAP) set amid a grandiose working
farm beside Lake Champlain.
Tennis, boating, fishing available. A
gem. **$$$$**

SHOREHAM

Shoreham Inn
51 Inn Street, 05770.
Tel: 802 897–5861/
800 255–5081.
11-room B&B in a personable
village farmhouse, with
sophisticated hosts. Near Larabees
Point on the southern end of Lake
Champlain. **$$**

STOWE

**Topnotch at Stowe Resort
and Spa**
Mountain Road, 05672.
Tel: 802 253–8585/
800 451–8686.
A luxury 105-room establishment
with a world-class spa, plus tennis
and stables. **$$$$**

Trapp Family Lodge
42 Trapp Hill Road, 05672.
Tel: 802 253–8511/
800 826–7000.
A modern 93-room replacement for
the original lodge, lost to fire;
2,000 acres with skiing and walking
paths. **$$$$**

Green Mountain Inn
Route 100, 05672.
Tel: 802 253–7301/
800 455–6629.
A rambling 1833 inn with 64 rooms,
nicely restored. **$–$$$$**

Inn at the Mountain
Route 108, 05672.
Tel: 802 253–3000/
800 253–4754.
A tastefully decorated motel-and-
condo complex with 40 rooms at
the foot of Mount Mansfield,
surrounded by state forest. **$$$**

Stowehof Inn
Edson Hill Road, 05672.
Tel: 802 253–9722/
800 932–7136.
A hilltop hotel with intentionally
eccentric decor in the 45 rooms
and an outdoor pool with the best
view in town. **$$–$$$**

Fiddler's Green Inn
Mountain Road, 05672.
Tel: 802 253–8124.
A homey seven-room 1820 lodge
with a congenial host. **$**

Mansfield Camp
Mountain Road, 05672.
Tel: 802 253–4010/
800 639–3390.
Two-dorm MAP. Basic bunk-bed

Snow Tours

The following places offer cross-
country ski tours led by ski
instructors, or guided
snowmobile tours:
● Killington, Wells and Post Mills
  in Vermont
● Bartlett, Colebrook, East
  Conway Littleton and Tamworth
  in New Hampshire
● Rangeley in Maine

lodgings in a Civilian Conservation
Corps hostel built in the 1930s;
with two hearty meals, the best
bargain in New England. **$**

VERGENNES

Basin Harbor Club
Basin Harbor Road, 05491.
Tel: 802 475–2311/
800 622–4000. Fax: 475 6545
www.basinharbor.com.
A classic lakeside summer colony,
built around an old farmhouse, full
of timeless pleasures. Most
accommodations (138 FAP) are now
in newer cottages, many with
fireplaces and refrigerators.
Located on a 700-acre property that
includes a beach, swimming pool,
golf course, tennis courts and a
playground. Extensive children's
activities. **$$$$**

WAITSFIELD

Inn at Round Barn
E Warren Road, 05673.
Tel: 802 496–2276.
Fax: 802 496–8832.
B&B. A luxuriously retrofitted
farmhouse B&B with 11 plush guest
rooms, some with whirlpool baths.
The unusual 12-sided Shaker-style
barn is used for summer concerts
and parties. **$$–$$$$**

Knoll Farm Inn
Bragg Hill Road, 05673,
Tel: 802 496–3939.
A functioning farmhouse offering
four rooms on 150 acres;
home-grown meals, and a pond for
swimming or skating. **$$**

Lareau Farm Country Inn
Route 100, 05673
Tel: 802 496–4949/
800 833–0766.
Fax: 802 496–7979.
13-room B&B. Authentic farmhouse
atmosphere, with country-style
rooms and a dining room with many
windows. On 67 acres of woods and
pasture, near the Mad River. **$–$$**

Mad River Barn
Route 17, 05673.
Tel: 802 496–3340.
A 1948 ski lodge with 15 MAP
rooms with a vintage game
room. **$$**

Price Categories

A very approximate guide to current room rates for a standard double per night is:

$$$$ = over $200
$$$ = $150–200
$$ = $100–150
$ = under $100

WATERBURY
Inn at Blush Hill
Blush Hill Road, 05676.
Tel: 802 244–7529/
800 736–7522.
Fax: 802 244–7314.
www.blushhill.com.
An exemplary B&B high on a hill with sweeping mountain vistas. Five cheerful rooms and gourmet breakfasts in a 1790s room with its original open hearth fireplace. **$–$$**

WEATHERSFIELD
Inn at Weathersfield
Route 106, 05151.
Tel: 802 263–9217/
800 477–4828.
Fax: 802 263–9219.
12-room MAP in a magical 18th-century country inn, where Early American style blends with modern amenities, with the promise of romance at every turn. Located south of Windsor. **$$$–$$$$**

WEST DOVER
Inn at Sawmill Farm
Route 100, 05356.
Tel: 802 464–3131/
800 493–1133.
Fax: 802 464–1130.
20-room MAP. An old farmstead jazzed up with bold decorative touches; country elegance at its best, plus superb regional cuisine. Convenient to Mount Snow and Haystack Mountain ski areas. **$$$$**

WEST TOWNSHEND
Windham Hill Inn
Windham Hill Road, 05359.
Tel: 802 874–4080/
800 944–4080.
Fax: 802 874–4702.
www.windhamhill.com.
An elegantly appointed 1825 farmhouse, cum cross-country ski center with 21 MAP rooms, set way back in the country. An extensive CD collection entertains music-loving guests. Pool, tennis courts, skating pond. Located 10 miles (16 km) north of Newfane and 10 miles (16 km) east of the Stratton Mountain ski area. **$$$$**

WILMINGTON
Trail's End
Smith Road, 05363.
Tel: 802 464–2727/
800 859–2585.
15 Lovely rooms and suites branch off from a cathedral-ceiling living room with fieldstone hearth in this B&B. Convenient to Mount Snow and Haystack Mountain ski areas. **$–$$$**

WINDSOR
Juniper Hill Inn
Juniper Hill Road, 05089.
Tel: 802 674–5273/
800 359–2541.
Fax: 802 674–2041.
A 100-year-old Greek Revival mansion B&B set on a broad lawn. 16 elegantly appointed rooms furnished with Queen Anne and Edwardian pieces. Near Ascutney Mountain. **$$–$$$**

WOODSTOCK AREA
Jackson House
37 Route 4 West, Woodstock, 05091.
Tel: 802 547–2065.
A lovingly restored 1890s clapboard house, now a 13-room B&B; five-course breakfasts, and hors-d'oeuvres with champagne. **$$$–$$$$**

Kedron Valley Inn
Route 106, South Woodstock, 05071.
Tel: 802 457–1473/
800 836–1193.
Fax: 802 457–4469.
Heirloom quilts line the walls and dress up the 27 prettily decorated rooms of this B&B, and the restaurant is exceptional. The ski lodge-style building behind the main inn attracts families, who also enjoy the swimming pond. **$$–$$$$**

Applebutter Inn
Happy Valley Road, Woodstock, 05091.
Tel: 802 457–4158.
Six-room B&B in a Federal house full of fluffy comforters; delicious breakfasts. **$–$$**

Three Church Street
3 Church Street.
Woodstock, 05091.
Tel: 802 457–1925.
11-room B&B in a gracious early 19th-century house near the common, with a tennis court and pool; well priced for this level of elegance. **$**

Woodstock Inn & Resort
14 The Green (Route 4),
Woodstock, 05091.
Tel: 802 457–1100/
800 448–7900.
Fax: 802 457–6699.
www.woodstockinn.com.
The Rockefellers' homage to country inns past, full of Americana. The decor is corporate/country with modern furniture and patchwork quilts. Facilities include 144 bedrooms indoor and outdoor pools, tennis courts, golf, health club, racquet ball and squash courts. **$$$–$$$$**

Where to Eat

ARLINGTON
Arlington Inn
Route 7A.
Tel: 802 375–6532.
A fairly formal candlelit restaurant creating French Continental dishes – rack of lamb, roast duck – all prepared with local meats and produce. **$$$**

West Mountain Inn
River Road (off Route 313).
Tel: 802 375–6516.
New American fare in a low-beamed paneled dining room at a romantic and family-friendly inn. **$$$–$$$$**

BENNINGTON
Four Chimneys
21 West Road (Route 9).
Tel: 802 447–3500.
Polished continental cuisine in a showpiece mansion. **$$$$**

Blue Benn Diner
Route 7.
Tel: 802 442–5140.
A classic 1940s diner serving

unconventional as well as traditional fare. **$**

BRATTLEBORO
Latchis Grill
Latchis Hotel, 50 Main Street.
Tel: 802 254–6300.
International fare and brews from the on-site Windham Brewery. **$$**
Mole's Eye Cafe
High Street.
Tel: 802 257–0771.
A local institution since the 1930s. A neighborly basement spot serving hearty homestyle fare. **$$**
Peter Havens
32 Elliot Street.
Tel: 802 257–3333.
The locals' favorite New American bistro. **$$**

BURLINGTON
The Ice House
171 Battery Street.
Tel: 802 864–1800.
Fresh seafood; refreshing views of Lake Champlain. **$$$**
Pauline's,
1834 Shelburne Road, (Route 7 S), South Burlington.
Tel: 802 862–1081.
Deft nouvelle American cuisine improbably plonked in a strip mall. **$$$**
Daily Planet
15 Center Street.
Tel: 802 862–9647.
World-beat cuisine: Mediterranean with Asian influences; the pulse center of town. **$$**
Dockside Restaurant on the Waterfront
209 Battery Street
Tel: 802 864-5266
Has deck overlooking Perkins Pier,

Lake Champlain, and the Adirondack sunsets. Has extended range from seafood to include beef, poultry and vegetarian dishes. **$$**
Sweet Tomatoes
83 Church Street,
Tel: 802 660–9533.
A boisterous trattoria with a wood-fired oven that turns out all manner of pizzas, as well as other Tuscan-inspired fare. **$$**
Trattoria Delia
152 Street Paul Street.
Tel: 802 864–5253.
Rustic Italian dishes. **$$**
Mirabelle's
198 Main Street.
Tel: 802 658–3074.
An inviting cafe/patisserie. **$**

CHESTER
Country Girl Diner
Route 11.
Tel: 802 875–2650.
A traditional 1950s diner on the western end of town. **$**

CRAFTSBURY
Craftsbury Inn
Main Street.
Tel: 802 586–2848.
Intriguing contemporary *prix-fixe* dinners prepared by a talented chef–owner. **$$$**

DORSET
Barrows House
Route 30.
Tel: 802 867–4455.
New American in an intimate setting; the tavern serves lighter fare. **$$$**
Chantecleer
Route 7A, East Dorset.
Tel: 802 362–1616.

Swiss and French provincial cuisine in an former dairy barn. **$$$**
Dorset Inn
Route 30.
Tel: 802 867–5500.
"Honest American cooking": a choice of formal dining or tavern feasting in a 1796 hostelry. **$$$**

EAST BURKE
Old Cutter Inn
Tel: 802 626–5152.
Chef-owner Fritz Walther's native Swiss specialties, including irresistible *rosti*. **$$**
River Garden Cafe
Route 114.
Tel: 802 626–3514.
Bruschetta and *tiramisu* come to the Northeast Kingdom, along with rack of lamb and local smoked trout. **$$**

GRAFTON
Old Tavern at Grafton
Route 121.
Tel: 802 843–2231.
Hearty New England dishes, perhaps venison stew or grilled quail, served in two dining rooms: one more formal, the other rustic tavern-style. **$$–$$$**

KILLINGTON
Cortina Inn
Route 4.
Tel: 802 773–3333.
Chefs from the New England Culinary Institute ensure deft and

Restaurant Guidelines

● **Prices** are approximate, but for a three-course meal for one (excluding beverages, tax and tip), the following guidelines may prove helpful:
$$$$ = over $40
$$$ = $28-40
$$ = $15-28
$ = under $15
● **Meal tax** varies from state to

state, but it is customary to tip 15 to 20 percent on the pre-tax total.
● **Credit cards** The more expensive establishments generally accept credit cards, but call ahead to check just in case.
● **Reservations** Most restaurants, except for the clearly casual, appreciate reservations (some require them).

Restaurant Guidelines

- **Prices** are approximate, but for a three-course meal for one (excluding beverages, tax and tip), the following guidelines may prove helpful:

$$$$ = over $40
$$$ = $28-40
$$ = $15-28
$ = under $15

- **Meal tax** varies from state to state, but it is customary to tip 15 to 20 percent on the pre-tax total.
- **Credit cards** The more expensive establishments generally accept credit cards, but call ahead to check just in case.
- **Reservations** Most restaurants, except for the clearly casual, appreciate reservations (some require them).

innovative fare. **$$$**
Hemingway's
Route 4.
Tel: 802 422–3886.
Inspired regional cuisine, consistently hailed as one of the nation's best. **$$$$**

LOWER WATERFORD
Rabbit Hill Inn
Route 18.
Tel: 802 748–5168.
Dazzling New American cuisine in a rural setting of understated elegance. **$$$**

LUDLOW
Nikki's
Route 103, Okemo Mountain.
Tel: 802 228–7797.
The decor is polished Hippie Deco, the New American cuisine delightful. **$$**

MANCHESTER
The Equinox
Route 7A.
Tel: 802 362–4700.
Spectacular regional cuisine in a formal barrel-vaulted dining room looking out on Mount Equinox; Marsh's Tavern serves more casual, but equally delicious fare. **$$$–$$$$**
Bistro Henry's
Route 11/30.
Tel: 802 362–4982.
A spacious dining room on the edge of town preparing authentic Mediterranean cuisine. Extensive wine list. **$$$**
Mother Myrick's Confectionery and Ice Cream Parlor
Route 7A.
Tel: 802 362–1560.

The place to indulge your sweet tooth with a slice of freshly baked pie, homemade fudge, or an ice cream treat. **$**

MIDDLEBURY
Swift House Inn
25 Stewart Lane.
Tel: 802 388–9925.
Elegant regional cuisine in a formal, paneled Federal dining room. **$$$**
Woody's
5 Bakery Lane.
Tel: 802 388–4182.
Unfussy regional American; congenial crowd. Looks out on Otter Creek. **$$$**

MONTGOMERY
Black Lantern
Route 118.
Tel: 802 326–4507.
Contemporary American fare at this inn restaurant near Jay Peak. **$$**

MONTPELIER
The Chef's Table
118 Main Street.
Tel: 802 223–9240.
This New England Culinary Institute enterprise is thoroughly elegant, and culinarily eloquent. **$$$**
Main Street Grill
118 Main Street.
Tel: 802 223–3188.
Adventurous grazing courtesy of the highly skilled students of the New England Culinary Institute. **$$**

NEWFANE
Four Columns Inn
230 West Street.
Tel: 802 365–7713.
Creative European/American cuisine, auberge-style. **$$$$**

PUTNEY
Curtis' Barbecue
Route 5 (no phone).
Good ol' barbecue, slow-cooked beside an old blue school bus; funky, but divine. **$**

QUECHEE
Parker House Inn
16 Main Street.
Tel: 802 295–6077.
Tasteful continental cuisine in a brick Victorian mansion with grand views. **$$$**
Quechee Inn at Marshland Farm
Clubhouse Road.
Tel: 802 295–3133.
Seasonal specialties in a tastefully restored tavern. **$$$**
Simon Pearce Restaurant
The Mill, Main Street.
Tel: 802 295–1470.
Fine country cuisine, with some Irish touches, in a modern café in an old riverside mill. Extensive wine list. **$$$**

RUTLAND
Back Home Cafe
21 Center Street.
Tel: 802 775–9313.
A second-floor café with wooden booths, exposed brick and an outdoor patio; simple, creative fare. **$–$$**
Royal's 121 Hearthside
37 N Main Street.
Tel: 802 775–0856.
A Rutland institution. Traditional fare – rack of lamb, prime rib, pan-roasted salmon – prepared behind an open hearth. **$$–$$$**

ST JOHNSBURY
Anthony's Diner
Railroad Street.
Tel: 802 748–3613.
Traditional diner meals. A St Johnsbury institution. **$$–$$$**

SHELBURNE
Inn at Shelburne Farms
Harbor Road.
Tel: 802 985–8498.
Reservations required. Gourmet dining (and breakfasting) in a Queen Anne-style manor overlooking Lake Champlain. **$$$**

STOWE

Ten Acres Lodge
Luce Hill at Barrows Road.
Tel: 802 253–7638.
Skilled regional cuisine, in handsome old farmhouse set amid a meadow. **$$$–$$$$**

Cliff House
Mount Mansfield.
Tel: 802 253–3000.
Board the world's fastest gondola for a culinary "peak" experience. **$$$**

Stowehof Inn
Edson Hill Road.
Tel: 802 253–9722.
Elegant and astute New American cuisine, with a dramatic view. **$$$**

Topnotch at Stowe
Mountain Road.
Tel: 802 253–8585.
A formal dining room and casual grill offer skilled contemporary cuisine, some calibrated for the health-conscious. **$$$**

Trapp Family Lodge
Luce Hill Road.
Tel: 802 253–8511.
Gemutlich treats with fine valley views from the Tea Room; formal dining too. **$$**

Blue Moon Cafe
35 School Street.
Tel: 802 253–7006.
A contemporary bistro with lots of charm, vivid cuisine, and great prices. **$$**

Miguel's Stowe Away
Mountain Road.
Tel: 802 253–7574.
Very convincing Mexican, for ski country. **$**

Trattoria La Festa
Mountain Road.
Tel: 802 253–8480.
Authentic Italian cuisine in an 1859 farmhouse. **$$**

WAITSFIELD

Tucker Hill Lodge
65 Marble Hill Road.
Tel: 802 496–3983.
Offers steakhouse fare in its restaurant, lighter fare in pub. **$$**

WARREN

Chez Henri
Sugarbush Village.
Tel: 802 583–2600.
An authentic romantic French bistro in the middle of a bustling ski resort. **$$$**

The Common Man,
German Flats Road,
Tel: 802 583–2800.
Country-sophisticate fare in an atmospheric old barn. **$$$**

Sam Rupert's
Sugarbush Access Road,
Tel: 802 583–2421.
Superb New American cuisine in a cozy, romantic setting. **$$$**

WATERBURY

Cold Hollow Cider Mill
Route 100.
Tel: 802 244–8771.
Freshly made apple cider and baked goods. Don't miss the cider donuts. A perfect place for a snack after skiing or leaf-peeping. **$**

WEATHERSFIELD

Inn at Weathersfield
Route 106.
Tel: 802 263–9217.
Fine regional fare in a library illuminated by candlelight, with two grand pianos offering accompaniment. **$$$**

WEST DOVER

Inn at Sawmill Farm
off Route 100,
Tel: 802 464–8131.
Cuisine superb in its seeming simplicity; the setting is elegant rusticity. **$$$$**

WEST TOWNSHEND

Windham Hill Inn
Windham Hill Road.
Tel: 802 874–4080.
Prix-fixe classic French cuisine in a romantically appointed inn. **$$$$**

WILMINGTON

The Hermitage
Coldbrook Road.
Tel: 802 464–3511.
Game birds raised on the grounds, and a legendary wine cellar. **$$$$**

Le Petit Chef
Route 100.
Tel: 802 464–8437.
Classic French cuisine in a refined farmhouse. **$$$**

WINDSOR

Juniper Hill Inn
Juniper Hill Road.
Tel: 802 674–5273.
A traditional dining room in a traditional inn where updated classics are served by candlelight. **$$$**

Windsor Station
Depot Avenue.
Tel: 802 674–2052.
Traditional Continental fare in a converted railroad station, where the booths were constructed from the depot's railroad benches. **$$**

WOODSTOCK AREA

Bentley's Restaurant
3 Elm Street, Woodstock.
Tel: (802) 457–3232.
Eclectic, antique-ish decor and international dishes; a popular spot. Live music (jazz or blues) on the weekends. **$$**

The Prince & the Pauper
24 Elm Street, Woodstock.
Tel: 802 457–1818.
Known for fine regional, seasonal fare, and fantastic desserts in a romantic Colonial setting. **$$$$**

Woodstock Inn & Resort
Route 4 on The Green, Woodstock.
Tel: 802 457–1100.
Regional and New American cuisine in an ultra-formal setting. **$$$**

Kedron Valley Inn
Route 106, South Woodstock.
Tel: 802 457–1473.
Chef Tom Hopewell is not just an artist, but a magician with regional ingredients. **$$$**

Culture

Call **Burlington City Arts** (tel: 802 865–7166, 802 865–9163) for up-to-the-minute information on what's happening in this hip and lively city.

CLASSICAL MUSIC

Marlboro Music Festival (tel: 802 254–2394, Marlboro Music Center) has one of the most renowned line-ups in New England; concerts are given in the summer.

Vermont Symphony Orchestra (tel: 802 864–5741) performs in Manchester, Woodstock and

Brattleboro in the summer and in the southwestern towns of Bennington, Arlington and Rutland in the winter.
Stowe Performing Arts (tel: 802 253–7792) puts on summertime jazz and classical performances at the Trapp Family Lodge.

OPERA
Opera North (tel: (603) 643–1946; Hanover, NH) fords the Connecticut River to perform a few operas yearly in Vermont's Upper Valley region.

FOLK
Vermont Pub and Brewery (tel: 802 865–0500; College and Street Paul Sts, Burlington), is one of the more popular places in this youthful college town, and hosts folk musicians.

THEATER
Street Michael's Playhouse (tel: 802 654–2281; Burlington) is Vermont's oldest equity playhouse; you can always count on them for quality productions.
Flynn Theater for the Performing Arts (tel: 802 863–8778; 153 Main Street, Burlington) is the big venue for big-name and big-audience productions.
Weston Playhouse Theater Company (tel: 802 824–5288; Weston) is home to Vermont's oldest summer theater.
Dorset Playhouse (tel: 802 867–5777; Dorset) stages professional performances in the summer, but in the winter a fine consortium of community folks takes to the stage.

CINEMA
Catamount Arts (tel: 802 748–2600; 60 Eastern Avenue, St Johnsbury) brings a little bit of everything to this remote corner of Vermont: art films, dance, classical music. Do stop by if you're in the area and something's on tap.

Nightlife

LIVE MUSIC
Club Metronome (tel: 802 865–4563; 188 Main Street, Burlington) has a beat all its own: reggae, blues, whatever the newest musical beat happens to be.
Mulligan's (tel: 802 297–9293) on Stratton has year–round music.
Common Ground (tel: 802 257–0855; 25 Eliot Street, Brattleboro) has jam dance bands on most weekends, while more mellow guitarists play during brunch.

LATE-NIGHT VENUES
All of the big ski mountains have a phalanx of nightly live music from which to choose. You're bound to find something to your liking.
Bentley's (tel: 802 457–3232; 3 Elm Street, Woodstock) has DJs on the weekends.

Outdoor Activities
BIKING
Many of the downhill ski areas turn into mountain biking centers after the winter season ends.
Mount Snow (tel: 802 464–3333), home to the first US mountain bike school, has 45 miles (72 km) of bike terrain and runs one-day coaching programs, leads mountain tours and hosts family bike weekends.

Vermont's Festivals

● **SPRING**
Over 90 varieties of lilacs offer a fragrant setting for family activities and musical entertainment at the **Shelburne Museum's Lilac Festival** (tel: 802 985–3346) in May.
 Also in May, artists across the state open their studios to visitors during the annual **Open Studio Weekend** (tel: 802 223–3380).

● **SUMMER**
The hills come alive with the sound of music as soon as summer arrives, starting with Burlington's **Discover Jazz Festival** (tel: 802 863–7992) in early June.
 In July, Marlboro College, on a bucolic hilltop, welcomes the month-long, internationally renowned **Marlboro Music Festival** (tel: 802 254–2394).
 Meanwhile, Burlington-area towns host the **Vermont Mozart Festival** (tel: 802 862–7352, (800) 639–9097).
 Circus Smirkus (tel: 802 744–6122) – the world's only international youth circus, with participants recruited from as far afield as Russia and China – raises its one-ring big top throughout Vermont mid-July to mid-August.
 Early in August, the quirky **Bread and Puppet Theatre** (tel: 802 525–3031) in West Glover mounts its annual Domestic Resurrection Circus, a mix of radical agitprop and simple celebration.

● **FALL**
The state's wide variety of autumn fairs and festivals includes the huge **Champlain Valley Fair** in Essex Junction (tel: 802 878–5545), the **Stratton Arts Festival** – the state's oldest and largest juried exhibition of contemporary crafts (tel: 802 297–3265), and **Killington's Vermont Sheep and Wool Festival** (tel: 802 828–2416).

● **WINTER**
Vermonters celebrate New Year's Eve with **Burlington's First Night** festivities (tel: 802 863–6005). Then in mid-January, the ski town of Stowe, which views the frigid weather as one more excuse to party, hosts the **Stowe Winter Carnival**, a week-long bash featuring dog-sled races, ice sculptures, and fireworks.
 Other ski areas also sponsor various special events to spice up the season.

For further details about events, contact the local tourist office.

At **Killington** (tel: 802 422–6232), mountain bikers can cruise 50 miles (80 km) of trails. Vermont is a popular destination for upscale inn-to-inn tours.

The Berkeley, California-based **Backroads** (tel: (800) 462–2848) offers several tours, as does **Bike Vermont** (tel: (800) 257–2226).

CANOEING/KAYAKING AND RAFTING

Vermont Canoe (tel: 802 257–5008; Brattleboro) rents canoes and kayaks and conducts guided paddling tours. Burlington-based **Paddleways** (tel: 802 660–8606) teaches kayaking fundamentals and runs kayaking trips, as does **True North Kayak Tours** (tel: 802 860–1910).

FISHING

Anglers flock to the trout-laded Battenkill River near Manchester, where **Orvis** (tel: 802 362–3622, (800) 235–9763) runs a program of popular two-and–a-half day fly-fishing classes.

Battenkill Anglers (tel: 802 362–3184) organize fly-fishing vacations and schools.

Fishing guides at **Strictly Trout** (tel: 802 869–3116) work all Vermont rivers but specialize in the Connecticut River.

HIKING

Vermont's topography offers everything from easy day hikes to multi-day mountain jaunts. Long-distance hikers gravitate to the **Appalachian Trail**, which cuts across southern Vermont, and to the **Long Trail**, a 445-mile (712-km) traverse across Vermont's highest peaks between the Massachusetts state line and the Canadian border.

Green Mountain Club (tel: 802 244–7037) has specific trail information and publishes the *Day Hiker's Guide to Vermont.*

To mix serious hiking with country-inn comforts, contact **Country Inns Along the Trail** (tel: 802 247–3300), which organizes inn-to-inn tours.

Hiking Holidays of Bristol (tel: 802 453–4816, (800) 537–3850)

also packages Green Mountain inn-to-inn tours.

SAILING

Lake Champlain and **Lake Memphremagog** are Vermont's principal sailing lakes.

Burlington Community Boathouse (tel: 802 865–3377) rents sailboats and runs charters and "bareboats" on Lake Champlain.

Winds of Ireland (tel: 802 863–5090; Burlington Boathouse) runs day and sunset sailing cruises.

On Lake Memphremagog, you can rent sailboats at **Newport Marine** (tel: 802 334–5911) and **East Side Landing** (tel: 802 334–2340).

SKIING

For many, Vermont is synonymous with New England skiing. In the south, the largest downhill mountains are:
Stratton (tel: 802 297–4000, (800) 787–2886; Jamaica),
Okemo (tel: 802 228–4041, (800) 786–5366; Ludlow)
and **Mount Snow** (tel: (800) 245–7669).

Killington (tel: 802 422–3261, (800) 621–6867; Rutland) is mammoth.

In the north, check out:
Stowe (tel: 802 253–3600),
Sugarbush (tel: 802 583–2381, (800) 537–8427; Warren)
and **Jay Peak** (tel: 802 988–2611, (800) 451–4449; Jay).

One of Vermont's largest cross-country skiing areas is **Craftsbury Nordic Center** (tel: (800) 729–7751), but Stowe also boasts several excellent centers, including **Edson Hill** (tel: 802 253–8954), **Topnotch** (tel: 802 253–8585), and **Trapp Family Lodge** (tel: 802 253–8511).

Serious Nordic skiers may ski the 280-mile (450-km) **Catamount Trail**, which runs nearly the entire length of the state; contact the Catamount Trail Association (tel: 802 864–5794; Burlington).

WHERE TO SHOP

Vermont's largest city, Burlington, has its most diverse and sophisticated offerings. The **Burlington Square Mall** on Church Street; **The Champlain Mill** (tel: 802 655–9477, Routes 2 and 7, north of the city); and the **Wing Building** on the waterfront have the greatest concentration of shops.

COUNTRY STORES

Vermont Country Store (tel: 802 824–3184; Route 100, Weston), the venerated institution that country stores all over the country aspire toward, might as well be a department store, for the range of merchandise you can get here. From Vermont-made food stuffs to folk remedies to flannel shirts.

Shelburne Country Store (tel: 802 985–3657; on the green, Shelburne) is a scaled-down version of the above, but a fine one at that.

MARKETS & FOODSTUFFS

Equinox Valley Nursery (tel: 802 362–2610; Route 7A south of Manchester) sells homegrown products; they always have a scarecrow display and other seasonal displays that make you want to take out your camera.

Harlow's Sugar House (tel: 802 387–5852; Route 5, Putney) takes kids and adults on horse-drawn sugaring rides. In the fall you can pick apples here, and in the summer, berries.

Cold Hollow Cider Mill (tel: 802 244–8771; Route 100, Waterbury Center) offers up glasses and cartons of fresh-pressed cider and other goodies grown in Vermont.

Green Mountain Chocolate Co. (tel: 802 244–1139; Route 100, Waterbury) sells the stuff of children's dreams and dentists' nightmares.

Cabot Creamery Annex (tel: 802 244–6334; Route 100, north of Waterbury), Vermont's largest cheese producer, offers free samples of smoked, aged, and sharp cheddar cheese. You can also tour of the state-of-the-art facility.

MARKETPLACES

Church Street Marketplace (tel: 802 863–1648; Main and Pearl Sts, Burlington) encompasses a pedestrian-only section of downtown lined with lively cafés and interesting shops.

Historic Marble Works (tel: 802 388–3701; Middlebury) is a warren of individual shops in a renovated marble factory.

FASHION & ACCESSORIES

Manchester is a Mecca for name-brand outlet shops, including Anne Klein, Giorgio Armani and Orvis.

Manchester Commons (tel: 802 362–3736; Routes 7 and 30) has the most outlets under one roof.

Johnson Woolen Mills (tel: 802 635–7185; Main Street, Johnson), an old-fashioned factory store, has old-fashioned discounted prices to match.

BOOKS

Chassman & Bem Booksellers (tel: 802 862–4332; 1 Church Street, Burlington) is an exceptional place, one of the best in New England.

Tuttle Antiquarian Books (tel: 802 773–8229; 28 S Main Street, Rutland) publishes its own fine booklist pertaining to Asia and things spiritual, but they also have a great selection of rare and out-of-print titles.

Northshire Bookstore (tel: 802

● **Lake Champlain Basin Science Center**
One College Street, Burlington. Tel: 802 864–1848.
Teaches youngsters and "oldsters" about the lake's history and ecology.

● **Montshire Museum of Science**
Montshire Road, Norwich. Tel: 802 649–2200.
Arguably second only to the Boston's Museum of Science, is a fine place to explore and discover the natural and man-made world.

362–2200; Main Street, Manchester) is one of the better shops in the state.

ANTIQUES

Danby Antiques Center (tel: 802 293–9984; off Route 7, north of Manchester) has a dozen rooms full of folk art and furniture.

See also page 255 for crafts in Vermont.

GLASS

Simon Pearce (tel: 802 295–2711; Main Street, Quechee), perhaps the most famous glass emporium in New England, employees a number of mastercraftsmen to carry out his vision and you can watch them work here. The shop sells first and second quality glassware and other fragile items.

Luminosity Studios (tel: 802 496–2231; Route 100, Waitsfield) sells stained glass from this former church.

GIFTS

Scotland by the Yard (tel: 802 295–5351; Route 4, Quechee) sells everything Scottish, and although you came to Vermont not the Highlands, you might just find a warrm sweater for an unusually early fall day.

ARTS AND CRAFTS

Vermont Artisan Design (tel: 802 257–7044; 115 Main Street, Brattleboro) is one of the state's best shops for handmade goods.

Bennington Potters (tel: 802 447–7531; 324 County Street, Bennington) sells seconds (as well as the best, of course) from the well-known (and expensive) Bennington Potters.

Newfane Country Store (tel: 802 365–7916; Route 30, Newfane) is the place to go for quilts.

Green Mountain Spinnery (tel: 802 387–4528; Exit 4 off I–91, Putney) offers home-grown, home-spun wool and mohair.

North Wind Artisans' Gallery (tel: 802 457–4587; 81 Central Street, Woodstock) carries a variety of excellent work.

By Vermont Hands (tel: 802

As well as producing over 30 "euphoric flavors" of ice cream, Ben Cohen and Jerry Greenfield plough back 7½ percent of their profits into social causes and half the proceeds of their factory tours go to Vermont charities.

● **Ben & Jerry's Ice Cream Factory**, Route 100, north of 1–89, near Waterbury.

635–7664; Route 15, Johnson) sells crafts made by almost 100 different local artisans. Johnson and nearby Jefferson are teeming with fine artists.

Bennington Potters North (tel: 802 863–2221; 127 College Street, Burlington), purveyors of their own very popular pottery, also offers a selective line of complementary housewares.

TOYS

Vermont Teddy Bear Company (tel: 802 985–3001; 2236 Shelburne Road, Shelburne), which sells furry handmade creatures for significant sums of money, turned a small cottage industry into a multi-million dollar enterprise.

New Hampshire

The Place

Known as: The Granite State.
Motto: Live free or die.
Origin of name: Named in 1629 by Captain John Mason of Plymough Council for his home county in England.
Entered Union: June 21, 1788, the ninth of the 13 original states.
Capital: Concord.
Area: 9,351 sq. miles (24,219 sq. km).
Highest point: Mount Washington, 6,288 ft (1,917 m).
Population: 1.1 million.
Population density: 119 people per sq. mile (46 per sq. km).
Economy: Manufacturing (industrial machinery, precision instruments, and electronic equipment) and services (including tourism).
National representation: two senators and two representatives to Congress.
Famous citizens: Mary Baker Eddy, Robert Frost, Horace Greeley and Daniel Webster

Where to Stay

BEDFORD
Bedford Village Inn
2 Old Bedford Road, 03110.
Tel: 603 472–2602/
800 852–1166.
Fax: 603 472–2379.
14 luxury suites, with four-poster beds and marble bathrooms, carved out of a three-story barn, south of Manchester. **$$$–$$$$**

BETHLEHEM
Adair
80 Guider Ln (at Route 302), 03574.
Tel: 603 444–2600/
800 441–2606.
Fax: 603 444–4823.
www.adairinn.com.
9 rooms. B&B. A 1927 mansion with 200 acres encompassing gardens and tennis courts. Common areas include a tap room with honor bar, fireplace, and vintage pool table. Guest rooms are furnished with elegant antiques or reproductions; all have either garden or mountain views. **$$–$$$**
Mulburn Inn
2370 Main Street, 03574.
Tel: 603 869–3389/
800 457–9440.
Fax: 603 869–5633.
7 rooms. B&B. A Tudor mansion built for Woolworths in 1913, with stained glass windows, ornately carved mantles, and imported fireplace tiles. Spacious individually decorated guest rooms. **$**

BRETTON WOODS
Mount Washington Hotel and Resort
Route 302, 03575.
Tel: 603 278–1000/
800 258–0330.
195 rooms. MAP. A grand hotel preserved in all its glory since 1902. Formal atmosphere (jackets required in the dining room in the evenings), but family friendly: kids' camp and other children's programs, along with swimming pools, tennis courts, horseback riding, movies, and a fitness center, keep the whole gang entertained. A 900-foot-long verandah looks out across the Presidential Range. **$$$$**

CENTER HARBOR
Red Hill Inn
Route 25B, 03226.
Tel: 603 279–7001/
800 573–3445.
Fax: 603 279–7003.
21 rooms. B&B. This early 20th-century red-brick summer home, plus a farmhouse and a stone cottage, once belonged to the inventor of the soda fountain. Fourteen of the rooms have either fireplaces or woodstoves. **$$–$$$**

CENTER SANDWICH
Corner House Inn
Main Street, 03227.
Tel: 603 284–6219.
Fax: 603 284–6220.
3 rooms. B&B. An old-fashioned Victorian cottage in a Currier & Ives town near Squam Lake. **$**

CONCORD
Wyman Farm
Wyman Road, Loudon, 03301.
Tel: 603 783–4467.
3 rooms. B&B. An 18th-century Cape on a 60-acre hilltop, about a 10-minute drive from Canterbury Shaker Village. **$**

Price Categories

A very approximate guide to current room rates for a standard double per night is:
$$$$ = over $200
$$$ = $150–200
$$ = $100–150
$ = under $100

DIXVILLE NOTCH
Balsams Grand Resort Hotel
Route 26, 03576.
Tel: 603 255–3400/
800 255–0600.
Fax: 603 255–4221.
www.thebalsams.com.
215 rooms. FAP. A fabulous 19th-century resort hotel, set in its own natural preserve. Activities include dancing and entertainment nightly, pool, tennis courts, skiing, fishing, children's programs. Opulent lunch buffets, creative dinners. **$$$$**

EATON CENTER
Inn at Crystal Lake
Route 153, 03832.
Tel: 603 447–2120/
800 343–7336.
Fax: 603 447–3599.
11 rooms. B&B. An 1884 Victorian in a sleepy lakeside village. Each room is named for a gemstone and decorated in that stone's color. Walk to the beach on Crystal Lake; inn keeps a canoe and paddleboat for guests' use. **$–$$**

New Hampshire Trivia

The longest wooden bridge in the US and longest two-span covered bridge in the world links Cornish, New Hampshire with Windsor, Vermont. It was built in 1866 and cost the princely sum of $9,000.

Rockhouse Mountain Farm Inn
off Route 153, 03832.
Tel: 603 447–2880.
15 rooms. MAP. A family resort on a 450-acre farm (with resident horses, llamas, cows, chickens, pigs, and others), since 1946. **$$**

ETNA

Moose Mountain Lodge
Moose Mountain Highway, 03570.
Tel: 603 643–3529.
12 rooms. FAP. A classic 1938 ski lodge, with stone hearth and dizzying mountain views. Located right off the Appalachian Trail, only 7 miles (11 km) from the Dartmouth College green. **$$$**

FITZWILLIAM

Amos A. Parker House
Route 119, 03447.
Tel: 603 585–6540.
Four-room B&B in a formal 18th-century home with superb gardens. Hallways and some rooms are decorated with elaborate flower murals. A short walk to Fitzwilliam Green, a short drive to Cathedral of the Pines. **$**

Fitzwilliam Inn
Route 119, 03447.
Tel: 603 585–9000.
Fax: 603 585–3495.
28 rooms. This 1796 stagecoach inn offers comfortable, nonpricy, atmospheric lodgings. The Vermont Transit buses between Boston and Montreal stop at the front door. **$**

FRANCONIA

Bungay Jar Bed & Breakfast
Easton Valley Road, 03580.
Tel: 603 823–7775.
6 rooms. B&B. An imaginatively retrofitted 18th-century barn on 8 private acres with great views. **$–$$**

Franconia Inn
1300 Easton Valley Road, 03583.

Tel: 603 823–5542/
800 473–5299.
Fax: 603 823–8078.
www.franconiainn.com.
34 rooms. MAP. A 19th-century inn-turned-complete-resort with 107 acres to explore on foot, by ski, or on horseback. Other amusements include a pool, hot tub, tennis courts, and ice skating. **$$$–$$$$**

Sugar Hill Inn
Route 117, 03580.
Tel: 603 823–5621/
800 548–4748.
16 rooms. B&B. An 18th-century country inn on the side of Sugar Hill. Comfortably appointed, country-style rooms in main house and cottages. **$–$$**

GLEN

The Bernerhof
Route 302, 03838.
Tel: 603 383–9131/
800 548–8007;
www.bernerhofinn.com.
9 rooms. B&B. A Victorian inn with some modern improvements, such as double whirlpools. Restaurant serves Continental "Middle European" fare. **$$**

Covered Bridge House
Route 302, 03838.
Tel: 603 383–9109/
800 232–9109.
6 rooms. B&B. A basic Colonial on the banks of the Saco River, near North Conway. Rooms are country-style with quilts, braided rugs, and rocking chairs. Guests can use the small beach on the river for swimming. **$**

GORHAM

Appalachian Mountain Club
Tel: 603 466–2727.
10 dorms. MAP. The AMC operates

Meal Guide

● **B&Bs** supply a complimentary full breakfast, often quite sophisticated.
● **MAP** (Modified American Plan) rates include breakfast and dinner
● **FAP** (Full American Plan) rates include all three meals

two roadside dorms and six high-mountain "huts" in the White Mountain National forest; reservations required. **$–$$**

GREENLAND

Captain Folsom Inn
480 Portsmouth Avenue, 03840.
Tel: 603 436–2662.
6 rooms. B&B. A Colonial tavern turned Federal country mansion, 10 minutes from Portsmouth. **$**

HANOVER

Hanover Inn
Main Street, 03755.
Tel: 603 643–4300/
800 443–7024.
Fax: 603 646–3744.
www.dartmouth.edu/~inn.
92 rooms. An integral part of the Dartmouth campus, a four-story, traditionally decorated Georgian brick house with rockers on a long porch overlooking the common. **$$$$**

HARRISVILLE

The Harrisville Squires' Inn
Keene Road, 03450.
Tel: 603 827–3925.
www.nhweb.com/squires_inn.
5 rooms. An 1840s farmhouse on 50 acres (with cross-country ski trails), near the historic mill town. East of Keene. **$**

HENNIKER

Colby Hill Inn
3 The Oaks, 03242.
Tel: 603 428–3281/
800 531–0330.
Fax: 603 428–9218.
16 rooms. B&B. A rambling late 18th-century inn with a perennial garden and swimming pool. Rooms furnished with antiques and Colonial reproductions; four rooms have fireplaces. Located west of Concord, near the Pat's Peak ski area. **$–$$**

HOLDERNESS

The Manor on Golden Pond
Route 3 and Shepard Hill Road, 03245.
Tel: 603 968–3348/
800 545–2141,
Fax: 603 968–2116.

21 rooms. MAP. A 1903 English manor-style stone mansion with a clay tennis court, swimming pool, and private beach. **$$$$**

JACKSON

Inn at Thorn Hill
Thorn Hill Road, 03846.
Tel: 603 383–4242/
800 289–8990.
Fax: 603 383–8062.
19 rooms. MAP. Stanford White designed this gambrel-roofed summer house, on a secluded slope with views of Mount Washington. Romantically decorated rooms. Adjacent to Jackson cross-country trail network. **$$$–$$$$**

Wentworth Resort Hotel
Route 16A, 03846.
Tel: 603 383–9700/
800 637–0013.
58 rooms. MAP. An 1869 grand hotel and rental houses adjoining an 18-hole golf course and cross-country ski center. **$$–$$$**

Whitney's Inn at Jackson
Route 16B, 03846.
Tel: 603 383–8916/
800 677–5737.
Fax: 603 383–6886.
31 rooms. B&B. A comfy inn (with three cottages) geared to families, at the foot of Black Mountain, a small-scale ski area. Simple country furnishings, pub, game room. **$–$$**

Wildcat Inn & Tavern
Route 16A, 03846.
Tel: 603 383–4245/
800 228–4245.
12-room B&B with charming if tiny suites in the social center of town. **$**

JAFFREY

Benjamin Prescott Inn
Route 124, 03452.
Tel/fax: 603 532–6637.
9 rooms. B&B. A sprawling 1820 house, decorated with handmade quilts and ship models, set amid a working dairy farm. Near Mount Monadnock. **$–$$**

KEENE

Carriage Barn
358 Main Street, 03431.
Tel: 603 357–3812.
www.nhweb.com/carriagebarn.

A Civil War-era barn, now simply furnished with antiques and handmade quilts in the four rooms. Across the street from Keene State College. No credit cards. **$**.

LINCOLN

Mill House Inn
Route 112, 03251.
Tel: 603 745–6261/
800 654–6183.
Fax: 603 745–6896.
95 rooms. A modern country-style inn complex built around three old paper mill buildings, adjacent to the Millfront Marketplace shopping center. Free transportation to Loon Mountain in winter. **$$**

LITTLETON

Beal House Inn
2 West Main Street, 03561.
Tel: 603 444-2661/
888 616–2325.
Fax: 603 444–6224.
13 rooms. B&B. An 1833 Federal-style farmhouse full of antiques. **$**

NEW LONDON

Maple Hill Farm
200 Newport Road, 03257.
Tel: 603 526–2248/
800 231–8637.
A family-friendly, comfortably furnished 1824 farmhouse/B&B near Little Lake Sunapee (canoes and rowboats available). Owners raise chickens, sheep and rabbits; younger guests may help gather eggs or watch yarn being spun. **$**

New London Inn
140 Main Street, 03257.
Tel: 603 526–2791/
800 526–2791.
A 27-room 1792 B&B inn with eclectic decor and an inventive chef/innkeeper. **$–$$**

Pleasant Lake Inn
Pleasant Street, 03257.
Tel: 603 526–6271/
800 626–4907.
12 rooms. A 1790 inn on 5 pastoral lakeside acres. **$–$$**

NORTH CONWAY

Farm By The River
2555 West Side Road, 03860.
Tel: 603 356–2694/
888 414–8353.

12 rooms. B&B. A 1785 classic country farmhouse set on 65 acres, with gardens, a sugar maple orchard, and a beach on the Saco River. Located on a back road parallel to Route 16/302, one mile (1.6 km) from Echo Lake State Park. **$–$$**

Stonehurst Manor
Route 16, 03860.
Tel: 603 356–3113/
800 525–9100.
24 rooms. A 100-year-old mansion with outdoor pool, hot tub, and tennis court. **$$**

The 1785 Inn
Route 16, 03860.
Tel: 603 356–9025/
800 421–1785.
Fax: 603 356–6081.
17 rooms. B&B. One of the oldest buildings in the Mount Washington valley, this colonial inn with spectacular mountain views is comfortably furnished with colonial, Victorian, and country-style pieces. **$$–$$$**

NORTH SUTTON

Follansbee Inn
Route 114, 03260
Tel: 603 927–422/
800 626-4221.
23 rooms. B&B. A cozy lakeside inn with 500 acres of woods to roam or ski. **$**

NORTH WOODSTOCK

Woodstock Inn
Main Street (Route 3), 03262.
Tel: 603 745–3951/
800 321–3985.
Fax: 603 745–3701.
19 rooms. Three Victorian inns in a bustling tourist town. Rooms vary from romantic to family-friendly. Outdoor hot tub. **$–$$**

PORTSMOUTH

Sise Inn
40 Court Street, 03801.
Tel: 603 443–1200/
800 267–0525.
Fax: 603 433–1200.
34 rooms. An 1881 Queen Anne inn
in the center of town. Amenities
include antique furnishings,
fireplaces, whirlpool baths, and
stereos in some rooms. **$$–$$$**

Inn at Strawbery Banke
314 Court Street, 03801.
Tel: 603 436–7242.
7 rooms. B&B. An 1800 captain's
house adjoining the historic
preserve. **$–$$**

Martin Hill Inn
404 Islington Street, 03801.
Tel: 603 436–2287.
7 rooms. B&B. An 1812 Colonial
main house and a country-style
1850 guest house across the
perennial gardens. Solicitous hosts
and lavish breakfasts. **$–$$**

Inn at Christian Shore
335 Maplewood Avenue, 03801.
Tel: 603 431–6770.
6 rooms. B&B. An antique
appointed 1800 Federal house,
near the historic district. **$**

SNOWVILLE

Snowvillage Inn
92 Stuart Road (off Route 153),
03849.
Tel: 603 447–2818/
800 447–4345.
18 rooms. Austrian motifs pervade
this high-perched aerie. Rooms are
in the New England farmhouse-style
main house, an old carriage barn,
and a new lodge. Located south of
Conway, near Crystal Lake. Tennis
courts, hiking trails, sauna, cross-
country skiing (including lessons),
snowshoeing. **$$–$$$$**

SUGAR HILL

Sunset Hill House
Sunset Hill Road, 03585.
Tel: 603 823–5522/
800 786–4455.
Fax: 603 823–5738.
30 rooms. B&B. Built in 1880, this
inn (with a 30-foot deck) sits on a
1,700-foot ridge with sweeping
views of the Presidential Range.
Homey rooms all have mountain
views, some have bay windowed
reading nooks. Pool, golf course,
cross-country ski trails. **$–$$$**

Hilltop Inn
Route 117, 03585.
Tel: 603 823–5695/
800 770–5695.
Fax: 603 823–5518.
7 rooms. B&B. A homey 1895
Victorian serving large country-style
breakfasts. Located 10 minutes
from Franconia Notch. **$–$$**

SUNAPEE

Dexter's Inn and Tennis Club
Stage Coach Road, 03782.
Tel: 603 763–5571/
800 232–5571.
17 rooms. MAP. A secluded yellow
clapboard 1801 house with three
all-weather courts and an outdoor
pool. **$$–$$$**

Seven Hearths Inn
Route 11, 03782.
Tel: 603 763–5657/
800 237–2464.
A 10-room B&B in an 1801
farmhouse, well refurbished. **$$**

TEMPLE

Birchwood Inn
Route 45, 03084.
Tel: 603 878–3285.
Fax: 603 878–2159.
7 rooms. B&B. An 1800 brick inn
with Rufus Porter murals. Guest
rooms each have a theme: the
Editorial Room is decorated with
newspapers (with noteworthy
headlines), the Train Room has
photos and models of trains (of
course). Convenient to Cathedral of
the Pines. **$**

WATERVILLE VALLEY

Waterville Valley Resort
Waterville Valley, 03223.

Whale Watching

Whale watching and cruises to
the nine Isles of Shoals are
some of New Hampshire's big
attractions. Companies offering
these include:
- **The Isles of Shoals** Tel: 800
  441–4620, 603 431-5500
- **New Hampshire Seacoast
  Cruises** Tel: 603 964–5545
- **Portsmouth Harbor Cruises** Tel:
  800 776–0915, 603 436-8084

Tel: 800 468-2553. Fax: 236 4174.
Over 700 rooms. A resort complex
cupped in a high valley, with skiing
in winter, hiking, tennis, and other
sports the rest of the year. **$–$$$$**

WEST CHESTERFIELD

Chesterfield Inn
Route 9, 03466.
Tel: 603 256–3211/
800 365–5515.
Fax: 603 256–6131.
www.chesterfieldinn.com.
13 rooms. B&B. A 1798 house,
originally a tavern, converted to a
luxurious bed and breakfast.
Antiques combined with modern
amenities: wet bars, whirlpool tubs,
fireplaces. **$$**

WHITEFIELD

Spalding Inn
Mountainview Road, 03598.
Tel: 603 837–2572/
800 368–8439.
45 rooms. B&B. A quiet but full-
scale country resort, operating
since 1926, with golf course, tennis
courts, heated pool. Famous for
lawn bowling. Accommodations in
the main inn, a lodge, and separate
cottages. **$$–$$$**

WOLFEBORO

Wolfeboro Inn
90 North Main Street, 03894.
Tel: 603 569–3016/
800 451–2389.
Fax: 603 569–5375.
49 rooms. A luxury lakeside inn
since 1812. Located a short walk
from the village, the inn has a
private beach, excursion boat, and
fishing. **$$–$$$$**

Where to Eat

BEDFORD

Bedford Village Inn
2 Old Bedford Road.
Tel: 603 472–2001.
Country club atmosphere in an updated 18th-century inn south of Manchester. Traditional New England menu often features lobster and Atlantic salmon. **$$$**

BETHLEHEM

Tim-Bir Alley
Adair Country Inn, 80 Guider Lane (at Route 302).
Tel: 603 444–6142.
Extraordinary sophistication for a small-scale restaurant. **$$$**

BRETTON WOODS

Mount Washington Hotel
Route 302.
Tel: 603 278-1000.
Old-fashioned fare in a formal dining room, but a fascinating glimpse of luxury past. **$$$**

CENTER HARBOR

Red Hill Inn
Route 25B.
Tel: 603 279–7001.
New American creativity in a red-brick summer estate. Ask about the signature vinegar pie. **$$–$$$**

CENTER SANDWICH

Corner House Inn
Main Street (Routes 109 and 113).
Tel: 603 284–6219.
Continental fare in a charming 1849 house. **$$**

DIXVILLE NOTCH

Balsams Grand Resort Hotel
Route 26.
Tel: 603 255–3400/
800 255–3400.
Reservations required. Lavish buffet spreads. **$$$**

FRANCONIA

Franconia Inn
1300 Easton Valley Road.
Tel: 603 823–5542.
Ambitious Continental cuisine in a formal mountainview dining room. **$$$**

Lovett's Inn
Profile Road.
Tel: 603 823–7761.
A mix of traditional favorites and more adventurous fare. **$$**

GLEN

The Bernerhof
Route 302.
Tel: 603 383–4414.
Alpine delights—including spaetzle and Provimi veal—ideal for ski country. **$$$**

HANOVER

The Hanover Inn
Main Street.
Tel: 603 643–4300.
A successful New American eating experiment, with many appetizers and wines by the glass, set in a bastion of traditionalism. **$$$**

HENNIKER

Colby Hill Inn
3 The Oaks, 0342.
Tel: 603 428–3281.
A late 18th-century inn with country views and Continental cuisine with New England accents. **$$$**

HOLDERNESS

The Manor on Golden Pond
Route 3 and Shepard Hill Road.
Tel: 603 968–3348.
Rich continental cuisine in a baronial setting. **$$$**

JACKSON

Wentworth Resort Hotel Dining Room
Route 16A.
Tel: 603 383–9700.
Exceptional Continental cuisine with New England ingredients in a fancy

Shaker Meals

Creamery Restaurant
Canterbury Shaker Village,
Tel: 603 783–9511.
Reservations required for the one seating. Authentic Shaker cuisine. **$$**

French Provincial dining room. The more casual lounge serves mountain specialties including raclette and fondue. **$$$**

Inn at Thorn Hill
Thorn Hill Road
Tel: 603 383–4242.
Reservations required. A four-course prix fixe menu of country-sophisticate cuisine in a handsome country house. **$$$**

Thompson House Eatery
Routes 16A and 16.
Tel: 603 383–9341.
Closed in winter. Innovative salads and sandwiches, luscious entrees, in an 1800s barn with flowery patio. **$$**

Wildcat Inn & Tavern
Route 16A.
Tel: 603 383–4245.
Owner/chef Marty Sweeney caters for gourmets and gourmands alike. **$$**

KEENE

One Seventy Six Main
176 Main Street.
Tel: 603 357–3100.
Upscale pub grub (burgers, pasta, seafood) with an extensive beer list. **$$**

Restaurant Guidelines

● **Prices** are approximate, but for a three-course meal for one (excluding beverages, tax and tip), the following guidelines may prove helpful:
$$$$ = over $40
$$$ = $28-40
$$ = $15-28
$ = under $15
● **Meal tax** varies from state to state, but it is customary to tip 15 to 20 percent on the pre-tax total.
● **Credit cards** The more expensive establishments generally accept credit cards, but call ahead to check just in case.
● **Reservations** Most restaurants, except for the clearly casual, appreciate reservations (some require them).

New Hampshire Festivals

● SPRING

The town of Lisbon, near Cannon Mountain, bids farewell to winter in May with the annual **Lilac Festival** (tel: 603 828–6336).

The **Sheep and Wool Festival** (tel: 603 763–5859) in New Boston (near Manchester) readies in a different way – with shearing, spinning and weaving, as well as border collie demonstrations.

● SUMMER

Portsmouth's **Market Square Days** (tel: 603 431–5388) in June draw over 100,000 people to an outdoor street fair with concerts, a 10km road race, and other festivities.

Later in June, the **Portsmouth Jazz Festival** (tel: 603 436–7678) showcases many New England performers.

Motorcycle fans may want to visit the **Laconia Motorcycle Rally and Race Week** (tel: 603 466–3988) for eight days in June.

For a different sort of excitement, the annual **Mount Washington Road Race** (tel: 603 466–3988) takes runners up the 6,288-foot (2,000-meter) peak along the historic Auto Road.

With about 200 artists exhibiting at Mount Sunapee State Park, the **League of New Hampshire Craftsmen's Fair** (tel: 603 244–3375) in August draws thousands of visitors interested in traditional New England crafts.

● FALL

In September, Loon Mountain looks like Scotland when the **New Hampshire Highland Games** (tel: (800) 227–4191), with Scottish music, dances and other cultural events, come to Lincoln.

During the annual **Hampton Seafood Festival** (tel: 603 926–8718), also in September, local restaurants takes their seafood creations to the streets for a two-day food fair.

● WINTER

Concord and Manchester host **First Night** (tel: 603 746–9555) celebrations on New Year's Eve.

In March, more than 50 sugarhouses statewide open their doors for syrup-making demonstrations (and free samples) during **Maple Weekend** (tel: 603 267–7070).

LITTLETON

Beal House Inn
2 West Main Street (Routes 302 and 28).
Tel: 603 444–2661.
European cuisine in a handsome carriage house. **$$–$$$**

MANCHESTER

Red Arrow Diner
61 Lowell Avenue.
Tel: 603 626–1118.
A 1903 luncheonette, open 24 hours. **$**

MOULTONBORO

The Woodshed
Lee's Mill Road.
Tel: 603 476–2311.
New England classics – clam chowder, scrod, Indian pudding –

plus a raw bar in an 1860s barn. **$$–$$$**

NEW LONDON

New London Inn
140 Main Street.
Tel: 603 526–2791.
Inventive nouvelle regional cuisine. **$$–$$$**

NORTH CONWAY

Stonehurst Manor
Route 16.
Tel: 603 356–3113.
Continental cuisine, plus stone-hearth pizzas. **$$$**

NORTH WOODSTOCK

Woodstock Inn
Main Street (Route 3).
Tel: 603 745–3951.
Continental cuisine in the Victorian

parlor; casual fare from meatloaf to fajitas in the Woodstock Station cafe; and microbrews in the Woodstock Inn Brewery. **$–$$$**

PINKHAM NOTCH

Appalachian Mountain Club
Pinkham Notch Camp, Route 16.
Tel: 603 466–2727.
Hearty dinner only for hikers. **$**

PORTSMOUTH

Library Restaurant at the Rockingham House
401 State Street.
Tel: 603 431–5202.
International cuisine (rack of lamb, filet mignon) amid carved mahogany paneling and masses of books in a former luxury hotel (now converted to condominiums). **$$$**
Dolphin Striker
15 Bow Street.
Tel: 603 431–5222.
A riverfront tavern specializing in New American seafood. **$$**
Karen's
105 Daniel Street.
Tel: 603 431–1948.
A tiny cafe, unusually creative – especially the breakfasts and the simple seafood dishes. **$$**
Porto Bello
67 Bow Street.
Tel: 603 431–2989.
Nuovo Italian, with a view of the harbor. **$$–$$$**
Portsmouth Brewery
56 Market Street.
Tel: 603 431–1115.
A microbrewery with international munchies. **$$**
Cafe Brioche
14 Market Square.
Tel: 603 430–9225.
Croissants, quiches and a friendly sidewalk cafe. **$**

SNOWVILLE

Snowvillage Inn
92 Stuart Road (off Route 153).
Tel: 603 447–2818.
Austrian specialties; unparalleled views. **$$**

SUGAR HILL

Polly's Pancake Parlor
Route 117.
Tel: 603 823–5575.

All-you-can-eat, maple-drenched pancakes, since 1938. **$**

WOLFEBORO
The Bittersweet
Route 28.
Tel: 603 569–3636.
An artifact-packed barn featuring local specialties, ranging from seafood to Chateaubriand. **$$**

Culture

CLASSICAL MUSIC
The Music Hall (tel: 603 436–2400; 28 Chestnut Street) features international classical musicians, while **Music in Market Square** is a classical summer series (tel: 603 436–9109, North Church); both are in Portsmouth.

ROCK AND POP
Gaslight Co (tel: 603 430–8582; 64 Market Street, Portsmouth) features local rock acts from mid-May to mid-October.

OPERA
Opera North (tel: 603 643–1946; Hanover, NH) performs operas in the area.

THEATER
Seacoast Repertory Theater (tel: 603 433–4472; 125 Bow Street, Portsmouth) features adult and children's productions from September to June.
Colonial Theater (tel: 603 352–2033; 95 Main Street, Keene) features live performances and films.
Palace Theater (tel: 603 668–5588; 80 Hanover Street, Manchester) showcases six productions a year, including dinner theater, by its resident company, **Stage One Productions**.
Hopkins Center for the Arts (tel: 603 646–2422; Dartmouth College, Hanover) stages multiple musicals and other theater productions.

CINEMA
Hopkins Center for the Arts (tel: 603 646–2422, Dartmouth College, Hanover) shows classic

and experimental films, while **Nugget Theater** (tel: 603 643–2769; S Main Street, Hanover) shows current films.

ART GALLERIES
Your best bets are in Portsmouth: **New Hampshire Art Association-Robert Lincoln Levy Gallery** (tel: 603 431–4230; 136 State Street) exhibits paintings, photographs and prints, while **Pierce Gallery** (tel: 603 436–1988; 105 Market Street) offers New Hampshire and Maine coastal scenics.

Outdoor Activities

BIKING
Several ski areas offer summer and fall mountain biking. **Loon Mountain** attracts novice through advanced riders to 21 miles (34 km) of trails, where lifts serve the steepest biking routes.
Nearby, the self-guided **Franconia Notch Bike Tour** starts at Echo Lake, passes the Old Man of the Mountain, and ends at the Loon Mountain ski area.
Near Mount Washington, **Great Glen Trails** (tel: 603 466–2333) offers learn-to-mountain-bike courses, ranging from a short introductory class to more in-depth skill-building.
If inn-to-inn touring is more your speed, contact Harrisville-based **Monadnock Bicycling Touring** (tel: 603 827–3925).

CANOEING, KAYAKING AND RAFTING
Saco Bound (tel: (800) 677–7238) runs a river kayaking school, and leads canoeing expeditions, guided kayak trips, and white-water rafting excursions at several New Hampshire and Maine locations.
North Star Canoe Rentals (tel: 603 542–5802), based in Cornish, conducts canoe trips on the Connecticut River.
Appalachian Mountain Club's New Hampshire chapter (tel: 603 466–2725; www.amc-nh.org) offers a **Spring Whitewater Canoe School** one weekend each April.

FISHING
Great Glen Trails (see *Biking* above) offers introductory fishing classes and arranges guided fly fishing excursions.
North Country Angler (tel: 603 356–6000), also based in the White Mountains, runs guided fly-fishing weekends.
For ocean fishing, several charter companies operate on the seacoast, including **Atlantic Fishing Fleet** (tel: 603 964–5220; Rye) and **Al Gauron Deep Sea Fishing** (tel: 603 926–2469; Hampton Beach).

HIKING
The 86 major peaks of the White Mountains provide plenty of hiking challenges. The **US Forest Service** (tel: 603 528–8721; Laconia) provides specific trail information.
The **Appalachian Mountain Club** (tel: 603 466–2725) has detailed hiking trail information, too. The AMC maintains a network of huts in the White Mountains providing overnight accommodations. For hut reservations, call (603) 466–2727).
For inn-to-inn hiking tours, contact **New England Hiking Holidays** (tel: 603 356–9696, (800) 869–0949) in North Conway or **Great Outdoors Hiking & Biking Tours** (tel: 603 356–3113, (800) 525–9100).

Live Music

Press Room
77 Daniel Street, Portsmouth.
Tel: 603 431–5186.
Has live folk, Irish and blues music, with a country-western jam session every Friday.
The Music Hall
28 Chestnut Street, Portsmouth.
Tel: 603 436–2400
Offers a variety of musical performances all year.
Hopkins Center for the Arts
Dartmouth College, Hanover.
Tel: 603 646–2422
Has live music on and off, all year round.

SAILING

Marinas abound on Lake Winnipesaukee, the state's largest lake. Although it's a popular power boating spot, some marinas rent sailboats, including **Fay's Boat Yard** (tel: 603 293–8000; Guilford).

SKIING

Major areas include:
Waterville Valley (tel: (800) 468–2553),
Loon Mountain (tel: 603 745–8111; Lincoln) and
Cannon Mountain (tel: 603 823–5563; Franconia).

Smaller areas include:
Attitash (tel: (800) 223–7669; Bartlett),
Bretton Woods (tel: 603 278–5000) and
Wildcat (tel: 603 466–3326, (800) 255–6439), both of which are in Jackson.

The state's largest cross-country ski centers are **Jackson Ski Touring Foundation** (tel: (800) 927–6697) and **Mt Washington Valley Ski Touring** (tel: 603 356–9920; off Route 16, Intervale).

South of the White Mountains you'll find the **Nordic Center** (tel: 603 236–4666; Waterville Valley) and **Franconia Village Cross Country Center** at the Franconia Inn (tel: 603 823–5542, (800) 473–5299)

WHERE TO SHOP

Shops fill Portsmouth's revitalized waterfront area near Market, Bow and Ceres Streets.

Route 16 in North Conway is a mecca of over 200 outlet shops.

MALLS

The 19th-century **Colony Mill Marketplace** (tel: 603 357–1240; 222 West Street, Keene) houses 33 stores.
Mall of New Hampshire (tel: 603 669–0433; 1500 S Willow Street, Manchester) has 88 shops and three department stores.

BOOKS

Book Guild of Portsmouth (tel: 603 436–1758; 58 State Street), which sells maritime and local books, and **Portsmouth Book Shop** (tel: 603 433–4406; 1 Islington Street), which sells local history, travel guides and maps, are two of this hip city's specialized bookstores.

Eagle Books (tel: 603 357–8721; 19 West Street, Central Square, Keene) specializes in writer's projects books, and **Toadstool Bookshop** (tel: 603 352–8815; Colony Mill, Keene) carries general titles and also has a large café. **Dartmouth Bookstore** (tel: 643–3616; 33 S Main Street, Hanover) stocks upwards of 130,000 titles.

ANTIQUES

Antique stores, including **Antiques at Colony Mill** (tel: 603 358–6343; West Street, Keene), which represents over 100 dealers, abound in the Monadnock region.

ARTS AND CRAFTS

League of New Hampshire Craftsmen (tel: 603 224–1471; 205 North Main Street, Concord) has a gallery of handmade crafts.

STEAM TRAIN JOURNEYS

Winnipesaukee Railroad (tel: 603 279–5253; S Main Street, Meredith) runs historic coaches around the eponymous lake.
Conway Scenic Railroad (tel: 603 356–5251; North Conway) offers excursions from the 1874 station.
Mount Washington Cog Railway (tel: 603 846–5404, (800) 922–8825) has the second-steepest railway track in the world.

THEATER

Hampton Playhouse (tel: 603 926–3073; Route 101E, Hampton) showcases children's productions on summer Saturdays.

Maine

Known as: The Pine Tree State.
Motto: *Dirigo* (I direct).
Origin of name: called after ancient French province.
Entered Union: March 15, 1820, when it was separated from Massachusetts to form the 23rd state.
Capital: Augusta.
Area: 35,387 sq. miles (91,653 sq. km).
Highest point: Mount Katahdin, 5,268 ft (1,606 meters).
Population: 1.23 million.
Population density: 35 people per sq. mile (13 per sq. meter).
Economy: services (including tourism) and manufacturing (paper and paper products, footwear and other leather goods, lumber), plus fishing, agriculture, and forestry.
Annual visitors: 8 million.
National representation: two senators and two representatives to Congress.
Famous citizens: Longfellow, Sir Hiram and Hudson Maxim and Edna Street Vincent Millay.

Many of Maine's hotels and inns are open only in summer.

BAR HARBOR

The Tides
119 West Street, 04609.
Tel: 207 288–4968.
barharbortides.com.
An 1887 Greek Revival manor B&B with views of Frenchman's Bay. Three elegantly appointed suites with working fireplaces and ocean vistas. $$$$
(See also Hulls Cove, *page 395*)

Breakwater 1904
45 Hancock Street, 04609.
Tel: 207 288–2313
800 238–6309.
A 39-room mock-Tudor mansion with
six bedrooms for B&B. **$$$–$$$$**

Nannau-Seaside Bed & Breakfast
Lower Main Street, 04609.
Tel: 207 288–5575.
Fax: 207 288–5421;
www.acadia.net/nannau.
Four–room B&B. A 1904 Shingle-
style summer "cottage" (read
"estate") set by the water, one mile
(1.6 km) from downtown. **$$–$$$**

Manor House Inn
106 West Street, 04609.
Tel: 207 288–3759/
800 437–0088.
Fax: 207 288–2974;.
www.acadia.net/manorhouse.
An 1887 Victorian inn with 14
bedrooms surrounded by gardens.
$–$$$

BATH

Inn at Bath
469 Washington Street, 04530.
Tel: 207 443–4294.
Fax: 207 443–429.
www.innatbath.com.
An elegant, comfortable antiques-
filled 1810 inn B&B with nine guest
rooms with wood-burning fireplaces
and whirlpool baths. **$–$$$**

Fairhaven Inn
North Bath Road, 04530.
Tel: 207 443–4391.
www.maincoast.com/fairhaven.
A 1790 Colonial inn B&B set in 20
acres overlooking the Kennebec
river. The eight guest rooms
furnished with four-poster beds and
handmade quilts. Trails for hiking
and cross-country skiing. **$**

BETHEL

Bethel Inn & Country Club
Village Common, 04217.
Tel: 207 824–2175/
800 654–0125.
www.bethelinn.com.
MAP with 57 rooms. A rambling
yellow clapboard 1913 country inn,
with tennis, golf, and a lake for
water sports. **$$$–$$$$**

Sunday River Inn
RR 3, Box 1688, 04217.
Tel: 207 824–2410.

Fax: 207 824–3181.
23-room MAP. A handsome ski
dorm with its own cross-country
center. **$$**

Telemark Inn
RFD 2, Box 800, 04217
Tel: 207 836–2703.
www.maineguide.com/bethel/
telemark.
A secluded 1900 Adirondack-style
lodge with six B&B rooms 10 miles
(16 km) west of Bethel. Outdoor
activities offered include llama
treks and "skijouring", cross-
country skiing pulled by dogs. **$–$$**

The Ames Place
46 Broad Street, 04217.
Tel: 207 824–3170.
Two-room B&B in a lovely 1850
home with personable hosts. **$**

Holidae House,
Main Street, 04217,
Tel: 207 824–3400.
A bargain seven-room B&B,
considering the in-town location. **$**

BLUE HILL

Blue Hill Inn
Union Street, 04614.
Tel: 207 374–2844/
800 826–7415.
Fax: 207 374–2829.
www.bluehillinn.com.
11-room MAP in an 1830s Federal-
style inn with six fireplaces one
block from Blue Hill bay in a lovely
village. **$$$**

John Peters Inn
Peters Point (off Route 176),
04614.
Tel: 207 374–2116.
www.johnpetersinn.com.
A columned 1815 mansion B&B on
25 shorefront acres with a
commanding view of the bay. 14
tasteful, traditionally decorated
rooms in both the main inn and a
carriage house. **$$–$$$**

Price Categories

A very approximate guide to
current room rates for a standard
double per night is:
$$$$ = over $200
$$$ = $150–200
$$ = $100–150
$ = under $100

● **Maine State Ferry Service**
runs ferries from the mainland to
most of Maine's major islands.
Tel: 207 596–2202.
● **Marine Atlantic**
operates a car and passenger
ferry from Portanld and Bar
Harbor to Yarmouth, Nova Scotia
and Canada.
Tel: 800 341–7981.

Blue Hill Farm Country Inn
Route 15, 04614.
Tel: 207 374–5126.
www.bluehillfarm.com.
A 14-room B&B in a rural retreat on
48 acres 5 miles (8 km) from Blue
Hill village. **$**

BOOTHBAY HARBOR AREA

Spruce Point Inn and Lodges
Grandview Avenue, Boothbay
Harbor, 04538.
Tel: 207 633–4152/
800 553–0289.
www.sprucepointinn.com.
A 100-year-old MAP inn and resort
(including cottages and
condominiums, totalling 67 rooms)
on a 100-acre peninsula. Activities
include swimming pool, tennis
court, fitness room, croquet,
badminton, putting green. Shuttle
bus into town. **$$$$**

Linekin Bay Resort
Wall Point Road, Boothbay Harbor,
04538.
Tel: 207 633–2494.
70 rooms FAP. An old-fashioned
seaside resort with complimentary
sailing instruction. **$$–$$$**

Five Gables Inn
Murray Hill Road, East Boothbay
04544.
Tel: 207 633–4551/
800 451–5048.
fivegablesinn.com.
15-room B&B in a spiffed-up 1865
summer hotel by the bay. Views of
Lineken Bay and the ocean from the
broad verandah (complete with
hammock). **$$–$$$**

Green Shutters Cottages
76 Bay Street.
Boothbay Harbor, 04538.

Tel: 207 633–2646.
800 272–1028.
A comfortable family resort; weekly rentals (MAP) in five cottages. **$**

BROOKSVILLE
Oakland House
Herrick Road, 0461.
Tel: 207 359–8521/
800 359–7352.
www.acadia.net/guest/
oaklandhouse.
A casual 1889 complex with waterside cottages offering 33 MAP rooms set in 50 acres near Blue Hill. **$$–$$$**
Buck's Harbor Inn
Route 176, South Brooksville, 04617.
Tel: 207 326–8660.
Hundred-year-old charm in a quiet seaside town just north of Deer Isle. Traditional country furnishings in the seven B&B rooms embellished with art from the owners' travels. **$**

BRUNSWICK
Captain Daniel Stone Inn
10 Water Street, 04011.
Tel: 207 725–9898.
An upscale Federal inn overlooking the Adroscoggin River. Many of the 34 rooms have whirlpool baths. **$$$**
Brunswick Bed and Breakfast
165 Park Row, 04011.
Tel: 207 729–4914/
800 299–4914.
Fax: 207 725–1759;
brunswickbnb.com.
An historic house decorated with handmade quilts, within walking distance to the Bowdoin College campus. Five simply furnished guest rooms. **$–$$**

Meal Guide

● **B&Bs** supply a complimentary full breakfast, often quite sophisticated.
● **MAP** (Modified American Plan) rates include breakfast and dinner
● **FAP** (Full American Plan) rates include all three meals

Bethel Point Bed and Breakfast
Bethel Point Road, 04011.
Tel: 207 725–1115,
888 238–8262.
Fax: 207 725–2901.
Three-room B&B in an 1830s farmhouse on Hen Cove, overlooking the sea. **$**

CAMDEN
Camden Harbor Inn
83 Bayview Street, 04843.
Tel: 207 236–4200/
800 236–4266.
www.4chi.com.
22 rooms. B&B. A porch-encircled 1874 Victorian. Rooms are furnished with period antiques; some have fireplaces and decks, balconies, or patios. **$$$–$$$$**
Norumbega,
61 High Street (Route 1), 04843.
Tel: 207 236–4646.
Fax: 207 236–0824.
www.norumegainn.com.
12 rooms. B&B. A grand 1880s Victorian stone castle overlooking the bay. Furnished like an English country house, the inn has a three-story turret and seven fireplaces. Much photographed. **$$$–$$$$**
Edgecomb-Coles House
64 High Street, 04843.
Tel: 207 236–2336.
Fax: 207 236–6227.
6 rooms. B&B. A plush, rambling 1890s summer home with water views overlooking Penobscot Bay. **$$–$$$**
Lodge at Camden Hills
P.O. Box 794, Camden, 04843 (Route 1)
Tel: 800 832-7058/207 236-8478
20 units, including suites and jacuzzi cottages, in park-like setting with views of woods. **$$**
Maine Stay Inn
22 High Street (Route 1), 04853.
Tel: 207 236–9636.
Fax: 207 236–0621.
www.mainestay.com.
8 rooms. B&B. An 1802 house with period furnishings, a five-minute walk from the town center. Two parlors have wood-burning fireplaces; a glass-enclosed porch overlooks the gardens. **$–$$**
Whitehall Inn
52 High Street (Route 1), 04843.

Tel: 207 236–3391/
800 789–6565.
Fax: 207 236–4427.
whitehall-inn.com.
50 rooms. MAP. A venerable 1834 home, turned inn in 1901. Rooms are small and simple, but have a literary charm. **$$**
Windward House
6 High Street, 04843.
Tel: 207 236–9656.
Antiques, an English garden and all-out breakfasts in this eight-room B&B. **$$–$$$**

CAPE ELIZABETH
Inn by the Sea
40 Bowery Beach Road (Route 77, 04107.
Tel: 207 799–3134/
800 888–4287.
Fax: 207 799–4779.
43 rooms. A superb inn and resort connected by boardwalk to Crescent Beach. Rooms, suites and cottage condominiums with Chippendale-style pieces, plus wicker and white pine. Pool and tennis courts. **$$$$**

CAPE NEDDICK
Wooden Goose Inn
Route 1, 03902.
Tel: 207 363–5673,
Fax: 207 363–5627.
www.woodengooseinn.com.
7 rooms. B&B. A Victorian inn serving sumptuous breakfasts and teas, north of York Beach. **$$**

CASTINE
Castine Inn,
Main Street, 04421,
Tel: 207 326–4365,
Fax: 207 326–4570.
20 rooms. B&B. A simply furnished 1898 clapboard inn; comfortable living room with a fireplace. Harbor and garden views and a distinguished restaurant. **$–$$**
Pentagoet Inn
Main Street at Perkins Street, 04421.
Tel: 207 326–8616/
800 845–1701.
16 rooms. B&B. A turreted Victorian beauty. **$$**
Village Inn
Main Street, 04421.
Tel: 207 326–9510.
Four nothing-fancy rooms, but

there's a wonderful in-house bakery in this B&B. **$**

CHEBEAGUE ISLAND
Chebeague Island Inn
Box 492, 04017.
Tel: 207 846–5155.
21 rooms. B&B. Built in 1925 after the original structure was destroyed in a fire, this three-story clapboard inn is a classic summer hotel, accessible only by ferry, just north of Portland. **$–$$**

DEER ISLE
Pilgrim's Inn
Main Street (Route 15A), 04622.
Tel: 207 348–6615.
15 rooms. MAP. A four-story 1793 inn with antique-filled guest rooms and seaside cottages. Overlooking the harbor and a mill pond. **$$–$$$**

EASTPORT
Weston House
26 Boynton Street, 04631.
Tel: 207 853–2907.
This 1802 Federal manse, at the easternmost town in Maine near Campobello Island, is now a five-room B&B. It once hosted the naturalist John James Audubon (1785–1851). **$**

FREEPORT
Bagley House
1290 Royalsborough Road (Route 136), 04222.
Tel: 207 865–6566/
800 765–1772.
5 rooms. B&B. A 1772 Colonial in the country, 10 minutes from town. Breakfasts are served in the kitchen with its massive brick fireplace and beehive oven. **$–$$**

Price Categories
A very approximate guide to current room rates for a standard double per night is:
$$$$ = over $200
$$$ = $150–200
$$ = $100–150
$ = under $100

Harraseeket Inn
162 Main Street, 04032.
Tel: 207 865–9377/
800 342–6423.
Fax: 207 865–1684.
www.harraseeketinn.com.
54 rooms. B&B. Luxury in a town of bargains. An 1850 Greek Revival home with modern appointments. **$$$–$$$$**

Isaac Randall House
5 Independence Drive.
Tel: 207 865–9295/
800 865–9295.
Fax: 207 865–9003.
www.isaacrandall.com.
Nine-room B&B in an 1823 Federal-style farmhouse, Freeport's first bed and breakfast. Rooms mix country-style and Victorian furnishings. The "Caboose" room, in a railroad car next to a playground, is designed for families. **$$**

GEORGETOWN
Grey Havens Inn
Reid Park Road, 04548.
Tel: 207 371–2616.
Fax: 207 371–227,
www.greyhavens.com.
14 rooms. B&B. A Shingle-style 1904 inn with a wraparound verandah on an oceanfront hillside near Bath. **$$–$$$**

GREENVILLE
Greenville Inn
Norris Street, 04441.
Tel: 207 695–2206/
888 695–6000.
www.greenvilleinn.com.
13 rooms. A lumber baron's opulent 1895 mansion, plus several simpler cottages, overlooking Moosehead Lake. Ornate woodwork and stained glass set a formal tone in the inn's common rooms. **$$–$$$**

Lodge at Moosehead Lake
Lily Bay Road, 04441.
Tel: 207 695–4400.
Fax: 207 695–2281.
lodgeatmooseheadlake.com.
8 rooms. B&B. An eminently civilized wilderness retreat in a 1917 summer estate. Rooms have four-poster beds and whirlpool baths, some have private decks and spectacular lake views. **$$$**

HULLS COVE
Inn at Canoe Point
Eden Street (Route 3), 04609.
Tel: 207 288–9511.
Fax: 207 288–2870.
www.innatcanoepoint.com.
5 rooms. B&B. A secluded 1889 Tudor mansion perched on a rocky point at Frenchmen's Bay near Bar Harbor. **$$$–$$$$**

ISLE AU HAUT
The Keeper's House
Stonington 04681.
Tel: 207 367–2261.
6 rooms. FAP. A 100-year-old lighthouse keeper's house, on an island off Stonington, accessible only by mailboat. No electricity—light comes from gas lamps—but indoor plumbing and hot water are part of the package. **$$$$**

ISLESBORO
Dark Harbor House
Main Road, 04848.
Tel: 207 734–6669.
Fax: 207 734–6938.
10 rooms. B&B. A waterside 1890s mansion with an elegant double staircase and spacious guest rooms. Set up on a hill on an island accessible by ferry from Lincolnville

Beach, on Route 1 north of Camden. **$$–$$$$**

KENNEBUNKPORT

Captain Lord Mansion
Pleasant and Green Streets, 04046.
Tel: 207 967–3141/
800 522–3141.
Fax: 207 967–3172.
16 rooms. B&B. In Kennebunkport's historic district, an elegant formally decorated 1812 inn topped by an octagonal cupola. **$$$–$$$$**

Inn at Harbor Head
Pier Road, 04046.
Tel: 207 967–5564.
5 rooms. B&B. Luxury lodgings and gourmet breakfasts, alongside quaint Cape Porpoise harbor. **$$$–$$$$**

Old Fort Inn,
Old Fort Avenue, 04046.
Tel: 207 967–5353/
800 828–3678.
16 rooms. B&B. Country decor in a converted barn and brick carriage house. **$$$–$$$$**

The Colony
Ocean Avenue and Kings Road, 04046.
Tel: 207 967–3331/
800 552–2363.
139 rooms. FAP. A coastal grand hotel built in 1914. **$$–$$$$**

White Barn Inn
Beach Street, 04046
Tel: 207 967–2321.
25 rooms. Relais et Château-level luxury. **$$–$$$$**

Bufflehead Cove
Gornitz Lane, 04046.
Tel: 207 967–3879.
5 rooms. B&B. A comfortably appointed early 20th-century summer home overlooking the Kennebunk River. Private dock with rowboats available for guests. **$$–$$$**

Captain Jefferds Inn
Pearl Street, 04046.
Tel: 207 967–2311.
15 rooms. B&B. An antique-filled 1804 Federal home, with three carriage-house suites. **$–$$**

Green Heron Inn
Ocean Avenue, 04046.
Tel: 207 967–3315.
11 rooms. B&B. Plain and pleasant lodgings; outstanding breakfasts. **$**

KINGFIELD

Inn on Winter's Hill
RR 1, Box 1272, 04947.
Tel: 207 265–5421/
800 233–9687.
Fax: 207 265–5424.
20 rooms. An 1895 Georgian Revival mansion with rooms in the main house and in the simply furnished former barn. Amenities include pool, tennis, hot tub and cross-country skiing. **$$$**

Sugarloaf/USA
RR 1, Box 5000, 04947,
Tel: 207 237–2000, (
800) THE LOAF.
New England's largest ski village with two hotels and hundreds of condominiums (with over 400 rooms) attracts hikers, mountain-bikers, and golfers when the snow subsides. **$$–$$$**

Herbert Hotel
P.O. Box 67, 04947.
Tel: 207 265–2000/
800 THE-HERB.
32 rooms. This columned hotel, heralded upon its 1918 debut as "A Palace in the Wilderness", is now the unofficial heart of town. **$**

Three Stanley Avenue
3 Stanley Avenue, 04947.
Tel: 207 265–5541.
6 rooms. B&B. Comfy, country-style rooms, a fine regional restaurant. Open only in the winter time. **$**

KITTERY

Gundalow Inn
6 Water Street.
Tel: 207 439–4040.
6 rooms. B&B. An 1889 brick Victorian overlooking Portsmouth Harbor and the Piscataqua River. Named for "gundalows", the sailing barges that worked the river for 250 years. **$$**

MONHEGAN ISLAND

The Island Inn
Ocean View Terrace, 04852.
Tel: 207 596–0371.
Fax: 207 594–5517.
45 rooms. MAP. Hundred-year-old simplicity on a painter's dream of an island. **$$**

Tribler Cottage
Monhegan 04852.
Tel: 207 594–2445.
5 rooms. Plain and appealing accommodations, including apartments with kitchens (and some with private decks). **$**

NEWAGEN

Newagen Seaside Inn
Route 27, 04552.
Tel: 207 633–5242/
800 654–5242.
26 rooms. B&B. An old-fashioned inn, with saltwater and freshwater pools, at the tip of Southport Island, south of Boothbay Harbor. **$$–$$$**

NEW HARBOR

Gosnold Arms
Northside Road, 04554.
Tel: 207 677–3727.
Fax: 207 677–2662.
www.gosnold.com.

Scenic Tours in and around Portland

● **Bus 1** takes passengers round the Eastern and Western Promenades and the rest of downtown Portland.
● **Bikes** Forest City Mountain Bike Tours operate guided two- to six-hour tours of Portland, South Portland, Cape Elizabeth and elsewhere.
51 Melbourne Street, Portland.
Tel: 207 780–8155.
● **Cruises** Casco Bay, to the east of Portland town, is the starting point for cruises to Maine's islands.
Casco Bay Lines (tel: 207 774–7871) runs mail/delivery motorboats that you can hop on for cruises of various lengths up to just under two hours. From the Ferry Terminal at 56 Commercial Street at Franklin Street.
Eagle Tours, Long Wharf, Commercial Street (tel: 207 799–6498) runs trips to Eagle Island and Portland Head Light.

Price Categories

A very approximate guide to current room rates for a standard double per night is:

$$$$ = over $200
$$$ = $150–200
$$ = $100–150
$ = under $100

25 rooms. B&B. Shoreside rusticity at Pemaquid Point since 1925. The inn's glassed-in dining room overlooks the water. Rooms are available in the main inn and in 14 cottages. **$–$$**

NORTHEAST HARBOR
Asticou Inn
Route 3, 04662.
Tel: 207 276–3344.
Fax: 207 276–3344.
www.asticou.com.
65 rooms. MAP. A cultured carryover from Bar Harbor's heyday as Society's summer playground. Elegant Victorian-style accommodations, views of Great Harbor. **$$$$**
Harbourside Inn
Northeast Harbor 04662.
Tel: 207 276–3272.
A Shingle-style 1889 inn with 14 guest rooms beside Acadia National Park. **$–$$$.**

OGUNQUIT
The Anchorage
55 Shore Road, 03907.
Tel: 207 646–9384.
A modern waterside resort offering 220 rooms with classic detailing.
$$–$$$
Cliff House
Shore Road (off Route 1), 03907.
Tel: 207 361–1000.
Fax: 207 361–2122.
www.cliffhousemaine.com.
164 rooms. A classic New England summer resort since 1872. Several buildings, plus swimming pools and tennis courts, set on 70 acres with ravishing ocean views. **$–$$$**
The Dunes on the Waterfront
Route 1, 03907.
Tel: 207 646–2612.
www.dunesmotel:com.
36 rooms. A 1930s cottage

complex on the tidal Ogunquit River, 200 yards from Ogunquit Beach. On the trolley line to the town center. Swimming dock, with rowboats.
$–$$
Gorges Grant Hotel
239 Route 1, 03907.
Tel: 207 646–7003/
800 646–5001.
ogunquit.com/gorgesgrant.
81 rooms. A sleek contemporary hotel with traditionalist furnishings, just north of the town center. **$$**
Morning Dove
30 Bourne Lane, 03907.
Tel: 207 646–3891.
7 rooms. B&B. A lovingly decorated 1860s farmhouse. **$–$$**
Sparhawk Resort
Shore Road, 03907.
Tel: 207 646–5562.
82 rooms. A luxury motel with beach views and private decks.
$$$–$$$$

PORTLAND
The Danforth
163 Danforth Street, 04104.
Tel: 207–879–8755/
800 991–6557,
Fax: 207–879–8754;
www.visionwork.com/danforth.
11 rooms. Three-story brick mansion restored to a first-class hotel three blocks from the Old Port. Inn has 12 fireplaces, a library, and a restored billiards room, as well as antiques-adorned guest rooms with two-line phones and other modern conveniences.
$$–$$$$
Pomegranate Inn
49 Neal Street, 04102.
Tel: 207 772–1006/
800 356–0408.
Fax: 207–773–4426.
9 rooms. B&B. An elegant art- and antiques-filled home in Portland's upscale residential West End.
$$–$$$
Portland Regency in the Old Port
20 Milk Street, 04101.
Tel: 207 774–4200/
800 727–3436.
Fax: 207 775–2150.
www.theregency.com.
103 rooms. A snazzily rehabbed 19th-century armory, centrally located. **$$**

Radisson Eastlake
157 High Street, 04101.
Tel: 207 775–5411/
800 777–6246.
Fax: 207 775–2872.
204 rooms. A 1927 hotel with modern amenities and harbor views. The rooftop lounge is a fine spot to watch the sunset. **$$**
(See also Cape Elizabeth, *page 394*, and Chebeague Island, *page 395*, and Prouts Neck, *below*)

PROUTS NECK
Black Point Inn
510 Black Point Road.
Tel: 207 883–4126/
800 258–0003.
www.blackpointinn.com.
80 rooms. FAP. An 1870s resort, on a peninsula favored by Winslow Homer. Located between Old Orchard Beach and Cape Elizabeth, 10 miles (16 km) south of the Portland airport. Facilities include an 18-hole golf course, 14 tennis courts, two beaches, indoor/outdoor pools, boating, nature trails, and a health club.
$$$$

RANGELEY
Country Club Inn
Mingo Loop Road, 04970.
Tel: 207 864–3831.
20 rooms. B&B. Picture-window views of the lake; swimming pool and golf course. A 1920s inn, plus 1950s-era motel units. The inn's grand living room has two fireplaces, a cathedral ceiling, and game trophies. **$$**
Rangeley Inn and Motor Lodge
Main Street, 04970.
Tel: 207 864–3341/
800 666–3687.
Fax: 207 864–3634.
An old-fashioned three-story lakeside inn with 50 guest rooms (built around 1907), with some modern motel units. **$–$$**

ROCKLAND
Captain Lindsey House Inn
5 Lindsey Street, 04841.
Tel: 207 596–7950.
9 rooms. An 1885 building that had most recently housed the Camden Rockland Water company. Now

transformed into an antiques-filled
inn with spacious guest rooms.
$$–$$$
Limerock Inn
96 Limerock Avenue, 04841.
Tel: 207 594–2257/
800 546–3762.
8 rooms. B&B. Elegantly decorated
Queen Anne Victorian on a
residential street near the Shore
Village and Farnsworth Museums.
Some rooms have whirlpool tubs
and private decks. **$$–$$$**

ROCKPORT
Samoset Resort
220 Warrenton Street, 04856.
Tel: 207 594–2511/
800 341–1650.
150 rooms. A full-scale, seaside
golf resort. Swimming pool, tennis
courts, too. **$$$–$$$$**
Sign of the Unicorn
191 Beauchamp Point Road,
04856.
Tel: 207 236–4042/
800 789–8789.
4 rooms. B&B. A comfortable
home, with children's loft. **$–$$**

ROCKWOOD
(MOOSEHEAD LAKE)
Maynard-in-Maine
Rockwood 04478.
Tel: 207 534–7703.
13 rooms. FAP. A classic hunting
camp, founded in 1919. **$$**
Rockwood Cottages
Route 15, 04478.
Tel: 207 534–7725.
8 cottages. Lakeside cottages with
screened porches and fully
equipped kitchens. Amenities
include a sauna and boating. **$$**
The Birches
off Route 15, 04478.
Tel: 207 534–7305.
33 rooms. B&B. A rustic 1940s

lakeside lodge with log cabins (with
wood-burning stoves or fireplaces).
Boating on the lake; sauna and hot
tub. **$**

SEARSPORT
The Homeport Inn
E. Main Street (Route 1), 04974.
Tel: 207 548–2259/
800 742–5814.
10 rooms, two cottages. B&B. A
cupola-topped 1860s captain's
house filled with Victorian
appointments in the "antiques
capital" of Maine. Some rooms
have private decks and views of the
bay. **$**

SOUTH CASCO
Migis Lodge on Sebago Lake
P. O Box 40, 04077.
Tel: 207 655–4524.
Fax: 207 655–2054/
www.migis.com.
32 rooms. FAP. A rustic/elegant
and old-fashioned 100-acre resort.
Rooms in the main lodge and in
cottages, all overlooking the lake.
Sailing, canoeing, waterskiing,
tennis. Dining room offers
traditional New England fare,
including steamers, clam chowder,
lobster. **$$$–$$$$**

SOUTHWEST HARBOR
The Claremont
P. O. Box 1371, 04679.
Tel: 207 244–5036/
800 244–5036.
Fax: 207 244–3512.
www.acadia.net/claremont.
41 rooms. MAP. Mount Desert
Island's oldest grand hotel, built in
1884. Rooms in the main inn, two
guest houses, and a dozen
cottages. Waterfront location for
swimming, boating. Also tennis and
croquet. **$$–$$$**
Inn at Southwest
371 Main Street.
Tel: 207 244–3835.
Fax: 207 244–9879.
www.acadia.net/innatsw.
9 rooms. B&B. Elegant, romantic
rooms with antique furnishings in
an 1884 Victorian home overlooking
the harbor. **$–$$**

SPRUCE HEAD
Craignair Inn at Clark Island
Spruce Head, 04859.
Tel: 207 594–7644/
800 320–9997.
Fax: 207 596–7124.
www.midcoast.com/~craignar.
28 rooms. B&B. A basic, cheerful
shorefront inn near a nature
preserve between Rockland and
Tenants Harbor. Originally built in
1928 to house workers from the
nearby quarries. The 20 rooms in
the main inn share baths, the
somewhat more upscale rooms in
the annex have private baths. **$–$$**

STOCKTON SPRINGS
The Hichborn Inn
Church Street, 04981.
Tel: 207 567–4183.
4 rooms. B&B. An Italianate
mansion in an old ship-building
village north of Searsport. **$**

STONINGTON
Inn on the Harbor
Main Street, 04681.
Tel: 20) 367–2420/
800 942–2420.
Fax: 207 367–5165.
13 rooms. Waterside lodgings with
a spacious deck in a scarcely
touristed harbor town. **$$**

SUNSET
Goose Cove Lodge
Deer Isle, 04683.
Tel: 207 348–2508/
800 728–1963.
Fax: 207 348–2624.
22 rooms. MAP. An informal family
resort with a rustic, simply
furnished lodge and cottages in a
remote natural setting. Overlooking
Penobscot Bay, adjacent to nature
conservatory land. **$$$–$$$$**

TENANTS HARBOR
East Wind Inn and Meeting House
Mechanic Street (Route 131),
04860.
Tel: 207 372–6366/
800 241–8439. Fax: 207 372–6320.
26 rooms. B&B. Plainly decorated,
harborside inn with a wraparound
porch in an unspoiled fishing village
south of Rockland. **$$–$$$**

VINALHAVEN

Tidewater Motel
Main Street, 04863.
Tel: 207 863–4618.
11 rooms. A simple harborside
motel – literally right on the water –
on a moneyed island ideal for
biking. **$**

WISCASSET

Marston House
Main Street, 04578.
Tel: 207 882–6010/
800 852–4137.
A small private carriage house with
two rooms, simply appointed with
Shaker- and Colonial-style
furnishings and fireplaces. No
public spaces, but a continental
breakfast is delivered to the
rooms. **$**
Squire Tarbox Inn
Route 144 (RR 2, Box 620),
04578.
Tel: 207 882–7693.
Fax: 207 882–7107.
11 rooms. B&B. A colonial country
farmhouse on a working farm where
the owners raise goats. Delicious
home-grown dinners feature the
farm's goat cheese. **$$–$$$**

YORK AREA

View Point Inn
229 Nubble Road, York Beach,
03910.
Tel: 207 363–2661.
10 rooms. On the rocky shore, with
views of Nubble Light. **$$$$**
Stage Neck Inn
off Route 1A, York Harbor, 03911,
Tel: 207 363–3850/
800 222–3238.
www.stageneck.com.
A contemporary seaside resort
known for its 60 low-key luxury.
Queen Anne-style rooms with
refrigerators, many with ocean
views. Indoor pool with whirlpool
spa. **$$$–$$$$**
York Harbor Inn
Route 1A, York Harbor, 03911.
Tel: 207 363-5119,
800 343–3869.
Fax: 207 363–7151.
A fresh seaside inn which accrued
around a 1637 sail loft. 33
Colonial-style rooms, some with

fireplaces or whirlpools. **$–$–$$$$**
Dockside Guest Quarters
Harris Island Road (off Route 103),
York, 03909.
Tel: 207 363–2868/
888 (860) 7428.
Fax: 207–363–1977.
www.docksidegq.com.
Classic 19th-century seacoast home
flanked by cottages (27 rooms). **$–$$**

Where to Eat

BAR HARBOR

Porcupine Grill
123 Cottage Street.
Tel: 207 288–3884.
Yacht-club spiffy, and culinarily up-
to-date. Offerings may include fish
with citrus relish, cornbread-stuffed
pork chops, and fresh pastas. The
wine bar has a lighter menu. **$$$**
Jordan Pond House
Park Loop Road.
Tel: 207 276–3316.
A classic spot for popovers and tea
(and other meals, too), with an
expansive mountain view within
Acadia National Park. **$$**
Lompoc Cafe
36 Rodick Street.
Tel: 207 288–9392.
A brew pub with international
accompaniments. **$$**

BATH

Beale Street Barbecue & Grill
215 Water Street.
Tel: 207 442–9514.
A comfortable, affordable barbecue
joint, with choices ranging from a
basic pulled pork plate to a New
York sirloin. **$–$$**
Kristina's
160 Center Street (Route 209).

Tel: 207 442–8577.
A popular café housed in a pair of
19th-century homes; don't miss the
sticky buns. **$**

BETHEL

Bethel Inn & Country Club
Village Common. 04217.
Tel: 207 824–2175.
Yankee classics; mountain views.
$$
Mother's
Upper Main Street.
Tel: 207 824–2589.
A cozy house serving homemade
soups and sandwiches, as well as
substantial dinners, including
steaks, pastas and crab
cakes. **$$**

BLUE HILL

Blue Hill Inn
Union Street.
Tel: 207 374–2844.
Creative preparations of Maine
seafood and local produce in a
Federal-style inn. **$$$**
Jonathan's
Main Street.
Tel: 207 374–5226.
A contemporary café serving
robust international dishes.
$$–$$$

BOOTHBAY HARBOR

Black Orchid
5 Byway.
Tel: 207 633–6659.
Mediterranean influences pervade
this harborside summer house with
roof deck. **$$–$$$**
Ebb Tide
67 Commercial Street.
Tel: 207 633–5692.
A stylish restored diner where you'll

Restaurant Guidelines

● **Prices** are approximate, but for
a three-course meal for one
(excluding beverages, tax and tip),
the following guidelines may prove
helpful:
$$$$ = over $40
$$$ = $28-40
$$ = $15-28
$ = under $15
● **Meal tax** varies from state to

state, but it is customary to tip 15
to 20 percent on the pre-tax total.
● **Credit cards** The more
expensive establishments
generally accept credit cards, but
call ahead to check just in case.
● **Reservations** Most restaurants,
except for the clearly casual,
appreciate reservations (some
require them).

find a variety of classic comfort foods. **$–$$**

BRUNSWICK

The Great Impasta
42 Main Street.
Tel: 207 729–5858.
A small storefront serving, yes, pasta of all types. **$–$$**

CAMDEN

The Belmont
6 Belmont Avenue.
Tel: 207 236–8053.
New American wizardry, in a peaceful setting. **$$$**

Camden Harbor Inn
83 Bayview Street.
Tel: 207 236–4200.
Fine continental dining overlooking Camden harbor. **$$$–$$$$**

Hi Bombay
31 Elm Street.
Tel: 207 230–0434.
When you just can't look at another lobster, this relaxed Indian spot serves up curries and tandoor-roasted meats. **$–$$**

Sea Dog
43 Mechanic Street.
Tel: 207 236–6863.
A brew pub in a former wool mill. **$**

CAPE NEDDICK

Cape Neddick Inn
Routes 1 and 1A.
Tel: 207 363–2899.
Ambitious seasonal cuisine in a neo-traditional setting, north of York Beach. **$$$–$$$$**

CASTINE

The Pentagoet Inn
Main Street.
Tel: 207 326–8616.

A stain on Maine

In the cemetery at Bucksport, Maine, the tombstone of town founder and judge Colonel Jonathan Buck has a strange dark blemish shaped like a woman's leg. Allegedly, it is impossible to remove and the perpetrator is said to have been a defendant sentenced for witchcraft.

A *prix fixe* dinner party in a turreted Victorian inn. Reservations required. **$$$**

Castine Inn
Main Street.
Tel: 207 326–4365.
Regional delicacies in a dining room painted to depict the town. Dinner only. **$$**

Dennett's Wharf
Sea Street.
Tel: 207 326–9045.
Casual harborside seafood. **$$**

DEER ISLE

Pilgrim's Inn
Route 15A.
Tel: 207 348–6615.
An exquisite *prix-fixe* menu in a rustic barn. **$$$$**

FREEPORT

Freeport Inn & Cafe
Route 1.
Tel: 207 865–3106.
Simple soups, salads, and sandwiches, plus breakfast all day, in this small spot south of the shopping district. **$**

Harraseeket Inn
162 Main Street.
Tel: 207 865–9377.
Fabulous local produce, seafood, and game; famed for its buffets. More casual fare – hamburgers, steamers, and simple fish dishes– in the hunting lodge ambiance of the tavern room. **$$–$$$**

Harraseeket Lobster Company
Main Street, South Freeport.
Tel: 207 865–3535.
Seafood basics in the rough: lobster dinners, fried clams, other fried seafood. Next to the town landing in South Freeport. Picnic tables outside for al fresco munching in fair weather. **$–$$**

GARDINER

A-1 Diner
Route 201.
Tel: 207 582–4804.
A 1946 Worcester diner, south of Augusta, serving the standards. **$**

GEORGETOWN

Robinhood Free Meetinghouse
Robinhood Road.
Tel: 207 371–2188.

An 1855 Greek Revival meetinghouse near Bath transformed into a simple yet elegant temple of classic and fusion cuisine. Think American bistro fare blended with Italian, Chinese, Thai, and Caribbean influences. The chef's signature dessert is "Obsession in Three Chocolates". **$$$–$$$$**

GREENVILLE

Greenville Inn
Norris Street.
Tel: 207 695–2206.
Bountiful dinners accompanied by giant popovers in an opulent mansion overlooking Moosehead Lake. **$$$**

KENNEBUNKPORT

Cape Arundel Inn
Ocean Avenue.
Tel: 207 967–2125.
Ocean views and an interesting menu. **$$$**

Kennebunkport Inn
Dock Square.
Tel: 207 967–2621.
Delightful regional cuisine with French accents. **$$$–$$$$**

Grissini,
27 Western Avenue (Route 9).
Tel: 207 967–2211.
Fine contemporary northern Italian fare – such as grilled lamb with Tuscan white beans, gnocchi (potato dumplings) grilled salmon served on sweet potato polenta – in a casually upscale room. **$$**

Seascapes
On the Pier, Cape Porpoise.
Tel: 207 967–8500.
Regional specialties prepared with international panache. **$$$**

White Barn Inn,
Beach Street, Tel: 207 967–2321.
$$$$. A beautifully appointed barn serving stellar nouvelle cuisine.

Windows on the Water, Chase Hill, Tel: 207 967–3313. **$$$$**.
Reservations essential. A modern restaurant known for its inventive treatments of lobster, which may appear in half-a-dozen succulent guises.

Restaurant Guidelines

- **Prices** are approximate, but for a three-course meal for one (excluding beverages, tax and tip), the following guidelines may prove helpful:
  $$$$ = over $40
  $$$ = $28-40
  $$ = $15-28
  $ = under $15
- **Meal tax** varies from state to state, but it is customary to tip 15 to 20 percent on the pre-tax total.
- **Credit cards** The more expensive establishments generally accept credit cards, but call ahead to check just in case.
- **Reservations** Most restaurants, except for the clearly casual, appreciate reservations (some require them).

KINGFIELD

The Herbert, Main Street, Tel: 207 265–2000. **$$**. Hearty regional dishes served in an airy Victorian dining room.
Longfellow's, Main Street, Tel: 207 265–4394. **$**. A casual riverside cafe with good dishes and good prices.
One Stanley Avenue, Tel: 207 265–5541. **$$–$$$**. The indigenous foods of Maine, artfully prepared.

KITTERY

The Friendly Toast, Bridge Street, Tel: 207 439–2882. **$**. Funky cafe overlooking the river serving playful roadhouse food, plus creative vegetarian options. Breakfast available all day.
Warren's Lobster House, Route 1, Tel: 207 439–1630. **$$**. On the water just north of Portsmouth, a local institution serving lobster and other seafood. Hefty salad bar, too.

LITTLE DEER ISLE

Eaton's Lobster Pool, Blastow Cove, Tel: 207 348–2383. **$$$**. Water views and fresh-off-the-boat seafood.

NORTHEAST HARBOR

Asticou Inn
Tel: 207 276–3344.
Yankee standards as well as welcome interlopers, in a grand old dining room overlooking the sea. **$$$$**
Redfield's
Main Street, 04662
Tel: 207 276–5283.
A summery café serving all three meals, New American-style. **$$$**

OGUNQUIT

Arrows
Berwick Road (off Route 1).
Tel: 207 361–1100.
Adventurous (and exquisite) international cuisine in an English-country-style farmhouse. Dinner only. **$$$$**
Barnacle Billy's
Perkins Cove.
Tel: 207 646–5575.
Classic seafood, right on the water. **$$$**
Ida Reds
Route 1.
Tel: 207 646–0289.
An upscale bistro next to the Playhouse, serving often-dramatically constructed contemporary dishes. **$$$**

PORTLAND

Back Bay Grill
65 Portland Street.
Tel: 207 772–8833.
Sophisticated decor, sensuous New American dishes. **$$$**
Cafe Uffa!
190 State Street.
Tel: 207 775–3380.
A casual, eclectic bistro emphasizing vegetarian dishes, as well as fish. (There's no meat on the menu.) Microbrews, too. **$–$$**
Cotton Street Cantina
10 Cotton Street.
Tel: 207 775–3222.
A lively spot serving creative preparations that get their soul from the flavors of South America, Mexico, and the Caribbean. **$$**
Street & Company
33 Wharf Street.
Tel: 207 775–0887.
Fresh fish and seafood served in the pan right on one of the dozen copper-topped tables. You can choose a vegetarian alternative if you must, but creatively prepared seafood is the reason to be here. **$$–$$$**

RANGELEY

Country Club Inn
Mingo Loop Road.
Tel: 207 864–3831.
Traditional white-tablecloth fare in a glassed-in dining room with lake and mountain views. Reservations required. **$$$–$$$$**

ROCKLAND

Jessica's
2 S Main Street (Route 73).
Tel: 207 596–0770.
European bistro-style cuisine – pasta, risotto, paella – served in four cozy dining rooms in a Victorian house. Located at the far southern end of town. **$$**
The Waterworks
Lindsey Street.
Tel: 207 596–7950.
A former waterworks turned funky pub serving comfort food – ranging from roast turkey and fish 'n' chips, through grilled sausages to meatloaf – and microbrews.
$–$$

ROCKPORT

Marcel's at the Samoset Resort
220 Warrenton Street.
Tel: 207 594–0774.
Million-dollar views, with eclectic cuisine priced to match. From rack of lamb and Chateaubriand to more contemporary fare with French and Italian influences. **$$$$**
Sail Loft
Rockport Harbor.
Tel: 207 236–2330.
Upmarket seafood classics served baked, sautéed, and fried with an ocean view. Lots of lobster choices. **$$$–$$$$**

ROCKWOOD

The Birches
off Route 15.
Tel: 207 534–7305.
Seafood, steaks, and pasta overlooking Moosehead Lake at this north woods resort. **$$$**

Restaurant Guidelines

● **Prices** are approximate, but for a three-course meal for one (excluding beverages, tax and tip), the following guidelines may prove helpful:

$$$$ = over $40
$$$ = $28-40
$$ = $15-28
$ = under $15

● **Meal tax** varies from state to state, but it is customary to tip 15 to 20 percent on the pre-tax total.

● **Credit cards** The more expensive establishments generally accept credit cards, but call ahead to check just in case.

● **Reservations** Most restaurants, except for the clearly casual, appreciate reservations (some require them).

SEARSPORT

Nickerson Tavern
Route 1.
Tel: 207 548–2220.
Superb regional cuisine (dinner only) in a former sea captain's home. **$$$**

SOUTHWEST HARBOR

Beal's Lobster Pier
Clark Point Road.
Tel: 207 244–7178.
A classic wharfside lobster shack. **$**

The Claremont
Clark Point Road.
Tel: 207 244–5036.
The formal dining room of this venerable 1884 inn has an ambitious modernist menu. Jackets required for men, "corresponding attire" for women. **$$$**

STONINGTON

Bay View Restaurant
Seabreeze Avenue.
Tel: 207 367–2274.
Great at-the-source seafood feasting. **$$**

WISCASSET

Le Garage
Water Street.
Tel: 207 882–5409.
Regional American fare in a picture-perfect town. **$$$**

Squire Tarbox Restaurant
Route 144.
Tel: 207 882–7693.
A colonial farmhouse serving home-raised delicacies, included the farm's own goat cheese. Dinner only. **$$$**

YORK AREA

Mimmo's
Route 1A, York.
Tel: 207 363–3807.
An unprepossessing café with an exuberant Tuscan chef. **$$**

The Restaurant at Dockside Guest Quarters
Harris Island Road (off Route 103), York.
Tel: 207 363–2868.
From seaside standards to modern innovations – fried clams and steamed lobsters to "swordfish Pacific Rim" and pesto chicken – all with a water view. **$$$**

York Harbor Inn
Route 1A, York Harbor.
Tel: 207 363–5119.
Well-considered continental /regional fare with a seafood focus in a "big night out" room. **$$$–$$$$**

Culture

CLASSICAL MUSIC

Portland Symphony Orchestra (tel: 207 842–0800; 20 Myrtle Street, Portland) performs year-round except in September.

MUSIC FESTIVALS

Bowdoin Summer Music Festival (tel: 207 725–3895; Brunswick) hosts a popular and renowned six-week series of concerts.

Kneisel Hall Chamber Music Festival (tel: 207 374–2811; Route 15, Blue Hill) has a developed a fine reputation for its summer concerts.

THEATER

Portland Performing Arts Center (tel: 207 761–0591; 25A Forest Avenue, Portland) is a multi-purpose venue offering space for music, dance, and theater. Also in Portland, check the newspaper for anything mounted by the **Portland Stage Company** (tel: 207 774–0465).

Ogunquit Playhouse (tel: 207 646–5511; Route 1, Ogunquit) stages musicals, theater, and plays during the summer only. It's one of the oldest playhouses in the country.

ART GALLERIES

Bayview Gallery (tel: 207 773–3007, (800) 244–3007; 75 Market Street, Portland) represents preeminent Maine artists.

Nightlife

LIVE MUSIC

Left Bank Bakery and Cafe (tel: 207 374–2201; Route 172, Blue Hill) brings folk music to the already-musical town.

GAY & LESBIAN VENUES

Le Club (tel: 207 646–6655; 13 Main Street, Ogunquit) primarily caters for a seasonal gay clientele.

In fact, Ogunquit has an increasing number of gay-friendly establishments; look for the rainbow flags.

Underground (tel: 207 773–3315; 3 Spring Street, Portland) is the city's gay and lesbian club.

LATE-NIGHT VENUES

It doesn't have to be late to pop into the **Sea Dog Tavern & Brewery** (tel: 207 236–6863; 43 Mechanic Street, Camden), which features its own microbrews in a lively setting within a former wool mill.

Sunday River in Bethel is a hoping kind of place (both slopeside and in town) during ski season. Check out the **Sunday River Brewery** (tel: 207 824–4253; Route 2) and **Bumps Pub** (tel: 207 824–3000; on the mountain), which both have rock bands.

DANCING

Zootz Nightclub (tel: 207 773–8187; 31 Forest Avenue, for the college set, and **Granny Killam's** (tel: 207 761–5865; 55 Market Street), for the post-college crowd, are two of Portland's better dance clubs.

Outdoor Activities

BIKING

When the snow melts after winter, the Sunday River Ski area turns into the **Sunday River Mountain Bike Park** (tel: 207 824–3000), where bikers can ride the lifts up and bike down.

Boston-based **Bike Riders' Tours** (tel: 800 473–7040) is one of several companies offering bicycle tours in the state of Maine. Their week-long Penobscot Bay trip stops off in Camden, Islesboro and Castine.

CANOEING/KAYAKING AND RAFTING

With more than 2,000 coastal islands and their protected waters, Maine has become a center for sea kayaking.

The **Maine Island Kayak Company** (tel: 207 766–2373, (800) 796–2373), operating from Peaks Island near Portland, runs a wide range of sea kayaking trips and instructional courses.

H2Outfitters (tel: 207 833–5257), on Orr's Island near Brunswick, offers one-day sea kayaking classes, as well as multi-day trips.

The Kennebec, Dead, and Penobscot Rivers offer some of New England's most challenging whitewater rafting. **North American Whitewater Expeditions** (tel: (800)

727–4379) organizes Maine river rafting trips for novices through experts. The Allagash Wilderness Waterway, a 92-mile (150-km) corridor of lakes and rivers from Baxter State Park to the Canadian border, is another canoeing and rafting destination.

Outfitters in this area include **Allagash Canoe Trips in Greenville** (tel: 207 695–3668), **Mahoosuc Guide Service** in Newry (tel: 207 824–2073), and **North Country Outfitters** in Rockwood (tel: 207 534–2242).

For more sedate paddling excursions, the **Maine Audubon Society** (tel: 207 781–2330) offers guided canoe trips and rentals in Scarborough Marsh, the state's largest salt marsh.

On Mount Desert Island, **National Park Canoe Rentals** (tel: 207 244–5854) has canoes for hire on Long Pond.

FISHING

The Rangeley area is a popular destination for those who fly-fish. For ocean fishing excursions, **Devils Den** (tel: 207 761–4466) runs half- and full-day trips from Portland. In Kennebunkport, **Chick's Marina** (tel: 207 967–2782) offers fishing cruises for up to six people.

HIKING

Baxter State Park (tel: 207 723–5140) in Maine's North Woods draws thousands of hikers annually who tackle the day-long climb to the summit of **Mount Katahdin**, the state's highest peak (5,267 feet, or 1,755 meters). Eighteen mountains in the park are taller than 3,000 feet (900 meters).

SAILING

The Camden area is Maine's center for windjammer cruising. The **Maine Windjammer Association** (tel: (800) 807–9463), headquartered in Blue Hill, represents a number of Camden-based windjammers that offer multi-day excursions.

Do-it-yourself sailors can contact **Manset Yacht Service** (tel: 207 244-4040), near Acadia National Park, to arrange sailboat rentals.

Maine Festivals

● **SPRING**
March may be the beginning of spring in other states, but Maine is still celebrating winter when Rangeley plays host to the annual **Sled Dog Races** (tel: 207 864–5364).

● **SUMMER**
Portland kicks off the summer season with the **Old Port Festival** (tel: 207 772–6828) in early June, while later in the month, Wiscasset hosts its **Strawberry Festival** (tel: 207 882–7184).

Other summer celebrations of Maine food include **Rockland's Lobster Festival** (tel: (800) 562–2529) in late July, and the mid-August **Wild Blueberry Festival** (tel: 207 255–6665) down east in Machias.

Also in late June, Maine shows off its distinctive on-the-water craft, both improvised and historic, at the **Great Kennebec Whatever Week** (tel: 207 623–4559) – including a river race of homemade rafts – and during **Windjammer Days** (tel: 207 633–2353) in Boothbay Harbor.

In July and August, musicians

assemble in Hamilton for the **Sebago-Long Lake Chamber Music Festival** (tel: 207 583–6747), while the **Bar Harbor Music Festival** (tel: 207 288–5744) comes to Mount Desert Island.

● **FALL**
Several towns honor the season's colors in October with **Fall Foliage Festivals**, including events in Camden (tel: 207 236–4404), Boothbay (tel: 207 633–4743) and York (tel: 207 363–4422).

Portland toasts the season in a different way at the annual **Maine Brewer's Festival** (tel: 207 767–5424).

● **WINTER**
For two December weekends, the Kennebunk area hosts holiday crafts fairs with tree-lighting and caroling during the annual **Christmas Prelude** (tel: 207 967–0857).

In January, all of the cross-country ski areas thumb their noses at winter throughout the statewide **Ski Fest** events (tel: 800 754–9263).

Boats can also be hired on Sebago and Long Lakes: try **Mardon Marine** (tel: 207 693–6264) or **Sun Sports Plus** (tel: 207 693–3867), both in Naples.

SKIING
Maine's largest areas for downhill skiing are:
Sunday River in Bethel (tel: 207 824–3000, 800 543–2754).
Sugarloaf/USA in Kingfield (tel: 207 237–2000/800 843–5623).
Saddleback in Rangley (tel: 207 864–5671).

Bethel is also home to several cross-country ski centers including:
The Bethel Inn Ski Center (tel: 207 824–2175).
Carter's Cross Country Ski Centers (tel: 207 539–4848).
Sunday River Inn Ski Touring Center (tel: 207 824–2410).

Other Nordic skiing spots include **The Birches Cross Country Center** in Rockwood (tel: 207 534–7305) and the **Harris Farm Cross Country Ski Center** in Biddeford (tel: 207 499–2678).

See also page 269.

Shopping
WHERE TO SHOP
Between the towns of Freeport and Kittery, Maine's cornered the market in outlet stores (see also page 153)

Between Kittery and Wells (literally), you'll find more outlet stores popping up on Route 1, too.

If heavy foot traffic is any indication of good shopping, it's readily apparent that the Dock Square area in Kennebunkport offers it in spades.

Kayak Tours
A tour with a difference – guided sea kayaking excursions are conducted in the Acadia area by two Bar Harbor-based companies:
● **National Park Kayak Tours** Tel: 207 288–0342.
● **Coastal Kayaking Tours** Tel: 207 288–9605.

Portland's Old Port Exchange area, a dense few blocks along Fore and Exchange Streets, is great for browsing and buying.

SHOPPING MALLS
Maine Mall (tel: 207 774–0303), 5 miles (8 km) south of Portland, has almost 150 stores, including large anchor department stores.

BOOKS
DeLorme's Map Store (tel: 207 846–7000; Yarmouth) stocks an outstanding range of Maine and New England specialty maps, as well as travel guides.
Owl and Turtle Boookshop (tel: 207 236–4769; 8 Bay View Street, Camden) has two floors of Maine maritime and children's books.
Port in a Storm (tel: 207 244–4114; Main Street, Somesville, near Acadia National Park), regardless of the weather, is one of the best bookstores on the Maine coast.

ANTIQUES
You can often find silver for the price of flatware at flea markets, if you know what you're looking for.

Route 1 through Searsport is lined with semi-permanent seasonal flea markets, as well as traditional antiques shops. You'll do well here.

CHINA AND GLASS
Stein Gallery Contemporary Glass (tel: 207 772–9072; 195 Middle Street, Portland) make modern functional and decorative glassware.

ARTS AND CRAFTS
Handworks Gallery (tel: 207 374–5613; Main Street) and **North Country Textiles** (tel: 207 374–2715), both on Main Street in Blue Hill, are just two of many shops in town that carry excellent hand-made crafts.

Also, don't miss **Rackliffe Pottery** (tel: 207 374–2297; Route 172) and **Rowantrees Pottery** (tel: 207 374–5535; Union Street), also both in Blue Hill.

Although you may visit studios by only appointment, many alumni of

Gifts and Souvenirs
For those must-have mementos, downtown Boothbay Harbor (along with Camden and Bar Harbor further north) is chock-a-block with shops that will draw the money from your pockets like magnets to steel.

the **Haystack Mountain School of Crafts** (tel: 207 348–2306; off Route 15 south of Deer Isle) have settled in the area and have their own studio/shops. Stop in at **Blue Heron Gallery & Studio** (tel: 207 348–6051; Church Street, Deer Isle) which sells Haystack faculty work. **Deer Isle Artists Association** (no phone; Route 15, Deer Isle) mounts revolving shows of area artists.

Edgecomb Potters (tel: 207 882–6802; Route 27) and **Sheepscot River Pottery** (tel: 207 882–9410; Route 1) are both in Edgecomb selling distinctive pottery. Sheeposcot also offers a wide range of other hand-crafted goods.

Children
THEME PARKS
Palace Playground (tel: 207 934–2001; Old Orchard Street, Old Orchard Beach) features an old carousel and Ferris wheel and lots of other rides.

ZOOS
Maine Aquarium (tel: 207 284–4512; Route 1, Saco) has underwater creatures you'd expect (sharks, seals, and penguins), but they also have land-roamers too. **Acadia Zoo** (tel: 207 667–3244; Route 3, Trenton) is small but it will occupy the kids.

STEAM TRAIN JOURNEYS
Belfast & Moosehead Lake Railroad (tel: 207 948–5500; Unity) operates two scenic trains: one passes along a river, another by villages. Kids will particularly like the open-air cars.
Seashore Trolley Museum (tel: 207

967–2800; Log Cabin Road, Kennebunkport) offers a 4-mile trolley tips aboard one of their restored antiques.
Maine Coast Railroad (tel: 207 882–8000; Route 1, Wiscasset) travels up to Newcastle on restored vintage trains.
Boothbay Railway Village (tel: 207 633–4727; Route 27, Boothbay) offers just a 1½-mile narrow-gauge steam train ride, but it's picturesque as it travels through a re-created New England village.

MUSEUM

Children's Museum of Maine (tel: 207 828–1234; 142 Free Street, Portland) is one of the best in New England. Highly interactive, it will keep even the most boisterous occupied for hours – hauling in traps on a lobster boat, broadcasting the news and making stained glass, and lots more. Admission is free on Friday 5–7pm.

Further Reading

Not all the books cited are currently in print, but it can be fun tracking them down in New England's atmospheric secondhand bookshops.

History & Culture

Battles of the United States, by Sea and Land by Henry B. Dawson. *New York,* 1858.
A Description of New England by Captain John Smith. Boston, 1865.
The Flowering of New England by Van Wyck Brooks. New York, 1936.
New England: Indian Summer, 1865–1915 by Van Wyck Brooks. New York, 1940.
New England Frontier: Puritans and Indians by Alden T. Vaughan. Boston, 1965.
The New England Mind: From Colony to Province by Perry Miller. Cambridge, 1953.
Nooks and Corners of the New England Coast by Samuel Adams Drake. New York, 1875.
The Spread of New England Settlement and Institutions to the The Hill Country of Northern New England by Harold Fisher Wilson. New York, 1967.

Landscape and Natural History

These Fragile Outposts: A Geological Look at Cape Cod, Martha's Vineyard and Nantucket by Barbara B. Chamberlain. New York, 1964.
A Guide to New England's Landscape by Neil Jorgensen. Barre, VT, 1971.

Architecture

Cityscapes of Boston: An American City through Time by Robert Campbell and Peter Vanderwarker. Boston, 1992.
Preserving New England by Jane Holtz Kay and Pauline Chase-Harrell. New York, 1986.

Fiction

Contemporary New England Stories by Michael C. Curtis, ed. Old Saybrook, CT, 1992.
String Too Short to Be Saved: Recollections of Summers on a New England Farm by Donald Hall. Boston, 1979.
Imagining Boston: A Literary Landscape by Shaun O'Connell. Boston, 1990.

Other Insight Guides

More than 190 *Insight Guides* cover every continent. In addition, a companion series of more than 100 *Insight Pocket Guides* provides selected, carefully-timed itineraries for the traveler with little time to spare and include a full-size fold-out map. And more than 100 *Insight Compact Guides* provide ideal on-the-spot companions, with text, maps and pictures all carefully cross-referenced.
Titles which highlight destinations in New England include:

Insight Guide: Boston (above) is a lavishly illustrated companion to the present book, and *Pocket Guide: Boston* provides recommendations and a full-size city map.

Boston, Cape Cod, and *Martha's Vineyard & Nantucket* are covered in detail by three Compact Guides.

ART & PHOTO CREDITS

Picture Spreads

INSIGHT GUIDE

New England

Cartographic Editor **Zoë Goodwin**
Production **Stuart A Everitt**
Design Consultants
Carlotta Junger, Graham Mitchener
Picture Research
Hilary Genin, Monica Allende

Maps Colourmap Scanning Ltd.
© 1999 Apa Publications GmbH & Co.
Verlag KG (Singapore branch)

Index

Numbers in italics refer to photographs

a

Abenaki tribe 24, 276, 303
Acadia National Park *see* **Mount Desert Island**
Adams, John 56, 150
Adams, John Quincy 112, 150, 232
Adams, Samuel 39, 147
  burial place (Boston) 114
Adamsville 229
African-Americans 58–9, 118, 197
Alcott, Bronson 148, 149, 187
Alcott, Louisa May 118, 148, 149
Algonquin tribes 24, 25, 30, 53, 54, 55, 175
  see also under individual tribe names
Allagash Wilderness Waterway 322
Allen, Ethan 56, 207, 266
  Ethan Allen Homestead Trust (near Burlington) 262
American Revolution *see* **Revolutionary War**
American Society of Dowsers (Danville) 259
America's Cup 77, 164, 237
America's Stonehenge (Mystery Hill) (North Salem) 282
Amherst *191*, 191–2
amusement parks
  Story Land (Glen) 295
  Weirs Beach (Lake Winnepesaukee) 286
Andros, Edmund Sir 35, 36, 210
Annisquam (Cape Ann) *136–7*, 141
Aptucxet Trading Post (Cape Cod) 160
aquariums
  Aquarium (Nantucket) 180
  Maritime Aquarium (South Norwalk) 215
  Mystic Marinelife Aquarium (Mystic Seaport) 222
  National Marine Fisheries Service Aquarium (Woods Hole) 170
  New England Aquarium (Boston) 110
  Oceanarium (Mount Desert Island) 320
Aquinnah (formerly Gay Head) 174
architects
  see also Bulfinch, Charles
  Brown, Joseph 232

architects cont'd
  Gropius, Walter 88, 149
  Gund, Graham 88
  Hund, Richard Morris 235, 236
  Johnson, Philip 123
  Kallmann, McKinnell and Knowles 112
  LeCorbusier 88, 129
  Lowell, Guy 124
  McKim, Mead and White 88, 230
  Packard, Lambert 259
  Pei, I.M. 112, 123, 124, 307
  Potter, Edward Tuckerman 212
  Richardson, Henry Hobson 88, 121, 123, 129, 130
  Saarinen, Eero 126, 199
  Stern, Robert A.M. 198
  Upjohn, Richard 211
  White, Stanford 199, 212, 236
  Wright, Frank Lloyd 282
architecture 81–8
  see also **historic houses**
Arlington 267–8
art collections *see* **museums and art collections**
Arthur, President Chester Alan 228
artists' galleries
  Northampton (NoHo) 192
  Putney 250
  South Norwalk (SoNo) 215
  Tyringham 197
artist's/writers' retreats/colonies
  Bread Loaf Writers' Conference 264
  Greensboro 260
  McDowell Colony (Peterborough) 284
  Old Lyme 218
  Provincetown 167
  Rockport 141
  Vermont Studio Center (Johnson) 258
Ascutney 251
Ashley, Colonel John 195
Ashley Falls 195
Astor, Mrs 236
Augusta 325
  Fort Western 325
  Maine State Museum 325
  State House 325

b

Barnum, Phineas (museum) 216
Barre 254
Bartholomew's Cobble (Ashley Falls) 196
baseball 125, 201
Bash Bish Falls 195

basketball 201
  Hall of Fame (Springfield) 193
Bath Iron Works 309
Battle of Bunker Hill 22, 35, 38, 109, 133
Battle of Concord *36*, 37
Battle of Lexington *37*
Battle Road (Lexington to Concord) sites 146–7
  Battle Road Visitor Center 147
  Ebenezer Fiske House Site 147
  Hartwell Tavern 147
  Munroe Tavern 147
  Museum of Our National Heritage 146
  Paul Revere Capture Site 147
beaches
  Children's Beach (Nantucket) *96*, 82
  Cisco (Nantucket) 182
  Coast Guard Beach (Cape Cod) 165
  Craigville Beach (Centerville) 169
  Dionis (Nantucket) 182
  First Encounter Beach (Eastham) 165
  Head of the Meadow Beach (Cape Cod) 166
  Herring Cove (Provincetown) 168
  Jetties (Nantucket) 182
  Long Sands Beach (York) *303*, 305
  Madaket Beach (Nantucket) 182
  Marconi Beach (Cape Cod) 165
  Martha's Vineyard 171
  Nauset Beach (Orleans) 168
  Nauset Light Beach (Cape Cod) *165*
  Ogunquit 305
  Point Judith (Galilee) 239
  Race Point (Provincetown) 168
  Sand Beach (Mount Desert Island) 319
  Scarborough State Beach (Narragansett) 239
  Surfside Beach (Nantucket) 182
Bean, L.L. 308–9
Belfast 315
Benchley, Robert 189
Bennington 268
  Battle Monument 268
  Bennington College 268
  Bennington Museum and Grandma Moses Gallery 268
  Old Bennington 268
  Old First Church 268
Berkshires 195–200
Berwind, Edward Julius 233, 235
Bethel 324

Bethel cont'd
  Bethel Inn 324
  Moses Mason House 324
Bethlehem 290
Bierstadt, Albert 259
Billings, Frederick 252
blacks 58, 59
Blaxton, Reverend William 115, 227
Block, Adrian 205, 238
Block Island 237–9
  beaches 239
  fishing 239
  Mohegan Bluffs *238*, 239
  Spring House 239
Blue Hill 317
Boothbay Harbor 310–11
Boothbay Railway Village 311
Boston 36, *44*, *45*, *47*, *72*, *98–9*, *105–30*
  see also **Battle of Bunker Hill,
    Boston Harbor islands,
    Cambridge, Harvard
    College (University)**
  Acorn Street *104*
  Back Bay *120*, 120–1
  Beacon Hill (The Hill) 85–6, 116–19
  Beacon Hill Historic District 86
  Beacon Street *118*
  Black Heritage Trail 118
  Boston Athenaeum 114
  Boston Center for the Arts 124
  Boston Common 114–16
  Boston Marine Society 109
  Boston Public Library, 42, *106*, *123*
  Boston Tea Party Ship 110, *111*
  Bostonian Society museum 112
  Brahmins 56, 57, 106
  Bunker Hill Monument 109
  Charles River 126
  Charles Street 119
  Charles Street Meeting House 119
  Charlestown 133
  Chestnut Street *88*, 119
  Children's Museum 110
  Christian Science Church Center *122*, 122–3
  City Hall 112
  Columbus Park 109
  Commandant's House 109
  Commonwealth Avenue (Comm Ave) *120*, 121
  Community Boating 164
  Computer Museum 110
  concerts 124, 125, 126
  Copley Place 121

Boston cont'd
  Copley Square 123–4
  Copps Hill Burying Ground 109
  Custom House Tower 111
  daytrips 139–53
  Downtown Crossing 113
  Duck Tour 123
  Emerald Necklace 115
  Esplanade 126
  Faneuil Hall 111, 112
  Faneuil Hall Marketplace *87*, 107, 111, *112*
  Fenway Park 125, *126*
  festivals, North End 108
  Filene's Basement (bargain store) 113
  First Baptist Church 121
  FleetCenter 126
  Freedom Trail 107, 109, 113, 132–3
  galleries 121
  George Washington statue *105*, 115
  Gibson House 121
  Government Center 107, 112
  Hancock Tower *89*, 123–4, *124*
  harbor cruises (Long Wharf) 109
  Harrison Gray Otis House *86*, 118
  Hatch Memorial Shell 126
  history 46, 105–6
  Isabella Stewart Gardner Museum *125*
  John Hancock Observatory 123–4
  King's Chapel 113
  King's Chapel Burying Ground 132
  Louisburg Square 118, *119*
  Mapparium 122
  Mount Whoredom 117
  MuSEAm Connection water shuttle 109
  Museum of Afro-American History 118
  Museum of Fine Arts 42, 124
  Museum of Science 126
  Museum Wharf 110
  New England Aquarium 110
  New England Holocaust Memorial 112
  Newbury Street 121
  Nichols House 118
  No. 85 Mount Vernon Street 118
  North End 107–9
  Old Corner Bookstore (Boston Globe Bookstore) *113*
  Old Granary Burial Ground *114*
  Old North Church (Christ Church) 108

Boston cont'd
  Old South Meeting House 83, 113, 133
  Old State House 112, *113*, 133
  Park Street Church 114
  Paul Revere House *108*
  Prudential Center (The Pru) 107, 121
  Public Garden 116
  public transportation 139
  restaurants 108
  Revere Mall 108
  Revolutionary (Freedom Trail) 132–3
  Ritz-Carlton Hotel 121
  Sears Crescent 112
  shopping 113, 119
  Skywalk 121
  Somerset Club 118
  South End 124–6
  sports teams 125, 126, 201
  State House *41*, 85, 116–18
  Symphony Hall 124
  The Fenway 124–6
  tours 123
  Trimount 117
  Trinity Church *89*, 123
  USS *Cassin Young* 109
  USS *Constitution* (Old Ironsides) *109*, 133
  USS *Constitution* Museum 109
  Waterfront District 109–11
  whale-watch cruises 110
Boston Brahmins 56, 57
Boston Harbor islands 105, 152
  getting there 152
  George's Island 105, 152
  National Recreation Area 152
  Nix's Mate Island 105
Boston Latin School 42, 63
Boston Marathon 124, 201
Boston Massacre 37
Boston Pops 42, 124, 126
Boston Symphony Orchestra (BSO) 42, 124, 199
Boston Tea Party 37, 133
Bowdoin College (Brunswick) 42, 309
Brandeis University (Waltham) 61
Brattleboro 249
  Brattleboro Museum and Art Center 249
  Latchis Building *249*
  Naulahka 249
  The Common Ground 249
Brewster 163
Bridgeport 216
bridges, covered 273, 279
  Brattleboro 250

bridges, covered cont'd
Sheffield 196
West Cornwall 214
Windsor-Cornish Covered Bridge 251, 279
Bristol 213, 239
Brookfield *252*, 253
Brown, Moses 40
Brown, Nicholas 64
Brown University (Providence) 42, 64, *232*
Brunswick 309
Bulfinch, Charles 84, 85, 86
Boston 116, 129
Hartford 210
Orford 285
Augusta 325
Bunker Hill *see* **Battle of Bunker Hill**
Burgoyne, General John 268
Burlington 262–3
Church Street Marketplace 262
Flynn Theater for the Performing Arts 262
University of Vermont (UVM) 262
Byrd, Admiral Richard E. 119

C

Cabot 258–9
Cabot, John 25, 303
Cambridge 64, 126–30
see also **Harvard College**
Brattle Street 130
Cambridge Common 130
Carpenter Center for the Visual Arts 129
Harvard Cooperative Society (Coop) 127–8
Harvard Square 127, *128*
John. F. Kennedy Library and Museum 127
John Harvard's Brew House 128
Longfellow House *130*
Massachusetts Institute of Technology (MIT) 126–7
musems *see under* **Harvard College**
Out of Town News 127, *128*
Radcliffe College 130
regatta *129*, 201
Camden *315*
Campobello Island 321
Canterbury Shaker Village *283*, 284
Cape Ann *36*–7, 141
Cape Cod 27, 157–70
getting there/around 157, 160
Trails 160

Cape Cod National Seashore 157, 165
Salt Pond Visitor Center 165
Cape Cod School of Art 167
Cape Elizabeth 306
Cartier, Jacques *25*
casinos
Foxwoods (Ledyard) 55, 222, 223
Mohegan Sun (Uncasville) 223
Cassatt, Mary 212, 213
Castine 311, 316
Cathedral Ledge (NH) 295
Cathedral of the Pines (Rindge) 284
Center Sandwich 286
Champlain, Samuel de 261
Chappaquiddick Island 173
Charlestown 284
Chatham 168
Cheeshahteaumuck, Caleb 30
Chester 219, 251
National Survey Charthouse 251
Chesuncook 322
Choate, Joseph 199
Christian Science 122–3
Church Center (Boston) 122
Christiantown 174
churches and meeting houses
architecture 86
Baptist Church (Providence) 83
Charles Street Meeting House (Boston) 119
Congregational Church (Litchfield) 213
Congregational Meetinghouse (Wethersfield) 212
First Baptist Church (Boston) 121
First Baptist Church (Providence) 232
New Haven 217
Old First Church (Bennington) 268
Old Indian Meetinghouse (Mashpee) 169
Old North Church (Christ Church) (Boston) 108
Old Ship Meetinghouse (Hingham) 82, 150
Old South Meeting House (Boston) 83, 113, 133
Old Whaling Church (Edgartown) 173
Park Street Church (Boston) 114
Trinity Church (Boston) *89*, 123
Trinity Church (Newport, RI) 234
West Parish Meeting House (near Barnstaple) *83*

Civil War 245, 262
clams/clambakes 68–9, 141
Columbus, Christopher 25
Conanicut Island 239
Concord (MA) 28, 146, 147–9
Concord Museum 148
Old North Bridge *149*
Orchard House 148
Ralph Waldo Emerson House 148
Sleepy Hollow Cemetery 148, 149
The Old Manse 149
The Wayside 147–8
writers 148, 149
Concord (NH) 282–3
Christa McAuliffe Planetarium 283
League of New Hampshire Craftsmen 283
Museum of New Hampshire Society 283
State House 282
Connecticut 28, 205–23
black population 59
history 58, 205–9
industry 208
Connecticut River *192*, 193, 205, 219
cruises 219
source 295
state boundary 249
Valley 284–5
Valley Railroad 219
Constitution State 205
Continental Congress 37, 38, 278
Conway Scenic Railway 295
Coolidge, President Calvin 57, 266
President Coolidge Birthplace and Homestead (Plymouth, VT) 265
Cornish 285
cotton mills 40, 41, 46
covered bridges *see* **bridges, covered**
crafts
Haystack Mountain School of Crafts (Deer Isle) 316
in Vermont 255
League of New Hampshire Craftsmen 283, 287
Putney 250
Vermont State Craft Center (Frog Hollow, Middlesbury) 255, 264
web site (Vermont) 255
Craftsbury Common 260
cranberries 69, 166
Crawford, Abel and 294

Crawford, Ethan Allen 294
Crawford Notch 288, 294
Curley, James Michael 45, *46*, 57
Cushing 314
Cushing, Caleb 139

d

Dairy Mill Hill 253
Dartmouth College (Hanover) 42, 64, *285*
Dawes, William 37, 132
Declaration of Independence 38, 133
Deep River 219
Deer Isle 316–17
Dennis 162–3
Desert of Maine 309
Dickinson, Emily 42, 191, 192
Homestead (Amherst) 191
Dixville Notch 295
Dorset 266
DuBois, W.E.B. 197
Dwight, Timothy 56

e

East Haddam *219*, 220
Eastham *154–5*, 165
Eddy, Mary Baker 122, 123
Edgartown *173*, *175*
education 42, 63, 64
Eisenstaedt, Alfred 174
Eliot, Charles W. 317
Emerson, Ralph Waldo 37, *66*, 67, 105, 149
burial place (Concord, MA) 148
House/study (Concord, MA) 148
Erikson, Leif 23
Essex *140*, 141, 219

f

fairs *see* festivals and fairs
fall, the *6–7*, 184–5, *196*, 261, 292
foliage hotline numbers 292
web site 292
Fall River 152
Battleship Cove 152
Factory Outlet (Heart) District 153
Marine Museum 152
Falmouth *169*, 170
Faneuil, Peter 111, 113
Farmington 212
farms
Shelburne Farms 263
UVM Morgan Horse Farm (Weybridge) 264

farms cont'd
Vermont Wildflower Farm (Charlotte) 263
Farnsworthy, "Aunt" Lucy 314
Farnum, Tom 312
festivals and fairs
see also music
Aston Magna Festival (Great Barrington) 199
Ben and Jerry's Folk Festival (Newport, RI) 237
Berkshire Theater Festival (Stockbridge) 199
Domestic Resurrection Circus (Bread and Puppet Theater) (Glover) 260
Eastern States Exposition (Big E) (West Springfield) 194
Jacob's Pillow Dance Festival (Becket) 199
JVC Jazz Festival (Newport, RI) 237
Marlboro Music Festival 249
Mozart and Shakespeare festivals (Burlington) 262
Stowe Winter Carnival 257
Vermont Maple Festival (St Albans) 262
Williamstown Theater Festival 199
Fisher, Dorothy Canfield 268
Martha Canfield Library (Arlington) 268
Fisher, Dr Daniel 173
Fisher, Jonathan 317
fishing 73, *76*, 77, 164, 261, 266, 267
food 68–71
food, gourmet/specialty 70
Ben & Jerry's Homemade Ice Cream Factory (Waterbury) 256
Cabot 258–9
Grafton Village Cheese Company 251
Polly's Pancake Parlor (maple syrup) (Sugar Hill) *290*
Waterbury 256
forests
Martha's Vineyard State Forest 173
White Mountain National Forest 279, 287
Fort Dummer 249
Fort Edgecoomb 310
Fort Good Hope 205
Fort Knox 316
Fort McClary 304
Fort Saybrook 218

Fort Western 325
Fort William Henry 311
Foxwoods High Stakes and Bingo (casino) 55, 222, 223
Franconia 289
Franconia Notch *270–1*, 289
Franconia Notch Bike Tour 164
Freeport 153, 308–9
French-Canadians 60, 282
L'Association Canado-Américaine (Manchester, NH) 282
French, Daniel Chester 149, 283
Chesterwood (near Stockbridge) 199
Frost, Robert 42, 264
grave (Bennington) 268
Interpretive Trail (Ripton) 264
Place (Franconia) 285

g

Gage, General Thomas 35, 37, 38, 149
Galilee 239
gambling 223
Garrison, William Lloyd 44, 67, 114
Gay Head *174*
Gehring, Dr John 324
geology 21, 170, 301
Gilbert, Sir Humphrey 26
Gillette Castle (Hadlyme) 219–20
Gillette, William 219, 220
Gloucester 142
Gorges, Sir Ferdinando 26, 29, 276, 303
Gosnold, Bartholomew 26, 158
Grafton 87, 250–1
Graniteville 253
Great Barrington 197
Greenville 322, 323
Griswold, Florence 218
Groton 220
Guilford 205, 218

h

Hadlyme 219
Hammond Castle (Gloucester) 143
Hancock, John 39, 114
Hancock Shaker Village 200
Hanover 285
Harrisville 88, 284
Hartford 29, 207, 209–12
Bushnell Memorial Auditorium 211
Bushnell Park 211
Connecticut State Capitol *210*, 211

Hartford cont'd
Constitution Plaza *211*
Harriet Beecher Stowe House
212
Mark Twain Memorial *212*
Observation Deck 211
Old State House 210
Phoenix Mutual Life Insurance
Building 211
State Library 211
Travelers Tower 211
Wadsworth Atheneum 42,
210–11
Hartford Insurance Company
209–10
Harvard College (University) 28,
42, 64, 128–30
Arthur Sackler Museum 130
Botanical Museum 130
Carpenter Center for the Visual
Arts 129–30
Fogg and Busch-Reisinger Art
Museums 130
Harvard Houses 129
Harvard Yard 128
Massachusetts Hall 129
Mineralogical and Geological
Museum 130
Museum of Comparative Zoology
130
Peabody Museum of Archaeology
and Ethnology 130
University Hall 129
Widener Library 129
Harvard, John 64, 129
Harvard (town) 187
Harvard, William 325
Harwich Port 168
Hassam, Childe 219, 282
Hawthorne, Charles Webster 167
Hawthorne, Nathaniel *66*, 67, 148,
149, 290
burial place (Concord, MA) 149
replica cottage (Tanglewood) 199
The Great Stone Face 289
Hingham 150
Hull Lifesaving Museum 150
Nantasket 150
Old Ship Meetinghouse 150
World's End Reservation 150
historic houses
see also **architecture**
Blithewold (Bristol) 239
Boston 118, 119, 120, 121
Capen House (Topsfield) 81
Captain Bangs Hallett House
(Yarmouth Port) 162
Castle in the Clouds (near
Moultonboro) 286

historic houses cont'd
Chester 251
Clark House (Wolfeboro) 286
Dexter Mill and the Hoxie House
(Sandwich) *81*, 161
Dr Daniel Fisher House
(Edgartown) 173
Falmouth 170
Forest Hall (the Barrett House)
(New Ipswich) 284
Grafton 250–1
Great House (Ipswich) 140
Gropius House (Lincoln) 88, 149
Guilford 218
Hancock-Clarke House
(Lexington) 147
Historic Deerfield 190, 191
Holley-Williams House (Lakeville)
214
Jeremiah Lee Mansion
(Marblehead) 145
Jericho House (South Dennis)
169
Kennebunkport 306
Litchfield 84, 213
National Landmark Historic
District (Nantucket) 178, 180
Newfane 250
Newport (RI) mansions 234, 235
(*see under* **Newport (RI)** for
mansions by name)
Old Deerfield 83, 190–1
Orford 285
Paper House (Rockport) 142
Plymouth 151
Portland (ME) 307
Portsmouth (NH) 83, 280, 281
Providence 231
Salem 144, 145
Sleeper-McCann (Beauport)
House (Gloucester) 143
Spencer-Pierce-Little Farm (near
Newburyport) 140
The Cushing House
(Newburyport) 139
Vincent House (Edgartown) 173
Wethersfield 212
Whipple House (Ipswich) *81*,
140
Wing Fort House (East Sandwich)
81
Winslow Crocker House
(Yarmouth Port) 162
Wiscasset 310
York 304
historical parks and historical sites
Adams National Historical Site
(Quincy) 150
Lowell National Historic Park 88

historical parks and historical sites
cont'd
Marsh–Billings National Historic
Park (Woodstock) 253
Minute Man National Historical
Park (Battle Road) 146
Saint-Gaudens National Historic
Site (Cornish) 285
Springfield Armory National
Historic Site 193
history 18–19
see also under individual states
prehistory–1670s 20–31
late 17th–19th centuries 35–42
20th century 44–7
Holmes, Oliver Wendell 105
Homer, Winslow 42, 307
Hooker, Reverend Thomas 28, 205
Housatonic River 197
Howells, William Dean 118, 262
Hudson River School of painters
187, 259, 317
Hutchinson, Anne 29, 30, 227
Hutchinson, Governor Thomas 36,
37
Hyannis 169
Cape Cod Melody Tent 169
John F. Kennedy Museum 169

i

Ice Age 21, 22
ice cream 71, 128, 256
ice, harvest/export 75, 253
ice-hockey 126
immigration 44, 59–61, 71, 208
Indians 24, 28, 31, 54 197, 198,
276, 277
see also **Algonquin tribes** *and*
under individual tribe names
industry 40, 46, 47, 75
see also under individual states
Ingram, David 313
insurance 47, 209, 210
Ipswich, 28, 140
Irish immigrants 44, 59–60, 106–7
Isla La Motte 262
Isle au Haut 317
Isles of Shoals 281
Italian immigrants 61, 71, 233
Ivy League colleges 217

j

Jackson 295
Jackson Falls 295
Jamaica 250
James, Henry 114, 284
Jamestown 239

Jarvis, Deming 161
Jeffersonville 258
Jewish immigrants 61, 227

k

Kancamagus Highway 288
Karlsefni, Thorfin 23
Keene 284
Kennebunkport 306
　architectural walking tour 306
　Brick Store Museum 306
　Kennebunkport Book Port 306
　Seashore Trolley Museum 306
　Wedding Cake House *306*
Kennedy, Edward 173
Kennedy, Joe 60
Kennedy, John F. Fitzgerald
　("Honey-Fitz") 60
Kennedy, John Fitzgerald *46*
Kezar Lake 324
King, Melvin 60
King Philip's War *31*, 277
Kingfield 323
Kipling Rudyard 249, 253
　Naulahka (house, Brattleboro) 249
Kittery 153, 303
Kopechne, Mary Jo 173

l

Lake Champlain 22, *261*, 261–2
　cruises 262
　Four Brothers Islands 261
Lake Memphrémagog 260–1
Lake Sunapee 286
Lake Waramaug 215
Lake Winnipesaukee 285
Lakes Region 285–7
Lakeville 214
leaf-peeping see fall, the
Lehr, Harry 233
Lenox *198*, 199
　The Mount 199
Lexington 146, 147
　Battle Green 147
　Buckman Tavern 147
　Hancock-Clarke House 147
libraries 42
　Athenaeum/Art Gallery (St
　　Johnsbury) 259
　Beinecke Rare Book and
　　Manuscript Library (Yale
　　University, New Haven) 217
　Boston Athenaeum 114
　Boston Public Library 42, *106*,
　　123
　John F. Kennedy Library and
　　Museum (Cambridge) 127

libraries cont'd
　Nantucket Atheneum 178–9
　presidential libraries 127
　Providence Atheneum 232
　Providence Atheneum 42
　Redwood Library and Atheneum
　　(Newport) 234
　Wadsworth Atheneum (Hartford)
　　42, 210
lighthouses 320
　Bass Harbor Head Lighthouse
　　(Mount Desert Island) 320
　Boston Light 150
　Brant Point (Nantucket) *96*, 181
　Cape Cod Light (Highland Light)
　　166
　Chatham Light 168
　Gay Head *174*
　Great (New Castle) Island 282
　Great Point Lighthouse
　　(Nantucket) *176*, 181
　museums 313, 314, 320
　Nauset Light Beach 165
　Nubble Light (York Beach) 305,
　　320
　Pemaquid Point Lighthouse *311*,
　　313, 320
　Portland Head Light (Cape
　　Elizabeth) *298–9*, 306, 320
　Stonington 222
　West Chop Lighthouse (Vineyard
　　Haven) 172
　West Quoddy Head Lighthouse
　　320
Lincoln (MA) 88, 146, 149
Lincoln (NH) 288
Litchfield 213–14, *214*
　houses 84, 213
　school of law 214
Litchfield Hills 213–15
Livermore 324
living history
　Fort at Number 4 (Charlestown)
　　284
　Mystic Seaport 221–2
　Norlands Living History Center
　　(Livermore) 324
lobsters and lobstering 68, 312
　guided lobstering trips 312
logging *277*, 321
Longfellow, Henry Wadsworth 38,
　42
　House (Cambridge) 130
　Wadsworth-Longfellow House
　　(Portland, ME) 307–8
　Wreck of the Hesperus 306
Lost River (North Woodstock)
　288
Lowell 88, 146

Lowell, Francis Cabot 40, 56
Lubec 320

m

Machias 320
MacMillan, Donald 309
Madison 218
Maine 301–25
　history 57, 301, 303
　leaf-peeping (fall foliage) 292
　Mid-coast 309–11, 313
　North Woods 321–3
　South Coast 303–6
Maine Maritime Academy
　(Castine) 316
Maine Photographic Workshops
　(Rockport) 314
Manasee tribe 239
Manchester (MA) 143, 245, 266–7
　American Museum of Fly Fishing
　　267
　Equinox hotel 266
　fishing 266, 267
　Hildene 267
　Norman Rockwell Exhibition 267
　outlet shopping 153, 267
　Skyline Drive 266
　Southern Vermont Art Center
　　267
Manchester (NH) 282
　Currier Gallery of Art 282
　L'Association Canado-Américaine
　　282
　Manchester Historical
　　Association 282
　Zimmerman House 282
maple syrup 69–70, 245, *290*
Marblehead 145
March, Sylvester 293
Marconi, Guglielmo 165
maritime tradition 39, 72–7
Marlboro 249
Marsh, George Perkins 252
Martha's Vineyard 170–5
　beaches 171
Mashanlucket Pequot tribe 223
Mashpee 169
Mason, Captain John 29, 276
Massachusetts 39, 105–95
　Boston 105–33
　Central 187–95
　industry 189, 195
　liquor laws 67
Massachusetts Bay Colony 28, 63
Massachusetts Institute of
　Technology (MIT) 126–7
Mather, Cotton 18, 30, 56, 65
　grave (Boston) 109

Mayflower 27, 72, 158
Mayflower Compact 35, 158–9
Mayhew, Thomas 170, 174
Mayhew, Thomas Jr 173
McIntire, Samuel 84, 85
meetinghouses 82, 83
see also under **churches**
Melville, Herman 42, 200
Menemsha 174
Merrimack Valley 282–4
Middlebury 264
Mill River 196
Millay, Edna St Vincent 315
Minute Man **statue (Concord, MA)**
149
Minutemen 37, 147
Mitchell, Maria 179
Mohegan tribe 53, 54, 239
Mohegan Sun (casino) 223
Mohican tribe 197, 198
Monhegan Island *313*, 313–14
Monomoy Island 168
Montpelier 254–5
New England Culinary Institute
255
Pavilion Hotel 254
Vermont Historical Society
Museum 255
Vermont State House *254*
Moosehead Lake 322, 323
Morgan horse 264
Morison, Samuel Eliot 199
Mosher, Howard Frank 258
Moultonboro 286
Mount Desert Island (Acadia
National Park) 317–20
Acadia Wild Garden 319
Bar Harbor 318
Bass Harbor Head Lighthouse
320
Cadillac Mountain 319
Oceanarium 320
Robert Abbe Museum 319
Sand Beach 319
Thuya Gardens 319
Trails 319
Visitor Center (Hulls Cove) 318
Mount Holyoke College (South
Hadley) 193
Mount Washington (hamlet) 196
Mount Washington (mountain)
290–1, 293
Cog Railway *291*, 293
Mount Washington Auto Road
291
Mount Washington Hotel *293*
Mount Washington Observatory
Museum 291
Tip Top House 291

mountains
see also **Mount Washington, ski**
resorts/areas
Appalachian system 21
Attitash Bear Peak 295
Baxter Peak 321
Berkshire Hills 21, 195–200
Cadillac Mountain 319
Equinox 266
formation of 21
Green Mountains 21, *242–3*,
255–8
Hoosac Mountains (Berkshire
Barrier) 195
Jiminy Peak 200
Knife Edge 321
Monument Mountain 197
Mount Ascutney 252
Mount Greylock 200
Mount Katahdin 301, 321
Mount Mansfield 256, 257
Mount Monadnock 21, 284
Mount Peg 252
Mount Willard 288
Mount Tom 252, 253
Pamola Peak 321, 322
Presidental Range 290
Taconic Mountains 21
White Mountains 21, *90–1*,
92–3, 270–1, 287–91, 293
museums and art collections
see also **libraries**
American Clock and Watch
Museum (Bristol) 213
American Museum of Fly Fishing
(Manchester, MA) 267
American Precision Museum
(Windsor) 251
Arthur Sackler Museum (Harvard,
Cambridge) 130
Athenaeum/Art Gallery (St
Johnsbury) 259
Barnum Museum (Bridgeport)
216
Basketball Hall of Fame
(Springfield) 193
Bennington Museum and
Grandma Moses Gallery 268
Billings Farm Museum
(Woodstock) 252
Boott Cotton Mills Museum
(Lowell) 146
Boston Center for the Arts 124
Boston Marine Society 109
Bostonian Society museum 112
Botanical Museum (Harvard,
Cambridge) 130
Brattleboro Museum and Art
Center 249

museums and art collections cont'd
Bread and Puppet Museum
(Glover) 260
Burnham Tavern (Machias) 320
Cape Ann Historical Association
(Gloucester) 142
Cape Cod Museum of Natural
History (Brewster) 163
Cape Cod Museum of Natural
History (Chatham) 168
Chatham Railroad Museum
168
Children's Museum (Boston)
110
Children's Museum of Maine
(Portland, ME) 307
Christa McAuliffe Planetarium
(Concord, NH) 283
Colonel John Ashley House
(Ashley Falls) 195–6
Colonial Pemaquid Restoration
311
Concord Museum (NH) 148
Connecticut River Museum
(Essex) 219
Connecticut Valley Historical
Museum (Springfield) 194
Currier Gallery of Art
(Manchester, NH) 282
Dairy Mill Hill (Mormon museum)
253
DeCordova Museum and
Sculpture Park (Lincoln) 149
Fairbanks Museum and
Planetarium (St Johnsbury)
259
Falmouth Historical Society
Museum 170
Farnsworth Art Museum
(Rockland) 314
Fishermen's Museum (Pemaquid
Point Lighthouse) 313
Florence Griswold Museum (Old
Lyme) 218–19
Fogg and Busch-Reisinger Art
Museums (Harvard,
Cambridge) 130
French Cable Museum (Orleans)
168
Fruitlands Museum (Harvard)
187
George Walter Vincent Smith Art
Museum (Springfield) 194
Henry Whitfield State Museum
(Guilford) 218
Heritage Plantation (Sandwich)
161
Higgins Armory Museum
(Worcester) 189

museums and art collections cont'd
Hill-Stead Museum (Farmington) 212
Hood Museum of Art (Hanover) 285
Hull Lifesaving Museum (Hingham) 150
Hyland House (Guilford) 218
Indian Museum (Harvard) 187
International Tennis Hall of Fame (Newport, RI) 235
Isabella Stewart Gardner Museum (Boston) *125*
John F. Kennedy Library and Museum (Cambridge) 127
John F. Kennedy Museum (Hyannis) 169
Kittery Historical and Naval Museum 304
Lake Champlain Maritime Museum (Vergennes) 261–2
Life Saving Museum (Nantucket) 179
Lumberman's Museum (Patten) 321
Maine Maritime Museum and Shipyard (Bath) 310
Maine State Museum (Augusta) 325
Maria Mitchell Science Center (Nantucket) 179
Marine Museum (Fall River) 152
Maritime Museum (Newburyport) 139
Maritime Museum and Albacore Park (Portsmouth, NH) 281
Mashantucket Pequot Museum and Research Center 222, 223
Mayflower Society Museum (Plymouth, MA) 151
Mead Art Museum (Amherst) 192
Mineralogical and Geological Museum (Harvard, Cambridge) 130
Montshire Museum of Science (Norwich) 285
Moosehead Marine Museum 322
Mount Washington Observatory Museum 291
Museum of Afro-American History (Boston) 118
Museum of Art (Brunswick) 309
Museum of Childhood (Wakefield) 286
Museum of Comparative Zoology (Harvard, Cambridge) 130
Museum of Fine Arts (Boston) 124

museums and art collections cont'd
Museum of Fine Arts (Springfield) 194
Museum of New Hampshire History (Concord, NH) 283
Museum of Newport History (RI) 234
Museum of Our National Heritage (Lexington) 146
Museum of Portland Head Light 306
Museum of Science (Boston) 126
Museum of Yachting (Newport, RI) 237
New England Fire and History Museum (Brewster) 163
New England Quilt Museum (Lowell) 146
New England Ski Museum (Cannon Mountain) 289
New England Ski Museum (Franconia) 269
New England Sports Museum (Lowell) 146
Newport Art Museum (RI) 235
Norman Rockwell Exhibition (Manchester, MA) 267
Norman Rockwell Museum (Stockbridge) 198
Ogunquit Museum of American Art 305
Old Constitution House (Windsor) 251
Old Lincoln County Jail and Museum (Wiscasset) 310
Old Schoolhouse Museum (Vineyard Haven) 172
Old Stone House Museum (Brownington) 260
Orgonon (Wilhem Reich Museum) (Rangeley) 324
Owl's Head Transportation Museum (Rockland) 314
Peabody Essex Museum (Salem) 144
Peabody Museum of Archaeology and Ethnology (Harvard, Cambridge) 130
Peary-MacMillan Arctic Museum (Brunswick) 309
Pejepscot Historical Society Museum (Brunswick) 309
Penobscot Marine Museum (Searsport) 315
Peter Foulger Museum (Nantucket) 178
Peterborough Historical Society and Museum 284

museums and art collections cont'd
Pilgrim Hall (Plymouth) 151
Portland Museum of Art (ME) 307
Provincetown Art Association and Museum 167
Provincetown Heritage Museum 167
Provincetown Museum 168
Rhode Island School of Design (RISD) Museum of Art (Providence) 232
Robert Abbe Museum (Mount Desert Island) 319
Salem Witch Museum 145
Sandwich Glass Museum 161
Science Museum (Springfield) 194
Seashore Trolley Museum (Kennebunkport) 306
Shelburne Museum 263
Shore Line Trolley Museum (East Haven) 217
Shore Village Museum (Rockland) 314
Sloane-Stanley Museum (Kent Falls State Park) 215
Smith College Museum of Art (Northampton) 192
Springfield Armory National Historic Site 193
Stanley Museum (Kingsfield) 323
Sterling and Francine Clark Art Institute (Williamstown) 200
Stillman Building (Mystic Seaport) 222
Storrowton Village Museum (West Springfield) 194
Strawbery Banke Museum (Portsmouth, NH) 280, *281*
The Sugar Hill Historical Museum 289
The Vineyard Museum (Edgartown) 173
Thomas Griswold House (Guilford) 218
Trayser Memorial Museum (Sandy Neck) 162
USS *Constitution* Museum (Boston) 109
Vermont Historical Society Museum (Montpelier) 255
Wadsworth Atheneum (Hartford) 42, 210–11
Webb-Deane-Stevens Museum (Hartford) 212
Whaling Museum (Nantucket) 178
Whaling Museum (New Bedford) 152

museums and art collections cont'd
Willowbrook at Newfield
(museum village) 325
Witch Dungeon Museum (Salem)
145
Worcester Art Museum (189
Worcester Historical Museum
189
Words and Pictures Museum
(Northampton) 192
Yale Center of British Art (New
Haven) 217
Yale University Art Gallery (New
Haven) 217
music 194, 199
see also festivals, Tanglewood
Mystic 221
Mystic Seaport 221–2

n

Nantucket *177*, 177–81
Aquarium 180
Brant Point lighthouse 181
Hadwen House 180
Jared Coffin House *180*
Jethro Coffin House 180
Life Saving Museum 179
Maria Mitchell Science Center
179–80
Nantucket Atheneum 178–9
National Landmark Historic
District 178
No. 99 Main Street 180
Old Goal 180
Old Mill 179
Old South Wharf 178
Peter Foulger Museum 178
Straight Wharf 178
Three Bricks 180
Two Greeks 180
Upper Main Street 177
Whaling Museum 178
Nantucket island 175–82
beaches 182
Nantucket Moors 182
Narragansett 239
Narragansett Bay 227, *229*
Narrangansett tribe 24, 29, 31,
53, 54, 55
National Historic Landmark
Portsmouth (NH) 281
Salem 85, 145
Native American 55–6, 174
see also Algonquin tribes,
reservations
Naumkeaq 199
Nauset tribe 24
Nevelson, Louise 314

New Bedford 152
New England
see also history
origin of name 26
people 53–61
states of 20
New Hampshire 273–95
history 58, 275–80
North Country 295
politics/Presidential primaries
273, 274, 275
Town Meeting/Day 274
New Haven 29, 207, 216–18
see also Yale College
(University)
churches 217
Shore Line Trolley Museum (East
Haven) 217
Yale Repertory Theater 217
New Ipswich 284
New London 220
New Marlborough 196
Newburyport *139*, 139–40
Newfane *78–9*, *245*, 250
Newman, Robert 108
Newport (RI) 233–7
beaches 237
Beechwood Mansion 236
Belcourt Castle 236
Bellevue Avenue 234
Brenton Point State Park 237
Château-sur-Mer 235
Cliff Walk 236
Fort Adams State Park 237
Historic Hill 234
Hunter House 234
International Tennis Hall of Fame
235
Kingscote 235
mansions 234, 235
Marble House 236
Museum of Newport History 234
Museum of Yachting 237
Naval War College 228
Newport Art Museum 235
Ocean Drive *234*, 237
Old Stone Mill 234
Redwood Library and Atheneum
234
Rosecliff Manor *224–5*, *226*,
236
The Breakers 235–6, *236*
The Elms 235
The Point 234
Theater 235
Touro Synagogue 234, 235
Trinity Church 234
Villa Marina *227*
yachting 164, 237

Newport (VT) 261
newspapers, early 42
Newtowne College 64
Niantic tribe 24
Nickerson, Roland 163
Nipmuc tribe 24, 31
Norfolk 214
North Conway 153, 295
North Salem 282
North Woodstock 288
Northampton (NoHo) 192–3
Norwich *259*

o

Oak Bluffs *171*, 172
Occum, Samson 54
Oelrichs, Mrs Hermann 236
Ogunquit 305–6
Marginal Way 305
Ogunquit Museum of American
Art 305
Ogunquit Playhouse 305
Perkins Cove 305
Old Deerfield 83, 190–1
Old Lyme 218–19
**Old Man of the Mountain (Profile
Lake)** *289*
Old Saybrook 207, *215*, 218
Old Sturbridge Village *186*, *189*,
190–1
Olmsted, Frederick Law 115, 150,
193, 263
On Golden Pond 286, 287
Orford 285
Orleans 168
Orvis, Charles and Franklin 266
Osterville 169
Otis, Harrison Gray 86
Otis, James 112, 132

p

Pairpoint Glass Works (Cape Cod)
160
Parker, Captain John 147
Parker, Daniel 118
Parrish, Maxfield 252
Patten 321
Pawtucket 239
Slater Mill Historic Site 239
Pearce, Simon 253
Peary, Admiral Robert 42, 309
Pemaquid Point 311
Colonial Pemaquid Restoration
(museum) 311
Fort William Henry 311
Lighthouse *311*, 313
Pennacook tribe 24, 276

Penobscot Bay *10–11*, 314–16
Penobscot tribe 55
Pequot tribe 31, 53, 55, 223
Perkins Cove, Ogunquit *305*
Peterborough 284
Philip (Wampanoag *sachem*) 31, 54
Phillips Academy (Andover) 64
Phillips, Dr John 64, 141
Phillips Exeter Academy (Exeter) 64
Phillips, Samuel 64
Phips, Governor General Sir William 66
Pierce, President Franklin 42, 278
Pilgrims 27, *28*, 72, 165
Pine Tree State 301
Pinkham Notch 288, 290, 294
   Visitor Center 294
Pioneer Valley 191
Pittsfield 200
Plant, Thomas Gustave 286
Plimoth Plantation *27*, *150*, 151
Plum Island 139–40
Plymouth (MA) 28, 72, 151–2
   Howland House 152
   Mayflower II, 151
   Mayflower Society Museum 151
   Pilgrim Hall (museum) 151
   Richard Sparrow House 151
   Rock 27, 151
Plymouth (VT) 265
Plymouth Colony (MA) 29
Plymouth Company 26, 27
Plymouth Rock (MA) 27, 151
Pocumtuck tribe 24, 190
Poe, Edgar Allen 42, 232
politics 46, 60
Pope, Alfred Atmore 212
Porter, Rufus 194, 324
Portland (ME) 306–8
   Calendar Islands/cruises 308
   Children's Museum of Maine 307
   Old Port Exchange 307
   Portland Museum of Art 307
   Victoria Mansion 307
   Wadsworth-Longfellow House 307
   Western Promenade 307
Portsmouth (NH) *280*, 280–2
   Isles of Shoals/cruise 281
   Maritime Museum and Albacore Park 281
   Moffat-Ladd House 281
   Portsmouth Passport (historic houses walking tour) 280
   Strawbery Banke Museum 280, *281*

Portsmouth (NH) cont'd
   Warner House 281
   Wentworth-Gardner House 83
   whale-watching trips 282
Portsmouth (RI) 239
   Green Animals Topiary Gardens 239
Portsmouth Navy Yard 303–4
Portuguese immigrants 61, 71, 167, 232
powwow 24, 55
Praying Towns 30, 54, 174
Precision Valley 251
Prescott, Colonel William 38, 147
Proctor 264
Profile Lake 287
Providence 29, 229–33
   1828 Arcade 87, *230*, 231
   artists 230
   Baptist Church 83
   Benefit Street *83*, *231*
   Brown University *232*
   College Hill 232
   Constitution Hill 230
   Customs House 231
   East Bay Bicycle Path 233
   Federal Hill 233
   First Baptist Church 232
   Fox Point 233
   John Brown House 232
   Kennedy Plaza 231
   Old State House 232
   Prospect Terrace park 232
   Providence Atheneum 232
   Providence Station 231
   Rhode Island School of Design (RISD) Museum of Art 232
   shopping 232
   State Capitol 230
   Superman Building 231
   Turk's Head Building 231
   Waterplace Park 230–1
Provincetown 166–8
   art colony 167
   art galleries 167
   beaches 168
   Exhibition Whydah 168
   gay population 166
   Pilgrim Memorial 168
   Province Lands Visitors' Center 168
   Provincetown Art Association and Museum 167
   Provincetown Heritage Museum *167*
   writers 167
Provincial Congress 37
Puritans 27, 28, 35, 56, 63–7
   see also school system

Putnam, General Israel 207
Putney 250

q
Quabbin Reservoir 190
Quakers 227
Quechee 253
Quechee Gorge 253
Quincy 150
Quincy, Edmund 57
Quisset Harbor *170*

r
racism/race riots 44, 59, 60
Rangeley 324
Red Paint People 303
Redcoats 36, 37, 38, 147
Reich, Wilhelm 324
religion 26–30, 56, 63
   camp meeting site (Oak Bluffs) *171*, 172
Remond, Charles 59
reservations 54, 55
   Crane Memorial Reservation 139
   Mashantucket Pequot Reservation 222, 223
   Wasque Reservation (Chappaquiddick Island) 173
   World's End Reservation (Hingham) 150
resorts 293
   Craftsbury Center Sports Resort 260
   Mount Washington Hotel 293
   Old Orchard Beach 306
   Stowe Mountain Resort 257
   The Balsams (Dixville Notch) 295
   Woodstock Inn and Resort 253
Revenue Act 1764 36
Revere, Paul 37, 38, 108, *132*, 147
   burial place (Boston) 114
   House (Boston) 133
Revolutionary War 36, 38, 176, 207, 268, 278, 320
   Freedom Trail (Boston) 132–3
Rhode Island 29, 30, 227–39
   beaches 239
   Constitution 39
   history 45, 227–30
   Yankees 58
Rhode Island College *see* Brown University
Rindge 284
Ripton 264
rock hunting 324
Rock, John Swett 59

Rock of Ages Quarry 253–4
Rockefeller, Laurence 252
Rockland 314
Rockport (MA) *141*, 141–2
Rockport (ME) 314
Rockwell, Norman 284
  Exhibition (Manchester, MA) 267
  Museum (Stockbridge) 198
Roosevelt, Franklin Delano
  house (Campobello Island) 321
Rutland 265

s

Sacred Cod 73, 117
Sagamore Bridge 160
Saint-Gaudens, Augustus 285
Salem 64, 143–5, 145
  architecture 84
  Chestnut Street 85, 145
  Gardner-Pingree house 84, 85
  House of the Seven Gables 144
  Peabody Essex Museum 144
  Salem Maritime National Historic
    Site 144
  Salem Witch Museum *144*, 145
  Salem Witch Trials Tercentenary
    Memorial 145
  Stephen Phillips Memorial Trust
    House 145
  web site 144
  Witch Dungeon Museum 145
  witches/witch trials 64–6, 144
Sandwich 161, *162*
Sandy Neck 162
Sargeant, John 197
Saugus Iron Works 145
Schoodic Peninsula 320
school system 42, 63
sea kayaking 164
Searsport 315
Sebago Lakes 325
Sedgewick, General John 245
Serkin, Rudolf 250
Seven Sisters colleges 217
Shakers 187, 197, 200, 283, 284
  Canterbury Shaker Village *283*,
    284
  Hancock Shaker Village 200
Shay's Rebellion 39
Sheffield 196
Shelburne 263
shopping
  factory outlet stores 153, 189,
    295
Siasconset 182
ski resorts/areas *244*, 269
  Ascutney 252
  Bromley Mountain 267

ski resorts/areas cont'd
  Burke 259–60
  Cannon Mountain 289
  Jay Peak 261
  Jiminy Peak 200
  Killington 265, 269
  Mad River Glen 255
  Mount Mansfield 257
  Mount Snow (including
    Wilmington and West Dover)
    250, 269
  New Hampshire 279
  Pico 265
  Smuggler's Notch 257, 269
  Stowe 256–7
  Sugarbush 255, 269, *323*
  Sugarloaf *323*
  Suicide Six (Woodstock) 253
  Sunday River 324
  Wachusett Mountain State Park
    187
  Wildcat (Pinkham Notch) 294
skiing 187, 200, *244*
  cross-country 257, 269
  Graduated Length Method 269
  snow report 269
  Sunday River Cross-Country Ski
    Center 324
Slater, Samuel 40
slavery 57, 58, 67
Sloane, Eric 215
Smith, Captain John 26, 282, 303
Smith, Joseph 253
Smuggler's Notch 257
snowboarding (snurfing) 269, 323
Society for the Preservation of
  New England Antiquities 86,
    149, 284, 310
South Norwalk (SoNo) 215–16
South Dennis 169
Southbury *202–3*
sporting activities 164, 201, 255
Springfield 193–4
  see also West Springfield
  Basketball Hall of Fame *193*
  Connecticut Valley Historical
    Museum 194
  George Walter Vincent Smith Art
    Museum 194
  Museum of Fine Arts 194
  Riverfront Park 193
  Science Museum 194
  Springfield Armory National
    Historic Site 193
  Springfield Museum Quadrangle
    194
  StageWest 194
  Student Prince and Fort
    Restaurant 194

Squam Lake 286, 287
Squanto 28
St Albans 262
St Anne's Shrine (Isla La Motte)
  262
St Johnsbury 259
Stamp Act 1765 35, 36
Standish, Captain Miles (Captain
  Shrimp) 27
Stanley, F.O. and F.E. 323
Stanley, William 197
Stark, General John 268
state and national parks
  Acadia National Park 317–20
  Baxter State Park 321–2
  Brenton Point State Park 237
  Camden Hills State Park 315
  Fort Adams State Park 237
  Hailbut Point State Park 141
  Hammonasset Beach State Park
    218
  Holyoke Range State Park 193
  Nickerson State Park 163
  Kent Falls State Park 214–15
  Mount Sunapee State Park 280
  Odiorne Point State Park 282
  Popham Beach State Park 310
  Quoddy Head State Park 320
  Wachusett Mountain State Park
    187
Stockbridge 197–8
  Mission House 198
  Norman Rockwell Museum 198
  Red Lion Inn 198
  Sargeant House *197*
Stonington 222, *317*
Stony Brook Mill (Dennis) 163
Stowe 256–7
  Stowe Recreation Path 256
  Trapp Family Lodge 256, 257
Stowe, Harriet Beecher 67, 309
  House (Hartford) 212
Sugar Hill 289
summer activities 164
surfing 182
Swift River Historical Society 190

t

Tanglewood 42, 199
tea 36, 37
Terryville 213
Thanksgiving 28
Thaxter, Celia 282
The Crucible 65
The Flume (Lincoln) 289
The Forks 323
theater 42, 199
  Bread and Puppet Theater 260

theater cont'd
Cape Playhouse (Dennis) 163
Dorset Playhouse 266
Flynn Theater for the Performing
Arts (Burlington) 262
Ogunquit Playhouse 305
St Michael's Playhouse
(Burlington) 263
Shakespeare & Co. (Lenox) 199
Yale Repertory Theater (New
Haven) 217
Thomas, Isaiah 189
Thomaston 213
Thoreau, Henry David 67, 148, 301
burial place (Concord, MA) 149
The Maine Woods 322
Walden 149
Townshend 250
Townshend Acts 36, 37
trails
Appalachian Mountain Club
(AMC) (Pinkham Notch) 288,
290
Appalachian Trail 164, 213
Atlantic White Cedar Swamp Trail
165
Boulder Loop Trail 288
Campobello Island 321
Cape Cod National Seashore
Trail 160
Cape Cod Rail Trail 160
Champney Falls Trail 288
Cranberry Bog Trail 166
Long Trail 164
Mohawk Trail 292, 200
Monhegan Island 313
Mount Katahdin 322
Mount Tom 253
Mount Desert Island 319
Stowe Recreation Path 256
White Mountain Guide 288
White Mountain National Forest
287, 288
transcendentalism 66, 67, 187
Triangular Trade 39, 73, 229
tribes *see* Algonquin tribes
Trinity Park (Oak Bluffs) 171, 172
Twain, Mark (Samuel Clemens)
Memorial (Nook Farm) (Hartford)
212
Twilight, "Uncle" Alexander 260
Tyringham 197

U

U-Mass (Northampton) 192
Uncle Tom's Cabin 67, 309
**US Coast Guard Academy (New
London)** 221

US Naval Submarine Base (Groton)
221
USS Constitution 109

V

Valley Railroad (Essex) 219
Vanderbilt, Cornelius II 236
Vanderbilt, William K. 236
Vermont 245–69
constitution 251
crafts 255
Northeast Kingdom 258–61
origin of name 265
Vermont Marble Exhibit (Proctor)
264
Vermonters 57, 245
Verrazano, Giovanni da 25, 229
Vikings 22, 23
Vinalhaven island 314
Vineyard Haven 171–2
vineyards 70
Vinland the Good 23

W

Wadsworth, Daniel 211
Wadsworth, John 205, 210
Waitsfield 255
Walden Pond 67, 148, 149
Wampanoag tribe 31, 53, 54
legal action 55
tribal lands 169
Ward, General Artemus 29, 38
Washington, George 130, 193
Gilbert Stuart portrait 230
state (Boston) 105, 116
Watch and Ward Society 45
Waterbury 256
Wauwinet 182
Webb, Electra Havemeyer 263
Webster, Noah 191
Weld family 56
Wellfleet 68, 165–6
Wentworth, John 277, 286, 294
West Barnstaple 83, 162
West Cornwall 214
West Paris 324
West Springfield 194–5
Eastern States Exposition (Big E)
194
Storrowton Village Museum
194–5
West Tisbury 173–4
Beetlebung Corner, Chilmark
Center 174
county fair 174
Granary Gallery 173
Wethersfield 29, 207, 212

Wetmore, William S. 235
Weymouth, George 26, 28
whale-watching trips 183
whaling 19, 38, 39, 73–4, 173,
175, 176, 220
Wharton, Edith 199
Wheelock, Eleazar 54, 64
Where the Rivers Run North 258
White River Junction 253
whitewater rafting 164, 322, 323
Whitfield, Reverend Henry 218
Whitney, Eli 208, 216
Wickle, Augustus van 239
wildlife
see also reservations
Cape Poge Wildlife Refuge
(Chappaquiddick Island) 173
Cedar Tree Neck Wildlife
Sanctuary (Gay Head) 175
Coatue-Coskata Wildlife Refuge
(Nantucket island) 181
Monomoy National Wildlife
Refuge 168
Plum Island (Parker River
National Wildlife Refuge)
139–40
Rachel Carson Wildlife Refuge
(near York) 305
Science Center of New
Hampshire (near Center
Sandwich) 286
Vermont Raptor Center
(Woodstock) 253
Wellfleet Bay Wildlife Sanctuary
165
Williams College (Williamstown)
200
Williams, Reverend Roger 29, 30,
65, 227
burial place (Providence) 232
Williamstown 200
Windsor (CT) 29, 207
Windsor (VT) 251
American Precision Museum 251
Catamount Brewing Co./tours
251
crafts 255
Old Constitution House
(museum) 251
Windsor-Cornish Covered Bridge
251
Winooski 262
Champlain Mill Mall 263
Winslow, Edward 28
Winter Harbor 320
Winthrop, Governor John 28, 35,
63, 105, 115
Winthrop, John Jr 145
Wiscasset 310

Wiscasset cont'd
  Castle Tucker 310
  Fort Edgecoomb 310
  Hesper 310
  Luther Little 310
  Musical Wonder House 310
  Nickels-Sortwell House 310
  Old Lincoln County Jail and
      Museum 310
witch trials (Salem) 64–6
Wolfeboro 286
women's colleges 67, 217
Woodbury, Charles 305

Woodman, Lawrence 141
Woods Hole 77, 170
  Marine Biological Laboratory 170
  National Marine Fisheries
      Service Aquarium 170
  Woods Hole Oceanographic
      Institute 170
Worcester 153, 187, 189
writers' retreats *see*
  artists/writers' retreats
Wyeth, Andrew 307, 314
Wyeth, Jamie 313, 314

y

yachting 77, 164, 237, 314
Yale College (University) 42, 64,
  216, 216–17
  Beinecke Rare Book and
      Manuscript Library 217
  tour 217
  Yale Center of British Art 217
  Yale University Art Gallery 217
Yale, Elihu 64, 216
Yankees 56, 57, 58, 208
Yarmouth Port 162

Boston Subway

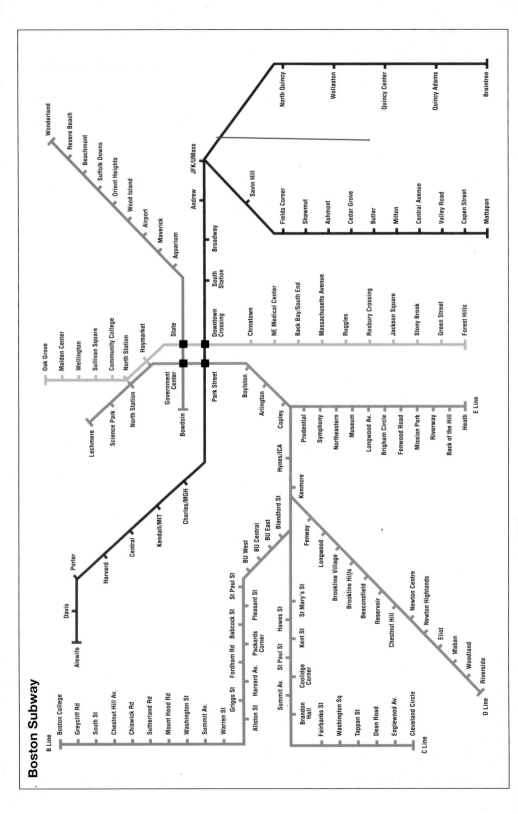